Semantic Theory

Studies in Language

Noam Chomsky and Morris Halle, Editors

Semantic Theory

Jerrold J. Katz
Massachusetts Institute of Technology

Harper & Row, Publishers
New York, Evanston, San Francisco, London

Semantic Theory

Standard Book Number: 06-043567-4

Library of Congress Catalog Card Number: 74-137801

The author gratefully acknowledges permission by the publishers to quote from these works: *Word and Object* by W. V. Quine; reprinted by permission of the M.I.T. Press, Cambridge, Massachusetts; copyright 1960 by the Massachusetts Institute of Technology; and *Translations from the Philosophical Writings of Gottlob Frege,* edited by P. Geach and M. Black; reprinted by permission of Basil Blackwell & Mott Ltd., Oxford, England; copyright 1952.

This book is dedicated to the person
from whom I learned about linguistics

NOAM A. CHOMSKY

Contents

Acknowledgments

I owe a special debt of gratitude to Noam Chomsky, who introduced me to linguistics, who over the years has been the most important influence on my research, and who served as reader for the manuscript of this book, providing many valuable comments and criticisms. I am also indebted to Hans G. Herzberger, who helped me see the relevance of aspects of philosophical logic to linguistic theory. Many of the ideas in Sections 1 and 2 of Chapter 4 dealing with statement-hood and presupposition were worked out jointly in the course of a study of the concept of truth in natural language (Herzberger and Katz (in preparation)). Another sizable debt is owed to Robert M. Harnish, who, as a member of the M.I.T. seminars in which portions of the manuscript of this book were used and as a frequent visitor to my office, made very many valuable contributions to the work, including the preparation of the index. I am much indebted to the philoso-phers and linguists who were members of those M.I.T. seminars and to Thomas Bever, John Dolan, Robert Hambourger, Gilbert Harman, D. Terence Langendoen, Harris Savin, Robert Schwartz, and Virginia Valian, who were members of a similar seminar that I gave at The Rockefeller University. I owe a considerable debt to Manfred Bierwisch, whose early support of semantic theory and later contributions to it have meant a great deal to me and to the progress of the theory. I wish further to acknowledge help from my friends, particularly Paul Postal, Sylvain Bromberger, Morris Halle, James Thomson, James Harris, Robert Ware, Bruce Fraser, Steven Davis, and Yuji Nishiyama. Assistance was received from the humanities and philosophy departments and the Research Laboratory of Electronics of M.I.T., as well as the philosophy and psycholinguistics groups at The Rockefeller University. And I thank Professors Harry Frankfurt and George A. Miller for the opportunity of presenting some of the material in this book at a seminar at The Rockefeller University during the spring of 1969.

I want to express my gratitude to Florence Warshawsky Harris, who was my editor (and much else besides), to her husband James Harris, who was both our courier and critic, and to Diane Kravif, who took over the copyediting at the page proof stage. I can imagine how the book might have gotten published without Florence Harris, but this is only because philosophical training develops one's ability to imagine all sorts of logical possibilities.

Finally, I'm deeply grateful to Virginia Valian.

This work was supported in part by the National Institute of Mental Health (Grant 5 P01 MH13390-05).

J. J. K.

November, 1971

There are constant references in contemporary philosophy, which notoriously is concerned with language, to a 'logical grammar' and a 'logical syntax' as though these were things distinct from ordinary grammarian's grammar and syntax : and certainly they do seem, whatever exactly they may be, different from traditional grammar. But grammar today is itself in a state of flux ; for fifty years or more it has been questioned on all hands and counts whether what Dionysius Thrax once thought was the truth about Greek is the truth and the whole truth about all language and all languages. Do we know, then, that there will prove to be any ultimate boundary between 'logical grammar' and a revised and enlarged *Grammar*? In the history of human inquiry, philosophy has the place of the initial central sun, seminal and tumultuous : from time to time it throws off some portion of itself to take station as a science, a planet, cool and well regulated, progressing steadily towards a distant final state. This happened long ago at the birth of mathematics, and again at the birth of physics : only in the last century we have witnessed the same process once again, slow and at the time almost imperceptible, in the birth of the science of mathematical logic, through the joint labours of philosophers and mathematicians. Is it not possible that the next century may see the birth, through the joint labours of philosophers, grammarians, and numerous other students of language, of a true and comprehensive *science of language*? Then we shall have rid ourselves of one more part of philosophy (there will be plenty left) in the only way we ever can get rid of philosophy, by kicking it upstairs.

J. L. Austin

Preface

Sciences tend to shy away from problems that look too difficult and to occupy themselves instead with ones that seem manageable. This is undoubtedly a wise research strategy, but, like anything else, it can be carried too far. This has happened in some areas of modern psychology and social science as the result of a general drift toward a high degree of professionalization.

When this otherwise sensible research strategy goes astray, the problems of a field of study come to be determined less by the inherent features of its subject than by the availability of precise methods for obtaining objective solutions. The focus of research shifts to manageable problems, and those that are found "unmanageable" recede further and further from the attention of the scientific community. Eventually, the field comes to be defined in terms of the problems which are amenable to solution through the application of precise methods developed by generations of professionals. Problems that are central to the structure of the subject may come to seem quite peripheral or end up being defined out of the field.

This, I think, is what happened to the classical problem of logical form over the course of the first half of this century in both of the fields to which it naturally belongs, linguistics and logic. The problem, that of explaining the consequence relations of sentences on the basis of the meaning of their constituents (without regard to syntactic category), all but disappeared from these fields up until quite recently. Even now, paradoxically, the problem has reappeared in distorted form in many instances because it is made to fit the conception of language and logic that caused its disappearance.

By concentrating on manageable problems, linguistics and (to a far greater extent) logic were able to achieve a large measure of success. This very success, however, made the trend toward professionalization harder to reverse since professionals could point with deserved pride to the scientific results obtained by the application of precise methods to manageable problems. Thus, attempts to reverse the trend ran up against the reluctance of the professionals to think that the successes in their field did not necessarily reflect the true degree of scientific advancement. Such attempts also ran up against a narrowing of perspective on the part of subsequent generations of practitioners whose conception of their field was acquired from professionals who, with succeeding generations, passed on less of an idea of the unprofessionalized subject.

By the early fifties, the point had been reached in linguistics and logic where only in histories could one find attempts to theorize about the full range of deductive relations in the sentences of natural languages. Both fields dealt with certain aspects or special cases of the problem, of course. Also, outside of these fields discussions of the general problem of logical form still went on—but in the field of philosophy, where unmanageable problems are stock-in-trade.

Professionalism alone was not responsible. Two other factors worked together with it, namely, the inherent difficulty of the problem of logical form in natural language and the influence of a renascent empiricism in these fields. Together, these three powerful factors led to an exaggeration of the differences between linguists and logicians. And as the problem of logical form, the common problem that relates these fields, came to occupy less and less of a central place within them, linguists and logicians came to look as different from each other as botanists and mathematicians.

What makes the problem of logical form in natural language difficult is that similarities in the overt grammatical form of sentences disguise their underlying logical differences. Thus, the valid arguments (1), (2), and (3) seem indistinguishable from the invalid arguments (4), (5), and (6), respectively:

(1)   (a) There is a fire in my kitchen
       (b) My kitchen is in my house
       (c) Hence, there is a fire in my house

(2)   (a) Today I ate what I bought at the store last week
       (b) I bought a(n) $\left\{ \begin{array}{l} \text{viviparous} \\ \text{expensive} \\ \text{small} \end{array} \right\}$ fish at the store last week

(c) Hence, today I ate a(n) $\begin{Bmatrix} \text{viviparous} \\ \text{expensive} \\ \text{small} \end{Bmatrix}$ fish

(3) (a) Every part of the toy is $\begin{Bmatrix} \text{gingerbread} \\ \text{silver} \\ \text{oily} \end{Bmatrix}$

(b) Hence, the toy (itself) is $\begin{Bmatrix} \text{gingerbread} \\ \text{silver} \\ \text{oily} \end{Bmatrix}$

(4) (a) There is a pain in my foot
(b) My foot is in my shoe
(c) Hence, there is a pain in my shoe

(5) (a) Today I ate what I bought in the store last week

(b) I bought a $\begin{Bmatrix} \text{raw} \\ \text{fresh} \\ \text{dirty} \end{Bmatrix}$ fish in the store last week

(c) Hence, today I ate a $\begin{Bmatrix} \text{raw} \\ \text{fresh} \\ \text{dirty} \end{Bmatrix}$ fish

(6) (a) Every part of the toy is $\begin{Bmatrix} \text{little} \\ \text{square} \\ \text{light} \end{Bmatrix}$

(b) Hence, the toy (itself) is $\begin{Bmatrix} \text{little} \\ \text{square} \\ \text{light} \end{Bmatrix}$

Faced with the fact that, at the very least, sentences of a natural language do not wear their logical form on their phonetic (or orthographic) sleeve, how is one to penetrate beyond surface similarities? This problem was severe enough to make one of the outstanding philosophers of this century despair. Wittgenstein (1922), who had tackled the problem of constructing a theory of logical form in the *Tractatus*, remarked:

> Language disguises thought. So much so, that from the outward form of the clothing it is impossible to infer the form of the thought beneath it, because the outward form of the clothing is not designed to reveal the form of the body, but for entirely different purposes (p. 63).

Thus, logicians and linguists had reason to look about for manageable problems.

Logicians turned to the construction of artificial languages, specially designed to incorporate a highly restricted (from the viewpoint of natural language) notion of logical form. Such artificial languages were constructed to make it possible to write formulas that do wear their logical form on their (notational) sleeve. Similarities in the overt grammatical form of these "sentences" were safe guides to similarities in logical form, for they were constructed with just this feature in mind.

Grammarians, on the other hand, occupied themselves with the linguistic features of the overt grammatical form of sentences of natural languages. This resulted in a disproportionate emphasis on phonetics, phonology, morphology, and surface syntax. By way of caricature, one can say that logicians entered the business of making highly intricate mannequins, while linguists took up tailoring, concerning themselves with the phonetic cut and the syntactic weave of the garment.

We have looked briefly at professionalization and at the difficulty of the problem of logical form in natural language. The third factor in the disappearance of the classical problem of logical form was the empiricist attack on the vestige of the rationalist doctrine of necessary truth found in the linguistic systems of Carnap and other positivists. One path pursued in this attack is now familiar as Quine's criticism of Carnap's and other positivists' attempts to draw the analytic-synthetic distinction. Another path, one not so easily recognized as leading to an attack on the same distinction, involved the development of the conception of logical form based on a prespecified list of so-called "logical particles" (sometimes "logical words"), which culminates in something like Quine's definition of logic (to which we shall return). That this development also is inimical to the notion of analyticity can be seen from the following considerations. First, the list of logical particles—which contains terms such as "or," "and," "not," "all," "is," and "if . . ., then . . ."—excludes such items as the nouns, verbs, and adjectives of a language from the category 'logical vocabulary' and assigns them to the limbo of 'extra-logical vocabulary.' Second, analyticities (in the straight Kantian sense) depend on logical relations like synonymy and meaning inclusion among the nouns, verbs, and other terms of the "extra-logical" vocabulary. For example, the analytic sentences (7) and (8) rest, respectively, on the synonymy of "bachelor" and "unmarried adult human male" and the meaning inclusion of "male" in "men":

(7)   Bachelors are unmarried adult human males

(8)   All men are male

If assigning terms like "bachelor," "adult unmarried human male," and "male" to the category of the extra-logical means anything, it is that relations such as synonymy and meaning inclusion are extra-logical; this, if it implies anything, implies that analyticity is an extra-logical and hence non-logical property.

Such a conception of logical form is based on an arbitrary distinction between the *form* and *matter* (*content*) of an argument. It comes about in something like the following way. One reflects on the validity of an argument like that in (9)–(11):

(9)   Every man is mortal

(10)   Socrates is a man

(11)   Hence, Socrates is mortal

One notices that the validity of this argument is independent of the particular choice of words "man," "mortal," and "Socrates." That is, if we choose any triple of words and replace each occurrence of "man" in (9)–(11) by one member of the triple, each occurrence of "mortal" by another, and each occurrence of "Socrates" by the remaining member, the result will also be a valid argument. Since the source of the validity of every argument constructed in this manner is the same, it is clear that the form of the argument (9)–(11) is expressed by (12):

(12)   Every x is y, and z is a x; hence, z is y

And the matter (or content) of the argument is "man," "mortal," and "Socrates"; for these terms, since they can be changed while the valid form remains unaltered, play no role in the deductive relation between (9) and (10) and (11). But the terms "every" and "is" cannot be so changed while preserving validity, and thus they enter into the form of the argument. Reflecting in this way on other arguments that turn on properties of connectives and quantifiers, one builds up a list of logical particles. In order to abstract from such cases and obtain a general distinction between form and matter, it is necessary, at some point, to decide that the list of particles is complete, that no further such reflection on other valid arguments can add substantively to the present stock of logical words. Given this decision, it is easy to see how a concept of form in contrast to content can be specified with respect to this list and how principles like (12) can be formulated to determine the validity of arguments (from their form alone).

But there is no nonarbitrary basis for making such a decision in a way that divides the words of the language into the familiar logical particles and everything else. For almost every term or expression excluded from the list of logical particles, one can find a valid argument (in exactly the same sense, namely, if its premisses are true, then its conclusion must also be true) in which that term or expression cannot be replaced systematically while preserving validity. For example, neither the term "man" nor the term "male" can be replaced in the argument (13)–(14) by another term selected at random from the same syntactic category:

(13)   Socrates is a man

(14)   Hence, Socrates is male

The paralogisms (4), (5), and (6) provide less trivial examples since they show that the terms "fire," "viviparous" ("expensive," "small"), and "gingerbread" ("silver," "oily") cannot be replaced in the arguments (1), (2), and (3) by terms randomly selected from the same syntactic category without incurring invalidity. Since arguments like (13)–(14) are just as much cases of the consequence relation (of deductive connection) as are arguments like (9)–(11), there can be no nonarbitrary criterion for deciding that the logical particles and only these should be included on the list of terms that play a role in logical form.[1]

The arbitrariness of the distinction between form and matter reveals itself in a number of other ways. First, the theory of logical form based on the logical

---

[1] See Section 5 of Chapter 2 for further discussion.

particles exclusively implies that the premisses and conclusions of arguments (1), (2), and (3) have the same logical structure as the corresponding premisses and conclusions of (4), (5), and (6).[2] Furthermore, although the list of logical particles was set up to contrast with the "extra-logical" terms of the language, the two actually overlap. There are sentences having the same range of logical relations and yet one sentence gains its potential to enter into consequence relations from a logical particle while the other gains exactly the same potential from a (so-called) extra-logical term. For instance, consider (15) and (16). Since "mortal" is an extra-logical term, consequence relations that can be handled in the case of (16) cannot be handled in the case of (15):

(15)   Animals are mortal

(16)   Animals do not live forever

Any attempt to base a theory of logical form exclusively on the logical particles of a language runs up against indefinitely many such cases where the same deductive relations are determined by the logical vocabulary and by terms excluded from it.

Of course, in practice, a word is included in the logical vocabulary if precise methods are available for specifying its contribution to inferences. Since logic has the means to formally specify the contributions of quantifiers and truth-functional connectives to inferences, it is no surprise that they appear on everyone's list of logical words. And, since very little has been done in logic proper toward developing the formal apparatus for representing the manner in which the nouns, verbs, adjectives, and so on enter into the logical form of sentences, it is no surprise that no one lists terms like "pain," "small," and "bachelor" in his enumeration of the logical vocabulary.

The conclusion of the professionalization process and of the empiricist influence was to enshrine in a definition of logic this practice of explicating logical form on the basis of those words for which there are precise rules to specify their contribution to valid argumentation. Thus, Quine characterizes logic as the discipline that seeks to discover all truths of the form (17) (where each such conditional corresponds to an argument form in the manner that (17) corresponds to (12)) in which only logical particles occur essentially:[3]

(17)   If every x is a y and z is a x, then z is a y

A definition such as Quine's proposes a theoretical characterization of the subject of logic. Judged as a theory about the nature of logic, it is more precise than the competing definition where the logical form of a sentence consists of *all* the grammatical features that determine valid inferences into which the sentence enters, but it is less faithful to the unprofessionalized subject. This, of course, is not to say that Quine's definition does not characterize a type of logical form, a

---

[2] See Quine (1941, p. 1).

[3] See Quine (1955, pp. 1–3). He also includes discourse about logical truths in his account of logic, but this aspect need not concern us here.

particular species of deductive relation. The criticism is that, as an account of what does and does not belong to logic essentially, Quine's definition is inadequate because it arbitrarily excludes indefinitely many inferences (such as the inference from (13) to (14) or from (15) to (16)) that are no less deductively valid than those that it includes (such as the inference from (9) and (10) to (11)). It also excludes indefinitely many propositions like (18) from the status of logical truths, even though they are as deserving of this status as are propositions like (17):

(18)   If x is a bachelor, then x is an unmarried adult human male

In taxonomic grammar, manageable problems also occupied the limelight, and very little was accomplished in the way of clarifying the logico-semantic structure of natural languages. Problems of articulatory phonetics, phonology, morphology, and syntax dominated the work of these linguists. Their textbooks sometimes touched on problems of meaning, but when they did it was quite clear, both from the relatively minor position accorded such problems and from the character of their treatment, that they were conceived of as being among the peripheral issues of the field. One finds no literature dealing with questions like the following: What is the semantic difference between "fire" and "pain" responsible for the fact that they exhibit different logical behavior, as in (1) versus (4)? What do terms like "viviparous," "expensive," and "small" have in common that contrasts them with terms like "raw," "fresh," and "dirty," as in (2) versus (5)? What is the nature of the semantic structure on which the validity of arguments like (13)–(14) rests? How do we know that the relation on which the argument (1) turns is transitive?[4]

The same three factors behind the neglect of semantic structure in logic were responsible for its neglect in linguistics—growing professionalism, the inherent difficulty of the problems, and the rise and eventual dominance of empiricism. The first two require no special comment here, but there is something to be said about the third.

The antimentalistic outlook of linguistics was typified by remarks such as that of Bloomfield (1936), the major figure of the period:

> Non-linguists (unless they happen to be physicalists) constantly forget that a speaker is making noise, and credit him, instead, with the possession of impalpable 'ideas'. It remains for linguists to show, in detail, that the speaker has no 'ideas', and that the noise is sufficient . . . (p. 93).

To avoid reference to mentalistic properties, Bloomfieldians adopted a physicalist conception of the subject matter of linguistics, on which the object of grammatical study is the corpus of actual utterances recorded by the linguist in field work. The study itself took on the character of library cataloguing. Like a library classification scheme, in which acquisitions are grouped into higher and higher categories until

---

[4] Clearly, these questions involve inherent features of the subject matter of both linguistics and logic: they involve meaning and syntactic organization, and they fall under the general problem of specifying the conditions under which a consequence can be deduced validly in arguments.

each is catalogued as a book, magazine, journal, or such, these grammars classified the phones and stretches of phones in utterances into the categories of phoneme, morpheme, word, phrase, clause, and, finally, declarative sentence, interrogative, imperative, or such. Since taxonomic grammars do no more than regroup and reclassify the speech sounds of an utterance, there is no place for meaning in their description of the grammatical structure of sentences, and, therefore, semantics must be thought of as something outside grammar. Bloomfield (1933) thus took the meaning of a sentence to be "the situation which prompts people to utter speech" and "the response which it calls forth in the hearer" (p. 139).

Recently, the situation has begun to change. The change is primarily the result of the change in outlook brought about by transformational grammar, in particular its return to the Cartesian conception of the subject matter of linguistics. With linguistics conceived of as studying the system of internalized rules that constitute the native speaker's linguistic competence (see Section 1 of Chapter 2), meaning has a place in grammatical structure, for now grammatical structure is no longer identified with surface structure and the reality of language is no longer identified with corpora of utterances.

Now linguists and some logicians are starting to pay serious attention to questions about the semantic structure of natural language. In some cases, this reflects a genuine change in outlook, a more realistic view to the basic problems of logical form in natural language, and a start toward interdisciplinary cooperation between linguists and logicians. In others, however, the changes are only superficial. True enough, linguists now generally acknowledge that semantic structure is part of the grammar of a sentence, and the range of words whose logical form is being investigated is now far wider than the class of logical particles. But these developments have in part taken place within the empiricist framework and therefore, in the case of some linguists and philosophers, do not reflect a change from empiricist assumptions.

A linguist like Lakoff (1969), for example, who would make semantic rules the basis of a grammar, makes syntactic and semantic structure a function of all sorts of factual beliefs of speakers, thereby removing any grounds for the rationalist distinction between logical (linguistic) truths and contingent ones. Lakoff thus tends to undo the work of overcoming the Bloomfieldian exclusion of semantics by subjecting semantic structure to a straightforward Quinean interpretation. A philosopher like Davidson (1967), who has done much to interest philosophers in a rigorous study of the logic of words not ordinarily thought of as belonging to the logical apparatus of a language, nonetheless constructs his program along Quinean lines: its explicit aim is to show that concepts of the theory of meaning can be dispensed with in favor of notions from the theory of reference and its methods preserve the old division of words into logical particles and extra-logical terms.

Thus, although problems of logical form and meaning are no longer as neglected as they were in the first half of this century, their return to linguistics and logic is not an unmitigated triumph for rationalist theories of language and mind. In a sense, then, the real problem has not been brought back at all in the case of neo-Quineans, since reframing it to fit in with empiricist assumptions changes it entirely. The problem, as these linguists and philosophers now see it, is essentially how to handle the logical contributions of descriptive words from natural languages on the basis of the formal machinery developed for handling the relatively more manageable problems about logical particles, making no use of notions from the theory of meaning or, what comes to the same thing, no distinction between a priori linguistic knowledge and a posteriori factual knowledge. Given that this is the problem that guides research in the semantic structure of the "extra-logical" vocabulary of natural languages, it is unlikely that such research will lead to a refutation of the empiricist theories of logic and language, particularly Quine's, that were developed on the basis of the restriction of systems of logic to those constructible with logical particles alone.

In order to refute these theories we need to do two things, both of which are facets of the program of carrying the transformationalist revolution to its logical conclusion. First, there is the critical task of exhibiting the origins and basis of such empiricist theories. Here, we need to see how empiricist theories of semantics and logic and taxonomic theories of language depend on each other for support. I think it can be shown, on the one hand, that Bloomfieldian structuralism depends completely on something like the Quinean theory of methodology or early positivist doctrines of physicalism and, on the other, that critical assumptions of Quinean extensionalism such as that there are no such things as meanings "over and against their verbal embodiments" (Quine (1960b, p. 76)) derive their only plausibility from Bloomfieldian conceptions of grammar that exclude meaning from grammatical structure.[5] Once these interconnections are established, the criticisms of physicalism can be directed against Bloomfieldian structuralism and the criticisms of the taxonomic model of grammar can be directed against Quinean extensionalism.

The second task involved in refuting the empiricist theories is a constructive one. Empiricists claim that concepts of the theory of meaning are unscientific, occult, or useless and should be banished from a scientific theory of language. They claim that there is no need for such concepts anyway because concepts of the theory of reference can do the work that has to be done in constructing a theory of language. Thus, the constructive task for the rationalist approach to the study of language is to reply to these claims in the only way that can ultimately discredit them, that is, by building a linguistic theory which demonstrates the scientific soundness of concepts such as sense, meaning, synonymy, analyticity, and so on, by showing that they are essential components in an empirically revealing systematization of the facts about natural languages.

The primary aim of this book is to advance the construction of such a theory. Its orientation is, of course, rationalist and intensionalist. It thus runs counter to the professionalization described previously in that it makes no distinction between what is logical and what is not, unless there is an undeniable difference in our logical intuitions about the validity of the cases. The book assumes the truth of Austin's suggestion in the epigraph that the philosophical notion of logical grammar is an essential part of the linguistic notion of empirical (or descriptive) grammar.

---

[5] I have begun such a study in "Logic and Language: An Examination of Recent Criticisms of Intensionalism" (to appear).

This is a programmatic thesis, to the effect that the study of grammatical structure in empirical linguistics will eventually provide a full account of the logical form of sentences in natural language.

      Chomsky's revival of the Cartesian conception of linguistics and his extension of grammatical theory by the introduction of transformational apparatus have shown that many of the differences between logical grammar and empirical grammar merely reflect superficial aspects of the surface form of sentences. Although Chomsky has blurred this artificial distinction, his work is only the first step toward the goal of showing that our conception of descriptive grammar can be expanded to the point where all differences between logical grammar and empirical grammar disappear. At present, it has only been shown that a certain range of questions relating to logical form, which could not be dealt with by empirical linguistics, can now be handled by transformational grammar. Achieving our goal requires the further step of showing how a representation of the logical form of sentences in natural language, which is adequate to the demands of logic, comes in as a natural component of a descriptive grammar's analysis of linguistic structure. At this point, the claim that transformational grammars include logical grammar is more of an optimistic prognosis about the future of transformational grammar than a fact already established by its findings. It may well take until the next century to see the birth of a "true and comprehensive *science of language*," to see philosophy "throw off some portion of itself to take station as a science" (of language).

      This book moves toward this next step. It proposes a conception of semantic representation that is designed both to reflect the logical form of sentences and to provide a basis for defining semantic properties and relations like synonymy, analyticity, ambiguity, and redundancy. The idea underlying this conception is that the logical form of a sentence is identical with its meaning as determined compositionally from the senses of its lexical items and the grammatical relations between its syntactic constituents. Such a conception is not wholly new, of course. It was set forth in an earlier and much less detailed form in a number of publications, beginning with Katz and Fodor (1963). Moreover, the more our approach was worked out, the more it was found to embody versions of Frege's principles. Fodor and I were originally unaware of the extent to which doctrines of ours were often replicas of Frege's. In the present book, I have tried to indicate some of the debt that empirical semantics (in our sense) owes to him.[6]

      The writing of this book was prompted and guided by two motives. One was to make available the results of research in semantics over the last few years. The other was to bring together a number of earlier discussions of semantic theory so that there would be available a single, reasonably comprehensive presentation of the theory. These motives proved to be interrelated in a natural way. To provide a reasonably comprehensive presentation of semantic theory, it was necessary to include much of the new research, while to provide the requisite background for

---

     [6] Frege's contributions to formal logic and the foundations of mathematics are certainly not neglected, but his contributions to a theory of the semantics of natural language are. As I see the situation, Frege's work in this area stands in much the same relation to current semantic work that Port-Royal work in syntax stands to transformationalist work in syntax. For some background on this analogy, see Chomsky (1966a).

the new research, it was necessary to include a good deal of material from earlier discussions of the theory. The book thus shows the effect of the new on the old in the way that new ideas change certain principles and formulations characteristic of earlier discussions, and it shows the effects of the old on the new in the way that the leading ideas of earlier work direct the course of more recent investigations.

The organization and content of the individual chapters were influenced by various motives. The motive behind the first chapter was the desire to get away from the manner in which semantic theory was originally presented, namely, as a means of completing the explanation, begun by phonological and syntactic theory, of how speakers of a natural language are able to understand and produce sentences that are novel to them: semantic theory is presented as a description of the semantic component of a grammar.[7] The subject matter of semantics is thus negatively characterized as that part of a speaker's competence to produce and understand novel sentences which is neither syntactic nor phonological. It is not that I now think this way of presenting semantic theory is wrong; rather, I think there is a better way.

In Chapter 1 semantic theory is presented in a way that is more closely related to our pretheoretical intuitions about meaning. Semantic theory is taken to be an answer to the question "What is meaning?" but one that also answers each of the subsidary questions to which the general question reduces, such as "What is sameness of meaning?" "What is multiplicity of meaning?" "What is the difference between meaningfulness and meaninglessness?" It is conceived of as an integrated body of definitions (or explications) of the semantic properties and relations about which such subsidary questions ask. This shift of emphasis from a negative definition of semantics to a positive one in terms of the kind of phenomena that a semantic theory ought to explain has a number of definite advantages. One is that it offers a better picture of the goal of semantic theory, namely, the explanation of the phenomena in the domain of semantics. The reason is that the notion of domain required to say what is a semantic phenomenon is now antecedently fixed, in large part, by our presystematic intuitions about whether the answers to particular questions like "What is sameness or difference in meaning?" are part of the answer to the general question "What is meaning?" A second advantage is that we can give a clearer conception of the empirical constraints on semantic representations. We can specify these constraints generally in terms of the formal structure that semantic representations must have in order to serve as the basis from which we make predictions about the semantic properties and relations of expressions and sentences. Another advantage is that it will be easier to determine the boundary between semantics and other areas of linguistic communication—phonology and syntax, on the one side, and extra-grammatical aspects of sentence use, on the other. This is because properties and relations that fall outside of semantics can be expected not to fit in simply and naturally with the already achieved systematization of clear cases of semantic properties and relations (in the way that new genuinely semantic ones do).

[7] See Katz and Fodor (1963, Sec. 3).

In Chapter 2 the theory to be constructed is outlined and its place in linguistic theory is sketched. This outline is intended to serve as a basis for the more wide-ranging and detailed discussions that occupy us in the rest of the book. The chapter also contains discussions of two critical notions. One is the now familiar but nonetheless ill-understood distinction between competence and performance. The other is the idea that natural languages are capable of providing a sentence to express any thought a speaker might wish to communicate, an idea which I call "effability." This notion is far less familiar, far more debatable, but, I think, just as important for the study of language.

Chapter 3 functions as a transition from the earlier discussions of semantic theory to the new material in this book. A fair-sized portion of the chapter is a revised and expanded version of "Recent issues in semantic theory" (Katz (1967a)), but it also contains new material, including improvements in previous formulations of constructs, a number of new constructs and principles, and some proposals for both syntax and semantics. Overall, the tenor of this chapter is atypically critical for this book (consisting of replies to various objections to doctrines on semantic theory in earlier publications, including objections by Weinreich, Bolinger, McCawley, Wilson, and others). Although I regret the emphasis on criticism here, I found such a dialectic the best way of making the transition from the earlier ideas about semantic theory to the new ones.

In Chapter 4 earlier discussions of the concepts of linguistic truth and analyticity are extended. The aim of the chapter is to link the earlier discussions with a number of traditional issues in philosophical logic (such as the sentence-proposition-statement distinction that intensionalists make and the concept of presupposition) and to provide an integrated treatment of these issues within the framework of semantic theory. The chapter contains some important revisions of earlier formulations of semantic concepts, in particular the concepts of analyticity and semantic entailment.

In Chapter 5 the ideas about linguistic truth developed in the previous chapter are carried over to the study of the logic of questions. Most of the material in this chapter is adapted from "The Logic of Questions" (Katz (1968a)). There are some significant changes and additions; in particular, there are suggestions about the further extension of these ideas to other sentence types, that is, suggestions about the prospects for a logic of requests and a logic of exclamations.

Chapter 6 is the most philosophically oriented chapter. In it we offer a defense (though by no means a comprehensive one) of intensionalist semantics. The first part deals with objections that Quine, Goodman, and philosophers influenced by them have made to intensionalist concepts, primarily their criticism of the analytic-synthetic distinction. The second part is a defense of an essentially Fregean account of the conditions under which valid inferences can be made by substitution into an opaque context. Included here is a critique of Quine's thesis of the indeterminacy of radical translation.

The issue of substitution into opaque contexts, although originally purely philosophical and logical, turns out also to be directly relevant to certain current questions in linguistic theory. If it is not possible to defend the intensionalist position on this issue, then it will follow that the semantic component must refer to aspects of the surface structure of sentences to determine their semantic interpretation. Besides the question of whether semantic interpretation applies exclusively to deep syntactic structures, this issue also concerns an aspect of the controversy between interpretive and generative semantics.[8]

Chapter 7 presents an extended investigation of the converse relation. It can be thought of as a case study showing the complexity that semantic representation has to take on to define a special case of even so apparently simple a relation as synonymy. The aim of the investigation is to determine the form of readings that represent constituents bearing the converse relation to each other, that is, to construct a definition of the converse relation that predicts, on the basis of the readings of constituents, which pairs of readings are converses. To do this, it was necessary to examine a number of semantic phenomena and to work out the general form for their semantic representation. Thus, in this chapter we formulate paradigms for treating state concepts, process concepts, temporal relations, semantic fields, and so on.

Chapter 8, the last chapter, offers a defense of the conception of the organization of grammars set forth in Katz and Postal (1964) and in Chomsky (1965), the position that Chomsky (1970a) now calls the "standard theory." In the last few years, this position has come under attack from two sides—from those who think that it is impossible to separate the syntactic and semantic components and to treat semantic analysis as an interpretive process, and from those who, although they accept a separation between these components, think that semantic interpretation cannot be restricted to underlying phrase markers. The alternative proposed by the former critics, the theory of generative semantics, is shown to be only a notational variant of the standard theory, but one that is forced to employ more complex treatments of grammatical phenomena due to its false assumption about the inseparability of syntax and semantics. The arguments used by the latter critics, those who think that surface structure plays a role in semantic interpretation, are inconclusive, in large part due to the use of too broad a notion of what counts as semantic. The conclusion of the attempt made in this chapter to assess these objections brought against the standard theory is that it stands up quite satisfactorily to them.

In the course of developing this line of defense, I consider the distinction between syntax and semantics in a quite detailed way and I also take up the complementary distinction between semantics and extra-grammatical aspects of sentence use. The examination of the generative semanticist's attack on the notion of deep structure leads to a rationale for the existence of a level of deep syntactic structure in natural languages, while the examination of the arguments against restricting semantic interpretation to underlying phrase markers leads us to recognize the need for a new interpretive component of the grammar that interprets surface structure in terms of aspects of style and rhetoric. We argue that the properties of surface

---

[8] Chomsky (1970a) argues that the surface differences between synonymous constituents (appearing in an opaque context) can affect the truth conditions of a sentence in ways that a generative semantics-type grammar cannot satisfactorily account for. If my defense is adequate, this argument against generative semantics is unsound.

structure that can no longer be regarded as semantic, once the critic's overly inclusive notion of semantics is suitably restricted, fall together with others to form a system whose import is clearly stylistic and rhetorical. Hopefully, the development of a theory of such a new component of generative grammars will make it possible to apply the syntactic (and phonological) apparatus of formal grammar more seriously to problems of rhetoric, style, and literary criticism.

The scope of semantics

If you have a lemon, make lemonade.

Dale Carnegie

Semantics is the study of linguistic meaning. It is concerned with what sentences and other linguistic objects express, not with the arrangement of their syntactic parts or with their pronunciation. Nearly everyone agrees on this. It is also generally agreed that the basic question of semantics is "What is meaning?" But at this point agreement ends and interminable controversies begin about what kind of thing meaning is. There is disagreement on issues of every sort, including the fundamental one of whether we can make something of the concept of meaning or whether we would be better off without it. Those who regard meaning as a worthless notion quarrel about how it can be eliminated, while those who consider it indispensable quarrel about how it is to be properly explicated. Furthermore, the particular problems that arise in discussions of this issue include deep-seated questions that have been debated since the very beginnings of philosophy. Accordingly, progress in the study of meaning, although significant in the direction of accumulating a richer and more extensive body of interesting facts, has been negligible in the direction of bringing order to these facts, that is, little has been accomplished in the way of revealing the general principles that underlie the organization of semantic phenomena.

It is no wonder, then, that in many quarters semantics has gained a reputation for being an irretrievably dreary discipline, the significance and stability of whose achievements is inversely proportional to the importance of its subject matter. Admittedly, there is much evidence from past experience to indicate that this reputation is not undeserved. But what is the source of the trouble? Where does the blame lie and where must we look to make changes? Anyone who would like to see semantics take its place as a reputable branch of empirical science, as well as anyone who would like to establish that this can never happen, must seek an answer to these questions. The alternatives are clear: the source of the trouble is either in the notion of meaning itself or in the approaches taken toward its study.

Those who say that the concept of meaning is at fault are, I think, saying that the unsavory reputation of semantics belongs to the concept of meaning much as the unsavory reputation of demonology belongs to the concept of a demon. Their skepticism rests on the view that meaning is not a suitable scientific notion, that it cannot, whatever we try to do to refurbish it, become the basis of a scientific theory that will succeed in explaining linguistic phenomena. Accordingly, if one believes, as I do, that the tragic history of semantics is instead a consequence of the failure to pursue a satisfactory approach to understanding meaning, he has no more nor less to do than to construct a theory that uses the concept of meaning to reveal underlying uniformities in language and to show how semantic phenomena reduce to them. It would be a mistake to believe that at this stage one can silence the skeptic in any other way. Advancing philosophical arguments against the principles on which his skepticism rests would just renew old debates. The only convincing argument consists in showing that the concept of meaning provides the basis for a theory that successfully accounts for semantic facts and in showing that without this concept no such basis exists.

Accordingly, we shall seek an approach to the explication of meaning that will provide a theory of meaning with the required explanatory power. We shall bypass the specific skeptical arguments of those who think that meaning is a worthless concept. If their arguments are sound, our investigations can lead no further than studies in demonology do. If, on the other hand, our investigations are successful, we will have shown that their arguments were not sound in the first place. Such skeptical arguments against semantics will take on the character that skeptical arguments against the justifiability of induction have when they are foolishly used to criticize scientific generalizations from observed cases of a phenomenon to unobserved ones.

We assume, then, that there is no fundamental trouble with semantics conceived as the study of meaning nor any difficulty with its basic question " What is meaning?" We assume that there has instead been some misconception about how the study of meaning should best proceed in trying to answer this question. This is not to deny that some linguists and philosophers were on the right track, but they simply never went far enough. They failed to bring about a consensus among serious workers concerning the proper approach to semantics.

The misconception, it seems to me, lies in the supposition that the question "What is meaning?" can be answered in a direct and straightforward way. The question is generally treated as if it were on a par with a question like "What is the capital of France?" to which the direct and straightforward answer "Paris" can be given. It is supposed that an answer can be given of the form "Meaning is this or that." But the question "What is meaning?" does *not* admit of a direct "this or that" answer; its answer is instead a whole theory. It is not a question like "What is the capital of France?" "When did Einstein retire?" "Where is Tasmania?" because it is not merely a request for an isolated fact, a request which can be answered simply and directly. Rather, it is a theoretical question, like "What is matter?" "What is electricity?" "What is light?"

Although these latter questions can really be answered only by theories, we can, of course, give "condensed answers." We can say, for example, that electricity is the property of protons and electrons by virtue of which they exert force on one another over and above their gravitational attraction. Such "condensed answers" make it all the more clear that genuine answers are full theories, for they make sense only in the context of a theory that explicates the theoretical terms used in their formulation.

Linguists and philosophers who have dealt with semantics have found it possible to give some sort of "condensed answer" to the question "What is meaning?" by equating meaning with something else—reference, dispositions to use words correctly, stimuli that elicit and control verbal responses, a body of Platonic archetypes, mental images so connected with words as to serve as their external sensible signs, and so on. Unlike scientists, however, they were satisfied to stop there. Instead of treating such direct answers as "condensed answers," as mere place-holders for a theory, they typically took them as sufficient direct answers and misunderstood the question itself as one that allows a "this or that" type answer. Few saw the necessity of going further, of taking the approach of theory construction, of attempting to work out an answer in the way that the Democritean answer to "What is matter?" was worked out.

This diagnosis seems to me to go quite far in explaining why so little has been accomplished toward constructing a theory that would establish the explanatory utility of the concept of meaning. In these terms it is not hard to understand why skepticism is still possible in semantics and why the interminable controversies that have been a constant feature of the history of semantics continue to rage.[1]

I do not insist, however, that this explanation be accepted as a piece of historical analysis. I can easily see the role of other factors in the continuation of the controversies but I have no desire to evaluate their relative importance. My diagnosis is, rather, put forth as the assessment of the situation that affected the choice of my own approach. It led me to begin with the assumption that "What is meaning?" is a request for a *semantic theory*. Furthermore, it influenced me to

---

[1] Frege is an exception to the general tendency to misconstrue the nature of the question "What is meaning?" Such exceptions have been extremely rare, however, and they have failed to significantly curb the tendency.

try to find an answer in the same manner that physical scientists found an answer to the question " What is matter ?"—to model my attempt to build a semantic theory on their mode of theory construction, insofar as this was possible. Thus, the approach taken here is as follows. We shall attempt to answer the question "What is meaning?" by constructing a theory that explicates the concept of meaning within the framework of a full systematization of the empirical facts about semantic structure in natural language. The goal is a theory of the underlying principles that will interrelate and thus organize the empirical facts within the domain of semantics, and we pursue this goal by following the example set by fruitful scientific cases of theory construction.

Physicists were in no position to say what matter was until they identified a wide range of phenomena exhibited in the behavior of matter and ascertained many of the significant empirical facts in each case. These various phenomena (diffusion, expansion, interpenetration, conduction, etc.) demarcated the domain for a theory of matter by bringing together the properties that such a theory had to explain. It then became possible to compare different conceptions of the nature of matter in terms of their explanatory adequacy within this circumscribed domain. We can say, therefore, that the Democritean theory was arrived at by the construal of the questions " What is diffusion (of matter)?" " What is expansion (of matter)?" " What is interpenetration (of matter)?" and so on as components of the question " What is matter?" This reflects the common practice in science of breaking down a large, general question into narrower, more specific ones. The answers to these questions then form integral parts of the answer to the general question because the phenomena about which they ask are within the appropriate explanatory domain.

To model our attempt to construct a semantic theory on this example, we should first seek to break down the general question " What is meaning?" into a number of narrower, more specific questions that are inherently part of the larger one. Here our pretheoretical intuitions about meaning can guide us. Clearly, an answer to " What is meaning?" presupposes answers to such questions as " What is sameness of meaning?" " What are similarity and difference of meaning?" " What are meaningfulness and meaninglessness?" " What is multiplicity or ambiguity of meaning?" " What is truth by virtue of meaning?" These questions are, then, the analogues to the subquestions of the question " What is matter?"

We can state at the outset the fifteen subquestions in (1.1)–(1.15):

(1.1)   What are synonymy and paraphrase?

(1.2)   What are semantic similarity and semantic difference?

(1.3)   What is antonymy?

(1.4)   What is superordination?

(1.5)   What are meaningfulness and semantic anomaly?

(1.6)   What is semantic ambiguity?

(1.7)   What is semantic redundancy?

(1.8)   What is semantic truth (analyticity, metalinguistic truth, etc.)?

(1.9)   What is semantic falsehood (contradiction, metalinguistic falsehood, etc.)?

(1.10) What is semantically undetermined truth or falsehood (e.g., syntheticity)?

(1.11) What is inconsistency?

(1.12) What is entailment?

(1.13) What is presupposition?

(1.14) What is a possible answer to a question?

(1.15) What is a self-answered question?

These questions pin down the domain of a semantic theory: any theory that offers an answer to "What is meaning?" must answer questions (1.1)–(1.15) and others like them, and any theory that answers such questions must offer an answer to "What is meaning?" In other words, the questions tell us what kinds of phenomena a semantic theory has to explain, namely, those in (1.16)–(1.30):

(1.16) the phenomena of *synonymy* and *paraphrase*, that is, the relation of sameness of meaning—for example, the fact that "fist" and "balled hand," "chocolate sprinkles" and "jimmies," and "John loves Mary's only sister" and "John loves the female sibling of Mary" are synonymous, and the members of the latter pair are paraphrases.

(1.17) the phenomena of *semantic similarity* and *semantic difference*—for example, the fact that such words as "aunt," "cow," "nun," "sister," "woman," "filly," "actress" are semantically similar in one respect, that is, there is a component common to the meaning of each, and the fact that "aunt," "dog," "stone," "leaf," "mote," "mountain," "car" are semantically similar in a respect (i.e., the meaning of each of these words contains the concept of a physical object) that contrasts with the respect in which "shadow," "mirror image," "reflection," "afterimage," "lap" are semantically similar.

(1.18) the phenomenon of *antonymy*, that is, semantic difference of a special sort, namely, incompatibility of meanings—for example, the fact that the members of the word pairs "open" and "close," "whisper" and "shout," "girl" and "boy" are antonymous.

(1.19) the phenomenon of *superordination* (and its inverse, *subordination*)—for example, the fact that "finger" and "thumb," "dwelling" and "cottage," "human" and "boy" are superordinate-subordinate pairs.

(1.20) the phenomena of *meaningfulness* and *semantic anomaly* (i.e., meaninglessness, full or partial)—for example, the fact that the expression "a smelly soap" is meaningful whereas "a smelly itch" is not, as well as the fact that the sentences "Jars empty quickly" and "The man is falling upside down" are both meaningful but the sentences "Shadows empty quickly" and "The hail is falling upside down" are semantically anomalous.

(1.21) the phenomenon of *semantic ambiguity*, that is, multiplicity of senses versus uniqueness of sense—for example, the fact that the words "button," "ball," "foot," "pipe" have more than one sense and the fact that the sentences "There's no school anymore," "I've found the button," "Take your pick" have two or more senses.

(1.22)   the phenomenon of *semantic redundancy*—for example, the fact that "my female aunt," "an adult unmarried male bachelor," "a naked nude" have senses that contain superfluous information, that is, the sense of the modifier is included in the sense of the head.

(1.23)   the phenomenon of *analytic truth*—for example, the fact that each of the sentences "Kings are monarchs," "Uncles are males," "Babies are not adults" is true just by virtue of the fact that the meaning of the subject contains the property expressed by the predicate.

(1.24)   the phenomenon of *contradictoriness*—for example, the fact that each of the sentences "Kings are females," "Uncles are women," "Babies are adults" is false just by virtue of the fact that the meaning of the subject contains information incompatible with what is attributed to it in the predicate.

(1.25)   the phenomenon of *syntheticity*—for example, the fact that the sentences "Kings are generous," "Uncles are verbose," "Babies are cute" are neither true nor false on the basis of meaning alone, that is, their truth or falsity is not settled by the language but depends on what is the case in actuality.

(1.26)   the phenomenon of *inconsistency*—for example, the fact that the sentences "John is alive" and "John is dead" are neither true together nor false together when they refer to the same individual but, rather, one must be true and the other false.

(1.27)   the phenomenon of *entailment*, that is, the relation between two sentences under which one follows necessarily from the other by virtue of a certain semantic relation between them—for example, the fact that the sentence "Monarchs are spendthrifts" entails "Queens are spendthrifts" and the sentence "The car is red" entails "The car is colored."

(1.28)   the phenomenon of *presupposition*—for example, the fact that the interrogative "Where is the key?" presupposes the truth of the declarative "The key is someplace" in the sense that the interrogative expresses a question only in cases where the declarative that expresses its presupposition is true.

(1.29)   the phenomenon of *possible answer*—for example, the fact that the sentences "John arrived at noon," "John arrived on Tuesday," "John arrived a minute ago," "John arrived on Christmas" are possible answers to "When did John arrive?" whereas "John loves to eat fruit," "John is Mary's brother," "Bill arrived yesterday" are not.

(1.30)   the phenomenon of a *self-answered question*—for example, the fact that the interrogatives "Is a spinster female?" and "What is the color of my red wagon?" express questions that are answered in the asking.

That the phenomena cited in (1.16)–(1.30) are semantic in nature and that together they provide us with a reasonable conception of what phenomena the subject of semantics is concerned with seems to me beyond serious doubt, although one or another of the phenomena cited might be shown to be nonsemantic *as the result of the elaboration of some semantic theory*. Having said this, let me add that I do not think that the examples given in (1.16)–(1.30) are nearly as uncontroversial as the phenomena they are intended to illustrate. I do regard them as fairly clear cases, however, at least clear enough to pin down our intuitions at the outset.

It thus seems to me quite natural to require that a semantic theory explain the phenomena just listed and predict the facts within the range of each. This is to say no more than that a linguistic construction's synonymy with another construction, its ambiguity, its semantic redundancy, and so on are due to its meaning. A semantic theory must explain why the meaning of a linguistic construction makes it a case of a certain semantic property or relation, makes it exhibit the phenomenon of synonymy, ambiguity, or redundancy, and so forth.

An answer to "What is meaning?" therefore cannot be given merely by equating the meaning of a linguistic construction with, say, what it names or refers to, or with dispositions according to which it is used correctly, or with the mental idea for which it is the sensible, external sign, or with the eliciting and controlling stimuli that produce it as a verbal response, or with the eternal Platonic archetype for which it stands. Whatever their merit as *leading principles* for the construction of a semantic theory, such equations, as argued previously, cannot by themselves be answers to the general question since they offer no answers to (1.1)–(1.15) and other questions that belong with them. Unless equations of the sort mentioned receive extensive elaboration and development in the form of a general semantic theory that explicates each of the subsidiary concepts in (1.1)–(1.15) as well as whatever other semantic concepts there are, they must remain at the level of first speculations about the answer to "What is meaning?" Whether any such equation provides an adequate basis for a theory to explain these semantic phenomena and predict the known facts in the range of each one is the test of whether it works as a leading principle.

The importance of these phenomena to semantics is revealed in the fact that the standard way of criticizing one or another of these equations is to cite cases where the explanation of one or more such phenomena is inadequate because false predictions are made about semantic properties and relations of linguistic expressions. Let us consider some examples.

First, there is the equation of meaning with reference. As a leading principle, this equation says that we should construct a theory based on the principle that the meaning of an expression is the entity, class of entities, event, class of events, and so on that the expression names (refers to, denotes, designates). Accordingly, the meaning of "Bertrand Russell" is the man named, the meaning of "men" is the class of adult male humans, the meaning of "Columbus' discovery of America" is the historic event of 1492, and so forth. The attraction of this equation seems to be that it brings meaning out into the open, making it something no more mysterious than the things, persons, places, and events of daily life. But Frege's well-known objection to the equation of meaning with reference dashes the hopes for such a simple explanation. His argument was a special case of the criterion that such equations as leading principles must successfully predict semantic properties and relations which are intuitively central to the domain of semantics. Specifically, he argued that the phenomenon of synonymy is inadequately handled on the reference theory. If the meaning of an expression is equated with all and only those things to which it refers, then two expressions must be said to have the same meaning in case they refer to the same things. On this account, Frege pointed out, nonsynonymous expressions like "the morning star" and "the evening star" (or "creature with a heart" and "creature with a kidney") are falsely predicted to by synonymous because, as a matter of contingent fact, they are coreferential. Furthermore, nonsynonymous expressions like "witch" and "warlock" would be taken to be synonymous: since both refer to nothing, it follows that anything one refers to the other does too.

Second, there is the equation of meaning with the system of dispositions determining use. As a leading principle, this equation says that the explication of the meaning of an expression is the explication of the distinctions underlying its correct use in the social art of language. Here, too, the equation fails the critical test. The members of pairs like "bunny" and "rabbit," "piggy" and "pig," "tummy" and "stomach" have different patterns of use: "bunny," "piggy," and "tummy" are appropriately used where the speaker is a young child or is addressing a young child and are inappropriately used in situations where the speakers are adults discussing matters of consequence, yet the meaning of "bunny" and "rabbit" is the same, the meaning of "piggy" and "pig" is the same, and the meaning of "tummy" and "stomach" is the same. Thus, the predictions about synonymy and entailment relations that follow from the equation under examination conflict with our ordinary intuitions.

Third, there is the equation of the meaning of an expression with the image or mental picture for which it is alleged to stand as an external, intersubjective sign. In this case, the distinction between meaningfulness and meaninglessness, that is, the phenomenon of semantic anomaly, is mishandled. Perfectly meaningful words like "possibility," "randomness," "chance," "infinity," "virtue," and a host of others which cannot be said to have a corresponding image or mental picture would be counted as meaningless. In addition to cases of meaningful words for which there is no image present in the mind of the speaker or hearer on occasions of their use, there are meaningless expressions which do conjure up such images. For example, nonsense expressions like Lewis Carroll's "slithy toves" often evoke images and thus would, on this equation, count as meaningful.

When an equation like one of the three just considered is found to conflict with strong pretheoretical intuitions about whether or not an expression or sentence has some linguistic property or relation, and when we take the conflict to be a criticism of the equation's account of meaning, then the particular property or relation concerned must be semantic. Thus, the connection between the general question "What is meaning?" and special questions like (1.1)–(1.15) is just the kind that has been suggested here. If one agrees that the preceding criticisms are relevant to any attempt to answer the question "What is meaning?" then this fact alone establishes the connection between the general question and special ones such as "What is synonymy?" "What is meaningfulness?" "What is semantic anomaly?" "What is entailment?" It also establishes that we have a far better presystematic conception of the domain of semantics than we are usually led to believe. The problem has been that we have not taken the trouble to articulate it. We have not explicitly canvassed our semantic intuitions to find the range of putatively semantic phenomena required to develop a true conception of the subject matter of semantics. Once such phenomena are brought to light by explicitly articulating our pretheoretical conception of this field, it becomes clear that the notion of meaning encompasses an extensive range of systematically related phenomena which, from the ordinary scientific perspective, invites theory construction.

An appreciation of the rich variety of phenomena in the field of semantics inclines us not only toward theory construction but also against skepticism. Many of the attempts to do away with the concept of meaning derive their initial plausibility from the supposition that there are very few, perhaps only one or two, semantic phenomena to be explained away by a program to eliminate the concept of meaning.[2] The emerging extensiveness of the domain of semantics thus undermines the initial plausibility of skepticism. So does the fact that this domain must be considered to be open-ended: clearly, once we have gone as far as enumerating the fifteen semantic properties and relations in (1.16)–(1.30), we can no longer think that we have reached the end, that we have found them all. From this perspective, it becomes quite clear how traditional skeptical efforts fail to come to grips with the problems that confront attempts to dispense with the concept of meaning. It also becomes obvious that much of the initial plausibility of such efforts depends on a narrow and oversimplified view of what a meaning-free linguistic theory would have to explain. No actual attempt to eliminate meanings has ever faced up to the difficulties posed for it by a realistic view of what has to be explained away; thus, none deserves to stand in the way of attempts to found a theory on the concept of meaning.[3]

Quine (1953b), though no friend of the concept of meaning, has defined the situation quite accurately:

> Pending a satisfactory explanation of the notion of meaning, linguists in semantic fields are in the situation of not knowing what they are talking about. This is not an untenable situation. Ancient astronomers knew the movements of the planets remarkably well without knowing what sort of things the planets were. But it is a theoretically unsatisfactory situation, as the more theoretically minded among linguists are painfully aware (p. 47).

The analogy with ancient astronomy is good. It suggests that we try to find out what sort of thing meaning is by going about our investigations in the spirit in which modern astronomers went about discovering what sorts of things planets

---

[2] See my paper "Logic and Language: An Examination of Recent Criticisms of Intensionalism" (to appear) for a discussion of some reasons why this supposition has been made by many contemporary philosophers.

[3] We shall show in Chapter 6 that the best and most influential skeptical arguments against the concept of meaning, namely, Quine's and Goodman's, reduce in the final analysis to nothing essentially more than a stark denial, unsupported by argument, that meaning is a tenable concept.

are. Corresponding to the phenomena of the movements of the planets, which demarcated the scope of explanation for early astronomy, in semantics there are such phenomena as those cited in (1.16)–(1.30), which demarcate the scope of explanation for a theory of meaning. They provide not an exhaustive but a fairly representative list of the types of phenomena that individually belong to the domain of semantics and collectively circumscribe it. While we have as yet no theory to appeal to in order to decide decisively what facts properly belong to semantics, we can take it for granted that the facts in (1.16)–(1.30) do. Ancient astronomy had no bedrock foundation either, only a rich history of careful data collection. As speakers of a natural language, our presystematic intuitions, together with the considerable body of data from traditional lexicography, enable us to identify the aforementioned phenomena as semantic in nature, thereby providing, not a bedrock foundation, but firm enough ground on which to erect a semantic theory. Astronomy found its answer to " What are planets ? " by constructing a theory that explained planetary motion on the assumption that planets are physical objects that obey standard mechanical laws. In the same spirit, once we construct a theory that can successfully explain a reasonably large portion of the semantic phenomena, we can base our answer to " What is meaning ? " on what the theory had to assume meaning was in order to provide its explanations.

On the general character of semantic theory

Everything in nature, whether in the animate or inanimate world, takes place *according to rules,* although we do not always know these rules. Water falls according to gravity, and animal locomotion also takes place according to rules. . . . All nature, indeed, is nothing but a combination of phenomena which follow rules; and *nowhere* is there *any irregularity*. When we think we find any such, we can only say that the rules are unknown.

The exercise of our own faculties takes place also according to certain rules, which we follow at first *unconsciously,* until by a long continued use of our faculties we attain the knowledge of them, and at last make them so familiar, that it costs us much trouble to think of them *in abstracto.* Thus, e.g. general grammar is the form of language in general. One may speak, however, without knowing grammar, and he who speaks without knowing it has really a grammar, and speaks according to its rules of which, however, he is not aware.

Immanuel Kant

Semantic theory, understood as a theory that answers questions such as (1.1)–(1.15) about semantic properties and relations, concerns the semantic structure of natural language in general. It is not a theory concerning the semantic structure of any particular natural language or languages to the exclusion of others. The answers to questions such as (1.1)–(1.15), like the answer to "What is meaning?" cannot be restricted to some limited group of the natural languages of the world. Asking "What is the semantic property P in English?" or "What is the semantic relation H in Chinese?" would be as foolish as asking "What is the biological property P for Englishmen?" or "What is the biological relation H for Chinese?" That is, asking "What is analyticity in English?" or "What is synonymy in Chinese?" is no less foolish than asking "What is a toothache for Englishmen?" or "What is the relation of being sicker than among Chinese?" Questions like (1.1)–(1.15) are thus not about the concepts of analyticity, synonymy, and so on conceived of as relative notions, to be explicated with respect to the particular structure of one or another natural language or some proper subset of the world's languages. Rather, they are to be conceived of as absolute notions, as semantic properties and relations exhibited by words, phrases, clauses, and sentences in each and every natural language. The empirical side of this claim is that, given a natural language which falls outside the proper subset of the world's languages to which such semantic properties and relations have been restricted, fluent speakers of that language can provide examples that exhibit each semantic property and relation in question. Another way of putting this is to say that a list of examples parallel to the list (1.16)–(1.30) for English can be provided for each natural language and, for any proper extension of (1.16)–(1.30), a parallel extension can be provided for each natural language. The philosophical side of this claim is that this linguistic universality is the basis on which the explications of semantic properties and relations in a semantic theory achieve the status of philosophical analyses.

Given that the answers supplied by semantic theory to questions like (1.1)–(1.15) must hold for language in general, the theory must be considered part of the theory of language universals, *linguistic theory* or *the theory of language*, as it has come to be known. This theory seeks an answer to the question " What is a natural language? " in the form of a definition of the concept ' natural language'. Such a definition must capture the essential features of all natural languages, rather than merely picking out natural languages from other forms of communication by citing one differentiating property.[1]

In this chapter we shall discuss some of the general features of the theory of language. Our aim in doing so will be to see to what extent general features of semantic theory can be determined from what we know about the theory of language and about the place semantic theory must occupy in the theory of language. Once we have pinned down in this way some of the general features of semantic theory, we shall present an account of the general makeup of semantic theory as determined by previous work in semantics.

1.   Theories about the objective reality of language

A definition of the concept ' natural language' would provide a theoretical account of the essential structure of natural languages. An attempt to construct such a definition must begin with a conception of the objective or empirical reality of natural languages since it must start with some idea of what is investigated in empirical studies of linguistic structure. The conception of the traditional rationalist theory of grammar, recently rediscovered in the theory of transformational grammar, is that the objective or empirical reality of a language consists in the internalized rules of grammar that constitute the fluency of its native speakers. This is the view of Humboldt and Arnauld. The opposing view of such empiricist linguists as Whitney and Bloomfield is that language consists in a vast stock of sound chunks classifiable into various phonological and syntactic categories, much

---

[1] Natural languages might be differentiated by saying that they are the primary form of communication among human beings, but this would be no more illuminating than saying that an even prime is an integer between one and three.

as the books of a library are classifiable into various fiction and nonfiction subject categories.

The question of the nature of the objective reality of language is by no means a purely speculative one in the metaphysics of linguistics. As the history of this conflict clearly shows, the position taken on this question strongly influences one's conception of what empirical investigations of language are as well as the limitations under which they proceed. When the objective reality of language is taken to be chunks of physical sound, then empirical investigations are conceived as being concerned with the construction and employment of procedures of segmentation and classification which sort concatenations of sound patterns into pigeonholes in a taxonomy. When, instead, language is taken as internalized grammatical rules, the conception of the nature of relevant investigations is quite different: the main concern is with the discovery of hypotheses about the mental capacities that underlie the complex chain of operations by which structures expressing the meaning of a sentence are related to its physical exemplifications. The former conception limits the aspirations of linguistic investigation to uncovering rather superficial facts about the aspects of sentence structure most directly related to properties of the physical speech signal; the latter allows linguistic investigation to concern itself with deeper properties of syntactic organization and semantic interpretation which have no physical realization in utterances. Thus, in retrospect, it is in no way surprising that the primary contribution of the empiricist linguists consisted in providing an enormous body of formally presented facts about phonology and surface syntax, which, however, does not constitute much of a scientific advance over the informal descriptions of encyclopedic grammarians like Jespersen; but the primary contribution of the rationalist linguists was to provide the revolutionary theoretical insight that sentences have a deep level of grammatical organization which determines their overt syntactic and phonetic form, on the one hand, and their semantic properties, on the other, and which makes it possible to explain grammatical properties that cannot be explained without an account of deep structure. Clearly, it was the commitment of the empiricist linguists to the external, material side of language that prevented their recognizing the mental reality that deep structure represents.

The rationale behind adopting the rationalist conception of the objective reality of language can best be appreciated if one first becomes acquainted with the problems inherent in other conceptions. For example, one may attempt to specify the objective reality of a natural language in terms of some set of its sentences that have occurred or will occur; in other words, one may claim that the objective existence of a language lies in speech. This attempt has to fail because the speaker's command of his language far outstrips anything in his own linguistic history or in the history of his language. Regarded apart from various psychological and practical factors, such as memory limitations, human mortality, available quantity of breath, muscle fatigue, tolerance for boredom on the part of hearers, and so forth, the speaker's ability to produce and understand sentences extends over an infinite range of sentential structures. But, due to these psychological and practical factors, infinitely many sentences can never occur. One does not have to be a professional linguist to recognize that there is no grammatical restriction on the number of modifying clauses that may be strung out in a sentence. This, coupled with the recognition that linguistically extraneous factors force us, sooner or later, to bring a sentence to completion, is what underlies the amusement children find in such "sentence stories" as (2.1):

(2.1)   This is the cow with the crumpled horn that tossed the dog that worried the cat that killed the rat that ate the malt ... that lay in the house that Jack built

In this connection, Postal (1964b) has stressed that the linguistically fundamental fact is that

> knowledge of a natural language provides a speaker in principle with knowledge of an infinite set of linguistic objects. Only this assumption, for example, makes it possible to explain why, as the limits on memory are weakened, as with the use of pencil and paper, a speaker's abilities to use and understand sentences are extended to those of greater length. It is no accident that traditionally, for example, written German involves lengthy and complex constructions not normally found in the spoken language. The analogy with arithmetic is appropriate here. One who has learned the rules of arithmetic is clearly capable in principle of determining the result of multiplying any two of the infinite set of whole numbers. Yet obviously no one ever has or ever could compute more than a small finite number of such multiples (p. 247).

Since a speaker can produce no more than a finite number of sentences and since the sum of the finite productions of the finitely many speakers in the history of a language is also finite, it follows that the history of a language contains only a finite sample of the infinite set of sentences that belong to the language.[2]

To do justice to the infinite nature of language while still retaining the idea that the objective reality of a language is a set of sentences, one might try, as many have, to say that the objective existence of a language is the set of sentences that *could* occur without eliciting oddity reactions from speakers. But this approach can succeed in grounding the study of linguistic structure in some objective reality only if the proposal is understood as saying that the objective existence of a language consists in the dispositions of speakers. Since there is no upper bound on sentence length, the sentences which are to constitute the empirical reality of a language are unactualizable possibilities, except for an arbitrary finite set of sentences, namely, those sufficiently short and sufficiently "fortunate" to occur in speech. There being nothing empirically real about unactualizable possibilities, it seems necessary to drop the idea that the objective existence of a language, the empirical reality investigated in its study, can be specified in terms of sentences given in speech; instead we must specify it in terms of the linguistic dispositions characteristic of a language community.

Speakers often respond appropriately to grammatical and to ill-formed strings of words. They will say, for example, that (2.2) is a well-formed part of English, but that its reverse, (2.3), is grammatical word salad:

[2] See Katz (1966, p. 121n).

(2.2)   Now is the time for all good men to come to the aid of their party

(2.3)   Party their of aid the to come to men good all for time the is now

But the idea of using such reactions as a guide to what is or is not in a language, of specifying the objective existence of a language in terms of the dispositions of speakers, is not adequate without qualification. Dispositions, thought of as tendencies to respond, vary with all sorts of linguistically irrelevant factors such as mood changes, beliefs, motives, mores, memory, health, brain conditions, nutrition, and drugs. Thus, although speakers exhibit reliable judgments about grammatical oddity, they exhibit unreliable ones, too. Obviously, then, we must qualify "dispositions" by making some distinction between factors that produce irrelevant variations in responses and those that do not. Otherwise every influence becomes tantamount to a change in the language. To specify the objective reality of a language in terms of linguistic dispositions of its speakers to make judgments about whether a string of words is grammatical, it is further required that there be a way of construing these dispositions so that, on the basis of finite data from the judgments obtained from speakers, we can inductively project distinctions between grammaticality and ungrammaticality over an infinite range of sentences and non-sentences. That is, the dispositions must be thought of as incorporating recursive mechanisms of sentence generation. Granting these two provisions, referring to dispositions is the same as saying that the empirical existence of a natural language lies in the linguistic rules internalized by its speakers.

Let us illustrate with a simple case, analogous to natural language. Suppose we encounter a black box with a device inside that "tells" us whether or not a given string in an alphabet whose only symbols are 'a' and 'b' is grammatical in the box language. The language has an infinite set of strings in this alphabet. If we make up a string of any number of occurrences of 'a's and 'b's and feed it into the black box, the device inside will return the string to us if it is grammatical in the language but will give no output if the string is ungrammatical. Now suppose that after a great number of trials, we have obtained the list of returned strings exemplified in (2.4):

(2.4)   *ab, aabb, aaabbb, aaaabbbb, aaaaabbbbb, aaaaaabbbbbb*, ...

We assume that the device has a theoretically infinite capacity to evaluate strings and that due to nonlinguistic factors this capacity is mapped onto a finite output. Now, we can say that the objective existence of the language in question is the box's disposition to make an oddity response (that is, to do nothing) when given an ungrammatical string and to accept when given a grammatical one, or we can say that it is a system of recursive rules defining the property of grammaticality in the box language, a system somehow built into the device. The trouble with talking about dispositions *simpliciter* is that attention is drawn away from the inherent structure of the language, making it appear as if there is nothing left to explain. This structure can, of course, be inferred for the box language from the data in (2.4): the grammaticality of a string consists in its taking the form of n occurrences of 'a' followed by n occurrences of 'b'. Still, one could always say that the box has the disposition to approve a string just in case it has the specified form. At this point, the distinction between dispositions and rules disappears completely. In either way of talking, we can simulate the output of the black box by a grammar that specifies its language as the set of strings L that is produced by the rules in (2.5):

$$(2.5) \quad E: \quad Z$$
$$F_1: \quad Z \rightarrow ab$$
$$F_2: \quad Z \rightarrow aZb$$

The advocate of dispositional description does not think that the box works by magic but thinks it contains some physical mechanism capable of producing the set of strings, some device that physically realizes the grammar (2.5). The advocate of rule description, on the other hand, does not talk about the actual physical form taken by the realization of the grammar (2.5) in the box. Both are supposing the existence of a physical mechanism inside the box with a structure suitable to producing the output, and neither commits himself to an account of the particular form of this realization of (2.5). Moreover, both would believe that the tendency to respond approvingly when and only when the input is a string generated by (2.5) is itself to be explained on the basis of a hypothesis about the structure of the device inside the box. Hence, both are saying the same thing, and we may regard talk about dispositions to be merely an oblique way of talking about internalized rules.

Thus, instead of taking the objective existence of a language to be the dispositions of the members of the community who speak it, we take it to be their internalizations of the linguistic rules that recursively define the language. Note that, on the interpretation just given, the claim that the objective existence of a language lies in internalized linguistic rules is no more ontologically ambitious than the claim that its objective existence consists in the dispositions of the members of the speech community.

It would be a mistake to go on now to identify a natural language like English with the actual internalized realizations of its rules. Such an error is made when, thinking of an idiolect as a single individual's linguistic rules, a natural language is equated with the class of idiolects of its speakers or, less directly, with the class of dialects, where each dialect is thought of as a collection of idiolects. The mistake in identifying English, or any natural language, with the concrete realizations of the linguistic rules in the heads of its speakers is akin to that of identifying arithmetic with the concrete realizations of the mathematical rules in the heads of those who can compute using positive real numbers. The error consists in conflating a language with its empirical exemplifications. This distinction is quite apparent in the expressions "living language" and "dead language," where the former means a language for which there are native speakers who use it as their means of communication and the latter means a language for which there are no such speakers. Nothing happens to the language itself when it becomes a dead language, but only to its speakers. Sanskrit, though dead, is still the same language as it was during the time of the Pānini grammarians. A language is not itself subject to the fate of the mortals who speak it. It is some sort of abstract entity, whatever it is that this means.

By conflating the distinction between language and the concrete realizations of rules in speakers' minds, we would define a language as the class of its empirical exemplifications or as what is common to them. But either definition would lead to an incorrect account of specific languages: in the former case the account would be too broad; in the latter, too narrow. The rub is that exemplifications suffer from imperfections of all kinds. Consider the parallel situation of the biological conception of human genetic endowment. This abstraction cannot be identified with the class consisting of the gene systems of each human being who has ever and will ever live, the particular gene systems that made you and me human beings rather than bears, beans, or bacteria. Nor can it be regarded as referring to whatever features such gene systems have in common. In the former case, the concept would be too broad, including many factors that have no place in a genetic definition of 'human being'; in the latter case, the concept would be too narrow, excluding many factors that have a place in this definition. The former would allow any of the idiosyncratic, or individual, characteristics which ought to be abstracted away in defining this concept, while the latter would disallow some general characteristics because there are freaks that do not share them. The concept of human genetic endowment is therefore an idealization, analogous to the physicist's perfect vacuum or ideal gas. Similarly, the concept of a natural language ought to be taken as an idealization which is exemplified empirically by its speakers. This is the view that Chomsky (1965) had in mind when he wrote:

> Linguistic theory is concerned primarily with an ideal speaker-listener, in a completely homogeneous speech-community, who knows its language perfectly and is unaffected by such grammatically irrelevant conditions as memory limitations, distractions, shifts of attention and interest, and errors (random or characteristic) in applying his knowledge of the language in actual performance. This seems to me to have been the position of the founders of modern general linguistics, and no cogent reason for modifying it has been offered (pp. 3–4).

A similar view was once espoused by Carnap (1937), with one significant exception. Carnap wrote:

> The direct analysis of [natural languages], which has been prevalent hitherto, must inevitably fail, just as a physicist would be frustrated were he from the outset to attempt to relate his laws to natural things—trees, stones, and so on. In the first place, the physicist relates his laws to the simplest of constructed forms; to a thin straight lever, to a simple pendulum, to punctiform masses, etc. Then, with the help of the laws relating to these constructed [idealized] forms, he is later in a position to analyze into suitable elements the complicated behavior of real bodies, and thus control them. One more comparison: the complicated configurations of mountain chains, rivers, frontiers, and the like are most easily represented and investigated by the help of geographical co-ordinates—or, in other words, by constructed lines not given in nature. In the same way, the syntactical property of a particular word-language, such as English, or of word-languages, or of a particular sub-language of a word-language, is best represented and investigated by comparison with a constructed language which serves as a system of reference (p. 8).

The exception, which distinguishes Carnap's approach from the linguist's, is that the "constructed language" of which Carnap speaks is not construed as an empirical theory about the structure of natural language but rather as an artificially invented system that may embody any set of principles, no matter how far they might diverge from those of the language for which the system "serves as a system of reference." These systems not only are under no empirical controls to insure that their principles reflect the regularities in natural language, but they are put forth with the express purpose of supplying principles to govern cases where, it is assumed, there are no regularities in natural language.[3] Thus, Carnap conceives of his constructed languages as idealizations for which the descriptive and explanatory goals of science are given up in favor of prescriptive standards whose purpose is to reform natural languages. On our view, on the other hand, linguistic theory is conceived of as an idealization for which the descriptive and explanatory goals of science are retained and serve as the standards for determining how well the theory accounts for the structure of natural language.

2.   Effability

The basic function of natural languages is to serve as vehicles of communication for their speakers.[4] But function does not distinguish them from "languages" of other sorts, for many types of systems serve as vehicles of communication. Therefore this distinction must be drawn in terms of the range of information that can be communicated and the manner in which it is communicated. The hypothesis that will be put forth in this section is that natural languages alone are unlimited

---

[3] It is with regard to this aspect, not Carnap's stress on idealization per se, that I have criticized his conception of the philosophy of language (see Katz (1966, pp. 62–68)). It should be pointed out here that, although Carnap's conception of a constructed language as an idealization of a natural language would appear to entail the need for empirical constraints, this is immediately contradicted by his rationale for such constructed languages, namely, that they are to supply semantic conventions that are absent in natural languages. If a natural language does not contain semantic regularities (of the sort that would enable us to mark "Caesar is a prime number" as deviant) and a constructed language must be introduced just to provide the missing semantic restrictions (according to which "Caesar is a prime number" is shown to involve a category mistake), then it is inconsistent to hold that a constructed language is an idealization in the usual scientific sense. For, if we understand the notion of an idealization in the way it is understood as a description of theories in physics, then, as an idealization, a constructed language must state (in idealized form, but, nonetheless, state) the regularities *in* the natural language of which it is an idealization. Carnap cannot have it both ways. Either he forgoes construing such languages as idealizations or he gives up the rationale for introducing them. Since this rationale is more basic to his program than is the particular interpretation of constructed languages as idealizations, it is clear that it was a mistake on Carnap's part to have taken over this interpretation of his constructed languages from physical theory. Yet the mistake leads to a far more fruitful conception of what a theory of language is than does Carnap's conception of it as a body of rigorously formulated prescriptive conventions.

[4] There is, however, a genuine qualification required for the claim that communication is the basic function of a natural language. As Sapir (1958) wrote: "The primary function of language is generally said to be communication. There can be no quarrel with this so long as it is distinctly understood that there may be effective communication without overt speech and that language is highly relevant to situations which are not obviously of a communicative sort.... It is best to admit that language is primarily a vocal actualization of the tendency to see realities symbolically, that it is precisely this quality which renders it a fit instrument for communication and that it is in the actual give and take of social intercourse that it has been complicated and refined into the form in which it is known today" (p. 15).

in the range of information that can be communicated through their sentences. Other communication systems can transmit messages that are transmittable by natural languages, but no other permits the transmission of any message whatever, unless, like a code, it is essentially parasitic on a natural language.

The principle on which this hypothesis depends, which I will call the *principle of effability*, was, to the best of my knowledge, first suggested by Frege (1963). He observed that the expressive capacities of a natural language are such that

> a thought grasped by a human being for the first time can be put into a form of words which will be understood by someone to whom the thought is entirely new (p. 1).

Frege's version of the principle might be explicated as follows: anything which is thinkable is communicable through some sentence of a natural language (because the structure of sentences mirrors the structure of thoughts). The principle of expressibility suggested by Searle (1969, pp. 19–21), that whatever a speaker might want to communicate can be said, and the principle of universality posited by Tarski (1956, p. 164), that natural languages can express whatever can be meaningfully spoken about, are other versions of the same principle. There are differences among these statements, but their essence is that each human thought is expressible by some sentence of any natural language. And, indeed, one does almost inevitably find a sentence in his language to express what he wants to say, even though the process may not always be easy and the final choice may not always be the best way to say it. Failure means the person is not sufficiently skillful in exploiting the richness of his language rather than that the language is not rich enough in expressive power. We have each had the experience of not being able to think of the proper sentence, only to find later that someone more skillful succeeded where we had failed. It would clearly be absurd for anyone to assert that he cannot communicate one of his thoughts because English has no sentence that expresses it, to try to shift the blame from himself to the English language. I take it as some empirical evidence for the claim that natural languages are effable that speakers almost always find appropriate sentences to express their thoughts, that difficulties in thinking of a sentence are invariably regarded as a failing on the part of the speaker rather than of the language, and that there is nothing to indicate that there is any type of information that cannot be communicated by the sentences of a natural language.

There is no point, in the present theoretical context, in trying to argue extensively on behalf of the claim that natural languages are effable. It is, I think, even somewhat premature to try to provide a fully precise formulation of effability. This will come in the course of the development of the theory of language. However, we can say a few things to sharpen the principle.

Some philosophers will criticize the principle as being unverifiable. They will argue that we can determine what is thinkable only in terms of what is sayable, so that there can be no case where the principle can be shown false, that is, no case of something thinkable but not sayable. Such an argument, like most appeals to verificationalism, fails to take account of the possibilities of indirect disproof.

One could refute the charge of unverifiability by considering science fiction situations involving nonlinguistic devices such as cerebroscopes for determining what someone thinks. However, it suffices to point out that it follows from the effability thesis that each natural language is capable of expressing the same body of thoughts and that this implies (but is not implied by) the claim that all natural languages are intertranslatable in the sense that, for any sentence of one natural language, there is at least one sentence in every other natural language that expresses the same proposition. Accordingly, if we find one sentence in one natural language that has no translation in some other natural language, the thesis is false.

Not only can we thus show the falsifiability of the thesis, we can also describe an alternative theory which fits the facts so far adduced in favor of the principle of effability. It seems reasonable enough, at first glance, to rest the plausibility of the effability thesis on the success of speakers in exploiting the expressive power of their language. However, the fact that speakers can say whatever they want to say in their language might not be due to the unrestricted richness of the language as much as to the degree of poverty of their cognitive faculties. This possibility will not appear strange if we recall that the relativity thesis of Sapir and Whorf tells us that a language shapes the categories and forms of thought of those who acquire it natively. The thesis need not be construed as denying that the innate intellectual equipment of people in different language communities is the same; rather, it should be construed as saying that the interplay between biological nature and linguistic nurture results in significant and immutable differences between the mature cognitive faculties of people in different language communities. On this view, it is quite reasonable to suppose that a language might actually be highly limited in the range of thoughts it can express (say, with respect to another language) but that, because learning the language has accordingly limited the cognitive faculties of its speakers, every thought of theirs is expressible in their language. Thus, we now have a new principle, which we may refer to as the *principle of local effability*, namely, for any thought T of a native speaker of a natural language L, there is a sentence of L whose sense expresses T, but for some thought T_1 of a native speaker of a natural language L_1 and some different natural language L_2, there is no sentence of L_2 whose sense expresses T_1. The general success of speakers of a natural language in expressing what they have to say in their language is accounted for by both our principle of effability and the principle of local effability.

The basic issue, then, is an empirical one of whether translation is always possible between any pair of natural languages. Given this formulation of the issue, there arises an immediate objection to the effability thesis, the consideration of which allows us to sharpen significantly its formulation. The vocabulary of the languages of what are sometimes called primitive peoples is far less rich than that of more technologically advanced people, especially in the area of terms that express the most subtle concepts of physical science. Thus, it may be asked what sense it makes to suppose that sentences of English that express complicated laws of modern physics can be translated into the language of some South Sea Island people who still think that inanimate objects are inhabited by spirits.

To make the effability thesis sharp enough to answer this question, let us suppose the following situation. A native of a primitive society comes to the United States and goes through a college program in physics. He is bilingual, but his society is not. On his return he is required to teach the elders of his society what he has learned, but the elders refuse to learn English. What he must therefore do is either use English words for concepts not in his language or else make up words that more readily fit into the phonology of the language. In either case he will have to introduce a large stock of new words, but he will rely on the already existing semantic structure of the native language to define them and on the already existing syntactic and phonological structure of the native language to make it possible to form sentences with them that express the laws of modern physics. If he can, in principle, perform this task of education, it follows that the native language is effable, in our sense of effability. We do not suppose that by so enlarging the vocabulary of his native language he has in fact changed the language essentially, just as we do not assume that English has changed essentially as a result of the increase in the number of vocabulary items brought about by the rise of science in the last hundred years, and we do not assume that modern Hebrew, with its highly modernized vocabulary, is not Hebrew. The concept of effability thus rests on the following principle about the conditions of linguistic stability and change: a language L cannot be said to have changed over the period from t_1 to t_2, even though the optimal grammar G_L at t_1 does not generate the set of sentences S and S is generated by the optimal grammar of L at t_2, if it is the case that merely the addition of a finite number of lexical items to G_L would enable it to generate S, where the notion of adding lexical items is understood as adding as yet unused phonological possibilities. The syntactic features governing the distribution of the new lexical item in sentences and its semantic representation are not new but already part of G_L. (For an example see Section 5 of Chapter 7.)

One might now be tempted to jump to the conclusion that the question at issue here is no more than a straightforward empirical matter of whether there will be general success in translating from one language to another. If the facts show that there will be such success, then Frege and Tarski are correct; if the facts show otherwise, then Sapir and Whorf are right. But the facts are not at all clear. While supporters of the view of Frege and Tarski can point to one well-translated book after another, supporters of Sapir and Whorf can point to many unresolved disputes about translations. The reason the issue cannot be settled as straightforwardly as one would expect in the case of a purely empirical matter is the same as the reason that disputes about translations continue, namely, the issue is not purely empirical. Rather, there is a serious conceptual problem involved as well, that is, there is the problem of specifying just what properties of sentences must be preserved in translation. Without a solution to this problem, we have no way to judge what would count as a real counterexample to a claim that one sentence is a translation of another. But the set of properties with respect to which we determine whether a sentence from one language has the same literal meaning as a sentence from another is exactly what determines sameness of meaning generally. Thus, if what we have argued in Chapter 1 about the prospects for a semantic theory is right, it follows that the conceptual problem standing in the way of a decision about effability can only be solved in the course of the development of semantic theory. I will thus assume that further clarification and justification of the effability thesis is tied in with the development of semantic theory as a whole. I am well aware that there are philosophical objections to any program that assumes it is possible to define the conditions under which sentences express the same proposition, have the same sense, or, in case they are from different languages, are translations of one another. I urge that these objections be set aside for the time being. I will devote Chapter 6 to an attempt to answer them.

Effability makes a very strong claim about natural languages. What is so important about this claim that one should take on its defense? First, there is the fact that without it there is no basis for an interlinguistic notion of proposition on which to base hypotheses about the relation of logic and language. Less obviously, it seems that effability alone offers a satisfactory basis for drawing the distinction between natural languages, on the one hand, and systems of animal communication and artificial languages, on the other.

Chomsky (1966a) has proposed that this distinction be drawn on the basis of the properties of creativity, stimulus freedom, and appropriateness. But, although these properties are certainly important ones for linguistics, they do not enable us to draw the distinction. Creativity is the property of a system of rules by virtue of which someone who knows them is able, in principle, to produce indefinitely many sentences and to understand new sentences produced by others on the basis of the same system. But this property is found in both communication systems of animals and in artificial languages. Any artificial language with recursion built into it, even one of a highly restricted form like the propositional calculus, will be creative in the appropriate sense. Moreover, creativity is also a feature of certain animal communication systems. For example, a scout bee can produce new dances that are immediately "understood" by other bees, and such new dances can be drawn from an indefinitely large, theoretically infinite domain.[5] Stimulus freedom, the second property cited by Chomsky, means freedom from the control of *external* stimuli in the production of verbal behavior. It cannot mean freedom from the control of internal stimuli as well. But in this sense, freedom is not a special property of someone's linguistic competence; rather, it is the result of the thought processes that intervene between external stimulus and behavioral response, whether verbal or not. Furthermore, we find stimulus freedom exhibited in behavior of one sort or another among a wide variety of animals. Finally, appropriateness, which is a property of an utterance in context, appears also not to be a property of linguistic competence. Whether an utterance is appropriate to the context in which it occurs depends not only on its grammar but also on the things in the context, the goings-on in the minds of the speaker and hearer, particularly what each knows about what is going on in the mind of the other, and so on. (Why this is so will be clarified in Section 5 of Chapter 8.) Furthermore, as far as we know, appropriateness too is a feature of animal communication systems (as, for example, in the case of social bees).

[5] See Von Frisch (1953) and Lindauer (1961).

Expressive power, on the other hand, seems to be the natural dimension on which to distinguish natural languages from communication systems of animals and from artificial languages. The "dance language" of social bees, which figured in the preceding discussion, is restricted in its expressive power to communicating information about the location of food sources and the quality, distance, direction, and perhaps elevation of nesting areas. Artificial languages, such as those with which we are familiar from the work of Carnap and others, typically are narrowly restricted in expressive power, and when they are not, they gain their new-found expressive power parasitically, that is, through the introduction of stipulative definitions that connect their symbols to words, expressions, and sentences of a natural language, thereby obtaining the senses of the latter by transfer.

It is not necessary to claim that effability is the distinguishing property of natural languages in order to differentiate them from animal communication systems and artificial languages, for every case of both of the latter systems is *sharply* limited in expressive power by comparison to natural languages. The question thus arises whether full effability is necessary, since natural languages might be expressively rich to an extent that exceeds these other cases without being able to express the totality of what is thinkable. But there is no way to set a limit at some point short of effability, at least as far as I can now tell.[6] Furthermore, it is reasonable to try the strongest, most informative hypothesis about expressibility first. And it seems natural that the creative intellectual capacities of human beings should have an instrument of communication that is suited to them. Biologically, then, the effability of human languages fits in well with the various degrees of ineffability found in animals with a more restricted intellectual makeup.

The basic problem of linguistic theory, from this perspective, is to provide a definition of 'natural language' that explains how the linguistic competence of

---

[6] Herzberger (1970) makes it look as if such a limit is necessary and as if we know something about the considerations that might set this limit. Herzberger writes: "This *universality thesis*, which Tarski offers by way of the semantic paradoxes, puts forward a striking claim which, if the means be available, deserves being put to the test. ... I propose to show that universality cannot be the spirit of natural language, inasmuch as every conceptual framework suffers the same kind of inherent limitations on expressive capacity that have long been recognized in connection with languages built upon quantification theory. The result ... has certain unsettling consequences for semantic theory and for the philosophical issue of the relation between language and thought" (p. 147). However, when we examine Herzberger's results, we find that he has not shown any need for restricting the claim that full effability is the essential feature of natural languages. The appearance to the contrary depends on failing to make two distinctions, first, between a language and a theory, only the latter of which has postulates, statements put forth as the basic truths about some domain, and second, between the effability thesis, which is defined in terms of the *senses* of sentences, and what we may call the *statability thesis*, which is defined in terms of the statements expressed by sentences. Making both these distinctions, we note that Herzberger's conclusion that "any linguisitic theory is either essentially inexpressible in natural language or else is essentially incomplete" (p. 167) in no way excludes the effability of natural languages, since his disjunctive conclusion is satisfied if the effability thesis is true and linguistic *theory* is incomplete. This means that the principles that cannot be added to this theory without rendering it inconsistent, but which are nonetheless necessary for its completeness, are expressed in the senses of sentences in natural languages. That is, nothing in Herzberger's argument precludes these or other thinkables from being so expressible, though, of course, the argument precludes them from being statable, i.e., from being statable under conditions that qualify them for statementhood. The statability thesis cannot be "the spirit" of natural language.

a speaker provides him with a rich enough range of sentence structures to express any of his thoughts, regardless of their degree of novelty. Such unrestricted communication clearly depends on the ability of the speaker and hearer to pair the same meaning with each sentence. Thus, a definition of 'natural language' that comes to grips with the problem of explaining effability must begin by explicating the principles of encoding and decoding by which speakers of a natural language find the appropriate words for expressing their thoughts and find out what thoughts are expressed by the words they hear.

3. Competence and performance

If we look at linguistic communication from an ordinary, common sense viewpoint, it is a process that involves the transmission of one person's thoughts to another by means of disturbances in the air which the first person creates for this purpose. Somehow the speaker encodes his inner thoughts in the form of external, observable acoustic events, and the hearer, perceiving these sounds, decodes them, thereby obtaining for himself his own inner representation of the speaker's thoughts. It is in this way that we use language to obtain knowledge of the contents of another's mind.

We can assume that the encoding, by which a thought is transformed into instructions for the muscles of the articulatory tract and then into a syntactically structured and acoustically realized pattern of sound, proceeds in part by the same principles as the decoding, by which such sound patterns are transformed back into a thought. If the way in which the speaker finds the words with which to express his thought is not, at least in part, the same way that his hearer recovers the thought from the articulated words, the fact that different speakers of the same language can freely exchange positions as speaker and hearer, always associating the same thought with the same sentence, would be incomprehensible. Therefore, the basic question to ask is what are these common principles for encoding and decoding.

But this question does not define the subject matter of linguistic theory. There are facets of an ideal speaker-hearer's ability to pair messages and signals that are in the domain not of linguistic theory but of other theories that, together with linguistic theory, comprise a general theory of linguistic communication. Accordingly, to characterize properly the subject matter of linguistic theory, we must distinguish those aspects of the speaker-hearer's ability that belong to the domain of linguistic theory from those that belong to theories outside linguistics and from those that belong to different theories inside linguistics.

When we study a complex mental ability, we initially face the problem of how to sort out the different aspects that interplay in its exercise so that each is parceled out to the particular discipline that treats of matters of that kind. In the special case of the ability to communicate in a natural language, as Chomsky has stressed repeatedly and as we have pointed out here, we must distinguish between the aspects that concern the speaker's *linguistic competence*, that is, what an ideal speaker knows about the grammatical structure of his language that makes it possible for him to communicate in it, and his *linguistic performance*, that is, how he utilizes his linguistic competence to communicate with his fellow speakers in actual speech situations. Hence, the general theory of linguistic communication is composed of two separate but related theories, one a theory of competence and the other a theory of performance.

In the theory of linguistic competence we seek to state the system of rules that formally represents the ideal linguistic structures that underlie the utterances of natural speech. We idealize away from the distortions and irregularities characteristic of natural speech and concern ourselves with the systematization of those aspects of natural speech that directly reflect the contribution of a speaker's fluency. The theory of linguistic performance, on the other hand, seeks to account for the principles that speakers use in actually producing and understanding natural speech. Accordingly, the study of performance assumes the contribution of competence and directs its attention to the manner in which the contributions of various psychological factors—e.g., memory limitations, attention shifts, distractions, brain damage, errors—interplay with linguistic factors to produce natural speech, with all its characteristic distortions and irregularities.

Confusion about the competence-performance distinction has sometimes arisen due to a failure to be clear about the related but different distinction between the *linguistic* and the *psychological*. The confusion arises because, on the one hand, linguists concern themselves with competence while psychologists concern themselves with performance, while, on the other hand, it is plain that psychologists cannot ignore competence in their psycholinguistic investigations and that linguists learn from observing performance. To avoid confusion, one must recognize that although both linguists and psychologists must concern themselves with competence they do so in different ways, and the difference is determined by the distinction between the linguistic and the psychological. The linguist's concern with competence is like the mathematician's concern with arithmetic, that is, he is interested in abstract relations between elements and structures of a timeless, logical realm. His concern with performance has to do only with obtaining facts about linguistic structure in the only place where such facts can be obtained, namely, from the verbal reports or other behavioral indications speakers give about their linguistic intuitions. The psychologist, on the other hand, is interested in the nature of the brain (or mental) mechanisms in which such abstract structures are empirically realized and whose operations causally underlie verbal behavior. What makes his concern with linguistic ability psychological is that he seeks to construct a real-time model of the brain (or mind) which describes the form in which the grammar and the auxiliary performance mechanisms are realized. Thus, given that, logically speaking, a grammar can be physically realized in indefinitely many ways, the linguist tries to formulate an abstract description of the information that can be realized in each of these ways while the psychologist tries to find out in which way it is actually realized.

A number of philosophers, chief among whom is Harman (1967; 1969), have taken issue with Chomsky's statement of the competence-performance distinction. I do not wish to take up this controversy, however, since, as one turns from initial criticism to rejoinder, from rejoinder to reply to the rejoinder, and from the reply to the rejoinder to its rebuttal,[7] it appears more and more a terminological matter. It seems to me that Chomsky is correct in contending that Harman mistakenly attributes to him the conception that competence is the "knowledge that the language is described by the rules of the grammar" (which makes the speaker into a superlinguist) and "knowing how to speak and understand a language." Moreover, it strikes me as being of little theoretical importance whether Chomsky's conception of linguistic competence as the tacit (or unconscious) knowledge that speakers have of the structure of their language fits into the Rylean categories of 'knowing how' and 'knowing that'. Harman says that such knowledge is neither 'knowing how' nor 'knowing that' and goes on to raise difficulties about the intelligibility of Chomsky's conception. Chomsky's reply is that these categories have not been shown to be exhaustive, and until they are, Harman's criticisms do not apply. I think it fair enough for Chomsky to give this reply, but it opens a communication gap between transformationalist linguists and philosophers who have grown up with these Rylean categories. Without more discussion than Chomsky provides in this dispute about the kind of knowledge he takes competence to be, and without the familiar 'knowing how' and 'knowing that' categories, there is bound to be much talking at cross-purposes. Finally, it is not clear that there is any necessity to grant Harman's premiss that competence should not be taken as a form of 'knowing that'. Let us consider this option.

What seems to bother philosophers when linguists use "know" as Chomsky does is the reference to something unconscious as knowledge. Can we say that a native speaker of English knows that an ordinary English adjective-noun construction is derived from an embedded sentential structure by assigning a *wh* to the subject noun phrase, replacing the NP so marked by a pro-form, deleting the pro-form together with the copula of the embedded sentence structure, and inverting the adjective and the subject NP of the matrix structure? Wouldn't we say, rather, that the speaker does not know this relative clause rule until he learns it (in a course on formal grammar or out of a text)? The answer is that the speaker does learn the rule but the rule only explicates his tacit knowledge: what he didn't know before and comes to know as a result of his studies is the grammarian's explication of the speaker's unconscious knowledge.

But, then, why should we say that the untrained speaker has any such tacit knowledge when we would not say that he has the chemist's knowledge of the structure of poisons because he responds differentially to poisons and nonpoisons? A linguist's knowledge of the relative clause rule constitutes part of an explanatory theory of grammaticality in English, just as the chemist's knowledge of poisons constitutes part of an explanatory theory of substances. Moreover, in both the case of the speaker responding to ungrammatical relatives and the person responding to poisons, the response can occur without conscious mediation. Since a human can be a barometer for distinguishing sentences from nonsentences and, at the physiological level, a barometer for distinguishing poisons from nonpoisons, there is no distinction at hand. But were we restricted to this level of description, we would be unable to say anyone knows anything. Thus, when we say that someone

---

[7] See Harman (1967), Chomsky (1969b), Harman (1969), and Chomsky (1969a).

knows something—for example, that two plus two is four—we assume another level of description, a level at which cognitive concepts apply. The same distinction is of course involved when we differentiate the speaker's response in making the intuitive judgment that a certain string of words is ungrammatical from his exhibition of a conditioned response (e.g., an eye blink) to an ungrammatical string (as a result of having a puff of air blown on his eye whenever he is presented with an ungrammatical string).

The critic can be expected to agree but to maintain that what we are discussing is still at the level of consciousness: we say someone knows that two plus two is four because we know he consciously apprehends this arithmetic truth. At this point psychology suggests an extension, namely, that knowledge consists of conscious knowledge plus what can be brought to consciousness under appropriate conditions, for example, the psychoanalytic situation. (See Nagel (1969).)

Consider the following experiment. After having spent a few minutes in an unfamiliar room, subjects are asked to list as many of the objects that were in it as they can remember. When they have made such a list (including about twenty to thirty objects in one such experiment), the first phase of the experiment is over. In the second phase they are hypnotized and again asked to list the objects. This time they are able to list many more than they could recall previously, in fact, almost ten times as many. Now, there is no hesitation in saying that a subject *knows that* there was an apple in the room when he correctly lists it in the first phase. But what about a statement made during the first phase of the experiment that the subject knows that there was a peach in the room when at that time he cannot recall seeing one? If during the second phase he correctly lists a peach (and his other new items are all correct), we are by no means stretching language when we say that the statement about his knowing a peach was in the room is true.

What is suggested by this experiment, when spelled out, is that knowledge encompasses conscious knowledge together with whatever is inherently indistinguishable from it save for being unconscious. Under appropriate conditions we can intuitively come to grasp the fact that we had a certain thought that we didn't consciously realize we had. The psychologist can say that the thought has been brought to consciousness because the hypothesized unconscious thought is identical to the now conscious one and bears the same causal relation to relevant behavior. The trouble with this interesting suggestion from psychology is that it does not go far enough. The critic is able to argue that explicit knowledge of the relative clause rule, like explicit knowledge of the chemistry of poisons, is simply acquired, not brought to consciousness in the manner of subliminal memories or repressed thoughts. We do not intuitively recognize abstract generalizations like the relative clause rule in the way that we do the grammaticality or ungrammaticality of a string of words. They are not the same and they do not bear the same relation to behavior. The situation with respect to the relative clause rule, rather than being like one encountered in psychology and psychoanalysis, is instead like Socrates' claim in the *Meno* about the slave boy's knowledge of geometry.

The bias on the part of the critic is not against unconscious knowledge per se; it is the empiricist's bias against unconscious knowledge of general principles, that is, a rejection of one of the two major assumptions of rationalism (the other being that in certain instances such principles are not learned). But rationalists have a clear sense of 'knowing that' which can be applied to the claim that a speaker of English knows the relative clause rule. Moreover, this sense, unlike the suggestion from psychology, does not block on the distinction between intuitions and generalizations expressing the principle underlying a set of intuitions. Rationalists would claim that if intuitions about some phenomenon can be explained only on the assumption that they reflect the employment of a rule that finitely specifies the theoretically infinite set of such intuitions (from which the actual intuitions are an arbitrary sample), then someone who knows the facts about this phenomenon on the basis of his intuitions must also know the rule. In other words, if supposing that someone knows a rule is the way to explain successfully how he can intuitively judge in the manner he does, then he must know the rule, and if he doesn't know it consciously, then we must suppose he knows it unconsciously, that is, has tacit knowledge of it. (Once the possibility of unconscious knowledge is granted, as it presumably is in connection with cases from psychology, then this argument can be seen as just a special case of the standard form of scientific inference from observable effects to unobservable causes.)

Let us now return to the exchange between Harman and Chomsky mentioned earlier in this discussion. Harman's challenge, as I understand it, comes down to this: given that we can say that speakers of a language know that certain sentences are ungrammatical, certain ones ambiguous, certain ones related in certain ways to others, and so on, what licenses us to go further and say that the speakers know (tacitly) the linguistic principles whose formalization in the grammar explain the noted ungrammaticality, ambiguity, sentential relations, and the like?

The remarks of the preceding paragraphs suggest the lines along which Harman's question is to be answered. We suppose that the grammar of a language L is the optimal theory to explain the linguistic facts about the sentences of L. We suppose also that the grammar is a component of a real-time model of speech production and speech recognition and that this model provides an acceptable simulation of the verbal behavior of speakers of L on the basis of which we say that they know that certain sentences are ungrammatical, certain sentences ambiguous, and so forth. Finally, we suppose that in the simulation of the verbal behavior of the speakers the output of the model is arrived at by a sequence of computations that makes essential use of the grammar.

On these suppositions, we can claim that the etiology of the speaker's behavior is not different in any relevant way from the etiology of the behavior of the machine that acceptably simulates it. Fodor (1968a) has made this point quite well:

> If machines and organisms can produce behavior of the same type and if descriptions of machine computations in terms of the rules, instructions, etc., that they employ are true descriptions of the etiology of their output, then the principle that licenses inferences from like causes to like effects must license us to infer that the tacit knowledge of organisms is represented by the programs of the machines that simulate their behavior (p. 640).

The crux of this argument is that such a causal explanation of the linguistic behavior of speakers would make no sense whatsoever if it did not claim that the formal rules of the grammar utilized in the computations of the machine have real counterparts in the causal processes going on in the heads of the speakers.

Cases in physics are exactly parallel. The radiation which is emitted when fast-alpha-particles bombard beryllium or boron nuclei is of far greater penetrating power than that of the original alpha-particles. Chadwick explained this fact by hypothesizing that this radiation consists of a new type of entity, which he called a "neutron," an entity that is uncharged and equal in mass to a proton. He reasoned that there would be no ionization as these entities passed through gas and no deflection by the electrical field around the bombarded nuclei, hence explaining the greater penetrating power of the radiation. Clearly, this explanation cannot make sense if the causal process that it proposes is not envisioned as leading back from real physical events in the laboratory to the behavior of equally real neutrons. Likewise, the explanations of production or recognition models cannot make sense if the causal processes that they propose are not envisioned as leading back from the real verbal behavior of speakers to equally real physical instantiations of the principles formalized in the grammar. It seems to me, therefore, that at this stage of the argument the only basis on which one might deny tacit knowledge of linguistic principles is to adopt some version of the fictionalist view that talk about theoretical entities in science is mere *façon de parler*, not talk about actual physical objects. But such fictionalism is incapable of doing justice to theoretical inference in physics and other sciences, and it is hardly a view that one ought to take seriously in linguistics.[8]

Hence, in ascribing tacit knowledge to speakers, we are stating the conclusion of a theoretical inference whose form, in all relevant respects, is the same as inferences to unobservables like neutrons. The license we have to draw the conclusion is that it posits a necessary antecedent in a causal chain culminating in the observable effects for which the account in question is the best explanation, and the account cannot make sense as an explanation unless the hypothesized antecedent is as real as these effects.

4. The structure of the theory of language

A theory of the ideal speaker's linguistic competence to relate acoustic signals to meanings is broader than a theory of language: the latter comprises only that branch of linguistics whose aim is to state the universals of language, those aspects of the ideal speaker's linguistic competence that the ideal speaker of every natural language shares; the former encompasses the particular features of the natural language in question as well as whatever is common to all natural languages. The implicit knowledge that an ideal speaker has about the idiosyncracies of his language and the implicit knowledge that he has about every language together constitute the grammar of the language.

The theory of language that transformational grammar is now attempting

[8] See Katz (in press), "On the Existence of Theoretical Entities," for further discussion.

to develop is a revival of the traditional rationalistic theory of *universal grammar* or *philosophical grammar*. Beattie, in the latter part of the eighteenth century, conceived its aim as follows:

> Languages ... resemble men in this respect, that, though each has peculiarities, whereby it is distinguished from every other, yet all have certain qualities in common. The peculiarities of individual tongues are explained in their respective grammars and dictionaries. Those things, that all languages have in common, or that are necessary to every language, are treated of in a science, which some have called *Universal* or *Philosophical* grammar.[9]

The qualification "that are necessary to every language" is somewhat vague, but it is clearly intended to exclude accidental linguistic regularities. A clarification of this vagueness in Beattie's characterization is provided by Chomsky and Halle (1968):

> The essential properties of natural languages are often referred to as "linguistic universals." Certain apparent linguistic universals may be the result merely of historical accident. For example, if only inhabitants of Tasmania survive a future war, it might be a property of all then existing languages that pitch is not used to differentiate lexical items. Accidental universals of this sort are of no importance for general linguistics, which attempts rather to characterize the range of possible human languages. The significant linguistic universals are those that must be assumed to be available to the child learning a language as an a priori, innate endowment. That there must be a rich system of a priori properties —of essential linguistic universals—is fairly obvious from the following empirical observations. Every normal child acquires an extremely intricate and abstract grammar, the properties of which are much underdetermined by the available data. This takes place with great speed, under conditions that are far from ideal, and there is little significant variation among children who may differ greatly in intelligence and experience. The search for essential linguistic universals is, in effect, the study of the a priori *faculté de langage* that makes language acquisition possible under the given conditions of time and access to data (p. 4).

One unique feature of the transformationalist conception of linguistic theory is that it is framed as a specification of the class of grammars, so that its statements of the universal properties of languages are given in the form of constraints on grammars. The formulation of linguistic universals as necessary conditions on a formal system qualifying as a grammar is an extremely important departure from their traditional formulation as direct predications about languages. Its importance lies not only in the ease with which a formal statement of universals can be given, but, more significantly, in the fact that it makes possible the statement of a wider range of universals, including, for example, the definition of grammaticality as generation in an optimal grammar.

The theory of language, then, is a definition of 'grammar' and, alternatively, a definition of 'natural language', where a grammar is any system of rules consistent with the specified constraints and a natural language is anything represented by a grammar. The constraints are of three types: *formal universals*, *substantive universals*, and *organizational universals*. Formal universals constrain

---

[9] Quoted in Chomsky (1965, p. 5).

the form of the rules in a grammar; substantive universals provide a theoretical vocabulary from which the constructs used to formulate the rules of particular grammars are drawn; organizational universals, of which there are two subtypes, *componential organizational universals* and *systematic organizational universals*, specify the interrelations among the rules and among systems of rules within a grammar.

The categories of formal, substantive, and componential organizational universals cross-classify with the categories of *phonological universals, syntactic universals*, and *semantic universals*. This is to say that the former group of universals can be about phonological, syntactic, or semantic features of language and, conversely, that such features of language can concern form, content, or organization. Accordingly, linguistic theory consists of three subtheories: *phonological theory, syntactic theory*, and *semantic theory*. The first states the formal, substantive, and componential organizational universals at the phonological level; the second states the universals at the syntactic level; and the third states them at the semantic level. Each of these subtheories of linguistic theory is, then, a model of one of the components of a grammar: phonological theory defines the notion 'phonological component', syntactic theory defines the notion 'syntactic component', and semantic theory defines the notion 'semantic component'. The formal and substantive universals in each of the subtheories specify the requirements on the form and content of the rules in the component of the grammar that the subtheory defines. The requirement that grammars contain transformational rules is a formal universal, while the requirement that the constructs out of which phonological rules are formulated be chosen from a fixed vocabulary of distinctive features is a substantive universal. The componential organizational universals in each subtheory specify the way in which the rules of each component are organized. They determine the ordering conditions under which rules of certain kinds within a component apply with respect to one another and with respect to rules of other kinds. For example, the relation of the base to the transformational subcomponent of the syntactic component and the ordering of transformational rules are universals of this type.

The systematic organizational universals specify how the three components of a grammar are related to one other. They are thus what makes linguistic theory a model of a grammar, and they are the principal part of linguistic theory's explanation of how different speakers of a language are capable of making the same systematic sound-meaning correlations. The most significant of such universals in current linguistic theory is stated in (2.6):

(2.6)   The syntactic component is the generative source of a grammar. Its output is the input to both the phonological component and the semantic component. Its output consists of an infinite set of structural descriptions, one for each sentence of the language. Each structural description consists of a set of underlying phrase markers and a single superficial phrase marker. The semantic component operates on the former to provide a representation of the meaning of the sentence; the phonological component operates on the latter to provide a representation of its pronunciation.

Various aspects of (2.6) are quite controversial at this time, and we shall examine some of the alternative views in Chapter 8. But if (2.6) is accepted, we obtain the following explanation of the sound-meaning correlations. The phonological component interprets superficial phrase markers in terms of speech sounds and the semantic component interprets underlying phrase markers in terms of meaning. The superficial phrase marker of a sentence is related to its underlying phrase markers by sequences of intervening phrase markers. These phrase markers are determined by sequences of transformations that generate the first intervening phrase markers from the underlying phrase markers, the next from the first intervening phrase markers, and so on, until the superficial phrase marker is obtained from the last intervening phrase markers. Thus, the interpretation of the sentence's pronunciation is related to the interpretation of its meaning by virtue of the mediating transformation relation between the syntactic objects of which they are interpretations.

If linguistic theory is to provide this or some form of this explanation of the correlation of semantic and phonetic interpretations, it must have a means of representing the phonetic shape of utterances, the common structure of phrase structure and transformational relations, and the meaning paired with phonetic objects by such relations. Thus phonological theory is required to provide a representation scheme for perceptual correlates of acoustic signals, a definition of the notion 'possible utterance in a language' in terms of a recursive enumeration of the set of phonetic representations for possible utterances of natural languages.[10] Syntactic theory is required to provide a representation scheme for the syntactic organization within a sentence. That is, it will contain a universal theory of constituent structure and grammatical relations in which the notion 'possible sentence in a language' is defined by a recursive enumeration of the set of possible sentence structures.[11] We also require a semantic theory to provide a representation scheme for meanings, that is, a universal theory of concepts in which the notion 'possible (cognitive) meaning in a language' is defined by a recursive enumeration of the set of possible senses.[12]

The problem of constructing a universal scheme for semantic representation is thus one of the primary goals of semantic theory, just as the problem of constructing a universal scheme for phonetic representation is one of the primary goals of phonological theory. A solution to the latter problem would be a system of universal phonology in which the notion 'phonetic representation' is defined, and a solution to the former would be a system of universal semantics in which the notion 'semantic interpretation' is defined. Given such systems, the two interpretive components of grammars would have available phonetic and semantic representations to map onto underlying and superficial phrase markers.

---

[10] On the present account of phonological theory, such representations take the form of two-dimensional matrices in which the rows stand for particular constructs (i.e., distinctive features) from the substantive universals of the phonological level and the columns for the consecutive segments of the utterance being represented. (See Chomsky and Halle (1968, pp. 5, 165).)

[11] See Katz and Postal (1964) and Chomsky (1965).

[12] See Katz and Fodor (1963).

Semantic theory must therefore contain (2.7):

(2.7)   A scheme for semantic representation consisting of a theoretical vocabulary from which semantic constructs required in the formulation of particular semantic interpretations can be drawn.

Semantic theory must also contain a model of the semantic component of a grammar which must describe the manner in which semantic interpretations are mapped onto underlying phrase markers. It must specify the contribution of both linguistic universals and language-specific information to this mapping. It must also explain the semantic competence underlying the speaker's ability to understand the meaning of new sentences chosen arbitrarily from the infinite range of sentences. This explanation must assume that the speaker possesses, as part of his system of internalized rules, semantic rules that enable him to obtain the meaning of any new sentence as a compositional function of the meanings of its parts and their syntactic organization. The model must prescribe that the semantic component of a grammar contain a dictionary that formally specifies the senses of every syntactically atomic constituent in the language. It must also prescribe rules for obtaining representations of the senses of syntactically complex constituents, which are formed from representations of the senses of their atomic constituents in the dictionary. The dictionary provides the finite basis and the rules provide the machinery for projection onto the infinite range. Thus, semantic theory must also contain (2.8):

(2.8)   A specification of the form of the dictionary and a specification of the form of the rules that project semantic representations for complex syntactic constituents from the dictionary's representations of the senses of their minimal syntactic parts.

To complete this explanation of compositionality, semantic theory will also need to include certain componential organizational universals that relate the components of the dictionary, that relate the dictionary to the projection rules, and that specify the manner in which these rules operate in the process of going from less to more syntactically complex constituents. Thus, semantic theory must also contain (2.9):

(2.9)   A specification of the form of the semantic component, of the relation between the dictionary and the projection rules, and of the manner in which these rules apply in assigning semantic representations.

Requirement (2.7) concerns the substantive universals at the semantic level. The semantic vocabulary that meets this requirement will contain the analogues of syntactic substantive universals such as the constructs 'S', 'NP', 'V' and phonological substantive universals such as the features [±consonantal], [±strident]. Requirement (2.8) concerns the formal universals at the semantic level. Their analogues are the formal characterizations of phrase structure and transformational rules. Requirement (2.9) concerns the componential organizational universals at the semantic level. Their analogues are the statements of the relation between the base and transformational component and the ordering conditions on transformational rules.

Beyond (2.7)–(2.9), which determine the role semantic theory plays in the explanation of sound-meaning correlations given by linguistic theory, semantic theory has a special task of its own. As stressed in Chapter 1, semantics is the area of linguistics that concerns itself with such phenomena as synonymy, semantic similarity, semantic ambiguity, antonymy, and meaningfulness and meaninglessness. The basic task of this theory, then, is to explain (explicate) each such semantic property and relation. Thus, (2.10) must be added as a requirement for a semantic theory:

(2.10) A set of definitions for semantic properties and relations such as those listed in (1.16)–(1.30).

5. Semantic theory's model of a semantic component

How does the conception of semantic theory as a body of explications which meets (2.10) relate to the conception of semantic theory as an account of the manner in which semantic interpretations are assigned to underlying phrase markers? How do these two conceptions fit together into one coherent conception of semantic theory?[13] The answer is straightforward, stemming from the almost trivial observation that linguistic expressions have the semantic properties and relations they do by virtue of their meaning. Thus, since semantic properties and relations are aspects of the structure of the senses formed in the compositional determination of meaning, there is no problem in coalescing the two conceptions of semantic theory into one coherent whole.

Since the semantic properties and relations of an expression are determined by its meaning and since its meaning is given by semantic representations, it follows that the definitions of semantic properties and relations must be stated in terms of formal features of semantic representations. If this is done, there will be an explanation of how the meaning of one expression makes it synonymous with another, or analytic, semantically ambiguous, semantically anomalous, and so on. It will be clear what features of its meaning determine that the expression has a particular semantic property or relation, because just these features will be the basis on which the definition of the particular property or relation will apply. Accordingly, the language-independent semantic properties and relations like those in (1.16)–(1.30) will be defined in terms of general features of semantic representations.

[13] This situation is not unique to semantics. It also arises in phonology. Phonological theory not only must determine the general form of phonetic representations and the principles by which they are assigned to syntactic representations of surface structure; it must accomplish its own special task, dictated by its own subject matter, of explaining such phonological properties and relations as alliteration, rhyme, internal rhyme, metrical forms, etc.

We will now try to spell out the requirements (2.7)–(2.10) in sufficient detail to make clear how a semantic component's description of a sentence represents its meaning as a compositional function of the meanings of its parts and how its semantic properties and relations are determined by this description, in conjunction with the definitions of the semantic properties and relations in semantic theory. (In subsequent chapters there will be a more detailed specification of (2.7)–(2.10).)

The most elementary syntactic components of a sentence are, in general, meaningful units of the language. These, the morphemes, can be divided into two types, grammatical morphemes, which are relatively rare and devoid of meaning, and the nongrammatical morphemes, each of which bears some fixed conceptual interpretation. The latter are meaningful in a sense which makes them contrast with nonsense syllables and nonce words. However, they cannot by themselves express full messages in linguistic communication, as do sentences, nor are they all meaningful in the same way. For example, common nouns like "boy," "table," and "car" are meaningful in a different way from affixes like "de-," "un-," and "-ed." This difference is sometimes described by saying that the latter are syncategorematic. We shall return to these two sorts of meaning at a later point.

Since morphemes are formed out of phonological elements having no intrinsic semantic content, and since higher level syntactic constituents are formed out of them, it is reasonable to think that the meaning of higher level syntactic constituents comes from the meanings of their component morphemes. If so, then a speaker's ability to understand any sentence depends in part on his knowing the meanings of its component morphemes. This can be seen from the fact that a speaker who does not know the meaning of certain morphemes in his language will miss something about the meaning of every sentence in which those unfamiliar morphemes appear—aside from cases where he can "guess" the meaning from the sentential or socio-physical context. That the incomprehensibility due to an unknown word can be transmitted to every constituent of the sentence of which that word is a part (up to and including the whole sentence) shows that the meaning of the sentence and each of its constituents containing the unknown word depends on the meaning of that word. This, in turn, shows that any constituent's meaning is a compositional function of the meanings of its parts and thus, ultimately, its morphemes. Idioms are the exceptions that prove this rule. Locutions like "shoot the breeze," "stir up trouble," "give hell to" make no sense whatever if construed compositionally.

The meaning of a complex constituent does not depend only on the meanings of its component morphemes, however. It also depends on syntactic structure, that is, the way the morphemes are syntactically related to one another in the complex constituent. The same set of morphemes can mean different things when put in different syntactic arrangements, as illustrated by (2.11), (2.12), and (2.13):

(2.11)   John thought he had left Mary alone

(2.12)   Mary alone thought he had left John

(2.13)   Had he alone thought Mary left John?

Rearranging the order of morphemes can also produce just a jumble of words, grammatical word salad such as (2.14):

(2.14)   Thought left John he Mary had alone

Such considerations clearly demonstrate the necessary role of syntactic organization in determining the meaning of complex constituents.

To explain how a speaker is able to understand sentences, we must explain how he goes from the meanings of morphemes in specific syntactic relations to each other to the meaning of sentences. We must reconstruct the semantic knowledge an ideal speaker-hearer has of the meanings of the morphemes in his language, the syntax of the sentences, and the compositional function that gives him the meaning of sentences in terms of both of these. This reconstruction attempts to formulate rules that formally reflect the structure of this knowledge by producing semantic representations of sentences from semantic representations of their elementary parts and the syntactic relations between these parts.

These considerations lead us to a first approximation of the internal organization of the semantic component. First, it is a device whose inputs are the underlying phrase markers produced by the syntactic component: the semantic component operates on underlying phrase marker(s) to obtain the syntactic information it requires about a sentence. Second, it is a device that contains a list of the meanings of the morphemes of the language (and the idioms). The meanings of the morphemes can be listed since there are only finitely many of them (and only finitely many idioms). Third, it is a device that contains rules that use information about the syntactic structure of a sentence and the meanings of its morphemes to assign the sentence a semantic interpretation that represents each semantic fact about it. Such semantic interpretations will be the outputs of the semantic component. In short, the semantic component consists of a list of the meanings of the morphemes of the language, which we will call a *dictionary*, and a set of rules that reconstruct the speaker's ability to project sentence meanings from morpheme meanings, which we will call *projection rules*. The inputs are underlying phrase markers and the outputs are *semantic interpretations*.

The process which ends with the assignment of a semantic interpretation to a sentence begins, as we have seen, with the assignment of a meaning to each of the morphemes of that sentence. The meaning of a morpheme is represented by what we shall call a *dictionary entry*. But many, perhaps almost all, morphemes are semantically ambiguous. We shall use the term *sense* in its customary usage to refer to one of the different meanings which a morpheme (or expression) may bear and reserve the term *meaning* for the collection of senses that a morpheme (or expression) has. Accordingly, the meaning of a morpheme, or, as we shall say, a *lexical item*, is the set of senses it has in the dictionary, and the meaning of a complex expression is the set of senses it has on the basis of the meanings of its parts and their mode of semantic composition. Thus, a dictionary entry will contain a semantic representation for each sense of its lexical item, and the semantic representation of the meaning of a lexical item will be taken to be the set of semantic representations of its senses.

We want a representation of a sense to formally distinguish it from other senses and to formally reflect the respects in which it is similar to other senses. The formal properties of a representation must be such that combinations of this representation with others will result in correct representations of the senses of complex expressions and sentences. To construct semantic representations that will satisfy these demands, it is essential to treat a sense neither as atomic nor as monolithic but as a composite of concepts that can be decomposed into parts and the relations in which they stand.[14] The representation of a sense must formalize the structure of a sense, reflecting in its formal structure the natural division of the sense into its conceptual parts and their interrelations. If these representations are built so that each is a formal analysis of the sense it represents, they will exhibit the structural complexity which displays the similarities and differences among senses and determines their compositional potentials.

We thus introduce a pair of technical terms that incorporate this design for the construction of semantic representations. We use the term *reading* to refer to a semantic representation of a sense of a morpheme, word, phrase, clause, or sentence. In addition, we use the term *semantic marker* to refer to the semantic representation of one or another of the concepts that appear as parts of senses. Semantic markers represent the conceptual constituents of senses in the same way in which phrase markers represent the syntactic constituents of sentences. They represent not only the atomic constituents of a sense, that is, the simplest concepts in the sense (analogous to the morphemes in a sentence), but also the complex ones. Accordingly, some semantic markers will have a highly complex internal structure, reflecting the highly complex internal structure of the concepts they represent. A reading, then, is a set of semantic markers. For present purposes, we make no distinction between semantic markers and distinguishers.[15] The latter constructs are treated as special cases of semantic markers. Finally, we differentiate between *lexical readings* and *derived readings*, the former being readings that occur in dictionary entries while the latter are formed from lexical readings by the operation of projection rules.

Let us consider the notion of a semantic marker further. First, it will occur to the reader that the semantic markers are collectively the theoretical vocabulary for semantic representation that was referred to in (2.7). This is roughly correct, except for two qualifications. One is that in a variety of cases semantic markers are introduced by the operation of projection rules. These rules can combine readings in such a manner that a semantic marker in one is fitted into a semantic marker in another or transformed into another, thus creating a partly new, partly old construct. Such semantic markers, which we discuss further at a later point, need not be included in the theoretical vocabulary of semantic theory. They are uniquely determined by the set of semantic markers occurring in dictionary entries and the projection rules. Moreover, they comprise an infinite set of semantic markers and so could not in principle be listed in the theoretical vocabulary. The

---

[14] For example, if we were to take the sense of a morpheme like "nude" as unanalyzable, we would then be unable to explain the semantic redundancy of an expression like "naked nude" as a case where the sense of the modifier is identical to a proper part of the sense of the head.

[15] See Chapter 3, Section 5.

other exception is those semantic markers that, although they occur in dictionary entries, can be defined in terms of primitives. This is a familiar case in theory construction. The treatment, too, is familiar: we include within our theoretical vocabulary only the *primitive semantic markers*. However, it must be clearly understood that an extensional distinction between primitive and defined constructs in semantic theory can be drawn only after semantic theory has reached a much more sophisticated state of formulation. Therefore, this distinction will be of little concern to us in these investigations. In the final statement of semantic theory, the theoretical vocabulary of semantic markers will consist of each and every primitive semantic marker that is required in the formulation of dictionary entries.[16]

We next turn to the question of the interpretation of semantic markers. As we have already indicated, a semantic marker is a theoretical construct which is intended to represent a concept that is part of the sense of morphemes and other constituents of natural languages. By a concept in this connection we do not mean images or mental ideas or particular thoughts. These, which we will refer to collectively as *cognitions*, form part of the conscious experience of some individual person, in the same way as do sensations, feelings, memories, and hallucinations. Cognitions are individuated in part by the persons who have them. If you and I both have the same thought that John will marry Mary, there are two cognitions, not one. Cognitions are datable: they occur within the time period marked out by their appearance and disappearance from the consciousness of the person who has them. Concepts, on the other hand, are abstract entities. They do not belong to the conscious experience of anyone, though they may be thought about, as in our thinking about the concept of a circle. They are not individuated by persons: you and I may think about the same concept. They are not, as Frege (1956) urged, elements in the subjective process of thinking, but rather the objective content of thought processes, which is " capable of being the common property of several thinkers." Nor are they datable: they cannot possess temporal properties or bear temporal relations.

Because abstract entities such as concepts and propositions differ in these ways from cognitions (and physical objects), they present a problem in regard to their individuation. How are we to decide when reference is being made to the same concept or proposition and when reference is being made to different ones? How do we differentiate one such abstract entity from others if it cannot be assigned differential spatio-temporal properties (as in the case of physical objects) and if it cannot be differentially related to persons who are antecedently individuated, in

---

[16] In this connection, note the following remark by Frege (1952a): "...my explanation is not meant as a proper definition. One cannot require that everything shall be defined, any more than one can require that a chemist shall decompose every substance. What is simple cannot be decomposed, and what is logically simple cannot have a proper definition. Now something logically simple is no more given us at the outset than most of the chemical elements are; it is reached only by means of scientific work. If something has been discovered that is simple, or at least must count as simple for the time being, we shall have to coin a term for it, since language will not originally contain an expression that exactly answers. On the introduction of a name for something logically simple, a definition is not possible; there is nothing for it but to lead the reader or hearer, by means of hints, to understand the words as is intended " (pp. 42–43).

part, spatio-temporally (as in the case of cognitions)? The answer is that natural languages accomplish such individuation. Speakers, after all, communicate without confusion of reference about particular abstractions and use them to investigate the characteristics of concrete objects. What enables them to perform such individuations is that concepts and propositions are senses of expressions and sentences. That is, senses are concepts and propositions connected with the phonetic (or orthographic) objects in natural languages. Since these objects have physical counterparts, we can look to the semantic and phonetic representations of sentences and the grammatical rules that systematically interconnect representations of meaning and sound to individuate concepts and propositions. If the grammar provides an account of the semantic content of each phonetic object in the language, then the pairing of sound and meaning will provide the required individuation in terms of phonetically specified features of stretches of speech. These features will differentiate the meanings with which they are correlated under this mapping. Therefore, the problem of individuating abstract conceptual entities is part of the general problem of grammar construction. Since the former problem is solved by speakers on the basis of their linguistic competence, the grammar's reconstruction of linguistic competence will have to explain their solution.

This, however, still leaves open the question of what the ontological status of concepts and propositions is, of what kinds of things senses and meanings are. This question will be left here without a final answer. The reason is twofold. On the one hand, the problem, pushed far enough, becomes the ancient philosophical puzzle about universals, which is best left out of attempts to carry on scientific investigations. On the other hand, even approximations to a serious solution cannot be developed until much more is known about semantic structure. The situation is comparable to the question in physics of what light is. Fruitful investigation into the structure of a phenomenon does not presuppose a definite knowledge of what that phenomenon really is, but, quite the reverse, eventually learning what that phenomenon is presupposes an extensive knowledge of its structure. Just as Maxwell's field theory explains many of the structural features of the propagation of light without explaining what light really is, so we can construct a semantic theory which explains the structure of complex meanings without resting this explanation on an ontological account of concepts and propositions.

It is quite unreasonable to insist at the outset, as some philosophers have,[17] that we provide a general definition of 'semantic marker' and 'reading' that clarifies the ontological status of the notions 'concept' and 'proposition' before these constructs are introduced, to insist, that is, on a clarification of the ontological underpinnings of the notions of concept and proposition as a precondition for accepting the explanations of semantic properties and relations given by a theory employing 'semantic marker' and 'reading'. The parody of this demand runs as follows. Mathematicians have defined notions like 'sum', 'product', 'square

---

[17] Wilson (1967) argues that I have defined "'analytic' in terms of 'semantic marker', and on this account . . . cannot honestly resist the demand for a general definition of 'semantic marker' and at the same time claim, as [I do], to have supplied a general definition of 'S is analytic in L'" (p. 67).

root' (the analogues of 'synonymy', 'semantic ambiguity', 'semantic anomaly', 'analyticity', etc.) in terms of 'number' (the analogue of 'proposition' and 'concept'). But no ontologically satisfactory definition of 'number' has been given, and so we must regard the definitions mathematicians give of 'sum', 'product', 'square root', etc., as suspect. How can mathematicians resist the demand for a definition of 'number' and at the same time claim to have supplied definitions of 'sum', 'product', 'square root'? This parody shows that such ontological clarifications, though highly desirable, are not preconditions for successful theory construction and theoretical explanation. A general definition of 'semantic marker' and 'reading' is, then, no more a prerequisite for definitions of 'semantic ambiguity', 'semantic anomaly', 'synonymy', and other semantic properties and relations than a definition of 'number' is a prerequisite for defining arithmetic operations.

Of course, there must be some progress toward an explanation of the construct of a semantic marker in terms of an extensional characterization of the notion 'x is a semantic marker'. This is exactly the task of building a semantic theory of natural language, since the values of 'x' would be the empirical spelling out of (2.7). Therefore, the demand that we provide a general definition of 'semantic marker' and 'reading' is unreasonable if laid down as a condition for accepting a semantic theory, since it insists on a complete semantic theory in advance of the empirical and theoretical work required to construct it.

Some further intuitive considerations will clarify the notion of a semantic marker. When we consider semantic markers in their role of representing senses of constituents, we find that there are a few ways to think of them. A reading provides a decomposition of the sense it represents by breaking down that sense into its component concepts. The structure of a conceptually complex sense is thus reflected in the form of semantic markers, which serve as the formal elements to make this analysis possible. For example, the most common sense of the English noun "chair" can be decomposed into a set of concepts which might be represented by the semantic markers in (2.15):

(2.15)   (Object), (Physical), (Non-living), (Artifact), (Furniture), (Portable), (Something with legs), (Something with a back), (Something with a seat), (Seat for one)

It is obvious that this analysis leaves out a considerable amount of information. Each of the concepts represented by the semantic markers in (2.15) can itself be broken into components. For example, the concept of an object represented by '(Object)' might be analyzed as *an organization of parts that are spatio-temporally contiguous which form a stable whole having an orientation in space.* On such further analysis, the semantic markers representing the concepts 'legs', 'back', and 'seat' could be formally related to the notion of parts in the analysis of the concept of an object so as to indicate that these are the parts of a chair. This would provide an aspect of the distinction between the meaning of "chair" and other closely related words like "table." Also, we might be able to formally represent the notion 'orientation in space' so that it could be specified here as

inherently vertical, thus providing a basis for the difference in meaning between
(2.16) and (2.17):[18]

(2.16) The chair is tall

(2.17) The cigarette is tall

As in the case of the concept ' object ', we shall often leave concepts without
a definition in terms of more primitive semantic markers. This means that certain
relationships that depend on the internal structure of the concept cannot yet be
formalized. Still, we can work with a reading that takes us part of the way toward
a full analysis of the sense and try to determine to what extent the semantic markers
found useful here are also useful in providing a means of representing senses of
other expressions and stating semantic relations between them.

Another way of thinking of semantic markers is as the elements in terms
of which semantic generalizations about senses can be made. Consider the word
"chair" in connection with the words "hat," "planet," "shadow," "car,"
"molecule" and contrast these with words such as "breath," "truth," "ripple,"
"thought," "togetherness," "feeling." The senses of the words in the first group
are in many ways quite different from one another, yet they are semantically
similar in a way in which the senses of the words in the second group are not:
each word in the first group contains the concept of an object as one component
of its sense while no word in the second group has a sense containing this concept.
The generalization about the intragroup similarities and intergroup differences
can be expressed using the semantic marker '(Object)' as an element in the lexical
reading of each of the words in the former group and excluding it from the lexical
reading of any word in the latter. In general, then, semantic markers, by their
inclusion or exclusion from readings in dictionary entries, enable us to state
semantic generalizations about words.

A third way of thinking about semantic markers is as symbols that mark
the components of senses of expressions on which inferences from sentences
containing the expressions depend. They are, in this case, thought of as marking
aspects of the logical form of the sentences in whose semantic representation they
occur. The sentence (2.18) entails (2.19)–(2.26):

(2.18) There is a chair in the room

(2.19) There is a physical object in the room

(2.20) There is something nonliving in the room

(2.21) There is an artifact in the room

(2.22) There is a piece of furniture in the room

(2.23) There is something portable in the room

(2.24) There is something having legs in the room

(2.25) There is something with a back in the room

(2.26) There is a seat for one person in the room

[18] See Bierwisch (1967) and Teller (1969).

The semantic markers in (2.15), which comprise a reading for "chair," mark the elements in the sense of this word on which the inferences from (2.18) to (2.19)– (2.26) depend. Moreover, the absence of other semantic markers, such as '(Female)', explains why certain other sentences, such as (2.27), are not valid inferences from (2.18):

(2.27)   There is a woman in the room

It is worth noting here that Frege (1952a) came close to having the notion of a semantic marker. He observed that instead of saying (2.28a,b,c), we can say (2.29):

(2.28)   (a) 2 is a positive number
          (b) 2 is a whole number
          (c) 2 is less than 10

(2.29)   2 is a positive whole number less than 10

Thus, 'to be a positive number', 'to be a whole number', and 'to be less than 10' are all, in Frege's terminology, *properties* of the number '2' and *marks* of the concept 'positive whole number less than 10'. If Frege had made the further observation—which, as far as I can tell, he did not make—that marks could be represented by formal symbols and that these symbols could be employed to provide a formal representation of the contribution that the senses of items in the descriptive vocabulary of a language make to the inference potentialities of sentences in which the items occur (Frege had the notion of compositionality), then he would have had the notion of a semantic marker. There is, after all, nothing basically different between this case of Frege's and cases where the relation 'is a mark of' holds between the subconcepts forming a composite concept, on the one hand, and that composite concept in the role of the sense of a syntactically simple noun, on the other—for example, between the subconcepts 'to be a physical object', 'to be human', 'to be male', 'to be an adult', and 'to never have married' and the composite concept 'physical object which is human, male, adult, and never married', which is the sense of the syntactically simple noun "bachelor."

Having considered the notion of a semantic marker in some detail, we return to our discussion of lexical and derived readings. Lexical readings are the basis of the compositional process which assigns semantic representations to syntactically complex constituents of sentences. Derived readings are the semantic representations that are assigned to syntactically complex constituents as a representation of the way their meaning is a function of the meanings of their syntactic parts. Succinctly, the process of forming and assigning derived readings works as follows. The phrase markers of a sentence that provide the information necessary for semantic interpretation are received as input by the semantic component. Its first operation is to assign lexical readings from the dictionary to each terminal element of the phrase marker that represents a meaningful element of the sentence. Lexical readings are then combined by the projection rule to form derived readings which are assigned to the lowest order syntactically complex constituents. The projection rule goes on to combine derived readings until a set of derived readings is associated with each syntactically complex constituent, including the whole sentence itself.

The process just sketched must not only construct readings, it must also prevent the construction of them. If we count the number of senses of lexical items in an ordinary fifteen- or twenty-word sentence and compute the total number of possible combinations that could be formed from these senses when they are paired up appropriately, the number of possible senses for the whole sentence usually runs into the hundreds. Since no sentence has anywhere near this many different senses, a rather severe form of selection must be at work in the process whereby derived readings are produced. Furthermore, the fact that some sentences have no sense, even though their individual words are meaningful, indicates that the absence of sense, i.e., meaninglessness, is the limit of whatever selectional process gives rise to multiplicity of senses, i.e., ambiguity. Both these considerations suggest that the account of this process of selection included in the semantic component of a grammar must be in terms of some mechanism that allows or blocks the formation of a derived reading.

Since the formation of derived readings begins with the combination of lexical readings, the latter must contain, besides a set of semantic markers, a *selection restriction*. This will state the condition under which the sense represented by the set of semantic markers can combine with other senses to form a sense of a syntactic complex constituent. The adjective "gold," for example, has at least two senses—that of being made of a certain malleable metallic element and that of having a deep yellowish color. Neither of these senses can combine with the senses of nouns like "truth," "thought," "virtue": expressions like "metal truth," "yellow thought," "yellow virtue" are senseless. The selection restriction reconstructs the distinction between the range of senses with which a given sense can unite to form a new sense and the range of senses with which it cannot unite. Whenever a constituent is formed from component constituents and the sense of one belongs to the range of senses excluded from combination with the sense of the other, then the constituent is meaningless (conceptually absurd) unless the component constituents have other senses that can combine. Both senses of "gold" can combine with the sense of "chair," giving the two senses of the semantically ambiguous expression "gold chair," namely, one of a metal chair and the other of a chair of a certain color. But only the first sense of "gold" can combine with the senses of the other constituents in "white-gold ring" to form a sense for the whole, whereas only the second sense of "gold" can combine with the sense of "mist" to form a sense for "gold mist." Were "gold" to have only the first sense, "gold mist" would be meaningless. Note, however, that were "gold" to have only the second sense, "white-gold ring" would not be meaningless but contradictory. The senses of words like "white," "red," "blue" are antonymous with "gold" in the sense of the color, as is "nongold," but they have the same range of combination with other senses that "gold" does. The same things that can be gold (in color) can be white, red, blue, etc., and the things that cannot literally be gold cannot literally be white, red, blue, etc. Thus there is something common in the senses of the words to which "gold," "white," "red," "blue," etc. apply that marks them off as a class from those words to which "gold," "white," "red," "blue," etc. cannot apply. This common semantic element will be stated in the selection restriction of "gold," "white," "red," "blue," etc., and the fact that each of these words has the same selection restriction will express this generalization about a common semantic element. Since, furthermore, as in the case of any element of a sense, such common semantic elements are represented by semantic markers, a selection restriction must be formulated as a requirement on the semantic marker content of readings. Thus the selection restriction in a reading specifies the semantic markers that other readings must have in order that they may combine with the first reading to form derived readings.

Let us consider a crude illustration of a dictionary entry. The adjective "handsome" appears to have one sense where it means 'beautiful with dignity', another where it means 'gracious or generous', and still another where it means 'moderately large'. The first applies to persons and artifacts, as in expressions like "a handsome woman" or "a handsome desk"; the second applies to some forms of conduct, as in the expression "a handsome welcome"; and the third applies to amounts, as in "a handsome sum of money." Thus, the dictionary entry for "handsome" might look like (2.30), where the semantic markers enclosed in angled brackets represent the selection restriction for that sense:

(2.30) *handsome*; [+ Adj, . . .]; (Physical), (Object), (Beautiful), (Dignified in appearance), ⟨(Human ∨ (Artifact)⟩

(Gracious), (Generous), ⟨(Conduct)⟩

(Moderately large), ⟨(Amount)⟩

One can see how, given something like (2.15) as the lexical reading of one sense of "chair," the derived reading for the noun "handsome chair" would be one on which the sense is 'a physical object which is a portable piece of furniture with legs, a back, and a seat which serves as a seat for one, and which is an artifact of beauty and dignity'. The other lexical readings of "handsome" would not combine with this lexical reading of "chair" because it contains neither the semantic marker '(Conduct)' nor the semantic marker '(Amount)'.

The dictionary consists of a complete list of dictionary entries, one for each lexical item in the lexicon of the syntactic component that represents a meaningful item of the language, and a list of what we may call *semantic redundancy rules*. These serve to simplify the formulation of dictionary entries by allowing us to eliminate any semantic markers from a lexical reading whose occurrence is predictable on the basis of the occurrence of another semantic marker in the same reading. The rules can be illustrated by (2.31):

(2.31) (a) (Furniture) → (Artifact)
(b) (Artifact) → $\begin{Bmatrix} \text{(Object)} \\ \text{(Physical)} \\ \text{(Non-living)} \end{Bmatrix}$

The rules in (2.31) would simplify the lexical reading for one sense of "chair" given in (2.15) by allowing the elimination of '(Object)', '(Physical)',

'(Non-living)', '(Artifact)'. There will, of course, be many other redundancy rules that eliminate semantic markers such as '(Physical)' and '(Artifact)' from the dictionary, as, for example, rules (a) and (b) of (2.32):[19]

(2.32)   (a) (Animal) → (Physical)
         (b) (Vehicle) → (Artifact)

The dictionary is the base from which the semantic component works in forming derived readings to account for the compositional meaning of syntactically complex constituents. The projection rules are the mechanism for forming the derived readings. Let us now examine how the dictionary and the projection rules work together to provide readings for each constituent of a sentence.

As has already been observed, the compositional account of the meaning of a sentence requires two types of syntactic information, namely, a specification of the syntactic atomic constituents (that is, the lexical items) and a specification of their syntactic organization (that is, which items go together to form constituents of the sentence and by what relations they combine). Although information of this sort is included in all of the phrase markers in the structural description of a sentence, the underlying phrase markers seem to give it in its most complete form. The other phrase markers result from transformations, and transformational operations of deletion and permutation eliminate information about both lexical items and constituent structure.[20] Therefore, if the semantic component is to have the syntactic information it needs, it seems reasonable to require that the input to the semantic component for a sentence S is the underlying phrase marker(s) of S generated by the syntactic component.

The first step in the process of providing readings for the constituents of a sentence is to assign appropriate lexical readings from the dictionary to the lexical items in the terminal string of the underlying phrase marker. This can be done on the basis of the following convention: an occurrence of a lexical item in the terminal string is paired with the set of lexical readings in the dictionary entry for this item on the condition that the syntactic markers in the lexicon entry categorize it in the same way that it is categorized in the underlying phrase marker. The simplest form of this convention would be the stipulation that the set of lexical readings paired with a lexical item in a dictionary entry is carried along with the lexical item when the lexical rule of the syntactic component inserts that item in a preterminal string.[21]

Once lexical readings are assigned to lexical items in an underlying phrase marker, the semantic redundancy rules can operate to fill out compressed lexical readings by supplying the semantic markers which were excluded for purposes of economy in the formulation of lexical readings in dictionary entries. These semantic markers must be introduced at this stage because they will be required to determine whether or not lexical readings can combine to form derived readings. For instance,

---

[19] For further discussion see Katz (1966, pp. 224–239).
[20] See Katz and Postal (1964, Chapters 3 and 4).
[21] See Chomsky (1965, Section 2.3.3. of Chapter 2).

the sense of "hard" meaning 'not easily penetrated' can combine with the sense of "chair" represented by the lexical reading given in (2.15) only if the semantic marker '(Physical)' appears in the reading of "chair" in an underlying phrase marker. But, as was mentioned with regard to rule (2.31), this semantic marker does not actually appear in the lexical reading of "chair." Hence, it must be introduced by a semantic redundancy rule prior to the point at which the projection rules would combine readings of "hard" and "chair" to obtain a derived reading for "hard chair."

Once the semantic redundancy rules have done their work, we have what we will call *lexically interpreted underlying phrase markers*. These constitute the domain of the projection rules. The principles expressing the order of the operation of the subcomponents—the assignment of lexical readings first, then the application of the semantic redundancy rules, and finally the operation of the projection rules—constitute the main semantic universals under (2.9), that is, the main componential organizational universals at the semantic level.

The projection rules finish the job of giving the readings for the constituents of a sentence by assigning all of the derived readings. They convert lexically interpreted underlying phrase markers into *semantically interpreted underlying phrase markers*. Each of the constituents of these underlying phrase markers is associated with an optimal set of readings, that is, each reading in the set represents one sense of the constituent to which it is assigned and each sense of this constituent is represented by one reading in the set.

The projection rules first combine expanded lexical readings. They next combine the derived readings formed from the combination of expanded lexical readings and continue combining derived readings until the process terminates with the assignment of derived readings for the whole sentence. When the lexical readings were assigned to terminal symbols, the semantic component used the underlying phrase marker for information about what lexical items occurred in the deep structure of the sentence and what syntactic categorization they received. At the point when the projection rules apply, the semantic component again uses the underlying phrase marker, this time for information about how the lexical items concatenate to form constituents, that is, information about the relation of subconstituent to constituent and about the syntactic categorization of constituents. The projection rules can then combine readings associated with subconstituents to form the readings for the full constituent. They do this by moving from smaller to larger constituents in accord with another semantic universal under (2.9).[22] In the course of their operation, the projection rules enforce selection restrictions at each step, thus preventing some readings from combining while allowing others to form derived readings which are assigned to constituents. In this manner, each constituent in an underlying phrase marker, including the whole sentence constituent, receives a set of readings to represent its meaning, and the lexically interpreted underlying phrase marker is converted into a semantically interpreted underlying phrase marker.

---

[22] The universal in question here states that projection rules apply first to the innermost labeled bracketings of the terminal string of an underlying phrase marker, then to the next innermost, and so on, until they reach the outermost. In other words they proceed from the bottom to the top of a tree.

Projection rules, as they have been formulated,[23] differ from one another by their conditions of application and by the operations they perform in producing a derived reading. A projection rule applies to a set of readings associated with an *n*-tuple of constituents just in case the *n*-tuple satisfies the grammatical relation in terms of which the projection rule is defined. There is, then, a different projection rule for each distinct grammatical relation—one for the attribution relation, one for the subject-verb relation, one for the verb–direct object relation, one for the verb–indirect object relation, and so on. Which projection rule applies in a given step in forming a semantically interpreted underlying phrase marker thus depends on the grammatical relation that holds among the subconstituents (of the constituent at that step), which already have readings assigned to them, and the full complex constituent that these subconstituents form, which does not as yet have any readings assigned to it. If, for example, the relation is that of modifier to head, then the projection rule applies whose conditions of application are defined by the modification relation; if the relation is verb-object, then the projection rule defined for that grammatical relation applies, and so forth. Each such rule, moreover, performs a distinct operation on the readings to which it applies. The projection rule that applies to readings of a modifier and readings of its head forms a derived reading by taking the Boolean union of the semantic markers in both readings, while the projection rule that combines readings of a verb with readings of its direct object forms derived readings by embedding the reading of the direct object in the reading of the verb at a fixed position. Of course, such combinatorial operations are performed only if the readings in the domain of a projection rule meet the selection restriction governing their combination. Thus, the projection rules associate types of semantic combination with particular grammatical relations. They specify the semantic import of the grammatical relations defined in syntactic theory. Their full characterization is, then, a main item under (2.8), that is, a prime formal universal on the semantic level.

We now define the notion 'semantic interpretation of a sentence'. What is involved here is the concept of the full set of statements that can be made about the meaning of the sentence. The set of semantically interpreted underlying phrase markers for a sentence does not by itself specify the semantic properties and relations that the sentence has. This is what the semantic interpretation of the sentence provides over and above representations of senses. Given definitions for each semantic property and relation (i.e., a complete specification of (2.10)) and semantically interpreted underlying phrase markers for a sentence S, it will be possible to enumerate the full list of *semantic predictions* about the semantic properties and relations of S. This list is the semantic interpretation of S.

6. Preliminary definitions of some semantic properties and relations

The definitions of semantic properties and relations in semantic theory can be thought of as formal explications of our ordinary notions about semantic concepts. For example, our ordinary notions of semantic similarity, ambiguity,

---

[23] See Katz and Fodor (1963) and Katz (1966).

meaningfulness, and synonymy are, roughly, that semantically similar expressions are ones whose senses share a feature, that an ambiguous expression is one that has more than one sense, that a meaningful expression is one that has a sense, and that two expressions are synonymous in case they have a common sense. To construct a semantic theory, we have to reformulate such ordinary, common sense notions within a formal theory of grammar which exhibits their interrelations and their connections to the expressions and sentences of natural languages. In each case the lines along which we are to construct the reformulation is to some extent suggested by the ordinary notion we are trying to explicate formally. But although these notions guide our efforts to arrive at formal definitions, they by no means determine them. As we shall see in the course of this study, the form in which the definitions are given is also influenced by considerations of other sorts, considerations having to do with the role these definitions play in semantic theory, their interrelations and their connection to other systematic aspects of the theory of language and semantic theory. The definitions to be presented in this section are the most direct conversion of our ordinary notions of semantic concepts into the formalism of semantic theory. This is so because, at the present early stage of theory construction, there is very little else available to influence the form such definitions take. Once we develop semantic theory more fully, other considerations will enter to change their statement. Accordingly, the definitions to be given here are called "preliminary" to acknowledge from the outset that they are not intended as final characterizations of semantic properties and relations.

We think of things as similar when they have some but not all features in common. Accordingly, we think of two expressions from a natural language as similar in meaning when their senses are built out of some of the same concepts. Since semantic markers represent the concepts out of which senses are built, we are immediately led to the definitions of 'semantic similarity' and 'semantic distinctness' in (2.33) and (2.34):

(2.33)   A constituent C_i is semantically similar to a constituent C_j on a sense just in case there is a reading of C_i and a reading of C_j which have a semantic marker in common. (They can be said to be semantically similar with respect to the concept ϕ in case the shared semantic marker represents ϕ.)

(2.34)   A constituent C_i is semantically distinct from a constituent C_j on a sense of C_i and a sense of C_j just in case the readings of these senses have no semantic markers in common.

Clearly, synonymy is the limiting case of semantic similarity: it is the case where two constituents are as similar as possible, where there is no difference in meaning between a sense of one and a sense of the other. Hence, the definition of 'synonymy' is as in (2.35) and of 'full synonymy' as in (2.36):

(2.35)   A constituent C_i is synonymous with another constituent C_j on a sense just in case they have a reading in common.

(2.36)   A constituent C_i is fully synonymous with C_j just in case the set of readings assigned to C_i is identical to the set of readings assigned to C_j.

Paraphrase can be taken as synonymy between sentences.

   Closely tied in with these relations is 'meaning inclusion', defined as in (2.37) and (2.38):

(2.37) A constituent C_i's sense is semantically included in a sense of a constituent of C_j just in case every semantic marker in a reading of C_i is also in a reading for C_j.

(2.38) A constituent C_i is fully included semantically in a constituent C_j just in case, for each reading of C_i, there is a reading of C_j such that the semantic markers in the former are also in the latter.

If two constituents are synonymous, then they are each semantically included in the other, but if one is semantically included in the other, it does not follow that the two are synonymous.

   The next semantic properties to be defined depend on the manner in which multiple senses of lexical items are carried up to constituents at higher phrase structure levels.

   Ambiguity, as ordinarily understood, is a case where there is a problem telling one thing from another, and, accordingly, a semantic ambiguity is a case where there are (at least) the two senses required to pose this problem. Furthermore, given that readings represent senses of constituents and that the number of senses of a constituent is its degree of ambiguity, it follows that the number of readings assigned to a constituent should correctly reflect its degree of ambiguity. Thus, we define 'semantic ambiguity' as in (2.39):

(2.39) A constituent C is semantically ambiguous just in case the set of readings assigned to C contains two or more members. (C's degree of ambiguity is given by the number of readings in the set.)

   Normally selection restrictions filter out some potential readings and allow others to form and to be assigned to the appropriate higher level constituents. In the extreme case, however, the selection restriction will block all combinations and the higher level constituents will receive no reading. The constituents are then represented as having no senses, as being meaningless or, as we shall say here, semantically anomalous.[24] Hence, the definition of 'anomaly' is as in (2.40):

(2.40) A constituent is semantically anomalous just in case it is assigned no readings (the set of readings assigned to it is null).

   If exactly one reading is assigned to a constituent, it is neither semantically anomalous nor semantically ambiguous. Thus the definition of 'uniqueness' is as in (2.41):

(2.41) A constituent is semantically unique just in case the set of readings assigned to it contains exactly one member.

[24] This term is chosen because "meaningless" has a stronger connotation than is desired.

The Kantian notion of analyticity is that of the vacuous assertion that results when the meaning of a predicate contains only attributes that are components of the meaning of the subject. Analytic sentences are thus trivially true by virtue of the fact that the determination of the things to which their subject refers already guarantees that these things will have the attributes their predicate asserts of them. Since semantic markers represent the conceptual components that form the meaning of a subject and a predicate, the primary condition for 'analyticity' can be stated, as in (2.42) and (2.43), in terms of the formal condition that the semantic markers in the reading of the predicate also appear in the reading of the subject.[25] (The further defining condition in (2.42) will be explained in Chapter 4.)

(2.42) S is analytic on a reading $R_{1,2}$ if and only if every noncomplex semantic marker in R_2 occurs in R_1 and for any complex semantic marker $((M_1) \vee (M_2) \vee \cdots \vee (M_n))$ in R_2 there is an (M_i), $1 \leq i \leq n$, in R_1;

(2.43) S is fully analytic if and only if S is analytic on each reading assigned to its sentence constituent; i.e., for each reading $R_{i,j}$ assigned to S, S is analytic (in the sense of (2.42)) on $R_{i,j}$;

where the symbol 'R_i' or 'R_1' stands for a reading of the subject of a sentence in the range of 'S', the symbol 'R_j' or 'R_2' stands for a reading of the predicate of such a sentence, and the symbol '$R_{i,j}$' or '$R_{1,2}$' stands for a reading of the whole sentence which results from the semantic combination of 'R_i' and 'R_j' and of 'R_1' and 'R_2', respectively.

Analyticity is the counterpart on the sentence level of the semantic relation of redundancy at the level of nonsentential constituents. The analyticity of " Mothers are female" is thus the counterpart of the redundancy of "female mother." This leads to the definitions (2.44) and (2.45) of 'redundancy':

(2.44) A constituent C is redundant on a reading $R_{i,j}$ if (a) C is syntactically formed from the constituents c_i and c_j, (b) c_i is a modifier and c_j is its head, (c) $R_{i,j}$ is a reading of C formed from R_i which is a reading of c_i and R_j which is a reading of c_j, (d) every noncomplex semantic marker in R_i occurs in R_j and for any complex semantic marker $((M_1) \vee (M_2) \vee \cdots \vee (M_n))$ in R_i, there is an (M_z), $1 \leq z \leq n$, in R_j.

(2.45) C is fully redundant if and only if C is redundant on each of its readings.

Analogously, contradiction is the counterpart, on the level of sentences, of the semantic relation of meaning incompatibility at the level of lower order constituents. We thus seek definitions which are constructed in such a manner that the similarity and difference between contradictoriness and incompatibility are explained. Further, these definitions must integrate with (2.42), (2.43), and the definitions of 'syntheticity' to provide the logical relationships among these concepts.

---

[25] We assume throughout the remaining definitions that the variable 'S' ranges over sentences that are determinable, which means, in the case of (2.42), that S is determinable on $R_{1,2}$. This notion and the reason for the requirement will be dealt with in Chapter 4, where the concept of determinability is presented.

Linguistically, the concept of incompatibility appears as antonymy, which is a relation between expressions. Under the general notion there are many specific types of antonymy relations. One example is the sex-antonymy relation that holds between a pair of expressions just in case their senses are identical except that where one contains femaleness as one of its component concepts the other contains maleness. Some instances of sex-antonymy are given in (2.46):

(2.46)   bride/groom, aunt/uncle, cow/bull, girl/boy, actress/actor, doe/buck

The general case for antonymy relations is not pairs, but *n*-tuples. For example, there are species-antonymous *n*-tuples, an instance of which is presented in (2.47):

(2.47)   child/cub/puppy/kitten/cygnet

Besides there being many other types of antonymy relations, the extension of any one, i.e., the set of all and only the *n*-tuples of expressions of the language that bear that type of antonymy relation to one another, is infinite, since the process of constructing further expressions from the simplest cases by syntactic rules is recursive and generally preserves the antonymy relation. Thus, the set of antonymous *n*-tuples that contains the words listed in (2.46) also contains the more complex expressions listed in (2.48):

(2.48)   the nervous bride/the nervous groom, several aunts who talk far too much/several uncles who talk far too much, our beloved old cow/our beloved old bull

Note that the importance of obtaining an explication of the concept of antonymy—here understood in the broad sense which goes beyond the lexicographer's usage where "antonymy" is usually applied only to the relation when it holds of words—has to do not only with explaining this semantic relation between words and expressions as in (2.46) and (2.47) but also with explaining various other semantic properties.

Consider the sentences in (2.49):

(2.49)   (a) John is well and Mary's not sick either
         (b) John is smart and Mary's not stupid either
         (c) John is well and Mary's not $\left\{ \begin{matrix} \text{in fair health} \\ \text{well, healthy} \\ \text{foolish} \\ \text{poor} \\ \text{dead} \end{matrix} \right\}$ either
         (d) John is smart and Mary's not $\left\{ \begin{matrix} \text{smart} \\ \text{bright} \\ \text{sick} \\ \text{dirty} \\ \text{alive} \end{matrix} \right\}$ either

The sentences represented in (a) and (b) of (2.49) are meaningful whereas those in (c) and (d) are semantically anomalous. The reason is clearly that when "either" operates together with a conjunction to conjoin a positive and negative sentence in order to say something about one person and then "ditto" about another, there is a semantic restriction that the expressions serving as predicates (the expressions that provide the content for what is said about the people) must be antonymous (members of the same antonymous n-tuple). Obviously, then, the formalism on which such semantic anomalousness is predicted and explained will require a definition of the antonymy relation.

The most natural way of defining the notion 'antonymous constituents' so that the definition will be adequate for antonymy sets containing infinitely many particular n-tuples of antonymous expressions is to group semantic markers into antonymous n-tuples on the basis of the incompatibilities they are supposed to represent. This can be accomplished by using some suitable formal device in the formulation of semantic markers in which they are so represented that the membership of any n-tuple of antonymous semantic markers can be uniquely determined on the basis of formal features of the symbols that comprise the semantic markers. For example, we could write the semantic markers that represent the concepts of maleness and femaleness, assuming them to be incompatible and jointly exhaustive of the sexual domain, in the form '(S^+)' and '(S^-)', respectively. Assuming, on the other hand, that the concepts are not jointly exhaustive (taking the term "hermaphrodite" into consideration, for example), we could write an antonymous n-tuple in the form '(S^m)', '(S^f)', and '(S^h)'. Actually, later we shall find reason to further modify this notation in certain ways, but, generally, the notation for X-antonymous n-tuples of semantic markers will be represented by a common base semantic marker with semantic marker superscripts that indicate the incompatible elements within the domain determined by the base semantic marker. Thus, the general form of an antonymous n-tuple of semantic markers is as shown in (2.50) and as specified in (2.51):

(2.50) $(M^{(\alpha_1)}), (M^{(\alpha_2)}), \ldots, (M^{(\alpha_n)})$

(2.51)   Two semantic markers belong to the same antonymous n-tuple of semantic markers if and only if one has the form $(M^{(\alpha_i)})$ and the other has the form $(M^{(\alpha_j)})$, where $i \neq j$ and $1 \leq i \leq n$ and $1 \leq j \leq n$.

We may now define 'antonymy' as in (2.52) and (2.53):

(2.52)   Two constituents C_i and C_j are antonymous (on a sense) if and only if they are not full sentences and they have, respectively, readings R_i and R_j such that R_i is identical to R_j except that R_i contains a semantic marker (M_i) and R_j contains a semantic marker (M_j) and the semantic markers (M_i) and (M_j) are distinct members of the same antonymous n-tuple of semantic markers.

(2.53)   Two constituents C_i and C_j are fully antonymous if and only if they are antonymous on every sense.

In earlier discussions,[26] we failed to single out the ordinary lexicographical notion of antonymy as we have done here. Instead, we included it under the general notion of incompatibility. Here we explicate the latter by (2.54) and (2.55):

(2.54) Two constituents C_i and C_j are incompatible (on a sense) if and only if they are not full sentences and they have, respectively, readings R_i and R_j such that R_i contains a semantic marker (M_i) and R_j contains a semantic marker (M_j) and the semantic markers (M_i) and (M_j) are distinct members of the same antonymous n-tuple of semantic markers.

(2.55) Two constituents C_i and C_j are fully incompatible if and only if they are incompatible on every sense.

Lumping both notions under one definition and using the label 'antonymous expression' (as the defined term) caused some unnecessary confusion about antonymy and incompatibility. Cases like "cow" and "cowboy," which are not antonyms in the strict lexicographer's sense, were regarded as antonymous expressions on the former usage (incompatible expressions on the present usage). This led some to think that we were unable to explicate the lexicographer's notion of antonymy. The distinction we now make explicit in (2.52) and (2.54) should eliminate the occasion for such confusion and show that both the notion of lexicographical antonymy and the notion of incompatibility can be explicated.

We may construct definitions for 'S is contradictory (on a sense)' and 'S is fully contradictory' that reveal the way in which these concepts reflect antonymy and incompatibility relations on the level of nonsentential constituents. Thus we have (2.56) and (2.57):

(2.56) S is contradictory on a sense represented by the reading $R_{1,2}$ if and only if the reading R_1 contains a semantic marker (M_i) and the reading R_2 contains a semantic marker (M_j) such that (M_i) and (M_j) are different semantic markers belonging to the same antonymous n-tuple of semantic markers.

(2.57) S is fully contradictory if and only if S is contradictory on every reading assigned to its sentence constituent.

What is asserted about a sentence when its semantic interpretation marks it as contradictory on a reading is that anything to which its subject refers possesses a property or properties incompatible with some property or properties attributed to it by the predicate. Thus, just as analytic statements are true by virtue of meaning alone, contradictory statements are false by virtue of meaning alone. The very condition that determines when something is correctly regarded as an instance of the subject concept guarantees the falsity of the predication.

In terms of the previous definitions, we can now define 'syntheticity' as in (2.58) and (2.59):

---

[26] See Katz (1964a; 1966, pp. 118–224).

(2.58)   S is synthetic on a sense if and only if there is a reading $R_{1,2}$ assigned to S's sentence constituent such that S is neither analytic nor contradictory on $R_{1,2}$.

(2.59)   S is fully synthetic if and only if S is synthetic on each of the readings assigned to its sentence constituents.

These definitions reconstruct the idea that a synthetic sentence is one whose truth or falsity cannot be decided on the basis of the meanings of its component words, but must be decided on the basis of consideration of whether or not what the sentence's subject refers to has the property that it is asserted to have.

Relative to the definitions of semantic properties and relations, the semantic component provides an explanation of how the semantic properties and relations of a constituent are determined by the senses of the constituents that comprise it. The form of such an explanation is as follows. A constituent of a sentence (perhaps the whole sentence itself) receives a set of readings in the semantically interpreted underlying phrase marker where the constituent occurs. Each reading in such a set formally represents one of the senses of the constituent in the sentence to which the semantically interpreted underlying phrase marker is assigned. Since the definitions of semantic properties and relations in semantic theory are formulated in terms of formal features of readings, whether a constituent C has the semantic property P or bears the relation H (to some other constituent) depends on whether the readings in the set assigned to C exhibit the formal features required by the definition for P or H. What explains the presence of the features of the readings in C's semantically interpreted underlying phrase marker by virtue of which C is marked as P (or H) are the projection rules, which reconstruct the way in which the meanings of complex constituents are a compositional function of the meanings of their component constituents, and the dictionary, which provides readings for noncomplex constituents of the language. Hence, what explains C being P (or H) is the application of the dictionary and the operation of the projection rules.

Not only do the definitions of semantic properties and relations complete the definition of the concept of a semantic interpretation, they also provide a basis for systematically testing the semantic component of a grammar. In accordance with these definitions, the semantic interpretation of a sentence S will contain a list of semantic predictions, each of which will say either that S has or does not have a certain semantic property P or that S does or does not bear a certain semantic relation H to some other constituent. These predictions can be tested against the judgments made by fluent speakers of the language. Fluent speakers make various judgments about aspects of the meaning of a constituent and the semantic interpretation makes predictions about the same aspects. If the judgments and predictions coincide, that is, if the statements in the semantic interpretation of the sentence about aspects of its meaning correctly predict the judgments of the speakers, then the semantic component from which the predictions come is confirmed; if not, it is disconfirmed. In this manner, the semantic component can be submitted to empirical tests that may either confirm or disconfirm its account of the meanings of expressions in the language. If there is confirmation over a wide range of empirical cases, it may be claimed that the semantic component reflects the linguistic competence of native speakers in regard to their knowledge of the semantic structure of their language. In the case of disconfirmation, the falsified predictions guide us in making suitable revisions in the dictionary or projection rules or definitions. Then the process of empirical test begins again.

As in the explication of any abstract concept, we assume in the explication of semantic properties and relations that we are, initially, in possession of a fairly representative set of the relevant facts. These take the form of examples of morphemes, words, phrases, and sentences of various natural languages that have one or another particular linguistic property or that bear one or another linguistic relation to some other construction. We assume, therefore, that such examples are substantiated on the basis of reliable linguistic intuitions on the part of fluent speakers of the language. That is, we assume that we can demonstrate, in one manner or another, that fluent speakers will make consistent intuitive judgments indicating that the example does exhibit the property or relation it has been taken to exhibit. Accordingly, these examples serve as clear cases for the explication of semantic concepts. We seek to construct a semantic theory that explains the clear cases in the simplest and most revealing way and to allow the theory to stand the challenge of predictive test as further clear cases are brought up. Not all cases will be clear cases. The unclear ones, those about which the intuitions of speakers are too weak or conflicting to determine linguistic properties and relations, have to be decided by the theory itself. This, however, is a familiar feature of explication. The fact that we can allow the theory to decide in some situations confers an enormous advantage on theory construction. It permits the linguist to postpone the obligation to provide a treatment of unclear cases until he has obtained the theoretical machinery for interpolating their treatment from the treatment he has given the available clear cases, thereby preventing unclear cases from standing in the way of further linguistic inquiry.

Aspects of semantic representation

I have yet to see any problem, however complicated, which
when you looked at it the right way did not become still more
complicated.

Paul Anderson

In this chapter we attempt to reply to various recent criticisms of
semantic theory. However, we shall also be concerned with setting the stage for the
succeeding chapters by providing a more up-to-date account of semantic representation than is available in earlier published work on semantic theory.[1]

1. Some historical remarks

Bolinger (1965) starts out by giving a false picture of the historical
background and sources of semantic theory as presented in the early publications.
According to Bolinger, the theory is an attempt to carry over the syntactic notion

---

[1] By "earlier published work" I refer to "The Structure of a Semantic Theory"
(Katz and Fodor (1963)), "Analyticity and Contradiction in Natural Language" (Katz (1964a)),
"Semantic Theory and the Meaning of 'Good'" (Katz (1964c)), etc. *An Integrated Theory of
Linguistic Descriptions* (Katz and Postal (1964)) also belongs to this period.

of a *marker* into semantics in essentially the same way as taxonomic linguistics was an attempt to carry over the phonological notion of the *eme* into morphology. This analogy, however, is quite misleading. Taxonomic linguistics sought to define morphemes as sequences of phonemes in order to show that linguistic units at any grammatical level ultimately reduce to physical segments of utterances.[2] In studies of semantics such as those referred to in note 1, there is no corresponding attempt to treat meanings (or senses) as classes of those syntactic elements represented by syntactic markers ('Noun', 'Verb', etc.) In fact, an aim of this work was to show that semantic elements are autonomous and relate to syntactic elements only by virtue of highly abstract connections between the systems into which they enter within a grammar. Thus, there is clearly no attempt to vindicate the taxonomic aim of reducing semantic units to syntactic units in a classificational analysis whose lowest level consists of physical segments of utterances.

Bolinger's analogy is a misrepresentation in another respect. It was not the syntactic notion of a marker (in the taxonomic sense or any other) that was borrowed, but only the label "marker." This was done so that linguistic theory might enjoy some standardization in the theoretical vocabulary employed for representation at the syntactic and semantic levels. The actual historical link between the new semantics and the slightly less new syntax is that the latter, in the form of generative, transformational grammar, provided for the first time an adequate formal object for semantic interpretation, namely, the underlying phrase marker. It also provided a conception of what the basic problem of semantic description might be, namely, the completion of the explanation, begun but not nearly finished by the syntactic component, of the speaker's competence to produce and understand new sentences of his language. It was precisely because taxonomic grammar, which gave syntactic analyses of surface structure only, was abandoned in favor of transformational grammar, which gave analyses of the more semantically relevant deep structure, that semantic interpretation had an appropriate object. And it was precisely because the study of deep structure showed the limits of syntactic analysis that semantic description could be conceived of as starting at the point where syntactic description leaves off and completing the account of grammatical competence.

Finally, Bolinger's historical discussion is highly provincial in that it neglects the philosophical sources of semantic theory. It says nothing about the methodological framework that was taken from the philosophy of science and served as a guide to theory construction both in syntax and semantics. It ignores the exceedingly significant impetus for the development of a semantic theory within formal grammar that was provided by critiques of positivist and ordinary language philosopher's attempts to handle meaning. It omits the basic problem common to every philosophical effort to gain some measure of clarity about the concept of meaning, namely, the problem of understanding logical form. And it neglects wholly the direction given to the development of semantic theory by the classical philosophical problems of analyticity, categories, and so on. In short, Bolinger fails to note that semantic theory was not simply a development within linguistics, but rather a joint development within both linguistics and philosophy.

[2] See Katz (1964b).

2. On explanatory goals in semantics

Both Bolinger and Weinreich misrepresent the explanatory goals of semantic theory. Bolinger (1965) characterizes these exclusively in terms of "what a dictionary does or ought to do to enable the rules of the theory—the 'projection rules'—to disambiguate a semantically ambiguous sentence" (p. 556). Weinreich (1966), after quoting a remark from Katz and Fodor (1963) about explanatory goals in semantics, a remark which contradicts his construal of these goals, says, "In actuality, KF is concerned with an extremely limited part of the semantic competence: the detection of semantic anomalies and the determination of the number of readings of a sentence" (p. 397).[3] These two accounts drastically mischaracterize the aim of semantic interpretation by describing the output of the semantic component, not as a semantic interpretation of a sentence (where this includes predictions about every semantic property and relation), but rather as an integer: 0 in case the sentence is semantically anomalous (the degree of ambiguity is zero), 1 in case it is unique, and 2 or greater in case it is two or more ways ambiguous. But it has been explicitly stated, both in our original article (Katz and Fodor (1963)), to which Bolinger and Weinreich refer, and in other places, that a semantic component is concerned with *every* facet of the speaker's ability to fathom the meaning of sentences compositionally and to determine the full range of their semantic properties and relations. Indeed, the very passage quoted by Weinreich clearly explains that we do not limit semantic description as he and Bolinger claim: the quotation includes the qualification that a semantic component must mark "every other semantic property or relation that plays a role in this ability." Hence, the misrepresentation of semantic theory in question here consists in taking two things that the theory demands of an adequate semantic component to constitute the only things that the component, on our conception of semantic theory, must do.[4]

[3] Weinreich says that Fodor and I only touched on the notion of paraphrase in passing and then concludes that paraphrase determination is not one of the concerns of semantic theory in our sense. We did more than just touch on it, however; we made it as central as the determination of anomaly and ambiguity, defining the paraphrase relation in terms of the identity of readings. This is neither more nor less than defining anomaly in terms of the absence of readings or ambiguity in terms of multiplicity of readings, and these he accepts as genuine concerns of our semantic theory.

[4] We have not merely listed a set of requirements on the predictive adequacy of a semantic component; we have also offered explanations of the semantic properties and relations which we require a semantic component to predict and a general method for arriving at such predictions based on these explanations. In other words, in each case, we have offered a definition of the semantic property or relation which explains what it is that the speaker's judgment is a judgment of, that is, the definition explains what structure is attributed to a sentence or one of its constituents when it is predicted to have a certain semantic property or to bear a certain semantic relation. Therefore, even in the case of the semantic properties that Bolinger and Weinreich concede to semantic theory, the theory attempts to do more than their accounts would suggest: it does not just express the degree of ambiguity of a constituent by determining the number of senses it has; it attempts to *explain* the semantic ambiguity, distinctness, or semantic anomaly on the basis of how the semantic representations of a constituent's parts are compositionally combined to form its semantic representation. Constituents that have two senses or exactly one sense or no senses can arrive at their degree of ambiguity in very different ways and for very different reasons. Such differences among constituents with the same number of senses must be reflected in the semantically interpreted underlying phrase marker of the semantic component as defined by semantic theory.

Note that, although we have not as yet given definitions for all the semantic properties and relations that play a role in the speaker's semantic competence, the present formulation of semantic theory commits us to the thesis that any other semantic properties and relations about which speakers can make reliable judgments can be defined in the same manner as the ones considered so far. That is—and this is a crucial point—our semantic theory is built on the principle that all such aspects of a speaker's semantic competence can be reconstructed and explained on the basis of definitions framed in terms of formal features of semantically interpreted underlying phrase markers. Thus, any aspect of the speaker's semantic competence that can be expressed in his judgments about the semantic structure of sentences can be predicted from such definitions and the appropriate semantically interpreted underlying phrase markers. One of the real tests of semantic theory lies in determining the truth of this claim.

Weinreich (1966) goes on to discuss the errors of a preoccupation with the concept of polysemy:

> But in assigning this concept so central a place, KF is guilty of two errors. In the first place, it takes no cognizance of the obvious danger that the differentiation of submeanings in a dictionary might continue without limit (p. 398).

This is all Weinreich says about the first of these two alleged errors at this point in his paper. Later he returns to it:

> When one considers the phrases *eat bread* and *eat soup*, one realizes that *eat* has a slightly different meaning in each phrase: in the latter expression, but not in the former, it covers the manipulation of a spoon. Continuing the procedure applied in KF to polysemous items such as *ball* and *colorful*, we would have to represent the dictionary entry for *eat* by a branching path, perhaps as in ...:

$$eat \to \cdots \to (\text{Action}) \to \cdots \to (\text{Swallow}) \nearrow^{(\text{Chew}) \to \cdots \langle(\text{Solid})\rangle}_{\searrow \cdots \to (\text{Spoon}) \langle(\text{Liquid})\rangle}$$

> ... But then the activity symbolized by *eat* is also different depending on whether things are eaten with a fork or with one's hands; and even hand-eating of apples and peanuts, or the fork-eating of peas and spaghetti, are recognizably different. It is apparent, therefore, that a KF-type dictionary is in danger of having to represent an unlimited differentiation of meanings (p. 411).

Weinreich here is entertaining the possibility that the submeanings, or senses, of a lexical item can be infinite in number, that differentiation of the senses of lexical items can involve infinitely many semantic distinctions. There are the best of empirical reasons for dismissing this possibility, however. The dictionary is a reconstruction of an aspect of the speaker's semantic competence. Since speakers are equipped with finite brains, the mechanism reconstructed by the dictionary can, in principle, *store* only finitely many bits of information about a particular lexical item. A language with a dictionary that has, for each (or any) lexical item representing an activity, a lexical reading for each of the infinitely many ways that the activity can be performed could not be acquired by creatures such as ourselves, whose brains are finite and function in real time. Thus, the fact that the semantic component is an explication of a human competence rules out the possibility of the danger cited by Weinreich. We therefore require in our statement of semantic theory that the dictionary be a finite list of entries, that each entry consist of a finite number of lexical readings, and that each lexical reading contain a finite number of semantic markers.

Rather, the danger lies in taking seriously the notion of infinite polysemy since no rule of grammar could enumerate each and every one of the respects in which the "activity symbolized by *eat*" can be "recognizably different" from case to case. Moreover, if the dictionary had to account for infinite polysemy, we would have to forget about trying to explain semantic relations. For example, consider the argument (3.1):

(3.1)   John ate meat with a knife and Bill ate meat with chopsticks

   (Therefore) John and Bill ate meat

The premiss of (3.1) clearly entails the conclusion, but we could not explain this on Weinreich's conception of the dictionary.

Weinreich here fails to make the important distinction between the meaning of words and a fully detailed description of the actual things, situations, activities, events, and such to which words refer. Various activities that can correctly be called "eating" may differ in the ways they are carried out, as Weinreich suggests. They may be performed with spoons, fingers, chopsticks, knives, shovels, or what-ever strikes one's fancy, but, nonetheless, they are instances of "eating" in the same sense of this term. The fundamental point is that, insofar as "eating" applies to each activity with exactly the same sense, they are equivalent activities. Meaning must be an abstraction from the variable features of the things referred to by a term: the meaning of a word must represent only the invariant features by virtue of which something is a thing, situation, activity, event, or whatever of a given type. Otherwise no word could ever be used again with the same meaning with which it is used at any one time, since there is always some difference in what is referred to from one time to the next.

Presumably, Weinreich's failure to distinguish semantically irrelevant referential features from genuine semantic considerations stems from his feeling that the distinction between them is hard to draw. Excluding semantically irrelevant referential features from being represented in lexical readings will, according to Weinreich,

> presuppose, as a primitive concept of the theory, an absolute distinction between true ambiguity and mere indefiniteness of reference. The difficulty of validating such a distinction empirically makes its theoretical usefulness rather dubious (pp. 411–412).

By parity of argument, one might hold that the distinction between virtue and vice, truth and falsehood, beauty and ugliness are of rather dubious theoretical usefulness since these are notoriously difficult to validate empirically. Obviously, no doubt is cast on the theoretical usefulness of a distinction simply because it turns out to be a hard one to draw empirically.

If the distinction between ambiguity and indefiniteness of reference is not drawn, any attempt to cope with semantic structure will die a death of "infinitely many qualifications," one qualification for each of the infinitely many respects in which things, situations, events, actions, and so on that are correcty referred to by the same term in the same sense can differ. Moreover, the distinction between true ambiguity and indefiniteness of reference is easily motivated by the simple consideration that each of the alternative senses of an ambiguous constituent is referentially indefinite in just the same way, though, of course, not with respect to the same features. Consider Weinreich's example of "eat" again. Besides the sense of "taking food through the mouth and swallowing," this word also has the sense of "destruction by gradual consumption," as in talking about the effect of acid on metals. Both senses of the ambiguous word "eat" are referentially indefinite, for just as we can eat with one or another implement, so acid can be applied by one or another means to one or another part of the chain; just as we can eat one or another food, so one or another acid can eat one or another substance, and so forth.

Let us now examine what Weinreich considers to be the second error that results from assigning a central place to the concept of polysemy. He writes:

> In the second place, one would think a scientific approach which distinguishes between competence (knowledge of a language) and performance (use of a language) ought to regard the disambiguation of potential ambiguities as a matter of hearer performance (p. 398).

The mistake underlying this criticism is a confusion of two different things under the expression "disambiguation of potential ambiguities." One is part of the theory of competence while the other is part of the theory of performance. First, there is the sort of disambiguation that is a matter of the internal semantic structure of a sentence, where various senses of certain of its constituents make no contribution to the meaning of the whole sentence due to their conceptual incongruity with senses of other constituents in the sentence. In Katz and Fodor (1963) internal disambiguation was explicated in terms of the operation of selection restrictions, enforced by projection rules, to prevent the assignment of derived readings to constituents whose component constituents have senses that are conceptually incongruous. We illustrated this sort of disambiguation with a variety of examples, one of which is given in (3.2):

(3.2)   The man hit the colorful ball

We argued that (3.2) has no meaningful interpretation on which "ball" has the sense of a social activity, even though this is one of its senses in the dictionary, because of the conceptual incongruity of making a social activity the object on which a physical action like hitting is performed. This type of disambiguation has as its limiting case semantically anomalous sentences such as (3.3):

(3.3)   The man hit the tea party with a hammer

Disambiguation of this sort is regarded as a necessary task for semantic components since it concerns the internal semantic structure of sentences and no extralinguistic considerations enter to decide such cases. Thus, semantic theory takes such disambiguation as a matter to be dealt with in the theory of competence.

The other type of disambiguation, on the other hand, is accomplished on the basis of extralinguistic considerations, particularly contextual information. Consider a semantically ambiguous sentence such as (3.4):

(3.4)   There is no school anymore

Such a sentence can occur in a situation where the hearer can decide that some of its possible senses do not apply but others do. For example, suppose an utterance of (3.4) occurs while we are looking at a school building, intact and undamaged. Then, the situation or context gives us the information we need to decide that the utterance uniquely means that there will be no more sessions at the teaching institution. The point becomes clearer when we compare this case with one where an utterance of (3.4) occurs while we are faced with the charred rubble of what was once the school. Such cases of external disambiguation were referred to in Katz and Fodor (1963) as "setting selection," and we took great pains to argue that they do not fall within the domain of semantic components. (For some idea of how setting selection might occur, see the discussion of Grice's work in Chapter 8, Section 5.)

Weinreich's criticism seems plausible on the surface because these two distinct types of disambiguation are confused with each other. The reader is, as a result, led to think that we require that external disambiguation be handled in the same theory in which we propose to handle internal disambiguation.

It should be pointed out also that Weinreich's statement that we "could not explain sentences that are meant by the speaker to be ambiguous" (p. 348) is not a criticism of our theory. No theory dealing exclusively with linguistic competence can be expected to explain the intentions of speakers in actual speech situations. Consider a parallel case in syntax illustrated by (3.5):

(3.5)   Visiting relatives can be annoying

A speaker could use (3.5) with the express intention of referring to annoyance that is caused by relatives who come to visit, or with the express intention of referring to annoyance caused by going to visit relatives, or with the express intention of uttering an ambiguous sentence (to confuse his hearer or refer to both annoyances at once). No one would say that the grammar of English has to explain that a particular utterance of (3.5) was meant by the speaker to be ambiguous and that another particular utterance of (3.5) was meant not to be. Weinreich fails to appreciate the fact that a theory of competence, whether at the semantic or grammatical level, abstracts away from features of utterance contexts and concerns itself exclusively with inherent features of the sentence type, of which utterances in context are just tokens. He misunderstands this aspect of the distinction between competence and performance, taking intention, which is one psychological variable influencing performance, to be a significant feature of competence.[5]

3. Some confusion about syntactic markers

Weinreich (1966) begins his discussion of the Katz and Fodor (1963) treatment of syntactic markers by saying that "the theoretical status of the syntactic markers in KF is not clear" (p. 400). He then goes on to say:

> It is probably fair to understand that the function of the syntactic marker SxM_i is to assure that all entries having that marker, and only those, can be introduced into the points of a syntactic frame identified by the category symbol SxM_i (p. 400).

Weinreich's manner of phrasing this matter makes it appear as if he is according us a better interpretation than our discussion deserves.[6] Actually, however, our treatment of the status and role of syntactic markers is formally much more satisfactory than his rephrasing of it.[7]

---

[5] Weinreich's further claim that a semantic description in our sense ". . . cannot represent the ambiguity between a grammatical and a deviant sentence " (p. 398) is false, as can be seen from the discussion of deviant sentences in my paper "Semi-sentences" (Katz (1964d)), where such a representation is given. Admittedly, the theory of semi-sentences is far from worked out, but it does offer a conception of how to represent ambiguities between deviant and nondeviant cases. On my theory, semi-sentences are provided with a semantic interpretation from the grammatical sentences related to them (as explicated by a semi-derivation). Hence, if a particular phonetic object has both a grammatical derivation and a semi-derivation, and these are connected with different semantic interpretations, the phonetic object will be represented as ambiguous. Weinreich, to support his claim that semantic theory cannot do what it is supposed to do in this case, would therefore have had to show that a semantic theory, together with a theory of deviance of this kind, is not adequate for marking the ambiguities in question. Because he neglected the theory of deviance, his claim is unsupported.

[6] Let us review the account of the status and utilization of syntactic markers as given in previous publications. A dictionary entry consists of a set of lexical readings associated with a phonological representation of a morpheme and a set of syntactic markers. These syntactic markers provide the information necessary to determine whether the lexical reading associated with a morpheme is to be assigned to an occurrence of that morpheme in an underlying phrase marker. We proposed that the assignment take place just in case the syntactic categorization of the morpheme in the underlying phrase marker ascribes to it exactly those syntactic markers that appear in the set of syntactic markers in the entry for the morpheme. Thus, syntactic markers in a dictionary entry provide a necessary and sufficient condition for assigning a lexical reading to occurrences of lexical items in phrase markers that have the requisite syntactic properties; the satisfaction of the condition is decided in any particular case on the basis of the purely formal operation of checking the symbols labeling nodes.

[7] Consider Weinreich's formulas presented in (2), page 401 of his article (1966). For one thing, the rule (2i), according to Weinreich, does not exhibit the fact that B and C are subcategories of A, but it can, since any rule of this form produces a configuration of symbols in a phrase marker in which either A dominates B or A dominates C. For another, he says (2ii) does show subcategorization. This is true, but it does so for exactly the same reason that (2i) does. In fact, these are formally the same cases, since A_1 and A_2 are just formally distinct single symbols like B and C. Weinreich thinks that the subscripts in (2ii) serve as subcategory designations, but actually all they do is formally distinguish A_1 from A_2 as different symbols, just as the difference in shape between the letters B and C distinguishes them as different symbols. Finally, (2iii) is not, as Weinreich claims, a feature notation. Rather, it is a rewrite rule, allowing us to add the line $A + [+F]$ or $A + [-F]$ when we already have the line A in a phrase structure derivation. It is not the inability of phrase structure rules to exhibit subcategorization that makes features necessary but rather the inappropriateness of subcategorization at the level of cross-classification.

Weinreich next observes, quite correctly, that the formulation of the syntactic portion of a dictionary entry in Katz and Fodor is given in terms of the type of syntactic theory presented in early works of Chomsky's.[8] In this theory, subclassification under a major category (Noun, Verb, etc.) and cross-classification with respect to subclasses were handled by using rewriting rules typical of what was then called the phrase structure subcomponent of the grammar. Chomsky (1965) has since discovered that rules of this sort are inappropriate to express a satisfactory systematization of cross-classificational phenomena at the syntactic level, for reasons which we discuss directly. But Fodor and I went along with other linguists prior to Chomsky's discovery in accepting the older theory in which cross-classificational properties and relations were treated as if they were subclassificational. Since the account we gave of syntactic markers was thus based upon an incorrect conception of the nature of the markers that represent the syntactic properties and relations involved in cross-classification under major categories, we cannot be accused of being unclear with regard to whether we understood such markers in terms of the older or newer type of syntactic theory.

The difficulty in using phrase structure rules to handle the phenomena of cross-classification is that their use expresses the mistaken hypothesis that the relation between a morpheme and the categories to which it belongs is the same as the relation between a phrase and the categories to which it belongs. But, as has been argued convincingly by Chomsky (1965), subclassification and cross-classification under major categories are not organized hierarchically in the way that phrases are categorized. Phrase structure rules thus serve as an adequate model of phrase structure organization but not as an adequate model of subclassification and cross-classification. Consider an example. An English noun can be subclassified as either *common* or *proper*, as "apple" versus "John." Independently, it can also be subclassified as *count* or *mass*, as "spoon" versus "blood." Further, it can be independently classified as *masculine*, *feminine*, or *neuter*, as "brother" versus "lady" versus "stone." Still further, it can be classified as *abstract* or *concrete*, as "truth" versus "house." And so forth. Now, if we try to handle cross-classification by rules of the form $A \rightarrow X$, we have to choose one of these distinctions—proper–common, count–mass, masculine–feminine–neuter, abstract–concrete, etc.—as the highest category division in the hierarchy, since rules of this form hypothesize that subclassification and cross-classification under major categories has, like phrase structure, a hierarchical organization. Suppose, then, we choose *proper–common* as most appropriate for the highest level distinction. Accordingly, with a further choice of the next highest distinction, another for the next highest, still another for the next, and so on, we might have rules like those in (3.6):

(3.6)   (a) Noun → Proper-Noun
      (b) Noun → Common-Noun
      (c) Proper-Noun → Count-Proper-Noun
      (d) Common-Noun → Count-Common-Noun
      (e) Proper-Noun → Mass-Proper-Noun
      (f) Common-Noun → Mass-Common-Noun

[8] For example, Chomsky (1957; 1962).

The trouble with such rules is the following. First, there is no motivation for the choices that we have to make about subclassificational distinctions as levels in the hierarchy. Second, symbols such as 'Count-Proper-Noun', Count-Common-Noun', and 'Mass-Common-Noun' are, formally speaking, as distinct from one another as the symbols 'A', 'B', 'C', etc. As a result, there is no way to express the relations between subcategories, for the formalism treats the subcategories represented by 'Count-Proper-Noun' and 'Count-Common-Noun' as bearing no more relation to one another than the subcategories represented by 'Proper-Noun' and 'Abstract-Noun'. Consequently, although it will be possible to state a transformational rule that applies only to proper nouns, for example, or one that applies only to common nouns, when it comes to a rule that must apply to count nouns or one that must apply to mass nouns, it must be stated in terms of the wholly unrelated subcategories of Proper-Noun or Common-Noun. Accordingly, we miss a generalization that would increase the simplicity and depth of the analysis. The seriousness of this failure is multiplied as we require further rules that apply to cases in terms of subcategories lower down in the hierarchy, for the lower we go the more we increase the number of unnecessary distinctions that must be imported whenever a rule requires a subcategory distinction. In summary, if we represent cross-classificational subclassification hierarchically, we have no motivation for the decisions about domination that we adopt, and we are unable to formulate transformational rules so that they make simple and revealing generalizations about the conditions under which they connect underlying and superficial structures.

To correct this situation, Chomsky developed a way of representing cross-classificational subclassification in syntax without imposing hierarchical ordering, modeling his treatment on the example of phonology.[9] Revising his early version of syntactic theory, he restricted the appearance of rewriting rules to what he calls the *categorial component* of the grammar, which handles just the phrase structure, and he introduced what he calls a *lexicon* to handle structure below the phrase level. The lexicon consists of an unordered set of entries; each entry is a set of syntactic features associated with a set of phonological features that specify the lexical item itself. The syntactic features are given in a *complex symbol* such as [+Noun, +Common, −Count, ...], where '+' indicates that the lexical item in question has the feature so marked and '−' indicates that it does not. The categorial component contains, for each major category A, a rule A →∆, where ∆ is a dummy symbol for which complex symbols will be substituted according to a fixed convention. The categorial component and the lexicon constitute the base component of the syntactic component of a linguistic description. The categorial component generates preterminal strings which consist of occurrences of ∆ and grammatical morphemes but contain no lexical items or subclassification markers. These strings are converted into terminal strings of the base component when complex symbols are inserted into the positions marked by occurrences of ∆ in accord with the general convention for substitution, which we turn to shortly.[10]

---

[9] See Chomsky and Halle (1968).

[10] The treatment given here is one of two approaches proposed by Chomsky (1965, pp. 75–127). At the present time, it is not known which of them is preferable, but for the purposes of our discussion they are not sufficiently different to warrant a comparison.

Thus, there is no longer a need for unmotivated choices because there is no longer the need for arranging the subclassification divisions into a hierarchy, and the transformational rules can now refer just to the feature(s) actually determining their application. This new theory not only avoids the problems encountered in trying to state cross-classificational relations in terms of a hierarchy system, but it turns out also to lead to a sizable number of extremely important additional results in syntax.

Fodor and I based our original conception of a dictionary entry on the early theory of syntactic subclassification and cross-classification and thus inherited the mistakes of that theory. However, it is because we did adopt the wrong conception then prevalent that it is not true, as Weinreich claims, that we were eclectic as between a category and feature interpretation of the syntactic markers in a dictionary entry. To quote Weinreich:

> Single, global syntactic markers would correspond to implicit notations, such as (2i); sequences of elementary markers, to a feature notation such as (2iii). The KF approach is eclectic on this point. The sequences of markers 'Verb-Verb Transitive' for their sample entry 'play' corresponds to principle (2iii); the marker 'Noun concrete' seems to follow the least revealing principle (2i) (p. 401).

There is no justification for Weinreich's claim that we regarded 'Verb-Transitive' as anything but a category symbol just like 'Noun-Concrete'. Of course, in line with Chomsky's recent revision I would now prefer to treat transitivity and concreteness as features rather than as categories in a hierarchy.

As a consequence of Chomsky's reinterpretation of syntactic markers at the subclassificational level as features, semantic theory faces the question of how to manage the association of readings with lexical items introduced into underlying phrase markers by lexical insertion. It will be recalled that an entry in the lexicon is now a pair (D, C), where D is a phonological distinctive feature matrix which specifies the spelling of a lexical item and C is a complex symbol which provides its syntactic features. This requires no change from earlier theory in the conception of the dictionary since a dictionary entry is an entry from the lexicon and a set of lexical readings, as before. The lexical rule allows us to replace occurrences of Δ in preterminal strings by entries of the form (D,C) from the lexicon.[11] If the set of readings for D is already associated with (D,C) in the dictionary, of which the lexicon is a part, then there is no reason for not allowing this set of readings to be carried along, so that after all lexical substitutions have been made, each lexical item in the underlying phrase marker will have been assigned its proper set of lexical readings. Thus, the most natural change to make in the conception of the semantic component to bring it in line with Chomsky's change in the syntactic component is to drop the convention (I),[12] since the lexical substitution rule already

---

[11] Chomsky (1965, pp. 84–106).

[12] Katz and Fodor (1963, p. 196). The convention (I) said that a lexical reading from a dictionary entry for a morpheme is assigned to an occurrence of that morpheme in a phrase marker if each symbol in the set of syntactic markers in the entry also occurs among the symbols that categorize the occurrence of the morpheme in the phrase marker.

performs the function for which (I) was designed. The postulation of (I) was necessary to fill a gap that existed in the earlier formulation of the syntactic component. Its removal can be thought of as involving not only an increase in the simplicity of the semantic component but also the elimination of a certain heterogeneity in the types of rules proposed in semantic theory. The status of (I) was always somewhat unclear. Was it a type of projection rule, different in kind from the others, or some type of semantic rule? The former interpretation complicated the general definition of the notion 'projection rule' and the latter complicated the general definition of the notion 'semantic rule'.

This brings up the matter of the elimination of type 2 projection rules.[13] In *An Integrated Theory of Linguistic Descriptions* (Katz and Postal (1964)) it was suggested that this type of projection rule (which we describe directly) could be eliminated from the semantic component on the basis of an elimination of generalized transformations from the syntactic component. Postal and I argued that singulary transformations do not make a contribution to the meaning of a sentence, that whatever contribution they may appear to make must be taken to come from some inherent feature of underlying phrase markers. We also argued that singulary transformations characteristically produce phrase markers that are too impoverished structurally to be the objects of semantic interpretation since they eliminate syntactic information that is essential for semantic rules to operate correctly. Thus, we concluded that semantic rules must operate exclusively on phrase markers that have not been produced by the application of singulary transformations. The syntactic function of generalized transformations is to embed a phrase marker within another phrase marker at a position already specified in the latter. Postal and I showed that the semantic function of such embedding is just to indicate with which readings of constituents in the matrix phrase marker a given reading of the whole embedded phrase marker can be combined by projection rules. On the basis of these conclusions, we suggested that the transformational subcomponent of the syntactic component be modified by eliminating all generalized transformations in favor of another way of generating phrase markers with phrase markers embedded in them. One way of thus dispensing with generalized phrase markers—the way that Chomsky adopts—is simply to introduce a new rewriting rule into the categorial subcomponent of the syntactic component, a rule which reintroduces the initial category symbol 'S' within a derivation. Then, phrase markers within phrase markers are generated by the application of rewriting rules of the form $A \rightarrow \ldots S \ldots$ and the application of the other rewriting rules of the categorial subcomponent to these internal occurrences of 'S'. Any phrase marker that can be produced by a set of generalized transformations operating on a sequence of phrase markers can also be produced in this fashion.

Chomsky (1965, pp. 128–147) established the validity of this revised account by showing that the elimination of generalized transformations leads to a simpler and empirically more successful syntactic theory. It was known that (a) the set of singulary transformations had to be strictly ordered with respect to priority of application, (b) the set of generalized transformations required no ordering

---

[13] See Katz and Fodor (1963, pp. 514–516).

whatever, (c) singulary transformations always applied to a constituent phrase marker before embedding, and (d) the only ordering required between the set of singulary and the set of generalized transformations was that in many cases certain singulary transformations had to apply to a matrix phrase marker after another phrase marker had been embedded in it. On the early conception of syntactic theory, it was necessary to state these facts as ad hoc requirements. But, as Chomsky points out, the elimination of generalized transformations automatically builds into the model of a syntactic component the only real possibility for ordering, namely, ordering among singulary transformations.[14] Thus, we tighten the constraints on the syntactic component and provide a means of organizing certain linguistic facts on far more general principles.

If there are no generalized transformations, there is no need for type 2 projection rules. The only service they performed for semantic interpretation was to connect an embedded phrase marker with a specific constituent of a matrix phrase marker so that the projection rules would amalgamate the readings of the embedded phrase marker with the readings of the proper constituent. This function is now performed by the constituent structure of underlying phrase markers generated by rules of the form $A \rightarrow \ldots S \ldots$.

The theoretical advantage in eliminating type 2 projection rules is the same as that obtained by the elimination of convention (I), namely, it is possible to make the definition of 'projection rule' less complicated because the collection of rules that it now covers is less heterogeneous. We can define 'projection rule' as a rule that operates on a partly semantically interpreted underlying phrase marker by combining readings assigned to grammatically related constituents when the governing selection restriction is satisfied and assigning the combination as a derived reading to the constituent that dominates the constituents whose readings were combined.

4.   The form of a dictionary entry

Weinreich (1966) contends that the normal form for a dictionary entry on our theory "does not discriminate between fortuitous homonymy and lexicologically interesting polysemy" (p. 402). By this he means that we provide the same normal form for representing "lexicologically interesting cases of polysemy" such as "land" meaning 'country' and "land" meaning 'real estate' (also, "cook" meaning 'one who prepares food for eating' and "cook" meaning 'to prepare food for eating') and for representing cases of "fortuitous homonymy" such as "rock" meaning 'back and forth movement' and "rock" meaning 'a concreted mass of stony material'. His criticism is that without different normal forms to distinguish these two types of cases, we cannot exhibit the relations between lexicologically interesting instances of polysemy.

Weinreich does suggest that we might try to exhibit the similarity among the senses in cases of lexicologically interesting polysemy by employing branching

---

[14] Given, of course, the principle that singulary transformations apply cyclically from most deeply embedded phrase marker constituent to least deeply embedded.

at the appropriate syntactic marker to indicate overlapping and divergent portions of their senses.[15] But then, Weinreich goes on, the two senses of "rock," which are not similar, would have to be handled in the same manner. Thus:

> KF would ... have to be extended at least by a requirement that conflated entries with branching of syntactic markers be permitted only if there is a reconvergence of paths at some semantic marker; only, that is, if the dictionary entry shows explicitly that the meanings of the entries are related as in ...

> But such makeshift remedies, feasible though they are, would still fail to represent class shifting of the type *to explore–an explorer a package–to package* as a (partly) productive process: the KF dictionary would have to store all forms which the speakers of the language can form at will (p. 402).

The remedy of having reconverging paths, which Weinreich himself disowns, is not only makeshift but depends on dictionary entries being in the form of tree diagrams, and this, although once entertained, is no longer accepted as the best form for dictionary entries. I will return to this point later and explain why this form was abandoned.

Assuming that Weinreich's distinction between "fortuitous homonymy" and "lexicologically interesting polysemy" is not based on diachronic considerations (in which case it would be irrelevant to a professedly synchronic theory of language such as ours), we can represent the semantic similarity in cases of the latter sort and the semantic dissimilarity in cases of the former sort in terms of semantic markers. No distinction in types of normal form is required to exhibit the semantic relations involved. The lexical readings for the two senses of "cook" will be virtually the same, except that in the case where "cook" refers to the one who does the preparing the lexical reading will contain the semantic marker '(Human)', whereas in the case where "cook" means the preparation itself the lexical reading will contain the semantic marker '(Process)'.[16] On the other hand, the lexical readings for the two senses of "rock" will have no semantic markers in common. The two senses of "land" represent a phenomenon that falls somewhere in between since the senses here are not as close in meaning as those of "cook" but not as different as those of "rock."

[15] Actually, there is a confusion in Weinreich's discussion here as a result of his erroneous assumption that the "cook" (meaning 'one who prepares food for eating') is a distinct lexical item. Rather, "cook" is an agentive noun with the morphophonemic peculiarity that it does not have "er" as a suffix but, like certain other agentive nouns such as "bore" ("He is a bore," not "He is a borer"), it has a zero suffix. Consequently, "cook" in this sense gets its meaning from a sentence structure such as "Somebody cooks something," not from a dictionary entry as in the case of the verb "cook." Having noted this oversight of Weinreich's, we adopt his suggestion for the sake of argument.

[16] This is one difference, but of course not the only one. The form of the lexical reading for the latter sense of "cook" will be dealt with in Chapter 7. The lexical reading for the former sense, in terms of Katz (1964c; 1966), will have (besides the semantic marker '(Human)') an evaluation semantic marker something like '(Eval$_{duty}$: (Make pleasurably tasting food by a process using heat)). This will account for the meaning of "good cook."

Such facts show that there is no simple dichotomy between "lexicologically interesting cases of polysemy" exhibiting similarity in meaning and cases of "fortuitous homonymy" exhibiting no similarity in meaning. Rather, there is a range of similarity in meaning, the limiting cases of which are synonymy, at the one extreme, and, at the other, complete difference in meaning. Weinreich's terminology makes it appear that there is a dichotomy calling for a two-way distinction in the notation of semantic theory when instead there is a scale of sense similarity in terms of which pairs of lexical items can be compared and their differences in degree of sense similarity estimated. Because he has oversimplified the problem, Weinreich fails to see that the semantic markers, together with the normal form which specifies that a lexical reading contains a set of semantic markers, provide the theoretical machinery for representing sense similarity.

Furthermore, Weinreich fails to notice that plausible instances of class shifting of the kind he discusses have a syntactic origin, as in the case of "refuse" to "refusal."[17] Our theory handles these cases nicely by providing a lexical reading for the base form which then enters into the reading for the sentence structure from which the derivative form comes transformationally. Consider, for example, (3.7):

(3.7)   John's refusal was accepted

The reading for "refusal" in this sentence comes from the lexical reading for the verb "refuse" in the underlying sentence structure for (3.8):

(3.8)   John refused something

Alternatively, one can handle cases that are not syntactically productive by having a separate dictionary entry for each form when, as in the case of "rock," the syntactic markers in the entries in the lexicon already specify a feature distinction. Thus it will be possible to interpret the dictionary as providing an explicit statement of the morphemes of the language in terms of a unique pair (D,C) in the lexicon, an explicit statement of the senses of each morpheme in terms of the set of lexical readings associated with its entry in the lexicon, and an explicit statement of the similarities and differences between senses, both within a dictionary entry and across dictionary entries, in terms of identity and distinctness of semantic markers in lexical readings.

Next, consider Weinreich's notion of a dictionary entry (p. 417). That dictionary entries consist of a set of phonological markers, a set of syntactic markers, and a set of semantic markers hardly counts as an improvement on our conception of semantic theory. On the other hand, Weinreich's stipulation that a particular dictionary entry not contain more than one lexical reading, so that the different senses of a lexical item must be represented by different entries, seems a departure from our conception of the dictionary. But the difference is merely terminological, a matter of alternative notation without any substantive significance. It cannot matter in the least whether the pair consisting of a distinctive feature

[17] See note 15 of this Chapter and Katz and Postal (1964, chapter 4, section 3).

matrix D and its associated complex symbol C is listed once in the dictionary with *n* lexical readings attached or the pair (D,C) is listed *n* times, each instance being associated with just one of the *n* lexical readings and each of the lexical readings being associated with just one of the *n* occurrences of (D,C). It seems to me, however, to be notationally more economical to adopt our account and not list (D,C) more than once, that is, our notation is a substantively equivalent way which avoids uneconomical repetitions. Furthermore, Weinreich's claim (p. 418) that his method of writing dictionary entries insures that underlying phrase markers are free of lexical ambiguities adds no support to his thesis that a lexical item with multiple senses should be represented in the dictionary by a distinct entry for each of its senses. This claim begs the question at issue: freedom from lexical ambiguities means nothing more than that the notation Weinreich advocates does not represent a lexical item with *n* senses in terms of a single entry whose (D,C) is associated with *n* lexical readings.

At this point Weinreich introduces ordering of semantic markers in lexical readings, exactly what he formerly wanted to do away with on grounds of simplicity. He does not want every set of semantic markers to be ordered but offers a rationale for ordering certain ones. Thus, he proposes to further characterize his notion of a dictionary entry by the condition that it can contain either clusters of semantic features, i.e., just unordered sets of them, or configurations of semantic features, i.e., ordered sets of them, or (?) both. By way of giving a rationale for introducing such ordering, he writes:

> Suppose the meaning of *daughter* is analyzed into the components '*female*' and '*offspring*'. Anyone who is a daughter is both female and an offspring; we represent the features 'female' and 'offspring' as a cluster. But suppose the meaning of *chair* is represented in terms of the features 'furniture' and 'sit'. Whatever is a chair is 'furniture', but it is not sitting: it is 'to be sat on'. We would represent this fact by saying that the features 'furniture' and 'sitting' form a configuration (p. 419).

In Katz (1964c), I proposed a way of handling this type of case, a way that does not make use of ordering; however, Weinreich never considered the proposal. In terms of the ideas in that paper, we can make the desired contrast between the semantic information that a chair is a piece of furniture and the semantic information that it is used as a seat for someone to sit on by rewriting the semantic marker '(Seat for one)' in (2.15) as the *evaluation semantic marker* shown in (3.9):

(3.9) $(\text{Eval}_{use}: (\text{Seat for one}))$

According to the conventions for interpreting the formalism here, the occurrence of this semantic marker in a reading such as (2.15) says that what falls under the concept it represents is normally evaluated in terms of how well it serves as a seat for one. Thus, Weinreich's claim that ordering among semantic features is necessary to represent such differences is false. Moreover, the sort of ordering Weinreich proposed is not even a suitable means of accomplishing this purpose. An ordering of symbols is an arrangement of them into a sequence in accord with some principle that provides an interpretation for differences in position within the sequence. In Weinreich's use of ordering, there is no linguistic interpretation for the positioning of symbols, no interpretation for the formal arrangement in which a symbol *a* precedes *b*, which may, in turn, precede *c*, and so forth, beyond the stipulation that a semantic feature so ordered is not to be taken in the straight-forward way that is suggested by the symbol that labels it. Thus, in the case of "chair," Weinreich's arrow is used as a conventional symbol to indicate that '(sitting)' should really have been '(to be sat on)'. He could have used '(to be sat on)' without the circumlocution and ordering.

With respect to these notions of clusters and configuration, Weinreich defines the notion 'linking'. The idea underlying this notion Weinreich calls "a basic tenet" of his approach, namely,

> that *the semantic structures of complex expressions and of simplex expressions are in principle representable in the same form.* ... This principle explains the possi-bility of freely introducing new words into a language L by stipulating their meanings through expressions couched in words of language L (p. 419).

This, however, is a restatement of our principle, incorporated in our definition of the notion 'reading', that derived readings have the same form as lexical readings. The definition of the notion 'reading' says that every reading is a set of semantic markers, with optional distinguisher, and a selection restriction. Since the semantic structure of the simplest constituents is represented by lexical readings and the semantic structure of syntactically complex constituents is represented by derived readings, and since both lexical and derived readings are covered by this definition, it follows that the semantic structure of both the simple and the complex con-stituents is, in principle, representable in the same form. Hence, the "basic tenet" of Weinreich's approach is a variant of one of our definitions.

Linking is a device for forming unordered sets of semantic features. The linking of the clusters and configurations in the semantic characterization of an expression E_1 with the clusters and configurations in the semantic characterization of another expression E_2 is just the Boolean union of these clusters and configura-tions. The resulting Boolean union is the semantic characterization of the compound expression (p. 419 of Weinreich (1966)). It thus looks as if the formalism of linking is a disguised version of projection rules. However, to fully appreciate what is going on, we must make a distinction between, on the one hand, the operation of forming the semantic representation of a compound constituent and, on the other, the formal structure of the semantic representation of a compound constituent which results from such an operation. In terms of this distinction, it is clear that linking is not a version of projection rules. Linking is actually part of a taxonomy of types of formal structures exhibited in semantic representations, and, as such, it describes one type of such representation. It cannot be compared with projection rules because there is no concept of rule built into it, that is, no concept of formal opera-tions for determining the structure of derived readings. Rather, from our point of view, linking is a purported description of the formal character of the output of some class of projection rules. Thus, Weinreich's approach here is the same as approaches in syntax which favor writing descriptions of the syntactic structure of sentences without generative rules. The inadequacy of such approaches is that, although they can say something about the speaker's knowledge concerning certain particular sentences, they cannot formulate a theory of his linguistic competence since they make no attempt to state rules.[18]

The influence that empiricism has had on current philosophical thinking (see the Preface) manifests itself most strongly in the attitude of philosophers toward the program of building a theory of meaning and, in particular, toward its concept of a dictionary entry. Wilson (1967) regards this program as doomed because "it rests on the archaic notion that dictionary entries in general give the 'meaning' of a word, that a sentence is analytic if it can be got from the dictionary" (p. 62). His claim is that a dictionary gives not the meaning of words but only factual information about their referents. Consider, in this regard, (3.10):

(3.10)   Mothers are females

According to Wilson, it would be false to say that (3.10) is analytic since femaleness is only contingently connected with the referent of "mothers" by dictionaries. He denies the possibility of drawing a distinction between semantic information about words and factual information about their referents.

Behind Wilson's claim that "there is no sharp line between what properly belongs in a dictionary and what properly belongs in an encyclopedia" (p. 63) is the theory that what are ordinarily thought of as components of the meaning of a word are in reality no more than factual beliefs about that to which the word refers.[19] Thus, statements about bachelors being unmarried and gold being a metal are fully on a par with statements about bachelors being over a foot tall and gold being a medium of exchange. According to Wilson, lexicographers, thus dictionary entries, "give you a bare minimum of ready-made factual beliefs about [something] and thereby enable you to tune in on conversations about [that thing]" (p. 64). What takes the place of a dictionary entry in Wilson's theory is a special sort of encyclopedia entry which presents the common core of factual beliefs about the referent of a word, presumably those beliefs about the referent shared by the members of the language community which suffice to identify the referent. Hence, it is not meanings but these common beliefs, and the knowledge on the part of the members of the language community that they are common property, that enable the participants in a conversation to understand what others are talking about.

Philosophers are not the only ones to come under this influence. Recently some linguists, in particular Lakoff (1969), have claimed that grammatical structure

---

[18] For a discussion of some of Weinreich's apparatus for semantic representation, see Katz (1967a, pp. 180–193). The major part of that discussion is not repeated in the present work.

[19] I put Wilson's theory in general form for two reasons, First, two of his examples, "Archimedes" and "Plato," are proper names and are thus dubious examples in this context since it is an open question whether proper names have meaning, and certainly no one who advocates a sharp line between semantic and factual information is committed to the view that they have meaning in the way common nouns do. Second, Wilson *is* setting up an opposing theory, not simply commenting on the unclear border between our ordinary notion of gold and the scientist's, for he is rejecting any distinction between semantic and factual information, any basis for the analytic-synthetic distinction.

is determined by the beliefs of speakers about matters of fact. (See Katz (in preparation).)

It is not clear by what means we are to determine the "bare minimum of ready-made factual beliefs" that constitute a "tune-in entry" for a word. We shall return to this point. But if the items in such an entry are factual beliefs about the extension of the word for which the entry is given, Wilson's theory faces a variety of objections. First, there are what may be called Frege-type objections. Suppose every member of the English-speaking community knows the contingent fact that creatures with hearts are creatures with kidneys and vice versa and, accordingly, has the same beliefs about creatures with hearts and creatures with kidneys. Then, lexicographers must provide the same entry for "creature with a heart" and "creature with a kidney," thereby predicting falsely that these expressions are synonymous. Again, an expression like "the least rapidly convergent series" (Frege's example) has no referent, and, hence, there can be no factual beliefs about its referent. Consequently, such a case will be falsely predicted to be meaningless.

It will not help to reply that our examples do not have tune-in entries because they are complex expressions, not lexical items. The same points apply if the account of how we tune in on their extension is obtained from the tune-in entries of their parts, since the tune-in accounts must consist exclusively of factual beliefs, too.

Another objection to Wilson's theory arises in connection with examples like (3.11):

(3.11)   There is something about which no one at present has any factual beliefs

The sentence (3.11) certainly expresses a true statement. But Wilson's theory cannot even account for how the extension of "something about which no one at present has any factual beliefs" could be tuned in on. Since this expression is meaningful, on Wilson's theory its tune-in account must be a non-null set of factual beliefs held by speakers of the language about the objects in its extension. But, then, the theory must say that its extension consists only of objects about which someone has some belief, and this is directly contrary to the fact that its extension consists only of objects about which no one has even one factual belief.

Furthermore, Wilson's theory implies that a large class of allegedly contingent statements are irrefutable by experience. Let us suppose that B is a set of factual beliefs in the tune-in entry for the word W, each member of B expressing a necessary condition for the application of W. We may suppose that W is the word "bachelor" and B contains beliefs such as those in (3.12):

(3.12)   (a) Bachelors are human
         (b) Bachelors are male
         (c) Bachelors are adult
         (d) Bachelors are unmarried

Each of these beliefs has the form 'Ws are P', and so one would expect that, since they are allegedly factual beliefs, they could be refuted by finding something which is a W but not P. However, an object that is not P will not be tuned in on in referential uses of the word W. That is, none of the statements (3.12a–d) can be disproved by finding someone to whom "bachelor" applies but who is not human or not male or not adult or not unmarried since anyone who is not all of these things cannot be someone to whom "bachelor" applies. If, therefore, the point of the claim that we tune in on the extension of a word on the basis of factual beliefs is that such beliefs are contingent and hence do not give rise to analytic statements, the claim must lose all point when it is recognized that the beliefs in question cannot be refuted by experience. Moreover, if the defender of the theory attempts to meet this objection by changing the form of the beliefs in tune-in entries so that they appear as conditions of the form 'W applies to something which is P', the theory itself becomes the theory it was meant to replace.

Some sense must be given Wilson's notion of "bare minimum" since otherwise the theory runs the danger of making all beliefs irrefutable. But the only thing that suggests itself as an explication of this notion is the idea that the beliefs in a tune-in entry should be restricted to those that speakers share about the referent of the word or those that are statistically frequent enough in the population of speakers. But if this is the criterion, then clear-cut contingent statements are explicated as a priori truths. Beliefs such as that bachelors are over an inch tall or that dogs exist and gremlins do not are as widely shared as any, even as widely shared as the beliefs that bachelors are male, dogs animals, and gremlins gnomes that interfere with airplane engines. Thus, by the criterion in question, statements like those in (3.13) must be counted as irrefutable by experience:

(3.13) (a) Bachelors are over an inch tall
        (b) Dogs exist
        (c) Gremlins are fictional beings

Moreover, on this criterion, words must be seen as changing their tune-in entry continuously, since each time a new discovery is made about the world and speakers come to know about it, their belief in the newly discovered fact must be added to some tune-in entries and a related belief must be added to most. For example, if a new planet is discovered and speakers are informed of the fact, then the tune-in entry for words like "bachelor" and "dog" will have to be revised to contain the belief that bachelors, dogs, and so on inhabit a world containing this newly discovered planet.

It might be replied at this point that "bare minimum" should be explicated not in terms of commonly held beliefs or frequently held beliefs but rather in terms of something like the narrowest set of commonly held or frequently held beliefs that suffices to determine the reference. Thus, we might rule out the belief that bachelors are over an inch tall and rule in the belief that they are male on the grounds that the former does not distinguish the reference of "bachelor" from the reference of other words whereas the latter does, in conjunction with the beliefs that bachelors are human, that they are adult, and that they are unmarried. This reply also avoids the objection by changing the theory into the one it was supposed to replace, since, from a purely empirical viewpoint, it makes little sense to try to make such distinctions between maleness and exceeding an inch in height in connection with tuning in on bachelors when bachelors are, each and every one of them, both male and over an inch tall.

Hence, if such difficulties are to be avoided, it is necessary to draw a distinction between information that warrants inclusion in a dictionary (or manual for tuning in on conversations, for determining extension, or whatever one wants to call it) and information that properly belongs in an encyclopedia, that is, contingent information about the things to which words refer that tells us something beyond what is used in picking them out linguistically. The question, then, is not whether there is such a distinction, but rather on what basis it is to be drawn. The proper question to ask is by what criterion are we to decide when a piece of information is correctly represented in the dictionary entry for a word as part of the dictionary's account of a sense of the word and when a piece of information is correctly excluded from lexical readings. In Chapter 6, I will go into this matter more deeply. Here, we need only indicate the nature of this criterion. The criterion can be thought of as an answer to the following question: how do we make a justified choice between two lexical readings R_1 and R_2 for the word W if they are exactly the same except that R_2 but not R_1 contains a symbol or symbols that (*ex hypothesi*) represent information of the sort that properly belongs in an encyclopedia entry for the thing(s) to which W refers, i.e., information of a factual and purely contingent nature about everything to which W refers? This question, then, is a reformulation in terms of semantic theory of the queries that Wilson put forth.[20] The answer, roughly, is that we are to choose R_2 over R_1 if the incorporation of R_2 in the dictionary of the semantic component as the lexical reading of W enables us to predict a range of semantic properties and relations of sentences (for example, their semantic ambiguity, synonymy, semantic anomaly, redundancy) that cannot be predicted by incorporating R_1 in the dictionary in place of R_2, and we are to choose R_1 over R_2 if the incorporation of R_2 in the dictionary entry for W does *not* enable us to predict anything that is not already predicted on the basis of R_1. What this criterion says, then, is that if the information represented in the symbol(s) that constitutes the only formal difference between R_2 and R_1 plays a role in predicting *semantic* properties and relations of sentences (see Chapter 1), then this information is dictionary information, information about meaning; but if we can simplify the dictionary entry for W by not including the symbol(s) that distinguish R_2 from R_1 without the semantic component's losing any predictive power, then this information is not dictionary information but encyclopedia information, factual information about the referent of W.

As pointed out in the Preface, attempts to understand deductive relations in terms of the concept of logical form based exclusively on logical particles assume we can justify drawing a distinction between the logical particles of the language and its extra-logical (or descriptive) vocabulary. Not all logicians who have accepted this distinction have been comfortable about their grounds for doing so. For example, Tarski (1956) wrote:

[20] Wilson's questions about the construction and justification of dictionary entries, namely, "Where does the dictionary entry come from?" and "Why do you put this rather than that item in a certain dictionary entry?" (p. 64) are thus the appropriate ones.

Underlying our whole construction is the division of terms of the language discussed into logical and extra-logical. This division is certainly not arbitrary.... If, for example, we were to include among the extra-logical signs the implication sign, or the universal quantifier, then our definition of the concept of consequence would lead to results which obviously contradict ordinary usage. On the other hand, no objective grounds are known to me which permit us to draw a sharp boundary between the two groups of terms. It seems to be possible to include among logical terms some which are usually regarded by logicians as extra-logical without running into consequences which stand in sharp contrast to ordinary usage. In the extreme case we could regard all terms of the language as logical. The concept of *formal* consequence would then coincide with that of material consequence (pp. 418–419).

What Tarski says here is right except for the last remark. Tarski and other logicians resist giving up on the attempt to draw this distinction, even though they appreciate the fact that there is no sound basis for it. They believe that if there is no such distinction then one has to abandon the distinction between a formal consequence and a material consequence and, with it, the distinction between logical and natural necessity. This, however, is not the case as long as semantic theory can draw a distinction between information that is legitimately part of the meaning of extra-logical terms and information that is nonsemantic, that is, information that is part of a scientific account of the structure and causal relations of what such terms refer to. But this, of course, is exactly the distinction we are able to make given the criterion put forth here. This criterion, coupled with the scientific ingenuity required to apply it, enables us to avoid the consequences that Tarski rightly but unnecessarily fears, for example, the inability to distinguish a material or causal connection such as the connection between an insult and the anger it provokes and a logical connection such as the connection between the concept of an insult and the concept of an injury to the dignity of another.

Our notion of a dictionary entry rests on a number of other distinctions beyond the distinction between semantic and factual information just discussed. One of these is the distinction between semantic information and syntactic information. Weinreich (1966) has explicitly rejected this. The first step in the formulation of his criticism is the assumption that syntactic classification and semantic classification of lexical items proceed according to the same principles. There is, however, little to recommend this assumption. Lexical classification in terms of syntactic features is introduced to explain and predict grammatical properties and relations arising from the manner in which constituents are syntactically organized to form sentences, for example, properties and relations like word order, inflectional form, sentence type, agreement, ellipsis; on the other hand, semantic classification is introduced to explain a different set of properties and relations, for example, semantic anomaly, redundancy, analyticity, synonymy.[21]

---

[21] It is worth observing here that generative semantics owes Weinreich a far larger debt than it has acknowledged. Weinreich was the first to propose a thesis that now much exercises generative semanticists, namely, the thesis that syntactic and semantic descriptions make use of the same constructs. I shall later indicate (Chapter 8, Section 2) some other ideas of generative semantics that can be traced back to Weinreich.

About semantic classification, Weinreich writes:

> A general criterion of economy would presumably require that there be as few markers (primes) as possible; hence, the analyst should aim to add markers only when failure to do so would result in a failure to mark ambiguities or anomalies of sentences. The general principle would seem to be that no semantic marker should appear in the path of any dictionary entry unless it also appears in the selection restriction of at least one other entry (p. 402).

Weinreich's misrepresentation of the goals of a semantic component causes him to draw the wrong conclusion here. Even if our conception of the goals was as he imagines it to be—just the marking of ambiguities and anomalies—his principle would not be a consequence of these goals, and, accordingly, it could not serve as a general requirement of economy which semantic theory imposes on the construction of semantic components. Suppose there is a semantic marker (M) that appears in no selection restriction of a semantic component. Can (M) appear in a lexical reading in the dictionary of this component? Yes, since (M) can still serve to distinguish senses of a number of words and expressions in the language. It is true that those senses which (M) helps to distinguish will never be eliminated by selection restrictions in the process whereby projection rules form derived readings, but this is obviously a possibility. Consequently, Weinreich's principle is incorrect even on the view that a semantic component only marks anomalous and semantically ambiguous sentences. Since the goals of a semantic component are actually far broader, Weinreich's principle is guaranteed rejection by virtue of the fact that its acceptance would prevent a semantic component from having the semantic markers it needs to represent other semantic properties and relations. If a semantic marker appears in a selection restriction, then it must also appear in some lexical reading, but the converse does not hold. Therefore, the classification effected by the introduction of a semantic marker into a lexical reading can be motivated by the need to predict any one of the large variety of semantic properties and relations.

About syntactic classification Weinreich writes:

> The reasons [for increasing the delicacy of subcategorization in syntax] turn out to be precisely the same as those for semantics: a subcategorization step is taken if failure to do so would make the grammar generate (a) ill-formed expressions or (b) ambiguous sentences (p. 403).

This is a misrepresentation, too. It is clear from a consideration of the concept of a transformation that the goals of the syntactic component which depend on subcategorization go far beyond just the marking of ill-formed expressions and ambiguous sentences. The syntactic markers that express subcategorization features such as [+Count], [+Common] provide part of the information which determines whether or not a given phrase marker satisfies the structural condition of a given transformation. From this it follows that subcategorization features partly control the assignment of derived constituent structure and thus determine the superficial phrase markers. Consequently, such features must be chosen and justified on the basis of the full range of predictions about sentences that are made by their superficial phrase markers. Weinreich would have a case if such predictions were restricted to ill-formedness and syntactic ambiguity, but they go well beyond these two cases, covering every aspect of the segmentation and classification of formatives. We can put the point in another, perhaps more revealing, way. If the prediction of ill-formedness and syntactic ambiguity were all that had to be determined from superficial phrase markers, as it is on Weinreich's account, then we could dispense with such phrase markers entirely. The output of the transformations could be just integers, 0 in case there is no superficial phrase marker (the sentence is ill-formed), 1 in case the sentence is syntactically unambiguous, and some integer n $(n > 1)$ in case the sentence is syntactically ambiguous n ways. But if a string of formatives is assigned only an integer i, we can say nothing about how it is segmented into continuous constituents and how these constituents are classified (which segments belong to the same categories, etc.)

Hence Weinreich's rationale for syntactic subcategorization misrepresents the considerations involved in choosing and justifying subclassification features in syntax in the same way that his rationale misrepresents the considerations involved in choosing and justifying semantic markers. He neglects all of the descriptive goals of a syntactic component except for the two which are similar to the two goals of a semantic component that he recognizes as our having set forth. Thus, it looks as if classification of lexical items proceeds according to the same principles and has the same function in syntax and semantics because Weinreich has made it appear as if both kinds of classification are carried out to reach the same goals.

Given this much, it is easy for Weinreich to say that we beg the question of drawing a line between syntactic and semantic markers when we argue that this line can be drawn in terms of the principles for their selection and the function they perform. Weinreich's criticism must be rejected once it is recognized that our claim is that syntactic and semantic markers can be distinguished in terms of considerations having to do with all of the goals of the syntactic component, on the one hand, and, on the other, all of the goals of the semantic component.

Any demarcation between syntactic and semantic markers defines a marker as syntactic just in case it appears essentially in a rule of the syntactic component and defines a marker as semantic just in case it appears essentially in a lexical reading of a dictionary entry of the semantic component. (A marker appears essentially if the successful operation of the rules requires the information it contributes. To say that the rules require such information means that that component cannot be better formulated without those rules.)

Although these definitions permit us to differentiate markers as syntactic and semantic, they do this only given an optimal linguistic description. Hence, they make no direct statement about the basis on which a marker is selected for inclusion in the formulation of syntactic and semantic rules or about the essential difference between markers selected for the former and for the latter types of rules. But it is easy to see what these are. The motivation for selecting syntactic subclassification markers for the complex symbol of an entry in the lexicon is that transformations require the information that they specify in order to generate superficial phrase markers that incorporate correct predictions about such things as segmentation cuts, constituent membership of the segments, stress, and other features of pronunciation. On the other hand, the motivation for selecting semantic markers for a lexical reading is that dictionary entries and projection rules require the information that they specify in order to generate semantically interpreted underlying phrase markers from which we can correctly predict semantic anomaly, semantic ambiguity, synonymy, antonymy, paraphrase, analyticity, contradiction, syntheticity, entailment, inconsistency, presupposition, and so on. Consequently, both the basis for selecting a marker and the function of the marker are different in the two cases.

Weinreich (p. 404) took our claim that semantic markers provide a means of representing the conceptual content of constituents to be a statement of a criterion for deciding whether a marker is syntactic or semantic. On our theory, however, the criterion governing such a decision has to do with predictive success, with whether a semantic component that treats a marker as syntactic by failing to employ it is more or less successful in predicting semantic properties and relations of sentences than one that treats the marker as semantic by employing it. Our claim that semantic markers provide a means of representing the conceptual content of constituents was intended to indicate that they represent components of the thoughts conveyed by acoustic realizations of grammatical concatenations of phonetic segments, not formal properties that determine the concatenation of phonetic segments and the underlying organization of these segments into grammatically related constituents.

Weinreich next argues as follows:

> It is proposed, for example, that *baby* be marked semantically as (Human), but grammatically as nonHuman (hence it is pronominalized by *it*), whereas *ship* is treated in the reverse way. The problem, however, has been solved in a purely grammatical way since Antiquity in terms of mixed genders or of double gender membership (p. 404).

Although the construct of mixed gender enables us to solve a problem, that problem has nothing to do with the one we raised about the equating of syntactic and semantic markers. Mixed gender concerns such facts as that the sentences (3.14), (3.15), and (3.16) are all syntactically well-formed:

(3.14)   The baby lost its rattle

(3.15)   The baby lost his rattle

(3.16)   The baby lost her rattle

We want to be able to construct the complex symbol for the lexical item " baby " in such a fashion that we can transformationally obtain any one of the forms "it," "he," or "she," their corresponding possessives, and their reflexives as pronominalizations of "baby." The construct of mixed gender solves this problem in that we can obtain such forms by introducing the syntactic features [+ Masculine], [+ Feminine], and [+ Neuter] into the complex symbol for "baby." In contrast, the problem we raised is not a purely syntactic question, as this one is, but a logical or conceptual problem. We argued that unless syntactic markers such as [+ Masculine] and [+ Feminine] are distinguished from semantic markers (which may have a similar distribution in the dictionary), the linguistic description will deal incorrectly with certain syntactic constructions or certain semantic constructions. Suppose that "baby" is entered in the lexicon with the features [+Masculine], [+Feminine], and [+Neuter] in order that the linguistic description can deal with (3.14), (3.15), and (3.16), and that the semantic markers '(Male)' and '(Female)' are equated with [+Masculine] and [+Feminine], respectively. This would force us to the absurd conclusion that the concept of a baby involves both maleness and femaleness and is thus internally contradictory, and we would be unable to state the semantic regularity that items such as those in (3.17) have meanings that put no condition of sex upon the being to which they can refer:

(3.17)   baby, parent, sibling, child, classmate, teacher, monarch

Our problem, too, has long been recognized. St. Anselm (Henry (1964)) wrote:

> grammarians assert one thing about a word considered as an exemplar, but quite another when it is considered in relation to the constitution of circumstances.
> After all, they tell us that "stone" is masculine in gender, "rock" feminine, but "property" neuter, ..., yet no one asserts that a stone is masculine, a rock feminine, or a property neither masculine nor feminine ... (p. 73).

To recognize that this is a logical matter, not simply a grammatical one, consider the case of "ship," which must receive the syntactic feature [+Feminine] so that sentences such as (3.18) will be marked as syntactically well-formed:

(3.18)   The ship met her doom on the rocks

It is entirely obvious that from (3.19) we cannot infer (3.20):

(3.19)   A ship collided with the rock
(3.20)   A female collided with the rock

That is, (3.19) does not entail (3.20). It is equally obvious that from (3.21) we can infer (3.20), that is, (3.21) does entail (3.20):

(3.21)   A spinster collided with the rock

By holding that only semantic markers express concepts which make up meanings, and thus distinguishing '(Female)' from the syntactic marker that expresses feminine gender, we can explain entailments such as that of (3.20) by (3.21) and prevent ourselves from being committed to treating an illicit inference such as that from (3.19) to (3.20) as a genuine entailment.

Weinreich argues further that it is unlikely that marking "baby" with '(Human)' would solve any semantic problems because "most things predicable of humans who are not babies could no more be predicated of babies than of animals (i.e. non-Humans)" (p. 405). It could be argued in reply to Weinreich that there are as many things predicable of babies and noninfant humans as there are things that cannot be jointly predicated of them since, in fact, there are infinitely many things predicable of both. It is less important to dwell on this than to reply directly to Weinreich's claim that so marking "baby" solves no semantic problems. The important question is whether or not the lexical reading for "baby" has to contain the semantic marker '(Human)': is there at least one case of a semantic property or relation that requires this item to be so marked in order for sentences exhibiting the property or relation to be correctly predicted by the linguistic description? Putting the question in this way, it is easy to show that marking "baby" with '(Human)' does indeed solve some semantic problems. For example, since '(Human)' is a member of the species-antonymous n-tuple of semantic markers, including it in the lexical reading for "baby" (assuming that appropriate other members of this n-tuple are included in the lexical readings for "puppy," "cub," "kitten," etc.) enables us both to predict the antonymy of items such as "baby," "puppy," "cub," "kitten" and to predict that sentences such as (3.22) are contradictory on a reading:

(3.22)   Babies are puppies

Finally, Weinreich makes the criticism that we fail to

> represent as a productive process the reference (especially by men) to lovingly handled objects by means of *she*. The patent fact is that any physical object can in English be referred to by *she* with a special semantic effect (p. 405).

This implies that a semantic component ought to reconstruct this sort of reference, which is a confusion about the competence-performance distinction. Weinreich has taken a purely psychological effect produced by uttering a deviant sentence under suitable conditions to be a feature of the speaker's semantic competence. No linguistic description can have a convention to the effect that any noun can have feminine gender or receive '(Human)' under conditions of reference such as those Weinreich imagines. This would mean that the application of syntactic or semantic rules would depend on information about the sex of the speaker, his attitude toward the object, and the sex of the object. But then the linguistic description would no longer be dealing with sentence types; it would be dealing with individual utterance tokens of sentence types.

Weinreich is also wrong in saying that any physical object can in English be referred to by "she." Compare the sentences (3.23) and (3.24):

(3.23)   John (the desk) is in the room but she will be gone soon

(3.24)   Sally (the ship) is in the room but she will be gone soon

The occurrence of "she" in (3.24) but not (3.23) can refer to the subject of the first clause as well as to someone else.

The discussion here does not, of course, do justice to the important question of how to distinguish between syntactic markers and semantic markers. The matter will be treated more fully in Chapter 8, Section 1.

5.   Semantic markers and distinguishers

Two further distinctions on which our notion of the form of a dictionary entry depends will be discussed in this section and the next. Here we shall examine criticisms by linguists of the distinction between the lexical information represented in semantic markers and that represented in distinguishers. In the next section we shall consider the distinction between the information represented in the semantic markers and distinguishers of a reading and the information represented in its selection restriction.

The introduction of the concept 'distinguisher' in Katz and Fodor (1963) was less than adequate in a number of respects, chief of which was that the two criteria for determining distinguishers failed to give the same results. We shall turn to this deficiency later and propose a remedy. Here, however, we shall consider some complaints on the part of linguists who either were misled by inadequacies in the original treatment of the concept of a distinguisher or failed to look beyond them to see what distinction we were trying to draw.

Weinreich (1966) makes a number of criticisms of this concept. His first objection is as follows:

> The hierarchization of semantic features into markers and distinguishers in KF does not seem to correspond to either of the conventional criteria (p. 405).

The two "conventional criteria" to which Weinreich is referring are meaning (or sense) and denotation (or reference). He goes on to argue that Fodor and I are caught in a dilemma. According to Weinreich, distinguishers are not motivated by considerations having to do with meaning because they do not express conceptual components of senses as do semantic markers, and distinguishers are not motivated by considerations having to do with reference because our semantic theory does not try to handle the problem of how linguistic constructions can refer to objects, actions, events, and so on in the world. The mistake in this argument is its false assumption that a theory of meaning which does not say everything about reference cannot say anything about it. There is no a priori reason to suppose that a semantic component is precluded from treating some aspects of reference and every empirical reason to suppose that it will treat some, for meaning and reference are closely related.

One of the more significant features of the distinction between competence and performance is that the explanation of how linguistic constructions relate to the world is a matter of formulating a psychological model which accounts for the way speakers employ their competence to refer to the furniture of the universe. Theories of competence cannot describe such uses of language, but they must specify all the purely linguistic information upon which referential uses of language depend. The syntactic component must represent some of the information presupposed in referential distinctions. Consider, for example, the sentence (3.25).

(3.25)   John tipped his hat and he left

The information about pronoun-noun relations that underlies the ambiguity of this sentence is certainly referentially relevant information that has to be represented in syntactic rules (Chomsky (1965, pp. 145–147)). Semantic markers themselves specify information that is relevant to referential distinctions, as can be seen from the fact that in readings they constitute conditions on the things to which linguistic constructions can refer. For example, as more semantic markers are added, say, in attribution, the newly formed constructions involve progressively tighter referential conditions, so that the denotation of the next construction is generally narrower than the one before. The denotation of "chair" properly includes that of "upholstered chair," which, in turn, properly includes that of "red upholstered chair," and so forth. Further, synonymous linguistic constructions must have the same denotation and antonymous ones must have different denotations unless they refer to nothing, as with "witch" and "warlock." Therefore, there is nothing strange or illicit in motivating distinguishers on the basis of referential considerations.

Distinguishers can be regarded as providing a purely denotative distinction which plays the semantic role of separating lexical items that would otherwise be fully synonymous. Unlike semantic markers, which represent conceptual components of senses of lexical items and expressions, distinguishers mark purely perceptual distinctions among the referents of conceptually identical senses. Presumably, a psychological theory of the mechanisms of (visual, auditory, tactile, and so on) perception will define the perceptual distinctions which distinguishers mark at the linguistic level. Consequently, only a general theory of linguistic performance, which incorporates and integrates accounts of linguistic competence and perceptual mechanisms, can connect the distinguishers in the vocabulary of semantic theory with the constructs in the vocabulary of perceptual theory that correspond to them. Only such a general theory can explain, *inter alia*, how it is that different color words refer to different colors.

When Fodor and I wrote that "distinguishers do not enter into theoretical relations" and that semantic markers "reflect whatever systematic relations hold between [a lexical] item and the rest of the vocabulary of the language" (the only remarks of ours about the contrast between distinguishers and semantic markers to which Weinreich refers (p. 405)), we meant that the inter-sense congruity relations that are reconstructed by selection restrictions hold only between conceptual components of senses. We argued at a number of points that selection restrictions are defined in terms of semantic markers, not in terms of distinguishers. We did not say that distinguishers have no role in marking semantic properties and relations such as semantic ambiguity, synonymy, paraphrase, analyticity, and so on.

This view led us to the conclusion that semantic ambiguities, in cases where the readings that differentiate the terms of the ambiguity differ only by distinguishers, could be represented in a semantic component but could not be resolved on the purely linguistic basis that is offered by the semantic component. I find no reason in anything Weinreich has said to change this position regarding the contrast between semantic markers and distinguishers.[22]

Weinreich also states:

> The whole notion of distinguisher appears to stand on precarious ground when one reflects that there is no motivated way for the describer of a language to decide whether a certain sequence of markers should be followed by a distinguisher or not (p. 406).

---

[22] The treatment given various examples in the early papers on semantic theory often errs in packing information into distinguishers that really belongs in semantic markers. However, we did warn that the examples were merely for the purposes of illustration and that their treatment was not to be taken as an account of their semantic analysis.

This seems a peculiar thing for Weinreich to say in light of the fact that he quotes an example of one of the things that does motivate the system of distinguishers for color words in English. That is, he cites my example of the need to mark sentences such as (3.26) as contradictory:

(3.26)   Red is green

But Weinreich makes it perfectly clear that he regards my treatment of cases such as (3.26) as contradictions due to distinguisher antonymy to be inconsistent with what Fodor and I said about distinguishers. According to Weinreich:

> The theory of distinguishers is further weakened when we are told (KF, fn. 16) that "certain semantic relations among lexical items may be expressed in terms of interrelations between their distinguishers." Although this contradicts the definition just quoted [see above], one may still suppose that an extension of the system would specify some special relations which may be defined on distinguishers. But the conception topples down completely in Katz's own paper [1964a], where contradictoriness, a relation developed in terms of markers, is found in the sentence *Red is green* as a result of the distinguishers! Here the inconsistency has reached fatal proportions (p. 406).

Contrary to Weinreich's claim, there is no inconsistency in our treatment of distinguishers. We hold that distinguishers do not enter into the system of inter-sense congruity relations reconstructed by selection restrictions, but, as we have shown, this claim is compatible with holding that distinguishers in the readings of semantically interpreted underlying phrase markers can play a role in marking semantic properties and relations of sentences. Thus, Weinreich's claim to have found a contradiction in our position rests on a confusion between these two quite different types of relations.

Weinreich's more basic criticism that there is no motivated way of deciding when we need a distinguisher in a lexical reading can also be shown to be false. Consider the case Weinreich refers to, namely, (3.26). We have to mark such sentences as contradictory. This means that their semantically interpreted underlying phrase markers must contain a reading for the subject which has a semantic marker or distinguisher that is antonymous with a semantic marker or distinguisher in the reading for the predicate. The only question that remains is whether the antonymous elements are semantic markers or distinguishers in the case at hand. They can be either on our conception of semantic theory, since Weinreich is wrong when he says that contradictoriness is defined over semantic markers only. If the elements concerned are semantic markers, then the distinction marked by these elements is a conceptual one. If, on the other hand, they are distinguishers, this distinction is a (linguistically reflected) perceptual one. In the case under considera-tion, we are clearly dealing with a perceptual distinction; thus, the elements between which the antonymy relation holds are distinguishers. Even if the case were not clear-cut, we could motivate our decision by an indirect empirical check on whether we have made the right choice in deciding that the elements are distinguishers. For example, if the elements here turn out to be required elsewhere in some selection restriction, we have not made the right choice. Determining whether they are required in the formulation of a selection restriction is a matter of constructing the semantic component to predict the semantic properties and relations, as discussed previously.

Hence, it is wrong for Weinreich to say that there is no motivated way to make decisions about the occurrence of distinguishers in lexical readings unless he accepts nothing as motivating such decisions that falls short of providing a discovery procedure. If he does insist on something that strong, he will be in the position of rejecting reasonable empirical constraints because they do not meet impossible demands.

Bolinger (1965) also finds fault with our distinction between semantic markers and distinguishers. His first worry is "whether the distinguisher will not keep receding toward the horizon until it vanishes altogether" as a semantic component is made more capable of accounting for the disambiguations that speakers make (p. 558). This may or may not be so. It is an empirical question that can be decided only after more empirical work has been done. My reasons for thinking that the question will be decided in favor of a place in semantic theory for distinguishers has been given, and nothing Bolinger says on the matter contradicts them. In fact, his lengthy list of examples of how certain distinguishers might be converted into "a string of semantic markers" is irrelevant to the question at issue, since his examples trade on cases that were not claimed to be distinguishers.

Bolinger's second worry is that distinguishers may be redundant. The point seems to be this: *if* there is a reading in which the concept of knighthood is coded as part of a distinguisher and that reading also contains the semantic markers '(Human)' and '(Male)', and *if* the distinguisher part representing knighthood can be replaced by the semantic markers '(Human)', '(Male)', and '(Member of lowest nobility)', then the reading will be redundant since the semantic markers '(Human)' and '(Male)' will each appear twice. This is hardly a redundancy inherent in the distinguisher concept. The duplication exists because some hypothetical semanticist, noticing that some other hypothetical semanticist mistakenly used a distinguisher where semantic markers were called for, failed to eliminate the duplication that resulted when he replaced part of the distinguisher by the appropriate semantic markers. The alleged redundancy is, therefore, an artifact of the way in which Bolinger sees the process of correcting readings when mistakes of this sort exist.

"The chief fault of the marker-distinguisher dualism," according to Bolinger, "is that it does not appear to correspond to any clear division in natural language" (p. 561). I think Bolinger says this because he mistakenly construes a semantic component to be a reconstruction of "what dictionary-makers have been doing all along." His criticism seems to be based on his observation that "The dictionary (in the ordinary Webster-type dictionary-makers sense) draws no line between markers and distinguishers" and the false conception of our theory as one that concerns itself with the reconstruction of the practice of such lexicographers. This leads Bolinger to fail to see that our distinction does have a "conspicuous objective counterpart" in natural language, though not in those parts of natural language that can be seen through the eyes of traditional lexicographers.

Consider, now, sentence (3.27):

(3.27)   Henry became a bachelor in 1965

Bolinger's attempt to make a place for distinguishers in the process by which speakers use knowledge of the world to disambiguate such a sentence on the basis of the knowledge that knighthood died out in the Middle Ages shows his confusion about the concept he is criticizing. If the sentence in question is ambiguous and one sense in the ambiguity is that John became a member of the lowest nobility in 1965, then the disambiguation of an utterance of that sentence on the basis of factual information about the age of knighthood is irrelevant to the semantic interpretation of the sentence type. If, on the other hand, this sentence is not ambiguous, then there is no such contextual disambiguation. In the latter case, no distinguisher is required, and in the former, one may be, depending on whether the semantic information concerned is fully idiosyncratic. In either case, if Bolinger's other criticisms were correct, we would be unable to find a place for distinguishers within an account of how speakers interpret utterances, tokens of sentence types. What Bolinger confuses is, on the one hand, the process of disambiguation in the sense of eliminating from a construal of a token certain senses that its sentence type bears and, on the other, the process of selection within the compositional determination of a sentence's meaning, wherein certain senses are excluded by selection restriction. Only the latter is involved in semantic theory as we have postulated it, but Bolinger has not distinguished that process from contextual disambiguation.

I shall conclude this section by offering my own criticism of the distinguisher concept. But, before doing so, I should point out that the extensive discussion this concept has received is a tempest in a teapot. If it turns out that distinguishers are unnecessary in semantic description, we would, of course, have drawn a spurious distinction. But giving up this distinction would not affect any other part of the theory.

As worked out in early discussions on semantic theory, the distinction between semantic markers and distinguishers was based on two criteria for the latter: (a) that they mark conceptually unanalyzable, purely perceptual qualities, and (b) that the distribution of each distinguisher in the dictionary is restricted to a single lexical item. We may observe now that it is possible that the set of semantic constructs that mark such qualities and the set whose members are constructs having such a restricted distribution are not identical.

It is hard to imagine that a color quality like redness is susceptible to conceptual analysis. Shape qualities like roundness or triangularity, which are perceived in more than one sensory mode, must be susceptible to some form of conceptual analysis since they *are* intermodally identified. A blind man is able to understand "round" and "triangular" and is able to identify their visual exemplifications on gaining sight, without special training in their visual appearance.[23] But color qualities are unique to one mode. A blind man does not "understand" red in the way a person with sight does even though the blind man may be able to use the word. Furthermore, there is no reason in principle to deny that there are

---

[23] See Gregory and Wallace (1963).

semantic elements with a minimal distribution in the dictionary. Given that neither the set of semantic constructs that mark purely perceptual qualities nor the set of semantic constructs that have a maximally restricted distribution is null, there are ways that the criteria (a) and (b) can yield nonidentical sets. First, constructs in the latter set might represent sensory qualities having a conceptual analysis, and, second, constructs in the former set might occur in more than one lexical reading. About the first possibility, nothing can be said at this stage of research. But we can find evidence to show that the second is more than just a possibility. For instance, there are pairs of color words, such as "red" and "scarlet," "green" and "viridescent," and "blue" and "azure," in which the second member refers to one of the shades of the color covered by the first. This can be brought out in analytic sentences such as (3.28), (3.29), and (3.30):

(3.28)   Scarlet objects are red

(3.29)   Viridescent objects are green

(3.30)   Azure objects are blue

But this means that words like "scarlet," "viridescent," and "azure" must have lexical readings that represent them as referring to a shade of color represented by the reading of the word paired with them. Consequently, semantic constructs that code information about particular hues will have to appear in more than one lexical reading. In light of the fact that the two criteria for distinguishers diverge, it now seems advisable to drop the criterion of minimal distribution: nothing is known about the class of semantic elements that are confined to one lexical reading in the dictionary, and the original marker-distinguisher distinction was introduced in order to differentiate between cases that are susceptible to definition in terms of conceptual analysis and cases that are not because the words serve as labels for purely sensory qualities. Thus, we shall use distinguishers only to mark the difference between cases of the former type and cases of the latter and to express, in the cases of the latter type, the particular facts about purely sensory distinctions that the language records but for which it provides no conceptual interpretation.

Leibniz (1951) wrote:

> we have not even nominal definitions of [sensible] qualities by which to explain these terms. The purpose of nominal definitions is to give sufficient marks by which the thing may be recognized; for example, assayers have marks by which they distinguish gold from every other metal, and even if a man had never seen gold these signs might be taught him so that he would infallibly recognize it if he should some day meet with it. But it is not the same with these sensible qualities; and marks to recognize blue, for example, could not be given if we had never seen it. So that blue is its own mark, and in order that a man may know what blue is it must be shown to him.
>
> It is for this reason that we are accustomed to say that the *notions* of these qualities are *clear*, for they serve to recognize them; but that these same notions are not *distinct*, because we cannot distinguish or develop that which they include (p. 356).

The concept of a distinguisher reflects the same point about language.

6.   Readings and selection restrictions

Weinreich (1966) says:

It seems safe to conclude that the distinction between paths and selection restrictions is as untenable as [our semantic theory's] other specifications of the format of dictionary entries (p. 407).

This conclusion comes as somewhat of a surprise insofar as the argument Weinreich offers on its behalf is based on a treatment of linguistic phenomena that reinforces the distinction drawn between the marker and selection restriction portions of a lexical reading. We will examine this matter in some detail. Our discussion, however, will not include Weinreich's example "pretty children" because his analysis of this case rests on the very dubious assumption that from the sentence (3.31) we can validly infer (3.32):

(3.31)   They are pretty children
(3.32)   They are girls

Weinreich describes cases in which, in order to represent the sense of a pro-form occurring in a sentence, it is necessary to transfer to the reading of a pro-form semantic markers from a selection restriction in the reading of another constituent in the sentence with which the pro-form is grammatically related. Consider the sentences (3.33) and (3.34):

(3.33)   It's addled
(3.34)   He is reading something

Clearly, an English speaker's understanding of the sentences involves information about the meanings of "it" and "something" in these sentences, information that is not available from the meanings of the pro-forms outside such sentential structures. Thus, the speaker knows that what is asserted to be addled in (3.33) is either an egg or somebody's brain and that what the person referred to in (3.34) is reading is something with characters of some sort appearing on it. This information cannot be in the lexical readings of the pro-forms since it is not contained as part of the sense(s) of the same forms in sentences like (3.35) and (3.36):

(3.35)   It is on the table
(3.36)   He has something

But exactly this information is represented by some of the semantic markers in the selection restrictions of the lexical readings for the verbs "addle" and "read" which are grammatically related to "it" and "something," respectively, in (3.33) and (3.34). The problem posed by these cases is, then, how to specify that such information in the meanings of constituents which are grammatically related to the pro-forms is also information about the meaning of the pro-forms, how to extract the information from the related constituent and transfer it to the pro-form.

Postal and I first raised this problem in *An Integrated Theory of Linguistic Descriptions* (1964). We noticed that it is generally the case that the sense a pro-form takes on contains the very same information that the related constituent makes use of to determine what senses can combine with its sense to form derived senses. Thus, we offered the following solution to the problem of how to utilize the presence of semantic markers in selection restrictions to provide the required characterizations of the sense of pro-forms. We introduced a new type of semantic marker, for which we invented the label '(Selector)', and we made it an obligatory element in the lexical reading of every pro-form. This marker was contextually defined to be the set consisting of all and only those semantic markers occurring in the selection restriction of the reading for the constituent grammatically related to the pro-form in a particular sentence. In accord with this definition, the selector semantic marker in a reading of a pro-form is replaced by the appropriate set of semantic markers prior to the amalgamation of the reading (by projection rules) with the reading of the constituent from whose selection restriction the members of the set came.

This solution still seems to me to be empirically adequate, that is, adequate in the sense that it provides a correct account of the senses that pro-forms take on when in construction with other constituents. However, later in this chapter, we shall see that it is unnecessarily complicated. As a result of the introduction of some new conceptual machinery, it will turn out that this generalization about the senses of pro-forms in construction can be expressed by a simple rule, thereby making it unnecessary to introduce '(Selector)' in the lexical reading of each pro-form of the language (see (3.77)).

Weinreich accepts our early solution,[24] but, with no further argument, concludes that it somehow undermines our distinction between lexical readings and selection restrictions. Not only is there nothing here to undermine this distinction, but the very concept of '(Selector)' presupposes it. This semantic marker is, in fact, defined in terms of the distinction between readings and selection restrictions: the operation performed by '(Selector)' converts one reading into a new reading by adding the semantic markers found in the selection restriction of another reading.[25] Without this distinction, we would not know which semantic markers from another reading are to be included in the reading that replaces '(Selector)'.

The concept of a selection restriction gives rise to the distinction between semantically anomalous sentences and false or contradictory ones. This distinction, as I have learned from experience, is by no means a clear one to many linguists and philosophers. Accordingly, it will be worth taking time to attempt to clarify the distinction.

The intuitive distinction we seek to draw is that between cases like those in (3.37), which we count as semantically anomalous, and cases like those in (3.38), which we count as contradictory:

[24] He considers the adoption of "a more powerful conception of the semantic interpretation process, in which features of a selection of a word Z would be transferred into the path of another word W, when it is constructed with Z." He then goes on to say, "This is the solution adopted by Katz and Postal . . ., and it is the general solution which we will elaborate . . . " (p. 407).

[25] See Katz and Postal (1964, pp. 81–84).

(3.37) (a) My red afterimage is waterproof
        (b) That truth is strawberry-flavored
        (c) Prepositions feel oily
        (d) He saw George and the point of the argument
        (e) That triangle is in love

(3.38) (a) My red afterimage is colorless
        (b) That truth is known to be false
        (c) Prepositions are not a part of speech
        (d) His remark is important and trivial
        (e) That triangle is square

The difference we want to make clear can be brought out more saliently by contrasting the components of each of the semantically anomalous sentences in (3.37) with the components of the corresponding contradictory sentence or contradiction (see Chapter 4, Section 5, for a discussion of the difference) in (3.38). For example, the components of (3.37b), given in (3.39a,b), contrast with the components of (3.38b), shown in (3.40a,b):

(3.39) (a) x is strawberry-flavored
        (b) x is a truth

(3.40) (a) x is known to be false
        (b) x is a truth

The cases (a) and (b) of (3.39) cannot be used to make inconsistent statements about something, since the categories that determine the range of the predicates are exclusive, whereas the cases (a) and (b) of (3.40) can since the category in these cases does not prevent them from being attributed to the same thing. Put another way, there are expressions like "that plane figure" which can be the subject of a sentence whose predicate phrase is "is square" and of a sentence whose predicate phrase is "is a triangle," and both sentences can make a true statement, but there are no expressions which can serve as the subject of a sentence whose predicate phrase is "is strawberry-flavored" and as the subject of a sentence whose predicate phrase is "is a truth" such that these sentences can both make a true statement.

The point here is that a concept has a range of predication specified as a category that determines the concepts with which it can combine in forming assertions. Thus, if, by virtue of the flexibility of the syntactic rules, a sentence is formed that puts a concept into combination with one outside its range of predication, as in the cases (3.37a–e), the sentence will be "conceptually absurd," "nonsense," "meaningless," "an instance of a category mistake," or, using our cover term for these more colorful descriptions, "semantically anomalous." As Ryle (1955) phrases the point:

> 'Saturday is in bed' breaks no rule of grammar. Yet the sentence is absurd. Consequently the possible complements must be not only of certain grammatical types, they must also express proposition-factors of certain logical types. The

several factors in a non-absurd sentence are typically suited to each other; those in an absurd sentence, or some of them, are typically unsuitable to each other. To say that a given proposition-factor is of a certain category or type, is to say that its expression could complete certain sentence frames without absurdity (p. 70).

Our notion of a selection restriction is, then, an attempt to provide a formal explication of the idea of suitability and unsuitability to which Ryle appeals.

Another feature of the distinction between semantic anomaly and falsehood or contradiction is that the former concept is a graded one while the latter concepts are absolute. A sentence can be more semantically anomalous or less semantically anomalous than another, but sentences cannot be more false or more contradictory than others. For example, it makes no sense to claim that any of the examples in (3.38) are more or less false or contradictory than any of the others, whereas it makes perfectly good sense to claim (though the claim may be incorrect) that some of the examples in (3.37) are more or less semantically anomalous than some of the others in the same set.

Still another feature of the distinction between (3.37) and (3.38) is that only in the case of contradictory sentences like (3.38) can we identify antonymous elements in the incompatible expressions responsible for the contradiction. In (3.38a), for example, "red afterimage" has a sense containing the element 'colored' which is antonymous with the sense of "colorless," but in (3.37a) the sense of "waterproof," namely, that water cannot penetrate through the surface from the outside to the inside of something, has no element antonymous with an element in the sense of "red afterimage." Of course, the something with a surface has to be a physical object. But this observation makes just the point we are trying to make, that is, that the property expressed by "is waterproof" has a category, namely, physical objects, that determines its range of predication. The requirement that the thing in question have a surface determines what the property can be attributed to rather than being a part of the attribution it makes. Since the category 'Physical object' is not a concept predicated of something in applying "waterproof" to it, the incompatibility between this concept and 'Perceptual object' as a conceptual component of the sense of "red afterimage" cannot have the form of a joint, inconsistent predication, as is found in (3.38a–e).

Semantically anomalous sentences differ from false or contradictory sentences in yet another way, a way that has to do with the semantic selection that operates in the process of forming senses of syntactically complex constituents from the senses of their parts. If we compute the total number of possible combinations of the lexical senses of an ordinary fifteen- or twenty-word sentence when these senses are paired up in accord with the grammatical relations in the sentence, we find that the number of senses that are possible for the whole sentence runs into the hundreds. Since no such sentence has anywhere near so many senses, we must conclude that a rather severe kind of weeding-out process is at work in the projection operations whereby syntactically complex constituents receive senses from those of their parts. As a consequence of this semantic selection, some sentences receive two or three senses, some more, some only one, and some no sense at all,

even though the words or lexical items that make them up are individually meaningful. Thus, ambiguity is the case where the weeding-out process stops short of the
limit. An ambiguous sentence or a semantically unique sentence is one where a
certain number of the senses that are possible on the basis of the various possible
combinations of lexical senses in the sentence are not removed by selection. Semantic anomaly is, then, the limit, the case where every possible sense is blocked at some
stage in the compositional process. Accordingly, semantic anomaly is the product of
the very same process which produces semantic ambiguity. And unless we accept
the distinction between semantic anomaly and contradictoriness, we will have to
make the absurd claim that every ordinary fifteen- or twenty-word sentence is
ambiguous in hundreds of ways with almost all of the multiplicity of its senses
being as contradictory as (3.38a–e).

This exhibits a difference between semantic anomaly and falsity or contradictoriness: the former but not the latter is related to ambiguity in the way just
described. Sentences that are false or internally inconsistent cannot be accounted
for as the extreme of the selection process where no sense remains for the whole
sentence. Such sentences have a sense, and their falsity or contradictoriness is
partly something internal to the structure of their sense, i.e., the expression of
truth conditions that cannot be satisfied.

Compare the sentences in (3.41) with those in (3.42):

(3.41) (a) The division was slaughtered by cannon fire
        (b) The seal dragged itself onto the beach to die
        (c) The knight dedicated himself to chivalrous conduct

(3.42) (a) Human children grow to over ten miles tall
        (b) Mice know all of quantum mechanics within a single day after their
            birth
        (c) Human beings and animals never die

Cases (a), (b), and (c) of (3.41) have certain possible but not actual senses,
among which are the sense of (a) on which "division" refers to the arithmetic
operation, the sense of (b) on which "seal" refers to a design-bearing device made
so that it can impart the impression of the design, and the sense of (c) on which
"knight" refers to the chess piece. The construal of semantically anomalous
sentences as (extremely) obvious falsehoods or contradictions would result in one
of two highly counterintuitive claims, namely, that the possible but not actual
senses of cases like (3.41a–c) are just as truly *senses* of the sentences as are the
senses of absurdly false sentences like (3.42a–c), or that the actual senses of
absurdly false sentences like (3.42a–c) are no more truly senses of the sentences than
are the possible but not actual senses of sentences like (3.41a–c).

Now consider the sentence (3.43):

(3.43) The man waterproofed something

Note that the interpretation of the pronoun here as referring to a physical object
also implies a distinction between the part of a reading that states the selection

restriction and the part that represents the rest of the sense. That is, only a part of the semantic content of "waterproof" is carried over to provide semantic content for the otherwise semantically empty pro-form "something," namely, the information that the referent of the pro-form, what is waterproofed, is a physical object. The remaining part of the semantic content of "waterproof," the information that someone or something makes something such that water cannot pass through its surface from the outside to the inside, must not be carried over but instead must function as the truth conditions of the sentence. Using the semantic marker '(Selector)' or some equivalent device in the lexical reading for a pro-form formalizes the process of "carrying over" part of the sense of such a verb. But the use of such a device depends on a prior distinction between the part of a reading that states the selectional condition and the part that represents the other information in the sense. This cannot be treated simply as a distinction between the semantic information from a verb that carries over to pro-forms and the information that does not, as a distinction with no relevance to matters of selection. The reason is that the semantic elements that "carry over" are the very elements that determine whether the sense of constituents that are not pro-forms can combine to form meaningful sentences, that is, they are the same elements that provide the selectional condition whose failure produces semantic anomaly. For example, the information that what is waterproofed must be a physical object functions also to determine the anomalousness of (3.44) and (3.45):

(3.44)   The man waterproofed the shadow (mirror image, reflection)

(3.45)   The man waterproofed virtue (seventeen, the itch)

There is yet another reason for having readings that distinguish a part of the sense of a constituent from the rest of that sense and express it as a condition for the meaningfulness of the sentences in which the constituent occurs. The relation 'x is a possible answer to the question q' will be discussed and defined in Chapter 5. Here we may introduce it by some examples: possible answers to the questions "What is it?" "When is it?" "Where is it?" and "Who is it?" are "It is a bear," "It is at midnight," "It is here," and "It is the president," respectively, but not in any other pairings. Now note that the question version of (3.43), namely, (3.46), does not have the declarative (3.47) as one of its possible answers:

(3.46)   What did the man waterproof?

(3.47)   The man waterproofed the shadow (afterimage, reflection)

Since the class of possible answers to a question includes false sentences as well as true ones, it cannot be on the basis of falsehood that (3.47) is not a possible answer to (3.46). What rules out (3.47) is, rather, the requirement on possible answers that the constituent in a declarative sentence that corresponds to the interrogative pronoun of the question have a reading that meets the selection restriction governing its occurrence in nonanomalous sentences. Thus, (3.47) is ruled out as a possible answer to (3.46) for the same reason it is deemed semantically anomalous, namely, the semantic marker '(Physical object)', which the selection restriction in the reading of the verb "waterproof" requires in the reading of its direct object, is absent from the relevant reading of "shadow."

Although a sentence like (3.37c), "Prepositions feel oily," has no *sub-sentential* constituent that combines a concept with one outside its range of predication, it is, nonetheless, semantically anomalous. In such cases where the sense of the subject does not belong to the category of the predicate, the conceptual incongruity is not a feature of any subsentential constituent but a feature of the whole sentence. However, the whole sentence is one of its own constituents. The semantic anomaly of sentences like (3.37c) is therefore entirely consistent with our claim that the occurrence of a conceptually incongruous constituent is a necessary condition of anomaly.[26]

But the presence of conceptual incongruity is not a sufficient condition for semantic anomaly: the fact that a sentence contains a semantically anomalous sub-sentential constituent does not guarantee that the sentence itself is semantically anomalous. This is shown by cases of sentences in which reference is made to one or another aspect of a sentence or its use, as in (a) and (b) of (3.48):

(3.48) (a) The sentence "Prepositions feel oily" is conceptually absurd (an instance of a category mistake, semantically anomalous)
  (b) We would think it queer if someone were to say that he smells itchy

Since (3.48a) simply reports a fact about an English sentence and (3.48b) simply describes the speaker's conception of how people would react to someone who said something absurd, both sentences are clearly meaningful, yet both contain a constituent that deviates significantly from full meaningfulness.

In the type of semantic theory being presented here, such sentences as (a) and (b) of (3.48) will have semantically interpreted underlying phrase markers in which one (or more) of their constituents is assigned no reading but the full sentence will receive at least one reading. This is dictated by the general decision to construct readings as representations of senses, from which it follows that constituents without a sense must be assigned no reading.

McCawley (1968b) has objected to this treatment of meaningful sentences that contain embedded sentences that are semantically anomalous. He writes:

> the position that the constituent in question has no readings in untenable, since that would mean that

(3.49) He says he smells itchy

(3.50) He says that he poured his mother into an inkwell

(3.51) He says that his toenail sings five-part madrigals

> would be synonymous. Moreover, if the embedded sentence in something like

(3.52) It is nonsense to speak of a rock having diabetes

> contains a polysemous item only one reading of which makes the sentence anomalous, then throwing away anomalies whenever they arise would give an

---

[26] See Katz (1966, pp. 160–161).

incorrect reading to the sentence. For example, if "king" is assumed to have the two readings 'monarch' and 'chess piece', Katz's procedure would mark

(3.53)   It is nonsense to speak of a king as made of plastic

as unambiguously meaning 'it is nonsense to speak of a chess king as made of plastic' and would exclude the normal interpretation, 'it is nonsense to speak of a monarch as made of plastic' (pp. 128–129).

McCawley's argument is that if the constituent representing the embedded sentence in each of (3.49)–(3.53) is assigned no reading, then the semantic component of a grammar, as it is conceived here, must mistakenly predict that the first three sentences are the same in meaning and the last is not semantically ambiguous. But this conclusion does not follow. If it did, we would be forced into the solution McCawley adopts, that of saying that the constituents representing the embedded sentences receive a reading. But if we had to accept McCawley's solution, we would face consequences just as bad as those he thinks follow from my account. If these constituents are assigned readings, they are marked as meaningful (i.e., as having a sense), which not only contradicts our agreed-upon judgments concerning them but leads to the absurd view that sentences like (3.48) are false. Accordingly, if this argument is sound, we face a dilemma: either we adopt a solution on which we are forced to make false predictions about synonymy and ambiguity or we adopt one on which we are forced to make false predictions about semantic anomaly and metalinguistic truth.

Although McCawley does not say this explicitly, it is clear that he is arguing that if the embedded sentences were meaningless they would make the same (null) contribution to the sentences in which they are embedded; therefore, since the sentences in which they are embedded are otherwise identical, these sentences would have to be the same in meaning. The fallacy in this argument is in its false assumption that only the reading of the full embedded sentence can contribute to the meaning of the sentence in which it is embedded. The fact that the whole embedded sentence in cases like (3.49)–(3.53) has no reading means just that the semantic interpretation cannot draw on readings of the *whole* embedded sentence. It does not mean that it cannot draw on the readings of the subsentential constituents. Moreover, when we attend carefully to the meaning of sentences like (3.49)–(3.53), it becomes clear that this is precisely what the semantic interpretation should make use of. The verb "say" has a number of senses, but the one of interest in this connection is the sense on which to say of someone that he said something is to say that he asserted that some object has some property or that some objects bear a relation to one another. For example, we naturally interpret (3.49) to mean that the person referred to by the subject of the whole sentence claims that the person referred to by the subject of the embedded sentence has a smell and the smell is itchy. Accordingly, the lexical reading of this sense of "say" must be formally constructed to distinguish between the semantic information in the embedded sentence that tells us who it is that the referent of the subject of "say" has made an assertion about and the semantic information in the embedded sentence that tells us what the assertion is. This means that the readings from the semantic interpretation of the embedded sentence that we want to use are the reading of the subject, the reading of the verb, and the reading of the adverb. These considerations are, I think, sufficient to show that McCawley's objection is baseless.

7.   The definition of 'suppressed sense'

As pointed out in the previous section, a sense of a constituent is prevented from entering into the compositionally formed senses of higher order constituents when it falls outside the categories that determine what senses can be combined with those of other constituents in the same sentence. The fact that there are senses that are excluded from forming derived readings in particular cases provides us with another semantic relation to be added to our list of semantic properties and relations, namely, 'is a suppressed sense of'. In this section we shall try to define this new relation so that we can add another definition to semantic theory.

The notion 'supressed sense' may be illustrated by the following children's riddle: why are cats longer at night than in the morning? The answer that is given is (3.54):

(3.54)   Because cats are taken in in the morning and let out at night

The joke here depends on the ability of the listener to identify the suppressed senses of "take in" and "let out" in (3.54), namely, 'to decrease length' and 'to increase length', respectively. These senses are suppressed because the category that determines their range of application is the category 'garments' in connection with their grammatical object. That is, since the object in (3.54) is "cat" rather than a kind of garment, the aforementioned senses of the lexical items "take in" and "let out" are suppressed in favor of the senses 'to bring in from the outside' and 'to put outside', respectively. The amusement of the riddle lies in the way it flaunts the violation of this semantic fact.

Consider the sentences (3.55) and (3.56):

(3.55)   The pike impaled George

(3.56)   George saw the pike

The word "pike" in (3.56) has a sense on which it means a spike, one on which it means a mountain peak, one on which it means a certain kind of fish, one on which it means a spearlike weapon, and one on which it means a main highway. Accordingly, (3.56) is five-ways ambiguous. The word "pike" in (3.55) does not have at least the last of these senses, that is, the sentence does not mean that a main highway impaled George. Yet "pike" lexically has a sense on which it means a main highway, and this must be represented by one of the lexical readings assigned to "pike" in the semantically interpreted underlying phrase marker for (3.55). Moreover, this lexical reading must be eliminated by a selection restriction in the reading of "impale."

We understand a suppressed sense of a subconstituent of a complex constituent to be one of its senses but not one that contributes to a sense of the complex constituent. Thus, it is quite natural to seek an explication of this notion in terms of the operation of selection restrictions whereby certain senses of subconstituents are eliminated. Suppose there is a suppressed sense of a constituent C. The reading of C that represents this sense will be eliminated when the other readings (there may also be no other readings) of C are combined with the readings of the constituent(s) with which C is grammatically related. It will be eliminated because it fails to satisfy the selection restrictions in the readings for the other constituent(s). And it will fail to satisfy them because it contains or does not contain certain semantic markers. Therefore, on the basis of selection restrictions, one can formally define, in terms of semantic markers, a property that each of the readings of a sense of C has but that no reading for a suppressed sense of C has, namely, the property of satisfying the disjunction of the selection restrictions in the readings of the constituents with which C is grammatically related in the underlying phrase marker. It is just this property that a suppressed sense must lack and an actual sense must have. We therefore have the definition (3.57):

(3.57) A sense σ is a suppressed sense of the constituent C in a sentence S relative to its underlying phrase marker U just in case the occurrence of C in U has the reading R representing σ and R does not satisfy the disjunction of the selection restrictions in the readings of the constituents in U to which C is grammatically related.

8. The structure of lexical readings

Weinreich (1966) argued that the ordering of semantic markers in lexical readings (provided by representing lexical readings as paths in a tree diagram) and the structure of lexical readings (provided by representing the dictionary entry for a lexical item as such a tree diagram) should be eliminated in favor of an account in which the semantic markers in a lexical reading are treated as a set and the lexical readings in a dictionary are treated as a set of such sets. There is no disagreement with Weinreich on this. In fact, I adopted the latter treatment as a result of certain systematic considerations that came to light after Katz and Fodor (1963) was published.[27] But Weinreich makes it appear as if there never was any theoretical motivation for ordering[28] when he claims that its elimination would be justified as a simplification of semantic theory. Such a claim could not be made without supporting arguments unless it were assumed that no theoretical justification had been given.

The original motivation for ordering semantic markers in lexical readings was to provide a formal means of stating such facts as that the concepts represented

---

[27] See Katz (1964c, p. 75; 1966, chapter 5).

[28] It must have occurred to Weinreich that we had some motivation for ordering the semantic markers in a lexical reading, for, in a footnote, he wrote: "The prospect that implicational relations among markers, such as those discussed by Katz and Postal . . . may automatically yield unique networks of features, is attractive, but it is unlikely to be borne out when nonanecdotal evidence is considered" (p. 409n).

by the semantic markers '(Human)', '(Plant)', '(Animal)', '(Artifact)', and so on are subsumed under the more abstract concept represented by the semantic marker '(Physical object)'. Facts such as this indicate a hierarchical organization in the system of concepts that underlies the semantics of natural languages. We sought to reconstruct this hierarchical conceptual organization by having semantic markers such as '(Physical)' and '(Object)' dominate semantic markers such as '(Human)', '(Plant)', '(Animal)', '(Artifact)' in each lexical reading where they occur.

Thus, the ordering of semantic markers was not gratuitous formalism but was intended to deal with certain types of facts. Weinreich puts the question of eliminating such ordering on the wrong basis, making it appear as if economy were the sole consideration. The question instead has to be posed in terms of whether or not ordering is the best method of describing the facts involved. In order to ask this question, then, there must be an alternative to the ordering of semantic markers. Without such an alternative, the question makes little sense. Thus, Fodor and I had to retain ordering as part of our theory until another means of describing the relevant facts came along.

It was with the development of semantic redundancy rules[29] that the question of whether ordering is the best descriptive method could first be seriously considered. Semantic redundancy rules were originally devised to simplify lexical readings in dictionary entries and to express generalizations about semantic structure at the lexical level. It was noticed that in many cases a semantic marker (M_i) must occur in a lexical reading if another semantic marker (M_j) occurs in that reading. That is, the occurrence of (M_j) in the lexical reading makes the occurrence of (M_i) redundant given a general representation of the regularity governing the occurrence of (M_i) with respect to the occurrence of (M_j). For example, if any of such semantic markers as '(Human)', '(Animal)', '(Plant)', '(Artifact)' occur in a lexical reading R, then R must also contain the semantic markers '(Physical)' and '(Object)'. Since the concepts represented by the former semantic markers are subsumed under the concepts represented by the latter, the occurrence of any of the former semantic markers in R makes the occurrence of the latter in R redundant. In order to avoid such redundancy and to obtain generalizations that express such regularities, as reflected in more economical lexical readings, it was proposed that the dictionary contain semantic redundancy rules of the form (2.31) and (2.32). These rules comprise a redundancy rule subcomponent of the dictionary.

Given that the dictionary contains a redundancy rule subcomponent, we can formulate an alternative to the ordering of semantic markers in lexical readings. Each redundancy rule in this subcomponent can be interpreted as specifying that the semantic marker on the left-hand side of the arrow represents a concept that is subsumed under the concept represented by the semantic marker on the right-hand side. On this interpretation, the hierarchy of concepts that we wish to describe falls out quite naturally by (3.58).

---

[29] See Katz and Postal (1964, pp. 16–18) and Katz (1966, pp. 224–239). See also Chapter 2, Section 5, of the present work for our initial mention of the need for rules that simplify lexical readings by formulating them without redundant semantic markers.

(3.58) (a) Those semantic markers appearing on the right-hand side of some semantic redundancy rules but not on the left-hand side of any such rules represent the most abstract concepts, the semantic categories, of the language.

(b) Those semantic markers appearing on the left-hand side of some semantic redundancy rules but not on the right-hand side of'any such rules represent the least abstract concepts of the language.

(c) Given the two semantic redundancy rules $(M_2) \rightarrow (M_1)$ and $(M_3) \rightarrow (M_2)$, the concept which is represented by (M_1) will be at a higher level in the hierarchy than that represented by both (M_2) and (M_3), the concept represented by (M_2) will be at the next lower level, and the concept represented by (M_3) will be at the level immediately below the concept represented by (M_2).

This interpretation of the semantic redundancy rules turns out to be quite superior to ordered semantic markers in lexical readings as a method of describing the hierarchical organization of concepts. Its superiority consists in this: semantic redundancy rules provide as adequate a description as the ordering of semantic markers, but, unlike such ordering, they are needed independently in the semantic component to express the most economical generalizations about the occurrence of semantic markers in lexical readings. Ordering serves no purpose other than to provide a reconstruction of the hierarchical organization of concepts. On these grounds we have strong motivation for altering the form of lexical readings so that the semantic markers are now taken to constitute an unordered set.

Given that the semantic markers in lexical readings are unordered, Weinreich levels another criticism. He considers the two sentences (3.59) and (3.60):

(3.59)   Cats chase mice

(3.60)   Mice chase cats

Weinreich then comments:

> The paths of (1) *cats*, (2) *chase*, and (3) *mice* ... although amalgamated in the order $1 + (2 + 3)$ in [(3.59)] and as $(2 + 1) + 3$ in [(3.60)], would yield the same unordered set of features {1 2 3}, as the amalgamated path; for, as we have seen, there is neither ordering nor bracketing of elements in a KF path. For similar reasons, the theory is unable to mark the distinction between *three cats chased a mouse* and *a cat chased three mice*, between (*bloody* + *red*) + *sunset* and *bloody* + *red* + *sunset*, and so on for an infinite number of crucial cases.
>
> For KF, the meaning of a complex expression (such as a phrase or a sentence) is an unstructured heap of features—just like the meaning of a single word. The projection rules as formulated in KF *destroy the semantic structure* and reduce the words of a sentence to a heap (p. 410).

This criticism is rather strange since it applies neither to the actual theory that Fodor and I held at the time nor to any modified version of that theory which we either would want to hold or would need to hold. On the one hand, the theory that we postulated, the one against which the criticisms throughout Weinreich's paper are directed, did contain the ordering of semantic markers in lexical readings, and this, of course, is sufficient to block Weinreich's criticism. On the other hand, the replacement of lexical readings in which semantic markers are ordered by lexical readings in which semantic markers form sets does not in fact lead to the unacceptable consequences that Weinreich posits. The source of his error is, I think, a misconstrual of both projection rules and the concept of a semantic marker.

The first misinterpretation is to identify the operations of projection rules with those of just one projection rule, namely, the rule referred to as (R1) in Katz and Fodor (1963, pp. 198–200), which was proposed to deal with cases of attribution. This rule does perform the operation of forming the Boolean union of the semantic markers in the readings to which it is applied. But, as was made clear from the earliest papers, the operation of producing derived readings in the form of a Boolean sum is by no means characteristic of other projection rules.[30]

The second misunderstanding is the treatment of semantic markers as if they were simple syntactic features. Syntactic and phonological features are binary, ternary, or *n*-ary distinctions that indicate that the items to which they are ascribed have one or another member of a set of exclusive simple properties. They have no internal structure and are not components in the formal structure of other markers of their kind. Semantic markers are thus not features because they have internal structure and can be components of other semantic markers. They are intended to reflect, in their formal structure, the structure of the concepts they represent. Some confusion may have resulted from the fact that many of the examples of semantic markers given in early papers did not exhibit formal structure of this kind. The reason is that at the time we were unable to state such structure and used only illustrations of semantic relations whose formalization did not depend on the internal structure of the concepts represented by semantic markers. Such semantic markers were regarded as terms that would eventually be defined away; their definitions, when available, were supposed to eliminate them in favor of formal structures that represented the complex internal structure of concepts. For example, '(Object)', although not definable then or even now, should eventually be replaced by some formal configuration of symbols whose internal structure reflects the structure of the concept represented.[31]

In order to see how a semantic component avoids the difficulty that Weinreich cites, consider the way that such a component for English could distinguish between the meaning of (3.59) and (3.60). The reading of the most familiar sense of "chase" is represented in (3.61).[32]

(3.61)

[30] Katz (1964c).
[31] See the discussion in Chapter 2 in connection with (2.15).
[32] The braces indicate a grouping which will be explained in Chapter 4, Section 3.

The semantic marker '(Activity)' in (3.61) distinguishes "chase" from *state verbs*, such as "sleep," "wait," "suffer," "believe," and from *process verbs*, such as "grow," "freeze," "dry." It classifies "chase" together with other *activity verbs*, such as "eat," "speak," "walk," "remember," which will also have '(Activity)' in their lexical readings. The semantic marker '(Physical)', together with the bracketing, indicates that the activity is qualified as to its nature, that is, that chasing is a physical activity. This distinguishes "chase" from verbs like "think," "remember," "imagine," which would be qualified in their lexical readings to indicate that they are mental activities. Notice that '(Activity)' does not encompass either the semantic marker '(Group)' or the semantic marker '(Individual)'. Thus, *inter alia*, "chase" can apply to either a group or an individual activity. In this respect, "chase" differs both from "mob," whose lexical reading would contain the semantic marker '(Group)' at a position parallel to that of '(Physical)' in (3.61), and from "solo," whose lexical reading would contain the semantic marker '(Individual)' at such a position. The need for such markers can be seen from the sentences (3.62) and (3.63):

(3.62)   Mary mobbed the movie star (all by herself)

(3.63)   They solo in the plane on Monday

The semantic marker '(Group)' would explain the contradictoriness of (3.62), while the marker '(Individual)' would explain the fact that (3.63) has the unique meaning that each of the persons referred to flies the plane by himself on Monday. Since "chase" is unmarked for either of these conceptual properties, it is represented as an activity that can be performed by a group or by an individual.

The semantic marker '(Movement)' indicates that chasing involves movement from place to place.[33] This movement necessarily occurs at a fast speed, as indicated by the semantic marker '(Speed)$^{(Fast)}$', which distinguishes "chase" from "creep," "walk," "trail," etc. Also, this movement is marked as having the character of following someone or something, which distinguishes "chase" from "flee," "wander," etc. No further semantic markers are encompassed by '(Movement)', which means that the movement is not specified as to manner. Of course, it can be so specified by putting "chase" in construction with a manner adverbial such as "on foot" or "by car." Furthermore, for someone to be chasing someone or something, it is not necessary that the person be moving in any specified direction. This is indicated by the absence of a qualification of the form '(Direction)$^{( )}$'. "Chase" is thus distinguished from "descend," "advance," "retreat," etc. But it is necessary that the person or group doing the chasing have the purpose of trying to catch the thing being chased, which is indicated by the semantic marker '(Purpose)', together with the semantic marker it encompasses. Therefore "chase" falls together with "pursue" and contrasts with "follow" and "trail." In previous publications the semantic marker '(Intention)' was used instead of '(Purpose)'. I think the present practice is preferable since activities have purposes but not intentions. It is

---

[33] That the person chasing must be moving is revealed by the contradictoriness of sentences such as "The man who is standing still is chasing the dog." See Chapter 4, Section 5.

left open as to what extent the persons engaged in an activity having a fixed purpose themselves have the associated intention. Note also that, although it is sometimes held that the person chased must be fleeing, this is a mistake. Consider the sentence (3.64):

(3.64)   The police chased the speeding motorist

Such sentences do not imply that the motorist is fleeing either from the police or from anything else.

   Finally, notice that "chase" is not an achievement verb in the sense of applying just to cases where the purpose is achieved: it is not necessary for the person or group to catch the one being chased. This is shown by the fact that (3.65a) is not contradictory but (3.65b) is:

(3.65)   (a) He chased him but did not catch him
         (b) He won against him but did not defeat him

Thus "chase" contrasts with "intercept," "trap," "deceive," etc.

   'X' and 'Y' in (3.61) are categorized variables. They designate the positions in readings at which other readings can be substituted by projection rules. 'X' is the variable for which readings of subjects can be substituted and 'Y' the variable for which readings of objects can be substituted. Thus, 'X' and 'Y' in (3.61) designate, respectively, the position for the readings of the subject of "chase" and the positions for the readings of the object of "chase." These variables and others are categorized in the sense that their range of values—the readings that may be substituted for one of them—is determined by the category of the variable. The category, which is defined in terms of a grammatical relation in syntactic theory, is formally designated by the orthographic shape of the letter chosen for the variable. Thus, the letter 'X' designates one category, that is, readings of subjects of the constituents in whose readings it appears; 'Y' another, namely, direct objects; 'Z', still another, say, indirect objects; and so forth.

   Given a variable A categorized for the grammatical relation H in a reading for a constituent C_i and a constituent C_j that bears H to C_i, the readings of C_j are the values of A. Any such readings may be substituted for A just in case they satisfy the selection restriction associated with the occurrence of A in H. Whenever the projection rules encounter a constituent whose reading contains a categorized variable, they determine which of the readings assigned to constituents in the underlying phrase marker that are values of the variable satisfy the selection restriction. These they substitute for occurrences of the variable, thus forming derived readings for the higher constituent.

   On the basis of such variables, therefore, we can have two projection rules, one for the verb-object relation and one for the subject-predicate relation. The former substitutes a reading of the object of a verb for the occurrences of 'Y' in the reading of the verb. The latter substitutes a reading of the subject of a verb for occurrences of 'X' in the reading of the predicate (which includes the reading for the verb, as determined by the first of these projection rules).

From this, it is clear that the derived readings for the sentences (3.59) and (3.60) will differ in a way appropriate to their difference in meaning. Weinreich's criticism that a semantic component designed in terms of our conception of semantic theory would assign the same semantic interpretation to sentences which differ in meaning is thus wrong. The operation of projection rules on the lexically interpreted underlying phrase markers for (3.59) and (3.60), both of which include (3.61) as a reading of their verb constituent, would give a reading for (3.59) in which the reading of "cats" occupies the 'X' position and the reading for "mice" occupies the 'Y' positions, and a reading for (3.60) in which the reading of "mice" occupies the 'X' position and the reading for "cats" occupies the 'Y' positions. We thus represent the fact that the difference in meaning between these two sentences is that (3.59) says that cats are the chasers and mice the chased while (3.60) says the reverse. (See the discussion in connection with (3.85) in the next section.)

9. Categorized variables, grammatical relations, and case grammars

The first part of this section presents a generalization of the idea of a categorized variable just discussed. This generalization will turn out to have important implications both for the theory of projection (see the next section of this chapter) and for semantic representation and the definition of semantic properties and relations (see Chapter 7).

In the discussion in the previous section, as well as in Katz (1967a), we assumed that semantic theory provided the letters 'X', 'Y', 'Z', etc., as symbols standing for distinct categorized variables. Each such variable was thought of as introduced into the theory by a special definition which differentiated the letter it defined from the letters that represent other variables on the basis of the grammatical relation specifying the category of the variable. The grammatical relation that determines the constituent whose readings provide the values for an occurrence of a categorized variable was thus not a part of the formalism of the symbol that stood for the variable but was indicated by a special definition.

We shall now change this by using complex symbols to represent the variables so that their categorizing grammatical relations are presented directly as part of the structure of these complex symbols. Thus, the letters previously used can now be thought of as abbreviations, serving to simplify a somewhat more complicated but far more clear and powerful notion.

We shall use the letter 'X' with brackets above it and angles below it. The brackets contain a specification of a grammatical function and, optionally, a semantic condition, while the angles contain a function of semantic markers. 'X', 'Y', 'Z', etc., are therefore each to be replaced definitionally by a complex symbol of the form (3.66):

(3.66) $$[B_1, B_2, \ldots, B_i] \ \& \ K$$
$$X$$
$$\langle F(M_1), (M_2), \ldots, (M_J) \rangle$$

The B's in (3.66) represent category symbols of the base of the syntactic component, and K is a semantic condition. The grammatical function appearing inside the brackets expresses the categorization of the variable, and the semantic condition, if there is one, restricts the range determined by the category. The semantic markers in the angles function as a selection restriction for the values of the variable.

Accordingly, the categorized variables to be used in semantic markers will be chosen from the enumeration (3.67):

(3.67)

$$\underset{\langle\ \rangle}{\underset{X}{[\text{NP, S}]}}, \quad \underset{\langle\ \rangle}{\underset{X}{[\text{NP, VP, Pred-Phrase, S}]}}, \quad \underset{\langle\ \rangle}{\underset{X}{[\text{NP, Prep-Phrase, VP, Pred-Phrase, S}]}}, \dots$$

'[NP, S]' in (3.67) is the grammatical function specifying the 'subject-of' relation, '[NP, VP, Pred-Phrase, S]' is the grammatical function specifying the 'object-of' relation, '[NP, Prep-Phrase, VP, Pred-Phrase, S]' is the grammatical function specifying the 'indirect-object-of' relation, and so on.[34] As Chomsky points out, grammatical relations can be defined derivatively in terms of grammatical functions. For example, the definition of the subject-verb relation can be given as the function of functions '[[NP, S], [V, VP, Pred-Phrase, S]]', where this notation is to be read as "the relation that the substring that is directly dominated by 'NP' which is directly dominated by 'S' bears to the substring that is directly dominated by 'V' which is directly dominated by 'VP' which is directly dominated by 'Pred-Phrase' which is directly dominated by 'S'." This is, in effect, what putting a grammatical function over 'X' within a reading does. Since an occurrence of a categorized variable from (3.67) appears in a reading assigned to a constituent in an underlying phrase marker, we may take the relation it expresses to be the relation between the substring it specifies and that constituent; for example, '[NP, S]' appearing over 'X' within a reading of a verb makes the same specification as '[[NP, S], [V, VP, Pred-Phrase, S]]' where 'V' directly dominates the verb in question. Thus, the first categorized variable in (3.67) has as its values the readings of the subject of the constituent in whose reading it occurs, the second has as its values the readings of the direct object of the verb constituent in whose reading it

---

[34] See (3.79)–(3.81) and the accompanying discussion for further clarification of such grammatical functions.

Here and in the rest of this discussion I rely on Chomsky's account (1965, pp. 63–74) of the definitions of grammatical relations. The definitions I give are, of course, to be taken as just as tentative as those of Chomsky's. However, there is reason for adopting the definition of 'indirect-object-of' given in (3.67) rather than one that assumes that the deep structure of sentences with indirect objects contains the indirect object as the first noun phrase following the verb. Preferring the structure in which the indirect object is found in a prepositional phrase in the verb phrase means that structures like "John gave Mary the book" are derived from structures like "John gave the book to Mary." One reason for this preference is that order of consituents should not enter into the definition of grammatical relations. Another is that there are verbs that, when they take an indirect object, do not have a form without the prepositional phrase, e.g., "declare," "state," "describe," "explain," "dedicate."

occurs, the third has as its values the readings of the indirect object of the verb constituent in whose reading it occurs, and so on.

We will discuss and illustrate the optional semantic condition K in Chapter 6, Section 2.

The angles under a categorized variable specify the selection restriction that determines whether or not a reading in the range of the variable can be substituted for an occurrence of that variable to form a derived reading. Consider the expanded version of the reading for "chase," as given in (3.68):

(3.68)

$(((Activity) (((Physical))$

$$((Movement) ((Speed)^{(Fast)} (Following \quad \begin{matrix} [NP, VP, Pred\text{-}Phrase, S] \\ X \\ \langle (Object) \rangle \end{matrix} \quad)))$$

$$((Purpose) ((To\ catch \quad \begin{matrix} [NP, VP, Pred\text{-}Phrase, S] \\ X \\ \langle (Object) \rangle \end{matrix} \quad)))))$$

$$\begin{matrix} [NP, S] \\ X \\ \langle (Human) \vee (Animal) \rangle \end{matrix} \quad)$$

The selection restriction for the variable categorized for the subject of "chase" requires that its reading have one of the semantic markers '(Human)' or '(Animal)' in order to be substituted. Thus, while the sentences (3.69a–c) are perfectly acceptable, the sentences (3.70a–c) are all semantically anomalous:[35]

(3.69) (a) The policeman chased the bandit
        (b) The dog chased the stick
        (c) The spider chased the fly

(3.70) (a) The reflection chased the bandit
        (b) The stick chased the dog
        (c) The tree chased the fly

The selection restriction for the variable categorized for the direct object of "chase" requires that its reading contain the semantic marker '(Object)'. Note that the reading of the object of "chase" does not require the semantic marker '(Physical)' but just the semantic marker '(Object)'. Thus, the sentences (3.71), (3.72), and (3.73) are not anomalous:

(3.71) The dog chased the cat's reflection

(3.72) The cat chased the image of the bird across the mirror

(3.73) The policeman chased the shadow of the bandit

---

[35] It may be possible to supply the selection restriction in this case by a redundancy rule that relates intentions with those beings that are capable of them, but this is not something that we can go into.

The sentences (3.74), (3.75), (3.76), on the other hand, are anomalous:

(3.74) The dog chased an itch

(3.75) The cat chased a virtue and a vice

(3.76) The policeman chased an English sentence

We will impose condition (3.77) as part of the definition of 'categorized variable':

(3.77) If there is no constituent available to provide a reading to serve as the value of an occurrence of a categorized variable or if the appropriate constituent is a pro-form, then the value of the categorized variable is the set of semantic markers X such that X contains (a) any semantic marker that appears as a conjunct of a condition in the selection restriction of the categorized variable; (b) $((M^{(\alpha)}) \lor (M^{(\beta)}) \lor \ldots \lor (M^{(\gamma)}))$ for any semantic markers $(M^{(\alpha)})$, $(M^{(\beta)})$, ..., $(M^{(\gamma)})$ that appear as the disjuncts of a condition; and, finally (c) $A/(M^{(\delta_i)})$ for any semantic marker that appears in a negative condition, i.e., as $\overline{(M^{(\delta_i)})}$.[36]

The condition (3.77) covers cases where such a variable cannot obtain an appropriate value because there is no constituent that stands in the specified grammatical relation to the constituent in whose reading it appears or because there is such a constituent but its meaning lacks the proper semantic information, that is, where no constituent satisfies the grammatical function which categorizes the variable or when a pro-form satisfies it. Note that (3.77) does not apply when there is such a constituent but it has no readings (i.e., is semantically anomalous) or when the readings of such a constituent do not satisfy the selection restriction governing substitutions.

Condition (3.77) enables categorized variables to do the work of the semantic marker '(Selector)', thereby allowing us to eliminate it from the vocabulary of semantic theory.[37] Consider a sentence such as (3.78):

(3.78) Something chased something

Given condition (3.77), this sentence receives a reading that represents the proposition that some human or animal chased some object, and the need for using '(Selector)' as a lexical reading of pro-forms no longer exists. We shall discuss this feature of categorized variables further in Chapter 7.

---

[36] Since the selection restriction on the categorized variable in the reading for "honest" (see Katz (1966, p. 160)) is $\langle$(Human) & $\overline{\text{(Infant)}}\rangle$ (where the bar over '(Infant)' means that this marker cannot occur in readings satisfying the selection restriction), the reading of the subject of the sentence "Someone is honest" will contain '(Human)' and the complex semantic marker '$((M^{(\delta 1)}) \lor (M^{(\delta 2)}) \lor \ldots \lor (M^{(\delta i - 1)}), (M^{(\delta i + 1)}) \lor \ldots \lor (M^{(\delta n)}))$, where $(M^{(\delta i)}) = $ (Infant).

[37] See Katz and Postal (1964, pp. 83–84).

Let us now examine some questions about the status of the grammatical relations which semantic theory makes use of in the formulation of categorized variables.

Consider a base component of the sort Chomsky presents (1965, pp. 106–107), with phrase structure rules such as those in (3.79):

(3.79) (a) S → NP⌒Predicate-Phrase
        (b) Predicate-Phrase → Aux⌒VP (Place) (Time)
        (c) VP → {
            Copula⌒Predicate
            V ((NP) (Prep-Phrase) (Prep-Phrase) (Manner))
            S′
            Predicate
            }
        (d) Predicate → { Adjective
                          (like) Predicate-Nominal }
        (e) Copula → be
        (f) Aux → Tense (Modal) (Aspect)
        (g) NP → (Det) N (S′)
        (h) Prep-Phrase → Direction, Duration, Place, etc.
        (i) Det → (pre-Article⌒of) Article (post-Article)

There will also be an appropriate completion in the form of rules such as 'N → CS', 'V → CS', '[+Det——] → [±Count]', 'Article → [±Definite]' and a lexicon with entries such as '(sincerity; [+N, +Det——, −Count, +Abstract, ...])'. As already mentioned with regard to (3.67), on the basis of such rules it is possible to define grammatical functions such as 'subject-of-the-sentence' and 'direct-object-of-the-sentence' as shown in (a) and (b) of (3.80), and also to define, in terms of the former definitions, the grammatical relations of 'subject-of-the-main-verb' and 'direct-object-of-the-main-verb' as in (a) and (b) of (3.81):

(3.80) (a) [NP, S]
        (b) [NP, VP, Pred-Phrase, S]

(3.81) (a) [[NP, S], [V, VP, Pred-Phrase, S]]
        (b) [[NP, VP, Pred-Phrase, S], [V, VP, Pred-Phrase, S]]

This account, however, as Chomsky (1965) correctly observes, is incomplete. Chomsky writes:

> We have no basis, as yet, for distinguishing the legitimate and traditionally recognized grammatical relation *Subject-Verb* . . . from the irrelevant pseudo-relation *Subject-Object*, which is definable just as easily in the same terms (pp. 73-74).

The problem is actually far more extensive than Chomsky here suggests. Besides the particular pseudorelation he cites, we can equally well define far more bizarre pseudorelations such as in (3.82):

(3.82) (a) [[Det, NP, S], [Det, NP, VP, Pred-Phrase, S]]
        (b) [[V, VP, Pred-Phrase, S], [Article, Det, NP, VP, Pred-Phrase, S]]

As a way out, Chomsky (1965, pp. 113–114) proposes that the true grammatical relations, like those in (3.81), be distinguished from the pseudorelations, like those in (3.82), by the fact that in the former case there are selectional restrictions governing the paired categories whereas in the latter there are none.

The selectional rule on which Chomsky (p. 107) bases his claim that (3.81a) defines the 'subject-of-the-main-verb' relation is that given in (3.83):

(3.83) $[+V] \rightarrow CS/\alpha \frown Aux$——$(Det \frown \beta)$, where α is an N and β is an N

This rule constrains the choice of a verb in terms of a free choice of certain syntactic features of nouns, but the nouns in question need not be the subject (or the object) of the main verb in question. Consider, for example, (3.84):

(3.84) Several happy boys with masks on their faces frightened an old lady who had thought that Halloween was over

In this sentence the selectional relation in the sense of (3.83) holds between the constituents "boys" and "frighten." However, the subject of the main verb "frighten" is "several happy boys with masks on their faces," not "boys." Moreover, Chomsky's proposal does not account for why, with regard to grammatical functions, cases like (a) and (b) of (3.80) define "legitimate and traditionally recognized" relations whereas cases like the functions '[Det, NP, S]' and '[Prep-Phrase, VP, Pred-Phrase, S]' define only "irrelevant pseudorelations" between a substring of the terminal string and the entire terminal string.

One can also find examples that seem to show that Chomsky's criterion for distinguishing true grammatical relations from pseudogrammatical relations fails in both directions. Examples of selectional rules that govern the choice of a verb in an embedded sentence structure in terms of a choice of a particular verb in the higher sentence would provide an argument that this criterion is too inclusive, that is, marks certain pseudogrammatical relations as true grammatical relations. Examples of cases where there is no selectional rule governing the choice of one constituent in terms of another but where, nonetheless, the relation between them is intuitively indistinguishable in any relevant respect from cases that are counted as grammatically related—for instance, the relation between the secondary indirect object and verb to be treated in Chapter 7—would provide an argument that the criterion is too exclusive, that is, that it marks certain true gramatical relations as pseudogrammatical relations. But I have so far been unable to find sufficiently strong examples to make a conclusive case against Chomsky's criterion. The reason has to do with the fact that the nature of the selection is highly debatable. The examples of higher to lower verb selection can be challenged by arguing that they are not instances of syntactic selection but, rather, instances of semantic restriction; the examples supporting the claim that the criterion is too exclusive can be challenged by arguing that certain of the alleged semantic restrictions which apply in these cases are instances of syntactic selection.

Even if the criterion were adequate in the sense that a pair of constituents is grammatically related when and only when there is an appropriate selectional relation that determines the choice of one in terms of a choice of the other, it would offer very little in the way of a full account of the traditional notion of grammatical relations, which is in part semantic. After discussing some of the syntactic tests for subjects and objects, Jespersen (1933) says:

> What is said in the preceding paragraphs is merely an aid to our grammatical analysis; but a much more important question is: What means does the English language possess to enable the man in the street, who is no grammarian and has no need of learned terms like subject and object, to understand the meaning of sentences? If he hears a sentence like "John saw Henry," it is, of course, necessary for him at once to know who was the seer and who was seen. How is this effected? (p. 98)

The question of paramount importance, as Jespersen suggests, is what role grammatical relations play in determining what sentences tell us about the persons, places, events, things, etc., with which they are concerned. As a first step toward answering this question, I wish to propose a criterion in place of Chomsky's. My proposal will attempt to provide a basis for deciding whether a formally definable relation (in terms of a set of rules such as (3.79)) is a real grammatical relation like (a) and (b) of (3.81) or a pseudorelation like (a) and (b) of (3.82) in terms of the way that the information given in a statement of a grammatical relation is used in determining what sentences tell us about the persons, places, events, things, etc., with which they are concerned.

Rules such as (3.79) provide vastly more information than is required for definitions of grammatical relations, so that isolating the information relevant to defining the true grammatical relations becomes a special problem. It is significant that the solution to this problem plays no real role in syntactic analysis: the base rules of the syntactic component cannot separate information that is relevant to defining grammatical relations from other information about deep structure, and the transformational component does not require the full statement of grammatical relations (that is, the structure indices of transformations do not appear to make essential use of this information). Accordingly, the definitions of grammatical relations would appear to play a role in grammar by providing information for the semantic component. Therefore, if we can formulate some hypothesis about where this information is used in semantic analysis and what use it has, we can state the grammatical relations as part of the formulation of the semantic rules that use them. The true grammatical relations will then be those that occur in the statement of the semantic rules in question.

It has been argued here that the semantic component must be a function F that is both *compositional*, in that F determines the semantic representations of a constituent (including a sentence) from the semantic representations of its subconstituents, and *general*, in that, for any constituent of the language, F recursively determines the semantic representations assigned to it with respect to the description it receives in the syntactic component. But to determine the right semantic representation for a constituent of some syntactic complexity, it will not be enough to know only what its subconstituents are: we must also know how they are related to one another as subconstituents of the constituent. This information is provided in the configuration of labeled bracketings that gives the syntactic description of the constituent within a phrase marker. We could try to specify F in terms of the full configurations of labeled bracketings for the constituents on which F will operate. This is equivalent to saying that F makes use of every piece of information in such configurations in assigning derived readings. But, as we shall try to show in the course of this book, this approach is both overly complicated and misses a significant generalization, namely, that *the form of semantic composition by which readings of subconstituents are amalgamated, insofar as it depends on syntactic information about these subconstituents, depends only on information about how they are grammatically related.* This is to say, then, that any information in the configurations of labeled bracketings beyond what is required to determine the grammatical relations of subconstituents is irrelevant to specifying the way the semantic component combines their readings to provide a reading for the constituent of which they are subconstituents. On the basis of this generalization, we propose the following criterion to distinguish between true grammatical relations and pseudogrammatical relations: an ordered *n*-tuple of grammatical functions is a grammatical relation just in case it is required in the semantic component as part of the statement of a specific type of combination that readings can undergo in the process of forming semantically interpreted underlying phrase markers from lexically interpreted underlying phrase markers. Thus, the potential forms of semantic combination that can be effected by the operation of a projection rule not only specify the semantic import of a set of *n*-tuples of grammatical functions, but, in so doing, also confer the status of genuine grammatical relations on the members of the set.

These reflections strongly suggest that Fillmore's (1968) proposal for a "case grammar" is based on a misconception about the function of grammatical relations in a grammar of the type described by Chomsky (1965). Fillmore's primary reason for criticizing Chomsky's account of grammatical relations as well as for proposing a case grammar is that Chomsky's account is not, in and of itself, an adequate account of semantic roles: the definitions it provides for grammatical relations like 'subject-of' and 'direct-object-of' are not answers to questions of the kind that Jespersen asked about the ability of speakers to determine semantic roles like 'agent' and 'recipient' from the meaning of sentences. Basically, Fillmore proposes to replace phrase structure rules such as (a), (b), and (c) of (3.79) with a system of case rules that analyzes the category 'Sentence' as 'Modality' plus 'Proposition' and expands the latter category in terms of 'Verb' plus one or more symbols chosen from a predetermined list of case markers ('A' for Agentive, 'D' for Dative, etc.); from such case markers, symbols like 'NP' can be developed, and these latter symbols can, in turn, be developed by familiar rules like (3.79g). Syntactic symbols like 'A' and 'D' also receive definitions expressing the essential characteristics of the semantic role common to the constituents they dominate.

To support this proposal, Fillmore has collected a great deal of evidence to show that grammatical relations assigned on the basis of phrase structure rules like (3.79a–i) do not pick out correctly the semantic roles expressed in sentences: the semantic role of the subject of a sentence is not always the agent (or any other particular semantic role), the semantic role of the direct object is not always the recipient (or any other particular semantic role), and so on; conversely, each semantic role correlates with a variety of grammatical relations. But this evidence by itself proves nothing. Fillmore's argument requires the premiss that the function of grammatical relations in Chomsky's account of grammar is to provide the full, formal basis for determining semantic roles. Unless Fillmore assumes this, he cannot make the criticism that Chomsky-type definitions of grammatical relations do not perform their function (as shown by the evidence) and then go on to claim, on this basis, that a case grammar is required to account for semantic roles.

But, as the considerations in this section show, such a premiss is false. The function of definitions of grammatical relations is to provide the most economical and abstract statement of the syntactic information required by the projection rule operations to construct derived readings compositionally. Without this function, one would wonder why grammatical theory should bother to define grammatical relations. One might then assume, as I think Fillmore does, that grammatical theory defines them in order to have a basis for predicting semantic roles. But, if the definitions of grammatical relations already have the function of providing the syntactic information needed for semantic interpretation, then there is no reason to burden them with the further function of providing the basis for predicting semantic roles. Moreover, the very evidence accumulated by Fillmore to show that there is no point-for-point correspondence between grammatical relations and semantic roles now provides a compelling argument against assigning the definitions of grammatical relations this further function.

Fillmore's argument for case grammar thus overlooks the most natural position for the defender of a Chomsky-type theory of grammar, namely, that the semantic roles expressed by a sentence are represented at the semantic level by its reading. On this position, the grammar's account of semantic roles is determined in part by the syntactic information contained in definitions of grammatical relations, but also in part by the inherent meaning of the lexical items of the sentence. Such an hypothesis explains, on the one hand, why traditional treatments of grammatical relations had some basis for linking them to semantic roles and, on the other, why semantic roles are not determined solely by grammatical relations.

Let us illustrate this position with some simple examples. Suppose we adopt the traditional notions of agent and recipient as, respectively, the instigator and performer of the action expressed in the verb and the receiver of this action. We might formalize the notions, roughly, as follows. A reading R denotes the agent if R substitutes for the categorized variable subscripted i in a reading of a predicate of the form (3.85), and a reading R denotes the recipient if R substitutes for the categorized variable subscripted j, where $i \neq j$:

$$(3.85) \quad (((Activity), (\ ), \ldots, (\ldots \underset{\langle\ \rangle}{\overset{[\ ]}{X_j}} \ldots), \ldots, (\ )) \underset{\langle\ \rangle}{\overset{[\ ]}{X_i}})$$

Applying these definitions to the readings that result from (3.68) for the sentences (3.69a–c), we would predict that the readings of "the policeman," "the dog," and "the spider" denote the agents referred to in (a), (b), and (c), respectively, and that the readings of "the bandit," "the stick," and "the fly" denote the recipients referred to in (a), (b), and (c), respectively. Moreover, as long as these definitions are applied to properly constructed readings, they will also predict the semantic roles in connection with sentences in which the grammatical subject is the semantic recipient and the grammatical object is the semantic agent. Let us imagine that there is a verb "esahc" that is the converse of "chase": "esahc" stands to "chase" as "receive" stands to "give." If the lexical reading of "esahc" were properly constructed, it would be exactly the same as (3.68) except that where the variable categorized for the 'direct-object-of' relation occurs in (3.68) the variable categorized for the 'subject-of' relation would occur in the lexical reading for "esahc" and where the variable categorized for the 'subject-of' relation occurs in (3.68) the variable categorized for the 'direct-object-of' relation would occur in the lexical reading for "esahc" (see Katz (1967a)). Thus, applying the definitions of 'agent' and 'recipient' to the readings of the sentences that result from replacing "chase" by "esahc" in (3.69a–c), we would make exactly the opposite predictions about their semantic agents and semantic recipients from those stated for "chase," which is precisely the desired result.

There are three sets of relations (defined over phrase marker structures) that can be distinguished in the theory of transformational grammar. First, there are the *grammatical relations* in Chomsky's sense. These are defined over underlying phrase markers. Second, there are the relations we have just tried to distinguish from grammatical relations, namely, the *semantic roles*, which Fillmore has brought to the attention of grammarians. These, we argued, are defined over semantic representations, or semantically interpreted phrase markers. And, looking ahead, there are relations similar to grammatical relations, which we will call *rhetorical relations* ('Topic' and 'Comment', for example). These will be defined over representations of surface structure.

We have argued that Fillmore's case grammar is based on a failure to distinguish the second type of relation from the first. In Chapter 8, Section 4, we shall argue that a large part of Chomsky's (1970a) claim that surface structure is relevant to semantic interpretation is based on a mistake similar to Fillmore's, namely, a failure to differentiate the third type of relation from the first. We shall propose that Chomsky's recent criticism of the Katz and Postal (1964) thesis that transformations play no role in semantic interpretation can, in part, be answered by distinguishing the function of relations in surface structure from relations in deep structure: if, as we shall claim, many of Chomsky's cases are rhetorical rather than semantic, then the fact that transformations introduce them is no argument against the thesis that transformations introduce no semantically relevant structure.

10. Projection

The introduction of categorized variables together with the elimination of type 2 projection rules makes it possible to reformulate entirely the original version of the theory of projection rules.[38] Without type 2 projection rules, there is only one type of projection possible, a projection rule that combines readings assigned to constituents in a single phrase marker to form a derived reading that is assigned to a constituent in the same phrase marker. Categorized variables, on the other hand, do away with the need to have different particular projection rules of this type in order to determine (a) the form of semantic combination required in connection with different grammatical relations, and (b) the point at which one reading will embed in another to form a derived reading: categorized variables determine both. Thus, it is possible to have only one type of projection rule, namely, one that combines readings of constituents in an underlying phrase marker, working from the lowest order constituents to the highest, and taking the readings of the subconstituents of a constituent to be the components of the derived reading of that constituent. This rule operates by substituting the reading of a constituent for a categorized variable in the reading of another constituent just in case the constituents bear a grammatical relation to each other and the governing selection restriction is met. It assigns the result of the substitution as a derived reading to the constituent whose subconstituents provided the substituent and the reading in which it was substituted.

The projection rule would thus be the general substitution rule (3.86):

(3.86)   Given an underlying phrase marker U in which there is a segmentation or bracketing that satisfies the conditions

(a) there is a node N that directly dominates the nodes N_i and N_j,

(b) the substring of the terminal string of U that is dominated by N_i bears the grammatical relation H to either the substring of the terminal string of U that is dominated by N_j or some constituent of it,

(c) either (i) N has no set of readings assigned to it but N_i and N_j have a maximal set of readings assigned to them, the sets R_i and R_j, respectively, or (ii) N has a maximal set of readings R_i assigned to it and there is an N_j that has a maximal set of readings R_j assigned to it,

---

[38] Type 2 projection rules were eliminated because generalized transformations were eliminated from the syntactic component (see Katz and Postal (1964, chapter 3) and Chomsky (1965, chapter 3)). The removal of this type of transformational rule from the grammar means, of course, that type 2 projection rules no longer have a function. The elimination of generalized transformations was accomplished by introducing rules of the form $A \rightarrow \ldots S \ldots$ into the phrase structure rules of the base of the syntactic component. Such rules permit the derivation of sentential structures within the derivation of a sentence and thereby transfer the recursive power of the syntactic rules from the transformational component to the phrase structure rules of the base. This means that sentential structures can be related *within* the confines of a phrase marker in precisely the manner in which they were formerly related within a T-marker. Since what was formerly a problem of combining readings of sentence structures in the same T-marker now becomes the problem of combining readings of constituents in the same phrase marker, the semantic effect of type 2 projection rules can be obtained by using type 1 projection rules alone.

Weinreich (1966, p. 412) was thus wrong in saying that type 2 projection rules were eliminated because all optional transformations were eliminated. The position adopted by Postal and myself and by Chomsky does eliminate *certain* optional transformations, namely, generalized transformations, and it does change the status of *certain* singulary transformations from optional to obligatory, but it does not do away with optional transformations. For example, singulary transformations that produce stylistic variants like "He looked the book up" and "He looked up the book" remain.

form the possible combination pairs of readings from the sets R_i and R_j, i.e., $(r_{i_1}, r_{j_1}), (r_{i_1}, r_{j_2}), \ldots, (r_{i_m}, r_{j_n})$, and then, for each such pair (r_i, r_j), replace each occurrence of the variable categorized for H in one with the other member of the pair just in case it satisfies the selection restriction contained in the angles under the categorized variable. In case there is no categorized variable in these readings, simply form the union of them. The result of doing this for each combination pair will be a set of *potential derived readings*. If N directly dominates nothing besides N_i and N_j, then assign the potential derived readings as derived readings of the constituent dominated by N. If N directly dominates another node N_k, repeat the process with the combination pairs whose first member is a reading from the potential derived readings and whose second is a reading from the set assigned to the constituents dominated by N_k. Repeat until all nodes dominated by N are exhausted.

The segmentations referred to in the statement of the conditions for the application of (3.86) are those that divide words into their component morphemes, for example, "re-" and "sell" in the verb "resell" and "in-" and "distinct" in the adjective "indistinct." For the sake of simplicity in the statement of (3.86), we are establishing the convention that there is a grammatical relation that holds between such components. Whether we need one grammatical relation connecting each of the components of a word or a number of grammatical relations (one for the relation of a prefix to a stem, one for the relation of a suffix to a stem, etc.) does not need to be decided here and now. If, as we argued earlier, the specification of a grammatical relation is a choice from among the set of possible relations among substrings of the terminal string of an underlying phrase that are formally definable on the basis of the rules of the base component, and if the choice is semantic in the sense that it depends on the requirements of the projection process whereby derived readings are formed, then such new grammatical relations are a natural extension of those already recognized. We shall see later (Section 5 of Chapter 7) that significant semantic combinations are found in connection with the senses of prefixes, suffixes, and stems.

Rule (3.86) is the only rule that is required by the semantic component in the way of projection machinery. From here on I shall proceed on the basis of this simplification of early accounts of semantic theory. Accordingly, former claims that there will be a different projection rule for each distinct grammatical relation must, strictly speaking, be taken as false. However, the substance of those claims, which was that there is a different type of semantic combination that corresponds to each different grammatical relation, has been incorporated into (3.86) in connection with the apparatus of categorized variables.

Furthermore, it would be a mistake to include the projection rule within the semantic component of a grammar.[39] By doing so, linguistic theory would be saying that projection rules are language-specific. If one such rule can serve for every natural language, then it is a linguistic universal, and, as such, it must be

[39] Katz (1967a).

stated once in linguistic theory, as part of that theory's formulation of the formal universals at the semantic level. The semantic components of particular grammars will not contain any projection rules but will consist only of a dictionary.

This simplification in the conception of a semantic component can be motivated by the following consideration. The only constructs that are used in the formulation of a projection rule are general, language-independent notions such as that of a grammatical relation, a constituent, a reading, a semantic marker, a selection restriction, and certain constructs from logic and mathematics. No language-particular notions appear in the statement of the projection machinery. Since only linguistic universals enter into the formulation of a projection rule, and since particular instances of them, i.e., particular constituents like "the man" and "went out," particular readings, particular selection restrictions, etc., will appear in every linguistic description generated by a grammar, it is reasonable to suppose that a projection rule is itself a linguistic universal. This does not imply that every grammatical relation appears in every language, but only that, for every language that a grammatical relation H appears in, there is the same definition of H in terms of a configuration of symbols in a phrase marker. Likewise, this does not imply that every language has the semantic operation for combining readings corresponding to H, but only that every language that has occurrences of H has the same semantic operation for the meanings of the constituents that bear H to each other. Finally, this does not imply that every language has the same readings, semantic markers, distinguishers, or selection restrictions, but only that the semantic structure of every language can be best described in terms of constructs that qualify as readings, semantic markers, distinguishers, and selection restrictions.[40]

In the theory as it now stands, there is one projection rule, namely, (3.86), and it is stated in semantic theory, not in any semantic component. It applies in the process of semantic interpretation carried on by the grammar of any language, whenever a process reaches the point at which the conditions of application of (3.86) are met.

---

[40] It is worth commenting in passing that, on the view that the projection rule is a universal, we obtain a very realistic picture of what happens in second-language learning. On this view, what we learn beyond phonology and besides transformations is a dictionary in which readings, most of which are already in the dictionary for the native language, are correlated with morphemes in the foreign tongue (i.e., a dictionary of the foreign language). We do not also learn a new set of projection rules, both according to this view and according to everyone's experience in such situations. Once the learner has mastered the phonology and transformations of the new language and can obtain the underlying phrase marker for a sentence, he can use the dictionary he has learned to obtain the meaning of the sentence because he already knows the right projection rule to apply.

Linguistic truth

I have no wish to incur the reproach of picking petty quarrels with a genius to whom we must all look up with grateful awe ; I feel bound, therefore, to call attention also to the extent of my agreement with him, which far exceeds any disagreement. To touch only upon what is immediately relevant, I consider Kant did great service in drawing the distinction between synthetic and analytic judgments.

Gottlob Frege

To many philosophers, the intensity and scale of the attack mounted in the fifties and sixties against the analytic-synthetic distinction seems disproportionately great compared to the modest philosophical significance of the distinction. Some have this reaction because they fail to see the real issues underlying the controversies engendered by the attack against this distinction. Since they found their own philosophical work unaffected by whether or not they could avail themselves of an absolute dichotomy between analytic and synthetic sentences, they came to regard this mountain of controversies as something concocted from a molehill-sized distinction. There are other philosophers who, although recognizing the deeper issues involved, also regard these controversies as conferring too much philosophical importance on the analytic-synthetic distinction, but for quite a different reason. They see that the attack launched by Quine, Goodman, and White was not what it might appear on the surface, namely, a new criticism of empiricism, but rather an internal conflict within empiricism. They correctly see it as a conflict between a European school of empiricism, calling itself "Logical

Positivism," which had compromised with rationalist doctrines of necessary truth by adopting the notion of linguistic truth, and a more extreme brand of American empiricism that was not willing to make the same compromise. Thus, even so attenuated a version of the doctrine of necessary truth as in the syntactic and semantic systems of Carnap came under strong attack at the hands of these latter empiricists. Yet many of the philosophers who understood that this attack constituted a new and far more thoroughgoing empiricist challenge to the rationalist conception of necessity nonetheless felt that the issue over necessity could be better addressed independent of the controversies about the analytic-synthetic distinction. Preoccupation with this distinction seems to them to narrow the types of necessity that enter into the discussion.

However, some of the issues underlying the controversies over the analytic-synthetic distinction seem best approached in the context of these controversies. One such issue, which is brought up in the Preface and elaborated on in Chapters 2 and 3, has to do with the nature of logic. We claimed that the concept of the logical form of a sentence has undergone an unfortunate change, that it no longer encompasses everything about the grammar of a sentence that determines the deductive relations it can enter into (the classical or Fregean notion) but now includes only those aspects of the grammar of a sentence that are features of the logical particles. Furthermore, we claimed that this change was brought about by a process of professionalization, wherein the availability of precise rules of formal deduction for the logical particles led to a focus on the development of such rules and, in turn, to a conception of logical form that reflects more the domain of these precise rules than the domain of necessary inference. From the perspective of these claims, it is clear, I think, that the controversy over the analytic-synthetic distinction constitutes another form of the question of which is the better theory about the nature of logic, the one that results from the process of professionalization, within which logic is defined in terms of the aforementioned new notion of logical form, or the classical theory based on the Fregean notion that the domain of logic includes any grammatical determinate of a necessary inference, regardless of whether the vocabulary involved is "logical" or "extra-logical." If the analytic-synthetic distinction can be drawn, there exist inferences that depend on the so-called "extra-logical" or descriptive expressions in their premises and conclusion, and these inferences can in no relevant way whatsoever be distinguished from inferences depending exclusively on logical particles. If there are analytic sentences, then there are logical relations between expressions belonging to what is called the descriptive vocabulary—in particular, the containment relation between the sense of the subject and the sense of the predicate of an analytic sentence—that are no less "really" logical than relations among logical particles such as those expressed by De Morgan's laws or rules of quantifier exchange, and, accordingly, these relations between extra-logical expressions can form the basis of logically necessary inferences. Hence, given an analytic sentence, there will be a corresponding necessary inference, based on the same containment relation. Therefore, the existence of analytic sentences in the full sense of an absolute dichotomy between them and synthetic sentences refutes any theory of logic based on the notion of logical form that is defined exclusively in terms of logical particles. It is not coincidental that

Quine, who (as noted in the Preface) put forth just such a theory of logic, should be the spearhead of the empiricist attack upon the analytic-synthetic distinction.

One aim of this chapter, therefore, is to defend the theory of the nature of logic based on the Fregean notion of logical form. As I see it, there are two lines of defense that have to be pursued in this regard. One is the presentation of a systematic formalization of the concept of analyticity within semantic theory. Accordingly, an attempt will be made in this chapter to show that the concept of analyticity (as well as contradictoriness and syntheticity) can be formally defined in a way that enables the theory of language to extend significantly its range of explanatory and predictive power. The other line of defense required to vindicate the analytic-synthetic distinction involves demonstrating that the criticisms raised in the empiricist attack, particularly those leveled by Quine and Goodman, are either invalid or inapplicable to the distinction as it is explicated in semantic theory. This second line of defense will be taken up in Chapter 6.

Another aim of this chapter is to distinguish among the different kinds of linguistic truth encountered in natural languages. This is crucial both in order to attain greater clarity about the essential features of each of the kinds of truth and to avoid certain philosophical mistakes about the relations among semantic theory, logic, and other theories.

The term *linguistic truth* refers to statements whose truth conditions are satisfied just on the basis of principles that enter into the structure of the language in which the statement is expressible. For example, statements of the form ' $p \vee \sim p$ ' or ' $\sim (p \cdot \sim p)$ ' constitute one kind of linguistic truth if the language is found to have a structure that makes it possible to express disjunctions, conjunctions, and denials of sentences without restriction as to their content. Our main concern, however, is not so much with identifying the aspect of the structure of language that is the source of any one kind of linguistic truth as with determining the differences in propositional structure that distinguish one kind from another. Accordingly, we shall try to uncover the essential differences between two kinds of statements—those that have the form of tautologies and quantificationally valid schemata, which, following standard practice, we call *logical truths,* and those that have the form of explicative predications, which, following Kant, we call *analytic truths.* The unfortunate practice of stretching the term *analytic* to cover logical truths goes back quite far in the history of contemporary linguistic philosophy, originating, to the best of my knowledge, with Frege himself.[1] We shall provide later on some examples of the confusions this practice has engendered. Here we simply stress the need to make the distinction in question explicit by insisting that we restrict the term *analytic* to the Kantian notion of a sentence whose predicate attributes no more to what its subject designates than is already (definitionally) contained in the subject.

We shall distinguish still a third kind of linguistic truth, which we call *metalinguistic truth.* As we shall see, the contrast between metalinguistic truths and

---

[1] See Frege (1953, section 3, pp. 3ᵉ–4ᵉ). After first connecting the term *analytic* to Kant's notion, and without any explanation, Frege goes on to characterize analytic truths as ones that are deducible from the laws of logic without the aid of truths belonging to special sciences. (I am indebted to R. M. Harnish for calling my attention to this passage.)

logical truths, on the one hand, and analytic truths, on the other, will help to clarify the difference between logical and analytic truths. We shall view these as three essentially distinct subcategories of linguistic truth, but we make no claim for their exhaustiveness.

In the broadest sense, our aim is to formulate the definitions of semantic properties and relations that characterize the logic of statements. In the present chapter, we deal with semantic properties and relations that characterize the logical features of assertive propositions; in the next chapter, we shall be concerned with those that characterize the logic of nonstatements, particularly questions.

1. General remarks on propositions and statements

Semantic properties and relations such as analyticity and contradiction can be defined so as to apply to sentences, but they apply naturally and most directly to the propositions expressed by sentences. The term *proposition* has come to be used in a wide variety of ways by philosophers. Here it is understood to refer to a sense of a sentence, where a sentence is a concatenation of words, phonetically or orthographically specifiable, that conforms to the syntactic rules of well-formedness for a natural language.

Sentences are frequently ambiguous, that is, they express more than one sense. Thus, we shall say that an *n*-way ambiguous sentence expresses *n* distinct propositions. (We have taken the term *meaning* to refer to the sum of the propositions expressed by a sentence or the sum of the concepts expressed by a subsentential constituent.) We also understand *proposition* to convey what synonymous sentences have in common by virtue of which they are synonymous. Sentences that are synonymous on a sense are thus said to express the same proposition, and fully synonymous sentences are said to express the same set of propositions. Semantically anomalous sentences express no proposition at all.

By introducing the notion of a proposition in this manner, we provide a unique object of reference in cases where we speak about one linguistic object implying, contradicting, confirming, supporting, etc. another or in cases where we apply predicates like "true," "false," "questioned," "refuted" to a linguistic object. The linguistic objects that we claim bear such relations or have such properties cannot be sentences because sentences are frequently ambiguous and thus do not provide the unique object required by such predications. Moreover, similar problems arise in connection with synonymous sentences and with meaningless sentences.

There is another standard way of introducing the notion of a proposition, namely, taking a proposition to be what is designated by a "that-S" clause appearing in a sentence as a complement of a main verb such as "asserts," "denies," "argues," "says," "discovers." I have not used this approach or any of its variants because it does not work by itself, that is, it must rely on the first approach. Once we notice that the sentences that occur as complements of the aforementioned verbs exhibit essentially the same range of ambiguities, synonymy relations, and semantic anomalies as sentences in general, it becomes immediately apparent that the approach taken here is basic.

This conception of propositionality is extended from the intra- to the interlinguistic case by saying, further, that translations of a sentence into different natural languages, as in (4.1), are synonymous, that is, express the same proposition(s):

(4.1)   (a) I am cold
          (b) Mir ist kalt
          (c) J'ai froid
          (d) Tengo frío

The legitimacy of this extension has been questioned.[2] In Chapter 6 I will try to answer the criticisms and to provide further motivation for the introduction of the notion of a proposition. Here I will simply cite, as a preliminary justification, the defense by Frege (1952a) of a language-invariant notion of a proposition:

> Nowadays people seem inclined to exaggerate the scope of the statement that different linguistic expressions are never completely equivalent, that a word can never be exactly translated into another language. One might perhaps go even further, and say that the same word is never taken in quite the same way even by men who share a language. I will not enquire as to the measure of truth in these statements; I would only emphasize that nevertheless different expressions quite often have something in common, which I call the sense, or, in the special case of sentences, the thought. In other words, we must not fail to recognize that the same sense, the same thought, may be variously expressed; thus the difference does not here concern the sense, but only the apprehension, shading, or colouring of the thought, and is irrelevant for logic. It is possible for one sentence to give no more or less information than another; and, for all the multiplicity of languages, mankind has a common stock of thoughts. If all transformations of the expression were forbidden on the plea that this would alter the content as well, logic would simply be crippled; for the task of logic can hardly be performed without trying to recognize the thought in its manifold guises. Moreover, all definitions would then have to be rejected as false (p. 46).

Traditional grammarians distinguish a small number of sentence types: for English, declaratives, interrogatives, imperatives, hortatories, and perhaps a few others. Philosophers, on the other hand, distinguish a large number of proposition types: besides assertions, questions, requests, and wishes, corresponding to declaratives, interrogatives, imperatives, and hortatories, respectively, they cite bets, claims, promises, offers, authorizations, warnings, resolves, threats, pleas, commands, implorings, and so on. Here the term *proposition* is used to cover the sense of any sentence type whatever, and propositions will be put into classes that correspond roughly to those enumerated by philosophers who make such distinctions.

---

[2] Together with the legitimacy of the intralinguistic notion. See Quine (1960, chapters 1, 2, 6).

Propositions are identified here with senses of sentences because talk about senses of sentences and talk about propositions seem to amount to no more than different ways of referring to the same thing. Although this is not the place to enter into a lengthy defense of this claim, some indication of the reasons behind it is called for.

When we talk in terms of propositions, we are able to refer to them independently of the various linguistic forms in which they are expressed. This is often desirable, since in many discussions about a proposition nothing hangs on the particular phonetic (or orthographic) and syntactic features of one or another of the sentences that express it. On the other hand, it is often desirable to refer to propositions in relation to the sentences through which they are expressed or to aspects of sentences that have to do with the manner in which propositions are expressed. In such cases we find talk about senses appropriate. Thus, from a theoretical viewpoint, we ought not to suppose that there are two distinct sorts of entities: in virtually all essential respects, talk about propositions and talk about senses of sentences are interchangeable except for perspective. The following considerations make this more plausible. Sentences that do not have a sense—semantically anomalous sentences—cannot be said to express a proposition; sentences that have *n* distinct senses will be said to express *n* distinct propositions; and pairs of sentences that share a sense will be said to express the same proposition. Consider the examples in (4.2) and (4.3):

(4.2)   John took my photograph

(4.3)   (a) John photographed me
         (b) John made off with a photograph belonging to me

The sentence (4.2) is ambiguous, having the sense of both (4.3a) and (4.3b), among others. If we were trying to call someone's attention to the sense of (4.2) on which it is synonymous with (4.3a), we might say that we are concerned with the sense of (4.2) on which it implies that John produced an image of me. Alternatively, we might call attention to the same entity by saying that we are concerned with that one of the propositions expressed by (4.2) that implies that John produced an image of me. In general, we make such distinctions by referring to properties of one sense or proposition which the other sense or proposition does not have, and the differentiating properties are the same whether we talk of them as applying to senses or to propositions.

Another point about our use of the term *proposition*, one that follows trivially from the way we have characterized the range of sentence types whose senses are to be referred to as propositions, is that the class of propositions cannot be identified with the class of statements, where statements are understood as the logical objects that are the bearers of truth values (i.e., as the objects that obey the law of excluded middle). The fact that our characterization of the class of propositions encompasses a multitude of nonassertive propositions (questions, requests, etc.), for which it makes no sense to talk about truth and falsity, makes this amply clear. But we cannot even identify the class of statements with the class of assertive propositions since a proposition with a token indexical element cannot have a fixed truth value. Consider, for example, (4.4):

(4.4)   I need medical attention

The proposition conveyed here contains an indexical element referring to the speaker of a token of (4.4) and another referring to the moment at which such an utterance occurs. Accordingly, different tokens of (4.4)—(4.4) uttered by different persons at the same time, different persons at different times, or even the same person at different times—can have different truth values. If we took propositions to be statements, some propositions like (4.4) would have to be taken to have variable truth values or to be jointly true and false. Since neither of these is a welcome consequence, we have to exempt some propositions from the status of statements.

Cartwright (1962) makes this proposition-statement distinction as follows:

> Consider, for this purpose, the words "It's raining." These are words, in the uttering of which, people often (though not always) assert something. But of course *what* is asserted varies from one occasion of their utterance to another. A person who utters them one day does not (normally) make the same statement as one who utters them the next; and one who utters them in Oberlin does not usually assert what is asserted by one who utters them in Detroit. But these variations in what is asserted are *not* accompanied by corresponding changes in meaning. The words "It's raining" retain the same meaning throughout.... The fundamental point is this. It is perfectly possible to know what the words "It's raining" mean. Any speaker of English knows what they mean. Probably many Russians do not know; but they can easily find out by consulting dictionaries, grammars, and speakers of English. But it is *not* possible to know what (one and only one) statement is made by assertively uttering those words. There is no such statement. They are used, without any alteration in meaning, to assert now one thing, now another (pp. 92–94).

Cartwright (p. 95) goes on to point out that, although this argument shows that statements cannot in general be identified with the sense of the sentences used to make them, it does not follow that statements never coincide with the sense of the sentence used to make them, that is, with the proposition expressed by the sentence used to make them. This reflection leads Cartwright to consider that we might identify the class of statements with that proper subset of the class of propositions that contains all and only those that make the same statement on every occasion of uttering the sentence that expresses them. Cartwright calls a sentence "incomplete" if its meaning is such "as to permit the utterances of the sentence to vary as to statement made" and "complete" if its meaning is such "that assertive utterances of it coincide as to statement made"; he then observes that it can be held that "for each statement that can be made by uttering some given incomplete sentence, there is (or in theory could be) a complete sentence having that statement as its meaning" (p. 96). We may take this last observation to be a consequence of the effability thesis: if the statements we make using sentences are, in theory, comprehensible, then if the effability thesis is valid, there is at least one sentence that expresses a proposition which includes in its propositional structure exactly the information to fully specify the statement made by the use of an incomplete sentence.

Cartwright, however, comes to reject his own proposal on the basis of an argument that statements, in principle, cannot be identified with propositions understood as senses of sentences. His argument runs as follows. If statements are to be identified with propositions, they must share all properties. But there are many properties of the former that do not apply to the latter. For example, there are many things, such as 'being asserted', 'being denied', 'being questioned', and 'being contradicted', which are predicable of statements but not of senses of sentences. Accordingly, statements cannot be identified with propositions.

I agree it makes no sense to speak of asserting (denying, etc.) the sense of a sentence in general, but this strikes me as due to the fact that it makes no sense to use such locutions in connection with propositions that can vary as to the statement they make. I see nothing wrong, however, with the restricted claim embodied in the propositionalist view. That is, I see nothing absurd about saying that the sense of a complete sentence is asserted, denied, questioned, or contradicted. We are unfamiliar with this way of speaking, which may make us uneasy, especially since we are accustomed to thinking of statements as distinct from propositions and to using predicates like "is asserted," "is denied" in reference to statements. But such uneasiness is typical in situations where a theoretical identification has occurred, and, as will be recalled, our proposal that propositions be taken as senses of sentences was put forth as a theoretical identification, in analogy with theoretical identifications in science such as the identification of water with H_2O or the identification of light with electromagnetic radiation (of such-and-such wavelengths). In these latter cases, we experience the same uneasiness when locutions ordinarily used in connection with the everyday term are used in connection with the new, technical term, as in "sipping H_2O," "diving into a body of H_2O," and "H_2Oing the grass," or "see to it that George has enough electromagnetic radiation (of such-and-such wavelengths) to read by." Cartwright's argument depends on the assumption that there is only one way to explain the uneasiness we feel in applying predicates like "is asserted" or "is denied" to senses, namely, by saying that our uneasiness reflects the logical inapplicability of such predicates to senses. Since we have found an explanation that does not assume the impossibility of such predications, however, Cartwright's argument does not prevent the identification of statements with propositions.

If Cartwright's proposal can be saved from his own criticisms, we will have a highly attractive doctrine of statementhood. On this proposal, the entities of which the laws of logic hold are ones whose structure is formally specifiable within grammar and ones that can be the objects of thought, the objects asserted, denied, questioned, etc., in the occurrence of speech acts, and logical objects even though never thought, asserted, denied, etc. Thus, it will be well for us to consider this proposal in greater detail and to specify further the proposition-statement distinction in terms of it.

We may divide propositions, in a manner similar to Quine's division of sentences, into three mutually exclusive and jointly exhaustive classes: *occasion propositions, standing propositions*, and *eternal propositions*.[3] The first class includes those that make different statements in different contexts as a matter of contingent fact; the second, those that make the same statement in different contexts, also as a matter of contingent fact; and the third, those that make the same statement regardless of contextual differences as a matter of logical necessity. Occasion propositions and standing propositions contain token indexical elements referring to contingent persons, places, times, things, etc., but the referential specifications in the latter are sufficiently complete to prevent the statement they express from varying. Eternal propositions, on the other hand, do not vary in the statement they make because of the absence of any token indexical element.[4] Eternal propositions meet the condition that, for any possible world W, every token of the same eternal proposition type has the same truth value in W. Standing propositions meet the condition that in the actual world every token of the same standing proposition has the same truth value but in other possible worlds they have different truth values. Occasion propositions meet the condition that, in the actual world, as well as in other possible worlds, there can be, and with sufficiently extensive use of the sentence in sufficiently different contexts are, tokens of the same proposition type that have different truth values. An example of an occasion proposition appeared in (4.4); an example of a standing proposition is given in (4.5) and of an eternal proposition in (4.6):

(4.5)   The Lyndon Baines Johnson who was born near Stonewall, Texas, on August 27, 1908, who was the son of Samuel Ealy and Rebekah (Baines) Johnson, and who married Lady Bird Johnson, was a president of the United States

(4.6)   The square of the hypotenuse of a right triangle is equal in length to the sum of the squares of its sides

We now propose to identify the class of statements with the class of non-occasion propositions so that statements can be individuated exclusively in terms of the formal distinctions in their propositional structure. The difficulties arising from variation in statement and truth value from one occasion of the use of a sentence to another cannot arise in connection with statements so understood: every statement is either a standing or eternal proposition, and both are immune from such variation. There is, of course, the problem of determining which propositions with token indexical elements are standing propositions, but this is not of concern here inasmuch as it is a matter of specifying the extension of the class

---

[3] Note that the usage of these terms diverges from Quine's. I have chosen to keep his triplet of adjectives instead of concocting a new set of terms because the basic idea here is not substantively different.

[4] Note that the use of a code or a similar device suspends the grammatical basis for assigning a meaning to a sentence, replacing it by the meaning of another sentence. Thus, standing and eternal *sentences* cannot be said to always make the same statement regardless of context, but standing and eternal *propositions* can. If the sentence "17 is a prime number" is code for "17 people are missing," the proposition used when this sentence is uttered is not that expressed by the former sentence but, rather, that expressed by the latter.

of nonoccasion propositions rather than of determining that the class is identical to the class of statements. The only relevant question that arises in connection with this proposal is, then, whether the class of statements outstrips the class of nonoccasion propositions, that is, whether among the indefinitely large number of statements that can be made using an occasion proposition such as the one expressed by the sentence (4.4), each individuated by contextual considerations like time of utterance, place, and identity of speaker, there are none that are not conveyed by some standing or eternal proposition. Accordingly, the Cartwright proposal can be understood to claim that each statement associated with an occasion proposition can be fully specified in the form of a standing or eternal proposition, the information from the context that serves to individuate the statement now being part of the structure of the proposition.

At this point, except for the issue about the dispensability of propositions, the Cartwright proposal is identical to the thesis of Quine's (1960) about the eternalization of sentences and the concept of statementhood based on it. Roughly, rephrased in our terms, Quine's idea is that a sentence expressing an occasion proposition that makes a statement in a given context can be expanded on the basis of the information in the context to provide another sentence that expresses a proposition that always makes the statement in question, no matter what the context of the utterance. The expansion consists of replacing each indexical element by an expression that has the same reference as the indexical element it replaces but whose referent stays fixed with variations in time, place, speaker, etc. The usual indexical tense indicator will be replaced by such a referentially unique time designation, devised with respect to some appropriate calendar and clock; indexical nominal elements like "I," "he," "it," and "John" will be replaced by precise specifications of the individuals or objects that include whatever information about their vital statistics is required to make the specifications resist changes in reference; and so forth. It does not matter whether one can actually carry out such an expansion, but only whether the expansion is always possible in theory on the basis of the expressive power of the language to formulate every statement within the class of nonoccasion propositions.

Lemmon (1966) has objected to Quine's thesis about eternalization on the grounds that "no such definite description or proper name, however 'complete', carries a *logical* assurance of context-free unique reference, which is what Quine's expansion seems to demand" (p. 102). This objection misses the point, however. Neither Quine's expansion nor any of the philosophical axes it is intended to grind demands such logical assurance. All that is required is that, for each case where such an expansion provides a standing or eternal proposition as the statement associated with a given sentence-proposition-context n-tuple, it is the case, *as a matter of contingent fact*, that the former proposition will always make the same assertion as was made in the utterance of the sentence in the given context.

On behalf of this conception, we can argue that any counterexample to the claim that a given proposed standing or eternal proposition is a proper eternalization of a sentence-proposition-context n-tuple would itself provide the amendment required to formulate another standing or eternal proposition that avoids it. For example, if there is another Lyndon Baines Johnson who was also born near Stonewall, Texas, etc., then (4.5) can be replaced by another sentence that includes a linguistic specification of whatever property was cited in the counter-example. If the alleged counterexample fails to cite a property that distinguishes Johnson from his near doppelganger, it can hardly count as a real counterexample to the claim that (4.5) expresses a standing proposition; and if the counterexample does cite such a property, its linguistic specification is readily available to serve as the feature that distinguishes the first Johnson. Either way, we are left with an unchallenged claim that there is an appropriate standing proposition. The only alternative to the conception of statementhood we are considering is thus a form of mysticism that claims that some things to which we can refer by the use of indexical elements are, in principle, beyond the range of unique description.

2. Presupposition

Just as some propositions vary in the statement they make from one speech situation to another and other propositions resist such variation and always make the same statement, so some propositions succeed in making a statement on some occasions but not on others and other propositions always succeed in making a statement. Moreover, the conditions responsible for a proposition making differ-ent statements in different speech situations are related to the conditions responsible for a proposition sometimes succeeding in making a statement and sometimes failing. The token indexical elements in a proposition are, as it were, at the mercy of the speech contexts in which a sentence expressing the proposition is used. One context may provide one thing as the referent of a token indexical element in a proposition, while another context may provide a different thing as its referent, and, in just the same way, still another context may provide no referent. Thus, the token indexical element for a third person singular masculine subject of a sentence whose predicate is, for example, "is a politician" may receive Richard M. Nixon as its referent on one occasion, Pablo Picasso on another, and nothing on still another. Accordingly, on the first occasion, the proposition would make the true statement that Nixon is a politician; on the second, it would make the false statement that Picasso is a politician; and on the third, it would not make a statement.

The conception of statementhood under consideration must not only guarantee that the objects taken to be statements can never be associated with more than one truth value but must also guarantee that they always have a truth value. Only if the conception explains how both of these can be insured will we be in a position to say that statements (when properly construed) are the objects of which the law of excluded middle holds, that statements are, of necessity, either true or false. But so far we have said nothing about this aspect of the theory of statementhood, nothing about what the conditions are under which a proposition has a truth value. Our conception takes the class of statements to be the union of the classes of eternal and standing propositions, but its characterization of a standing proposition as one whose truth value is not subject to variation simply stipulates that standing propositions have a truth value. We are left, then, with the question of how to tell whether a noneternal proposition is a candidate for the status of a standing proposition, whether it has a truth value at all.

This question is a far-reaching one, and an attempt at a full answer cannot be made within this work. The reason is that only one aspect of the answer has to do with the structure of propositions. The distinction between occasion propositions and standing propositions, on the one hand, and eternal propositions, on the other, does reflect a difference in the structure of propositions, namely, the presence versus the absence of token indexical elements. But the distinction between occasion propositions and standing propositions reflects no grammatical difference. Rather, it reflects a difference in the way that grammatically specifiable objects fare in the real world. Whether a noneternal proposition, that is, one containing an occurrence of a token indexical element, is a candidate for the status of a standing proposition by virtue of having a truth value is mainly a matter of how grammatically specifiable objects fare in the world. All grammar can do is to explicate the conditions that token indexical elements in a proposition impose on things in the world in order for some of them to qualify as the referents of these elements.

The aspect of the question to which grammar addresses itself is, therefore, what, on the basis of the propositional structure of a sense of a sentence, are the conditions to be satisfied by the world in order for the proposition expressed by a sentence to bear a truth value. Putting the question in its more traditional form, what is the presupposition of the proposition. Determining that the presupposition of a proposition is satisfied on occasions of its use, that is, determining that the proposition is a statement, is, on the other hand, an extragrammatical problem, belonging to a theory of sentence use.

The concept of a presupposition is that of a referential condition, expressed in the meaning of a sentence, under which a noneternal assertive proposition has a truth value (and, as will be made clear shortly, under which noneternal propositions of other types have properties corresponding to that of bearing a truth value). Eternal propositions, such as the generic proposition expressed by (4.7), can be thought of as being distinguished, in part, by the fact that they have no presupposition:[5]

(4.7)   The dog is domesticable

We will say that a noneternal proposition is *indeterminable* in case, logically, it cannot have a satisfied presupposition, and we will say that a noneternal proposition is *determinable* if, logically, it is possible for it to have a satisfied presupposition. Determinable propositions will be classified into *indeterminate* and *determinate* ones, the latter being those that, given the way the world is, do have a satisfied presupposition, and the former being those that, given the way the world is, do not. Consider the examples (4.8)–(4.10).

---

[5] See Section 5 of this chapter, particularly the textual discussion of (4.116) and footnotes 27 and 28.

(4.8)   The present female king of France is bald

(4.9)   The present king of France is bald

(4.10)   The last king of France was bald

The proposition in (4.8) is indeterminable. The propositions in (4.9) and (4.10), on the other hand, are both determinable, but (4.9) is indeterminate while (4.10) is determinate.

The conception of presupposition that we have adopted is essentially Frege's (1952b):

> If anything is asserted there is always an obvious presupposition that the simple or compound proper names used have reference. If one therefore asserts " Kepler died in misery," there is a presupposition that the name "Kepler" designates something; but it does not follow that the sense of the sentence "Kepler died in misery" contains the thought that the name "Kepler" designates something. If this were the case the negation would have to run not

(4.11)   Kepler did not die in misery

but

(4.12)   Kepler did not die in misery, or the name " Kepler " has no reference

> That the name "Kepler" designates something is just as much a presupposition for the assertion

(4.13)   Kepler died in misery

> as for the contrary assertion. Now languages have the fault of containing expressions which fail to designate an object (although their grammatical form seems to qualify them for that purpose) because the truth of some sentences is a prerequisite. Thus it depends on the truth of the sentence:

(4.14)   There was someone who discovered the elliptic form of the planetary orbits

> whether the subordinate clause "whoever discovered the elliptic form of the planetary orbits" really designates an object or only seems to do so while having in fact no reference. And it may appear as if our subordinate clause contained as a part of its sense the thought that there was somebody who discovered the elliptic form of the planetary orbits. If this were right the negation would run:

(4.15)   Either whoever discovered the elliptic form of the planetary orbits did not die in misery or there was nobody who discovered the elliptic form of the planetary orbits (p. 69–70).

Frege wants to show that the use of a name (in sentences such as (4.13)) presupposes that the name designates. His thesis is that such sentences express propositions that contain a condition that referential occurrences of names designate and that this condition is not a part of their assertion. In the case of (4.13), the presuppositional condition is that the occurrence of the name "Kepler" has a referent, and the assertion (whose statementhood depends on "Kepler" having a referent) is no more than that the referent is someone who died in misery.

It is perhaps best to specify the presupposition of (4.13) as something like the condition that Kepler exists (or existed), rather than to follow Frege in taking the presupposition to be (4.14). The condition (4.14) in no way follows from the meaning of (4.13) without adding Frege's rather tenuous doctrine about the senses of proper names, which we will find reason to reject when we reach Chapter 8. If we specify the presupposition as I am suggesting, we admit the possibility that it can be satisfied on the grounds that there exists one and only one individual who bears the name " Kepler " and he is a German wurst-maker now living on the Lower East Side of New York. But this detail is not relevant to the question at issue.

That question is Frege's claim that the condition that Kepler exists is not part of the assertion that (4.13) makes. The alternative to Frege's view is that this condition is a component of the assertion of (4.13), that is, one of its truth conditions. On this alternative (4.13) is, according to Frege, to be analyzed as having the logical form 'Kepler exists and Kepler died in misery'. Frege contends that this analysis, which fails to distinguish the presupposition of the proposition from its assertion, runs into trouble in trying to account for the negation of (4.13). His argument seems to be something like this. Since (4.13) is treated as a conjunction, the negation of (4.13) must be the disjunction (4.12). But this is absurd: the negation of (4.13) is (4.11), which is not equivalent to (4.12). To claim that (4.11) is equivalent to (4.12) is to claim that the proposition that the name " Kepler " has no reference is a logical falsehood, since only if 'q' is a logical falsehood are 'p' and '$p \vee q$' materially equivalent. The absurdity of this claim is, I think, what leads Frege to believe that the alternative to his view is wrong.

The term *presupposition* will be used here in a sense close to Frege's. The presupposition of an assertion will be taken to be a condition found in the meaning of the sentence expressing the proposition. It expresses a referential requirement whose satisfaction is the condition under which the proposition can make a statement, that is, the condition under which the proposition is either true or has a true negation. Determinate propositions are those that have a truth value; indeterminate ones are those that do not. In saying that there are presuppositions we undertake to defend the view that not all nongeneric propositions expressed by well-formed declarative sentences are either true or false. We call this *Frege's view*. The opposing view we call *Russell's view*.

These two views differ on the specification of the class of statements. Russell's view takes the grammatical well-formedness of a declarative sentence to be the condition for its being true or false, while Frege's view takes this condition to depend on considerations beyond grammar. Although on Frege's view the presuppositional condition for statementhood is determined from the grammatical structure of sentences, the condition itself is not, in general, satisfied on the basis of features of grammatical structure. Such conditions, except in cases of metalinguistic sentences, apply to the nonlinguistic world, and their satisfaction is an extralinguistic question, to be settled, broadly speaking, on the basis of fact. The facts that determine which presuppositions are satisfied determine which grammatically well-formed declarative sentences express statements. Thus the two views give different specifications of the class of statements, Frege's view giving a far narrower class just because indeterminate but grammatically well-formed declaratives do not count as statements while on Russell's view they do.

To further clarify the differences between these two views, let us consider how each treats the case (4.9). Following Frege, the existence of an individual who is unique in being king of France at the time of utterance is logically prior to and taken for granted in the statement, which is the assertion that that individual is bald. If there is no such individual, then there is no such statement since there is no one of whom the predication "is bald" or "is not bald" can hold. Russell's thesis is that the existence of such an individual is part of the statement expressed by (4.9). On this view, the falsity of the proposition that there is such an individual thus implies the falsity of the proposition expressed by (4.9).

Russell's thesis derives from his treatment of definite descriptions in his famous paper "On Denoting" (1956). A definite description like (4.16) or (4.17) is an expression in which the definite article indicates the uniqueness of the thing satisfying the description:

(4.16)   the president of the United States
(4.17)   the present king of France

The definite description (4.17) denotes nothing since there is no unique individual who now occupies the position of king of France. It might be thought that this renders (4.9) nonsense. But consider, in this regard, (4.18):

(4.18)   The president of the United States is under six feet tall

If we are encouraged by the grammatical similarity of (4.18) and (4.9), we may be inclined to treat the predication in (4.9) on the model of the one in (4.18). But, if we say that (4.18) is about Richard M. Nixon, whom do we say that (4.9) is about? Of whom is baldness predicated when (4.9) is used? It might be concluded, then, that (4.9) is nonsense. However, (4.9) cannot be nonsense in the usual sense of this term since it is not like either (4.19) or (4.20):

(4.19)   of the quickly is bald
(4.20)   The virtue of charity is bald

Thus, to avoid conflating (4.9) with cases like (4.19) and (4.20), Russell argued that (4.9) should be counted as a false statement.

To carry this through, he introduced a contextual definition of definite descriptions which permits their contribution to the meaning of sentences to be determined but which treats them as meaningless outside the context of a sentence. On this definition, sentences of the form 'The so-and-so is P' are to be understood as a conjunction with essentially three conjuncts: 'There is something which is a so-and-so', 'It is unique in being a so-and-so', and 'It has the property P'.

With respect to this syncategorematic analysis of the character of definite descriptions, both (4.18) and (4.9) can be taken to have the same logical form without assuming (4.9) to be nonsense. Sentence (4.9) is regarded as the assertion (4.21), while (4.18) is regarded as the assertion (4.22).

(4.21)   There is something which is a present king of France and which is unique in being such and which is bald

(4.22)   There is something which is president of the United States and which is unique in being such and which is under six feet tall

Each sentence asserts three things—an existential claim, a uniqueness claim, and a property ascription. The whole sentence, being interpreted as a conjunction, is true just in case all three claims are true, and false in case one claim is false. Therefore, (4.9) is simply false insofar as its existential claim is false.

The Fregean thesis agrees with the Russellian on the treatment of true statements since both imply (4.23) and (4.24):

(4.23)   *'The so-and-so is P' is true* implies *There is exactly one so-and-so*

(4.24)   *'The so-and-so is not P' is true* implies *There is exactly one so-and-so*

But the Fregean thesis disagrees on the treatment of false statements since it would also claim (4.25) and (4.26), which the Russellian thesis would deny:

(4.25)   *'The so-and-so is P' is false* implies *There is exactly one so-and-so*

(4.26)   *'The so-and-so is not P' is false* implies *There is exactly one so-and-so*

There is no inherent disagreement over the numerical interpretation of the definite article. I am treating the Fregean thesis as if it incorporates Russell's account of the interpretation of the definite article. It need not, of course, but there is no harm in provisionally assuming it does, and this assumption helps to bring the opposition of the two views into sharper relief. Further, both views can agree to accept ungrammaticality or semantic anomaly as conditions under which a sentence fails to express a proposition, and both can also agree that the class of statements is a subset of the class of propositions. The essential disagreement is that the Russellian thesis takes this subset to be the set of (assertive) propositions, whereas the Fregean thesis takes it to be a proper subset of the set of (assertive) propositions. This disagreement leads to the introduction of analyses such as (4.21) and (4.22) into the Russellian thesis, which in turn leads to disagreement over the treatment of false statements.

Russell gave no argument to show that the categories of nonsense and statementhood are exhaustive alternatives with respect to the class of declarative sentences. It seems as if he just assumed that there is no other possibility and thus begged the question of why there should not be at least a subset of the propositions which are neither true nor have true negations. Given that the Fregean view provides in the concept of a presupposition the concept of a necessary and sufficient condition for a proposition to fail of statementhood, there is no need to say that propositions such as (4.9) must be false in order to avoid classifying them incorrectly as nonsense. They can be classified as not about anything.

In favor of Frege's view over Russell's, it can be said that Frege's thesis allows us to maintain the commonsensical conceptions of denotation, predication, and falsehood. A Fregean analysis says that the three conjuncts that form "separate but equal" components in a Russellian analysis of a definite description like (4.21) and (4.22) are *ordered*. They are not each on a par with one another as individual clauses in the formulation of the truth conditions; rather, the first two components, the existential and the uniqueness clauses, jointly comprise a condition that is ordered logically prior to the third component, the predicative clause, and forms the condition under which it can express a true or false assertion. This can be seen from the fact that the natural way to state the truth conditions for a simple subject-predicate sentence is to say that it is true just in case what its subject refers to has the property expressed by its predicate and it is false just in case what its subject refers to lacks this property; for example, (4.9) is true if there is a bald king of France and (4.9) is false if there is a nonbald king of France. If no king of France exists at all, the condition under which truth or falsity applies is not met. There is nothing for the assertion of baldness to be about and hence nothing truly or falsely asserted. If we take the proposition in such cases to have no truth value, then we get a division of sentences into meaningful and meaningless, of meaningful sentences into assertive, requestive, etc. propositions, of assertive propositions into those that bear a truth value and those that do not, and, finally, a division of the former, i.e., of statements, into truths and falsehoods. We thus preserve the symmetry in (4.23)–(4.26). We do not have to take the predicate "is false" to apply in cases other than those in which something does not have the property it is predicated to have. We do not have to take "is false" to be synonymous with "is not true."

Geach (1950) provides a variant of this type of argument:

On Russell's view "the king of France is bald" is a false assertion. This view seems to me to commit the fallacy of 'many questions'. To see how this is so, let us take a typical example of the fallacy: the demand for "a plain answer—yes or no!" to the question "Have you been happier since your wife died?" Three questions are here involved:

1. Have you ever had a wife?
2. Is she dead?
3. Have you been happier since then?

The act of asking question 2 presupposes an affirmative answer to question 1; if the true answer to 1 is negative, question 2 *does not arise*. The act of asking question 3 presupposes an affirmative answer to question 2; if question 2 does not arise, or if the true answer to it is negative, question 3 *does not arise*. When a question does not arise, the only proper way of answering it is to say so and explain the reason; the "plain" affirmative or negative answer, though grammatically and logically possible, is *out of place*. This does not go against the laws of contradiction and excluded middle; what these laws tell us is that *if* the question arose "yes" and "no" *would be* exclusive alternatives.

Similarly, the question "Is the king of France bald?" involves two other questions:

4. Is anybody at the moment king of France?
5. Are there at the moment different people each of whom is a king of France?

And it does not arise unless the answer to 4 is affirmative and the answer to 5 negative.... If either of those answers is false, the affirmative answer "yes, he is bald" is not false but simply out of place (p. 33).

What Geach shows is that the notion of presupposition has a crucial place in the theory of questions. Because of the parallelism of questions and assertions, his conclusions transfer directly to assertions. A yes-no question like "Is the king of France bald?" is just a request to be told whether a proposition like (4.9) is true or false: the answer is affirmative just in case the assertion is true and negative just in case it is false. Thus, the case where a question does not arise must coincide with the case where its corresponding assertion is neither true nor false.

In fact, one can make a more general point. The propositions expressed by a declarative, its corresponding interrogative, corresponding imperative, corresponding hortatory, etc., are, respectively, a statement, question, request, wish, etc., by virtue of the satisfaction of the *same* condition. Consider, for example, (4.27):

(4.27) (a) The king of France is healthy.
        (b) Is the king of France healthy?
        (c) Make the king of France healthy!
        (d) Oh, were the king of France healthy!

The sentences in (4.27) can be used, respectively, to make a statement, ask a question, issue a request, and express a wish on the basis of the same condition, namely, that there is someone who is king of France at the moment of utterance and who is unique in being such. Hence, if one were to agree with Geach and yet still try to defend a Russellian account of propositional form in connection with declaratives, one would have to tolerate a wholly unmotivated asymmetry in the treatment of different sentence types since, if there is no king of France at the moment of utterance, the utterance of (4.27a) is counted as making a false statement but the answer to (4.27b) is not correspondingly "no" but rather "can't be answered either way." A further problem arises when it is recognized that (4.27a) is, in fact, one of the possible answers to (4.27b) while the negation of (4.27a) is the other. Since "yes" is equivalent to (4.27a) and "no" is equivalent to the denial of (4.27a), Russell's thesis about the logical form of declaratives implies that answering (4.27b) negatively can express the claim that there is no present king of France. But it is quite clear that a negative answer to (4.27b) does not mean that there is no king of France. What it means, rather, is that there is one and that he is sick. This problem appears perhaps even more sharply in connection with other sentence types like (4.27c). In this case, what corresponds to a negative answer to (4.27b) is a refusal to comply with the request conveyed by (4.27c), as in (4.28):

(4.28)   I will not make the king of France healthy

A sentence such as (4.28) implies that (4.27a) is false, just as (4.27c) does, yet it does not imply that there is no king of France.

Geach's point about interrogatives may be further supported in the following way. Consider the sentences in (4.29).

(4.29)   (a) Yes, I have been happier since she died
         (b) No, I have not been happier since she died
         (c) But I never had a wife (But she is still alive)
         (d) But I have been happier since she died
         (e) But I have not been happier since she died

      Sentences (4.29a) and (4.29b) are answers to Geach's question "Have you been happier since your wife died?" On the other hand, (4.29c) is not a possible answer but, as it were, a rejection of the question. What it says is that the question cannot receive an answer because one of the conditions for answering it is not met. This difference between (a) and (b) of (4.29), on the one hand, and (c), on the other, is quite dramatically brought out when the positive and negative answers are cast in the role of a rejection of the question, as in cases (d) and (e), which, taken in this way, make no sense at all. (We shall consider in Chapter 5 the explication of the relations 'possible answer to a question' and 'rejection of a question'.)

      Another difference between the presuppositional and assertive aspects of propositional form emerges when we ask about the possible questions to which a declarative can be an answer. It is clear that (4.27a) is a possible answer to (4.27b), and it is also clear that (4.27a) is a possible answer to a question such as (4.30):

(4.30)   Who is healthy?

But (4.27a) is not a possible answer to a question such as (4.31):

(4.31)   Does there exist someone who is presently the king of France and is unique
         in being such?

      This illustrates the general fact that, although the whole of the assertion of a declarative sentence can be questioned, and often many of its parts, neither the whole of the presupposition nor any of its parts can be questioned. Moreover, besides not being questionable, the presupposition, again unlike the assertion, is not negatable. When a sentence is negated, the presupposition is not denied, and the denial of a sentence does not deny its presupposition. The presupposition of a sentence and the presupposition of its negation are the same. Consider, for example, the sentences in (4.32):

(4.32)   (a) John remembers (realizes, knows) that he made the appointment
         (b) John does not remember (realize, know) that he made the appointment
         (c) John couldn't remember (realize, know) such a thing because he never
             made the appointment
         (d) How could John remember (realize, know) such a thing when he never
             made the appointment?
         (e) John couldn't remember (realize, know) such a thing because he is
             unaware that he made the appointment
         (f) How could John remember (realize, know) such a thing when he is
             unaware that he made the appointment?

The presupposition of cases like (a) of (4.32), namely, that John did make the appointment, is also the presupposition of cases like (b). This shows that the presupposition is refractory to the operation of negation but that the assertion is not, that is, that the distinction between presupposition and assertion must be drawn in order to state the scope of negation in such cases. Further support is provided by the fact that (4.32c) and (4.32d), which, like (4.29c), express rejection of the presupposition, are appropriate replies, whereas (4.32e) and (4.32f), like (4.29d) and (4.29e), are inappropriate.

The basic form of these arguments is that there are certain linguistic properties, such as being a rejection of a question, not being questionable, being outside the scope of negation, that hold of the part of the proposition that Fregeans distinguish as the presupposition and do not hold of the part that they take as the assertion. Therefore, in order to state the regularities that express the domain of application of these properties, it is necessary to differentiate between the presuppositional and the assertive parts of a proposition.

Another argument for drawing this distinction can be made on the basis of some far more abstract considerations. The argument from an Epimenidean sentence to the alleged contradiction, as Tarski (1952, pp. 348–349) runs it, is as follows. Consider (4.33):

(4.33)   (a) The sentence (4.33a) in this book is not true
         (b) 's' is true if and only if the sentence (4.33a) in this book is not true
         (c) 's' is identical with the sentence (4.33a) in this book, *viz.*, "The sentence (4.33a) in this book is not true"
         (d) 's' is true if and only if 's' is not true

For convenience, the sentence (4.33a) can be designated 's'. We can immediately assert (4.33b) since this is an instance of a convention which says that a sentence is true just in case what it asserts is the case. By inspection, we know that (4.33c) is true. But if we substitute 's' for the subject term of the right-hand side of (4.33b), as (4.33c) permits us to do, we obtain the contradiction expressed by (4.33d).

Tarski (1956) shares our view that natural languages are effable:

A characteristic feature of colloquial language (in contrast to various scientific languages) is its universality. It would not be in harmony with the spirit of this language if in some other language a word occurred which could not be translated into it; it could be claimed that 'if we can speak meaningfully about anything at all, we can speak about it in colloquial language' (pp. 164–165).

He therefore takes the contradiction expressed by (4.33d) to mean that natural languages are logically incoherent:

If we are to maintain this universality of everyday language in connection with semantical investigations, we must, to be consistent, admit into the language, in addition to its sentences and expressions, also the names of these sentences and expressions, and sentences containing these names, as well as such semantic expressions as 'true sentence', 'name', 'denote', etc. But it is presumably just this universality of everyday language which is the primary source of all semantical antinomies, like the antinomies of the liar and of heterological words. These antinomies seem to provide a proof that every day language which is universal in the above sense, and for which the normal laws of logic hold, must be inconsistent (p. 164).

But it is not clear that the semantic antinomies provide a proof of the inconsistency of natural languages on the assumptions that natural languages are effable and that the normal logical laws hold for them. The entire argument (4.33) can be recast as a *reductio* of a further assumption Tarski required, namely, that the Epimenidean sentence (4.33a) expresses a statement, i.e., is true or false. If (4.33a) expresses a statement, then the Tarski convention (roughly, ' X is true if and only if p ', where ' X ' is the name of a sentence and ' p ' is the sentence that ' X ' names) applies to it and we can obtain (4.33b). If, on the other hand, (4.33a) does not express a statement, then there is no reason to accept (4.33b) and the argument to (4.33d) does not carry through. If we take the Tarski convention to read ' If X expresses a statement, then X is true if and only if p ', the *reductio* runs as follows. Suppose that (4.33a) expresses a statement. Then (4.33b) is true. Furthermore, (4.33c) can be verified by inspection, so it is true. But (4.33b) and (4.33c) are inconsistent, as is demonstrated by the deduction of (4.33d). Hence, our supposition has led to a contradiction. From this contradiction, we infer that our supposition is false and, thus, that (4.33a) does not express a statement.

This way out of the Epimenidean paradox costs something. It commits us to the claim that there is a class of sentences which are both syntactically well-formed and semantically meaningful but which, nonetheless, do not make statements, and (4.33a) belongs to this class. But this is no more than what we pay for in a theory of presupposition. Because such a theory provides a category of nonstatements which are expressed by well-formed, meaningful sentences, we can explain why the sentence (4.33a) does not express a statement by saying that its presupposition is not satisfied.

Note, further, that on Tarski's way out of the paradox, which assumes a Russellian rather than a Fregean analysis of propositional form, we pay a price, too. Tarski's approach requires us to adopt the view that, to the extent that the sentences of natural languages and the rules by which we assign truth conditions to them are exactly specifiable, natural languages are logically incoherent. That is, if the notion of consistency can be given a precise meaning in the case of natural languages, then they are inconsistent, and, if it cannot be given a precise meaning, then these languages are, ipso facto, too vague and amorphous. Either way they are incoherent. But we can give a fairly precise meaning to the notion of consistency for natural languages. We can take the sentences of a natural language and their truth conditions to be specifiable in their structural descriptions in an optimal grammar of the language, and, following Herzberger (1965), we can say that a natural language is consistent just in case the set of its linguistic truths does not contain a member of the form ' p ' and another of the form ' not p '. Given this way of adapting the notion for application to natural languages, on Tarski's approach, natural languages must be considered inconsistent systems.

This price for a way out of the contradiction is, I think, staggering. It must then remain an eternal mystery as to how natural languages serve us in conducting our most important pieces of reasoning, whether in empirical science, everyday life, mathematics, or metamathematics. Since contradictions imply anything, any valid conclusion that we draw using a natural language can be paralleled by another validly drawn conclusion (from the Epimenidean sentence) which states something inconsistent with the first conclusion. Even the reconstruction that Tarski imagines, whereby a natural language is replaced by an infinite sequence of formalized languages, each bearing the relation 'metalanguage to object language' to its immediate predecessor, must be carried out in an inconsistent language. And, as has been observed in connection with Russell's theory of types, it will be impossible to make purely general statements about semantical properties like truth since each such statement has to be relativized to some finite set of languages in the sequence.

In reckoning which way out comes at the best price, we must also consider that the cost of a theory of presupposition is reduced by the independent need for such a theory, which has already been argued here. The only real cost, then, is the extension of the theory from sentences that are about persons, places, events, etc., to sentences that are about sentences. We shall require a theory that associates presuppositions with metalinguistic sentences and in this way explains why Epimenidean sentences express indeterminate propositions.[6] Tarski's way out, on the other hand, comes at a far higher price.

The other available approach, namely, denial of the effability assumption made both here and by Tarski, would require us to deny not only the strong form of the effability thesis proposed in Chapter 2, but even the weaker thesis that natural languages contain the apparatus for forming Epimenidean sentences and for forming a pair of sentences for each sentence, one of which says that the sentence is true and the other of which says that it is not true. Since at least the weaker thesis is true, this approach rests on an empirically false claim. In sum, then, it seems that the way out offered by the extension of a Fregean analysis to metalinguistic sentences is to be preferred over the other two possibilities.

If this is so, then we have another argument against Russell's account of the propositional form of sentences. As we have observed, there is an intimate relationship between the situation posed by the Epimenidean paradox and the issue between Russell and Frege about the proper way to treat the structure of propositions. Our way out of the paradox assumes Frege's presuppositional analysis of propositional structure (carried over to metalinguistic sentences), while Tarski's assumes Russell's form of analysis. Thus, although Russell's position on the desirability of a nonpresuppositional analysis of propositional form at first looks as if it costs nothing, it turns out to entail a price, which is the same price that has to be paid for adopting Tarski's approach. Accordingly, this price is an argument against Russell's position and in favor of Frege's: the latter provides us with theoretical machinery to work out an alternative to the view that natural languages

---

[6] This is the task undertaken in Herzberger and Katz (in preparation). A number of the ideas in the argument here come from this joint work, but, of course, Herzberger is not responsible for their present application.

are inconsistent, whereas the former forces us to accept (4.33b) as a valid instance of the Tarski schema and hence as a statement from which, given what appear to be undeniable facts about the expressiveness of natural languages, we can conclude that natural languages are inconsistent.

It seemed possible to Russell to escape the need to regard certain propositions as neither true nor false, that is, to avoid the problem of specifying the conditions under which a proposition is either true or false, by means of a harmless, linguistically neutral terminological device. Russell (1957) wrote:

> For my part I find it more convenient to define the word "false" so that every significant sentence is either true or false. This is purely a verbal question; and although I have no wish to claim the support of common usage, I do not think that he [Strawson] can claim it either (pp. 388–389).

Of course, the policy of using the term "false" in a broad sense to mean "not true" has certain initial advantages if it is recognized as terminological (see Quine (1960)). But the original problems involved in Russell's thesis do not disappear with this terminological sleight of hand. In the new terminology, the need to specify the condition under which a proposition is either true or false takes the form of a need to specify the condition under which a sentence, in Russell's nomenclature, is significant.

Although one might wonder, initially, whether this is a pressing issue, it can be shown that it is, and that considerations from linguistic theory, if not from common usage, can be brought to bear on the question about truth value gaps that Russell took to be purely terminological. These considerations revolve around theorem 14.22 of *Principia Mathematica* (Whitehead and Russell (1935, p. 182)), given here as (4.34):

(4.34) $E!(\imath x)(\phi x) . \equiv . \phi(\imath x)(\phi x)$

The commentary on this theorem is:

> Thus such a proposition as "The man who wrote Waverley wrote Waverley" does not embody a logically necessary truth, since it would be false if Waverley had not been written or had been written by two men in collaboration (p. 182).

Here Russell is merely arguing from his own theory. All that he is entitled to say is that (4.35) is not a theorem of his system:

(4.35) $\phi(\imath x)(\phi x)$

There are well-known difficulties with regard to (4.35) which Russell pointed out in his criticism of Meinong, who apparently held it to be a logical truth. Within a Fregean theory of presupposition, however, none of these difficulties arises, and (4.35) can be taken as a logical truth if it is understood that its instances are restricted to statements.

Since serious technical difficulties are encountered in attempting to carry the Fregean view through on a purely syntactical basis, Russell's theory, with the weaker theorem (4.35), might appear to be an attractive compromise that skirts such difficulties. Let us consider what is involved in representing the semantic structure of English sentences in accord with (4.35).

Sentences (4.36) and (4.37) are instances of (4.35) in English which have a consistent predicate:[7]

(4.36)   The author of *Principia Mathematica* is an author of *Principia Mathematica*

(4.37)   The present king of France is a king of France at present

Another instance is Russell's own example, given here as (4.38):

(4.38)   The man who squared the circle squared the circle

These instances of (4.35) are analytic sentences, like the familiar cases in (1.23) and (4.39):

(4.39)   The present king of France is male

That is, in such propositions the meaning of the predicate is already contained in the meaning of the subject so that a vacuous condition is imposed upon the world that cannot but be met. The notion of analyticity implies that all analytic *statements* are true. Since cases like (4.36)–(4.39) are each analytic and are each instances of (4.35), and since, on Russell's theory, instances of (4.35) can be true only if there is exactly one thing x such that ϕx is true,[8] (4.36)–(4.39) are statements and hence true only if there is exactly one author of *Principia Mathematica*, exactly one king of France, exactly one man who squared the circle (and/or exactly one first circle squarer). Therefore, one who holds (4.35) must acknowledge that (4.36)–(4.39) are not statements, since the condition that there exists exactly one thing x such that ϕx is true does not obtain in any of these cases. The problem of specifying the conditions under which a proposition is true or has a true negation, consequently, is reflected in the problem of specifying the conditions under which an analytic proposition is true. Moreover, such conditions, even on Russell's theory, may involve matters of fact (the existence of one and only one author of *Principia Mathematica*, of one and only one king of France, etc.)[9] Hence, perhaps the most significant advantage claimed for Russell's theory, namely, that the

---

[7] There is another kind of instance of (4.35), namely, one with an inconsistent predicate, e.g., "The round square is a round square." Russell pointed out such cases and said that they could not be true since they are contradictions. On the Fregean view, however, examples such as "The round square is a round square" would not be statements at all (and hence not logically false ones). This would account for their not being true, which is all that Russell needed to account for. In general, we consider propositions such as "The round square is round" or "The round square is a round square" to be indeterminable. (See Katz (1966, pp. 211–220).) Accordingly, the condition within the Fregean framework that excludes such cases from statementhood becomes in semantic theory the condition that for a proposition to be a statement it must be determinable. We shall consider this more fully later.

[8] Since this is just what (4.34) says.

[9] We will spell this out directly, when we try to clarify further Frege's conception of presupposition as well as ours.

conditions of statementhood can be identified with the purely grammatical conditions of significance, goes by the board.

Let us look back at the problem which Russell's terminology allegedly permitted one to avoid, namely, that of specifying the conditions under which a proposition is true or false in the ordinary sense (i.e., has a true negation). Russell's theory provides at least a partial answer to this problem in theorem 14.21, given here as (4.40):[10]

(4.40) $\psi(\imath x)(\phi x) . \supset . E!(\imath x)(\phi x)$

Thus, a necessary condition for a singular sentence to be a statement is that its subject expression, when in referential position, denotes exactly one thing. This condition, of course, is the one which we just previously considered, and the same one put forth by the Fregean theory as the condition on which such propositions are statements. The statementhood of propositions, on either Russell's or Frege's theory, becomes a contingent matter, resting on a question of fact. Therefore, the alleged advantage of Russell's theory, which is supposed to compensate for its artificiality, disappears.

Finally, let us consider one further difficulty which again robs Russell's thesis of an advantage it claims to have over Frege's, namely, that it does not require us to distinguish within a proposition between the presupposition and the assertion. The simplest account of the meaning of the definite article would take it to have only one sense and, therefore, the same sense in both referential and nonreferential positions. Intuitively, this seems correct, as the examples in (4.41) and (4.42) show:[11]

(4.41)   The president of France is bald

(4.42)   The president of France does not exist

These propositions, however, have quite different entailments. The first but not the second entails that the president of France exists. On a Fregean theory, presupposition is separated from assertion and given a suitably different representation, which permits it to have a different treatment. This treatment allows the problems posed by cases like (4.41) and (4.42) to be dealt with in a straightforward way. But with no such separation, the facts concerning referential and nonreferential occurrences of the definite article cannot be handled straightforwardly. Given the entailment relations of cases like (4.41) and (4.42), a theory that does not distinguish between presupposition and assertion is forced to treat the definite article as having a different sense for each of these different contexts. In effect,

---

[10] Whitehead and Russell (1935, p. 174).

[11] On some theories of referential position, (4.42) is counted as a referential position, e.g., Quine's (1960b, chapter 5, section 38). Nevertheless, the subject of (4.42) is clearly not referential since the sentence truly says that "the president of France" does not succeed in referring. Accordingly, (4.42) is a counterexample to any such theory, that is, to any theory that takes sameness of truth value after substitution of coreferential expressions as a sufficient condition for the referentiality of the substitution position. This point was suggested to me by H. G. Herzberger.

"the" must be treated as ambiguous, quite contrary to linguistic intuition. This is precisely what Russell does in his theory of descriptions. He gives one definition of the definite article in contexts of predication, that is, in referential positions,[12] and a separate definition for the definite article in contexts that are nonreferential.[13]

The fact that a Russellian theory is not equipped with the conceptual machinery to represent linguistic data of this sort is evidence for a presuppositional part of a proposition, logically distinct from the predicative part. This evidence is of the same kind as that presented by Frege in his arguments supporting the distinction between sense and reference.[14]

Assuming that considerations of the kind just discussed provide adequate grounds for accepting the presuppositional analysis of propositional form proposed by Frege, it is necessary for us to clarify some of the differences between Frege's full conception of presupposition and statementhood and the one being put forth here. The fact that grammatical form does not distinguish between those expressions that succeed in designating and those that do not, according to Frege (1952b) arise:

> from an imperfection of language, from which even the symbolic language of mathematical analysis is not altogether free; even there combinations of symbols can occur that seem to stand for something but have (at least so far) no reference, e.g., divergent infinite series.... A logically perfect language should satisfy the conditions, that every expression grammatically well constructed as a proper name out of signs already introduced shall in fact designate an object, and that no new sign shall be introduced as a sign without being secured a reference (p. 70).

It is, I think, a mistake of Frege's to regard the failure of grammatical form to distinguish designating from nondesignating expressions to be an imperfection of natural languages or symbolic languages of mathematics. Rather, it is a necessary feature of any language that is both reasonably rich in expressive power and presuppositional. In this context, there is no need to argue for the advantages of a language's having presuppositional structure. There are also clear advantages to a language that can employ expressions which have no referent or which have not been secured a referent. A language limited in expressive power so that it does not employ such expressions will be useless for the scientifically critical tasks of theory construction and verification. We surely want our language to leave open for its users the possibility of constructing theories which hypothesize the existence of such things as phlogiston, ether, and animal spirits and which state principles about their behavior and causal effects. Without the option of employing proper names for which the question of a referent is left open, scientific development would certainly be hamstrung.

[12] Whitehead and Russell (1935, 14.01, p. 173).

[13] Whitehead and Russell (1935, 14.02, p. 174).

[14] Russell's counter to this, that singular terms are syncategorematic, is based on a notion of meaning wherein meaning is denotation. It thus does not support his theory against the objection given here. Sense for Russell is logical form. Within his theory, singular terms have logical form, even though they do not have denotation, and are thus syncategorematic in this quite restricted sense. On Russell's treatment "the ϕ" has no denotation and at least two senses, two logical forms, which make their separate appearance in separate contexts.

As a consequence of the advantages of expressiveness and presupposition, a language will also have the feature that statementhood turns on a matter of fact. The grammar cannot incorporate a list of all the truths about the world and so cannot formally mark off the expressions that succeed in designating. If a language is effable, then, for every proposition, there will be a sentence expressing it. Without advance knowledge of the truths, there will have to be sentences in the language which express propositions with false presuppositions (i.e., indeterminate propositions) since a false presupposition is a false proposition playing the part of what is taken for granted in the assertion of another proposition.

Frege's approach to presupposition may thus seem to differ significantly from that taken here in that, for him, the formulation of a theory of presupposition determining which propositions are statements is part of the construction of an ideal, logically perfect language. On the approach taken here, however, it is part of a more general theory of the grammar of sentence structure in natural languages, that is, part of linguistic theory. But big as this difference may look since the work of Carnap and his followers, it does not come to much in this case. As I read Frege, I can find nothing to prevent us from construing principles of his theory as principles of linguistic theory rather than as blueprints for an ideal language. Both views seek to construct a formal representation of the logical form of thoughts (in Frege's sense). Both are sensitive to the grammatical structure of sentences in natural language, which is the object of formalization and the check on its correctness. Both proceed from the same general assumptions about language, particularly the assumptions about effability, the distinctness of sense and reference, the compositional structure of complex constructions, the desirability of a realistic framework, etc. The so-called "imperfections" that Frege (1952b) refers to in the passage last quoted, which continues as follows, can be handled in a grammar:

> The logic books contain warnings against logical mistakes arising from the ambiguity of expressions. I regard as no less pertinent a warning against apparent proper names having no reference (p. 70).

If grammars achieve their descriptive aims, they will mark the ambiguities of sentences in terms of the readings assigned to them. Thus, the warnings of the logic books will be heeded, since readings, not sentences, will serve as representations of propositions, and they have no troublemaking ambiguities. In essence, my contention is that the logically perfect language Frege sought can be regarded as a natural language understood in terms of an empirically optimal linguistic theory and an empirically optimal grammar.

We can now turn to the definitions of the notions 'determinate proposition', 'indeterminate proposition', 'determinable proposition', and 'indeterminable proposition'. The first two of these constructs can be defined as in (4.43) and (4.44):

(4.43)   A proposition is determinate just in case it is determinable and its presupposition is true.

(4.44)   A proposition is indeterminate just in case it is determinable and its presupposition is false.

These constructs can be thought of as belonging properly to the theory of reference, since the question of whether one or the other is satisfied in the case of an arbitrary proposition is not decidable on the grounds of its reading alone but requires that we know something about the world. The statements of a language are, given these definitions, the union of the class of eternal propositions and the intersection of the class of determinate propositions and the class of standing propositions.[15]

The notions 'indeterminable proposition' and 'determinable proposition', which must be given to complete (4.43) and (4.44) and which are crucial for the definitions of other semantic properties and relations to be discussed in this chapter, will be presented in stages. Provisionally, we define them as in (4.45) and (4.46):

(4.45) A proposition is indeterminable just in case it is represented by a reading R which is the reading of a sense of a sentence and, moreover, the reading of the subject of this sentence, which is a component of R, contains two distinct semantic markers from the same antonymous n-tuple.

(4.46) A proposition is determinable just in case it is represented by a reading R which is the reading of a sense of a sentence and, moreover, the reading of the subject of this sentence, which is a component of R, does not contain distinct semantic markers from the same antonymous n-tuple.

We add to these the definitions (4.47)–(4.50):

(4.47) A sentence S is indeterminable on a sense just in case there is a reading of S that satisfies (4.45).

(4.48) A sentence S is fully indeterminable just in case every reading of S satisfies (4.45).

(4.49) A sentence S is determinable on a sense just in case there is a reading of S that satisfies (4.46).

(4.50) A sentence S is fully determinable just in case every reading of S satisfies (4.46).

These definitions constitute the theory of determinability as it was first introduced in Katz (1966, pp. 211–220). Neither of the two basic definitions (4.45) and (4.46) is adequate. As we shall see shortly, the first is too narrow and the second is too broad. After first considering some properties of these notions, we shall discuss the difficulties and offer modifications that avoid them.

First, it is clear that these definitions and any that may replace them, unlike (4.43) and (4.44), belong to the theory of meaning.[16] Second, such definitions

---

[15] We cannot attempt here to set up the grammatical machinery that would be needed to formally characterize actual presuppositions of sentences. This machinery has to do mainly with the syntactic and semantic structure of the determiner system, which is not at all well understood. To embark on such an attempt would thus take us too far afield.

[16] We take definability exclusively in terms of readings to be a sufficient condition, in general, for a notion to belong to the theory of meaning.

apply only to the senses of nonconjoined, simple sentences, that is, sentences that are not conjunctions, disjunctions, conditionals, etc., or complex. Separate definitions will be required for each type of conjoined or complex sentence which specify the determinableness or indeterminableness (also the determinateness or indeterminateness) of a proposition expressed by a conjoined or complex sentence as a function of the semantic character of the connecting constituent and the determinableness or indeterminableness (also determinateness or indeterminateness) of the connected sentences. I will not attempt to give such definitions here, but it is easy to see the lines along which they must run. For example, since a conjunction is true just in case both its conjuncts are true, and since determinableness is a necessary condition for truth, both conjuncts of a conjunction must be determinable in order that the whole conjunction be determinable. Again, since a disjunction is true just in case one of its disjuncts is true, only one disjunct of a disjunction must be determinable in order that the whole disjunction be determinable.

The idea behind (4.45) is the following extension of the presuppositional approach. Given the fact that a logically contradictory concept cannot, under any circumstances, succeed in designating, if a clause of the presupposition of a proposition involves such a concept, the presupposition cannot, of necessity, be satisfied. Consider (4.51):

(4.51) The female king is handsome

Being indeterminable, (4.51) cannot have a true presupposition, for the extension of the concept expressed by "female king" is empty. The proposition expressed by (4.51) is logically precluded from statementhood. Indeterminableness is the linguistic (or logical) counterpart of indeterminateness (and determinableness is the linguistic counterpart of determinateness). In the case of indeterminableness, presupposition fails for purely conceptual reasons, whereas in the case of indeterminateness it fails for purely contingent reasons.

In Katz (1966, pp. 211–216), I drew an unnecessary distinction between indeterminableness and indeterminateness by requiring that the former but not the latter be disjoint from the categories of analytic, contradictory, and synthetic propositions. I argued that if we allow the class of indeterminable propositions to overlap with the analytic propositions or the contradictory propositions, then a proposition like the one expressed by (4.52) must be counted as both analytic and contradictory, and hence as both true and false:

(4.52) A female king is male

On the one hand, the concept of maleness expressed by the predicate of (4.52) is included in that of a king (since a king is a male monarch), and, accordingly, we would be committed to holding that (4.52) is analytic. On the other hand, the concept of maleness expressed by the predicate of (4.52) is incompatible with the concept of femaleness, and, accordingly, we would also be committed to holding that (4.52) is contradictory. Thus, in Katz (1966), the class of indeterminable sentences is made disjoint from both the class of analytic and the class of contradictory sentences by including in the definitions for the semantic properties of analyticity and contradictoriness the condition that the subject's reading not contain distinct semantic markers from the same antonymous *n*-tuple.

This distinction is unnecessary, however, because a sentence like (4.52) can be allowed as both analytic and contradictory without any danger of being both true and false. The reason is that since such sentences are indeterminable, they are, of necessity, never true and never false.

Indeterminable propositions, unlike semantically anomalous ones, have readings and can therefore bear semantic relations to other propositions. Consider, for example, the pairs of sentences (4.53)–(4.54) and (4.55)–(4.56):

(4.53)   A female king knighted John

(4.54)   John was knighted by a female king

(4.55)   A male sister of Bill's committed murder

(4.56)   A sister of Bill's murdered someone

Sentences (4.53) and (4.54) are genuine paraphrases, while (4.56) is entailed by (4.55).

We now turn to the reasons for the inadequacies in the previous definitions of determinateness and determinableness.[17] The question, quite simply, is why these definitions treat the readings of subject noun phrases differently from those of object noun phrases, that is, why the contradictoriness of the concept expressed by the subject is the only condition of a proposition's being indeterminable, and, correspondingly, why the failure of the subject to refer is the only condition of a proposition's being indeterminate. By way of further sharpening the question, it may be remarked that sentences with contradictory predicates, such as (4.57)–(4.59), should not be considered indeterminable:

(4.57)   The table top is both round and square in shape

(4.58)   John is a female king

(4.59)   Mary is crying copiously and exiguously

These sentences express straightforward contradictions, that is, they succeed in referring to the things they are about but make incompatible assertions concerning them. On the other hand, why should we not say that sentences with an object noun phrase whose meaning involves an inconsistency can no more succeed in making a statement than ones with such a subject noun phrase? In particular, what is the rationale for distinguishing between cases like (4.60) and (4.61)?[18]

---

[17] I am indebted to P. Postal (in correspondence) for first raising this issue with me.

[18] Postal (in correspondence) pointed out that in Katz (1966) the distinction between cases like (4.60) and (4.61) rests on the asymmetry of subject and predicate. Postal then observed that "this is purely syntactic and does not yield the conclusion if the object NP in the deep syntactic structure is not part of any predicate as I suggest. Again I emphasize that it is not the question of the distinction between indeterminable and contradictory which is at issue but rather whether this distinction necessitates an asymmetry between one NP in a deep structure and all others. This latter is, I am suggesting, not a semantic fact but a syntactic error, albeit a widespread one."

(4.60)   Bertrand Russell visited the female king

(4.61)   The female king visited Bertrand Russell

I now think that what was said in Katz (1966) about the special status of readings of the subject noun phrase of a sentence in the definitions of determinableness and indeterminableness and in the definitions of determinateness and indeterminateness was incorrect. The reason is not the fact that many speakers are unable to find an intuitive basis for distinguishing between cases like (4.61) and (4.60), although this is certainly disturbing, nor is it the fact that some grammarians can offer proposals about the syntactic relations in deep structure on which object noun phrases are not constituents of a predicate, which is also disturbing, though less so. What really points up the error of the earlier treatment is the fact that there is a direct argument to show that in cases like (4.60) and (4.61) one sentence cannot be construed as contradictory and the other indeterminable.

In Chapter 7, an explanation will be offered for the fact that sentences with converse main verbs that have the form of those in (4.62) are synonymous:

(4.62)   (a) NP_1 sold the NP_2 to NP_3
          (b) NP_3 bought the NP_2 from NP_1

However, this fact alone establishes that the definitions in question wrongly treat readings of subject noun phrases differently from those of object noun phrases. Consider instances of (4.62a,b) such as (4.63) and (4.64):

(4.63)   A female king sold the castle to Mary

(4.64)   Mary bought the castle from a female king

From the synonymy of these sentences we can conclude that either both must be determinable or both must be indeterminable since, given that a pair of propositions cannot be synonymous if one but not the other has a certain semantic property, both terms of a synonymy relation have to belong to the same semantic category. Hence, insofar as (4.45) and (4.46) say that for cases such as (4.63) and (4.64) there is at least one pair of semantic categories where synonymous sentences do not fall in the same category, these definitions must be rejected in favor of definitions that take both sentences in such pairs to be indeterminable. The two sentences cannot belong to the category of determinable propositions without doing so severe an injustice to the facts as to undermine the empirical tenability of the category of indeterminableness, for (4.63) is clearly indeterminable if any sentence is.

The definition (4.45) for 'indeterminable proposition' must be changed, therefore, to include sentences with a contradictory object (direct, indirect, etc.), as well as sentences with a contradictory subject, while still excluding sentences like (4.57)–(4.59), that is, sentences without objects and with consistent subjects. And the definition (4.46) for 'determinable proposition' must also be changed accordingly. The revised definitions will be of the form (4.65) and (4.66).

(4.65)   A proposition is indeterminable just in case the reading that represents it contains a component reading R* that has two or more semantic markers from the same antonymous *n*-tuple of semantic markers.

(4.66)   A proposition is determinable just in case the reading that represents it does not contain any component reading R* that has two or more semantic markers from the same antonymous *n*-tuple of semantic markers.

We cannot complete these definitions at this point because the required definition of the symbol 'R*' cannot be stated. For the time being, we can think of 'R*' as a reading for the subject, direct object, indirect object, or other constituent of a sentence whose meaning contributes a condition to its presupposition. We will soon take steps to define 'R*' in terms of the formal structure of the readings in semantically interpreted phrase markers. These, of course, will also be steps toward defining the term "presupposition" which appears in the definitions (4.43) and (4.44).

Wilson (1967) failed to understand the relation between indeterminacy and analyticity (contradiction, and syntheticity) because he neglected the distinction between a proposition's failure to express a statement for inherent, logical reasons, as in the case of indeterminableness, and its failure to do so on occasion for contingent reasons. Concerning the discussion of indeterminableness in Katz (1966), he wrote:

> From page 208 one would infer that
>
> (4.67)   The present king of France is a present king of France
>
> is analytic; from page 214 one would infer that it isn't even true. At this point, the exegete gives up in despair (p. 62).

The first of Wilson's two pieces of exegesis is, of course, correct. The second is not. On page 214, and in the rest of that discussion, I said that indeterminable propositions are neither true nor false. Although I did not explicitly introduce the two categories 'determinate' and 'indeterminate,' I never said that sentences like (4.67) were indeterminable, only that they were *similar* to indeterminable ones in the sense that the subject does not denote anything. Therefore sentences like (4.67) cannot be either true or false, there being nothing for the attribution of the property expressed by their predicates to be true or false of. In Katz (1966), I went on to point out the dissimilarity:

> But, note that in the case of indeterminable sentences semantic considerations alone suffice to decide that the subject of the sentence cannot denote, whereas in the case of such synthetic sentences this decision is a matter of fact (p. 214).

The point, then, is that the subject of (4.67) does not express a contradictory concept, as does, for example, the subject of the indeterminable sentence (4.68):

(4.68)   The present female king of France is a king of France

Sentences like (4.67) are similar to sentences like (4.68) in that in certain situations, like the circumstances of France at the present time, their subjects fail to denote. They fail to denote for contingent reasons, and this leads me to say that they are similar only up to a point: some tokens of types such as (4.67) are like tokens of types such as (4.68), but here the similarity ends, since some tokens of types such as (4.67) can be true whereas no tokens of types such as (4.68) can be either true or false on a theory of presupposition.

From these considerations, what it means to say that a proposition like (4.67) or any occasion proposition is analytic is that tokens of that type whose presupposition is satisfied are true. That is, tokens of analytic propositions, if they make a statement, make a true one. They are linguistically secured against falsehood. What it means to say that such a proposition is contradictory is that tokens of that type whose presupposition is satisfied are false. That is, tokens of contradictory propositions, if they make a statement, make a false one. Finally, what it means to say that an occasion proposition is synthetic is that tokens of that type whose presupposition is satisfied are either true or false, depending on what is the case.

McCawley (1968a) has put forth the proposal, which he attributes to Fillmore, that selection restrictions are not requirements that the senses of lexical items impose on other constituents but are rather "presuppositions about the intended referents of those constituents":

> I regard this as the most worthwhile proposal which has yet been made about selection restrictions. First of all, it explains why under the earlier proposals a selection restriction could require the absence but could not require the presence of a 'semantic marker'... Secondly, Fillmore's proposal (unlike earlier proposals) requires no modification to make it consistent with the conclusion ... that the lexical material of a noun phrase may originate in a 'higher' sentence than the one in which it appears, e.g.
>
> John denies that he kissed the girl who he kissed
>
> which is most normally interpreted with "the girl who he kissed" not being part of John's denial but being the speaker's description of the girl who John was talking about. Third, as pointed out by Fillmore, this proposal allows an item to impose a selection restriction 'on itself' in the sense that "bachelor" may be regarded not as meaning 'human, male, adult, unmarried' but rather as having the meaning 'unmarried' and the 'selectional restriction' (presupposition concerning the intended referent) 'human, male, adult', which fits well the fact noted by Fillmore that one may apply the word "bachelor" to someone known to be a male adult human in order to express that he is unmarried but not apply "bachelor" to someone known to be an unmarried adult human in order to express that he is male (p. 267).

This proposal is a medley of confusions and mistakes. A presupposition of a sentence is a condition whose satisfaction is both necessary and sufficient for the sentence to be capable of making a statement, issuing a request, etc., whereas a selection restriction is a condition whose satisfaction is necessary and sufficient for a constituent of a sentence to be meaningful. Thus, there are a number of essential differences between the two notions that make nonsense of any proposal to assimilate the latter notion to the former. The first difference to be mentioned is that in the case of a presupposition, the condition is sometimes satisfied by something in the world, while, in the case of a selection restriction, the condition is always satisfied by a sense of a constituent (in the same sentence as the constituent in whose sense the selection restriction figures). Another difference is that the failure of a presupposition renders a token of a sentence indeterminate, i.e., it can make no statement, issue no request, etc., while the failure of a selection restriction (except in special cases like (3.48)) renders a sentence type semantically anomalous. Still another difference is that there are certain kinds of sentences, namely, generic sentences, which do not have presuppositions but which can be semantically anomalous, for example, "The average American is a strawberry-flavored prime number," "A perpetual motion machine is the square root of a number," "Witches are implied by the axiom of choice."

The alleged justifications that McCawley offers provide further instances of confusions and mistakes in the proposal he is defending. His first is that Fillmore's proposal remedies a defect in my account of selection restrictions, namely, that selection restrictions cannot require the presence of a semantic marker. A glance at Katz and Fodor (1963, p. 191) or Katz (1964, p. 525) shows that this is simply a mistake about what was said. McCawley's second and third justifications depend on a confusion between the conditions under which it is appropriate to use a token of a sentence type and the respect in which such conditions incline hearers to a preferred interpretation, on the one hand, and the conditions under which a sentence type has a given meaning, on the other. McCawley's example would normally be used and interpreted in the way he suggests, but this is no argument to show that this example does not have a contradictory sense. Likewise, it is probably true that "bachelor" is normally used to express the fact that someone is unmarried, rather than to make the point that someone is male, but this does not show that the property of maleness is not attributed to someone when we predicate "bachelor" of him. It would thus seem that what we are being offered here is just a warmed-over version of the use theory of meaning. Finally, it is, I think, empirically clear that the sense of "bachelor" must contain the concept of maleness as a component of the assertion it makes when used predicatively. Consider the sentence (4.69):

(4.69)   All unmarried adult people are bachelors

This sentence is obviously synthetic and false. But if maleness were only presupposed in the application of "bachelor," we would have to say that (4.69) is analytic and true. According to the view under consideration, the presupposition of (4.69) is that the objects of predication are unmarried adult males while the assertion of (4.69) is that such objects are unmarried. As we shall see in Section 5 of this chapter, analyticity has to be defined as the inclusion of the content of the assertion in the content of the presupposition.

3.   Propositional type and propositional content

The distinction between the presupposition of an assertive proposition and its assertion is easily generalized to apply beyond assertive propositions. Consider the sentences in (4.70).

(4.70) (a) Someone stole the British crown jewels.
       (b) Who stole the British crown jewels?
       (c) Someone, steal the British crown jewels!
       (d) Oh, were someone only to steal the British crown jewels!

The presupposition in each case in (4.70) is the same, namely, the conditions that someone exists and that there exists something that is the British crown jewels and is unique in being such. If this presupposition is satisfied, then, under normal circumstances, (a) of (4.70) makes a statement, (b) makes a request for information, (c) issues a request for action, and (d) expresses a wish. If the presupposition is not satisfied, then, under normal circumstances, (a) fails to make a statement, (b) fails to make a request for information, (c) fails to issue a request for action, and (d) fails to express a fulfillable wish. Thus, the same kind of distinction that is drawn between the presupposition and the assertion of an assertive proposition can also be drawn between the presupposition and what corresponds to the assertion in the nonassertive proposition types in (b)–(d) of (4.70). In the case of propositions expressed by interrogatives, the distinction is to be drawn between the presupposition and the question; in the case of imperatives, it is to be drawn between the presupposition and the request; in the case of hortatories, it is to be drawn between the presupposition and the wish.

Besides having a common presupposition, the propositions expressed by (4.70a–d) share another component of propositional form. If we abstract away the fact that the proposition expressed by (a) is assertive, (b) erotetic, (c) requestive, and (d) covetive, we see that they each involve the same predicate, namely, the relation 'x steals y at time t'. We will say that these propositions have the same *condition* (as well as having the same presupposition). We will use the term *propositional content* to refer to the presupposition and the condition of a proposition. Thus, the propositions expressed by (4.70a–d) have the same propositional content. We will use the term *propositional type* to refer to the component of propositional structure with respect to which these cases differ from one another. We shall say that (a) of (4.70) is of the *assertive type*, (b) of the *erotetic type*, (c) of the *requestive type*, and (d) of the *covetive type*. Roughly, the propositional type of a proposition expressed by a sentence determines the illocutionary force of its utterances insofar as this is determined by the grammatical structure of the sentence.

We may analyze the structure of propositions in terms of these categories and their subcategories. For example, at the most general level, a proposition has a propositional type and a propositional content. At the next level, its type can be subcategorized as assertive, erotetic, requestive, covetive, or some other such type, and its propositional content can be broken down into a presupposition and a condition. Moreover, as we have seen in the previous section, the presupposition can be subcategorized as determinable or indeterminable. Its condition can be a *truth condition*, an *answerhood condition*, a *compliance condition*, a *fulfillment condition*, or some other such subcategory.

The subcategory of the condition of a proposition is a function of its propositional type. The propositional type determines the subcategory to which the condition belongs quite straightforwardly: if a proposition is of the assertive type, its condition is a truth condition; if the proposition is of the erotetic type, its condition is an answerhood condition; if a proposition is of the requestive type, its condition is a compliance condition; and if a proposition is of the covetive type, its condition is a fulfillment condition. Shortly, we will say more about the nature of these types and conditions and also more about how the former determine the latter.

It should be noted that our treatment of semantic theory is not committed to any specific claim about the variety of propositional types found in natural languages. Those mentioned so far will seem far from exhaustive to many philosophers, who will want to add further propositional types corresponding to greetings, promises, warnings, apologies, commands, entreaties, welcomes, and so on, including most of the cases usually considered in discussions of speech acts.[19] But the fact that one distinguishes a number of speech acts does not imply that there is a corresponding number of distinct propositional types. Commands and entreaties may be different speech acts, but the type of proposition expressed by the sentences normally conveying them may be requestive. The difference may lie in the fact that commands require the agent to have authority over the addressee while entreaties require the agent to have something like the opposite relation to the addressee. This distinction, however, may have nothing whatever to do with proposition type, even though it plays a role in the meaning of "command" and "entreat."

Sentence type does not by itself determine propositional type. For example, (4.71) and (4.72) are, respectively, of the same propositional type as (b) and (c) of (4.70), namely, erotetic and requestive, even though they are not expressed by an interrogative and an imperative:

(4.71)   I ask you who stole the British crown jewels

(4.72)   I request that you steal the British crown jewels

(4.73)   I promise to steal the British crown jewels

(4.74)   He asked who stole the British crown jewels

(4.75)   He requested that you steal the British crown jewels

(4.76)   He promised to steal the British crown jewels

When we extend our consideration to additional propositions, this fact becomes all the more clear. For example, (4.73) is a declarative but it does not express an assertive proposition. Thus, we have to say that the meaning of the main verb of a sentence determines propositional type when this is not determined by the sentence type. We may grammatically distinguish the class of performative verbs from other verbs by the fact that they play this role in the determination of propositional type.

As examples (4.73) and (4.76) show, however, the meaning of a performative main verb determines proposition type only if certain other constituents of the sentence have certain meanings. Thus, although (4.73) and (4.76) both have the

---

[19] See, in this connection, Austin (1961; 1962) and Searle (1969).

performative "promise" as their main verb, only (4.73) would characteristically be used to perform the speech act of promising. The sentence in (4.76) expresses instead an assertive proposition about someone's act. The critical difference is that the former has a first person subject and is in the present tense while the latter has a third person subject and is in the past tense. Since speech acts are the speaker's acts performed at the moment of utterance, we can accept the following generalization of this difference. The propositional type of the proposition(s) expressed by a declarative sentence with a performative verb occurring as the main verb is determined as nonassertive and as belonging to the subcategories specified in the meaning of the performative verb just in case the subject of the declarative is in the first person and the tense of the auxiliary is present.

Therefore, we will think of the propositional type of a proposition as being specified in the semantic representation of the syntactic elements that determine sentence type (e.g., the symbols 'Q' for interrogative and 'Imp' for imperative) in those cases where propositional type is a function of sentence type and as being specified in the semantic representation of the performative verb in those cases where propositional type is a function of the choice of a performative verb and the appropriate subject and tense constituent. We must consider the lines along which the reading of a performative verb will be constructed so as to embody the generalization of the preceding paragraph and specify the proper propositional type for the proposition(s) expressed by a sentence.

We now introduce one of the notational conventions that we will use to represent formally the structural organization of propositions. This is the convention for representing the distinction between the part of a reading that represents information about propositional type and the part that represents information about propositional content. For this purpose, a pair of "double" parentheses will be used—'(' and ')'. The part of a reading that is enclosed in such parentheses is the semantic representation of the propositional type and the part outside them is the semantic representation of the propositional content. In the next section, we will introduce another similar notational convention for distinguishing within a reading between the semantic representation of the presupposition and the semantic representation of the condition.

Information about propositional type is of two sorts. First, there is information about the nature of the illocutionary act that a speaker normally performs in uttering the sentence in appropriate circumstances, and, second, there is information that determines the conversion of the condition into one of the proper kind. For example, the propositions expressed by interrogative and imperative sentences are requestive, so that the illocutionary act in question is a request on the part of the speaker. But, although both are requestive, the condition in the case of the proposition expressed by an interrogative sentence becomes an answerhood condition while the condition in the case of the proposition expressed by the imperative sentence becomes a compliance condition. The condition in (b) and (c) of (4.70) is the same, namely, 'x steals the British crown jewels at some time t', but the propositional type of (b) converts it into an answerhood condition whereas the propositional type in (c) converts into a compliance condition. The chart in (4.77) illustrates roughly what is to be understood by these two sorts of information found in the semantic representation of propositional type.

(4.77)

PROPOSITIONAL TYPE	ILLOCUTIONARY FORCE	CONVERSION OF CONDITION
Assertive	Speaker asserts that x	x = the object(s), couples of objects, etc., that satisfy the presupposition satisfy the UCC
Requestive (Erotetic)	Speaker requests x of A	x = an utterance token of a sentence that is both a possible answer to the UCC and true
Requestive	Speaker requests x of A	x = A perform the act specified in UCC
Requestive (Apologetic)	Speaker requests x of A	x = A forgive speaker for the act specified in UCC
Promissory (?)	Speaker undertakes an obligation x for A	x = speaker to perform the act specified in UCC if A wants it performed

In (4.77) 'A' stands for the addressee and 'UCC' for the unconverted condition (i.e., the condition as found in the representation of the propositional content). We note that this chart is not intended to provide actual semantic analyses of the propositional types listed but only to illustrate what we take propositional type to be, that is, to indicate the kind of distinction we wish to draw between propositional type and propositional content and the kind of information that propositional type contains.

The readings that represent erotetic and requestive propositional types can be taken as lexical readings of the symbols 'Q' and 'Imp', respectively. Whatever information about the illocutionary force and conversion of the condition expresses the propositional type of propositions conveyed by hortatory sentences can be thought of as represented in the lexical reading of the symbol(s) that determine this sentence type. In the case of declarative sentences, the reading of the main verb would appear to carry the information about propositional type. If the main verb of such a sentence is not a performative, the proposition is generally assertive. If it is a performative, the proposition can be any of the different propositional types, including assertive, that enter into the meaning of such verbs.

We can indicate, roughly, how information about propositional type can be represented in the lexical reading of a performative verb. Consider the verb "warn." Part of its lexical reading will contain a set of semantic markers representing the illocutionary force of the proposition expressed by appropriate sentences with "warn" as their main verb. Perhaps these semantic markers represent the notion of someone's informing the addressee of something. Another part of this lexical reading will represent the information necessary to convert the condition, perhaps information that the addressee is informed of the event specified in the UCC and of its being somehow disadvantageous to him.

There are two selection restrictions on categorized variables in the lexical reading of a performative verb that determine the proposition type of the proposition expressed by the sentence in which this verb occurs. One is on the variable categorized for the subject–main verb relation and the other is on the variable categorized for the tense–main verb relation (see Chapter 7). The selection restriction on the first of these categorized variables requires its values (readings of the subject) to contain a semantic marker or markers representing the concept 'speaker of the sentence' (or something equivalent). The selection restriction on the second of these categorized variables requires its values (readings of the tense constituent) to contain a semantic marker representing the moment of utterance or speech point (see, again, Chapter 7). If either selection restriction is not satisfied, the proposition will be assertive; if both are satisfied, it will be of the type specified in the sense of the particular performative verb, that is, requestive if the verb is "apologize," promissory if the verb is "promise," etc. Moreover, we may note in this connection that such a selection restriction is the inverse of that for causative verbs. The selection restrictions for verbs in this corresponding class require that values of the variable categorized for the tense–main verb relation *not* contain semantic markers representing the moment of utterance. This feature helps to explain not only the difference between causative verbs and performative verbs but also semantic anomalies like that found in sentences such as (4.78):

(4.78)   I persuade you to return the five dollars

In concluding this section, let me mention a matter of theoretical interest which arises from these considerations concerning the representation of certain speech act information in semantic components. Some philosophers believe that speech act information belongs to a special theory of speech acts. Here it has been assumed, on the contrary, that information about illocutionary force and conversion of the condition belongs in the grammar, particularly in its account of semantic structure. The reason for this assumption is that such information derives in many cases as much from syntactic structure as does information about propositional content. For example, the request force of an interrogative or imperative or of a present tense sentence with a first person subject and a main verb such as "request" is clearly derivative from the meaning associated with these sentential moods or the meaning of such a verb (as contrasted with "promise," "warn," etc.) Also, the conversion of the condition of a proposition expressed by a sentence whose main verb is "promise" is different in one way from the conversion of the condition of a proposition expressed by a sentence whose main verb is "apologize" and in another way from the conversion in the case of a sentence whose main verb is "warn," but each such difference is inherent in the lexical senses of these verbs. Moreover, by taking such information to be part of the meaning of the appropriate lexical items and to effect propositional form by virtue of the compositional construction of propositional form from the meanings of lexical items, we can explain how in cases like (4.73) and (4.76) the same piece of information, e.g., the lexical information that the person to whom a promise is made wants what he is promised (see Searle (1969, p. 58)), can be a condition on the occurrence of the speech act in one case and part of a truth condition in the other. Therefore, our position so far follows Searle's (1969) suggestion that rules for performing a speech act like promising "attach to some output of the combinatorial operations of the semantic component" (p. 64).

On the other hand, there is speech act information that does not belong to semantic theory but to some theory beyond grammar. To see this, let us consider the viewpoint of the linguist and that of the speech act theorist. The linguist looks at a communication situation rather selectively. His attention focuses on the grammatical structure of the sentence type that the speaker's utterance exemplifies. He is concerned to explicate this structure in terms of a theory about the linguistic competence which the participants in the situation share by virtue of being able to speak the same language. The speech act theorist has a broader viewpoint. He focuses on the speech act that occurs when the speaker utters an appropriate sentence in an appropriate context. Thus, he must take account of not only grammar but also a wide range of other factors that contribute to the performance of the act. It is clear that the same sentence can be used to perform different illocutionary acts and that different sentences can be used to perform the same illocutionary act, depending on such nongrammatical factors as the speaker's and hearer's knowledge of each other's intentions, their beliefs, and their morals. Accordingly, one would expect that a theory of speech acts has to take account of any regularities in the way such nongrammatical factors bring about the occurrence of different illocutionary acts in connection with utterances of the same sentence or the occurrence of the same illocutionary act in connection with utterances of different sentences.

For example, of the rules that Searle (1965) gives for the function-indicating device of promising, some seem to be part of the grammar's account of the propositional type of sentences (e.g., the main verb is "promise," the subject is first person, and the tense is present), while other rules seem to be part of an independent theory of speech act performance. Thus, one of Searle's rules says that a condition on the illocutionary act of promising is that the sentence be uttered only if it is not obvious to both speaker and hearer(s) that the speaker will perform the promised act in the normal course of events. This rule does not seem to derive from any aspect of the grammar of the sentences in question, but rather seems a consequence of a more general convention about when actions are unnecessary. We find similar results in connection with acts of communicating information (see Chapter 8, Section 4), warning, ordering, etc. As a consequence of such a convention, Searle's rule seems to formulate a condition under which the hearer(s) may assume that the speaker is communicating the proposition expressed by the sentence he used or performing the illocutionary act normally associated with the use of the sentence. If the condition is violated, the hearer(s) may assume that some special interpretation is called for. Consider the case where someone, exasperated by the superfluity of his friend's praise for the joys of camping in the White Mountains, delivered while they are preparing to go camping there, finally says to the friend, "I promise to go camping in the White Mountains." Here the utterance is not a performance of the illocutionary act of promising. It is simply a way of telling the friend to shut up.

Searle's rules 1, 2, and 5 seem to be part of the grammar's account of the propositional type of the sentences in question, while his rules 3 and 4 seem to be part of a theory of speech act performance that goes beyond the contribution of grammar to speech acts. In the final chapter of this book, I will discuss Grice's theory of conversational implicature, which I take to be a theory of the latter sort and to be the proper place to state rules like Searle's rules 3 and 4. If this is so, speech act theory is a hybrid, composed of two parts, one of which naturally belongs to semantic theory and the other to some more encompassing pragmatic theory like Grice's.

4.   Antonymy and negation

Our taxonomy of types of propositions does not include categories for negative and affirmative propositions. In this we follow Frege (1952c):

> For logic at any rate such a distinction [between affirmative and negative thoughts] is wholly unnecessary; its ground must be sought outside logic. I know of no logical principle whose verbal expression makes it necessary, or even preferable, to use these terms. In any science in which it is a question of conformity to laws, the thing that must always be asked is: What technical expressions are necessary, or at least useful, in order to give precise expression to the laws of this science? What does not stand this test cometh of evil.
>
> What is more, it is by no means easy to state what is a negative judgment (thought). Consider the sentences "Christ is immortal," "Christ lives forever," "Christ is not immortal," "Christ is mortal," "Christ does not live forever." Now which of the thoughts we have here is affirmative, which negative? (p. 125)

In excluding the distinction between affirmative and negative propositions from our account of propositional types, we do not, of course, deny the existence of negative and positive *sentences*. The absence of such a distinction among propositions extends the distinction between syntax and semantics (see Section 1 of Chapter 8) by exhibiting relevant differences between corresponding syntactic and semantic objects.

Philosophers and logicians who accept the notion of logical form based on the distinction between the logical and extra-logical (or descriptive) vocabularies treat negation as a feature of the logical vocabulary somehow apart from negative elements in the meaning of extra-logical terms and accept the doctrine that validity is a function of logical form in the narrow sense in which it is determined by logical particles. They thus commit themselves to the existence of differences among inferences corresponding to this distinction in treatment. But examples like those in (4.79)–(4.81) clearly establish the incorrectness of this implication.

(4.79)　(a) Christ lives forever
　　　　(b) Christ does not live forever
　　　　(c) Christ is mortal

(4.80)　(a) The design of the robot is perfect
　　　　(b) The design of the robot is not perfect
　　　　(c) The design of the robot is flawed

(4.81)　(a) John became shorter last year
　　　　(b) John did not become shorter last year
　　　　(c) John's height increased or stayed the same last year

　　　　In each of these cases, (b) and (c) are negations of (a)—just as (a) is a negation of (b) and (c)—but (b) and (c) are themselves synonymous. Thus, extra-logical terms in a sentence can contribute to its logical form in exactly the same way as logical terms. There are no differences among inferences corresponding to the distinction the aforementioned philosophers and logicians have to make between cases (b) and (c).
　　　　Conceptions of negation developed by such philosophers and logicians usually are asked to meet only the condition of adequacy that negations of a true statement are false and negations of a false statement are true (i.e., for any pair of determinate propositions which are negations of each other, one is true and the other false). Our conception of negation, which underlies the apparatus of the antonymy operator to be discussed in this section, is developed to meet the further condition that the reading of the negation of a sentence S_i, say S_j, must represent S_j as having the same sense as any sentence synonymous with S_j: for example, the readings of the (b) and (c) cases in (4.79)–(4.81) must be identical. This condition of adequacy is simply a consequence of the fact that semantic structure, and hence all semantic properties and relations of sentences, is determined by the compositional combination of the senses of the constituents out of which sentences are built.
　　　　Given these considerations, the apparatus introduced into semantic theory to represent the contribution of the particle "not" to the logical form of a sentence (as in the (b) cases of (4.79)–(4.81)) is required also to present the semantic contribution of negative elements in the meaning of items from the so-called extra-logical vocabulary (as in the (c) cases of (4.79)–(4.81)). It is exactly for such a uniform treatment of negation that the antonymy operator is intended, that is, it is to be used, without distinction, both as a means of defining "not," "no," negative prefixes and suffixes, etc., and as a means of specifying the incompatibility relations among semantic elements into which the senses of words decompose.
　　　　Such incompatibility relations are often identified lexicologically as *antonymic relations*. But the lexicologic term *antonym* is a broad cover term, spanning a range of cases that includes examples falling into a number of distinct logical categories. Among the cases that dictionaries (of the ordinary sort) call antonyms, we find at least the types in (4.82).

(4.82)   (a) CONTRADICTORIES: perfect / flawed, imperfect
                               mortal / immortal
                               alive / dead

         (b) CONTRARIES: superior / inferior
                               rich / poor
                               warm / cool
                               parsimonious / prodigal
                               destitute / opulent

         (c) CONVERSES: husband / wife
                               taller / shorter
                               buy / sell
                               employer / employee

All three types are, broadly, antonyms in that their senses are so opposed that the members of a pair of antonyms are mutually exclusive in their application (to the same thing, at the same time, and in the same respect). *Contradictories*, however, admit of no possibility between them. They divide a common range of significance that is exhaustive as well as mutually exclusive. *Contraries*, on the other hand, admit of possibilities between and beyond them. They mark out regions on their range of significance that are incompatible but do not jointly cover the whole range. *Converses* are taken up in Chapter 7, and thus I will not discuss them here.

The contraries might be divided into *extreme contraries* and *local contraries*. Extreme contraries are cases where the language admits no greater divergence, with respect to the property in question, than is expressed by the terms. They are diametrical opposites, as, for example, "parsimonious" and "prodigal," "destitute" and "opulent." Local contraries are cases where opposition occurs between an extreme and some nonextreme, such as "destitute" and "comfortable," or between two nonextremes, such as "warm" and "cool." Furthermore, these cases can be overlapping or disjoint, as can be seen from a comparison of "moist" and "wet" with "needy" and "comfortable." These are obviously semantic relations that call for explication, but we shall not attempt to offer definitions here.

The notion of a range of significance requires some comment. Intuitively, we understand this notion as the domain picked out by the common component in the senses of an n-tuple of antonymous constituents. For example, the antonymous words "male" and "female" have senses that share the component 'bodily organs for the function of reproduction', the ascription of "male" saying that the function is begetting offspring and the ascription of "female" saying that the function is bearing offspring; the antonymous words "rich" and "poor" have senses that share the semantic component 'the possessions one has already or can obtain with one's present resources', the ascription of "rich" saying that such possessions are well in excess of what is needed for normal subsistence and the ascription of "poor" saying that such possessions are well below what is needed for normal subsistence. This suggests that any n expressions that form an antonymous n-tuple will have the same range of significance but will make incompatible ascriptions to objects in the domain, while n-tuples of different antonymous expressions can have different ranges. It was to account for these relations that we introduced the conceptual machinery for constructing antonymous n-tuples of semantic markers, where a particular antonymous n-tuple of semantic markers is to represent mutually incompatible predictions over a fixed domain by virtue of having the formal structure specified in (2.50). Thus, in an antonymous n-tuple of semantic markers, the common base symbol represents the common range of significance, and the differing superscripts represent the incompatible ascriptions within the domain. In this manner, the formal structure of semantic markers given in the theoretical vocabulary of semantic theory makes it possible to group them mechanically into antonymous n-tuples, as is required for applying the definitions of semantic properties and relations.

It is clear from the discussion of the examples "male"/"female" and "rich"/"poor" that the base symbol and the superscript of any antonymous n-tuple can be semantic markers of any degree of internal complexity. Thus, although at an earlier point in our discussion we represented the concepts of maleness and femaleness by '(S^m)' and '(S^f)', a deeper analysis would take the form '(Possesses bodily organs$^{\text{(Function: Begetting offspring)}}$)' and '(Possesses bodily organs $^{\text{(Function: Bearing offspring)}}$)', respectively. A superficial analysis such as our earlier one must be considered a stage in the process of arriving at a deeper, more sophisticated analysis.

To obtain a reading for a negative sentence, we will develop a definition of an operator that we refer to as the *antonymy operator*, symbolized '$A/\ldots$', where the operand, indicated by the dots, is a reading and the operation converts the operand into another reading whose form is determined by the clauses in the definition of the antonymy operator. The readings for negative constituents, e.g., "not," will be formulated out of the antonymy operator.

One finds considerable conflict of intuitions on the part of speakers when they make judgments about the proper interpretation of negative sentences such as those in (4.83):

(4.83)   (a) The table is not blue
              (b) The boy does not like the girl

Some speakers judge that (4.83a) means that the table in question is some color other than blue and that (4.83b) means that the boy has either an aversion to the girl or an attitude of indifference toward her. Other speakers judge the former sentence to mean that the table belongs to the complement of the set of blue things, that is, is either some other color or is colorless, and judge the latter to mean that the girl is in the complement of the set of things that the boy likes, that is, is either something he dislikes, something he is indifferent to, or simply something toward which he has no attitude whatever. Moreover, it is difficult to find a general argument that decides this issue one way or the other. In this situation, then, it is wise not to formulate semantic theory to favor one set of intuitions. Thus, the first clause in the definition of the antonymy operator can be either rule (a) or (b) of (4.84), where $(M^{(\alpha_1)})$, $(M^{(\alpha_2)})$, $\ldots$, $(M^{(\alpha_n)})$ is the full antonymous n-tuple to which the operand, $(M^{(\alpha_i)})$, belongs, where $A/A(M^{(\alpha_i)}) = (M^{(\alpha_i)})$, and where $A/(M)$ will be specified directly:

(4.84) (a) $A/(M^{(\alpha_i)})$ for $1 \leq i \leq n = (M^{(\alpha_1)}) \vee (M^{(\alpha_2)}) \vee \ldots \vee (M^{(\alpha_{i-1})})$
$\vee (M^{(\alpha_{i+1})}) \vee \ldots \vee (M^{(\alpha_n)})$
     (b) $A/(M^{(\alpha_i)})$ for $1 \leq i \leq n = (M^{(\alpha_1)}) \vee (M^{(\alpha_2)}) \vee \ldots \vee (M^{(\alpha_{i-1})})$
$\vee (M^{(\alpha_{i+1})}) \vee \ldots \vee (M^{(\alpha_n)}) \vee A/(M)$

We call the result of this operation a *complex semantic marker* and note that complex semantic markers function exactly like ordinary semantic markers with respect to their behavior under projection, that is, when they are combined with other readings to form derived readings.

We observe now that, for the purposes of the definitions of contradiction and so on in (2.52)–(2.57), we take the condition that (M_i) and (M_j) be distinct members of the same antonymous n-tuple of semantic markers to be satisfied also if it is the case that one is of the form $(M^{(\alpha_i)})$ and the other has the form of the right-hand side of (a) or (b) of (4.84).

Case (b) of (4.84) is not completely specified as yet, since '$A/(M)$' is not determined. To take care of this, we give the rule (4.85):

(4.85) $A/(M) = (M^{(-)})$

Here '(M)' is to be understood as an abbreviation for '$(M^{(+)})$' and the symbol '$(-)$' is to be understood as the logical complement of (M) within the superset determined by the semantic markers in the selection restriction for the reading in which '(M)' appears. This will be referred to as the *selected complement*. The reason for using the notion of selected complement rather than simply logical complement is that both the sentence "The stick and the stone agreed on all issues of public policy" and the sentence "The stick and the stone did not agree on all (any) issues of public policy" are regarded as semantically anomalous. Thus, we take the selection restriction common to the verb phrase with the negative constituent and the verb phrase without it to determine the domain with respect to which complementation is performed.

It is important to note that rule (4.85) would be required even if the data unequivocally established (4.84a). Thus, let us assume we can adopt (4.84a) and go on to consider the role that (4.85) plays as a clause of the definition of the antonymy operator.

Each of the sentences (4.79b), (4.80b), and (4.81b) will be interpreted as saying that the object(s) to which its subject refers belong to the (selected) complement of the set picked out by the sense of the verb phrase in the corresponding sentence in (a). But this will be a consequence of the fact that the set picked out by the reading of the verb phrase *is* the selected complement of the sense of the verb phrase in the corresponding (a) sentence. This reading is the reading of the verb phrase in the corresponding sentence in (c). For example, (4.80c) says that the object to which its subject refers is in the set of flawed things, and the set of flawed things is the set of things in the selected complement of the set of perfect things (and hence the synonymy with (4.80b).

However, not all semantic markers will be written in the form '$(M^{(\alpha_i)})$'. Many will not have superscripts that represent the concepts that are minimally incompatible with them. Such semantic markers may, nevertheless, be or be part of the reading of some expression in the language, and such an expression may be in the scope of a negative in a sentence. Accordingly, semantic markers that do not belong to an antonymous n-tuple can be in the range of the antonymy operator, and it is for just such cases that (4.85) will be required even if (4.84b) is ultimately rejected.

Consider the sentence (4.86):

(4.86)   The store is not a pizzeria

The reading of "a pizzeria" is a case in point. The semantic marker(s) that represent the definitional features of "pizza" cannot be supposed to belong to an antonymous n-tuple whose other members each represent the definitional properties of some other commodity whose sale characterizes a unique type of store and where the members of this n-tuple are exhaustive (i.e., every type of store falls under one of these concepts). Nonetheless, the reading of a sentence like (4.86) must somehow be obtained as a function of the application of the antonymy operator to the reading of "a pizzeria." Moreover, the reading of (4.86) will have to represent the proposition that says that the store is in the selected complement of the class of things that are pizzerias. Rule (4.85) gives such a reading. The derived reading that results from applying clause (4.85) of the reading for "not" to the reading of "a pizzeria" will say that whatever falls under the concept represented by this derived reading is in the selected complement of the set of things falling under the concept represented by the reading of "a pizzeria."

The difference between cases to which (4.85) applies and cases to which the other clauses of the definition of the antonymy operator apply is that in the former the derived readings specify only the bare fact of incompatibility while in the latter the derived readings specify the nature of the incompatibility. This is to say, in effect, that (4.85) groups semantic markers into antonymous n-tuples which are not so grouped in the statement of the theoretical vocabulary for semantic theory because the information they represent does not itself suffice to determine a range of incompatibility.

The introduction of the clause (4.85) to the definition of the antonymy operator requires that we say something about the treatment of evaluation semantic markers.[20] The use of the symbols '$(+)$' and '$(-)$' with regard to (4.85) might cause some confusion in connection with the same symbols employed in earlier works in stating the manner in which the senses of "good" and "bad" operate. Consider, for example, the sentences in (4.87):

(4.87)   (a) This is a watch
         (b) This is a good watch

---

[20] See Katz (1964c; 1966, pp. 283–317).

Since we are assuming $(M) = (M^{(+)})$, there might be some question as to whether (a) and (b) of (4.87) are predicted to be synonymous. It might be supposed that to avoid this prediction we should take steps to differentiate the symbols '$(+)$' and '$(-)$' employed in the readings of " good " and " bad " from the symbols '$(+)$' and '$(-)$' used in connection with (4.85). But we will not do this because the coincidence of symbols here suggests that, by taking both cases to be employments of the same symbols, a new generalization can be stated, namely, that " good " and " bad " are the same cases of non-negative and negative form that we encounter with ordinary negations. Thus, by not differentiating two sets of plus and minus signs, we can bring the treatment of the meaning of sentences containing " good " and " bad " under our treatment of negation.

There is, fortunately, a simple notational change that permits us to state this desired generalization and also to avoid the undesirable consequence of predicting that (a) and (b) of (4.87) are synonymous. In Katz (1964c; 1966) there was a contextual rule that took '$(+)$' and '$(-)$' from the readings of " good " and " bad " and incorporated them into an evaluation semantic marker in the reading of a noun. Here, instead, we write an evaluation semantic marker in the form (4.88):

(4.88) $(\text{Eval}_x : (\ )^{\langle (+) \vee (-) \rangle \begin{subarray}{c} [\gamma] \\ X \end{subarray}})$

In (4.88) the categorized variable occurs as a superscript of the semantic marker that expresses the standard of evaluation in question. The function γ in the square brackets defines the modification relation (i.e., the relation that an adjective bears to its nominal head, that an adverb bears to its verbal head, etc.). The selection restriction is that the substitution of a reading for the variable can be made on the condition that the reading contains either the semantic marker '$(+)$' or the semantic marker '$(-)$'. This specification removes any appearance of a duplication of the plus-minus symbolism, states the semantic generalization that relates evaluation with " good " and " bad " to ordinary non-negativeness and negativeness, and, furthermore, avoids a prediction that (a) and (b) of (4.87) are synonymous. The reading for the predicate nominal in (4.87a) will now be as in (4.89):

(4.89) (Physical) (Object), (Artifact) ... ( ),

(Eval$_{\text{use}}$: (Keeps time reliably under normal conditions)$^{\langle (+) \vee (-) \rangle \begin{subarray}{c} [\gamma] \\ X \end{subarray}}$)

The reading for the predicate nominal in (4.87b) will be the same as (4.89) but with the superscript variable replaced by '$(+)$'.

We also wish to account for the semantic properties and relations of the sentences in (4.90):

(4.90) (a) This is not a watch
      (b) This is a bad watch
      (c) This is not a good watch
      (d) This is not a bad watch

We take it that (b) and (c) of (4.90) are synonymous and that (d) is synonymous with (4.87b) on a sense. We will not consider here the possible senses of (c) and (d) of (4.90) represented by (4.91) and (4.92), respectively:

(4.91)   This is not such a good watch (but it is not such a bad one, either)

(4.92)   This is not such a bad watch (but it is not such a good one, either)

The reading for (b) of (4.90) is straightforward. It will be the same as that for (4.89) except that the categorized variable appearing in the superscript on the semantic marker specifying the use of a watch will be replaced by '$(-)$'. Thus, (4.87a) will be represented as saying that the thing referred to is an artifact that is evaluated on the basis of its ability to keep time reliably under normal conditions, (4.87b) will be represented as saying that the thing referred to is adequate to serve this use, and (4.90b) will be represented as saying that the thing referred to is not adequate to serve this use. To obtain the reading for (4.90a), we bring in here the principle governing the conversion of a set of semantic markers into its antonymous form. In previous studies, this principle was formulated as part of the lexical definition for the constituent 'Neg', but now we shall include it as a clause in the definition of the antonymy operator, where it more naturally belongs. Thus, we have (4.93) and (4.94):

(4.93) $A/\{(M_1), \ldots, (M_k)\} = \{A/(M_1) \vee \ldots \vee A/(M_k)\}$

(4.94) $A/\{A/(M_1) \vee \ldots \vee A/(M_k)\} = \{(M_1), \ldots, (M_k)\}$

By virtue of the operation of the reading for 'Neg' in (4.90a), which includes (4.93) because it is given in terms of the antonymy operator, the reading will say that the thing referred to is either not physical or not an object or not an artifact or . . . or not something evaluated on the basis of its reliability in keeping time under normal conditions, that is, it lacks at least one of the definitional features of the word "watch."

In order to predict the fact that (c) and (d) of (4.90) are synonymous with (4.90b) and (4.87b), respectively, the members of the former pair must have the same reading and the members of the latter pair must have the same reading. This can be obtained by adding the further condition to (4.85) that when '(M)' is '$(+)$' the result of the operation is '$(-)$' and when '(M)' is '$(-)$' the result is '$(+)$', and by so specifying the scope of negation in the verb phrase that the clauses of the antonymy operator in the reading of the constituent 'Neg' apply only to the verb phrase of the relative from which the preposed adjective comes. The addition to (4.85) is a natural way of completing this clause. The latter specification on the scope of negation simply reflects a quite general fact about the meaning of sentences in which negation applies to a constituent with a modifier. Consider the sentences in (4.95):

(4.95)   (a) The man is not a *trustworthy* congressman
         (b) He is not a man *who cares for humanity*
         (c) She doesn't like ice cream *that has nuts*
         (d) We will not support an *arbitrarily chosen* candidate
         (e) The boy is not running *fast*

In each of these cases, it is the sense of the modifier alone (i.e., the italicized constituent) that the negation operates on. The first of these sentences does not deny that the individual in question is a congressman, the second does not deny that the individual is a man, the third does not deny that the individual likes ice cream, and so on. If the scope of negation is so specified that it operates on the verb phrase of such relative clauses (if there are any, otherwise on the verb phrase in whose auxiliary the occurrence of " not " appears), then the reading of " good " in (4.90c) will be converted to '(−)' and the reading of "bad" in (4.90d) will be converted to '(+)'. Consequently, the former will receive the same reading as (4.90b) and the latter will receive the same reading as (4.87b).

A further supplement to the definition of the antonymy operator is required for the cases where it must apply inside the structure of compound semantic markers, that is, semantic markers that contain other semantic markers as components of their internal organization. Previously, this feature had been left out of the discussion of the antonymy operator because very little had been determined about the structure of compound semantic markers. Even now we have far less information about this important matter than we require. Thus, we shall attempt only a partial characterization of this feature of the operation of negation. Its completion will be left as a matter for further investigation into the nature of compound semantic markers.

Consider the reading for the verb "chase" presented in (3.61), which has the form (4.96):

(4.96)

The parenthesization marked "2" indicates that the individual(s) referred to by the reading that is the value of the categorized variable ' $\begin{smallmatrix} [NP, S] \\ X \\ \langle \, \rangle \end{smallmatrix}$ ' engages in an activity. The parenthesization marked "3," which has the parenthesizations marked " 4," " 5," and " 7 " as components, indicates that this activity is physical, involves movement, and is purposeful. The parenthesizations marked " 5 " and " 6 " indicate that the movement involved is fast and is guided in its course by the trajectory of the object(s) chased. The parenthesizations marked " 7 " and " 8 " indicate that the purpose of the activity is to catch the individual(s) being followed, i.e., what is referred to by the value of ' $\underset{\langle\ \rangle}{\overset{[\text{NP, VP, PP, S}]}{X}}$ '. The heavy parentheses enclosing the categorized variables in (4.96) will be explained directly.

This information can be thought of as assuming the form it would take were one summarizing the knowledge he had acquired in the course of a game of Twenty Questions: someone or some animal is engaged in an activity; the activity is physical, it involves movement which is fast and which takes the form of following something, and it has a purpose, which is to catch whomever or whatever is being pursued. The point of the parenthesization is to represent what is predicated and what it is predicated of. The entire complex configuration enclosed by the parentheses numbered " 3 " represents a second-order predicate on the predicate that is represented by " (a)," which itself is a predicate of individuals, *viz.*, of the things that satisfy the condition given by the reading that will be the value of the variable inside the outermost heavy parentheses. The application of " (a) " by itself to the reading that is the value of this variable would say that these things are engaged in some type of activity, and the application of " (b) " by itself would say that this activity is of a physical type (as opposed to, say, a mental one, such as thinking). Accordingly, the parenthesization that relates " (c) " to " (b)," " (d) " and " (e) " to " (b)," and so on represents higher order predictions whereby certain concepts qualify others by specifying them further.[21]

By itself (4.96) does not represent the full semantic structure of the sense of " chase." The semantic markers (a)–(g) do not, of course, reflect the rich internal structure of the concepts 'activity', 'physical', etc. We fully expect that such internal structure will be uncovered as a result of further work in semantic analysis and that ultimately the semantic markers listed here will be replaced by others that formally exhibit the full structure of the concepts for which they stand. Of special interest is the formal structure of the semantic markers that must eventually replace '(Activity)' and '(Movement)'. As things stand now, there is no indication that the sense of " chase " expresses a relation among a chaser, a chasee, a distance covered in the chase, and a time at which the chase took place.

To account for such facts, we suggest that '(Activity)' and '(Movement)' will eventually be replaced by semantic markers such as (4.97) and (4.98), respectively, where the categorization of the variables in (4.97) is given in terms of grammatical relations between the tense constituent and the verb within the same predicate phrase and between temporal adverbials and the verb within the

---

[21] Instead of such parenthesization, we could use the standard notation of predicate calculi (see Bierwisch (1969)). In certain cases, however, the parenthesis notation far better reflects the structure of the complex concepts (e.g., the representation of processes, discussed in Chapter 7), and, in general, the parenthesis notation is more convenient for the statement of rules.

same predicate phrase[22] and the categorization of the variables in (4.98) is given in terms of grammatical relations between locative adverbials and the verb within the same predicate phrase:

(4.97)   (Performs a sequence of related acts from $\begin{smallmatrix} [\ ] \\ X \\ \langle\ \rangle \end{smallmatrix}$ to $\begin{smallmatrix} [\ ] \\ X \\ \langle\ \rangle \end{smallmatrix}$)

(4.98)   (Covers the distance from $\begin{smallmatrix} [\ ] \\ X \\ \langle\ \rangle \end{smallmatrix}$ to $\begin{smallmatrix} [\ ] \\ X \\ \langle\ \rangle \end{smallmatrix}$)

The "heavy parentheses" '**(**' and '**)**' that enclose the categorized variables in (4.96) are, like the "double parentheses" of the preceding section, a notational convention for representing the structural organization of propositions. These parentheses are used in a reading to distinguish the argument places of a predicate that constitute referential positions from those that do not (e.g., from those that constitute opaque contexts—see Section 3 of Chapter 6). Thus, the configuration in (4.96) represents a predicate whose places, indicated by the categorized variables, are inherently transparent or referential contexts, i.e., ones whose transparency is a lexical feature of the verb—"chase" in this case—that expresses the predicate. Cases where categorized variables are not enclosed by heavy parentheses, so as to indicate a lexically determined opaque context, are the variables categorized for the 'direct-object-of' relation appearing in verbs like "imagine" or "want."
Readings that appear inside a pair of heavy parentheses represent clauses of the presupposition while readings that do not appear inside such parentheses, whether arguments of a predicate or components of a predicate's internal structure, represent parts of the condition. This being so, we can take a step toward specifying the symbol 'R*' in definitions (4.65) and (4.66) and thus toward completing the account of determinability. We stipulate that the range of 'R*' includes any sub-reading in the reading of a proposition which occurs inside a pair of heavy parentheses. We leave open the question of whether the range of 'R*' will have to include other kinds of presuppositional conditions. Thus we offer no definition of the notion 'presupposition' and leave incomplete the definitions of determinacy and indeterminacy in (4.43) and (4.44).
The introduction of heavy parentheses was delayed until this point since here the notational device can be independently justified in terms of its utility in establishing a suitable domain for the operation of the antonymy operator. The distinction between heavy and standard parentheses (and between these and double parentheses), which marks the distinction between components of the presupposition and the truth conditions of assertive propositions, permits us to add a further clause to the definition of the antonymy operator, expressing the generalization, discussed in Section 2 of this chapter, that negation does not affect the presupposition of a proposition. Clause (4.99) states this generalization and thus guarantees

---

[22] These relations and the readings of constituents expressing temporal information will be discussed in some detail in Chapter 7.

that the presupposition of a proposition and its negation are the same:

(4.99) $A/\{(M_1), (M_2), \ldots, \mathbf{(M}_i\mathbf{)}, \ldots, (M_n)\}$
          $= \{\mathbf{(M}_i\mathbf{)}, A/(M_1), (M_2), \ldots, (M_{i-1}), (M_{i+1}), (M_n)\}$

Another way in which parenthesization creates a suitable domain for the antonymy operator can be seen when we consider the operation that should be performed if an instance of (4.96) is in the scope of an occurrence of the antonymy operator. On the basis of clause (4.93), we have already taken care of cases where configurations of the form '$((d)(e))$' fall within the scope of the antonomy operator: $A/((d)(e)) = (A/(d) \lor A/(e))$. Now we require the introduction of a clause in the definition of the antonymy operator for the case of configurations of the form '$A/((f)((g)))$'. We therefore add (4.100):

(4.100) $A/((M_i)((M_j))) = (A/(M_i) \lor ((M_i) (A/(M_j))))$

We assume, of course, $A/(A/(M_i) \lor ((M_i) (A/(M_j)))) = (A/((M_i)((M_j))))$.
       Let us now apply clause (4.100) in connection with the component semantic marker '$((f)((g)))$' of (4.96). This case expresses another one of the possibilities for a statement that someone is chasing someone else to be false, namely, either these is no purpose to the former person's activity or there is a purpose but it is not that of catching the latter person (e.g., the purpose might be to stay exactly ten feet behind, say, to win a game they are playing).
       Together, clauses (4.93) and (4.100) enable us to handle cases of configurations of the form '$((c)((d)(e)))$' in the scope of the antonymy operator. Clause (4.100) says that $A/((c)((d)(e)))$ is $(A/(c) \lor ((c) (A/((d)(e)))))$ and (4.93) says that the second disjunct is $((c) (A/(d) \lor A/(e)))$.
       Consider the sentence in (4.101):

(4.101)   John is not chasing Bill

This calls for an application of the antonymy operator whose scope is the full reading of "chase" (with its categorized variables replaced by appropriate readings from the subject and object). The reading of (4.101) that results from this application represents the truth conditions of the proposition expressed by (4.101) as follows: either John is not engaged in an activity at the specified time and place or, if he is, then that activity is not physical, movement, and purposeful, or, if it is, then either the movement is not both fast and following (of Bill) or the purpose of the activity is something other than to catch Bill.[23]

---

[23] The specification of the antonymy operator is not complete. As we shall see in Chapter 7, it will be necessary to make provision for an infinite set of antonymous semantic markers. This complication, however, is best left until we reach the point in our discussion where we can utilize empirical considerations to motivate so broadening the treatment of antonymous n-tuples.

The dictionary entry for 'Neg' will be a rule which applies the antonymy operator to readings in its range. I shall not try to construct the actual entry because too little is known about the syntactic and semantic considerations that determine the proper range. Instead, I will deal with some of these considerations themselves and suggest some of the main problems that lie in the way of a full statement of the rule for applying the antonymy operator to appropriate readings of constituents to which 'Neg' is grammatically related.

Sentential negations can be formed by a variety of different syntactic devices. For example, besides introducing an occurrence of "not" in the usual position in the predicate phrase of a sentence, we can form negations by embedding a sentence within such frames as those in (4.102):

(4.102)　(a)　It is not true that ——
　　　　　(b)　That —— is not true
　　　　　(c)　"——" is not true
　　　　　(d)　"——" is materially equivalent to something not true

However, we should be careful to distinguish the cases in (4.102) from those in (4.103):

(4.103)　(a)　It is false that ——
　　　　　(b)　That —— is false
　　　　　(c)　"——" is false
　　　　　(d)　"——" is materially equivalent to something false

Each of the cases in (4.102) is a paraphrase of each of the others and each of the cases in (4.103) is a paraphrase of each of the others. But corresponding cases from (4.102) and (4.103)—e.g., (4.102a) and (4.103a)—are not synonymous.[24]

Returning now to forms of negative sentences, it is clear that negative simple sentences in English most commonly have "not" after the copula or before the verb, as illustrated in (4.104):

(4.104)　(a)　All baseballs are not new
　　　　　(b)　Both teams did not win their games
　　　　　(c)　Many did not hear the lecture
　　　　　(d)　Much blood was not spilled
　　　　　(e)　Every coin is not silver

The sentences in (4.104) are ambiguous, however, having one sense on which they are synonymous with their counterparts in (4.105) and another on which they are not.

---

[24] For example, substitute "Who loves everyone?" in both (4.102c) and (4.103c). I am indebted to H. G. Herzberger for clarification of this distinction.

(4.105) (a) It is not true that all baseballs are new
        (b) It is not true that both teams won their games
        (c) It is not true that many heard the lecture
        (d) It is not true that much blood was spilled
        (e) It is not true that every coin is silver

For example, (4.104a) can be read as saying that the class of baseballs is not composed only of new ones (cf. "All that glitters is not gold") and also as saying that the class of baseballs contains only non-new ones (cf. "All dictators are not human"). On the former sense, such sentences are also synonymous with those in (4.106):

(4.106) (a) Not all baseballs are new
        (b) Not both teams won their games
        (c) Not many heard the lecture
        (d) Not much blood was spilled
        (e) Not every coin is silver

The grammar of English must account for these synonymy relations, and here, as in other cases, there are two ways in which this may be done. One way is to construct base rules so that the underlying phrase markers for the sentences in question contain the same constituents with the same grammatical relations among them. The other way is to construct lexical readings for the morphemes of the sentences such that the operation of the projection rule results in the same readings, even though the constituents and the grammatical relations among them differ to a certain extent. On the first approach, we must suppose that on the sense where (4.104a), (4.105a), and (4.106a) are synonymous, the occurrence of 'Neg' in the underlying phrase markers has the same range in each case. Were we in possession of an adequate statement of the grammatical relation that specifies this range, it would then be a relatively easy matter to formally define sentential negation in terms of a component of the lexical reading for 'Neg'. This component would simply say that the antonymy operator applies to the part of the reading of the constituent to which 'Neg' bears the grammatical relation that is not within heavy parentheses. On the second approach, the situation is more complicated. We must suppose that the occurrence of 'Neg' in the underlying phrase markers for the synonymous sentences in question does not have the same range. We must determine the grammatical relation that specifies the range in each different case, and we must then formulate appropriate components of the lexical reading for 'Neg'. But here we encounter the first of the problems standing in the way of a full statement of the dictionary entry for 'Neg', namely, we do not have a sufficiently reliable syntactic treatment of the nature of the structures in underlying phrase markers where 'Neg' occurs.

    One might think that the first way could be made to work for cases like (4.104a) and (4.106a) but that there is little hope for carrying it over to cases like (4.105a). That is, it would seem that in the latter case 'Neg' must occur as a constituent of a higher sentence that refers to an embedded sentence while in the former case 'Neg' occurs in a nonembedded sentence that is otherwise the same as the embedded sentence. From this, one would conclude that the occurrences of 'Neg' in (4.105a), on the one hand, and (4.104a) and (4.106a), on the other, must enter into different grammatical relations. But there is a line of thinking on the part of some recent grammarians that would call this apparently obvious assumption into question.[25]

Even with an adequate account of the grammatical relation(s) into which 'Neg' enters in the cases considered thus far, there would still remain major gaps in syntactic theory to cause problems. For example, as noted earlier, the range of 'Neg' in sentences like (4.95a–e), that is, sentences in which the reading in the scope of 'Neg' contains a reading that has been derived from a reading of a modifier and a reading for its head, is just the reading of the modifier. To handle this complexity, we would require a formulation of the modifier-head relation in syntactic theory. Needless to say, we are still rather far from having a definition of this important grammatical relation.

Another problem has to do with the identification of negative forms by the criterion that they are derived from deeper constituents with an occurrence of 'Neg' in them. The difficulty here is that in very many instances the syntactic analysis of such cases is in error. Even Klima's (1964) careful treatment of such forms contains a number of mistakes. For example, on his account forms like "few" and "little" are derived, respectively, from constituents like 'Neg + "many"' and 'Neg + "much,"' and so they are regarded as negative. But such an analysis must be incorrect, since it implies that (4.107) and (4.108) are inconsistent sentences, which clearly they are not:

(4.107) A moderate amount of fat in the diet is better than much or little fat

(4.108) Don't buy just a few donuts and don't buy many, but get something in between

It would not be difficult to extend significantly this list of problems standing in the way of a complete dictionary entry for 'Neg', especially considering the wide variety of constructions into which negation can enter and the present very early stage of research in generative grammar. The problems already mentioned are, I believe, enough to indicate the sort of obstacles that need to be overcome by further research in syntax and semantics.

5. Analyticity and entailment

With the richer apparatus for representing propositional form we now have at our disposal, we are in a position to extend and refine the definitions for 'analyticity', 'contradictoriness', 'syntheticity', 'entailment', etc., given in earlier publications and in Chapter 2.

[25] I have in mind the extensive use of higher sentence structures to derive surface constituents which is characteristic of the analyses of grammarians who work within the framework of generative semantics (see Chapter 8).

In Katz (1966, pp. 207–210), separate definitions of these semantic properties and relations were given for copulative and noncopulative sentences, i.e., for sentences generated by the 'Copula-Predicate' option in the phrase structure rules (3.79), on the one hand, and for sentences generated by the 'Verb-...' option, on the other. This falsely suggested that in some sense the notions of analyticity, contradictoriness, and syntheticity are different for these different types of sentences. Consider, in this regard, the pairs of sentences in (4.109), (4.110), and (4.111):

(4.109) (a) Cows are female
       (b) Animals that pass the winter sleeping in close quarters hibernate

(4.110) (a) Kleptomaniacs are persons who steal out of a persistent neurotic impulse, without economic motive
       (b) Kleptomaniacs steal out of a persistent neurotic impulse, without economic motive

(4.111) (a) Southpaws are left-handed pitchers
       (b) Southpaws pitch with their left hand

While the (a) cases are typical copula sentences, the (b) cases are noncopula sentences. However, both members of each pair are analytic by virtue of the fact that the predicate contains only semantic information already found in the subject. For example, (a) and (b) of (4.109) can be regarded as sentences whose propositional form is that of a one-place predicate ("are female" in the one case and "hibernate" in the other) being applied to a term ("cows" and "animals that pass the winter sleeping in close quarters," respectively) which, because of the term's semantic structure, includes the sense of the predicate as one of the conditions that determines its extension. Clearly, then, copulative and noncopulative sentences manifest no essential differences with regard to the property of analyticity, and the reformulations of the definitions of 'analyticity', 'contradictoriness', etc., must recognize the irrelevance of this syntactic distinction.

Another consideration to be taken into account is that there are analytic (noncopulative) sentences in which some expression other than the subject contains the semantic information that makes the predication redundant. Consider the sentences in (4.112):

(4.112) (a) John buys from those who sell to him
       (b) John sells books to those who buy them from him
       (c) John accepts offers that he doesn't hesitate to take
       (d) John remembers things he does not forget
       (e) John wants to have the things that he desires

Sentences such as these suggest that the subject-predicate distinction, as well as the copulative-noncopulative distinction, is a syntactic distinction which is irrelevant in this case, that is, the subject-predicate relation is not what determines which constituents of a sentence manifest a sense inclusion that renders the sentence analytic. In other words, the sentences in (4.112) suggest that subject-predicate sense inclusion is really just a special case of some more general relation. Thus, it was a mistake in previous discussions of analyticity to depend only on the subject-predicate relation to determine which constituents of sentences figure in decisions about analyticity. This error was strongly encouraged by adhering too closely to the traditional discussions of analyticity. This mistake, moreover, also influenced our treatment of analytic noncopulative sentences (Katz (1966, pp. 208–210)). That the resulting analysis was too narrow is shown by examples of the sort given in (4.112), which fall outside previous definitions of analyticity because the analyticity in cases like (4.112) arises from redundancy with respect to objects of the verb, not subjects as in the case of (4.109), (4.110), and (4.111).

We have already found that our preoccupation with copulative sentences led to an overly restrictive notion of determinability and determinateness. Moreover, we found that to correct this difficulty, it was necessary to take account of the fact that objects as well as subjects can contribute to the presupposition of sentences. Now, if this is so, and if, furthermore, analyticity is a function of semantic redundancy with respect to objects also, it ought to be that analyticity, in the general case, is the situation where the assertion of a proposition involves no more information than is already contained in its presupposition.

This idea is, in fact, inherent in the previous, more restricted treatment of analyticity that appeared in earlier publications. If the analyticity of a (copulative) sentence consists in its predicate's sense containing just information that is already contained in the sense of the subject to which this predicate is applied, and if the sense of the subject expresses the presupposition of the sentence, as specified in our earlier doctrine that determinability and determinateness are defined in terms of semantic properties of the subject exclusively, then the analyticity of such sentences depends on their assertion, determined by the predicate, being included in their presupposition, determined by the subject. Moreover, according to our previous treatment, this connection between the assertion or truth conditions and the presupposition explained why analytic sentences are insured against falsehood, namely, if they are analytic, then their presupposition includes their truth conditions, so that satisfaction of the former implies satisfaction of the latter and failure of the former to be satisfied implies no truth value. Therefore, the previous view already contained the doctrine that the constituents of a sentence that contribute to its presupposition are identical to those constituents, or at least to some proper subset of them, that form the domain of the sense inclusion relation which produces analyticity. The present view, and the reformulation of the definitions based on it, merely extend this previous one by adding that the domain of the constituents in question is no longer restricted to the subject of the verb, but encompasses also direct objects, indirect objects, and certain other constituents bearing appropriate grammatical relations to the verb. What we are proposing now is simply a generalization of the previous account of analyticity that takes into consideration the more general theory of presupposition.

The basic conception of analyticity that emerges from this generalization is as follows. Analytic propositions are secured against falsehood (and contradictory propositions are secured against truth). Determinate analytic propositions are thus necessarily true. The reason for their being so is that their presupposition is both the condition whose satisfaction accords the proposition a truth value and the condition that guarantees that the things to which the proposition refers have the properties that satisfy the truth condition, i.e., make it a true statement. Accordingly, if an analytic proposition is determinate, then the things designated by its referring terms must, simply on the basis of the way they are picked out to be the designata by the senses of the referring terms, have the properties predicated of them in the assertion; and if the proposition is not determinate, it does not have a truth value and so cannot be false. We now propose a new definition for analyticity based upon this conception.

The term *analytic* applies directly to *senses* of sentences, that is, to the *propositions* expressed by sentences, not to sentences themselves. But it does not apply to all propositions, only to what we have called *assertive propositions*.[26] Accordingly, our definition will make use of the formal distinction between the part of the reading of a sentence within double parentheses and the part outside them, the former representing the propositional type and the latter representing the propositional content. The definition will use this distinction to restrict the class of analytic propositions to assertive propositions.

Given the considerations about presupposition and analyticity just discussed, the definition of analyticity must also depend on the formal distinction between the parts of the reading of a sentence that are enclosed within heavy parentheses and the parts not enclosed within such parentheses, since the former represent components of the presupposition and the latter represent the (truth) condition. In order to use this distinction in the definition, let us introduce some additional notation. We think of the propositional content of a proposition as taking the form of an n-placed predicate $P_{x_1, x_2, \ldots, x_n}$, with each place x_i filled by the corresponding term t_i from a sequence of terms $t_1, t_2, \ldots, t_n$. The part of the reading of a sense of a sentence that represents the propositional content can be analyzed into what we will call a *reading schema*, which we indicate as $\Phi_{x_1, x_2, \ldots, x_n}$, and a sequence of readings $r_1, r_2, \ldots, r_n$. The reading schema represents the predicate $P_{x_1, x_2, \ldots, x_n}$, and the sequence of readings represents the sequence of terms to which the predicate is applied. The sequence of readings $r_1, r_2, \ldots, r_n$ is obtained from the reading of the propositional content by choosing those of its subreadings that occur within heavy parentheses. The reading schema results when each pair of heavy parentheses in the propositional content part of the reading for the sentence is replaced by a variable, with heavy parenthesis pairs having the same reading in them being replaced by the same variable and heavy parenthesis pairs having different readings in them being replaced by different variables. Thus, each r_i in the sequence $r_1, r_2, \ldots, r_n$ normally represents a component of the presupposition while the schema $\Phi_{x_1, \ldots, x_n}$ represents the (truth) condition. Finally, we use the notation '$\alpha \sqsubset \beta$' to say that α is a part (but not necessarily a proper part) of β, where 'α' and 'β' stand for semantic markers or sets of semantic markers.

---

[26] In the next chapter we shall discuss the counterpart of analyticity in the case of propositions of other types, e.g., questions.

We now state the definition of 'analyticity' as in (4.113):

(4.113) A proposition or sense of a sentence is analytic, i.e., a sentence S is analytic on the reading R of S, if and only if
  (a) the part of R inside double parentheses marks the proposition represented by R as assertive in type,
  (b) the part of R outside double parentheses contains at least one r_i of the form $\Pi_{r_{i_1}, r_{i_2}, \ldots, r_{i_m}}$ such that $\Phi_{x_1, x_2, \ldots, x_n} \sqsubset \Pi_{x_1, x_2, \ldots, x_m}$, and
  (c) for each r_j of the sequence $r_1, r_2, \ldots, r_n$, $r_j \neq r_i$ (where r_j occupies the jth place in $\Phi_{x_1, x_2, \ldots, x_n}$), either $r_j \sqsubset \Pi$ or there is an r_{i_j} (where r_{i_j} is a reading that occupies the jth place in the part of $\Pi_{x_1, x_2, \ldots, x_m}$ to which $\Phi_{x_1, x_2, \ldots, x_n}$ is identical), $r_j \sqsubset r_{i_j}$.

We will first illustrate the application of this definition and then discuss one of its logical features (see (4.114), p. 176).

The diagram in (4.114) describes the application of the conditions (a), (b), and (c) of (4.113).[27] We will now illustrate, using the analytic proposition in (4.112e). Here the n is 2; r_1 is the reading of the subject "John," and r_2 is the reading of the expression "the things that John desires"; $\Phi_{x_1, x_2, \ldots, x_n}$ is the reading schema of the verbal "wants to have." It is immediately obvious that condition (a) is satisfied, since the propositional type of (4.112e) is assertive. Condition (b) will also be satisfied, with reading r_2 being the r_i in question. The relation 'x wants-to-have y' is identical to part of the relation 'x desires y' insofar as "desires" can be analyzed as 'wants to have very badly'. Thus, the reading schema $\Phi_{x_1, x_2, \ldots, x_n}$ will be identical to a part of $\Pi_{x_1, x_2, \ldots, x_m}$, where this is the reading schema of the direct object of (4.112e). Condition (c) requires that each of the readings representing components of the presupposition (of the whole proposition), except for the one picked out in (a), be included in some reading that represents one of the terms of the relation found in the reading chosen in connection with (b). Here, $m = 2$, and r_{i_1} is the reading of "John" and r_{i_2} is the reading of "the things." Since the only reading in question in $r_1, r_2, \ldots, r_n$ is the reading of "John" and since this is identical to r_{i_1} (we are not considering the sense of (4.112e) on which the pronoun is not coreferential with the subject), condition (c), too, is satisfied. Hence, the reading of the sentence in (4.112e) satisfies every condition of the definition (4.113) and the sentence is marked as expressing a proposition whose presupposition is contained in its (truth) condition.

We note that simple subject-predicate analytic sentences such as those for which our original definition of analyticity was given (Katz (1964a; 1966)), that is,

---

[27] We here pick up from our earlier discussion the treatment on which the assertive propositional type is indicated by a reading that says each conjunct in the presupposition succeeds in designating and that the object(s) or sequence of them that are thereby designated satisfy the truth condition. The ordinary philosophical notion of a referential presupposition, i.e., the condition that each of the terms in transparent contexts within a predicate refer, is thus here represented by this feature of the reading of propositional type. We shall see shortly how this ties in with what we have said about generic propositions. Propositional types other than assertions— e.g., questions, requests—involve the same clause about the presupposition but are distinguished from assertions by further information in the reading of the propositional type that indicates the kind of speech act they are normally used to make.

(4.114)

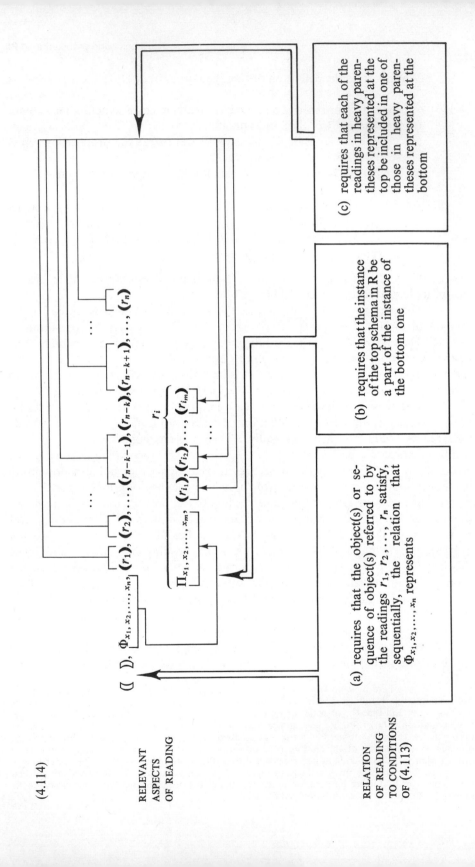

$(\llbracket \ \rrbracket, \ \Phi_{x_1, x_2, \ldots, x_n}, \ (r_1), \ (r_2), \ldots, \ (r_{n-k-1}), \ (r_{n-k}), \ (r_{n-k+1}), \ldots, \ (r_n)$

$\Pi_{x_1, x_2, \ldots, x_m}, \ (r_{i_1}), \ (r_{i_2}), \ldots, \ (r_{i_m})$

r_i

RELEVANT
ASPECTS
OF READING

RELATION
OF READING
TO CONDITIONS
OF (4.113)

(a) requires that the object(s) or sequence of object(s) referred to by
the readings $r_1, r_2, \ldots, r_n$ satisfy,
sequentially, the relation that
$\Phi_{x_1, x_2, \ldots, x_n}$ represents

(b) requires that the instance
of the top schema in R be
a part of the instance of
the bottom one

(c) requires that each of the
readings in heavy paren-
theses represented at the
top be included in one of
those in heavy paren-
theses represented at the
bottom

sentences such as (4.109a), fall under (4.113) by virtue of the fact that the senses of their subject noun phrases, such as "the P," "some P," "(all) P's," will receive readings representing them as having the form (a) 'there is something x such that x is P and x is unique (in the context?) in being such', (b) 'there is something x such that x is P', (c) 'the class of all and only the things x such that x is P is nonnull', respectively. As suggested in Section 2 of this chapter in connection with our account of how Russell's explication of the definite article would be used in a propositional analysis, these readings would provide a statement of the contribution that such noun phrases make to the presupposition of the sentences in which they occur. Thus, in connection with an example like (4.109a), Π is a reading containing the semantic markers '(Physical)', '(Object)', '(Animal)', '(Bovine)', '(Adult)', and '(Female)', Π_{x_1} is a component (of type (c)) of the presuppositional part of the reading, and Φ_{x_1} is the reading that represents the condition that what satisfies the presupposition is female. Accordingly, $\Phi_{x_1} \sqsubset \Pi_{x_1}$, and since the only r_j is Π itself, the condition (c) of (4.113) is trivially satisfied.

The sentences in (4.115), in contrast, are not analytic:

(4.115) (a) Does the king want to have what he desires?
        (b) The queen wants to have what she needs
        (c) The king wants to have what the queen desires

Sentence (a) is requestive and so fails condition (a) of (4.113). The reading for sentence (b) has no reading in heavy parentheses that qualifies as an r_i according to condition (b) of definition (4.113) because neither "the queen" nor "what she (the queen) needs" expresses a relation that includes 'x wants-to-have y'. Finally, in sentence (c) there is a reading in heavy parentheses in the reading of the whole proposition that is not the reading chosen as r_i and that is not included in some reading representing a term of the relation found in the reading chosen as r_i. Hence, this sentence fails condition (c) of (4.113).

We have characterized generic propositions as those that have no referential presuppositions, as propositions whose statementhood does *not* depend on the satisfaction of a referential presupposition. We also note that the definition of 'analyticity' (4.113) involves reference to readings appearing within heavy parentheses and, furthermore, that we have thus far gone on the provisional assumption that such readings represent components of the presupposition of a proposition. Now, we point out that there are analytic generic propositions, for example, those expressed by the sentences in (4.116):

(4.116) (a) A carpenter builds or repairs wooden artifacts
        (b) The crow is a bird

Since such sentences must be marked as analytic (on a sense) by our definition of analyticity, it looks as if either the characterization of genericness presented earlier or the definition (4.113) has to be modified. The question before us, then, is how we can maintain our characterization of generic propositions without making drastic changes in (4.113) and the doctrine on which it is based.

We note, first, that (4.113) refers only to readings within heavy parentheses, *not* to components of presuppositions. These components are determined by an appropriate definition in semantic theory. Thus, our assumption thus far that readings within heavy parentheses represent components of the presupposition need not be taken as a basis for the definition in semantic theory that specifies the components of the presupposition of a proposition (and how they collect to form the presupposition as a whole). We can state the definition for presupposition so that readings in heavy parentheses are taken to be components of the presupposition if and only if the proposition is nongeneric. Genericness can be explicated as a semantic function that operates in some way on the information about the propositional type, modifying it so that the relation represented by $\Phi_{x_1, x_2, \ldots, x_n}$ does not have to be satisfied by the referents of the readings in heavy parentheses. This is to say that the sense of an expression in what is in other respects a referential position does not contribute to the presupposition of the proposition unless its truth conditions are stated in terms of the referent of the sense of the expression. Thus, the new definition of 'presupposition of a proposition' says, in effect, that the terms in referential position in the proposition must successfully refer *if* the truth condition of the proposition is framed as a predication about their referents, but not otherwise. This change enables us to retain both our treatment of generic propositions and (4.113) as the definition of the concept of analyticity.[28]

We now turn to a definition for contradictory sentences such as those in (4.117):

(4.117) (a) Kleptomaniacs steal only out of economic motives
       (b) John sells things to those who don't buy them from him
       (c) John does not like whomever he fancies
       (d) John accepts offers he refuses
       (e) John remembers things he always forgets
       (f) John craves what he does not want

We want to define 'contradictory' so that the range of cases that the definition picks out corresponds to the range of cases picked out by the definition

---

[28] Perhaps a few more remarks are in order here about the reason why we want to represent generic propositions as having no referential condition on their statementhood. One notes, in the first place, that a generic proposition can be true or false even though there are no things corresponding to the referents of the terms occurring in it, as, for example, "The dodo (unicorn) is an animal (quadrupedal)." Rather, its truth or falsity seems to have to do with aspects of certain natural kinds. Note that the existence of owls that are no longer nocturnal due to an injection does not disconfirm the generic statement that owls are nocturnal. Also, note that when the subject does not express a natural kind, e.g., "The weed is an epigeous plant," the generic sense is blocked. (My thanks to J. Thomson for this point.) Moreover, it seems that biologists might some day establish a theory about genetics that states that the crossing of a cat and a dog would yield offspring, call them "cat-dogs," that meow but don't bark. It might also be discovered that cats and dogs cannot be crossed, yet the theory still remains true and clearly establishes the truth of the generic statement that the cat-dog meows. I propose the following hypothesis about the truth conditions for generic propositions. They are true in case their predication is contained in the account of their subject found in a true scientific theory or they are analytic. They are false if their predication is inconsistent with some feature of such an account or they are contradictory. Otherwise they are indeterminate.

(4.113) in the same way that the cases in (4.117) correspond to the cases in (4.112). To obtain such a definition, we must frame the definiens to reflect not only the basic similarity between contradictory propositions and analytic ones but also the basic difference between them. They are similar in that both are linguistically secured against one truth value and are such by virtue of a logico-semantic relation between their presupposition and their assertion. They differ in that this relation is a form of inclusion in the case of analytic propositions and a form of incompatibility in the case of contradictory propositions.

As we recall, analytic sentences can be said to be true (or necessarily true) only if they are determinate. That is, if they ever make a statement, they make a true one. Thus, analytic propositions are semantically secured against falsehood. Contradictory propositions, on the other hand, are semantically secured against truth. For exactly the same reasons, we can say that if a contradictory proposition ever makes a statement, it makes a false one.

In the case of analyticity, this security was explicated in terms of the condition that the presupposition of a proposition includes its truth condition. Correspondingly, then, the security of a contradictory proposition ought to be explicated in terms of the condition that its presupposition is logically incompatible with its truth condition. If this is the condition under which a proposition is contradictory, then a contradictory proposition either makes no statement and has no truth value or it makes a statement and is false, since, by virtue of the fact that the presupposition is incompatible with the truth conditions, the object(s) or sequence of objects that satisfies the presupposition cannot satisfy the truth conditions.

It is quite clear that the appearance of one member of an n-tuple of antonymous semantic markers in the reading that represents the truth condition and the appearance of another member of the same n-tuple in the reading that represents the presupposition is a necessary condition for contradictoriness. But it is not sufficient. Consider the propositions expressed by the sentences (4.117c–f) on the senses where their pronouns do not refer anaphorically and also the sentences in (4.118):

(4.118) (a) The thief stole from the kleptomaniac only out of economic motives
(b) John, who never buys anything, sold something to someone who never sells anything

The further condition that is required, therefore, is that the incompatibility occur between some component of the truth condition that constitutes a predication and the component of the presupposition to whose extension this predication applies. Thus, given that there is one member of an antonymous n-tuple of semantic markers in the reading of the truth condition of a proposition and another member in the reading of its presupposition, the proposition will be contradictory if the first semantic marker appears in the part of the reading of the truth condition that represents the attribution of something to the referent of the reading in which the other semantic marker appears.

To formalize this condition, we need appeal to nothing other than the components of the reading of the propositional content that provide the information about what place in a predicate a given term occupies and what components of the predicate make attributions to the referent of terms occupying that place. Accordingly, we need to consider components of the reading of the propositional content taking the form represented in (4.119):

(4.119) $(((\alpha_1)(\alpha_2) \ldots (\alpha_n))(\!(\beta_1)\!)(\!(\beta_2)\!) \ldots (\!(\beta_m)\!))$

The readings enclosed within heavy parentheses, i.e., 'β_1', 'β_2', ..., 'β_m', represent the terms; the readings not enclosed within heavy parentheses and thereby distinguished from the former readings as part of the representation of the internal structure or logical constitution of the predicate, i.e., 'α_1', 'α_2', ..., 'α_n', represent the attribution; and the bracketing of these two sets of symbol complexes with respect to each other (see the discussion of (4.96)) represents the application of the latter to the former. Thus, the α's represent the properties attributed to the extensions of the terms represented by the readings indicated by β's. We can now define 'contradictory' as in (4.120):

(4.120) A proposition or sense of a sentence is contradictory, i.e., a sentence S is contradictory on the reading R of S, if and only if
    (a) the part of R inside double parentheses marks the proposition represented by R as assertive in type, and
    (b) R contains a component of the form (4.119) and there is an α_i and a β_j, $1 \le i \le n$ and $1 \le j \le m$, such that α_i and β_j belong to the same antonymous n-tuple of semantic markers.

'Synthetic' can be directly defined in terms of the definitions of 'analytic' and 'contradictory', as in (4.121):

(4.121) A proposition or sense of a sentence is synthetic, i.e., a sentence S is synthetic on the reading R of S, if and only if
    (a) the part of R inside double parentheses marks the proposition represented by R as assertive in type, and
    (b) R satisfies neither (4.113) or (4.120).

Note that the concept of syntheticity does not imply that every synthetic proposition is contingent in the sense that its truth or falsity is exclusively a matter of empirical fact. Both linguistic truths and linguistic falsehoods, necessary truths and necessary falsehoods, will be found in the category of synthetic propositions determined by (4.121) since the concepts 'analytic', 'contradictory', and 'synthetic' describe relations found in propositional structure, that is, they refer to the constitution of senses, not to their connection with the world.

The definition of 'contradictory' (4.120) leaves open the possibility of noncontradictory, linguistically necessary falsehoods because it does not include the condition (4.122) in its definiens:

(4.122) (a) There is an α_i and an α_j, $1 \le i \le n$ and $1 \le j \le n$, such that α_i and α_j are distinct semantic markers belonging to the same antonymous n-tuple of semantic markers, or

(b) there is an α_k which is of the form $(\dots(\alpha_1')\dots(\alpha_t')((\alpha_1')\dots(\alpha_u')))$ or of the form $(\dots(\alpha_1')\dots(\alpha_t')\dots)$ and either there is an α_i' and an α_j', $1 \le i \le t$ and $1 \le j \le t$, such that α_i' and α_j' are distinct semantic markers from the same antonymous n-tuple, or there is an α_r' and an α_s', $1 \le r \le u$ and $1 \le s \le u$, such that α_r' and α_s' are distinct semantic markers from the same antonymous n-tuple, or, finally, there is an α_i' and an α_r' such that they are distinct semantic markers from the same antonymous n-tuple.

Sentences with a reading that has a component meeting the condition (4.122) will be called *contradictions*, where this term is understood in its basic logical sense, namely, the attribution of a property or relation that cannot apply to any object(s) or n-tuple of objects. Some examples are given in (4.123):

(4.123) (a) John has a hairy bald head
     (b) John shouted silently
     (c) John is always courageous and cowardly
     (d) John coaxed Bill into agreeing by terrorizing, intimidating, and browbeating him
     (e) The towel soaked the floor without wetting it

Such cases of contradiction predicate properties or relations that cannot be instantiated in a possible world; cases of contradictory sentences, on the other hand, predicate properties or relations that can be instantiated, but not under their conditions of determinateness. Let us compare (4.123a) with (4.117a). The property in the latter case, that of stealing only out of economic motives, can be exemplified in a possible world, but not, of course, in the class of kleptomaniacs, which is the reason why (4.117a) is contradictory and not synthetic. The property in the former case, that of having a hairy bald head, can never be exemplified in a possible world, which is why (4.123a) is a contradiction.

The definition of 'analytic' in (4.113) leaves open the possibility of non-analytic necessary truths, that is, cases where the property or relation in question holds of every object or n-tuple of objects to which its application makes sense. (Another way of saying this is that such cases are true in every possible world in which there exists an object or n-tuple of objects that fall under the concepts expressed by the semantic markers in the selection restriction(s) associated with the property or relation in question.) It thus seems proper to call these cases *logical truths*. Examples are, of course, very familiar and include those in (4.124):

(4.124) (a) John is destitute or not destitute
     (b) John is not both alive and dead

Analytic propositions differ from such cases of logical truths in a way analoguous to that in which contradictory propositions differ from contradictions. The property or relation in question in the case of an analytic proposition does not hold of any object or n-tuple of objects to which its application makes sense but, rather, holds only of those objects or n-tuples that, as a matter of contingent fact, possess the property or bear the relation to one another. The question of whether an analytic proposition is instantiated in a possible world that contains the relevant objects or *n*-tuples of objects, namely, those objects that fall under the concepts expressed by the semantic markers in the selection restriction(s) associated with the property or relation, is a contingent one, whereas the question of whether a logical truth is instantiated in such a possible world is not.

In summary, then, by 'synthetic proposition' we mean a proposition whose conditions of statementhood are neither such that their fulfillment insures truth nor such that their fulfillment insures falsehood. Synthetic propositions, including contradictions and logical truths, differ from analytic and contradictory propositions in that their presuppositions are not semantically related to their assertions in any general way.

The distinctions just considered are an important aspect of the main thesis of this chapter, namely, that language gives rise to a variety of truths (and falsehoods) whose status as such depends on language alone and, hence, that analytic truths (contradictory propositions) represent but one of several types of linguistic truth. We shall return to this thesis in the next section. Here, it is worth pausing to examine a recent example of the way in which distinctions among types of linguistic truth have been ignored.

In an interesting study of convention, Lewis (1969, Chapter 5) proposes to develop the grammatical concept of semantic interpretation in terms of the referential semantics of Tarski and Carnap. He thinks that the intensionalist line of development taken in Katz (1963) and extended here "leads to a semantic theory that leaves out such central semantic notions as truth and reference." I must confess to being puzzled by this allegation. As I see it, the criticism trades on an ambiguity of the term "semantic." On the one hand, semantics (as understood by lexicographers and some philosophers) is the study of meaning (in natural languages), and, on the other (as understood by logicians and other philosophers), it is the study of the relations between objects of one sort or another and the expressions of a language (usually an artificial language) that speak about them. The basic constructs in a theory of semantics in the former sense are 'synonymy', 'ambiguity', 'anomaly', etc. (see Chapter 1 of this book), while those in a theory of semantics in the latter sense are 'truth', 'satisfaction', 'denotation', etc. Now, the first part of Lewis' allegation is that my theory leaves out notions such as 'truth', and the second part is that leaving out such notions is a defect because they are "central semantic notions." Supposing we grant the first part, then how are we to understand the second? If "semantics" is construed in the latter way, as having to do with reference as opposed to sense, then the omitted notions are clearly central to semantics; however, the subject matter to which they are central is not the one that my semantic theory is or was ever intended to be about. If "semantics" is construed in the former way, as having to do with sense as opposed to reference, then the notions in question are *not* central to semantics and so there can be no claim that my theory has left out something central. In either case, there is no charge that the theory is defective.

Although Lewis doesn't say so explicitly, his position might be that semantics in these two senses are really one and the same discipline, and, moreover, a discipline that is not divided into two areas so that its theory separates naturally into parts, one of which is a theory of sense and the other a theory of reference. Furthermore, he might hold that the theory of this discipline uses notions like 'truth' as its central concepts and takes the notions regarded as basic constructs of the theory of sense to be derivative and definable in terms of the central concepts from the theory of reference. What encourages me to think that this might be Lewis' underlying position is his attempt to define 'analytic', 'contradictory', and 'synthetic' on the basis of the central concepts from the theory of reference. Let us consider Lewis' attempt at a definitional reduction of these intensional concepts to the central concepts in the theory of reference.

Lewis defines 'analyticity' as truth in all possible worlds, 'contradictoriness' as falsehood in all possible worlds, and 'syntheticity' as truth in some possible worlds and not in others. Lewis' argument to reduce 'analyticity' (and other intensional concepts) to concepts from the theory of reference requires only the further assumption that the notions of truth, falsehood, world, and possibility are concepts of the theory of reference with no taint of the theory of meaning. One can easily quarrel with this assumption on the grounds that the latter two concepts cannot be unpacked in a way that is adequate for natural language without the conceptual richness of the theory of meaning. But I don't intend to pursue this line here.[29] Lewis' argument is more directly vulnerable at its definitional base.

As we observed at the very beginning of this chapter, there are two senses of "analytic" in philosophical usage. First, there is the sense that this term received when it was originally introduced, the Kantian sense in which an analytic proposition is one whose predicate attributes nothing more than is already contained in the meaning of the subject. Second, there is the sense of "analytic" later introduced by Frege, on which an analytic proposition is one that is deducible from the laws of logic without any appeal to premises from the special sciences. In terms of the distinction we have drawn, this second sense we call *logical truth*. The fallacy in Lewis' argument emerges when, with reference to these two senses, we ask how we are to understand the occurrence of the word "analytic" in Lewis' definition saying that analyticity is truth in all possible worlds. If we understand it on the second of the senses, the definition comes to express a Leibnizian view about truths of reason. We have no need to take issue with the definition on this interpretation, since now it is totally irrelevant to the question of whether intensional concepts like 'analyticity' can be reduced to extensional ones like 'truth' and 'possible' and 'world'. On the other hand, if we understand the occurrence of "analytic" in Lewis' definition on the first of these senses, the definition comes to express the claim that the defining characteristic of the Kantian notion of analyticity is truth in all possible worlds. On this interpretation, the definition is relevant to the question at issue since the definiendum now refers to one of the concepts about which the issue of reduction arises. But the definition is not adequate because it is too broad: the class of propositions whose truth conditions are included in their presupposition is only a proper subset of the class that is picked out by the definiens. We can put the point this way: *mutatis mutandis*, with respect to the

---

[29] For further discussion, see Katz (to appear).

qualification that their presuppositions are satisfied, every proposition that is analytic on the present interpretation of "analytic" is true in every possible world, but not every proposition that is true in every possible world is analytic on this interpretation of "analytic." Consider sentences like those in (4.125), which are instances of the definiens but not of the definiendum:

(4.125) (a) Someone is either alive or not alive
         (b) Harry does not have both fever and chills if and only if he has neither
             fever nor chills

The essential distinction between a logical truth and an analytic proposition cannot concern what they, and perhaps other kinds of propositions, have in common, namely, the fact that they must be true in any possible world in which the presupposition is satisfied, but, rather, has to do with the difference in the reasons each must be true in any possible world in which the presupposition is satisfied. The reason that a logical truth like (a) of (4.125) is true in every such possible world is that its predicate is universally satisfied: everything is such that either it is alive or not, so that, as long as there is something in a possible world, and thus its presupposition is satisfied for that world, the proposition is going to be true in that world. On the other hand, the reason that an analytic proposition like (4.109a) is true in every such possible world is that its truth condition is included in its presupposition, so that, as long as there is an entity, entities, or sequence of entities that satisfies the presupposition, the proposition's truth conditions will also be satisfied in that world. But note that the predicate of an analytic proposition is *not* universally satisfied in every nonempty world. For example, the predicate of (4.109a), "female," is not satisfied in every possible world containing objects to which it can be applied, as is the predicate of (a) in (4.125), "either alive or not alive." In the case of analytic propositions, security against falsehood derives from the relation between the truth condition and the presupposition, while in the case of logical truths, such security derives from the structure of the truth conditions alone, from the fact that their structure imposes a vacuous requirement that cannot help but be met in any nonempty world.

We now turn to the concept of semantic entailment. The explicandum of this concept can be characterized as a relation between one proposition and another on the basis of which one follows logically from the other but *not* by virtue of any law of logic. That is, there are no steps from the premiss to the conclusion and hence no reason to invoke a law of logic. The validity of such arguments depends on the logical form of the conclusion being part of the logical form of the premiss. Therefore, they are the counterpart of analytic propositions in the case of arguments. Their justification—the guarantee that they preserve truth—rests on the meaning relations among the descriptive expressions in the sentences expressing their premiss and conclusion rather than on the existence of a law of logic connecting their premiss and conclusion in a truth-preserving way. Simple examples of semantic entailment are provided by the inferences from (4.126) to (4.127) and from (4.128) to (4.129).

(4.126) Mary had a nightmare

(4.127) Mary had a dream

(4.128) John is a bachelor

(4.129) John is male

The validity of such an argument cannot be exhibited in quantification theory by itself. The quantificational representation of (4.128)-(4.129) would be something like (4.130), where 'a' is an individual constant used to denote John, the predicate letter 'B' is used for the predicate expressed by "is a bachelor," and the predicate letter 'M' is used for the predicate expressed by "is male":

(4.130) B_a

M_a

Such a representation, however, does not distinguish the valid argument (4.128)-(4.129) from the invalid argument (4.131):

(4.131) (a) John is a banker

(b) John is mean

Using, for purposes of illustration, the same predicate letters 'B' and 'M' for the predicates expressed by "is a banker" and "is mean," respectively, (4.131) could also be rendered as (4.130). This situation led Carnap (1956) and others to introduce the device of meaning postulates in order to try to handle semantic entailments as cases where rules of logic justify inferring a conclusion from its premiss. In order to explain the validity of (4.128)-(4.129), the Carnapian introduces into the representation of the argument (4.129) a meaning postulate taking the form (4.132):

(4.132) $(x)(B_x \supset M_x)$

Thus the argument (4.128)-(4.129) is now rendered by the valid argument form (4.133):

(4.133) B_a
$(x)(B_x \supset M_x)$

M_a

But this move accomplishes nothing, simply because it is totally ad hoc. First, we are given no reason whatever as to why (4.133) does not show that (4.131) is valid. Presumably, (4.133) expresses a semantic relation between the predicates of the premiss (4.128) and conclusion (4.129), not one between the predicates of the premiss (a) and conclusion (b) of (4.131); but there is no semantic theory behind this exercise of linguistic intuition that might inform us about how we extrapolate principles to govern the choice between competing semantic analyses.[30] Why not the meaning postulate (4.134) for (4.128)-(4.129)?

(4.134) $(x)(M_x \supset B_x)$

For an approach like Carnap's, which has not given up the distinction between logical particles and extra-logical vocabulary as well as the doctrine of logical form based on it, there is no semantic theory (nor even a means of arguing from semantic intuitions) to provide a reason for (4.132) and the schematization (4.133). Any such theory or argument would violate Frege's requirement that the analysis of a logical argument can make no appeal to statements from a special science: the basis for accepting (4.132) is surely statements from linguistics.

Second, an account like (4.133) cannot even be claimed to represent the argument it is alleged to render in the idiom of quantification theory. The meaning postulate (4.132) is intended to state the proposition expressed by the sentence (4.135):

(4.135) Bachelors are male

Thus the account in (4.133) in fact represents not the argument (4.128)-(4.129) but rather the argument (4.136):

(4.136) (a) John is a bachelor

      (b) Bachelors are male

      ―――――――――――

      (c) John is male

It appears to me that the reason an appeal to meaning postulates turns out to be ad hoc is that the problem they are meant to solve is an impossible one. The philosopher or logician who makes this appeal recognizes that there is no non-arbitrary way to draw the line between the logical and extra-logical vocabulary of a language and that arguments like (4.128)-(4.129) are as valid as any that turn on logical particles. But, he does not go further and challenge the professional-ization of logic, and consequently it is necessary for him to try to cope with semantic relations like those on which the validity of arguments like (4.128)-(4.129) depend on the basis of apparatus designed to explicate inferences depending on logical particles exclusively. Those who appeal to meaning postulates thus recognize that semantic relations among descriptive expressions are as much a part of logical inference as any of the relations among logical particles dealt with in quanti-fication theory, but because these philosophers still stay within the professionalized framework that defines logic today, they are restricted to apparatus that is unsuited to the job.

---

[30] See the further discussion of this point in Section 1 of Chapter 6 in connection with Quine on the translation of sentences into canonical form.

Our definition of semantic entailment is an attempt to explain the validity of inferences like (4.128)-(4.129) directly in terms of the semantic relations underlying them. Thus semantic theory and this definition can be thought of as a supplement to quantification theory in the sense in which quantification theory supplements propositional logic. Semantic theory adds both to the stock of logical forms for arguments constructed out of sentences from a natural language and to the stock of inference rules for the definition of validity. Hence, the additional contribution that semantic theory makes to the formal reconstruction of valid inference as given in quantification theory is of the same kind as the additional contribution that quantification theory makes to this reconstruction as given in propositional logic: the readings of constituents and sentences given by the semantic component of a grammar supplement the stock of logical forms, and the definitions of entailment and analyticity given by semantic theory supplement the stock of rules for defining 'valid argument'. Consider (4.137) and (4.138):

(4.137) There is someone who is bald

(4.138) It is not the case that everyone is not bald

The inference from (4.137) to (4.138) can be rendered in propositional logic only by the invalid form (4.139):

(4.139) $\dfrac{P}{Q}$

But in quantification theory it can be rendered by the form (4.140), whose validity is expressed by the rules for quantifier exchange:

(4.140) $\dfrac{(\exists x)(B_x)}{\sim (x) \sim (B_x)}$

Similarly, although the logical form of the argument from (4.128)-(4.129) is not expressed by the schema (4.130), it is represented by the readings for the sentences (4.128) and (4.129) and its validity is expressed by the definition of entailment to be given directly. Thus, the analysis of the semantic structure of "bachelor" and "male" in terms of sets of semantic markers provides an account of the logical form of (4.128)-(4.129) just as the analysis of the referential structure of logical particles such as "all," "some," and "not" gives (4.140) as an account of the logical form of the argument from (4.137) to (4.138).

The point is that just as quantification theory is a step beyond propositional logic, so semantics is a step beyond quantification theory. Propositional logic takes propositions to be unanalyzed with respect to their internal structure, while quantification theory goes into the internal structure of propositions wherever logical particles play a role in determining the validity of inferences. But quantification theory takes predicates and terms to be unanalyzed with respect to their internal structure, while semantics goes into the internal structure of predicates and terms wherever meaning relations among expressions from the extra-logical vocabulary play a role in determining the validity of inferences. Quantification theory takes its point of departure from the limitations on the analysis of propositional form within propositional logic, for example, from inferences such as (4.137) to (4.138). Semantic theory takes its point of departure from limitations on the analysis of propositional form within quantification theory. If a sentence like (4.137) receives a complex representation of its logical form such as that in the premiss of (4.140), then, for just the same reason, a sentence such as (4.128) ought to have as complex a logical form as needed to explain cases like (4.128)-(4.129) as semantic entailments. Complex analyses of the semantic structure of nouns, verbs, and so on must be part of any complete theory of propositional form and inference.

The definition of the entailment relation is a generalization over the meaning relations formalized in the representations of semantic structure provided by readings. This generalization singles out a certain formal relation that can hold between a pair of readings as the condition under which any sentence with one of those readings entails any sentence with the other. We want this formalization to reflect the common relation of meaning inclusion that determines the connection between the presupposition and the assertion of an analytic proposition, on the one hand, and the connection between an entailing proposition and the proposition it entails, on the other. The representation of this common feature is as much a requirement on semantic theory as is either the representation of analyticity or of entailment by itself.

Whereas in the case of an analytic proposition there is a single presupposition and a single assertion, in the case of an entailment we have a presupposition and an assertion for the entailing proposition and a presupposition and an assertion for the entailed proposition. In the former case, linguistic truth arises from the content of the assertion being included in the content of the presupposition. But the latter case is somewhat more complicated since the entailment can come off both the presupposition and assertion of the entailing proposition or the presupposition alone. Accordingly, the definition has two parts. Let 'R_1' and 'R_2' be the readings of the entailing and entailed propositions, respectively, and let 'R_1'' and 'R_2'' be the parts of R_1 and R_2, respectively, that represent their propositional content. The definition of 'entailment' is then as in (4.141):

(4.141) A sentence S_1 entails a sentence S_2 on the readings R_1 (of S_1) and R_2 (of S_2) (i.e., the proposition represented by R_1 entails the proposition represented by R_2) if and only if either

(a) R_1' is of the form $\Phi_{a_1, a_2, \ldots, a_n}$ and R_2' is of the form $\Psi_{b_1, b_2, \ldots, b_m}$ and $\Psi_{b_1, b_2, \ldots, b_m} \sqsubset \Phi_{a_1, a_2, \ldots, a_n}$ and the part of $\Phi_{a_1, a_2, \ldots, a_n}$ to which $\Psi_{b_1, b_2, \ldots, b_m}$ is identical is of the form $\Upsilon_{a_{i1}, a_{i2}, \ldots, a_{i_k}}$ (where $1 \leq i \leq n$ and $k \leq n$) and for each b_j ($1 \leq j \leq m$) there is a corresponding a_{i_j} such that if both are particular, $b_j \sqsubset a_{i_j}$, and if a_{i_j} is universal, then $a_{i_j} \sqsubset b_j$, or

(b) R'_1 is of the form $\Phi_{a_1, a_2, \ldots, a_n}$ and R'_2 is of the form $\Psi_{b_1, b_2, \ldots, b_m}$ and there is an a_i $(1 \le i \le n)$ of the form $\Pi_{c_1, c_2, \ldots, c_g}$ and $\Psi_{b_1, b_2, \ldots, b_m} \sqsubset \Pi_{c_1, c_2, \ldots, c_g}$ and the part of $\Pi_{c_1, c_2, \ldots, c_g}$ to which $\Psi_{b_1, b_2, \ldots, b_m}$ is identical is of the form $\Upsilon_{c_{i_1}, c_{i_2}, \ldots, c_{i_k}}$ $(1 \le i \le g$ and $k \le g)$ and for each b_j $(1 \le j \le m)$ there is a corresponding c_{i_j} such that if both are particular, $b_j \sqsubset c_{i_j}$, and if c_{i_j} is universal, then $c_{i_j} \sqsubset b_j$.

Part (a) of definition (4.141) treats the case where the entailment comes off the presupposition and assertion of the entailing proposition, and part (b) treats the case where the entailment comes off the presupposition of the entailing proposition. Thus the first part of the definition accounts for the entailment in (4.142a), while the second part acconts for that in (4.142b).

(4.142) (a) A spinster assassinated a bachelor; hence, a woman killed a man
(b) The killers disposed of John's corpse; hence, John is dead

The distinction between the case where both terms are particular and the case where the term of the entailing proposition is universal and the omission of the case where the term of the entailing proposition is particular and the corresponding term of the entailed proposition is universal are intended to reflect the fact that the arguments (a) and (b) in (4.143) are valid but the arguments (c) are not:

(4.143) (a) (i) All females are dangerous motorists; hence, all (some) spinsters are dangerous motorists
  (ii) All females are geniuses; hence, all (some) spinsters are intelligent
  (iii) All principals are spinsters; hence, all (some) principals are females
 (b) (i) Some bachelors are rich; hence, some males are rich
  (ii) Some bachelors are kings; hence, some males are monarchs
  (iii) Some bachelors are kings; hence, some bachelors are monarchs
  (iv) John is a king; hence, John (someone) is a monarch
 (c) (i) Some females are dangerous motorists; hence, all spinsters are dangerous motorists
  (ii) Some females are geniuses; hence, all spinsters are intelligent
  (iii) Some principals are spinsters; hence, all principals are females
  (iv) Sally is a queen; hence, everyone is a monarch

Note that in our theory there is no need to consider an independent assumption concerning the existential import of the terms of a universal proposition in connection with arguments like those in (a) since either the propositions that occur as premisses are determinate or else the proposition that occurs as conclusion has no truth value. Hence, we will not be able to infer a false conclusion from true premisses when our assumption concerning the existential import of the terms of a universal proposition fails.[31]

In Chapter 6 we shall consider the application of the definition of entailment (4.141) to the problem of characterizing the conditions under which valid inferences can be made by substitution into a referentially opaque context. We shall argue, among other things, that, because (4.141) explicates the concept of an inference that does not depend on a law of logic but instead on the inclusion of one logical form within another, we can characterize such inference conditions by the requirement that the proposition resulting from the substitution be entailed by the one into which the substitution is made.

Part (a) of definition (4.141) is formulated so that the part inclusion required to hold among readings that represent terms is required to hold for pairs whose members occupy corresponding places in the common part of the readings representing relations. Part (b) of (4.141) and definition (4.113) both formulate the condition that there is a containment of the assertion in the presupposition in terms of the requirement that there be at least one reading representing a term that includes the semantic representation of the relation underlying the assertion and the other readings that represent terms of the relation. Why, it might be asked,[32] did we not choose the requirement that the conjunction of the readings representing the terms, the reading that represents the full presupposition, include the semantic representation of the relation underlying the assertion and the other readings that represent terms of the relation? The answer is that our requirement is the strongest condition that handles the cases which need to be covered. The only kind of case that seems to be handled by the broader and thus weaker requirement just suggested and not by our requirement is that illustrated by the argument (4.144a) and the necessary truth (4.144b):

(4.144)   (a)   Ralph is John's son
           _____
           Ralph is the grandson of John's father

           (b)   John's son is the grandson of John's father

Suppose we take the relation in these cases to be ' x is-the-son-of-the-son-of y '. In the case of the inference as well as the necessary truth corresponding to it,

---

[31] Note further that (4.141) does not itself account for the validity of arguments such as "Some bachelors are kings; hence, some monarchs are males." We think that this is as it should be, since we take the account of such inferences to be the joint task of this entailment definition and quantification theory. The entailment definition marks the entailment from the premiss of (4.143bii) to its conclusion, and quantification theory licenses the step from the conclusion of (4.143bii) to the proposition expressed by "Some monarchs are males." This is one example of the way in which the entailment definition supplements quantification theory by covering cases quantificational rules do not cover and the way in which quantification theory supplements the account of entailment by covering cases which cannot be handled by the entailment definition. In these latter cases, the logical form of the conclusion does not form part of the logical form of the premiss, that is, the truth conditions of the conclusion are not included in those of the premiss so that the inference is not immediate. Rather, the inference depends on the step(s) from the premiss to the conclusion being in accord with the laws of logic.

[32] Thanks to my colleague G. Boolos for asking this.

an inferential step justified by the logical law of transitivity is needed, namely, from a statement asserting that Ralph is the son of John, taken together with another asserting that John is the son of someone, to the conclusion that Ralph is the son of the someone such that John is his son. But we do not want to cover cases such as (4.144) under our definitions (4.141) and (4.113) since to do so would make our explications of the concepts in question too broad. Thus we had good reason in choosing to formulate the relevant clauses of (4.141) and (4.113) as we did.

The definition of 'entailment' enables us to explicate the so-called fallacy of 'arguing in a circle', the *petitio principii*. Elementary logic texts and introductory philosophy books often include a section treating informal fallacies in reasoning, listing the *petitio principii* among others. Copi (1961) describes it as follows:

> If one assumes as a premiss for his argument the very conclusion he intends to prove, the fallacy committed is that of *petitio principii* or begging the question. If the proposition to be established is formulated in exactly the same words both as premiss and as conclusion, the mistake would be so glaring as to deceive no one. Often, however, two formulations can be so different as to obscure the fact that one and the same proposition occurs both as premiss and conclusion (p. 65).

Consider (4.145):

(4.145) (a) An act done without the exercise of the agent's will should not be punished
(b) An involuntary act should not be punished

Although this argument is circular, it is not, strictly speaking, a fallacy, since it is valid in the customary sense (i.e., its premiss cannot be true and its conclusion false). Yet such an argument gives no grounds for its conclusion of the sort arguments are supposed to give for their conclusions:

> the premiss is logically irrelevant to the purpose of proving the conclusion. If the proposition is acceptable without argument, no argument is needed to establish it; and if the proposition is not acceptable without argument, then no argument which requires its acceptance as a premiss could possibly lead anyone to accept its conclusion (p. 65).

This is roughly correct, except that a qualification is necessary in connection with the last remark: one can imagine someone who refuses to accept (b) of (4.145) but, when presented with (a) and told that an involuntary act is just one done without the exercise of the agent's will, readily accepts (b). The necessary qualification is that the acceptance of the proposition as a premiss could not possibly lead an ideal speaker-hearer (*someone who knows the language perfectly*) to accept its conclusion.[33]

Failing to notice this qualification results in confusion about how the boundary is to be drawn between circular arguments and very trivial noncircular arguments, for example, arguments of the form '$p \cdot q$, therefore, p', or arguments

---

[33] See also Chapter 6 of this book.

of the form 'p, therefore $p \vee q$'. Sometimes this confusion leads to the doctrine that all logical reasoning is circular. Cohen and Nagel (1934) write in their section on circularity:

> There is a sense in which all science is circular, for all proof rests upon assumptions which are not derived from others but are justified by the set of consequences which are deduced from them ... the circle of theoretical science is so wide that we cannot set up any alternative to it (p. 379).

If one fails to distinguish circularity from trivial argument, then one proceeds, small step by small step, from more trivial argument to imperceptibly less trivial argument, to the conclusion that all argumentation is circular. But it is perfectly clear that in the sense of explicative argument in which a circular argument functions to explain meaning, and where such an argument is out of order if a proof not a meaning analysis is what is wanted, it is not the case that all reasoning is circular. To carry this term over from the domain where its use makes good sense to a domain where it makes no sense merely creates a pseudo-profundity like the thesis that all science is circular, which is revealed as either true but trivial or interesting but false once the proper distinction between domains of use is drawn. Here the distinction can be drawn in terms of the definition (4.146):

(4.146) An argument is circular just in case its conclusion is entailed (see (4.141)) by one of its premisses.

The relation of *meaning inclusion* is the counterpart at the level of subsentential constituents of the relation of semantic entailment at the level of full sentences. The including term, *superordinate*, is the counterpart of the entailing sentence, and the included term, *subordinate*, the counterpart of the entailed sentence. Examples of this relation are found between the words in (a) and those in (b) of (4.147):

(4.147) (a) human, dwelling, male, digit, stone
       (b) dilettante, cottage, boy, index finger, pebble

The relation of meaning inclusion can be defined in terms of definition (4.141) as in (4.148) and (4.149):

(4.148) A subsentential constituent C_1's meaning includes the meaning of the subsentential constituent C_2 on the readings R_1 (of C_1) and R_2 (of C_2) if and only if either (a) or (b) of (4.141) holds.

(4.149) Given that (4.148) applies to a pair C_1 and C_2, C_1 is called the superordinate and C_2 the subordinate.

We now turn to the topic of logical properties of relations. We shall try to sketch the manner in which such properties can be incorporated into semantic representations and to show, on the basis of such an incorporation, how certain logical consequence relations that depend on logical properties of relations can be subsumed under the definition of entailment. We shall not be able to consider at this point all the generally referred to cases of logical properties of relations. Some are outside the scope of this book, and others require too lengthy a discussion. A case of the latter type is the converse relation, which will take up most of Chapter 7.

The existence of a logic of relations, generally recognized as such, must count as yet another argument against Quine's conception of logic and logical form based on a division of the terms of a language into the logical particles and the nonlogical vocabulary. The reason is that the properties of relations (such as those to be discussed here) on which such a logic is framed can be nothing other than properties of the so-called "nonlogical" vocabulary.

The first properties we shall deal with are 'symmetry', 'asymmetry', and 'nonsymmetry'. A relation H is said to be symmetrical just in case (4.150) holds:

(4.150) For all x and all y, xHy implies yHx.

A relation H is said to be asymmetrical just in case (4.151) holds:

(4.151) For all x and all y, xHy implies $\sim y$Hx.

And a relation H is said to be nonsymmetrical just in case (4.152) holds:

(4.152) It is not the case that, for all x and all y, xHy implies yHx, and it is not the case that, for all x and all y, xHy implies $\sim y$Hx.

An example of a verb that expresses a symmetrical relation is "box," in the sense of engaging in a boxing match. Thus, (4.154) follows from (4.153):

(4.153) John boxed Bill in the main event
(4.154) Bill boxed John in the main event

An example of a verb that expresses an asymmetrical relation is "win against," in the sense of gaining a victory over someone in a contest. Thus, (4.156) follows from (4.155):

(4.155) John won the match against Bill
(4.156) Bill did not win the match against John

Examples of verbs that express an asymmetrical relation are "chase," "love," "annoy."

Before considering the semantic representation of these logical properties of relations, let us consider an attempt to characterize them syntactically. Lakoff and Peters (1966) claim that verbs taking NP* subjects are necessarily symmetrical. An NP* noun phrase is one introduced by some phrase structure rule of the form (4.157).

(4.157) NP → and (NP)^n, $n \geq 2$

NP*'s are cases like the subject of (4.158) but not like the subject of (4.159):

(4.158) The man and woman are acquainted
(4.159) The man and woman are foolish

That is, they are conjunctions in which the constituents conjoined are simple nouns, not reduced versions of two or more sentences. I am prepared to grant the truth of Lakoff and Peter's claim in cases like (4.158) since all it amounts to here is that conjunction is commutative, although there is still some room for doubt. However, their claim fails for the interesting cases of verbal forms such as "are similar" and "are identical." Lakoff and Peters' thesis is that sentences of the form 'X and Y are similar (with respect to K)' and 'X is similar to Y (with respect to K)' have the same underlying phrase marker and sentences of the form 'X and Y are identical' and 'X is identical with (to) Y' have the same underlying phrase marker. If this were so, it would explain the alleged symmetry since sentences of the latter form would be derived transformationally from ones of the former form and hence would have the same semantic interpretations. But such pairs cannot have the same underlying phrase marker because they are not synonymous. Consider the examples in (4.160) and (4.161):[34]

(4.160) If a tall man and a short man were identical in height, then the tall man would be short
(4.161) If a tall man and a short man were identical in height, then the short man would be tall

Neither of these is an acceptable inference, although (4.162) is, perhaps, acceptable:

(4.162) If a tall man and a short man were identical in height, then either the tall man would be short or the short man would be tall

On the other hand, the sentence (4.163) is a perfectly good inference:

(4.163) If a tall man were identical in height to a short man, then the tall man would be short

Sentence (4.164), however, is no better than (4.160) or (4.161):

(4.164) If a tall man were identical in height to a short man, then the short man would be tall

The difference in meaning seems to be that, in constructions of the form 'if X were identical (similar) in K to Y', Y plays a different role from X, serving

[34] These examples have been adapted from Quine (1959, p. 15).

as what determines the property which X, counter to fact, is assumed to have. In constructions of the form 'if X and Y are identical (similar) in K', on the other hand, the commutativity of conjunction prevents one of these constituents from assuming the special role played by Y in constructions of the first form. Thus, corresponding cases of these forms cannot have the same deep structure, and the Lakoff-Peters account of symmetry must be given up. As a result, it is worthwhile to explore the possibility of providing a semantic account of such logical properties of relations.

The symmetrical relation expressed by a verb can be represented in the formal structure of its lexical reading by having the categorized variables for the subject and the object placed together within the same semantic marker (with understood logical conjunction). Thus, the lexical reading of a verb expressing a symmetrical relation will contain the two categorized variables $X_{\langle\ \rangle}^{[NP,\,S]}$ and $X_{\langle\ \rangle}^{[NP,\,VP,\,PP,\,S]}$ (or the categorized variable for the constituent whose reading is the other term of the relation) wherever the reading of a verb contains an occurrence of $X_{\langle\ \rangle}^{[NP,\,S]}$. In the case of a verb that expresses a nonsymmetrical relation, there will be no occurrences of $X_{\langle\ \rangle}^{[NP,\,VP,\,PP,\,S]}$ where $X_{\langle\ \rangle}^{[NP,\,S]}$ occurs. Thus, the lexical reading of the verb "box" will have the form shown in (4.165):

$$(4.165)\quad (((\text{Activity})(\dots))\textbf{(}\ X_{\langle\ \rangle}^{[NP,\,S]}\ \textbf{)(}\ X_{\langle\ \rangle}^{[NP,\,VP,\,PP,\,S]}\ \textbf{))}$$

The lexical reading for "chase," on the other hand, will have the form shown in (4.166):

$$(4.166)\quad (((\text{Activity})(\dots))\textbf{(}\ X_{\langle\ \rangle}^{[NP,\,S]}\ \textbf{))}$$

The asymmetrical relation expressed by a verb can be represented in the form of its lexical reading, too, by having the categorized variable for the subject and the categorized variable for the object or indirect object (whichever is the other term) be components in semantic markers that belong to the same antonymous n-tuple. Thus for "win against" we might have a lexical reading like that in (4.167):

$$(4.167)$$
$$((\text{Contest})(((\text{Outcome})^{(\text{Victory})}\textbf{(}\ X_{\langle\ \rangle}^{[NP,\,S]}\ \textbf{)})((\text{Outcome}^{(\text{Defeat})}\textbf{(}\ X_{\langle\ \rangle}^{[NP,\,VP,\,PP,\,S]}\ \textbf{))))}$$

With such lexical readings, the inferences that are supported by the symmetry or asymmetry of the relations in question are reconstructed by the definition of entailment. Sentence (4.153) entails sentence (4.154) since both have the same reading.

The next logical properties of relations to be considered are 'reflexivity', 'irreflexivity', and 'nonreflexivity'. A relation H is said to be reflexive just in case (4.168) holds:

(4.168)   For all x, xHx.

A relation H is said to be irreflexive just in case (4.169) holds:

(4.169)   For all x, $\sim xHx$.

And a relation H is said to be nonreflexive just in case (4.170) holds:

(4.170)   It is not the case that, for all x, xHx, and it is not the case that, for all x, $\sim xHx$.

Examples of reflexive relations are exceedingly hard to come by. Logicians often cite 'is identical to' and 'is coexistent with'. But there are more common cases in natural languages, such as the one expressed by the verb "perjure." Examples of irreflexive relations are those expressed by "assassinate," "divorce," and "fornicate with," and examples of nonreflexive relations are "criticize," "like," "talk to."

The meaning of "perjure" as given in the dictionary gives us a clue to the treatment of constituents expressing reflexive relations. Webster's says that this word means 'to tell what is false when sworn to tell the truth'. I am not concerned with the correctness of this definition—for instance, whether *any* conditions under which one swears to speak the truth but does not do so count as perjury. What is of concern is that according to Webster's, semantically, "perjure" is a one-place predicate (omitting the question of time designation). Therefore, the occurrence of syntactic objects in sentences like (4.171a,b) has to be treated as a nonlogical matter of syntactic form:

(4.171)   (a) John perjured himself
          (b) John perjured someone, guess who?

Thus, we arrive at the general structure in (4.172) for readings of reflexive verbs:[35]

$$\begin{array}{cc} \text{[NP, S]} & \text{[NP, VP, PP, S]} \\ \end{array}$$
$$(4.172) \quad (((\ )(\ )\dots(\ ))(\quad X \qquad\qquad X \qquad)) \\ \qquad\qquad\qquad \langle\ \rangle \qquad\qquad \langle\ \rangle$$

---

[35] We include a categorized variable for the object of "perjure" in order to take account of further information about the agent that comes from the object noun phrase in sentences like "John perjured his mother's only son."

The treatment of irreflexive and nonreflexive cases is now quite straight-forward. Both have readings in which there is a pair of heavy parentheses enclosing only the categorized variable $\begin{matrix} [\text{NP, VP, PP, S}] \\ X \\ \langle\ \rangle \end{matrix}$. But the selection restriction in the case of a verb that expresses an irreflexive relation must contain a condition to the effect that no reading can be substituted for the variable it appears under that is identical to the reading of the subject of this verb. Accordingly, sentences like (4.173)-(4.175) are semantically anomalous:

(4.173)   John assassinated himself

(4.174)   John divorced his mother's only son

(4.175)   John fornicated with the person referred to by the subject of this sentence

The selection restriction in the case of a verb that expresses a nonreflexive relation will, of course, contain no such condition.

The properties of 'transitivity' and 'intransitivity' do not lend themselves to explication along the same lines as the properties just considered. Moreover, the problems to be faced in providing an explication of these properties are extensive. Accordingly, no attempt will be made to deal with them here.

6.   On the scope of the notion 'linguistic truth'

As remarked early in this chapter, there has been an unfortunate tendency in twentieth-century philosophy, beginning with Frege's departure from Kant's sense of "analytic," to stretch the term "analytic" to cover any sentence whose truth is guaranteed by considerations of meaning alone. This tendency, together with the failure to try to work out a precise, linguistically defined concept of analyticity, has concealed the existence of types of linguistic truth that do not have the form of analytic truths. The whole affair has the air of a self-fulfilling prophecy: the neglect of the study of other forms of linguistic truth, in turn, allowed the stretched usage of "analytic" to persist and become ingrained. In the preceding section, we sought to counteract this tendency by distinguishing between analytic propositions and logical truths. In this section, we shall seek to further rectify the situation by showing that the concept of linguistic truth is broader than that of both analyticity and logical truth. To demonstrate this, we shall provide examples of linguistic truths that are neither analytic propositions nor logical truths.

Linguistic truths are determinate propositions whose truth is secured on the basis of the principles of natural language, whereas analytic truths are the case of linguistic truths that obtain their security on the basis of redundant predication and logical truths are the case that obtain theirs on the basis of universally satisfiable predication. Thus, our examples will be cases where the principles of a language secure truth for a class of propositions in some way other than by according them the form of redundant or universally satisfiable predications.

One such type of linguistic truth is 'metalinguistic truth' (see Katz (1966, pp. 220–224), which arises from the power of natural languages to construct sentences about some sentence or expression of the same or of another natural language. The most conspicuous apparatus of this sort is direct quotation. Direct quotation presents a sentence or expression within another sentence in a position where it is the object of a predication. But direct quotation is supplemented by other devices. One is a class of metalinguistic expressions that provide a variety of predications to be made of linguistic objects. Another is a class of noun phrases—e.g., "the sentence," "the sense of the sentence," "the utterance," "the orthographic form," "the word"—which focus on the proper object of predication. Clearly, direct quotation can present only a token of a sentence type, though, equally clearly, reference is often to the type itself or to its meaning.[36]

Given the general applicability of direct quotation, it should not be surprising that there will be metalinguistic sentences that predicate something exclusively semantic of the sentence or expressions presented in them and that the semantic structure of the presented sentence or expression is such as to make the prediction true. Such metalinguistic sentences are the metalinguistic truths. Some examples are given in (4.176):[37]

(4.176) (a) "I like Indians without reservations" is semantically ambiguous
 (b) "Don't walk on the grass" is meaningful
 (c) "Sportswear" is synonymous with "clothing suitable for wearing while engaging in one or another sports activity"
 (d) "Male nephew" is redundant
 (e) "Kings are monarchs" is analytic
 (f) "Sick people always recover" is inconsistent with "Sick people never get well"
 (g) "John is sweating" entails "John is excreting moisture through pores in his skin"
 (h) "Nephews are female" is contradictory
 (i) "Don't empty the shadow" is meaningless
 (j) "Dream" is a superordinate of "nightmare"

Such metalinguistic truths come under the heading of linguistic truths because their truth conditions are satisfied on the basis of semantic considerations alone, that is, their truth conditions are satisfied in the same way as the truth conditions of analytic propositions, by virtue of semantic considerations in grammar and independently of extralinguistic fact. Note, however, that sentences like (4.176a–j) are not analytic either in the strict Kantian sense or in the sense explicated

---

[36] The *how* of such reference is, of course, a complex question, involving various theories about the nature of the object enclosed within quotation marks. We cannot enter into this question in the present context and have no need to, since we make no assumption about how an object enclosed in quotation marks is related to a sentence.

[37] Strictly speaking, the sentences (4.176a–j) should have more complex subjects and predicates. Their subjects should contain a noun phrase like "the sentence," and their predicates should contain a qualifying expression like "in English."

in the previous section. Their truth does not derive from their assertion being included in their presupposition. Rather, such sentences are linguistic truths because the semantic structure of the presented sentence or expression has the features that the metalinguistic predicate predicates of it. Hence, these sentences are linguistic truths that are distinct from the analytic linguistic truths.[38]

There are also metalinguistic falsehoods, distinct from contradictory sentences. Some examples are given in (4.177):

(4.177) (a) "Don't empty the shadow" is semantically ambiguous
(b) "Waterproof shadows" is meaningful
(c) "Sportswear" is synonymous with "clothing suitable for wearing in the rain"
(d) "Rich nephew" is redundant
(e) "Kings are myopic" is analytic
(f) "Sick people always recover" is inconsistent with "Sick people always get well"
(g) "John is sweating" entails "John is a big coward"
(h) "Nephews are male" is contradictory
(i) "Don't walk on the grass" is meaningless
(j) "Nightmare" is a superordinate of "dream"

Metalinguistic falsehoods are cases where the presented sentence or expression does not have the semantic structure to make the predication true. But since they are not cases where the predication is inconsistent with the presupposition, they cannot be considered contradictory in the sense related to analyticity. Such sentences are false because the semantic structure of the presented sentence (or expression) is not what the metalinguistic predicate says it is. A metalinguistic sentence which says of an expression like "rich uncle" that it is redundant is not false because of a conceptual incompatibility reflecting antonymy relations, but is false simply because the sort of semantic repetition found in cases of redundancy is not present in this case.

Furthermore, the concepts of metalinguistic truth and metalinguistic falsehood, unlike the concepts of analyticity and contradiction, do not have a third option, an analogue to syntheticity. A metalinguistic sentence is either metalinguistically true or metalinguistically false since its quotationally presented sentence or expression either does or does not have the property attributed to it by the metalinguistic predicate.[39]

We can handle these cases by introducing as a lexical reading for a metalinguistic predicate such as 'ambiguous', 'contradictory', 'analytic', 'synthetic', 'redundant' conditions on the semantically interpreted underlying phrase marker for the constituent sentence which require that it have the formal features that satisfy the definition for the appropriate metalinguistic property. Thus, the lexical

[38] Note further that such sentences are different from ones that employ metalinguistic predicates without quotation, e.g., "Ambiguous sentences are meaningful" (which is analytic).

[39] Note that a sentence like "The English noun 'Sätze' is semantically ambiguous" is indeterminate.

reading for the predicate 'contradictory' would be the condition that defines the notion 'contradictory sentence' in the theory of language; the lexical reading for 'nonsense' or 'anomalous' would be the condition that defines 'anomalous sentence' in semantic theory; and so forth. We also introduce the two definitions in (4.178) and (4.179):

(4.178) The sentence S is metalinguistically true (on a sense) if and only if the reading(s) that represent the linguistic object(s) about which S makes a predication have the formal structure to satisfy the condition that is expressed in the reading of the metalinguistic predicate of S.

(4.179) The sentence S is metalinguistically false (on a sense) if and only if the reading(s) that represent the linguistic object(s) about which S makes a predication lack the formal structure to satisfy the condition that is expressed in the reading of the metalinguistic predicate of S.

A logical truth is a proposition whose logical particles and their relations are such that its truth conditions must be satisfied in every possible world (where its presupposition is satisfied), but, unlike the case of analytic propositions, the truth of its presupposition does not entail the satisfaction of its truth conditions. Consider as an example the sentence in (4.125a). Its presupposition is presumably that there exists someone, and its truth conditions are that this person either is or is not alive. The truth of the presupposition does not entail that someone is either alive or not; rather, the truth of (4.125a) in each possible world arises from the logical fact that everything is either alive or not, Analytic truths, on the other hand, make true statements because the condition under which they make a statement, their presupposition, entails the satisfaction of their truth conditions, the conditions under which they make true statements. But their truth conditions themselves are not satisfied in every possible world. Metalinguistic truths differ from both logical truths and analytic truths. Their truth is a function of the fact that their truth conditions express a predication about a linguistic object to which the predication applies. They are linguistic truths because nothing more than linguistic considerations is required to determine their truth.

The logic of questions

"Why do you sit out here all alone?" asked Alice, not wishing
to begin an argument. "Why, because there's nobody with me!"
cried Humpty Dumpty. "Did you think I didn't know the answer
to *that*? Ask another."

Lewis Carroll

      In this chapter we turn from declaratives to an explication of some
logical properties and relations of interrogatives, thereby extending the range of
semantic properties and relations that semantic theory defines. At the same time
we shall seek further support for the approach to the philosophy of language that
is assumed throughout this work, namely, the search for the solutions of classical
philosophical problems in terms of the theoretical constructs developed for the
statement of grammatical universals in linguistic theory.[1] In particular, we shall
try to show that theoretical constructions introduced into semantic theory in order
to treat certain logical properties and relations of questions also contribute to our
understanding of the nature of logic in general.

      Accordingly, if we are to show that questions have genuine logical
features, we must provide clear examples of two kinds. First, we must provide

---

[1] This approach was first formulated in Katz (1965) (reprinted with some revisions in Rorty (1967)) and set forth at greater length in Katz (1966).

questions that have a property analogous to that of being a linguistic truth and so can serve as parallels if determinate propositions whose truth can be determined without appeal to premises (referring to matters outside language). Second, we must provide pairs of questions between which some sort of entailment relation holds so that they can serve as parallels of pairs of assertive propositions where by virtue of a deductive relation one (the conclusion) is true just in case the other (the premiss) is true. But it might be argued that any hope of finding such parallels on which to erect a logic of questions is foredoomed owing to the difference between statements and questions. That is, one might argue as follows. What admits of truth and falsity are statements, which are true when what they assert is the case and false otherwise. Since questions do not assert anything, but instead request information, truth and falsity cannot be properties of questions. If this is so, it makes no sense to speak of deductive connections between questions, of one question logically implying another. And speaking of a question as a logical truth is equally absurd, if not more so. Consequently, there cannot be a logic of questions any more than there can be a barber who shaves all and only those who do not shave themselves.

But this skeptical conclusion does not follow from the admittedly true assumption that questions do not have truth values. For it does not follow that there can be no deductive connections between questions, and so no logic of questions, unless the argument contains the further assumptions that a relation between propositions is deductive if and only if truth is inherited under it and that logic is concerned solely with those relations between premises and conclusions of arguments on which the truth of the former necessitates the truth of the latter. But there is no reason to grant either of these further assumptions. In the case of the first, there is nothing to prevent our claiming that there are deductive connections between questions. Only the standard truth-functional interpretation of such connections in the case of statements—that truth is inherited under them—does not apply to deductive connections in the case of questions. Nothing precludes the possibility of questions having genuine logical properties and relations under some non-truth-functional interpretation of deductive connections. The second assumption begs the question at issue. That logic is concerned solely with relations that preserve truth is not something that one can assume in dealing with the issue of whether objects that do not have truth values can have logical properties and relations.

One purpose of this chapter will be to disprove these critical assumptions, thereby providing a foundation for the logic of questions. To achieve this purpose, we must show two things. We must demonstrate, first, that deductive connections hold between entities that do not bear truth values (i.e., that questions have logical properties and relations) and, second, that there is a motivated and well-defined non-truth-functional interpretation for deductive connections between questions. The former will be shown by means of appropriate examples, ones fully on a par with those that have long served to establish that statements have logical properties and relations. The latter will be shown by constructing an appropriate non-truth-functional interpretation for validity on the basis of definitions from semantic theory and demonstrating that these definitions and the interpretation based on them explain the appropriate examples in a fully acceptable manner. This type of argument will be the same as the one on which the case for the truth-functional interpretation of validity for statement arguments rests.

Once this has been accomplished, we will turn to the question of what the existence of a logic of questions tells us about the nature of logic in general.

1.   Some examples of logical properties and relations

Questions that are parallels of linguistic truths ought to break down into types in the same way that linguistic truths do. Accordingly, there ought to be parallels of analytic statements, parallels of metalinguistic truths, and parallels of logical truths. This is indeed the case.

The questions that are parallels of analytic statements are those in (5.1) and (5.3).[2] (Question (5.2) will be discussed shortly.)

(5.1)   Is a spinster a female?

(5.2)   Is a spinster a male?

(5.3)   (a) Who killed the man who was killed by John?
         (b) What is the color of the red wagon?
         (c) Where is the hat that is on my head?
         (d) What time is it at exactly twelve midnight?
         (e) How many pages are there in a one-hundred-page book?

Questions that are parallels of metalinguistic truths are exemplified in (5.4). ((5.4b) will be discussed shortly.)

(5.4)   (a) Is the sentence "Bachelors are males?" analytic?
         (b) Is the sentence "Bachelors are males?" contradictory?
         (c) Is the expression "male parent" synonymous with the word "father"?
         (d) Does the sentence "William is a king" entail the sentence "William is a monarch"?

Questions that are parallels of logical truths are cases like those in (5.5) and (5.7). ((5.6) will be discussed shortly.)

(5.5)   Is John not both married and not married?

(5.6)   Is John both married and not married?

(5.7)   Is something circular if everything is circular?

Questions like (5.5)–(5.7) have been discussed widely in the literature of erotetic logic,[3] and their treatment is fairly straightforward given the well worked

---

[2] These are questions of the "Who's buried in Grant's tomb?" variety made famous by Groucho Marx.

[3] See the bibliography in Bromberger (1966, p. 597). See also Prior and Prior (1955).

out theory of propositional logic and quantification. Questions like those in (5.4) can be dealt with directly on the basis of a treatment of the other types without special complications. Thus, although we shall take such cases into consideration, it is questions like (5.1)–(5.3) that will be used as our primary examples.

As examples of question pairs that are parallels of entailments, we have cases such as those in (5.8):

(5.8)   (a) Is John a bachelor?   (b) Who stole a cat?

          Is John male?   Who stole an animal?

"Question arguments" such as these are parallels to arguments from one statement to another just as (5.1)–(5.3) are parallels of statements that can be asserted without premises. Except for cases like (5.2), (5.4b), and (5.6), the questions in (5.1)–(5.7) correspond directly to analytic statements, metalinguistic truths, and logical truths, as indicated, where the corresponding statement can be gotten simply by converting the interrogative into its obvious declarative counterpart, for example, (5.1) into "A spinster is a female," or (5.3b) into "The color of the red wagon is red." The question arguments in (5.8) correspond to statement arguments in the same sense, for example, (5.8b) corresponds to the argument from "Someone stole a cat" to "Someone stole an animal." The cases (5.2), (5.4b), and (5.6) correspond to contradictions, metalinguistic falsehoods, and logically false statements, respectively. The whole set of questions (5.1)–(5.7) corresponds to statements whose truth value is linguistically fixed.

In this connection, we should also note the interesting case of "mixed arguments," that is, arguments that involve propositions of different types. For example, consider the argument in (5.9):

(5.9)   Who killed Cock Robin?

          Cock Robin is dead

The premiss in (5.9) is a question and the conclusion is a statement which is true if the request for information expressed in the question can be fulfilled by an answer specifying "who." Such cases illustrate the inherent involvement of the logic of questions and the logic of statements.

I do not intend to provide any argument for the fact that these examples show that questions have logical properties and relations. It seems to me quite uncontroversial that they do.

2. Linguistic background

Before proceeding to an explication of the examples offered in the preceeding section, it is necessary to review certain aspects of linguistic theory that enter into the semantic account that will be proposed.[4]

---

[4] I have stayed with the analysis of sentence types in Katz and Postal (1964) instead of adopting an analysis on which declaratives, interrogatives, and other types are specified by features assigned to the main verb of the topmost matrix-structure in an underlying phrase marker. I find the so-called "performative" analysis as argued for by Ross (1970) unable to stand up to the criticisms of Anderson (1970) and Fraser (in preparation).

The underlying phrase marker for an interrogative sentence is like the underlying phrase marker for a declarative except that its first (i.e., leftmost) terminal symbol is 'Q' and it contains one or more noun phrases (i.e., substrings of the string of terminal symbols which are dominated by the symbol 'NP') to which an occurrence of the symbol '*wh*' is attached.[5] Q marks a question: it makes the application of question transformations obligatory. *Wh* is a scope indicator for Q. Its attachment to a noun phrase indicates that the noun phrase is questioned: syntactically, the noun phrase is transformed into an interrogative pronoun. In general, the noun phrases to which *wh* can be attached are pro-forms such as "someone," "something," "some time," "some place," "some way," and the corresponding interrogative pronouns which occur in the phonetic or orthographic realization are "who," "what," "when," "where," "how," and so on.

For example, the underlying phrase marker for (5.10) is (5.11):

(5.10)   What did John eat?

(5.11)

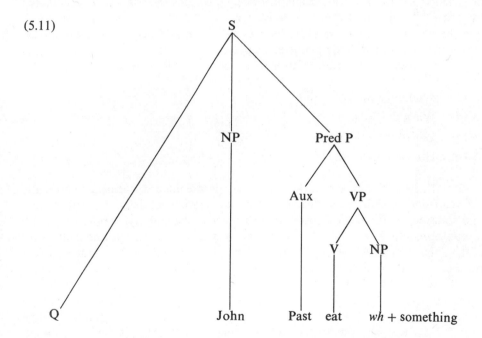

[5] Interrogatives are closely related to imperatives and may even be a form of the imperative type. In Katz and Postal (1964, pp. 79–120) interrogatives are seen to be semantically related to imperatives. They both express propositions of the same semantic type, namely, requests —requests for a certain kind of linguistic object (i.e., an answer) in the case of questions, and requests for behavior of some sort in the case of ordinary imperatives. This view was formulated in terms of suitable lexical readings for 'Q' and 'Imp'. However, there is some evidence that suggests that the relation may go deeper, that there is also a syntactic connection between imperatives and interrogatives.

The superficial phrase marker which specifies the interrogative form of the sentence that (5.11) underlies is simply (5.12):

(5.12)

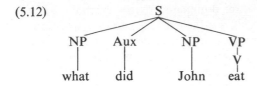

The superficial phrase marker (5.12) is transformationally derived from (5.11) by formal operations characteristic of the generation of interrogatives. To give a rough summary, Q is deleted and the constituent "*wh* + something" is moved to the position vacated by Q. The constituent dominated by "Aux" is inserted between "*wh* + something" and the subject noun phrase "John." An occurrence of "do" is introduced immediately preceding the constituent dominated by "Aux." Then "do + Past" is converted into "did" and "*wh* + something" into the interrogative pronoun "what."[6] Finally, (5.12) is operated on by phonological rules which provide its phonetic shape.

Consider, now, interrogatives like those in (5.13)–(5.16):

(5.13)   Who did John eat with?

(5.14)   When did John eat?

(5.15)   Where did John eat?

(5.16)   How did John eat?

In each of these cases, the superficial phrase marker is transformationally derived from the underlying phrase marker by operations of deletion, permutation, and addition similar to those just described. Each of the underlying phrase markers is appropriately different from the others in a way that reflects the differences among the interrogatives they underlie. That is, although each contains Q and occurrences of *wh* attached to noun phrases, different noun phrases in each have *wh* attached to them and these noun phrases occur in constituents of different syntactic types. For example, in (5.13) the *wh*'d noun phrase is "someone" in the prepositional phrase "with someone"; in (5.14) it is the noun phrase "some time" in the temporal adverbial "at some time"; in (5.15) it is the noun phrase "some place" in the locative adverbial "at some place"; and in (5.16) it is the noun phrase "some way" in the manner adverbial "in some way." The pattern of variation on the interrogative theme is thus clear: each distinct type of interrogative

---

[6] Notice that *wh* functions somewhat like bracketing in a quantification formula in that it determines which noun phrases in the terminal string of an underlying phrase marker are "captured" by Q. Just as not all occurrences of a particular variable need to be in the scope of a given qualifier, so not all noun phrases need to be questioned, nor even all pro-forms, in an interrogative: for example, consider "Who did something to John?" "Who did what to Howard?" "Who did what to whom?"

arises, transformationally, from a different *wh*'d noun phrase forming part of a different but, for its type, characteristic syntactic category. "Which" interrogatives, "how much" interrogatives, "why" interrogatives, "whoever" interrogatives, and other types also fall into place in this pattern.[7]

Jespersen and other grammarians distinguish between interrogatives of the sort just considered and what are commonly referred to as "yes-no" questions. Jespersen (1933) writes:

> There are two kinds of questions: "Did he say that?" is an example of the one kind, and "What did he say?" and "Who said that?" are examples of the other. In the former kind—*nexus-questions*—we call in question the combination (nexus) of a subject and a predicate.... In questions of the second kind we have an unknown quantity x, exactly as in an algebraic equation; we may therefore use the term *x-questions*. The linguistic expression for this x is an interrogative pronoun or pronominal adverb (pp. 304–305).

Semantically, this is a crucial distinction, but, syntactically, nexus-interrogatives are just another variant in the pattern shown by the different cases of *x*-interrogatives we have been discussing. They also arise from a specific constituent belonging to a distinct syntactic category which falls in the scope of the question marker 'Q'. This may not seem right at first glance because of the important semantic difference Jespersen mentions, yet it can easily be shown that nexus-interrogatives are also derived from *wh*'d constituents.

Wh interrogatives, regardless of type, appear as embedded questions in almost their standard interrogative form, as illustrated in (5.17)–(5.22):

(5.17)   John asked which Mary went

(5.18)   John asked where Mary went

(5.19)   John asked when Mary went

(5.20)   John asked how Mary went

(5.21)   John asked why Mary went

(5.22)   John asked who went

But so do nexus-interrogatives, as in (5.23):

(5.23)   John asked whether Mary went

This and other evidence establishes that there is a *wh*'d constituent underlying the word "whether" whose morphemic shape is "*wh* + either."

But to show that all nexus-interrogatives are derived from *wh*'d constituents in their underlying phrase marker, it must also be shown that when a nexus-interrogative occurs by itself as a full sentence—rather than as a nominalization within another sentence—its underlying phrase marker contains a *wh*'d constituent.

---

[7] For a more detailed and complete discussion, see Katz and Postal (1964, pp. 144–147, 177–184).

That is, it must be shown that "*wh* + either" occurs not only in the underlying phrase marker for a sentence such as (5.23) but also in the underlying phrase marker for a question such as (5.24), whose phonetic shape does not contain "whether":

(5.24) Did Mary go?

Note, to begin with, that such nexus-interrogatives are derived from underlying phrase markers that are disjunctive in form. Consider in this regard (5.25)–(5.28):

(5.25) Did Mary go or didn't Mary go?
(5.26) Did Mary go or didn't she?
(5.27) Did Mary go or not?
(5.28) Did Mary or didn't Mary go?

Clearly, the underlying phrase markers for these interrogatives are disjunctive in form.[8] Consequently, if (5.24) has the same underlying phrase marker as any of these nexus-interrogatives, its underlying phrase marker will also be disjunctive in form. Now, the nexus-interrogatives (5.25)–(5.28) are synonymous with one another, and, moreover, (5.24) is equivalent in meaning to them. Each of the cases (5.24)–(5.28) questions the truth of the statement that Mary went. In cases like (5.29) and (5.30), the synonymy relation can be accounted for on a strictly semantic basis:

(5.29) John is a bachelor
(5.30) John is an unmarried adult male

This is not so, however, with regard to (5.24)–(5.28), since here the synonymy relations do not hold between sentences with different morphemic content which through semantic interaction express the same meaning. Hence, these synonymy relations must be explained on the grounds that all of the interrogatives in question have the same underlying phrase marker. Sentences with the same underlying phrase marker receive the same semantic interpretation and are marked as paraphrases of one another.[9]

---

[8] Also, contrast these with the ungrammatical "Who went or not?" Furthermore, the tag question "Mary went, didn't she?" differs in meaning from (5.24)–(5.28) in that the former embodies the assertion that Mary went whereas the latter do not. We can explain this by deriving the tag question as a complex sentence whose deep main clause takes the form of the declarative structure 'Mary Past go' and whose deep subordinate clause is (5.31). Transformations delete the first coordinated structure of (5.31) on identity with the main clause and put the second in interrogative form, pronominalizing its subject.

[9] We assume, of course, that transformations make no contribution to the meaning of a sentence. See Katz and Postal (1964) and Chomsky (1965).

Let us assume, then, that the underlying phrase marker for (5.24)–(5.28) is something like (5.31):

(5.31)

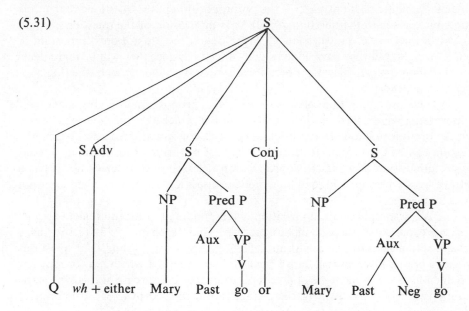

The interrogatives in (5.24)–(5.28) (or, rather, their superficial phrase markers) are each derived transformationally from (5.31) by a familiar ellipsis pattern in which repeated elements can be deleted.[10] This sort of derivation provides an explanation not only for the syntactic and semantic relations between (5.24)–(5.28), but for much else as well. To begin with, it explains the synonymy of (5.23) and (5.32):

(5.32)   John asked whether Mary went or not

Moreover, it explains why interrogatives like (5.24) express the same question as nexus-interrogatives like (5.33) even though the latter are negative forms of the former:[11]

(5.33)   Didn't Mary go?

Finally, on this treatment, when a nexus-interrogative occurs by itself, as a full sentence, "wh + either" is phonetically realized in the form of a stressed initial occurrence of "do" (or "will," "can," "should," "be," "have," etc.).

[10] See Chomsky (1965, pp. 144–147, 177–184).
[11] Of course, even though the negative and positive forms of a nexus-interrogative ask the same question, they are normally appropriate in different contexts. The former is used in cases where it is reasonable for the speaker to presume that the person referred to did not do the thing in question. Hence the secondary use of negative forms, as in the case where a husband and wife are going out and the wife is taking her time dressing, so the husband says "Aren't you coming?" See Jespersen, (1933, p. 304) and Chapter 8, Section 5.

In terms of this conception of the grammar of interrogatives, in particular the treatment of their underlying syntactic structure, it is possible to define the syntactic-semantic relations (a) 'x is the presupposition of the question q'; (b) 'x is a possible answer to the question q'; (c) 'x is an evasion of the question q'; and (d) 'x is a rejection of the question q'. These definitions are not only important in their own right, but they have added significance here since they will be ingredients in our definitions of logical properties and relations upon which the logic of questions depends.

The presupposition of a question is a proposition (or conjunction of propositions) whose truth is the condition under which the question expresses a request for information. More specifically, it is the condition under which the question can be used to put forth such a request by virtue of its meaning. Just as the presupposition of an assertive proposition determines whether or not it has a truth value, the presupposition of an erotetic proposition determines whether or not it has an answer.

A question has a presupposition corresponding to the requirement that its referring expressions succeed in designating. Thus, each of (5.13)–(5.16) has a presupposition in connection with its referring expression "John." But questions also have presuppositions that derive from clausal structures which may or may not be reducible to the former type of presupposition. The classic case of this type is the presupposition of (5.34), namely, the proposition expressed by (5.35), where (5.35) is thought of as used under the same utterance conditions as (5.34):

(5.34)   When did you stop beating your wife?

(5.35)   You stopped beating your wife at some time

We shall talk primarily about these presuppositions in our discussion of the presuppositions of questions because, as things will turn out, they will be defined in such a way as to include each of the more restricted presuppositions arising from referring expressions. Thus, for example, two components of the presupposition of (5.34) are the propositions expressed by (a) and (b) of (5.36), and each is a component of the presupposition expressed in (5.35):

(5.36)   (a) There is an addressee of the sentence (5.34) on the occasion in question
          (b) There is someone who is the wife of the addressee of (5.34) on the
              occasion in question

We now define the notions 'presupposition of the question q' and 'component of the presupposition of the question q'. These definitions should be thought of as clauses of the definition for the notion 'presupposition of the sentence S'.

(5.37)   A proposition p is the presupposition of the question q (i.e., of the sense of an interrogative) just in case p is represented by the reading of a sentence which has the same underlying phrase marker as that for q except for the absence of the symbol 'Q' and occurrence of the scope symbol 'wh' and which contains semantic markers inside double parentheses that express illocutionary force information marking it as an assertive proposition.

(5.38)   A proposition p' is a component of the presupposition of the question q just in case p' is represented by the reading of a sentence entailed by the presupposition of q.

On the basis of (5.37), the presupposition of (5.10), "What did John eat?" is the proposition expressed by both (a) and (b) of (5.39):[12]

(5.39)   (a) John ate something
(b) Something was eaten by John

And (5.35) is the presupposition of (5.34) while (5.40) is a component of the presupposition of (5.34):

(5.40)   You have beaten your wife at some time

Similarly, the presuppositions of (5.13)–(5.16) are the propositions which are expressed by (5.41)–(5.44):

(5.41)   John ate with somebody

(5.42)   John ate at some time

(5.43)   John ate at some place

(5.44)   John ate in some manner

The presupposition of the nexus-interrogative (5.24) and its paraphrases (5.25)–(5.28) and (5.33) is the proposition expressed by (5.45):

(5.45)   (Either) Mary did go or Mary did not go

Of course the presupposition of (5.24) is vacuous since it is an instance of a logical truth, but this is not the case for all types of nexus-interrogatives. The case (5.46) has the nonvacuous presupposition (5.47):

(5.46)   Did Mary go home or did Mary go to school?

(5.47)   (Either) Mary went home or Mary went to school

The notion 'possible answer' is analogous to the notion 'lawlike statement'.[13] Just as a lawlike statement is a statement that has all the characteristics of a law except for possibly being false, so a possible answer has all the characteristics of an answer except for possibly being false. True lawlike statements are genuine

---

[12] That is, (a) of (5.39) is the passive of (b), and passives are synonymous with their active counterparts. See Katz and Postal (1964, pp. 72–74) and Katz and Martin (1967).

[13] This is a familiar notion in the philosophy of science. See, for example, the discussion in Goodman (1965, p. 22).

laws, and, analogously, true possible answers are correct answers. Accordingly, the notion of a possible answer is that of a sentence (or the statement it expresses) that would satisfy the request for information if it were true.

Our definition of this notion treats nexus-interrogatives and x-interrogatives differently, in the manner suggested by Jespersen's remarks: semantically, the questions expressed by the former request information as to the truth or falsity of a statement (or set of statements, as in (5.46)), while those expressed by the latter request information about some unknown x. Thus we have the definition (5.48):

(5.48)   The proposition expressed by the sentence x is a possible answer to the question q just in case q is not indeterminable and (a) q is a nexus-interrogative and x's underlying phrase marker is the same as one of the two proper parts of the underlying phrase marker for q whose topmost node is labeled 'S' and is directly dominated by the topmost node in that phrase marker; or (b) q is an x-interrogative and x's underlying phrase marker is the same as that of the presupposition of q (see (5.37)) except that, for each noun phrase NP_i in x corresponding to a *wh*'d noun phrase in q, NP_i is replaced in the semantically interpreted underlying phrase marker for x by a noun phrase NP_j such that the reading for NP_j has more semantic markers than the reading for NP_i and satisfies the selection restriction governing nonanomalous occurrences of NP_j; or (c) x is a paraphrase of (on the appropriate sense, i.e., has the same reading as) some sentence satisfying either (a) or (b).

By this definition, in the case of both nexus-interrogatives and x-interrogatives, a possible answer provides information beyond what is contained in the meaning of the questioned constituent(s). However, in the former case this information is provided by a choice from among the disjuncts in the question. Jespersen (1933) put the matter in terms of questioning "the combination (nexus) of a subject and a predicate" (p. 304). But since questioning the combination actually takes the form of posing alternatives, one of which expresses its correctness and the other its incorrectness, if a possible answer is a particular choice from among the alternatives posed in the question, it will express a claim about the correctness of a predication. Accordingly, the questioning of a sentence adverbial requests information beyond what is given in the reading of the disjunction of sentences. The reading of one (in certain cases more than one) of the disjuncts provides this information. Thus, possible answers to (5.24) are (5.49) and (5.50):

(5.49)   Mary did go

(5.50)   Mary did not go

"Yes" is a stylistic variant of possible answers such as (5.49), and "No" is a stylistic variant of possible answers such as (5.50), but only when the superficial form of the interrogative is that represented in (5.24). Such variants of cases like (5.49) and (5.50)—including the bureaucratic uses of "affirmative" and "negative"

—cannot be possible answers when the superficial form of the interrogative is like that represented in (5.25)–(5.28) or when its underlying form is like that represented in (5.46).

In the case of x-interrogatives, the questioning of a noun phrase requests information beyond that given in the reading of the noun phrase questioned. Part (b) of definition (5.48) captures this in its requirement that the appropriate noun phrases in a possible answer have a reading that contains more semantic markers than appear in the reading for their corresponding *wh*'d noun phrases in the question. These additional semantic markers in the relevant noun phrases of a possible answer provide the further information requested.[14] Accordingly, some possible answers to (5.10) are those in (5.51)–(5.53):

(5.51)   John ate sticks and some stones

(5.52)   John ate food

(5.53)   John ate something he had in his pocket

The definition (5.48) provides an explication of the conversion of the condition of an erotetic proposition. In the chart (4.77), we indicated that the condition of an erotetic proposition is converted into an answerhood condition as a function of the propositional type, but at that point we were able to describe the converted condition only by the informal phrase "an utterance token of a sentence that is both a possible answer to the UCC and true." Now, however, we can say that the propositional type of an erotetic proposition, besides carrying the illocutionary force information specifying that interrogatives are used by the speaker to make requests, contains a specification of the notion 'possible answer' for the erotetic proposition in terms of the application of (5.48) to the semantically interpreted underlying phrase marker of the erotetic proposition.

The nature of the request embodied in the asking of a question is thus explained: the request is that the person addressed supply the speaker with the sort of information that is determined by the grammar of the question and the conditions expressed in (5.48).[15]

Possible answers must be distinguished from two closely related things: *evasions of a question* and *rejections of a question*. As grammatical notions, 'evasion' and 'rejection' are indirectly specified. That is, an evasion is a sentence whose information content is restricted to the information contained in the question for which it is used as a response or to part of the information contained in the question; a rejection is a sentence whose information content is restricted to something that conflicts with the information contained in the question for which it is used as a response. Evasions repeat the question's presupposition, or some part of its presupposition, while rejections assert the falsity of the question's presupposition. Thus we have the definitions (5.54) and (5.55).

---

[14] Thus, continuing Jespersen's algebraic analogy, such semantic markers are the analogues of expressions such as "y^2," "17," "$5y + 8z^3$" which "x" may equal in an equation.

[15] See Katz and Postal (1964, pp. 85–91).

(5.54)   The proposition expressed by the sentence x is an evasion of the question q just in case this proposition is the presupposition of q or identical to some conjunct of the presupposition of q.[16]

(5.55)   The proposition expressed by the sentence x is a rejection of the question q just in case this proposition entails the denial of the presupposition of q.

By definition (5.54), the sentence (5.56) is an evasion of the question (5.10):

(5.56)   John ate something

And (5.41)–(5.44) are, respectively, evasions of the questions (5.13)–(5.16). Also, (5.35) and (5.57) are evasions of the question (5.34):

(5.57)   You have a wife

By definition (5.55), the sentences (5.58) and (5.59) are rejections of the question expressed by (5.10):

(5.58)   John did not eat anything
(5.59)   John ate nothing

Also, (5.60a–c) are all rejections of the question (5.34) since each entails that the presupposition of (5.34) is false:

(5.60)   (a) I never stopped beating my wife
         (b) I never beat my wife at any time
         (c) I do not (even) have a wife

Similarly, (5.61a) is an evasion of (5.24), while (5.61b) is a rejection of (5.47):

(5.61)   (a) Mary did go or Mary didn't go
         (b) Mary did not go home and Mary did not go to school

Note, however, that sentences like (a), (b), and (c) of (5.62) are not possible answers or evasions or rejections of the questions (5.10), (5.13), and (5.15), respectively, but are simply confessions of ignorance.[17]

(5.62)   (a) I don't know what John ate
         (b) I don't know who John ate with
         (c) I don't know where John ate

---

[16] I am indebted to Sylvia Schwartz for pointing out the need for this second disjunct.

[17] The same is true for the abbreviation "I don't know," as well as many other forms such as "I don't know the answer." Confessions of ignorance are analogous to responses to imperatives (requests for action) such as "I am unable to do it."

It is clear, I think, that responses like (5.62a–c) are not evasions or rejections of their respective questions. To show that they are also not possible answers, we observe that they are responses not to the content of the question but to a presumption created in the context by the circumstances under which the interrogative is used. This is the presumption of the speaker that the addressee has the answer to his question. What the addressee says in uttering a token of a type like (5.62a–c) is that this presumption is false. We can compare this to the case where someone asserts (5.63) and someone else replies with (5.64):

(5.63)   The treasure is hidden under the house

(5.64)   That's a lie!

A person who responds in the manner of (5.64) is responding to the contextual presumption that the speaker believes what he asserts. If it were part of the semantics of a declarative sentence that the speaker believes the proposition it expresses, we could not use assertions to lie, whereas if it were part of the semantics of an interrogative that the addressee has the answer, we could not use questions to baffle and confound. Responses like (5.62a–c) are not related to the content of the questions, except in the case of quite different questions like those in (5.65) and (5.66):

(5.65)   Do you know what John ate?

(5.66)   Do you know who John ate with?

Thus the responses in (a), (b), and (c) of (5.62) cannot be considered possible answers to the questions (5.10), (5.13), and (5.15). Answers, as we have seen, supply information of the sort requested in the questions themselves.

Shortly we shall define the notion 'linguistically answerable question' as, roughly, one whose presupposition *can* be true, that is, one whose presupposition is neither indeterminable nor contradictory nor a contradiction. According to this natural definition, simple nexus-interrogatives like (5.24), as opposed to those like (5.46), always produce linguistically answerable questions if the referring expressions in them, those noun phrases occurring in referential positions, succeed in denoting appropriate objects in the contexts where the interrogatives are used. Hence, the questions expressed by these nexus-interrogatives cannot, in principle, be rejected on the basis of a true statement. We can account for this feature. If the referring expressions in such an interrogative do not succeed in denoting, then there cannot be a true, or for that matter even a false, rejection of the question expressed by the interrogative since then the corresponding expressions in the "rejection" will also fail to denote in that context. On the other hand, if these expressions succeed in denoting, the putative rejection must be a logical falsehood since, first, it is inconsistent with the presupposition of the question and, second, the presuppositions of such nexus-interrogatives are, as observed earlier, logical truths. Thus, on the account we have proposed for nexus-interrogatives, there is a natural explanation of why we can reject a question like (5.46) by denying its full presupposition, that is, by asserting that Mary neither went home nor to school, but we can reject a question like (5.24) not in this way but only by denying a component of the pre-supposition, for example, by asserting that the Mary in question does not exist (she is one of the children's imaginary playmates, for example).

This raises the question of whether (5.55) might be more adequate if the definiens were replaced by the condition that x is an internally consistent proposition that entails the denial of the presupposition of q. This condition would imply that there are no rejections of simple nexus-interrogatives like (5.24) which take the form of negations of their full presupposition since such propositions are inconsistent. I find this alternative less attractive than the definition as it now stands because it seems consistent with other terminology to allow inconsistent rejections of a question rather than to restrict rejections so that they are necessarily consistent propositions. After all, there are inconsistent statements, inconsistent answers, inconsistent questions, and so on.

Note, finally, that the notion of an answer that we have defined is that of a *direct* (possible) answer. We might also define a notion 'indirect answer', say, as any determinable proposition that entails a (direct) answer. Similarly, we might further define indirect versions of the other notions defined previously.[18]

3. Two basic questions about questions and answers

To explain the examples (5.1)–(5.8), it is necessary to answer two basic questions. First, what property do questions like (5.1) have that allows them to stand as parallels to analytic statements, and, further, what property do questions like (5.2) have that allows them to stand as parallels of contradictions? In general, what is the property that both kinds of questions have by virtue of which they parallel statement cases that have a linguistically determined truth value? How can such properties be like analyticity (and contradiction) without conferring truth (and falsity)? Second, what is the relation between the questions in pairs like (5.8a) and like (5.8b)? If valid statement arguments preserve truth, what do valid question arguments preserve? Also, what is the relation between the question and the statement in the pair constituting the argument in (5.9)? Since question arguments cannot be taken to preserve truth, how is it that, in cases such as (5.9), the truth of a statement can be inferred from a question? The two basic questions are, then, first, what is the direct analogue of declarative sentences expressing statements that are necessarily true or false for linguistic reasons alone, and, second, what is the direct analogue of statements that are necessarily true if certain premises for them are true?

Let us begin with the first of these questions. As has already been observed, cases like (5.1) cannot be taken to be analytic since, being questions, they express requests for information, not true assertions; and, likewise, cases like (5.2) cannot be taken as contradictory since, being questions, they make no assertion and hence no false assertion. Nevertheless, as is intuitively quite clear, they are very much like linguistically determined truths and falsehoods. Their similarity to and difference

---

[18] Thus, an indirect evasion or rejection might be defined as a proposition that is determinable, consistent, and entails a proposition that is an evasion of the question or a proposition that is a rejection of the question.

from sentences that have a linguistically determined truth value can be put as follows. Just as analytic and contradictory sentences express assertions whose truth and falsity are guaranteed by their meaning, so such interrogatives express questions whose affirmative answer, negative answer, or answer is given by their meaning. Since such questions are parallel to statements with a linguistically determined truth value, let us call them *self-answered questions* or *linguistically answered questions*. We have to show how the property of being a linguistically answered question can be defined in semantic theory.[19]

Since a question is either a nexus-question or an *x*-question, we have only to define the notions 'self-answered nexus-question' or 'linguistically answered nexus-question' and 'self-answered *x*-question' or 'linguistically answered *x*-question'. Let us consider the former case first. A nexus-question, as (5.1) and (5.2) show, can be 'linguistically answered in the affirmative' or 'linguistically answered in the negative'. Accordingly, we may begin with (5.67):

(5.67)   A nexus-question *q* is self-answered or linguistically answered just in case *q* is linguistically answered in the affirmative or linguistically answered in the negative.

There are two types of nexus-questions, those like (5.24), which we may call *simple nexus-questions*, and those like (5.46), which we may call *complex nexus-questions*. Simple nexus-questions have underlying phrase markers of the form shown in (5.68):

(5.68)

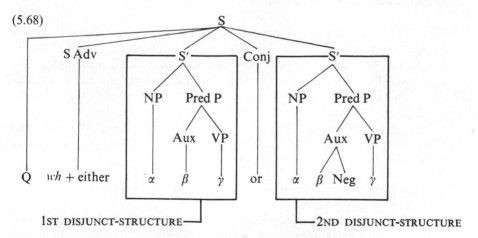

Complex nexus-questions have underlying phrase markers of the form shown in (5.69).

---

[19] It might be asked why a question like "Who saw the man who was seen by John?" is not linguistically answered whereas the quesions in (5.3) are. Like "Who's buried in Grant's tomb?," "Who saw the man who was seen by John?" is ambiguous. Just as Groucho Marx's question can be taken either to mean 'who is buried in the tomb known as the place of Grant's interment' or to mean 'who is buried in the tomb where Grant is interred', so the latter question can mean 'who else (besides John) saw the man who was seen by John' or simply 'who saw him.'

(5.69)

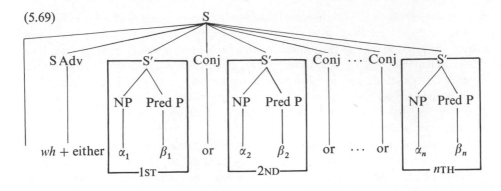

To simplify matters, I will introduce the terms *first disjunct-structure, second disjunct-structure,* and, in the case of complex nexus-questions, *third disjunct-structure, fourth disjunct-structure,* and so on. A *disjunct-structure,* as shown in (5.68) and (5.69), is a proper part of an underlying phrase marker for a nexus-interrogative: its topmost node is labeled 'S' and is directly dominated by the topmost node in the whole underlying phrase marker, and its terminal string is bounded by occurrences of the morpheme " or " or, in the case of the first and *n*th, respectively, by " *wh* + either " and " or " and by " or " and the sentence boundary. The leftmost such proper part is referred to as the *first disjunct-structure,* the next as the *second disjunct-structure,* and so forth. We can define the operative notions in the definition (5.67) as follows:

(5.70)   A nexus-question q is linguistically answered in the affirmative (on a sense) in case either
(a) q is a simple nexus-question and the semantically interpreted first disjunct-structure of q represents an analytic proposition, i.e., satisfies (4.113), or represents a metalinguistically true proposition, i.e., satisfies (4.178), or
(b) q is a complex nexus-question and there is one semantically intepreted disjunct-structure of q that represents an analytic proposition or one that represents a metalinguistically true proposition.[20]

(5.71)   A nexus-question q is linguistically answered in the negative (on a sense) in case either
(a) q is a simple nexus-question and the semantically interpreted first disjunct-structure of q represents a contradictory proposition, i.e., satisfies (4.120), or represents a metalinguistically false proposition, i.e., satisfies (4.179), or
(b) q is a complex nexus-question and every semantically interpreted disjunct-structure of q represents a contradictory proposition or every

---

[20] We leave open the possibility of further clauses—e.g., one for the conditions under which a nexus-question is self-answered by virtue of the meaning of its logical particles—that is, the possibility of expanding the definitions to encompass the question counterparts of logical truths and contradictions, and also mixed cases where each disjunct-structure represents a linguistic truth but not the same kind in each case.

semantically interpreted disjunct-structure represents a metalinguistic-ally false proposition.[21]

Thus, (5.1) is marked as linguistically answered in the affirmative and so is (5.4a), whereas (5.2) is marked as linguistically answered in the negative and so is (5.4b). All four of these simple nexus-questions are marked as linguistically answered questions (or self-answered questions) by (5.67). Now consider the complex nexus-questions in (5.72)–(5.75):

(5.72)   Is a spinster female or unmarried?

(5.73)   Is a spinster female or male?

(5.74)   Is a spinster male or married?

(5.75)   Is a spinster male or rich?

Questions (5.72) and (5.73) are both marked as linguistically answered in the affirmative, and (5.74) but not (5.75) is marked as linguistically answered in the negative. Accordingly, (5.72), (5.73), and (5.74) are marked as linguistically answered questions, while (5.75) is not.

(5.76)

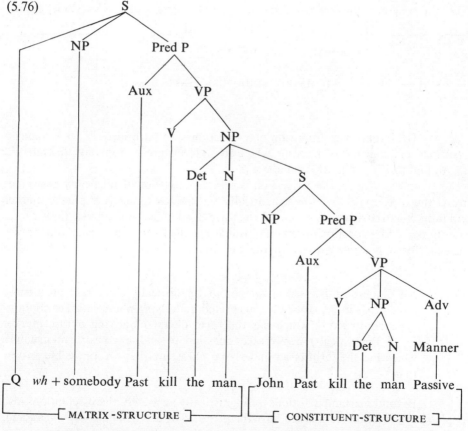

[21] Again, we leave open the possibility of further clauses, and also mixed cases where each disjunct-structure represents a linguistic falsehood but not the same kind in each case.

(5.77)

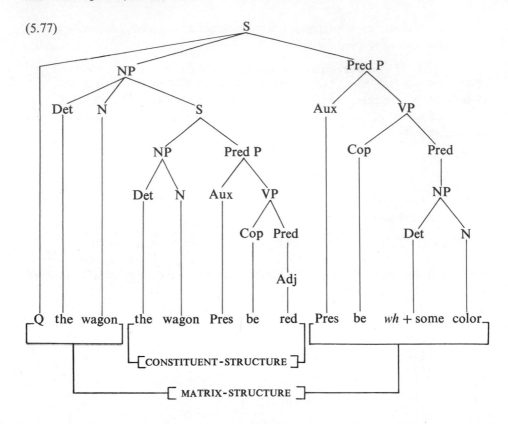

To simplify our discussion of x-questions, we introduce the terms *matrix-structure* and *constituent-structure*, where these terms are to apply as illustrated in (5.76) and (5.77) (see p. 219 and above):

In these cases, the x-question is self-answered (or linguistically answered) by virtue of the fact that the semantically interpreted underlying phrase marker contains a matrix-structure which has the form of an underlying phrase marker for a question q' and a constituent-structure which has the form of an underlying phrase marker for a possible answer to the question q'. Thus we have the definition (5.78):

(5.78)   An x-question q is self-answered (or linguistically answered) on a sense just in case its semantically interpreted underlying phrase marker contains a matrix-structure which has the form of an underlying phrase marker for a linguistically answerable question q' and a constituent-structure which has the form of an underlying phrase marker for a possible answer to q'.

Beyond marking questions as linguistically answered, these definitions also explain why questions so marked have the property of being linguistically answered. For nexus-questions the explanation is as follows. As we have observed, such questions query the truth of a statement: for example, (5.24) asks about the truth of the statement that Mary went. The first disjunct-structure of such nexus-questions represents the statement whose truth is asked about in the asking of the question (and the second helps state the query by posing its denial as an alternative). Thus, if a nexus-question is marked linguistically answered in the affirmative, the first disjunct-structure in its underlying phrase marker will represent an analytic statement. So, by virtue of the fact that the statement whose truth is queried is a linguistic truth, the query is answered. If a nexus-question is marked linguistically answered in the negative, the first disjunct-structure in its underlying phrase marker will represent a contradictory statement. So, by virtue of the fact that the statement whose truth is queried is a linguistic falsehood, the query is again answered. In either case, then, the query is answered.

In the case of x-questions, the explanation is this. If an x-question is linguistically answered, then the constituent-structure in its underlying phrase marker represents a possible answer to the question represented in the matrix-structure of that underlying phrase marker (see (5.48b)). This possible answer is also part of the presupposition of the whole question (see (5.37)). If the use of such an interrogative sentence expresses a request for information, its presupposition must be true, since the truth of the presupposition of an interrogative is a necessary condition for it to express a question. Consequently, this possible answer, being part of the presupposition, must itself be true, and so this possible answer is a (correct) answer to the question of which it is a part. Therefore, the whole question gives its own answer. Its request for information is made and met, as it were, in one and the same breath.

Since we have found parallels in the case of questions to statements whose truth and falsity are linguistically fixed, we should push the analogy further and try to find other logical properties of questions. It will be recalled from the previous chapter that semantic theory distinguishes two sorts of senses that nonanomalous declarative sentences can have, as exemplified in (5.79) and (5.80):

(5.79) The rich queen is unhappy

(5.80) The male queen is unhappy

The proposition expressed by (5.79) is determinable, that is, it can be used to make a statement because, as a matter of logical possibility, there can be an individual for its subject expression to designate. In contrast, the proposition expressed by (5.80) is indeterminable, that is, it can never be used to make a statement because there cannot be anyone designated by a contradictory expression such as "male queen."

The interrogatives in (5.81) and (5.82) correspond directly to these declarative cases: (5.81) is determinable and (5.82) is indeterminable:

(5.81) Is the rich queen happy?

(5.82) Is the male queen unhappy?

Since we cannot say that a determinable sense of an interrogative can make a statement and an indeterminable sense does not make a statement, we shall say that the former is *linguistically answerable* and the latter is *linguistically unanswerable*. Further examples of linguistically unanswerable questions are given in (5.83) and (5.84):

(5.83)   Who did the living corpse fall on?

(5.84)   Who will kill the corpse?

Cases like (5.82) and (5.83) can no more express linguistically answerable questions than their declarative counterparts can express true or false statements. The presupposition of (5.82) is that there is someone who is a male queen and is unique in being so and is either unhappy or not, and the presupposition of (5.83) is that there is something which is both living and a corpse, i.e., not living, that fell on someone. Both these presuppositions are indeterminable, and hence neither can be true. Since the truth of the presupposition of a question is a necessary condition for it to express a request for information, no tokens of an indeterminable question can express such a request. There is nothing for their answers to give the requisite information about. In the case of (5.84), although there can be something for the question and its answer to be about, nonetheless, the condition under which interrogatives express a question, namely, that their presupposition be true, cannot be met. The presupposition of (5.84) is that someone will kill the corpse, and the condition that this be true cannot be met because the presupposition is contradictory. To cover both types of cases, we give (a) and (b) of (5.85):

(5.85)   (a) A question q is linguistically unanswerable just in case the presupposition of q is either indeterminable or contradictory.

(b) A question q is linguistically answerable just in case the presupposition of q is neither indeterminable nor contradictory.

Since linguistically answered questions are parallels of necessary truths and necessary falsehoods and linguistically unanswerable questions are the parallel of propositions that make no statement, it follows that the class of erotetic propositions that are not linguistically answered but are linguistically answerable is the parallel to the assertive propositions that are synthetic truths or falsehoods. Thus we have (5.86):

(5.86)   A question q is contingently answerable just in case q is not linguistically answered but is linguistically answerable.

This completes our answer to the first of the two basic questions underlying the logic of questions. In short, parallel to statements that are validly assertable without premises are linguistically answered questions, questions that require no independent answer.

We now turn to the second of the two questions with which we are concerned in this section, namely, the problem of what property is preserved in valid question arguments. Or, to put the question another way, what sense does it make to say that the premisses in cases like (5.8a,b) entail their conclusions?

In the case of arguments involving statements, a conclusion that can be validly asserted on certain premisses is so assertable because its relation to its premisses is one that always preserves truth. Since the parallel of linguistically determined truth, which is what makes a statement assertable without premisses or on any premisses, is linguistically determined answerhood, by analogy, the property preserved in the case of arguments involving questions ought to be sameness of answer or simply answerhood. We shall now try to show that this analogy does indeed provide the solution to the problem at hand.

Consider the following question arguments involving nexus-questions that are, case by case, counterparts of the statement arguments presented in (i), (ii), (iii) of (4.143a) and (i), (ii), (iii), (iv) of (4.143b):

(5.87)   Are all females dangerous motorists?
_____
Are all spinsters dangerous motorists?

(5.88)   Are all females geniuses?
_____
Are all spinsters intelligent?

(5.89)   Are all principals spinsters?
_____
Are all principals females?

(5.90)   Are some bachelors rich?
_____
Are some males rich?

(5.91)   Are some bachelors kings?
_____
Are some males monarchs?

(5.92)   Are some bachelors kings?
_____
Are some bachelors monarchs?

(5.93)   Is John a king?
_____
Is John a monarch?

By the definition of entailment given in Chapter 4, each of the arguments (5.87)–(5.93) is an entailment, just like its statement-argument counterpart, for the definition of entailment is given for propositions, not for assertive propositions.

What is preserved in a valid question argument involving nexus-questions is *affirmative answerhood*. That is to say, if A is an affirmative answer to the premiss question Q_1, and Q_1 entails Q_2, then A is necessarily an affirmative answer to Q_2. For example, (5.94) is an affirmative answer to the premiss of (5.90).

(5.94)   (Yes) Some bachelors are rich

But (5.94) is necessarily (implies) also an affirmative answer to the conclusion of (5.90). Moreover, corresponding to the fact that in a valid deduction from one statement to another the falsity of the conclusion implies the falsity of at least one of the premisses, if N is a negative answer to Q_2, then N is necessarily (implies) also a negative answer to Q_1. For example, (5.95) is a negative answer to the conclusion of (5.90):

(5.95)   (No) No males are rich

And it is also a negative answer to the premiss of (5.90). Notice, however, that a negative answer to the premiss in a valid nexus-question argument is not an answer to the conclusion. For example, a negative answer to the premiss of (5.93) is not an answer to its conclusion. This can be shown quite easily. Consider (5.96):

(5.96)   Is John male?

Both (5.96) and the conclusion of (5.93) are entailed by the premiss of (5.93). Yet, given that the answer to the premiss is negative, these two questions can have opposite answers: the answer to one can be affirmative and the answer to the other negative. Furthermore, an affirmative answer to the conclusion of a valid nexus-question argument is not an answer to the premiss. For example, the answer to the conclusion in (5.93) can be affirmative while the answer to the premiss in (5.93) is negative.

In valid arguments involving x-questions like (5.8b), answerhood is preserved in the direct sense that anything that is an answer to the premiss question is itself an answer to the conclusion question. Consider, for example, (5.97):

(5.97)   The little old lady stole a cat

If (5.97) is the answer to the premiss question of (5.8b), it is the answer to the conclusion question of (5.8b) as well. But, of course, an answer to a conclusion question in such arguments is not necessarily an answer to the premiss question.

Finally, in valid arguments from questions to statements such as (5.9), we can say that if the premiss question has an answer then the conclusion is true. But, of course, the truth of the conclusion in such cases does not imply that the premiss question has an answer. Thus, Cock Robin might have died of natural causes, in which case, even if it is true that Cock Robin is dead, it does not follow that someone killed Cock Robin; but, since this is the presupposition of the premiss of (5.9), if it is not true then the question has no answer.

In the discussion in this section we have tried to formulate the property that the conclusion of a valid question argument inherits from its premiss, namely, affirmative answerhood in the case of nexus-questions and answerhood in the case of x-questions. Moreover, we have offered an explanation of the formal conditions under which such arguments are valid—under which they preserve answerhood— namely, that given in (4.141) and the apparatus of semantic theory on which it depends. It should be recognized, however, that this discussion is only a prolegomenon to the study of this extremely complex subject.

4. Applications: practical and theoretical

I do not wish to claim extensive practical applications for the logic of questions, that is, cases for which a logic of questions can serve as a proper standard of acceptable inference. But it is necessary to show that there are at least some practical applications. The following is a typical example. Consider a cross-examination in the course of a trial. The prosecuting attorney asks the witness the question in (5.98):

(5.98)   Did the victim murmur anything before dying?

The defense attorney objects that the witness need not answer this question on the grounds that it is entailed by a previous question, namely, (5.99), which the victim answered negatively:

(5.99)   Did the victim utter any sound before dying?

We could regard the logic of questions as providing an explanation of the defense attorney's inference that the prosecuting attorney's question had already been answered: since (5.98) is marked as entailing the previously (negatively) answered question (5.99), by the interpretation of deductive connections between questions, the answer to (5.98) is already determined, without the witness needing to reply.

The theoretical application I wish to discuss concerns the nature of logic in general. The conception of logic that makes the notion of a logic of questions seem paradoxical is the view that the proper domain of logic is restricted to entities that bear a truth value. "Logic," as Quine (1941) succinctly puts it, "studies the bearing of logical structure [of statements] upon truth and falsity" (p. 1). The business of logic, on this view, is to construct a theory of logical structure that sorts out those statements that are true just by virtue of their logical form from those that are not.[22] But, although this conception of the nature of logic is more precise than the definition of logic as the science of necessary inference, it is also less accurate.

[22] See Quine (1959, p. xi, first paragraph).

We have shown that logic concerns the logical properties and deductive relations of questions as well as statements. We have shown, further, that there is a suitable non-truth-functional interpretation of validity for question arguments that parallels the truth-functional interpretation of validity for statement arguments. Accordingly, it can be no more correct to say that logic studies the bearing of logical structure on truth than it would be to say that logic studies the bearing of logical structure on answerhood. Logic studies something more general than either what is preserved in valid statement arguments or what is preserved in valid question arguments. Neither the preservation of truth or answerhood is common to all and only cases of necessary inference; what is common are the deductive relations by virtue of which both truth and answerhood are preserved.

Suppose it is argued that the logic of statements is basic and the logic of questions derivative from it, so that, once we have a logic of statements, we can define logical relations between questions indirectly in terms of a one-to-one mapping given by the grammar of declaratives onto interrogatives. Then it could easily be replied that the logic of questions can make the same claim to priority: once we have a logic of questions, we can define logical relations between statements indirectly in terms of the same one-to-one grammatically determined mapping of interrogatives onto declaratives. That is, suppose one were to claim that there is a one-to-one mapping M that pairs arguments such as that from (5.100) to (5.101) with arguments such as (5.93):

(5.100) John is a king

(5.101) John is a monarch

And, therefore, we can characterize a valid question argument as one whose image under M is a valid statement argument, that is, one that preserves truth. It can then be replied to this claim that we can also proceed the other way around. We can characterize a valid statement argument as one whose image under M is a valid question argument, that is, one that preserves answerhood. Thus, the complete symmetry that obtains here leads to the conclusion that neither truth nor answerhood by itself should occupy the privileged position of providing the basis for a definition of logic.

Once again. The entailment relation that is explicated in (4.141), and the property of redundant predication explicated in the definitions of an analytic proposition and a linguistically answered question are sufficiently general to be features of both the meaning of declaratives and the meaning of interrogatives, and so they are independent of the different interpretations of validity for statements and questions. Therefore, the doctrine this discussion implies is that what is common in all and only cases of necessary inference and what logic in any of its forms studies is the semantic structures defined in such definitions as that of 'analyticity', 'contradiction', 'entailment', and metalinguistic truth', together with definitions expressing the rules of propositional logic and quantification, insofar as these are broad enough to represent all the logical aspects of the logical particles. The semantic structures characterized in these definitions determine necessary truth, on the one hand, and necessary answerhood and inherited answerhood, on the other. Logic, on this hypothesis, is an attempt to give a systematic theory of the semantic structures in natural language that determine valid inferences, a theory stating the conditions for deductive relations with respect to all interpretations that say what is necessary or necessarily inherited under them.

5.   Prospects for a logic of requests and exclamations

At this point it is natural to ask about the prospects for a logic of requests and a logic of exclamations. Let us consider briefly whether our treatment of interrogative sentences can be extended to imperatives and hortatories in the manner in which our treatment of declaratives was extended to interrogatives.

It is clear that there are entailments of one imperative by another and entailments of one hortatory by another. For example, the imperative (5.102) entails the imperative (5.103):

(5.102) Don't make any sound!

(5.103) Don't whisper (murmur, shout, etc.) anything!

And the hortatory (5.104) entails the hortatory (5.105):

(5.104) Oh, were I only a bachelor!

(5.105) Oh, were I only not married!

These cases fall directly under the definition of 'entailment'. It is clear that what is inherited or preserved in valid request arguments are obedience conditions in the sense that the obedience conditions of the entailed sentence are part of those for the entailing sentence and that what is inherited (or preserved) in valid exclamatory arguments is a desire expressed in the entailing sentence. There are no special problems here, and so these cases require no special discussion.

However, a problem does arise in connection with the possibility of a parallel for linguistic truths and self-answered questions in the cases of imperatives and hortatories. There are analogues of tautologies, as illustrated in (5.106) and (5.107):

(5.106)   Eat the dessert or don't eat it!

(5.107)   Oh, were I rich or not rich!

The analogues in the case of imperatives are empty requests, ones whose obedience conditions cannot but be fulfilled no matter what the person in question does. The analogues in the case of hortatories are empty yearnings, ones that cannot but be satisfied no matter what the future brings. But there appear to be no parallels of analytic declaratives and self-answered questions among these sentence types.

Consider the following facts. First, an imperative has a second person pronoun as its subject (i.e., "you" alone or "you" with some relative or apposition, such as "you who are standing around doing nothing").[23] Second, an imperative expresses a request (command, order, etc.) issued by the speaker and addressed to the person(s) to whom the subject of the imperative refers. Third, a request (command, order, etc.) makes sense only if it is logically possible for the person(s) to whom it is addressed to perform the act requested. The addressee must be *able* to act in such a way as to comply with the request. Accordingly, the use of a token of the sentence (5.108) does not convey a request that makes sense:

(5.108)   Stop taking up space!

From these considerations, it seems reasonable to conclude that there is no parallel to analytic declaratives or self-answered questions in the case of imperatives. The first two facts exclude examples in which the speaker addresses his request to himself and the request is one whose conditions on compliance are satisfied by the utterance of the imperative sentence expressing this request. The third excludes examples of imperative sentences with a semantic structure similar to that of analytic declaratives and self-answered questions, as in (5.109)–(5.111):

(5.109)   You who are doing nothing do nothing!
(5.110)   You children that are dirty get dirty!
(5.111)   Everyone who is now seated be seated!

Such imperatives are sentences whose predicate's meaning is contained in the meaning of their subject. Since the reading of their subject already contains this semantic information, the person(s) to whom the subject refers will, because this information determines the condition for assigning someone to the extension of the subject, already be or be doing what he (they) are requested to become or do. Hence, the request is nonsensical because it explicitly addresses itself to people who are the very opposite of those of whom the request can be made.

Calling such requests "nonsensical," however, does not explain their semantic character: it merely says that they are peculiar in some way. I propose the following explanation of the way in which sentences like (5.109)–(5.111) are peculiar.

We take the concept of request to express someone's asking someone else to bring something about at some time after the asking. Let us assume that a sentence like (5.109) has an underlying phrase marker like that in (5.112):

---

[23] See Katz and Postal (1964, pp. 74–79).

(5.112)

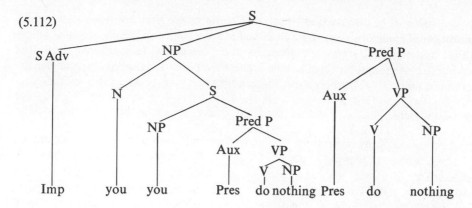

Then we treat the concept of request as entering the meaning of an imperative from the inherent semantic content of the symbol 'Imp'.[24] We may take (5.113) as a rough schema for the reading of 'Imp':

$$(5.113) \quad (((\text{Speaker}))((\text{Asks})((\begin{smallmatrix}[NP, S]\\X\\\langle\,\rangle\end{smallmatrix}))((M_1),(M_2),\ldots,(M_k))$$
$$\lor (\text{Bring about } (\text{State}_1), \ldots, (\text{State}_n))))$$

The first semantic marker in (5.113) represents the fact that it is the speaker of a token of an imperative who makes the request, and the second semantic marker represents the request he makes, namely, asking the person(s) referred to by the grammatical subject of the imperative sentence to do something or to bring about a certain change in the present state of something or someone. This change is represented as the transition from an initial state of a process to its terminal state. The representation of the terminal state is a characterization of the compliance conditions for the request. Take, for example, a case like (5.114):

(5.114) Take off your shirt!

Here the process will be that of removing one's shirt, the initial state will be that of the addressee's having a shirt on, and the terminal state will be that of his being shirtless. The specification of the addressee's being shirtless constitutes the compliance condition of the request conveyed by (5.114).[25]

---

[24] See Katz and Postal (1964, pp. 74–79).

[25] The reading for the question symbol 'Q' will be the same as (5.113) except that the unspecified action in (5.113) is specified as producing some token of a sentence type that is an answer to the question in whose underlying phrase marker the occurrence of 'Q' appears, where the relation of 'answer to a question' is spelled out as in a true sentence bearing the relation defined in (5.48) to the question.

As will be discussed at length in Chapter 7, we shall analyze a state as the condition of some object at some time and a process as a sequence of states whose initial and terminal states are given by their temporal designations, the initial having the lowest and the terminal the highest temporal designation. We enclose the semantic marker '(Speaker)' and the reading that will be the value of the categorized variable '$\underset{\langle\,\rangle}{\overset{[\text{NP, S}]}{X}}$' within heavy parentheses because they contribute to the presupposition of the imperative, that is, to the condition under which an utterance of it will succeed in making a request. Roughly, the condition here is that there is a speaker, an addressee, and an object (in the cases X are considering this is the addressee himself). That these semantic representations determine the presupposition seems clear enough, so I will not bother to show that they meet the tests discussed in the previous chapter. I do not include in the presupposition any condition that requires that what is requested be possible or that it be possible to comply with the request by possible means. Thus, sentences like (5.115) and (5.116) are taken to be capable of making requests if used in the proper context, but we shall take them to make *impossible requests*.

(5.115) Square the circle!

(5.116) Demonstrate your intelligence by squaring the circle!

States can be represented by semantic markers of the form (5.117), where '(Condition), ( ),..., ( )' specifies the condition, '$\underset{\langle\,\rangle}{\overset{[\ ]}{X}}$' is a categorized variable whose value specifies the object in this condition, and 't' specifies the time at which the object is in the condition:

$$(5.117)\quad ((\text{Condition}), (\,), \ldots, (\,)\mathbf{(}\underset{\langle\,\rangle}{\overset{[\ ]}{X}}\mathbf{)}\text{ at }t)$$

We note that the initial condition in the cases we are dealing with is always a function of the terminal state as given by the meaning of the verb phrase of the imperative. For instance, the VP of (5.114) specifies the terminal state as the condition of shirtlessness of the addressee, and, hence, the initial condition must be that of his wearing a shirt. Accordingly, we can use the antonymy operator as defined in the previous chapter to serve as the function that determines the initial state on the basis of the terminal state. Thus, for one range of cases, we can further specify (5.113) by replacing '(State$_1$)...(State$_n$)' by (5.118), where 't^0' represents the speech point (or point at which the utterance occurs) and 't^{0+k}' represents some point in the future with respect to the speech point:

$$(5.118)\quad ((\text{A}/\underset{\langle\,\rangle}{\overset{[\text{VP, PP, S}]}{X}})\mathbf{(}\underset{\langle\,\rangle}{\overset{[\text{NP, S}]}{X}}\mathbf{)}\text{ at }t^0 \ldots ((\underset{\langle\,\rangle}{\overset{[\text{VP, PP, S}]}{X}})\mathbf{(}\underset{\langle\,\rangle}{\overset{[\text{NP, S}]}{X}}\mathbf{)}\text{ at }t^{0+k}))$$

If we now reflect upon how derived readings for sentences like (5.109)–(5.111) are obtained by the projection rule from the readings of 'Imp' and the other constituents of such sentences, we see that the semantic marker which represents the initial state must contain an inconsistency between the assertion and the presupposition. In the case of (5.111), the semantic marker representing the initial state assumes the form (5.119):

(5.119) $((A/(\text{Seated}))(\!((\text{Seated addressees})\!)$ at $t^0))$

Because the inconsistency occurs between the representation of a property attributed to the extension of a term and the representation of the term itself, by (4.120), we conclude that these sentences express contradictory propositions. Hence, the way in which these sentences are peculiar is that the requests they make cannot be complied with under the conditions where their presuppositions are satisfied. Accordingly, we distinguish them from cases like (5.120) and (5.121) because these cases are indeterminable:

(5.120) Anyone who is both overweight and underweight be seated!

(5.121) The person who is an infant and an adult chew gum!

And we distinguish them from cases like (5.122) and (5.123), which are the counterparts of contradictions, and which we refer to as *logically impossible requests*:

(5.122) Become overweight and underweight at the same time!

(5.123) Be a spinster who is married!

Accordingly, the natural reaction of a native speaker to an utterance of (5.111) is to suppose that the person who uttered it did not succeed in saying what he intended to say. Thus the hearer may impose an "interpretation" on the utterance, perhaps by construing it to have the meaning of some closely related sentence like (5.124):

(5.124) Everyone who is now seated remain seated!

Such sentences differ in this respect from those like (5.115), (5.116), (5.122), and (5.123). In the latter cases, a native speaker is unlikely to suppose that the person who uttered the sentence failed to say what he intended to say. Rather, he would suppose that this person is confused or ignorant about the considerations that show that the task in question is physically or logically impossible.

The situation with hortatories is, I think, essentially the same. Consider (5.125)–(5.127):

(5.125) Oh, were I who am doing nothing doing nothing!

(5.126) Oh, were I who am now seated only sitting down!

(5.127) Oh, were bachelors only unmarried!

Such hortatories are direct parallels of the cases (5.109)–(5.111). We might thus offer the following explanation. A hortatory sentence such as (5.128) and a declarative sentence such as (5.129) are very close, if not identical, in meaning:

(5.128) Oh, were you only more generous to me

(5.129) I wish you were more generous to me

Thus, it seems that the semantic information that is expressed by the representation of the propositional type of the proposition conveyed by a hortatory must include the semantic information expressed by the lexical reading of the verb "wish."[26] Accordingly, the hortatory (5.128) can be taken to express the speaker's desire for the addressee to increase his present degree of generosity toward the speaker. More generally, it would seem that the proposition conveyed by a hortatory expresses the speaker's desire for some state of affairs to change in such a way that it conforms to the fulfillment conditions of the proposition. This implies that part of the presupposition of a hortatory is the condition that the state of affairs in question does not conform to the fulfillment conditions of the proposition at the time of utterance. But if the proposition has an analytic structure, as do examples (5.125)–(5.127), the state of affairs in question must conform to the fulfillment conditions at the time of utterance. Therefore, such hortatories must have fulfillment conditions that cannot be met under any circumstances where their presupposition is satisfied, and they must convey contradictory propositions.

---

[26] This is not an unfamiliar situation. It is directly parallel to the case of the representation of the propositional type for imperatives and the sense of the verb "request."

A discussion of analyticity and opacity

What provides the lexicographer with an entering wedge is the fact that there are many basic features of men's ways of conceptualizing their environment, of breaking the world down into things, which are common to all cultures. Every man is likely to see an apple or breadfruit or rabbit first and foremost as a unitary whole rather than as a congeries of smaller units or as a fragment of a larger environment, though from a sophisticated point of view all these attitudes are tenable. Every man will tend to segregate a mass of moving matter as a unit, separate from the static background, and to pay it particular attention. . . . As long as we adhere to this presumably common fund of conceptualization, we can successfully proceed on the working assumption that our Kalaba speaker and our English speaker, observed in like external situations, differ only in how they say things and not in what they say.

W. V. Quine

Underlying the issues taken up in this chapter is the controversy between the doctrines of extensionalism and intensionalism. Extensionalism, as we are using this term, is a version of skepticism about the scientific feasibility of attempting to explicate the concept of meaning (see the discussion in Chapter 1). According to the extensionalist position, the logical form of sentences and expressions in natural languages can be accounted for on the basis of the concept of extension, without recourse to the concept of meaning. On the intensionalist position, on the other hand, the concept of meaning (sense, intension, etc.) is viewed as necessary for this task. Adherents of either position can accept the theory of syntactic structure presupposed in this book, and they can easily agree that sentences and expressions have extensions in the customary sense and that considerations of reference play an indispensable role in the analysis of logical form. The extensionalist, however, wishes to stop at this point, while the intensionalist believes that not to go further would, in principle, preclude the achievement of a full theory of the logical structure of natural languages.

The philosophical problems of analyticity and opacity are taken up in this chapter because of the crucial role they play in the controversy between extensionalism and intensionalism in twentieth-century philosophy. But before dealing directly with these two problems, it will be worthwhile to set them in perspective against the controversy which is their background. Thus, the first section of this chapter will be concerned with aspects of the extensional-intensional controversy, and the two sections that follow will take up, in turn, the problems of analyticity and opacity.

1.   Extensionalism and intensionalism

The intensionalist position that there is an independent level of semantic structure in natural languages involves both (a) the claim that we find relations at this level that determine, in part, the denotation of expressions, the truth conditions of declarative sentences, the answerhood conditions of interrogatives, etc., and (b) the claim that these relationships are not reducible to those found at other levels of grammatical structure. Thus, one line of attack open to the extensionalist is to argue that intensional relationships can be reduced to extensional ones in every case so that the theory of reference absorbs the theory of meaning in roughly the way that statistical mechanics absorbs classical thermodynamics. The theory of reference, on this line of argument, is the reducing theory and the theory of meaning the reduced theory. The relation between the two theories, as in the case of other instances of reduction in science,[1] is that the reducing theory permits us to derive the empirical generalizations or laws of the theory which reduces to it, including those that contain concepts in the reduced theory that do not appear in the reducing theory. Since the benefits of unification and simplification which result from genuine reductions in science are not to be questioned, the extensionalist has but to show that semantic properties and relations can be defined in purely extensionalist terms (as was attempted by Lewis (1969), for example—see the discussion here in Section 5 of Chapter 4). This line of argument is also taken by extensionalists who maintain that meaning can be directly equated with reference. The naive version of this equation attempts to identify the semantic relation of synonymy with the referential relation of sameness of extension and the semantic property of meaningfulness with having a referent. But it fails because of cases of identical reference without sameness of meaning and cases of meaningful expressions that do not refer (see Chapter 1). The failure of this naive version of the reducing theory, however, does not show that correspondences like that of sameness and difference of meaning with sameness and difference of extension cannot be established on the basis of a more sophisticated concept of reference.

One attempt to provide such a sophisticated concept of reference is made in Goodman (1952). He acknowledges the shortcomings of the naive version of the

---

[1] See Nagel (1961, chapter 2) for a general discussion of the problem of reduction in science.

referential equation but resists adopting intensionalism because he regards this alternative as a

> return to the dismal search through never-never land for some ghostly entities called "meanings" that are distinct from and lie between words and their extensions (p. 70).

Thus, he is led to propose the following more sophisticated version of referential theory:

> Although two words have the same extension, certain predicates composed by making identical additions to these two words may have different extensions. It is then perhaps the case that for every two words that differ in meaning either their extensions or the extensions of some corresponding compounds of them are different. If so, difference of meaning among extensionally identical predicates can be explained as difference in the extensions of certain other predicates. Or, if we call the extension of a predicate by itself its *primary* extension, and the extension of any of its compounds a *secondary* extension, the thesis is formulated as follows: two terms have the same meaning if and only if they have the same primary and secondary extensions.... If the thesis is tenable, we have answered our question by stating, without reference to anything other than terms and the things to which they apply, the circumstances under which two terms have the same meaning (p. 71).

The counterexamples to the naive referential theory fail as counter-examples to Goodman's version. The difference in meaning between "the morning star" and "the evening star" can be accounted for in terms of a difference in their secondary extension since, for example, "picture of the morning star" and "picture of the evening star" differ in their primary extension, i.e., the former applies to some cases that the latter does not, and vice versa. The same point can, of course, be made in connection with "witch" and "warlock," "unicorn" and "Santa Claus," and so forth.

After demonstrating how the traditional Frege-type objections to the naive referential theory can be evaded by his sophisticated theory, Goodman proceeds to try to show that every difference in meaning can be reflected by a difference in primary or secondary extension. His first step is to point out that the compounds which determine the secondary extension of an expression "P" can include, besides "picture of a P" or "P-picture," "P-diagram," "P-symbol," and "P-description," as well as any number of other such compounds. Thus, Goodman argues,

> given any two predicates whatsoever, say "P" and "Q," do we not have in an inscription of the phrase "a P that is not a Q" something that is a P-description and not a Q-description? Clearly, the predicate "Centaur-description" applies while the predicate "unicorn-description" does not apply to an inscription of a "centaur that is not a unicorn" (p. 72).

It can be objected that this argument is unacceptable because it has the absurd consequence that no two words can have the same meaning. Consider the case of "rabbit" and "bunny." We have an inscription of the phrase "a rabbit that is not a bunny" which is a rabbit-description but not a bunny-description, and hence "rabbit-description" applies to it whereas "bunny-description" does not. To guard himself against this objection, Goodman denies that this consequence is absurd unless one already accepts (6.1):

(6.1)   There are synonymous expressions in English (or any other natural language).

Goodman is certainly right in claiming that the consequence of his argument that no two expressions can have the same meaning is innocuous enough if (6.1) is false, for this consequence is equivalent to the denial of (6.1). Since the denial of (6.1) is *prima facie* strongly counterintuitive, Goodman claims that the principle (6.2) represents a condition that any satisfactory account of synonymy must meet and also implies the denial of (6.1):

(6.2)   If P and Q are synonymous, then one may be replaced by the other in any nonintensional context without changing the truth value.

His argument runs as follows. Consider (6.3):

(6.3)   a P that is not a Q

This phrase is a case of a P-description and not a case of a Q-description. Thus, if we assume that (6.1) is true and that "P" and "Q" are the expressions on the basis of which it is true, then (6.4) must also be true:

(6.4)   'A P that is not a Q' is a P-description

But replacing "Q" for "P" in the predicate of (6.4) takes us from the true sentence (6.4) to the false sentence (6.5):

(6.5)   'A P that is not a Q' is a Q-description

Consequently, if (6.2) is to be accepted as a reasonable condition, then (6.1) must be rejected, and hence we must hold that no two different expressions can have the same meaning.

This argument, however, is not sound: it rests on a false premiss. We can agree that if (6.1) and (6.2) are incompatible, then (6.2) should be saved. But are they incompatible? It seems that we might answer offhand that they are not. Goodman's argument that in accepting (6.2) we are forced by (6.1) to infer false cases of (6.5) from true cases of (6.4) can, it would seem, be flatly denied. Nothing prevents us from claiming, contrary to Goodman, that when "P" and "Q" are synonymous a case of the form (6.3) *is* a Q-description, and so the corresponding case of (6.5) is true. Presumably, Goodman's answer must be that descriptions of the form (6.3) are, by their form, not Q-descriptions. But this raises the question of whether Goodman's argument leads to the absurd conclusion that "triangle" differs in meaning from "triangle" since, apparently, it is the case that "a triangle that is not a triangle" both is and is not a triangle-description. Goodman's reply (p. 72) is that this is not the case because "a triangle that is not a triangle" is contradictory and hence no description. Presumably, he means that in cases where a description of the form (6.3) is inconsistent, it cannot itself be considered a description since there cannot be anything which it describes.

This suggests a line of argument against Goodman's claim that (6.1) and (6.2) conflict. Let us suppose that (6.1) is true because the expressions "balled hand" and "fist" are synonymous in English. On this supposition, Goodman has to argue that (6.2) is, then, violated. He has to say that (6.6) is a balled-hand-description but not a fist-description:

(6.6)   a balled hand that is not a fist

To this, we can reply that if "balled hand" and "fist" are really synonymous, then (6.6), like "a triangle that is not a triangle," is contradictory and hence not a description. But if this is so, then (6.1) and (6.2) do not conflict because the expression (6.6) is neither a P-description nor a Q-description. Since it is no description at all, holding (6.1) does not force us to infer a false statement of the form (6.5) from a true statement of the form (6.4).

Goodman's argument is enthymemic, assuming the further premiss (6.7):

(6.7)   An expression can be asserted and a synonymous one denied of the same thing without contradiction.

Thus, his argument comes down to the claim that any two distinct expressions can substitute for "P" and "Q" in a case of (6.3) without producing inconsistency because there are no synonymous expressions. Goodman's argument begs the question: (6.7) is simply another way of saying that there are no synonymous expressions.

Goodman's argument is seen to rest simply on a refusal to accept semantic relations like synonymy and incompatibility of meanings. One is, of course, free to refuse to recognize the existence of such properties and relations, but such a decision ought not to be confused with an argument. Goodman's position, at first glance, looks as if it were an argument *demonstrating* that (6.1) is false. But we have seen that, on closer scrutiny, it turns out that the criterion of sameness of primary and secondary extension cannot give the result that no two distinct expressions can have the same meaning unless, in deciding whether something acknowledged to be a P-description is not a Q-description, we assume that there are no synonymous expressions or that synonymy is governed by a condition that makes nonsense out of sameness of meaning. Hence, the general reductionistic claim that we are considering can derive no comfort from Goodman's work. The supporter of such reduction may refuse to recognize the properties and relations in semantics, but this can have no bearing on the question of reduction. The sort of success that would attend a "reduction" of the theory of meaning that does no more than simply deny the phenomena characteristic of the theory is the sort of success that is more ordinarily called failure.

The proposal by Lewis (1969) for a reduction of the theory of meaning to the theory of reference, which was criticized in Chapter 4, is typical of what appears to be something of a trend among philosophers who have no faith in intensionalism but some reluctance to go along with Quine's attempt to undermine it by attacking the viability of the central properties and relations of semantics. This is the predisposing cause of the trend. The precipitating cause is the recent revival of interest in modal logic. With this work freeing modal logic from the stigma of sinfulness,[2] it couldn't take very long before these two causes conspired to produce the idea that the theory of meaning, with all its philosophical troubles, could be replaced by the philosophically unproblematic (except to Quine) theory of reference by taking the former to be just a theory of reference set up on the basis of work in modal logic. Hintikka (1970, p. 111n) cites a number of philosophers who he says are working on this approach.

Hintikka writes:

> The references, not the alleged meanings, of our primitive terms are thus what determine the [truth value] of first-order sentences. Hence the introduction of 'meanings' of singular terms and predicates is strictly useless: In any theory of meaning which serves to explain the information which first-order sentences convey, these 'meanings' are bound to be completely idle (p. 88).

Of what use are meanings, granting for the sake of argument that the only thing we require of a semantic theory is that it state the truth conditions for each sentence of the language?[3] Hintikka himself says:

> it seems to me in any case completely hopeless to try to divorce the idea of the meaning of a sentence from the idea of the *information* that the sentence can convey to a hearer or reader, should someone truthfully address it to him. Now what is this information? Clearly, it is just information to the effect that the world is such as to meet the truth-conditions of the sentence (p. 88).

The notion of sense adopted here, which seems to me reasonably close to Frege's, is nothing more than that of information grammatically connected with lexical items and other constituents which, under the principles of compositional projection, determine the extensions, primary and secondary (see the discussion toward the beginning of this chapter), of the expressions of a language and the truth conditions of its sentences (again, granting the assertive propositions). On everyone's story, including Hintikka's, there are truth conditions, which may be satisfied or not; hearers and readers discover something about the world or can do so from knowledge of their satisfaction. But what is satisfied or not, the truth conditions, contain the information that tells us how the world has to be to render a sentence that contains them true of the world. The information to the effect that "the world is such as to meet the truth conditions of the sentence" is something we learn from learning that the sentence is true. Distinct from this, and common to false sentences,

---

[2] See Quine (1963).
[3] Of course there is also the following fallacy in Hintikka's argument. References determine the truth value of a first-order sentence, as Hintikka says, but they do so only relative to its truth conditions. Hence, in order to make any conclusion about the idleness of meanings or intensional concepts, one must first show that they are not needed to explain truth conditions. Hintikka does not try to show this.

are the truth conditions themselves. According to the theory presented in this book, they are grammatically determined by a compositional process from lexically specified information; knowledge of them is part of knowledge of the language, or linguistic competence; and they are known independently of knowing the actual truth value of the sentences with which they are associated. If there is no disagreement with this, then the proposals of Hintikka and the other philosophers concerned imply programs that, nomenclature notwithstanding, are no different in the final analysis from the program of constructing a semantic theory in my sense. There is no real difference between, on the one hand, individuating functions à la Hintikka (pp. 99–106) and other apparatus for purposes of reference and predication and, on the other, readings of various kinds designed for the same purpose. The reason the theory of meaning is so badly treated by such philosophers is that, not understanding that this theory is involved with the same problems (and in the same way) as the theory of reference, and being misled by standard characterizations of the theory of reference into thinking that it has no obligation to explain semantic properties and relations, they have come to conceive of the theory of meaning as autonomous, irrelevant, and, hence, useless.

There are two lines of argument against attempts to reduce the theory of meaning to a theory of reference, where the latter is thought of as the theory of the logical particles *plus* the notions 'possible' and 'world'. Both stem from considerations already mentioned in our criticism of Lewis (1969) in Chapter 4, and both show that the distinction between the theory of meaning and the theory of reference, as now conceived, needs reconsideration for exactly the reasons that we have been arguing that the distinction between logical particles (and logical powers) and descriptive (or extra-logical) expressions (and semantic powers) does.

The first line of argument reverses the above approach to the claim that there is no distinction between the theory of meaning and the theory of reference, understood not in terms of the type of conceptual apparatus now used but in terms of their ultimate explanatory aims, of the sort that has been assumed by philosophers such as Hintikka. The differences in the conceptual apparatus reflecting the logical–extra-logical distinction are taken as the essential difference between the theories, and there is an attempt to show that, in order to meet criticisms, the theory of reference will have to be extended to encompass more and more of the theory of meaning. Recall that in our criticism of Lewis (1969) the definition of 'analytic' in terms of truth in every possible world was shown to be too broad and that, because this is not the defining property of 'analytic', there is a failure to draw the proper distinction between analytic truths, on the one hand, and logical truths (mathematical truths, etc.) on the other. It is not hard to see how this objection can be met by constructions that exhibit how truth in every possible world comes about differently in the case of sentences like (6.8) and (6.9):

(6.8)   Women are female

(6.9)   Women are such that either they are alive or not

That is, in (6.8) the function that identifies women contains a clause that picks out only females, while in (6.9) the truth conditions are so represented as to show that they are satisfied by the object(s) picked out by any identifying function. At this point, differences in terminology notwithstanding, the referential theorist and the semantic theorist are saying the same thing, assuming the referential theorist's reply is systematically worked out within a framework that demands that the conceptual apparatus function as part of an account of the compositional structure of sentences and as part of an account of semantic properties and relations.

Let us look at this the other way around. Senses, on my account, and I believe on Frege's, too, are conditions that determine extension.[4] As I conceive it, the construct 'sense' is introduced not only to say what synonyms have in common and what is referred to by an expression in an opaque context but also to provide part of the explanation of how extensional relations come to hold between linguistic expressions and objects in the world. That is, 'sense' has to do with that part of the relation that is determined by inherent features of the expressions as opposed to that part that is determined by aspects of the nonlinguistic context. For example, any referent of the subject of (6.8) is at once female and under one million miles tall, but the former is so because of inherent features of "woman" and the latter because of inherent features of the physical universe. This aspect of the construct of 'sense' becomes clearer when we recognize that our account of truth in natural language has to be formulated in terms of principles that locate the source of the various components of the truth conditions of sentences, and the referential conditions of expressions, in the denotational potentialities of the grammatically determined constituents of the sentences. For example, a full account of how extensional relations come to hold between linguistic expressions and objects in the world has to distinguish between the presence of a denotational contribution of "in-" in "insoluble liquid" and the absence of any contribution in a case like "inflammable liquid": the account has to explain why "inflammable liquid" denotes the same class of things as "flammable liquid," while "insoluble liquid" denotes the complement of the class denoted by "soluble liquid" with respect to the class of liquids. The story we shall have to tell about the adjectivization of the verb "inflame" to "inflammable" and the noun "flame" into the verb "flammable," on the one hand, and, on the other, the absence of a verb corresponding to "inflame," so that "in-" in "insoluble" is the negative prefix, must involve principles that trace the extensional difference between "insoluble" and "inflammable" back to a lexicographically fixed denotational feature of the negative prefix. Whatever we choose to call the constructs we use in such principles, whatever we name the conglomerate

---

[4] I put the point in this somewhat loose manner because there is some reason to think that a theory of meaning cannot be restricted to dealing solely with the conditions on the extension of sentences and their parts. Consider a sentence such as "Someone is a female spinster." The truth condition of this sentence is that there exists at least one individual who is human, adult, female, and unmarried. A semantic theory might succeed in stating this condition and still fail to capture the full meaning of the sentence because it failed to account for the redundancy of the modification in the predicate phrase. That a theory can capture the truth conditions of such sentences without saying anything about a number of their semantic properties and relations seems to be grounds for claiming that there is more in the theory of meaning than is necessary for reference, for such a theory would be an inadequate semantic theory no matter how adequate as a theory about extension. But it is not clear that there can be such a theory insofar as the semantic structure underlying a relation like redundancy is clearly involved in the explanation of semantic properties like analyticity in connection with sentences like "Spinsters are female," and presumably a theory that handles reference cannot ignore a semantic property like analyticity.

of such features of words, the name clearly refers to something over and above the phonetic or orthographic forms of the language and clearly is distinct from the extensions of such forms.

The peculiar thing is that many philosophers regard a sense as smelling less sweet by *that* name than by others. Thus, we find philosophers condemning senses and meanings, on the one hand, and constructing theories containing terms referring to them, on the other. This bias against senses and meanings receives its main impetus from the claims of Quine (1953) that they are "obscure intermediary entities" (p. 22) and accordingly otiose. According to Quine's argument (pp. 11f, 22, and 48f), which seems to have been uncritically accepted by a large number of philosophers, the status of senses or meanings as "obscure intermediary entities" comes from the fact that they are neither words nor the world but constructs of a theory (the theory of meaning) which is distinct from the theory that relates words and the world (the theory of reference). The fallacy of Quine's argument is that the distinctness of these theories does not follow from the quite correct distinction between meaning and reference. The claim that we are making, that the theory of meaning is the part of the theory of reference that concerns the linguistic sources of extensional relations, is entirely consistent with the distinction between meaning and reference. The Quinean claim that there are two theories, one well-founded, sound, and a paradigm of virtue, and the other "foggy," "mysterious," and a den of vice (pp. 137–138) is, in fact, just another form of the extreme professionalization of logic that we described in the Preface of this book.

We now turn to the second line of argument against attempts to reduce the theory of meaning to this kind of theory of reference. We begin with the observation made in Chapter 4 that the primitive notions of the theory of reference, particularly 'possibility' and 'world', must not be unpacked using notions from the theory of meaning or else the entire attempt at a reduction is vitiated. Curiously enough, it is Quine and Goodman who stressed the intimate involvement between notions of possibility and meaning [5] and provided us with the right arguments to show that a theory of reference based on these modal notions cannot offer a noncircular reduction.

Goodman (1952) expresses the involvement as follows:

> The notion of possible entities that are not and cannot be actual is a hard one for many of us to understand or accept. And even if we do accept it, how are we to decide when there is and when there is not such a possible that satisfies one but not the other of two terms? We have already seen that we get nowhere by appealing to conceivability as a test of possibility. Can we, then, determine whether two predicates "P" and "Q" apply to the same possibles by asking whether the predicate "is a P or a Q but not both" is self-consistent? This is hardly helpful; for so long as "P" and "Q" are different predicates the compound predicate is logically self-consistent, and we have no ready means for

---

[5] The involvement can be seen in the far more mundane point from elementary logic courses about adequate definition: there is no difference between the requirement that the definiens and definiendum be the same in meaning and the requirement that each apply to the same possible cases by virtue of their meaning. (The qualification "by virtue of their meaning" is necessary insofar as "even prime" and "two" apply to the same possible cases but are not synonymous.)

determining whether it is otherwise self-consistent. Indeed the latter question amounts to the very question whether "P" and "Q" have the same meaning (p. 68).

Quine (1953d) expresses it in this way:

This account [Carnap's account of analyticity or necessary truth as truth under every state-description] is an adaptation of Leibniz's "true in all possible worlds." But note that this version of analyticity serves its purpose only if the atomic statements of the language are, unlike 'John is a bachelor' and 'John is married', mutually independent. Otherwise, there would be a state-description which assigned truth to 'John is a bachelor' and 'John is married', and consequently 'No bachelors are married' would turn out synthetic rather than analytic under the proposed criterion. Thus the criterion of analyticity in terms of state-descriptions serves only for languages devoid of extra-logical synonym-pairs, such as 'bachelor' and 'unmarried man' (p. 23).

What both Quine and Goodman show is that for a language with the rich extra-logical vocabulary of a natural language and, accordingly, with semantic relations like synonymy holding among the elements of such an extra-logical vocabulary, the concepts of possible and world, possible object, etc., cannot be specified without some independent account of the meaning of these vocabulary elements and the complex expressions and sentences that result from them under compositional projection. Consider (6.10):

(6.10) (a) is palmistry or chiromancy but not both
        (b) No practice of palmistry is a practice of chiromancy

The question of whether there is a possible world such that the predicate in (6.10a) applies to something in it or a possible world such that the sentence (6.10b) is true is no different from the question of whether, assuming ordinary quantification theory, the extra-logical expressions "palmistry" and "chiromancy" have the same meaning.

Such attempts at reduction are not only circular, they are also too broad as explications of the concepts they seek to reduce. Expressions like "even prime" and "two" are true of exactly the same things in every possible world but they are not the same in meaning. This is because semantic relations are not the only ones that give rise to connections that hold in all possible worlds.

Because of problems like those mentioned here, certain extensionalists prefer to challenge the legitimacy of semantic properties and relations rather than to accept them and try to show that they can be reduced to extensional ones. Quine is typical of those who have thus sought to deny the validity of semantic distinctions. The focus of this attack on intensionalism has been the arguments Quine put forth against an absolute analytic-synthetic distinction. The question of whether these arguments can be answered is one of the issues to which we turn shortly. We shall argue that Quine's criticisms of the analytic-synthetic distinction as drawn by previous philosophers, particularly Carnap, does not apply to the distinction as drawn within semantic theory.

Another attack open to the extensionalist is to admit that there are legitimate semantic properties and relations, to leave open the question of whether they are reducible to extensional ones, but to argue that there are insurmountable problems facing any attempt to explicate such semantic properties and relations on the basis of a systematic theory of meaning in natural language. One form of this objection is taken up as the other topic which we shall consider in this chapter.

Davidson (1967) posed an objection of this sort when he wrote:

> Suppose we have a satisfactory theory of syntax for our language, consisting of an effective method of telling, for an arbitrary expression, whether or not it is independently meaningful (i.e., a sentence), and assume as usual that this involves viewing each sentence as composed, in allowable ways, out of elements drawn from a fixed finite stock of atomic syntactical elements (roughly, words). The hopeful thought is that syntax, so conceived, will yield semantics when a dictionary giving the meaning of each syntactic atom is added. Hopes will be dashed, however, if semantics is to comprise a theory of meaning in our sense, for knowledge of the structural characteristics that make for meaningfulness in a sentence, plus knowledge of the meanings of the ultimate parts, does not add up to knowledge of what a sentence means. The point is easily illustrated by belief sentences. Their syntax is relatively unproblematic. Yet, adding a dictionary does not touch the standard semantic problem, which is that we cannot account for even as much as truth conditions of such sentences on the basis of what we know of the meanings of the words in them (pp. 307–308).

Since we accept a compositional account of sentence meaning within a theory that is framed in terms of the organizational universal (2.6) which says that the semantic component of a grammar operates exclusively on underlying phrase markers, the problem of inference in connection with opaque contexts is crucial. We shall try to show that Davidson's objection and others like it depend on a very narrow conception of what is involved in specifying the meaning of syntactic atoms in the dictionary and that, on a more realistic conception, opacity is no obstacle to the proper formulation of the truth conditions for belief sentences (and others containing opaque contexts).

2. Analyticity and its critics

Quine's criticisms, as I see them, are sound objections to the conceptions of analyticity (particularly Carnap's) against which they were originally directed. This section will be an attempt to prevent philosophers from adopting the mistaken assumption, unfortunately encouraged by Quine himself,[6] that Quinean arguments are conclusive objections to *any* basis for drawing the analytic-synthetic distinction.

The primary reason that Quinean arguments do not apply to the analytic-synthetic distinction drawn within the framework of a semantic theory such as the one developed here is that this framework puts the whole question of definition and

---

[6] As Quine (1953d) puts it: "But, for all its a priori reasonableness, a boundary between analytic and synthetic statements simply has not been drawn. That there is such a distinction to be drawn at all is an unempirical dogma of empiricists, a metaphysical article of faith" (p. 37).

explication of meaning on a basis quite different from that assumed by Quine's criticisms. Quine (1953d, pp. 24–27) makes it clear that he considers only three types of definitions germane in connection with analyticity: *lexical definition*, which provides a paraphrase of the definiens of an appropriate sort; *explication*, which provides a definiens that preserves some aspects of the meaning of the definiendum but "improves" upon its meaning in some way; and *notational definition*, which functions merely to introduce a new notational convention for purposes of abbreviation.

I agree with Quine that the first two depend on prior semantic relations, full synonymy of definiens and definiendum in the first and identity of some components of the meaning of definiens and definiendum in the second. Because lexical definitions and, in the relevant respects, explications, too, rest on antecedent meaning relations, by themselves they are suspect as answers to questions about the nature of these relations. I also agree that notational definition has little to do with the analytic-synthetic distinction. But I disagree with Quine's underlying assumption that these three types are exhaustive and contend that his catalogue omits the very type that is required for a sound analytic-synthetic distinction, namely, what I will call *theoretical definition*.

Theoretical definition comes closest to lexical definition. Like the latter, it avoids the inherent difficulty with explications, i.e., that no way has yet been devised to determine when a departure from the meaning of the explicandum is a genuine improvement and when it is simply a failure on the part of the explicatum to capture a significant aspect of the meaning of the explicandum. Also like lexical definition, it is an attempt to describe empirical facts about a natural language by expressing them in the form of confirmable hypotheses. But unlike lexical definition, theoretical definition does not define a term by other terms or expressions with which it is synonymous in the same language. Rather—and this is the significant difference—theoretical definitions define terms *on the basis of constructs from linguistic theory*, that theory in empirical linguistics which expresses what is common to natural languages in the form of a definition of the notion 'natural language'. That is, a term from a natural language is defined by a dictionary entry which represents each one of its senses in the form of a theoretical construction, a *reading*, that is composed, not of words from that language, but of symbols expressing language-independent constructs, *semantic markers*, drawn from the theoretical vocabulary of empirical linguistics.

There are several reasons why the semantic component of a grammar must employ theoretical definition rather than lexical definition. First, defining words by pairing them with synonymous expressions in the same language (or even a different one—it makes no difference here) cannot provide an account of their meaning. Such pairings say no more than that the meaning of this or that word is the same as the meaning of some expression without at all saying what the meaning of either is. They are thus no more illuminating about meaning than the statement that two species have the same sensory organ is about the nature of that organ. Furthermore, being expressions in the same natural language (or in different ones—again it makes no difference), the definientia of lexical definitions will have, in general, the same semantic properties and relations that other words and expressions do. In particular, given the fact that practically every word in a natural language is ambiguous—which one can easily verify by consulting any standard reference dictionary—practically every definiens of a lexical definition will be ambiguous, too. Accordingly, lexical definitions cannot give *the* meaning of their definienda. To do this would require some way of disambiguating the definiens antecedently, some way of identifying the proper sense from among the various senses of the definiens and indicating that it alone is the sense of the definiendum; and this cannot be done by further lexical definitions for just the reason that disambiguation is required in the first place. Consequently, a semantic component based on lexical definition must beg the significant questions in semantics, for it is capable of accounting for semantic properties like synonymy and ambiguity only by some independent means of representing and marking them.

These and other reasons make it necessary to resist the extension of lexical definition, which has its proper place in ordinary reference dictionaries, to the-oretical semantics. These reasons also show, though I cannot argue it here, that the rationale used by Quine (1953, pp. 11–12, 48–49) for endorsing lexical definition, namely, his view that all talk about meaning can be dispensed with in favor of just talk about meaningfulness (significance) and synonymy, is inadequate.[7] Therefore, theoretical definition is employed here instead of lexical definition because it defines a sense of a word in terms of a vocabulary of theoretical constructs (semantic markers), each of which is devised to represent uniquely a specific component in the senses of words and to combine with other such constructs to form semantic representations (readings) that unequivocally specify a sense of a word, phrase, clause, or sentence.

This has the following consequence. Synonymy relations are not affirmed by the institution of a definitional connection between one term or expression from a natural language and another, as is the case in lexical definition. Rather, synonymy relations are affirmed on the basis of sameness of semantic representation, i.e., formal identity between the readings correlated with the two terms or expressions. Formal relations on the basis of which we affirm or deny that a particular linguistic construction has one or another semantic property or relation provide the abstract conditions that serve as definienda for the general semantic concepts 'is synony-mous with', 'has its meaning included in that of', 'is analytic', and so on.

Quine's remarks on the possibility of defining synonymous constructions as constructions that are interchangeable *salva veritate* are, in my opinion, quite correct. Something stronger is needed, and it is interchangeability *salva analyticitate*. But, since the notion of analyticity is what we sought to explain in studying the notion of synonymy, we cannot accept a proposal to define synonymy that rests on the unexplained notion of analyticity.

By employing theoretical definition, however, we are able to avoid the circularity of trying to define analyticity in terms of logical truth and synonymy, and synonymy in terms of interchangeability *salva analyticitate*. For now, "analy-ticity," "synonymy," "meaning inclusion," etc., do not themselves appear as

---

[7] In Katz (to appear), I argue that Quine's "reduction" of semantic concepts to the two concepts 'meaningful' and 'same in meaning' is based on nothing more than the Bloomfieldian taxonomic theory of grammar and so is subject to the same transformationalist criticism.

terms in the definienda of any such semantic concepts. As indicated, each semantic concept is defined on the basis of certain formal features of the readings for sentences and their constituents—more precisely, on the basis of formal conditions on semantically interpreted underlying phrase markers. For example, with no appeal to such terms as "synonymous," we defined an analytic sentence as a sentence that has a reading that satisfies (4.113).

It is important to notice that this method of defining semantic properties and relations is general: every semantic property and relation will be defined on the same basis, that is, in terms of a configuration of symbols in semantically interpreted underlying phrase markers. Thus, semantic theory defines a sentence or constituent as semantically anomalous just in case it receives no readings, as semantically ambiguous just in case it receives two or more readings, and so forth. Of course, as things presently stand, there are semantic properties and relations that have not been so defined within semantic theory. But I do not make the claim that semantic theory is complete. Rather, my claim is that this conception of semantic theory offers a conceptual apparatus for representing semantic structure which is sufficiently rich to enable us, with enough ingenuity, to set up adequate definitions for all semantic properties and relations.

Even though semantic properties and relations are not defined in terms of one another but rather on the common basis of formal features of semantically interpreted underlying phrase markers, different semantic properties and relations are interconnected by virtue of interrelated formal features of such phrase markers, which reflect uniformities in the semantic structure of the sentences the phrase markers describe. Consider, for example, (6.11) and (6.12):

(6.11)   The shadow hit the ground with a loud thud

(6.12)   A shadow is not a physical object

The lexical reading of "shadow" that enables us to mark (6.11) as semantically anomalous also enables us to mark (6.12) as analytic. This type of interconnection between semantic concepts makes it possible to obtain indirect evidence for a prediction about a given sentence having a given semantic property or relation by considering successful predictions about other semantic properties and relations that can be derived from the same representations of semantic structure. We shall return to this point later.

The conception of semantical rules (and meaning postulates) set forth by Carnap (1947) is criticized by Quine on essentially two counts. First, there is what I shall refer to as the *generality criticism*: the notion that should be defined is 'S is analytic for L' for variable "S" and "L," but Carnap does not define this. Second, there is what I shall call the *explanation criticism*: besides a specification of the analytic statements of a language, we require some account of just what is attributed to them by marking them as analytic, and Carnap does not offer this.

Neither of these criticisms carries over to the treatment of analyticity, synonymy, etc., being presented here. The generality criticism does not hold because, on the present account, semantic properties and relations are defined within linguistic theory. Accordingly, their definitions have the status of hypotheses about what all languages have in common, and, hence, each semantic property or relation is defined for variable "L."[8] Furthermore, unlike Carnap's account, where some analytic statements qualify as such by virtue of being listed under the heading "analytic," on this account, the concept 'analytic' is defined in terms of a formal condition such that *any* sentence whose semantically interpreted underlying phrase marker satisfies it is analytic. The same is true of other semantic properties and relations, and, hence, semantic concepts are defined for variable "S," too.

The explanation criticism does not carry over to the present treatment, either. Quine (1953d) rightly says of Carnap's semantical rules that "the rules contain the word 'analytic', which we do not understand! We understand what expressions the rules attribute analyticity to, but we do not understand what the rules attribute to those expressions" (p. 33). On my treatment, however, 'analytic' is defined in a way that tells us what is attributed to a sentence so marked, namely, the property of having truth conditions that are identical to clauses of its presupposition, so that the satisfaction of the latter is sufficient for the satisfaction of the former and the sentence is thus absolutely secured against falsehood (and in the case of generics, guaranteed as truths).

Our approach eliminates the need for such ad hoc devices as meaning postulates and semantical rules of the Carnapian variety. The reason that Carnap originally proposed them is clear. Logic reconstructs inferences formally on the basis of rules governing manipulation with "logical symbols," propositional connectives, quantifiers, etc. But some inferences also depend on the meaning of the "descriptive symbols" of a natural language, for which no formal representation is available. Consider in this regard (6.13) and (6.14):

(6.13)   Someone is a bachelor

(6.14)   Someone is a male

The inference from one to the other of these is formalized improperly by the invalid argument schema (6.15) unless the meanings of "bachelor" and "male" are taken into consideration by introducing the meaning postulate (6.16) as a further premiss in (6.15). But then we are no longer symbolizing the inference (6.13)–(6.14).

(6.15) $\dfrac{(\exists x)(Bx)}{(\exists x)(Mx)}$

(6.16) $(x)(Bx \supset Mx)$

Our approach, on the other hand, renders such ad hoc, inadequate devices unnecessary because it provides a formal representation of the inherent semantic structure

---

[8] These definitions are not restricted to any particular language since a linguistic description, or generative grammar, of a natural language describes each of its sentences in terms of a set of semantically interpreted underlying phrase markers, and the formal features referred to in the definitions of semantic properties and relations are features of readings and semantic markers in general (rather than specific symbols that might appear in some but not all descriptions). Of course, in order to obtain predictions about the semantic properties and relations of particular sentences in a given natural language, these definitions must be applied to the semantically interpreted underlying phrase markers for those sentences, but this is only a matter of specifying the values of the variables "S" and "L" in a particular case.

of descriptive symbols, i.e., morphemes, words, and expressions. Thus, the semantic markers in the readings for "bachelor" and "male" break up their meaning into component concepts, representing each separate component by a distinct formal symbol in the readings. On this basis, the inference from (6.13) to (6.14) can be properly reconstructed as an entailment by (4.141).

The introduction of meaning postulates and semantical rules constitutes a recognition on Carnap's part of the need for formally distinguishing the inherent semantic features of different words in a language in order that the representation of inferences be able to incorporate aspects of the meaning of words on which the validity of the inferences depends. But the device of meaning postulates and semantical rules is ad hoc because it provides a basis for dealing only with certain special cases of semantic properties and relations, in particular, "analytic," "entails," and some other logically related notions; in contrast, representation of the inherent semantic features of words on the basis of lexical readings in a dictionary provides a basis for dealing with all semantic properties and relations—for instance, "anomalous" and "ambiguous" in addition to "analytic," "entails," etc. As an example, consider a case such as (6.11) and (6.12), where Carnap can lay down a meaning postulate to mark (6.12) as analytic but where that meaning postulate does not suffice to mark (6.11) as semantically anomalous. Contrast Carnap's approach with that set forth here, where the dictionary characterizes "shadow" and "mirror image" as perceptual but not physical objects and where this characterization suffices to mark (6.11) as semantically anomalous as well as (6.12) as analytic.

Moreover, the device of meaning postulates and semantical rules does not meet the need for which it was originally introduced, because, as Quine (1953d) has shown, the meaning postulates and semantical rules are given only for a particular language and then just stipulated under one or another empty label.[9] Our approach, on the other hand, dispenses entirely with such pointless, relativized notions by proposing a general, language-independent concept of analyticity and by providing, for each distinct language, a semantic component for its grammar that assigns semantically interpreted underlying phrase markers to each sentence in the language.

We will now consider Quinean-type criticisms of the analytic-synthetic distinction. But so as not to attribute to Quine a position that he does not actually hold, let us distinguish between "Quine of the printed word" and "Quine of legendary fame."[10] Henceforth, unless otherwise indicated, I will be talking only about the latter.

We have taken the position that the semantic component of a grammar and semantic theory are empirical theories whose hypotheses are related as integrated parts of a system and can therefore be tested in various indirect as well as direct ways. (The more interconnections of the system are used to move from hypothesis

---

[9] Quine (1953d) writes, "Alternatively we may, indeed, view the so-called rule [Carnap's semantical rule for analytic sentences] as a conventional definition of a new simple symbol "analytic-for-L_0," which might better be written untendentiously as "K" so as not to seem to throw light on the interesting word "analytic" (p. 33).

[10] By "Quine of legendary fame" I do not refer to Quine. I use this device as a way of referring to certain prevalent views, some stemming from misinterpretations of Quine, which are now part of the folklore of our subject.

to observational prediction, the more indirect the confirmation.) The sort of argument that might be used to show that one of the lexical readings for "bachelor" requires the semantic marker '(Male)' could thus be that such a lexical reading provides the best basis for the rest of the dictionary and the projection rule to predict the semantic intuitions of speakers on questions about sentences containing "bachelor." For example, since '(Male)' and '(Female)' are antonymous semantic markers, this lexical reading for "bachelor" will lead to the grammar's marking (6.17) as contradictory on one of its senses:

(6.17)   My mother is a bachelor

Furthermore, because '(Male)' helps to distinguish different senses of "bachelor," it helps to mark (6.17) as semantically ambiguous. Also, it helps us mark (6.14) as entailed by (6.13). Since this lexical reading contributes to the marking of these and other types of semantic properties and relations, there is certainly empirical evidence for the claim that one reading of "bachelor" should have '(Male)' in it, and this evidence is, in turn, also evidence that (6.18) is analytic:

(6.18)   Bachelors are males

We might suppose that we can rest our case with the observation that this treatment of "bachelor" can serve as a model for the treatment of any other examples about which the same methodological question is raised. But for the Quine of legendary fame this straightforward answer will not do. He will not allow us to take for granted the facts that were assumed. "How do you know," he will ask, "that (6.17) is semantically ambiguous and contradictory on one of its senses, or that (6.13) entails (6.14), or that (6.18) is analytic?" To this, we would answer that such facts are obtained from intuitive judgments speakers make about the sentences; these judgments constitute our data. Now, Quine's rejoinder will concern how we obtain such data, and he will ask two questions about the claim to have such data.

First, he will want to know how we deal with cases that are unclear because speakers are unable to make definite judgments about them. For example, we can expect speakers to be somewhat confused about whether or not (6.19) is analytic, or even expect the possibility of a wrong judgment about this case:[11]

(6.19)   Whales are fish

But here we can reply that, as previously indicated, we do not need to have clear-cut judgments about a given case to have sound evidence on which to assert its analyticity, since we can bring indirect evidence to bear on it. That is, the virtue of semantic theory is that it interrelates semantic concepts and, thus, permits us to decide on the character of an unclear case by theoretical triangulation from clear cases of sentences having other semantic properties and relations. Let us illustrate this in connection with (6.19). We assume that "fishing" and "whaling" are, respectively,

---

[11] Goodman (1951) says, "To most of us 'fish' unquestionably applies to whales; if the biologist says that whales are not fish, his use of 'fish' differs from ours" (pp. 5–6).

an activity in which one tries to catch fish and an activity in which one tries to catch whales, so that "fishing" and "whaling" differ semantically in just the way that "fish" and "whale" do. Now, "but"-conjunction is governed by a semantic restriction that the conjoined expressions contrast semantically if the whole conjunction is to avoid semantic anomaly. Consider, for example, (6.20) and (6.21):

(6.20)   I went fishing but caught a fish (bass, pike, etc.) instead

(6.21)   I went whaling but caught a whale (baleen, sperm, etc.) instead

These sentences are both semantically anomalous because the object of the second clause in each is something that is of the same type as the thing that the speaker was trying to catch, or a subtype of that type. To avoid semantic anomaly, the type indicated by the object in the second clause must be a contrasting one. Thus, (6.22) and (6.23) are both nonanomalous sentences:

(6.22)   I went fishing but caught an old shoe instead

(6.23)   I went whaling but caught an octopus instead

But (6.24) and (6.25) are also nonanomalous:

(6.24)   I went fishing but caught a whale instead

(6.25)   I went whaling but caught a fish instead

We can thus conclude that, from the viewpoint of English, whales are not a type of fish. This can be reflected in the lexical reading for "whale" only if that reading does not contain the semantic markers that represent the concept of a fish, and, hence, (6.19) will be marked as not analytic, even though there may be no clear-cut judgment to this effect about (6.19) per se.[12]

The second question Quine will ask about data obtained from questioning speakers is: "Must speakers understand the meaning of such technical terms as 'semantically ambiguous', 'contradictory', 'entails', and 'analytic' before they can answer reliably?" The answer to this question is a categorical no. It is possible to obtain the relevant data without invoking such technical terms in framing the questions that are put to speakers. One test that avoids such circularity is this. We present speakers with short lists of sentences. List A contains only sentences that are clear cases of what we would regard as analytic. Lists, B, C, D, etc., contain clear

---

[12] Another case of the same kind is the following:

(a) John caught a sperm and Bill caught a whale also
(b) John caught a bass and Bill caught a whale also

or

(c) John caught a whale and Bill caught a whale also
(d) John caught a whale and Bill caught a fish also

"Also" in such constructions has the semantic requirement that the object of the second sentence structure has a reading identical to the reading of the object in the first or one that is included in the reading of the object in the first. Hence, (b) and (d) are both semantically deviant, and this fact is further evidence for the claim that (6.19) is not analytic.

cases of sentences that are not analytic, but, respectively, synthetic, contradictory, anomalous, etc. Then, we give the speakers a batch of sentences of all sorts and ask them to place these on the lists to which they belong. Each sentence is to be put on the list whose members it is similar to. If this experiment is conducted properly and if the predictions that the semantic component of the grammar makes match the actual sorting performed by the speakers (cases that are put on list A are those and only those that are predicted to be analytic, and so on), then we can claim that we have evidence, obtained in a quite unobjectionable fashion, in favor of the semantic component, as a result of its successful predictions about the data. However, the qualification that the experiment be conducted properly is extremely important. If the controls used in the experiment insure that the members of the short lists A, B, C, etc., are sufficiently different from one another in the appropriate respects, then there will be no spurious common features that might lead speakers to classify sentences on the basis of irrelevant linguistic properties (e.g., in the case of list A, on the basis of some linguistic property other than analyticity). Positive results in this experiment can be interpreted to mean that the judgments of the speakers reflect a recognition of the analyticity of the sentences concerned. We can say, then, that our definition of analyticity, which enabled us to predict the outcome of the experiment, describes the concept of analyticity employed by the speakers as their implicit criterion for identifying analytic sentences, i.e., for differentiating those of the test sentences that are similar to the members of list A from those that are not similar to them. We can say this on the grounds that assuming that this is their criterion provides us with the best explanation of the behavioral data obtained in the experiment. Since these grounds are the same as those on which other theories in other sciences are justified, they should satisfy even the Quine of legendary fame.[13]

Quine (1967) has commented on my objections to his criticisms of the analytic-synthetic distinction. Quine's main objection is that my characterization of analyticity does not succeed in defining the notion 'S is analytic in L', where "S" and "L" are variables. His argument runs as follows: (a) Katz's characterization is the criterion that a sentence is analytic if a (representative) sample of speakers uniformly classifies it together with acknowledged clear cases of analytic sentences; (b) for each new language (each possible value of "L"), a new list of acknowledged clear cases from the language is needed to apply the criterion; (c) "no linguistically general method is offered for making such lists" (p. 53); (d) analyticity is defined for variables "S" and "L" only if such a method is given, and, therefore, (e) Katz's characterization fails to define 'S is analytic in L'.

If this argument were sound, it would have a consequence even worse than (e): it would show that my characterization of analyticity also runs afoul of Quine's explanation criticism. For, if my characterization were the criterion set forth in (a), it would concern only the sorting of sentences on the basis of speakers' intuitions about their similarity or dissimilarity to other sentences. Thus, my account of analyticity would not rise above the level of data collection and so could offer no explication of what property is attributed to those sentences listed as analytic.

---

[13] At this point we drop the device of referring to the Quine of legendary fame.

But my characterization is *not* the criterion set forth in (a). Therefore, Quine's argument is unsound; his premiss (a) is false. My characterization is a definition; it says a sentence is analytic just in case it meets (4.113).[14] The sorting test, out of which Quine concocted the criterion in (a), was proposed as a way of meeting the objection that it is necessary to utilize technical terms from semantic theory, like "analytic," in framing questions put to native speakers when trying to elicit their linguistic judgments. It was originally mentioned only to show that such terms need appear only in the theory that predicts these linguistic judgments.[15] Quine (1967) ignores my definition, saying that it is "some of the apparatus that ... can be set aside as inessential to the central issue" (p. 53). Worse yet, he makes it appear as if I encouraged the reader to disregard the definition of analyticity: "Katz happily cuts through all this and epitomizes his approach by suggesting a direct test of analyticity with a minimum of auxiliary constructions" (p. 54). But, of course, I did no such thing, as should have been clear from earlier papers.[16]

As I see it, Quine's reply is irrelevant to the crucial issue that my defense of my definition of analyticity poses, namely, whether my *definition* succeeds in escaping his generality and explanation criticisms. What makes this issue crucial is that the truth of my claim that my definition does avoid Quine's criticisms is a very strong argument in favor of an acceptable analytic-synthetic distinction. Quine fails to address himself to *this* issue because he mistakenly takes my sorting test to be a proposal for a behavioral criterion for analyticity.

But why does Quine overlook my definition? The only explanation I can come up with is the following. Quine (1967) and I agree that "a satisfactory version of analyticity would have to carry with it some approximate behavioral criteria" (p. 53). Quine has long fought the good fight on this and can rightly count me among his converts. But his mistake—one quite typical of prophets—lies in construing conversion on one point of doctrine as conversion on all. I regard behavioral tests as indispensable, but I regard them as indispensable for *testing* the empirical adequacy of definitions of theoretical terms such as that of analyticity. Quine, on the other hand, regards them as indispensable for *defining* theoretical terms. He fails to make this distinction, and, as a consequence, interprets my agreement on the need for clarifying the relation between a linguistic concept and observable behavior of speakers as agreement with him that the definition of the concept should be given in terms of a behavioral criterion.

Quine also disavows my statement that he endorses lexical definition, a form of definition in which the meaning of an expression is given by pairing it with a synonymous expression from the same (or another) natural language. The reason is that he does not think I take account of the fact that, in many cases of sufficiently short expressions, definitions can take the form of contextual rules that indicate how sufficiently long expressions containing these shorter ones are to be para-

[14] Or a definition such as (D6) from the early paper (Katz 1964a).

[15] Indeed, the test itself presupposes an independent definition of analyticity, since it is the definition that gives the predictions and that receives confirmatory evidence when these predictions are borne out by the way that speakers sort sentences in the course of the test.

[16] See Katz and Fodor (1963) and Katz (1964a; 1966).

phrased (or translated).[17] True enough, such rules are not lexical definitions, but their function is to make lexical definitions possible for other cases. Quine endorses lexical definition for all expressions and sentences except those elementary sentences which appear explicitly as clauses in the recursive definition of meaning, and these are defined contextually so as to provide such lexical definitions. Hence, in forming equivalence classes of synonymous cases among the former expressions and sentences, lexical definition is primary and contextual definition is just a means to this end. Accordingly, my statement, though lacking a significant qualification, is basically correct.[18]

To my criticism that lexical definition cannot provide a general means of specifying the meaning of locutions because the extensive ambiguities of words and ambiguity-producing mechanisms in sentence formation make it impossible for us to guarantee that an expression proposed as the definiens in a lexical definition is free of unwanted senses, Quine replies that ambiguity can be made to dwindle in many cases. This is undoubtedly true, but there is no reason to think that ambiguity can be made to disappear entirely from the range of cases from which we must select defining expressions and every reason to think that in many instances " as we move out to sentences and longer sentences " we find ambiguity preserved or even increased. For the syntactic mechanisms that increase the length of sentences often create ambiguities, as is illustrated in (6.26)–(6.29):

(6.26)   Relatives can be annoying

(6.27)   Visiting relatives can be annoying

(6.28)   Ducks are often in danger

(6.29)   Sitting ducks are often in danger

My criticism that the pairing of two locutions does not provide the meaning of either is not answered by Quine's (1967) remark that this " seems of little consequence as long as we understand one of the pair of equated expressions " (p. 54). I was not denying the usefulness of lexical definition for practical purposes such as that to which it is put in the use of ordinary reference dictionaries. Rather, my point was that lexical definition fails for theoretical purposes just because, for such purposes, we cannot assume a speaker's competence to understand. The point would be the same if it were argued that we require no formal analysis of arguments in logic because one argument whose validity is in question can be

---

[17] Quoting Quine (1967) on his own behalf: "We may continue to characterize the lexicographer's domain squarely as synonymy, but only by recognizing synonymy as primarily a relation of sufficiently long segments of discourse" (p. 54).

[18] The absence of the qualification should not have been misleading since my contrast of lexical definition with theoretical definition was clearly presented as a contrast between definition by equating locutions each from a natural language and definition by representing the meaning of such locutions in terms of the constructs of linguistic theory. In the former case, synonymy relates definiendum and definiens, while in the latter the relation of synonymy is itself defined, holding between two locutions when the grammar assigns them the same semantic representation. Thus, it ought to have been clear that the feature of Quine's chosen form of definition to which I was calling primary attention was the use of a synonymous expression from natural language to serve as definiens as opposed to the use of constructs from a theory.

shown valid merely by pairing it with another whose validity is intuitively recognized by competent reasoners. The speaker's command of the semantic principles of his language, which he exercises to obtain the meaning of a locution from its phonetic or orthographic tokens, is just what the linguist (or linguistic philosopher) must provide a theory of, and the rules of such a theory must fully reconstruct these principles formally. To the extent that aspects of these principles are not represented by formal features of such a theory, to the extent that aspects are left out of the formal representation so that appeal to the understanding of competent speakers is required, the theory fails to do its job of reconstructing the semantic competence of the speakers of the language.

In conclusion, I wish to present a more concrete, empirical rationale for the claim that meanings have to be represented by the technical constructs of a theory of linguistic structure. The argument I will now try to develop seeks to show that theoretical definition, not lexical definition, is the proper general form in which to represent descriptions of the sense of expressions and sentences. I will try to establish this by showing that, in at least one significant range of cases, the most revealing and simplest description of sense makes explicit use of technical constructs of semantic theory not available outside the theory.

Adjectives divide into two kinds semantically, which I will call *relative adjectives* and *absolute adjectives*. Examples of the former kind are given in (6.30):

(6.30)   big, little, small, large, heavy, light, tall, short, expensive, cheap, thick, thin

Examples of absolute adjectives are given in (6.31):

(6.31)   carnivorous, speckled, sick, red, living

This distinction is, of course, found among the words of other major categories: for example, the determiner "many" and the adverb "fast" are both relative in our sense while the determiner "seventeen" and the adverb "with unerring accuracy" are absolute. But we shall restrict ourselves to adjectives in this discussion.

The difference between relative adjectives and absolute adjectives appears clearly in connection with inferences from comparative sentences. From the premiss (6.32) we cannot draw the conclusion (6.33):

(6.32)   The mountain is higher than the building
(6.33)   The mountain is high

But from the premiss (6.34) we can draw the conclusion (6.35):

(6.34)   The tablecloth is more spotted than the place mat
(6.35)   The tablecloth is spotted

The reasons are clear. Sentence (6.32) says that a certain mountain exceeds a certain building in height. Sentence (6.33) says that the mountain in question is high relative to mountains in general. Since the latter assertion may be false while the former is true, there is no valid inference from (6.32) to (6.33). Sentence (6.34), on the other hand, says that the number of spots on a certain tablecloth exceeds the number of spots on a certain place mat. Sentence (6.35) says that the tablecloth in question has some spots on it. Since the latter cannot be false when the former is true, the inference from (6.34) to (6.35) is valid.

Another form in which the difference between relative and absolute adjectives appears is the following. The sentence (6.36) is certainly not contradictory:

(6.36)   A small elephant is big

It means that an elephant which is small for an elephant is big for an animal. But corresponding sentences in which an absolute adjective and its antonym occupy the positions occupied in (6.36) by the relative adjective "small" and its antonym "big" are contradictory, as, for example, (6.37):

(6.37)   A carnivorous (sick, dead) elephant is herbivorous (healthy, alive)

The conceptual difference which shows up in these contrasts is that a relative adjective *relativizes* the judgment of the thing in question to the appropriate feature of *things of that kind generally*. The expression "small elephant" and the expression "high mountain" express judgments about the size of the referent of their nominal heads which is relative, respectively, to the size of elephants and mountains generally.[19] We note, further, that even in sentences where the subject is an individual the judgment is still relative. For example, (6.48) says that Jumbo is small for an elephant:

(6.38)   Jumbo the circus elephant is small

This relativized comparison is also found in other uses of the positive form of relative adjectives, as in (6.39):

(6.39)   Skyscrapers are high
(6.40)   Texans are tall
(6.41)   Fleas are little
(6.42)   Oceans are large
(6.43)   Tarantulas are big
(6.44)   Compact cars are small

[19] Relative adjectives divide further into various subtypes—size, weight, cost, height, and so on. We will concentrate on relative adjectives of size and height. The treatment given them will apply *mutatis mutandis* to the other subtypes.

The relativeness shows itself fully when cases (6.39)–(6.44) are rendered, respectively, with the riders in (6.45)–(6.50):

(6.45)   for buildings

(6.46)   for human beings

(6.47)   for insects

(6.48)   for bodies of water

(6.49)   for spiders

(6.50)   for automobiles

We note that elephants are compared with animals, skyscrapers with buildings, Texans with human beings, and so forth. Such implicit comparisons cannot be explained as transformationally produced ellipses, since this would mean that a sentence like (6.39) is derived from a structure whose terminal string is, roughly, that in (6.51) by a transformational deletion of "for buildings":

(6.51)   Skyscrapers are tall for buildings

Such an operation would violate the principle of recoverable deletion, unless there were a form like that in (6.52) underlying (6.51):

(6.52)   Skyscrapers are buildings which are tall for buildings

But this would just push the problem back to how the first occurrence of "buildings" got deleted without violating recoverable deletion. Moreover, such an explanation would not account for why (6.39) is not understood to mean that skyscrapers are tall for all physical objects.[20] Thus, we must look for a semantic explanation.

We observe, first, that sentences like those in (6.53) are analytic:

(6.53)   (a) Skyscrapers are buildings

(b) Texans are human beings

(c) Fleas are insects

(d) Oceans are bodies of water

(e) Tarantulas are spiders

(f) Compact cars are automobiles

Hence, the concept that represents the class of things with which the group specified by the subject is compared is part of the meaning of the subject. Accordingly, the reading of the subject, or, more generally, the reading of the expression used to designate the group about which the relative judgment is made, will contain the

---

[20] Assuming, of course, that the meaning of "buildings" in (6.52) contains the concepts 'Physical' and 'Object' in addition to those concepts that distinguish the meaning of "building" from the meaning of other physical object terms.

semantic marker that represents the concept which determines what the judgment is relative to.

There are two problems to be dealt with in order to represent the semantic structure of sentences with relative adjectives. One is how to pick out the particular semantic marker representing the concept to which the judgment is relative from among all the semantic markers to be found in the reading of the expression that designates the group about which the relative judgment is made. This semantic marker will rarely be the only one in this reading. When it isn't, we cannot end up rendering the meaning of a sentence such as (6.39) as expressing the assertion that skyscrapers are high for physical objects in general or a sentence such as (6.41) as expressing the assertion that fleas are little for animals, even though '(Physical)', '(Object)' are in the reading for "skyscraper" and '(Animal)' is in the reading for "flea." Consider, also, the examples in (6.54):

(6.54) (a) Skyscrapers are low
        (b) Fleas are big

To deny such sentences, one cites, respectively, examples of low buildings and big insects; one does not cite planets in the one case and horses in the other.

The other problem is how to formulate the readings of relative adjectives so that they express the fact that these adjectives fix the object to which they are attributed *at some position* on a scale of possible sizes (weights, costs, etc.) whose calibration is determined by the vocabulary of the language used to express the units of size (weight, cost, etc.). We cannot, of course, take the judgments conveyed by cases like (6.39)–(6.44) to express numerically exact positions on such scales. Rather, they express estimates, or rough approximations. Furthermore, the assignment of the group about which the judgment is made to a position must be determined on the basis of a prior assignment of the comparison class to some position on the same scale. Thus, we must ask, first, what is the position of the comparison class, and, second, what is the function that assigns the group to a position in terms of the position that the comparison class occupies on the scale.

Heretofore, we have spoken loosely of buildings, human beings, insects, bodies of water, spiders, and automobiles generally. To answer the question of what the position of the comparison class is on the appropriate scale, we must be more specific. Thus we set the comparison class at the portion of the scale representing the average or mean for the property scaled. We do not suppose that there have to be any things (buildings, human beings, insects, etc.) that actually are average with respect to the property in question, but just that there is, crudely, an average degree of the property.

The second question, namely, what the function is that assigns the group designated by the subject to a position on the same scale on the basis of the estimate of the average degree of the property for the comparison class, has a straightforward answer. The function is given in the meaning of the relative adjective in question. For example, "high" not only specifies a scale of vertical size but expresses a function which assigns what it is predicated of to some position exceeding that of the comparison class. Accordingly, a sentence of the form (6.55) makes a size judgment about the referent of its subject to the effect that this group is greater in vertical size than the average member of the relevant broader class of things:

(6.55)   NP is high

In general, then, the function will be specified by the meaning of the particular adjective but will vary from one adjective to another.

A full solution to the problem under discussion is not possible at this stage, since some of the required theoretical apparatus has yet to be developed. Nonetheless, we can provide the general form of the semantic markers for readings of relative adjectives like those in (6.30). These we call *relative semantic markers*, and we give an illustration in (6.56), where the braces indicate choices that differentiate cases like "high" from cases like "long":

$$
(6.56) \quad (((\text{Size})(\begin{Bmatrix} \text{Vertical} \\ \text{Horizontal} \\ \vdots \end{Bmatrix} \text{ spatial orientation) of } \begin{matrix} [\text{NP, S}] \\ X \\ \langle\ \rangle \end{matrix}) >
$$

$$
((\text{Size})(\begin{Bmatrix} \text{Vertical} \\ \text{Horizontal} \\ \vdots \end{Bmatrix} \text{ spatial orientation) of (Average } \Sigma)))
$$

The symbol 'Σ' will be a dummy symbol so defined that it is replaced just by the appropriate semantic marker from the reading of the subject. The solution to the first problem, that is, the problem of how to select the semantic marker that represents the concept to which the judgment is relative, is a definition of this symbol; such a definition will specify what differences in the meaning of nominal subjects are reflected in differences in the meaning of sentences with the same relative adjective.

The lexical reading for a relative size adjective like "big" will contain a relative semantic marker, which in this example will express the relation that the entities referred to by the subject of the sentence are greater in size than the average member of the class of entities with which it is compared, the class picked out by the value of 'Σ'. The question is how to determine 'Σ' in a general way so that, for any reading of a subject noun, the right class is selected.

We take 'Σ' to be a special case of (3.66) where $[B_1, B_2, \ldots, B_i]$ is the grammatical function [NP, S] and where 'K' is a chosen option. Taking $[B_1, B_2, \ldots, B_i]$ to be [NP, S] expresses the fact, which we already know, that the value of 'Σ' is one of the semantic markers in the reading of the subject of the sentence. The specific K that we select must be a semantic condition that picks just the semantic marker (in the reading of the subject) that determines the proper class for comparison, for, as just observed, further information is needed to provide the required semantic marker since, in general, the reading of the subject contains more than one semantic marker.

Our hypothesis about the semantic condition is that the proper semantic marker is the one representing the lowest order category of any represented by semantic markers in the reading of the subject. Given the reconstruction of 'category' here, this hypothesis can be rephrased as the condition that the appropriate semantic marker is the semantic marker in the reading of the subject which renders other semantic markers in the reading (if there are any) redundant but which is not itself rendered redundant by any semantic marker in the reading.

Sentence (6.57) expresses the proposition that chairs are greater in size than the average piece of furniture:

(6.57)   Chairs are big

Therefore, the appropriate class for comparison in this particular case is the class of furniture. This is also demonstrated by the fact that, to refute (6.57), one would not cite just any objects whose average size exceeds that of chairs but only those belonging to the class of furniture, as, for example, couches, beds, dining room tables. Now, the lexical reading for "chair" (or as close to it as we need come), namely, (2.15), can be simplified if the dictionary contains the redundancy rules (2.31), which, for the sake of convenience, we repeat here as (6.58):

(6.58)   (a) (Furniture) → (Artifact)

(b) (Artifact)   → $\left\{\begin{array}{l}\text{(Object)}\\\text{(Physical)}\\\text{(Non-living)}\end{array}\right\}$

These redundancy rules allow us to rewrite (2.15), the lexical entry for "chair," as (6.59):

(6.59)   (Furniture), (Portable), (Something with legs), (Something with a back), (Something with a seat), $(\text{Eval}_{\text{use}}: (\text{Seat for one}))$

According to the hypothesis under discussion, none of the semantic markers '(Object)', '(Physical)', '(Non-living)', '(Portable)', '(Something with legs)', '(Something with a back)', '(Something with a seat)', and '$(\text{Eval}_{\text{use}}:$ (Seat for one))' is appropriate to determine the proper class for comparison since none of these renders another semantic marker in (2.15) redundant. The only semantic markers in (2.15) that render others redundant are, then, '(Furniture)' and '(Artifact)', but the latter is ruled out because it is itself rendered redundant by the former, as indicated by (6.58a). Therefore, our hypothesis chooses the semantic marker '(Furniture)', which coincides with our intuition about the proper class for comparison in connection with (6.57). Moreover, application of our hypothesis to cases like "skyscraper," "Texan," "flea," "ocean," "tarantula," and "compact car" yields, respectively, '(Building)', '(Human)', '(Insect)', '(Body of water)', '(Spider)', and '(Automobile)' as the semantic markers that determine the proper comparison classes, and these results accord with the senses of (6.39)–(6.44) as explicated in (6.45)–(6.50).

Hence, it seems reasonable to adopt our hypothesis and take the value of an occurrence of 'Σ' to be the semantic marker representing the lowest level category of those represented by semantic markers in the reading of the subject in question. Accordingly, we construe the symbol 'Σ' to be a defined symbol, eliminable by (6.60), where K is a function that takes as input a reading R of the constituent picked out by the grammatical function with which K is conjoined (here the subject of the adjective in whose reading 'Σ' occurs) and that yields, as a value of 'X', the semantic marker from R that occurs on the left-hand side of one of the redundancy rules applicable to R but not also on the right-hand side of any of these rules.

(6.60) $\Sigma = \begin{array}{c} \text{[NP, S] \& K} \\ X \\ \langle \, \rangle \end{array}$

As further support for our treatment of the meaning of relative adjectives (adverbs, etc.), we note that it allows us to explain inferences like those in (6.61) and (6.62):

(6.61)   (a) This man is tall and that man is short
   _____
         (b) This man is taller than that man

(6.62)   (a) This horse runs fast and that horse runs slow
   _____
         (b) This horse runs faster than that horse

The relative adjectives "tall" and "short" and the relative adverbs "fast" and "slow" express a comparison between the height and speed, respectively, of the object to which their subject refers and the height and speed of the average member of the lowest order category to which this object belongs. It therefore follows that the propositions conveyed by the conjuncts of (6.61a) are, respectively, that the first man's height exceeds the height of the average man and that the second man's height falls below the height of the average man and that the propositions conveyed by the conjuncts of (6.62a) are, respectively, that the first horse's speed is greater than the speed of the average horse and that the second horse's speed is not as great as the speed of the average horse. The conclusion, in both cases, is that the first object referred to exceeds the second in the relevant respect. Therefore, our treatment supplies the missing middle term which is required to obtain the conclusions as inferences based on the transitivity of the relations.

If this treatment of the meaning of relative adjectives is essentially correct, it is reasonable to conclude that lexical definition, wherein the sense of a word is expressed by pairing it with a synonymous expression from a natural language, will not generally provide the best means of stating the meaning of words when the purpose is linguistic description. For this purpose, theoretical definition is needed because the meaning of certain words, particularly relative adjectives, adverbs, etc., cannot be stated in the most revealing way unless their definitions explicitly make use of or refer to principles of semantic theory (such as the redundancy rules of the dictionary and the condition defining the notion 'lowest order category'). Since theoretical constructs and principles of a theory must figure in the statement of the meaning of words and the sentences in which they occur, it is impossible to define every word and sentence in the ordinary lexicographer's fashion, independently of a semantic theory.[21]

3. Referential opacity

3.1 The problem

New theories ought to handle problems that plague the old theories from which they descend and whose general assumptions they preserve. Therefore, I want to show that semantic theory, particularly on the basis of its definition of the entailment relation, can handle what is perhaps the outstanding problem plaguing the theory of sense and reference set forth by Frege (1952b), namely, the problem of characterizing valid inference in cases of substitution into certain referentially opaque contexts.

A context is *referentially opaque* if substitutivity of identicals fails,[22] that is, if (6.63) holds:

(6.63)   A context ' X——Y ' is referentially opaque in case, given a true identity statement, say, '$a = b$ ', the statements ' $Xa\,Y$ ' and ' $Xb\,Y$ ' can have opposite truth values.

I will use the term "opacity" in a broader, not quite kosher sense, to cover also contexts where substitutivity of truth-functionally equivalent statements cannot be relied on to preserve truth, that is, contexts defined as in (6.64):

(6.64)   A context ' X——Y ' is referentially opaque in case, given a true truth-functional equivalence, say, ' $P \equiv Q$ ', the statements ' $XP\,Y$ ' and ' $XQ\,Y$ ' can have opposite truth values.

Let us illustrate with (6.65) and (6.66), which we shall suppose to be both true:

(6.65)   the girl living above John = the ugliest girl in the world

(6.66)   John has one wife ≡ John has as many wives as there are even primes

---

[21] Given a semantic theory, we can, of course, translate it into the vernacular and thereby provide some sort of paraphrase in the vernacular for the lexical reading of a word. But, in this sense, any theoretical definition from any science can, with sufficient complication, be phrased in the vernacular. This possibility, however, shows no more than that natural languages are effable.

[22] See Quine (1953c).

But sentences (6.67) and (6.68) can have opposite truth values, as can (6.69) and (6.70):

(6.67)   Bill wants to marry the girl living above John

(6.68)   Bill wants to marry the ugliest girl in the world

(6.69)   Bill believes John has one wife

(6.70)   Bill believes John has as many wives as there are even primes

Thus the contexts (6.71) and (6.72) are referentially opaque:

(6.71)   Bill wants to marry ——

(6.72)   Bill believes ——

Another type of opaque context, which will shortly be distinguished from the type just illustrated, is a sentence form which involves quotation. For example, the form (6.73) is a referentially opaque context since (6.74) is true whereas (6.75) is false:

(6.73)   "——" contains five words

(6.74)   "The girl living above John" contains five words

(6.75)   "The ugliest girl in the world" contains five words

A context is nonopaque, or *referentially transparent*, if the statements formed from this context by first filling the blank with one term of a true identity statement and then filling it with the other will have the same truth value. For example, the context (6.76) is transparent since, given the truth of (6.65), (6.77) and (6.78) are either both true or both false:

(6.76)   Bill kissed ——

(6.77)   Bill kissed the girl living above John

(6.78)   Bill kissed the ugliest girl in the world

We will also call a context transparent if the statements formed from this context by corresponding substitutions from a true truth-functional equivalence will have the same truth value.

Hence, if two sentences formed from the same transparent context differ only in that the expression occurring in such a context in one sentence is replaced in the other by a different description that denotes the same object or has the same truth value, these two sentences must themselves have the same truth value. The importance of transparency for the characterization of valid inference is thus clear. Linguistic differences between descriptions play no role in the statement of conditions under which valid inferences can be drawn by substitution of one description for the other. If we have an occurrence of an expression (or sentence) in a transparent context, we can characterize such conditions in a fully extensional way. If the premisses (6.79) are true, then we can infer the truth of (6.80):

(6.79) (a) $a = b$
       (b) X——Y is transparent
       (c) XaY
(6.80) XbY

And if the premisses (6.81) are true, then we can infer the truth of (6.82):

(6.81) (a) $P \equiv Q$
       (b) X——Y is transparent
       (c) XPY
(6.82) XQY

One of the strongest arguments intensionalists can bring against extensionalists is Frege's argument that extensional relations do not suffice to characterize fully the conditions under which substitution gives rise to valid inferences. Frege (1952b) claimed that substitution into an opaque context results in a valid inference if the meanings of the terms involved are appropriately related and not otherwise. If Frege is correct, extensionalism cannot account for validity in this class of arguments. But to be sustained, this objection to extensionalism must be supported by a solution to the problem of specifying the semantic relation in question.

The problem is as follows. If we have an occurrence of an expression or sentence in an opaque context of the form 'X——Y', what relation must 'a' bear to 'b' in order that we can infer the truth of 'XbY' from the truth of 'XaY' and the fact that 'a' bears that relation to 'b', and what relation must 'P' bear to 'Q' in order that we can infer the truth of 'XQY' from the truth of 'XPY' and the fact that 'P' bears that relation to 'Q'?

3.2 Frege's solution

Frege's solution to the problem just posed, and also in essence the solutions of Carnap (1956, pp. 56–64) and Church (1954), is that the sought-after relation is synonymy, or sameness of sense. For example, (6.83) is synonymous with (6.84):

(6.83) the girl whom John is living below
(6.84) the girl living above John

Then, from the truth of (6.67), we can infer the truth of (6.85):

(6.85) Bill wants to marry the girl whom John is living below

And given (6.86), we can infer the truth of (6.87):

(6.86) Bill believes that John is a bachelor
(6.87) Bill believes that John is an adult human male who is not married

Although this solution applies to the type of opaque context created by verbs of propositional attitude, such as "believe," "hope," "know," "doubt," it does *not* apply to the type created by direct quotation. Consider (6.88):

(6.88)   "The girl whom John is living below" contains five words

Clearly (6.88) and (6.74) have opposite truth values in spite of the fact that (6.83) and (6.84) are synonymous expressions. But quotational contexts are not of much interest here because, quite clearly, ordinary predicates which apply to a string of words bounded by quotes—"contains five words," "is a palindrome," etc.— attribute a property not to the denotation of the string in quotes but to the quoted string itself. The interest of nonquotational opaque contexts arises from the con- troversy centering about Frege's proposal to use the identity of the senses of the expressions or sentences occurring in such contexts as the condition under which inferences from one to another of two sentences involving these contexts can be validly drawn. Therefore, we shall ignore quotational contexts for the time being.

Accordingly, we rephrase Frege's solution as follows: if 'X——Y' is an opaque context that is not quotational, and if 'XaY' and 'XPY' are true, then it is necessary and sufficient for the truth of 'XbY' that 'b' be synonymous with 'a' and necessary and sufficient for the truth of 'XQY' that 'Q' be synonymous with 'P'. The important insight embodied in this proposed solution is simply that contexts of substitution divide on the basis of the kind of condition that deter- mines substitution in them.

A significant advantage of Frege's solution is that it automatically and quite naturally avoids the crucial difficulty found in any attempt to use the notion of logical consequence (say, as developed in any standard extensional system of propositional calculus or quantification theory) as the relation that determines valid inference in opaque contexts.[23] The problem is this. Suppose that T_1 and T_2 are truths (say, theorems) and that they are logically equivalent or T_2 is a logical consequence of T_1. Given the truth of the sentence (6.89), (6.90) may very well be false:

(6.89)   John knows that T_1
(6.90)   John knows that T_2

The reason may be one of several. First, John may never have heard of the theorem T_2. Second, although he may be acquainted with it, he may not understand it. Third, he may understand it but not know it because he does not know any of its proofs, including its (*ex hypothesi*, long and complicated) proofs as deductions from T_1. What makes counterexamples of this sort possible are two things: (a) a statement that implies another statement can be formulated out of concepts that do not occur in the statement it implies (and, hence, equivalent statements can be formulated out of different concepts), and (b) although such pairs of statements can be formulated out of exactly the same concepts, they can incorporate these

---

[23] See Mates (1952, p. 124) and Church (1954, p. 66) for a discussion of this difficulty.

concepts with different relations between them, for example, instances of $((p \supset q) \supset p) \supset p$ and corresponding instances of $q \supset (p \supset q)$. Thus, T_1 could be constructed out of concepts taught in freshman mathematics, whereas T_2 could be constructed out of concepts taught only when one reaches graduate mathematics, so that John, who is a normal undergraduate, is familiar with the concepts in T_1 but not those in T_2. Or, (6.89) might be the statement that a certain small child knows that two is less than ten and (6.90) might be the statement that the same child knows that the even prime is less than ten. Thus (6.89) could be true and (6.90) false because the child has no understanding of the concept of an even prime. Hence, attempts to employ the consequence relation (or the equivalence relation) to determine when substitutions can be made for sentences (or expressions) in opaque contexts must run afoul of counterexamples because of (a) or (b) or both.

But this difficulty cannot arise on Frege's view. Since the sentences T_1 and T_2 are merely (different) orthographic representations of the *same* proposition, there can be no differences of the sort responsible for the counterexamples against the criterion of logical consequence (or equivalence). Hence, it will not matter that John may never have encountered the unique form of words that is 'T_2'. He has encountered the proposition expressed by 'T_2' conveyed by the synonymous form of words 'T_1'. Nor will it matter that he may not understand 'T_2' when he encounters it, for he understands 'T_1'. He knows what proposition 'T_1' expresses and he understands that proposition. Finally, there can be no difficulty of the sort that arises in the case of logical consequence because of a failure to understand a long and complicated deductive connection (e.g., between T_1 and T_2), since there can be no such connection if the propositions expressed by T_1 and T_2 are one and the same. Thus, on Frege's view, since knowing a sentence is knowing the proposition it expresses, if someone knows 'T_1', he ipso facto knows 'T_2', insofar as the proposition he must know to know 'T_2' is the proposition expressed by 'T_1', which, *ex hypothesi*, he knows.

3.3   A revision of Frege's solution

As it stands, Frege's solution is too narrow, however. It fails to mark as valid indefinitely many inferences that are essentially the same as those whose validity it does mark. This is, of course, also true of Carnap's (1956) explication in terms of intensional isomorphism and Church's (1954) explication in terms of synonymous isomorphism. Synonymy, however explicated, cannot serve as the relation that determines valid inference in opaque contexts of indirect discourse because any criterion based exclusively on synonymy will have to reject valid inferences of the form '$Xa\,Y$' to '$Xb\,Y$' and of the form '$XP\,Y$' to '$XQ\,Y$' where the meaning of 'b' is included in the meaning of 'a' and 'Q' is entailed by 'P' but where neither 'a' is synonymous with 'b' nor 'P' with 'Q'. Thus, the type of example that is not accounted for by Frege's solution is the inference from (6.91) to (6.92):

(6.91)   Bill wants to marry someone's sister

(6.92)   Bill wants to marry a person who is not an only child

Or from (6.93) to (6.94):

(6.93) Bill wants to marry a spinster

(6.94) Bill wants to marry a woman

Or the inference from (6.86) to (6.95):

(6.95) Bill believes that John is unmarried

Surely, if there were no serious philosophical objections to inferences such as these in cases where 'a' is synonymous with 'b' and 'P' is synonymous with 'Q', or if those that exist could be answered satisfactorily, there could hardly be any objection to such inferences in cases where the meaning of 'b' is included in the meaning of 'a' or in cases where 'Q' is entailed by 'P'.

Roughly, my proposal is to take the relations of meaning inclusion and entailment, instead of synonymy, as the basis for a criterion of valid inference in opaque contexts of indirect discourse. When this proposal is worked out, it will constitute a generalization of Frege's, since, as we shall see, synonymy of expressions can be defined as mutual meaning inclusion and paraphrase can be defined as mutual entailment.

I do not regard this proposal for a revision as merely a correction of an oversight in Frege's, Carnap's, and Church's proposals. For their position as stated provides them with no means for making the proper adjustment. Within their position, the only appropriate relation weaker than synonymy is some version of the consequence relation. But the use of this relation, as we have seen from the previous section, leads to an insurmountable difficulty. Thus, appealing to the consequence relation to avoid the difficulty in connection with examples (6.89) and (6.90) would only exchange too narrow an explication for one that is too broad.

Not only is this revision a correction and generalization of Frege's solution, it is, further, an explication of it that brings it into the framework of linguistic theory. Frege provided no analysis of synonymy. Carnap's (1956, pp. 222–229) intensional isomorphism, a relation that holds between two sentences just in case they are built up in the same manner out of designators and corresponding designators are L-equivalent, begs all the important questions with which an explication should deal. Church (1954, pp. 66–67) makes certain minor modifications in Carnap's explication and one major one, which is to replace the concept of L-equivalence by the concept of synonymy, itself unanalyzed in Church's treatment. The trouble with both of these explications of Frege's proposal is, then, that they are based on notions that are almost wholly unexplicated in reference to natural languages. The notion 'sentences being built up in the same way out of designators' is merely a place-holder for a whole theory of grammatical structure; and the notion 'L-equivalence' (or for that matter the notion 'L-implication') is a place-holder for a whole theory of semantic structure. Bringing a Frege-type solution into linguistic theory provides concepts that are explicated in reference to natural languages, as required.

The concept of entailment defined in semantic theory avoids the dilemma within the Frege-Carnap-Church position of having to choose between synonymy and a too narrow explication, on the one hand, and logical consequence and a too broad one, on the other. Being an explication of the traditional notion of an immediate inference whose validity rests solely on meaning relations among the nonlogical (or descriptive) expressions in the premises and conclusion of an argument, entailment is appropriately broader than synonymy in applying to cases like the inference from (6.93) to (6.94) or the inference from (6.86) to (6.95), but, at the same time, narrower than logical consequence (or equivalence) in not applying to inferences from cases of the form (6.89) to ones of the form (6.90). Accordingly, the definition of entailment (4.141) offers a ready-made solution to the dilemma.

3.4 An old objection

Before we can proceed to the formulation of a criterion for inference in opaque contexts, we must consider an objection to Frege's solution that carries over to the revision just proposed. Mates (1952), who was first to present this objection, argues as follows:

> it [the proposal that synonymy, or some explication such as intensional iso-morphism, be chosen as the relation governing inference in opaque contexts] has, along with its merits, some rather odd consequences. For instance, let "D" and "D'" be abbreviations for two intensionally isomorphic [synonymous] sentences. Then the following sentences are also intensionally isomorphic [synonymous]:

(6.96)   Whoever believes that D, believes that D

and

(6.97)   Whoever believes that D, believes that D'

> But nobody doubts that whoever believes that D believes that D. Therefore, nobody doubts that whoever believes that D believes that D'. This seems to suggest that ... if anybody even doubts that whoever believes that D believes that D', then Carnap's explication is incorrect [and the same for synonymy under any explication] (p. 125).

And the same, of course, for any solution based on entailment. For, on such a solution, it must be held that if D entails D', then from the truth of (6.96) we can infer the truth of (6.97).

Two points about this objection. First, it can be put in a variety of ways. Thus, it is essentially the same objection to argue that everyone surely believes (6.98) and that "oculist" is synonymous with (thus includes the meaning of) "eye doctor," but, nevertheless, someone can have doubts about, and hence not believe, (6.99):

(6.98)   Oculists are oculists

(6.99)   Oculists are eye doctors

Moreover, it is the same objection to argue that (6.96) is true and (6.97) false where "D" and "D'" are, respectively, either (6.100) and (6.101) or (6.102) and (6.103):

(6.100) John gave the book to Bill

(6.101) John gave Bill the book

(6.102) John drives cars better than Bill

(6.103) John drives cars better than Bill drives cars

The point is that any difference in the orthographic form of a pair of expressions or sentences filling the same opaque context in otherwise identical sentences, i.e., any difference in their surface structure,[24] makes it possible, so this objection runs, to entertain some doubt, however slight, about one of the sentences in question while at the same time believing the other sentence. The crux of the objection is, then, that the object of belief, doubt, knowledge, etc., varies with variations in aspects of the orthographic form (the surface structure) of sentences.

The second point to be made about Mates's type of objection is that it should not be construed as merely saying that someone can affirm (6.96) but not affirm (6.97) since an affirmative response can be given by someone who does not believe and a negative response can be given by someone who does. In fact, what one says about his beliefs ought not to enter at all. Thus, it is a mistake on Carnap's part to find fault with Mates's objection on the grounds that it involves an illicit transition from an affirmative response to the existence of a belief or from the withholding of an affirmative response to the absence of a belief.[25] Even if it be granted that no such transition can be made, still it seems logically consistent for someone to believe (6.98) and not (6.99).

3.5 Church's suggestion

Church (1954) suggested a way out of this objection. He used the examples (6.104a,b) as instances of Mates's cases:

(6.104) (a) Whoever believes that the seventh consulate of Marius lasted less than a fortnight believes that the seventh consulate of Marius lasted less than a fortnight

(b) Whoever believes that the seventh consulate of Marius lasted less than a fortnight believes that the seventh consulate of Marius lasted less than fourteen days

---

[24] This includes even cases of alternative pronunciations (or spellings) of the same word.

[25] Carnap (1954) says: "Church pointed out to me that Mates' paradoxical result . . . disappears if we give up [the] view [that an affirmative response to D is a conclusive indication of a belief in D]. We may then take [(6.97)] as logically true, just like [(6.96)]. If somebody responds affirmatively to D but negatively to D', we shall merely conclude that one of his responses is nonindicative, perhaps due to his momentary confusion" (pp. 129–130).

As Church phrased his suggestion:

> It must be understood that those who are supposed to have doubted that [(6.104b)] without doubting that [(6.104a)] are supposed also to have had a sufficient knowledge of the English language so that the doubt was not, for example, about the meaning of the word 'fortnight' in English.
>
> Nevertheless, it is natural to suggest as a means of overcoming Mates's difficulty that it is after all not possible to doubt that [(6.104b)] without doubting that [(6.104a)]; and that the doubt which has been or may have been sometimes entertained by philosophers in considering the question of the criterion of identity of belief is not the doubt that [(6.104b)], but a doubt that does have reference to linguistic matters, namely, the doubt that [(6.105a)].

(6.105) (a) Whoever satisfies in English the sentential matrix 'x believes that the seventh consulate of Marius lasted less than a fortnight' satisfies in English the sentential matrix 'x believes that the seventh consulate of Marius lasted less than a period of fourteen days'.
  (b) Whoever satisfies in English the sentential matrix 'x believes that the seventh consulate of Marius lasted less than a fortnight' satisfies in English the sentential matrix 'x believes that the seventh consulate of Marius lasted less than a fortnight' (p. 69).

Church goes on to say:

> If this suggestion can be supported, the difficulty urged by Mates disappears, as [(6.105a)] is clearly not synonymously isomorphic either to [(6.104a)] or to [(6.105b)] (p. 69).

Church's support for his suggestion is that the German translations of (6.104a) and (6.104b) are identical, whereas the German translation of (6.105a) is different from the German translations of (6.104a) and (6.104b) because the sentential matrices occurring in (6.105a) retain their English orthography in the German translation. This seems to show that the doubt about (6.105a) can be regarded as a doubt about a linguistic expression rather than a doubt about what a linguistic expression is used to mean, and so it need not be regarded as a doubt about (6.104b).

I think that the spirit of Church's suggestion is correct and that it indicates a way out of Mates-type objections. But Church's own defense of his suggestion is not adequate and thus needs to be replaced by one that can show that Mates-type objections should be treated as doubts that refer exclusively to linguistic matters.

Note, in the first place, that Church's support for his suggestion does not establish that the Mates-type doubt *is* a doubt that (6.105a). This crucial point is assumed, not proven. His "support" seeks to show only that if it is a doubt that (6.105a), then this doubt is one that refers to linguistic matters. Second, on the basis of a Frege-Church conception of semantics, it cannot be the case that a doubt about (6.105a) is a doubt that refers to linguistic matters in the sense Church intends: in other words, the doubt must be the same as the alleged doubt about (6.104b). On this conception, sentences are distinguished from the propositions they express, the latter being taken as the object of belief. The predicate expressions "believes that the seventh consulate of Marius lasted less than a fortnight" and

" believes that the seventh consulate of Marius lasted less than a period of fourteen days" are synonymous, that is, express one and the same concept. Moreover, applying each predicate expression to the same name must result in synonymous sentences, sentences that express the same proposition. Accordingly, whoever satisfies the first sentential matrix of (6.105a) must satisfy the second sentential matrix of (6.105a). Therefore, a doubt that (6.105a) cannot be distinguished from a doubt that (6.104b).

We might conjecture that what Church intended to use instead of these sentential matrices were, respectively, "x believes that the sentence 'The seventh consulate of Marius lasted less than a fortnight' is true" and "x believes that the sentence 'The seventh consulate of Marius lasted less than a period of fourteen days' is true." In this case, the doubt in question would be a doubt that refers to linguistic matters in the sense intended. However, now Church's translation argument no longer goes through because the translation of (a) and (b) of (6.104) is the same German sentence, but the translation of (6.105a) and the translation of the sentence that results from substituting the new matrices in (6.105a) are different both from the translation of (6.104a,b) and from each other.

Church's argument assumes that (6.105b) cannot be synonymous (or synonymously isomorphic) to either (6.104a) or (6.105a). The reason he gives is that the quoted elements in (6.105b) are names, and a name can never be synonymous with another name or with an expression used instead of mentioned.[26]

But this is certainly open to dispute. Whereas one can certainly agree that "John" and "Johannes" are not synonymous in anything like the way in which the English noun "man" and the German noun "Mann" are, it is not at all clear that "names" formed by quotation of synonymous sentences can never be synonymous. Let us assume that the objection to regarding (6.105a) and (6.105b) as synonymous is that if one takes quotations to be synonymous when the sentences or expressions enclosed in quotes are synonymous, one risks arriving at false conclusions from true premises, as, for example, with the inference from (6.74) to (6.88). But this difficulty does not arise in cases like (a) and (b) of (6.105) because they involve the relation of satisfaction. In general, the danger of such fallacious inferences does not exist with predicates from the theory of reference like "is true," "names such-and-such," or "satisfies" since, as Quine has observed, these predicates "have the effect of undoing the ... quotes."[27] A predicate from the theory of reference ascribes a property to the thing to which its subject expression refers or expresses a relation between the things to which its argument expressions refer. For example,

---

[26] According to Church (1954), "*names* of two different sentences are not synonymous in any sense, ... even though the sentences themselves be synonymously isomorphic" (p. 72n).

[27] Quine, (1953c): "It would not be quite accurate to conclude that an occurrence of a name within single quotes is *never* referential. Consider the statements—(6) 'Giorgione played chess' is true. (7) 'Giorgione' named a chess player—each of which is true or false according as the quotationless statement—(8) Giorgione played chess—is true or false. Our criterion of referential occurrences makes the occurrence of the name 'Giorgione' in (8) referential, and must make the occurrences of 'Giorgione' in (6) and (7) referential by the same token, despite the presence of single quotes in (6) and (7). The point about quotation is not that it must destroy referential occurrence, but that it can (and ordinarily does) destroy referential occurrence. The examples (6) and (7) are exceptional in that the special predicates 'is true' and 'named' have the effect of undoing the single quotes ..." (p. 141).

the sentence "The person who satisfies 'x is Bertrand Russell's mother' is Katherine Louisa Stanley" says that it is true of the person to whom 'Bertrand Russell's mother' refers that she is Katherine Louisa Stanley. Since synonymous expressions necessarily refer to the same thing, the substitution of an expression synonymous with one occurring in quotes preserves truth value if the predicate in question is one from the theory of reference. The reason is that the attribution expressed by the predicate of the sentences is asserted of the thing referred to by the expression within quotes, and if the expression substituted for it necessarily refers to the same thing, the two sentences must make the same statement about it. Thus, substituting the expression 'x is the female parent of Bertrand Russell' for 'x is Bertrand Russell's mother' cannot produce a sentence whose truth value is different from that of "The person who satisfies 'x is Bertrand Russell's mother' is Katherine Louisa Stanley."

There is, then, no objection to regarding sentences like (6.105a) and (6.105b) as synonymous, since the quoted constituent sentences in them are synonymous, and the relation involved is that of satisfaction. But, if (a) and (b) of (6.105) can be regarded as synonymous, Church's defense collapses, since it is essential to his argument that the doubt in question cannot be that (6.105a) if it is believed that (6.105b) and if (6.105b) is synonymous with (6.105a).

The spirit of Church's suggestion is that an alleged doubt that (6.104b) is really not a doubt that (6.104b) but is taken as such due to a linguistic error or confusion. This can be clarified on the basis of an analogy between a code and the case in natural language. Suppose a spy ring adopts a secret code for the purpose of transmitting a finite set of messages. In the code, each message has two cryptograms, and no cryptogram is the coding of more than one message. The code book is a finite list of entries, each of which consists of a message paired with two cryptograms. Decoding and encoding involve nothing more than looking up the cryptogram or message to find what it is paired with in its entry. Now, suppose that the message is that the sending agent will be captured momentarily, and for this the code book gives the cryptograms in (6.106):

(6.106) (a) tsawbcm
        (b) mcbwast

It is clear that any spy who believes (6.106a) *must* also believe (6.106b) if he is to avoid inconsistency. If a spy were to affirm his belief in (6.106a) but deny belief in (6.106b), we could still say he believes (b) and explain his refusal to affirm his belief in it on the grounds that he must not know the code book well enough, for it is a necessary condition of understanding it that one know that (6.106a) and (6.106b) encode the same message.

The viewpoint underlying Church's suggestion is as follows. The situation in natural language with regard to inference and opacity is isomorphic to this code case, with synonymous sentences being different ways to express the same proposition just as cryptograms in the same entry of the code book are different ways to encode the same message.

The sentence-proposition distinction which provides the basis in natural language for this analogy with the code case is a distinction between sentence types and propositions in Frege's restricted construal of them as senses of sentence types. This distinction is straightforward enough (see Chapter 4, Section 1). It is clear that a single sentence type can have more than one sense, as in the case of semantically ambiguous sentences like (6.107):

(6.107) John was shocked because he didn't know the rail was alive

And some sentence types do not have even one sense, as in the case of meaningless sentences like (6.108):

(6.108) The elderly thought smells like a prehistoric itch

These empirical facts establish a sentence-proposition distinction by themselves. However, it is quite natural to go on and say that just as some sentences express no proposition and the same sentence can express different propositions, so different sentences can express the same proposition, as in the case of paraphrases like those in (6.109)–(6.111):

(6.109) (a) John likes Mary's bachelor brother
 (b) Mary's unmarried adult male sibling is liked by John
(6.110) (a) He painted the inside of the box one color and the outside another
 (b) He painted the outside of the box one color and the inside another
 (c) He painted the inside and outside of the box different colors
(6.111) (a) He shaved off his beard
 (b) He removed his beard by shaving it off

But, however natural, it is not necessary to thus go on in order to draw the appropriate sentence-proposition distinction. This is vital, since the question of whether synonymy can serve as a standard of identity for propositions is just what is at issue. Accordingly, the thing that needs to be stressed here is that the distinction between sentences and propositions does not depend on how this question is decided. Furthermore, for the purposes of this discussion, it is not necessary to make any assumption about the ontological character of propositions. Semantic theory distinguishes between sentences, clauses, phrases, etc., on the one hand, and their senses, on the other, taking the former to be orthographic or phonetic entities and the latter to be abstract entities of some sort. But here there is no need whatever to posit propositions and concepts as entities over and above sentences and expressions. Any argument in defense of Church's suggestion can be carried through even if we take propositions as equivalence classes of sentences and concepts as equivalence classes of expressions. On this interpretation, there is still a sentence-proposition (and expression-concept) distinction, namely, the distinction between a sentence and the appropriate equivalence class (which is not itself a sentence) to which it belongs.

We have taken the object of a verb like "believes" as an assertive proposition rather than either a sentence or a statement. The reason is the following. Such a verb, when used as the main verb with an appropriate complement, says something about someone's confidence in the truth of something. To say, for example, that someone believes that the moon is made of green cheese is to say that he has enough confidence in the moon's being made of green cheese for him to accept this as true. Thus, the object of belief (doubt, etc.) has to be the kind of thing to which predications of truth (or falsity) apply. Consider ambiguous sentences like those in (6.112):

(6.112) (a) The parts of the thing were found cleaved
         (b) The gunman took care of the child
         (c) It is true for a bachelor to say that it is true for his father to say that he is married
         (d) *Homer est sacer* (Homer is sacred; Homer is profane)

Such ambiguous sentences, where the senses in each case are inconsistent, show that sentences are not the kind of thing to which predications of truth (or falsity) apply directly. Consider, further, sentences like those in (6.113):

(6.113) (a) My little son believes that Santa Claus wears a red suit trimmed in white fur
         (b) Some primitive people believe that evil demons cause their misfortunes

The fact that such sentences can state truths about little boys and primitive peoples, even though their complement sentences are indeterminate, shows that it is not statements either that are the objects of belief (doubt, etc.). In (6.113a,b) the verb "believe" has the interesting property of converting what would be the presupposition of the complement sentence were it an independent sentence (respectively, the condition that there exists someone who is Santa Claus and is unique in being such and the condition that there are evil demons) into a component of the assertion the whole sentence makes about the beliefs of the individual(s) to which the subject refers. Thus, the assertion of (6.113a) is that the speaker's little son believes that there is someone who is Santa Claus and that that person wears a red suit trimmed in white fur. (A highly interesting general discussion of this property appears in Langendoen and Savin (1971).)

Assuming that sentences are to languages what cryptograms are to codes and that propositions (however analyzed) are to sentences what messages are to cryptograms, we can amplify our construal of Church's suggestion. It is left open whether there are two sentences that express the same proposition, just as there might or might not be more than one cryptogram that encodes the same message. If there are no cases where two or more sentences express the same proposition, then no application of a Frege-type criterion will license an inference by substitution into an opaque context, and if there are such cases, then an application of a Frege-type criterion will license such inferences. In the former case, there is no problem about the correctness of such a criterion, although there is a problem about its utility. In the latter case, there is no problem of utility, but there is a problem of correctness. Hence, an adequate defense of a Frege-type criterion must make it reasonable to think that such a criterion both has utility and is correct. Church's suggestion is directed to the problem of correctness. It is a reply to someone who thinks that there are synonymous expressions and sentences and that " D " and " D' " stand for such sentences but who is encouraged by the Mates objection to think that a Frege-type criterion will license invalid inferences in cases like that from (6.96) to (6.97). The reply shows that such an attitude is based on adopting an explanation of a fact that is not in dispute. The fact to be explained is how someone can affirm that he believes (6.96) and also affirm that he does not believe (6.97), be sincere in both affirmations, and yet not be contradicting himself in the blatant way that he would be were he, in the same breath, to both affirm and deny a belief in the truth of one and the same sentence. The supporter of Mates's objection explains this fact by supposing that (6.96) does not imply (6.97). Church (p. 71) offers an alternative explanation by supposing that, although on a literal interpretation such a person is contradicting himself, there is here, as in the code case, a charitable interpretation, namely, to say that the person has made a linguistic error, just as in the code case we said that someone who affirmed (a) of (6.106) yet denied (b) thereby exhibited ignorance of the code.

Suppose someone makes the linguistic error of thinking that " oculist " means " doctor of the occult." Then that person will think that (6.98) is true while (6.99) is not. However, the doubts that make the person unwilling to affirm (6.99) are really doubts about the truth of the proposition expressed by (6.114):

(6.114)   Doctors of the occult are eye doctors

Hence, these doubts are actually not doubts about the truth of (6.99).

The same sort of case arises when someone thinks that (6.99) expresses a different proposition from (6.98) or is unsure that it expresses the same proposition, even though he may not have confused the proposition expressed by (6.99) with a different one. Such cases, according to Church, are paradigmatic of the sort of linguistic error that makes it possible to affirm a belief in (6.96) and withhold belief in (6.97), be sincere, and yet not be blatantly contradicting oneself.

To sum up, Church's suggestion is that such linguistic errors or confusions are failures to take into account that D' is synonymous with D or entailed by D. If no such failure occurs, the person in question must, at least tacitly, realize that D and D' express the same proposition or that D' expresses one already affirmed by him in affirming D. If he realizes this, is willing to assert it, and yet disavows belief in D' while claiming to believe in D, he is contradicting himself. If, on the other hand, such a failure occurs, then his expression of doubt in connection with D' reflects an inadequacy in his linguistic knowledge, one that falsifies the assumption that the doubt is about the proposition actually expressed by D'. This being so, his judgment about D' must be irrelevant to the issue of whether or not he believes the proposition D' expresses.

3.6   A new criterion for inference in connection with opacity

Up to this point, we have preserved a convenient fiction because it simplified the discussion. We have assumed that the criterion for inference by substitution of one expression or sentence for another occurring in an opaque context of indirect discourse takes the form of a specification of the relation that an expression 'a' must bear to an expression 'b' in order that we can validly infer 'XbY' from 'XaY' and of the relation that a sentence 'P' must bear to a sentence 'Q' in order that we can validly infer 'XQY' from 'XPY'. First, we argued that the relation cannot be logical consequence, or some notion based on it, because the resulting criterion is too broad. Next, we considered the narrower relation of synonymy, but found it too narrow. Finally, we proposed the entailment relation (and meaning inclusion) because it is neither too inclusive nor too exclusive. But if we were to preserve the form of the criterion by simply specifying entailment rather than logical consequence or synonymy as the relation between the sentence appearing in the context and the sentence to be substituted for it, we would not obtain the correct result in all cases of opaque contexts. Although the new criterion would work for cases like the inference from (6.86) to (6.95), it would fail in cases like the inference from (6.115) to (6.116):

(6.115)   John doubts that his neighbor is a bachelor

(6.116)   John doubts that his neighbor is a male

Opaque contexts created by verbs like "doubt" are somehow different from those created by verbs like "believe" and "know," and we will mark this difference by coining a new term for opaque contexts of the former type and for the verbs that create them. We will call such contexts *translucent contexts* and call the verbs *translucent verbs*.

Up to this point, we have continued to use the form of the criterion for substitutions of one expression or sentence for another in an opaque context that Frege, Carnap, and other intensionalists introduced. Now, however, we must reconsider criteria of this form, for we note that they make the claim that the sole determinant of whether such substitution preserves truth is the semantic relations holding between the sentence appearing in an opaque context and the sentence to be substituted for it, and this claim seems to be undermined by the existence of translucent opaque contexts. It seems, then, that we must look for a different form for our criterion.

The difference between sentences involving translucent contexts and sentences involving nontranslucent opaque contexts is that in the former the semantic structure of the translucent verb contributes essentially to the object of the propositional attitude and thus to the determination of what inferences by substitution are valid. Thus, to take account of the contribution of translucent verbs, it is necessary to replace the type of criterion that applies the entailment condition to the expression or sentence appearing in an opaque context (where such an expression or sentence is treated independently of the full sentence in which it occurs) by a new type of criterion that applies the entailment condition to the full sentence itself. In this way, the criterion can take into account both the sense of the translucent verb and the sense of its complement sentence.

Accordingly, the criterion we seek for inferences in cases of opaque contexts of indirect discourse receives its simplest, most natural, and most general form as the principle that 'XbY' can be validly inferred from 'XaY' and 'XQY'

can be validly inferred from 'XPY' just in case 'XaY' entails 'XbY' and 'XPY' entails 'XQY', where entailment is understood in the sense of (4.141). This criterion takes into consideration both the sense of the translucent verb and the sense of its complement sentence because the entailment requirement is imposed on the readings of a whole sentence and they are formed by projection from the readings of the main verb and the readings of the complement sentences in the range of cases in question.

Let us now consider how we can avoid the problem posed by fallacious inferences like (6.115) to (6.116). Suppose the lexical reading for "doubt" represents the concept of having a reason that inclines one to accept a contrary of the proposition that is the object of doubt. Thus, to say that someone doubts that snow is white means that he has some reason that inclines him to accept the truth of the proposition that snow is blue or that snow is yellow or some other contrary. This concept can be represented by a lexical reading that takes the form (6.117):

$$(6.117) \quad ((\text{Has reason inclining him to accept } ((A/V_2)V_1))(\underset{\langle\,\rangle}{\overset{[NP, S]}{X}}))$$

Here "V_1" is a variable whose values are readings of the subject of a complement sentence, "V_2" is a variable whose values are readings of the predicate phrase of a complement sentence (i.e., V_1 is $\underset{\langle\,\rangle}{\overset{[NP, S, NP, VP, PP, S]}{X}}$ and V_2 is $\underset{\langle\,\rangle}{\overset{[VP, PP, S, NP, VP, PP, S]}{X}}$ — see Rosenbaum (1967, p. 34)), and the symbol 'A/' is the antonymy operator.

In the semantic interpretation of (6.115), after the projection rules have substituted a reading of the subject of the complement sentence and a reading of its predicate phrase for the variables "V_1" and "V_2," respectively, the antonymy operator will convert the reading of "is a bachelor"—'(Physical), (Object), (Human), (Adult), (Male), (Unmarried)'—into the semantic marker '(A/(Physical) ∨ A/(Object) ∨ A/(Human) ∨ A/(Adult) ∨ A/(Male) ∨ A/(Unmarried))', which represents a contrary of the proposition expressed by the complement sentence in (6.115). The same antonymy operation in connection with (6.116) will convert the reading of the predicate phrase "is a male" into 'A/(Male)'. But, although 'A/(Male)' appears as one of the semantic markers in the reading of (6.116), it is not one of the semantic markers in the reading of (6.115): in the reading of (6.115), 'A/(Male)' is merely a component of a semantic marker. Thus, when the entailment definition is applied to the readings of (6.115) and (6.116), the former will not be marked as entailing the latter.

We may note at this point that our distinction between translucent and nontranslucent opaque contexts and the revised criterion we have framed to take account of it provides a way of extending Frege's theory that does not suffer from the consequence cited by Linsky (1967, pp. 33–35), namely, that no two singular referring expressions can be synonymous. Linsky's argument uses the opaque context created by the verb "deny (explicitly)," which, of course, is a translucent verb of the same type as "doubt." The critical step of Linsky's argument is the premiss that, on Frege's theory, the proposition expressed by "Jones denied explicitly that $t = t'$" logically implies the proposition expressed by "Jones denied explicitly that $t = t$." On our revision of Frege's theory, this step would have to take the form of a claim that the former proposition entails the latter, but this claim is false because the context in question is translucent and hence our definition of entailment says that the former proposition does *not* entail the latter.

"Doubt" and "deny" are only two of the many examples of translucent verbs. "Reject," "disagree," "question," "refute," etc., are essentially like "doubt," and the treatment of "doubt" just given is intended to suggest the lines along which other translucent verbs of this type are to be dealt with. Another type of translucent context is that created by verbs or constructions like "rhymes with" or "is the acronym of" or by quotation. The fact that opaque contexts created by quotation (such as (6.73)) are also translucent explains why inferences like that from (6.74) to (6.75) are not valid.

It is, of course, not possible for us to show how to handle every different type of translucent verb, nor is it necessary. But we do have to consider the case where a verb utilizes some aspect of the way that a proposition is expressed in the complement sentence, that is, some aspect of the manner in which the complement sentence is formulated, to make its contribution to the determination of the object of the propositional attitude involved in the whole sentence. I know of no fully convincing example of such a verb in English.[28] However, not only might there be such examples, but also we can easily construct them. Thus, let us introduce the verb V*, which, with a complement sentence, expresses the assertion that the referent of its subject knows that the verb phrase constituent of its embedded sentence applies to the referent of the subject of the embedded sentence. Accordingly, the sentence (6.118a) does *not* entail the sentence (6.118b):

(6.118) (a) John V*s that Bill is an adult human male who has not yet married
         (b) John V*s that Bill is a bachelor

The reason is that the assertion that is made by (6.118a) is that John knows that the term "is an adult human male who has not yet married" applies to Bill whereas the assertion that is made by (6.118b) is that John knows that the term "is a bachelor" applies to Bill. That is, the object of knowledge in the former case is the proposition that Bill is someone to which "is an adult human male who has not yet married" applies and in the latter the proposition that Bill is someone to which "is a bachelor" applies. Hence, (6.118a) no more entails (6.118b) by (4.141) than the first of these propositions entails the second by (4.141).

3.7 Correctness: a new defense

In this section, we shall try to establish the correctness of our new criterion for valid inference in opaque contexts, leaving the discussion of its utility to the next section. We are allowed to assume that the opaque context in question is not a translucent one since, if it were, our criterion would not predict an entailment and

---

[28] Chomsky (1970), as I interpret him, claims that "realize" is such a verb.

thus no Mates-type objection would arise. Furthermore, we are allowed to assume that inferences based on entailment which do not involve substitution into an opaque context are unobjectionable, since the issue at hand is correctness, not utility. That is, we can assume that an inference such as that from the complement sentence of (6.87) by itself to the complement sentence of (6.86) by itself is valid on the basis of the synonymy of "an adult human male who is not married" and "a bachelor." The question of correctness here, then, is whether or not our assumptions enable us to infer that the complete sentence (6.87) entails the complete sentence (6.86). This is as general a form of the question as is possible so long as we consider the referent of (6.87) and (6.86) to be an *arbitrary* person, anyone you like. If, then, it can be shown that (6.87) entails (6.86) on the basis of these assumptions and without making use of any special feature of the verb "believes" or any idiosyncratic fact about the referent of the subject of (6.87) and (6.86), then it follows that, for appropriate choices of "D" and "D'," whoever believes (knows, etc.) D, believes (knows, etc.) D'. Hence, any reservations or doubts one might have about (6.97) will be rightly taken to reflect a confusion, to be dealt with along the lines suggested by Church and amplified here.

Given that (6.87) is true, Bill believes the proposition expressed by the complement sentence of (6.87), which is the proposition that there is an individual denoted by "John" and that individual has the properties represented by the semantic markers '(Physical)', '(Object)', '(Human)', '(Adult)', '(Male)', '(Unmarried)'. Since the complement sentence of (6.87) is synonymous with the complement sentence of (6.86), the proposition expressed by the complement sentence of (6.86) *is* the proposition expressed by the complement sentence of (6.87). Now, since (6.86) asserts that the same individual who is the referent of the subject of (6.87) believes the proposition expressed by the complement sentences of (6.87) and (6.86), and since, given that (6.87) is true, we already know he believes this proposition, then it follows that (6.86) must also be true.

To put the argument in terms of Mates's case, if it is true of the proposition expressed by D that it is believed by everyone who believes D, then, since the proposition expressed by D' is the proposition expressed by D, it must also be true of the proposition expressed by D' that it is believed by everyone who believes D. Thus, it follows from our assumptions that, if D' is synonymous with D, (6.96) and (6.97) must be true together, and that doubts about (6.97) do not provide a reason for denying that synonymy or entailment are the relations we want to govern inference in connection with substitution for an expression or sentence in an opaque context.

The same argument can be made to show that entailment in one direction is also sufficient as a condition for valid inference in such cases. If D entails D' (but not conversely), then D' expresses one of the propositions expressed by D. That proposition, call it "G," is clearly believed by everyone who believes D, since belief in G is a necessary condition for belief in D. But then G is the proposition expressed by D', and, hence, the proposition expressed by D' has the property of being believed by whoever believes D. Thus, (6.97), which says this, must be true.

The cases D and D' either are different orthographic or phonetic codings of the same proposition or the latter is an orthographic or phonetic coding of one of the propositions orthographically or phonetically coded by the former. In either case, the truth of (6.96) implies the truth of (6.97), for anyone who believes a proposition under one of its linguistic codings believes that proposition, even if he doesn't recognize another of its linguistic codings. The proposition has the property of being believed by the person(s) in question no matter how it is coded in a sentence that expresses their belief.

Let us consider the logic of this reply to a Mates-type objection. We are given a pair of sentences S_1 and S_2 of the form 'NP$_i$–V$_j$–that–S$_a$' and 'NP$_i$–V$_j$–that S$_b$', respectively, where 'V$_j$' creates a context that is opaque but not translucent and where, *ex hypothesi*, S$_a$ entails S$_b$. On this basis, the entailment definition predicts that S_1 entails S_2, and thus we are committed to the claim that the truth of S_1 is sufficient for the truth of S_2. A Mates-type objection takes the form of a denial that S_1 entails S_2 *on the grounds that*, as a matter of fact, S_1 is true but S_2 is false. Therefore, our reply is against the claim that S_2 is false (while S_1 is true): it is an argument to show that it is impossible for S_1 to be true and S_2 false. Notice, then, that our argument does not pretend to establish that S_1 entails (or is synonymous with) S_2. This is something that semantic theory and the grammar together predict by virtue of their account of the compositional structure of the meaning of S_1 and S_2. The argument seeks only to establish that any claim that there are counterexamples to this account must have its facts wrong.

We are therefore arguing that the intuitions upon which such claims are made are better explained on the supposition that the person in question, the person referred to by the subject of S_1 and S_2, is somehow deficient in his comprehension of the meaning of S$_a$ and S$_b$ than on the supposition that S_1 and S_2 can differ in truth value, since the latter explanation involves the logical incoherence (if our argument is sound) of claiming that something, S_2, which *must* be true on certain assumptions is not true even though these assumptions hold (*viz.*, that S$_a$ entails S$_b$, that V$_j$ creates a nontranslucent but opaque context, that the proposition expressed by the sentence in an opaque context is the object of the belief, etc., attributed to the person who is referred to by the subject of S_1 or S_2 when it makes a statement, and that S_1 is true).

Thus, we argued that if Bill is unwilling to affirm a belief in the proposition expressed by the complement sentence of (6.87), though he readily affirms a belief in that expressed by the complement sentence of (6.86), this can only be because he does not realize or take into consideration that the English word "bachelor" is synonymous with the English expression "adult human male who is not married." Not recognizing this is not, on our assumptions, a failure to recognize that bachelors are adult human males who are not married, which is simply a contingent fact. It is rather a linguistic failure. Such errors must not be allowed to enter the picture at all, since if they do, the fact that someone does not affirm a belief in the proposition expressed by the complement sentence in (6.87) because he quite genuinely "has his doubts" is totally independent of the question at issue, namely, the question of whether, in fact, he believes this proposition. Allowing the possibility that the person referred to might be making a linguistic error completely undermines a Mates-type objection since, unless such a possibility is excluded, we can always defeat the objection by replying that, although this person may think he doubts or does not believe the proposition expressed by the complement sentence in (6.87), this is *not* a proposition which he has doubts about or from which he has withheld belief. That this is actually so follows from the fact that, as expressed by the complement sentence in (6.86), the proposition is one that we already know he believes.

The point can be made another way by saying that, if S_a entails S_b, then an *ideal speaker* (i.e., someone who makes no linguistic errors, is in no way confused about the language, has a perfect grasp of the relevant grammatical facts, etc.) believes S_b if he believes S_a. I understand this notion of an ideal speaker in the same way as it is understood when a grammar is explained as the formal theory of the linguistic competence of an ideal speaker, but here it represents the first of three stages of inferential competence. After the ideal speaker, who knows exactly what sentences are the entailments of a given sentence, there is, at the second stage, the *ideal logician*, someone who knows all the logical consequences of any specific set of sentences he is given as premises. At the third stage, there is the *ideal combinator*, who, if B_1 and B_2 are any two sets of his beliefs, believes any consequence that can be validly inferred from the union of B_1 and B_2. Just as, for example, the notion of an ideal logician determines the concept of logical consequence, so the notion of an ideal speaker, *not* the deficiencies of actual or hypothetical speakers, determines the concept of entailment.

3.8　Utility

The correctness claim argued in the previous section is a conditional: *if* there are cases of expressions or sentences that are the same in meaning (or one's meaning is included in that of the other), and *if* there are two sentences which are identical except that one of the cases appears in one sentence and the other appears in the other sentence, and *if* the context in which these cases appear is opaque but not translucent, *then* the sentences cannot have different truth values. In our argument we sought to prove that the antecedent of this conditional implies the consequent on the basis of a few reasonable assumptions. Now, if the conditional is true, the denial of the claim that someone who believes D must believe D′ must be a denial of one of the antecedents of this conditional. Thus, such a denial must assume one of the forms (6.119) or (6.120):

(6.119)　An objection to the effect that there are no cases of synonymous expressions or synonymous sentences and no cases of meaning inclusion or entailment.

(6.120)　An objection to the effect that there are no opaque nontranslucent verbs, i.e., no constituents that create nontransparent and nontranslucent contexts.

These, I take it, are the only possibilities, since no one would deny that we can construct sentences that are identical except for the appropriate substitutions. Objection (6.119) is Quine's, and it will be considered in the latter half of this section. Objection (6.120), which seems to me less serious, will be taken up now.

If there are any opaque and nontranslucent contexts—even one—then the demonstration of correctness presented in the preceding section provides a definitive solution to the problem about inference in connection with substitution into opaque contexts. If there are no such contexts, then we forgo a powerful argument for the intensionalist viewpoint.

We observed earlier that extensional identity cannot be a criterion for inference in opaque contexts since, for example, someone's knowing that two is less than ten is not sufficient for us to say that he knows that the even prime is less than ten. If there are nontranslucent, opaque contexts, we cannot explain valid inferences by substitution exclusively on the basis of extensional relations but must invoke intensional relations. The need to invoke intensional relations like entailment in order to complete the theory of valid inference can, then, be used as a decisive argument against the extensionalist viewpoint, if, as we have also argued, synonymy, etc. cannot be reduced to extensional relations. If, on the other hand, there are no nontranslucent opaque contexts, then this argument for semantic relations, over and above extensional ones, does not go through, since extensional identity will serve as a criterion for inference in transparent contexts and inferences by substitution in translucent contexts are invalid.

Now, there is no argument against the possibility of there being one such context, as there is an argument, namely Quine's, against propositional or concept identity. Thus, it is not a question of refuting an argument against the utility of our criterion but rather one of giving reasons to think that there are contexts that establish the utility of our criterion. We have given "believe" as an example of an opaque but nontranslucent verb. As contrasted with "doubt," the verb "believe" appears to be a clear-cut case of a verb that creates an opaque but nontranslucent context. However, it might be denied that this is so. Consider, for example, (6.121) and (6.122):

(6.121) I believe that the culprit is an uncle of mine

(6.122) I believe that the culprit is a brother of one of my parents or a husband of one of my aunts

It might be claimed that a sentence such as (6.121) does not entail a sentence such as (6.122) because "believe" changes the propositional object of belief as a function of the syntactic and/or phonological differences between the synonymous expressions "uncle" and "brother of one's parent or husband of one's aunt." This is the only possible explanation of the claim that "believe" is translucent in cases like (6.121) and (6.122) since, *ex hypothesi*, "uncle" and "brother of one's parent or husband of one's aunt" are synonymous, differing only in their syntactic and/or phonological form. Accordingly, someone who claims that "believe" is translucent is claiming that what is believed in a case like (6.121) is different from what belief is withheld from in a case like (6.122). But if the object of a belief is a proposition and propositions are identical when the sentences expressing them are synonymous, then, since the claim cannot be that one thing can be identical to another and yet different from it, the claim must be either a denial that propositions are the objects of belief or a denial that synonymous sentences express the same proposition. Both of these claims, however, are gratuitous ones against which we have already given strong counterarguments.

But before leaving this topic, it is worth pointing out some of the undesirable empirical consequences that follow from the view that "believe" is translucent. Consider the sentences (6.123)–(6.125):

(6.123) I believe that the culprit is one of my uncles but *not* that the culprit is a brother of one of my parents or a husband of one of my aunts

(6.124) I believe that the culprit is one of my uncles who is a brother of one of my parents or a husband of one of my aunts

(6.125) I can believe that the culprit is one of my uncles just as long as I do not have to believe that the culprit is a brother of one of my parents or a husband of one of my aunts

Now contrast these with the sentences (6.126)–(6.128):

(6.126) (a) I believe that the culprit is one of my uncles but *not* that the culprit is a brother of one of my parents
     (b) I believe that the culprit is one of my uncles but *not* that the culprit is my lodge brother

(6.127) (a) I believe that the culprit is one of my uncles who is a brother of one of my parents
     (b) I believe that the culprit is one of my uncles who is a lodge brother of mine

(6.128) (a) I can believe that the culprit is one of my uncles just so long as I do not have to believe that the culprit is a brother of one of my parents
     (b) I can believe that the culprit is one of my uncles just so long as I do not have to believe that the culprit is one of my lodge brothers

Sentence (6.123) is contradictory, in contrast to both (a) and (b) of (6.126). Sentence (6.124) is semantically redundant, in contrast to both (a) and (b) of (6.127). Sentence (6.125) is semantically anomalous, in contrast to both (a) and (b) of (6.128). But someone who takes the view that "believe" is translucent in connection with the examples (6.121) and (6.122) must predict these facts incorrectly.

Further evidence for the conclusion that "believe" is not translucent comes from the fact that when the verb "believe" in (6.123)–(6.125) is replaced by a genuine translucent constituent the semantic properties and relations of the resulting sentences correspond to those of (6.126)–(6.128). Thus, consider the sentences (6.129)–(6.131):

(6.129) I understand what is meant when it is said that the culprit is one of my uncles but I do not understand what is meant when it is said that the culprit is a brother of one of my parents or a husband of one of my aunts

(6.130) I understand what is meant when it is said that the culprit is one of my uncles who is a brother of one of my parents or a husband of one of my aunts

(6.131) I can understand what is meant when it is said that the culprit is one of my uncles just as long as I do not have to understand what is meant when it is said that the culprit is a brother of one of my parents or a husband of one of my aunts

Sentence (6.129) might be continued "because I don't know the words 'brother' or 'husband'"; (6.130) might be continued "but it's redundant"; and (6.131) might be continued "because the latter confuses me to a point where I no longer understand the former." These cases, unlike (6.123)–(6.125) and like (6.126)–(6.128), are, respectively, noncontradictory, nonredundant, and nonanomalous.

We now turn to (6.119), the denial of utility (that is, to Quine's positive arguments against propositional identity). It will be recalled that we did not assume that there are sentences that express the same proposition. The virtue of not making this assumption is that the argument given as a defense of our criterion's correctness did not have to depend on this often debated point. The vice is that if it is false that there are sentences that express the same proposition, then the criterion is only vacuously correct.

There are certain fairly strong considerations in favor of the claim that there are sentences that express the same proposition (and sentences that express one of the propositions expressed by another). These considerations are of both an empirical and a theoretical nature. On the empirical side, making this assumption enables us to explain an indefinitely large class of sentence (and expression) relations, namely, paraphrase relations of the sort exhibited in cases like (6.109) and (6.110). On the theoretical side, as was mentioned earlier, this assumption renders contexts of propositional attitude transparent, thus dissolving the problems that they are alleged to pose for logic. It would thus seem clear, in the absence of any philosophical objections to the assumption, that it comes quite highly recommended.

However, those familiar with Quine's objections to synonymy as a standard of identity for propositions well know that there are objections, ones which, if they are sound, imply that our thesis about inference in opaque contexts is merely a vacuous truth. Therefore, to defend our thesis against such trivialization, I wish to try to show that none of Quine's objections hold against the use of synonymy (or entailment) to determine if and when different sentences express the same proposition.

Part of Quine's argument against an absolute notion rests on his criticisms of the analytic-synthetic distinction in "Two Dogmas of Empiricism" (1953d). I have replied to these in the previous section. The other part consists in his four objections to synonymy serving as a standard of identity for propositions, discussed in Section 42 of *Word and Object* (Quine (1960b)). Basically his argument is that there can be no sharp, absolute notion of synonymy so that we must have recourse only to a graded notion, and this offers us no help in connection with opacity. He says:

> there is no objection to a graded notion of synonymy or of analyticity, supposing it made reasonably clear; but it is unlikely to contribute directly or indirectly to a standard of identity of propositions. For propositions have to be the same or distinct absolutely; identity, properly so-called, knows no gradations (p. 203).

I agree that a graded notion of synonymy (or entailment), such as the one he goes on to formulate based on his own concept of stimulus-synonymy,[29] is wholly unsuited to the job of individuating propositions and so is unsuited to deal with inference in opaque contexts. Thus, the critical issue is whether or not Quine's arguments show that an absolute notion is unobtainable.

The first of Quine's (1960b) four objections to synonymy is as follows:

> The transformability of one sentence into another by the logic of quantification and truth functions can elude even the specialist in logic for indefinite periods; there is no general limit to the length of the inquiry that may be required (p. 204).

The reply to this is that the transformability of one sentence into another with respect to the relations of synonymy and entailment defined in semantic theory does not depend on the full power of the consequence relation defined in general quantification theory. Therefore, the fact that there is no decision procedure for general quantification theory cannot be used to disqualify propositions as objects of belief. As we have already pointed out, it is necessary to formulate synonymy and entailment relations within the bounds of immediate inference, just in order to avoid disqualifying propositions as objects of belief on somewhat different grounds.[30]

Quine's second criticism is that any means for individuating propositions based on stimulus synonymy of general terms will be too loose to provide the desired results. This is certainly correct, but, of course, it holds only for a graded notion.

Quine's next objection runs as follows:

> Whether a general term in a sentence of ordinary language survives in a canonical paraphrase of the sentence, or disappears in favor of a more minute analysis, depends only on one's momentary purposes in paraphrasing.... Nor should we care to meet this objection by specifying or imagining some absolute vocabulary of simple general terms, as canonical all-purpose elements of paraphrase. If the positing of propositions as objects is serious, any such arbitrary assembled groundwork for propositional identity must be seen as gratuitous (pp. 204–205).

The basic assumption of this argument is that there is no fixed standard for determining a canonical paraphrase, or for justifying any other kind of representation of the logical form of a sentence from natural language. Quine's reference to the dictates of "one's momentary purposes in paraphrasing" is no more than Carnap's principle of tolerance, to which the correct reply is that such tolerance is restricted by the grammatical facts about sentences that any representation of their logical form must heed. But facts by themselves often underdetermine the treatment of a case and require the use of a theory to provide an unequivocal treatment. Accordingly,

---

[29] Quine (1960b): "sentences in . . . canonical form of notation are synonymous if one can be transformed into the other by transformations of the logic of quantification and truth functions together with substitution of general terms for stimulus-synonymous general terms" p. 204.

[30] To put this reply in another way, the transformability of one sentence into another by the apparatus of quantification theory concerns the competence of an ideal logician but propositional identity concerns only the competence of an ideal speaker. See Section 3.2 of this chapter.

Quine's further point, that there is no nonarbitrary way of setting up a theoretical vocabulary to serve as a basis for a scheme for representing the logical form of sentences, must be answered. It is not hard to see this point as a direct denial of the possibility of a semantic theory, since such a theory claims to provide such a scheme in the form of a theoretical vocabulary of semantic markers. Quine's objection reaches its full form in a further remark:

> For if the posit of propositions is to be taken seriously, eternal sentences of other languages must be supposed to mean propositions too; and each of these must be identical with or distinct from each proposition meant by an eternal sentence of our own.... Surely it is philosophically unsatisfactory for such questions of identity to arise as recognized questions, however academic, without there being in principle some suggestion of how to construe them in terms of domestic and foreign dispositions to verbal behavior (p. 205).

Quine's claim is, then, that there is no nonarbitrary way of setting up a theoretical vocabulary for representing the propositions expressed by sentences in natural languages because there is no empirically motivated means for deciding when sentences (within a language or across languages) express the same proposition and when they express different ones. But this is just false. Semantic theory offers just such a means in the form of a principle telling when a piece of information is part of the meaning of a lexical item, as opposed to being a factual comment on its referent. Given such a principle, each piece of information that qualifies as semantic by the principle enters the semantic representation of that item in the form of a semantic marker in one of the lexical readings in its dictionary entry. The set of primitive semantic markers, chosen from the full set of semantic markers used in formulating lexical readings in the dictionaries for all natural languages according to the usual canons for setting up the extra-logical basis of a system,[31] is the theoretical vocabulary for semantic theory. They are, in Quine's terms, an "absolute vocabulary of simple general terms," and they serve as "canonical all-purpose elements of paraphrase" in the sense that synonymy relations can be picked out as cases where different lexical items, expressions, or whole sentences, in the same or different languages, receive the same semantic representation in terms of these elements from the theoretical vocabulary.

This principle, then, must decide how to choose between two lexical readings R_1 and R_2, which are the same except that R_2 contains (*ex hypothesi*) a component, putative semantic marker μ that represents *factual* information and R_1 does not contain μ. If we transpose to physics this question of how to decide that a certain concept does not belong to the descriptive apparatus of a certain theory, we can see more clearly the sort of methodological considerations that eliminate extraneous information from the generalizations in a science. These can then be brought into semantics to provide a rationale for choosing between R_1 and R_2. Suppose, therefore, that someone were to propose changing Archimedes' law that a body is buoyed up with a force equal to the weight of the displaced fluid by adding a further clause to the effect that the word "body" is an English noun. It is perfectly clear that physicists would resist this absurd addition on the grounds that it is of no

[31] Goodman (1951, chapter 3).

help whatever in explaining why ice floats on water or any other hydrodynamical phenomena. The failure to increase the explanatory power of the law is, thus, the rationale for saying that being an English noun is not a hydrodynamical property. Now, transposing this rationale to semantics, it must be equally clear that linguistics should resist the addition of any information to a lexical reading if its inclusion would fail to increase the predictive or explanatory power of the lexical reading and thus of the dictionary. Since what must be predicted and explained by a dictionary, as part of the semantic component of a grammar, are the semantic properties and relations of anomaly, ambiguity, synonymy, analyticity, entailment, etc., by showing that R_2 does not predict or explain any of these properties or relations that are not already predicted and explained by R_1, it will be shown that μ, which is the only difference between R_1 and R_2, represents factual, not semantic, information.

The principle whose existence falsifies the basic assumption of this argument of Quine's is thus as follows. If we cannot eliminate information from the lexical reading of a word W without losing predictions and explanations of semantic properties and relations of expressions and sentences in which W occurs, then such information belongs in the dictionary entry for W and is hence rightly deemed semantic; and if we can simplify the entries of the dictionary by excluding a certain piece of information from all of them, then it is rightly deemed nonsemantic.

Quine's final objection is that to have a relation of synonymy defined generally for the sentences of distinct natural languages it is necessary to suppose

> that among all the alternative systems of analytical hypotheses of translation ... which are compatible with the totality of dispositions to verbal behavior on the part of speakers of the two languages, some are "really" right and others wrong on behaviorally inscrutable grounds of propositional identity (p. 206).

Thus, Quine's principle of the indeterminacy of radical translation—namely,

> rival systems of analytical hypotheses can fit the totality of speech behavior to perfection, and can fit the totality of dispositions to speech behavior as well, and still specify mutually incompatible translations of countless sentences insusceptible of independent control (p. 72)

—is brought in here to rule out the possibility of a synonymy relation appropriate for the role of a standard of propositional identity. This principle, as we now learn, is to have its polemical use in Quine's attempt to eliminate any viable interlinguistic notion of a proposition. As Quine puts it, "The very question of conditions for identity of propositions presents not so much an unsolved problem as a mistaken ideal" (p. 206). Accordingly, the question of the effability thesis discussed in Chapter 2 and the question of utility with which we are concerned in this section both hinge completely on the untenability of Quine's doctrine of the indeterminacy of radical translation.

This doctrine amounts to skepticism about the prospects for the successful development of the sort of linguistic theory contemplated in this book. The prospects of such a theory can be seen to rest wholly on the question of whether human beings, by virtue of their biological makeup, have a rich enough set of innate concepts to prevent the diversity of their experience from dividing them from one another by incommensurate ontologies. The doctrine of the indeterminacy of radical translation claims that the genetically fixed concepts with which men organize their experience are insufficient to prevent differences in sensory stimulation from dividing them not only in " how they say things but in what they (can) say." If this claim is correct, the highest hopes for linguistic theory are doomed to be unfulfilled. If, on the other hand, man's innate biological makeup contains a sufficiently rich set of conceptual forms, then, if satisfactorily developed, linguistic theory will formulate syntactic and semantic universals strong enough to constrain translations so that there is no area of indeterminacy.

It would seem that whether or not there is such a rich set of innate conceptual forms is a purely empirical question. Hence, it is certainly a logical possibility that linguistic theory might fail to achieve its aims because of incommensurate differences in the conceptual systems underlying different languages. But, looked at in this way, it is also logically possible that linguistic theory will achieve its aims, and the situation reduces to the banal truth that linguists who espouse these aims take the same inductive risks as other scientists who put their hopes on strict uniformity of nature. However, Quine's doctrine is *not* intended as a helpful reminder to linguists that they are in the same boat as other empirical scientists. According to Quine, these aims are a " mistaken ideal." His doctrine is not that linguists have to take full account of ordinary, garden variety inductive risks, nor that there is inductive evidence to show that betting on the success of linguistic theory is a poor risk, but that the bet *cannot* be won because, no matter what system of analytical hypotheses one chooses to bet on, there is no rational means to determine that it is better than the others. Quine's doctrine thus depends on a distinction between *ordinary inductive risk* and *indeterminacy*. In the former case, our finite sample underdetermines any generalization we might base on it. Thus, our generalization goes beyond our sample and may go astray because it falsely predicts unobserved cases in the population. In the latter case, the population underdetermines the truth of any generalization we might make about it. Thus, we cannot avoid going astray if we commit ourselves to the truth of a generalization because, whatever we assume the possible data to be, an equally good case can be made for inconsistent generalizations on the very same assumption.

I shall argue that this distinction is untenable and that, as a consequence, Quine's doctrine has nothing to recommend it beyond its being a logical possibility. The critical point is whether analytical hypotheses can be objectively right or wrong, as statements of linguistic fact. Quine is surely correct in observing that there are always conceivable alternatives to any hypotheses about linguistic structure, that is, rival systems of hypotheses that are equally consistent with the total available evidence. But, of course, the same can be said about any empirical hypotheses, in any science. In particular, the same thing can be said about generalizations concerning the stimulus meaning of observation sentences and translations depending only on truth-functional connectives, both of which Quine regards as unproblematic cases. These cases are taken to involve only normal inductive risk and thus to be beyond the range of skepticism. But generalizations concerning the semantic structure of nonlogical expressions, particularly generalizations about semantic relations like synonymy, are regarded as well within the range of skepticism. They involve not just ordinary inductive uncertainty but full indeterminacy.

Why not treat the former cases in the same way as the latter case? According to Quine, truth functions such as negation, conjunction, and disjunction can be radically translated without worrying about indeterminacy. His approach for translating such alien expressions as negation, conjunction, and disjunction is to provide a "semantic criterion" for each of these concepts. For example:

> The semantic criterion of negation is that it turns any short sentence to which one will assent into a sentence from which one will dissent, and vice versa. That of conjunction is that it produces compounds to which ... one is prepared to assent always and only when one is prepared to assent to each component. That of alternation is similar with assent changed twice to dissent (pp. 57–58).

Quine continues:

> This approach ill accords with the doctrine of "prelogical mentality." To take the extreme case, let us suppose that certain natives are said to accept as true certain sentences translatable in the form 'p and not p'. Now this claim is absurd under our semantic criteria. And, not to be dogmatic about them, what criteria might one prefer? Wanton translation can make natives sound as queer as one pleases. Better translation imposes our logic upon them, and would beg the question of prelogicality if there were a question to beg (p. 58).

One is tempted to reply to Quine by saying that the existence of a prelogical community is an empirically real possibility and that, therefore, there is a question begged when we impose our logic on them just as much as when we translate "Gavagai" as our word 'rabbit'. But a more telling reply is to say that the more serious question-begging occurs when an assumption is made about the existence of a prelogical mentality in connection with the translation of "extra-logical" words while no such assumption is made in connection with the translation of the logical words: treating these two translation domains differently is not based on any distinction between logical and extra-logical words.

Either both domains are susceptible to indeterminacy or neither is. If we were to enrich the criteria of translation by adding to Quine's criteria those that could be obtained from a fully worked out semantic theory of the kind we have sketched, there is no reason to think there would be indeterminacy of translation. But it is just such machinery that is excluded from translation on Quine's view. No wonder, then, that there seems to be indeterminacy in the case to which this machinery is primarily applicable, the case of translating the nonlogical vocabulary of alien languages. This point can perhaps be made more dramatically by inverting it. If we were to keep truth-function logic out of the criteria for translating truth functions, we would find ourselves in a parallel situation of indeterminacy. For then, deprived of our knowledge of what truth functions are, we are no longer able to decide if the expressions of an alien language express them. Likewise, deprived of our knowledge of what innate conceptual constraints fix the ontological categories of a language, we are no longer able to decide if the expressions of an alien language are subject to them.

It is in this sense that Quine's view is truly a case of skepticism in the traditional sense. He, like the radical skeptic about inductive inferences from the past to the future, rules out the use of the very criteria that must be used if knowledge of the phenomena in question is to be had, and then goes on to argue that we cannot show that any claim to knowledge is better than any other.

Therefore, the central point on which Quine's doctrine of the indeterminacy of radical translation rests, the distinction between ordinary inductive uncertainty and full indeterminacy, proves to be a distinction without a difference to support it. Quine, however, believes there is a difference, namely, that in the cases of stimulus meaning and truth functions there are theories to which decisions between competing hypotheses can be referred (i.e., conditioning theory and truth-functional logic), whereas in the case of nonlogical expressions, there is none. In terms of the preceding discussion, we may reply that there is none only because the situation has been set up precisely to exclude such a theory.

But there is a further reply, namely, that the question at issue is not whether there is at present a suitable theory, but whether, in principle, there could be. Quine cannot assume that there could be no such theory because this assumption is, as we have seen, equivalent to the doctrine of the indeterminacy of radical translation, and this is just what is to be established.

To avoid the possible circularity here, Quine goes on to argue:

> The indefinability of synonymy by reference to the methodology of analytic hypotheses is formally the same as the indefinability of truth by reference to the scientific method (p. 75).

But this again is a distinction without a difference. Some sort of basis for settling questions of truth is granted to conditioning theory, truth-functional logic, and physics. Whatever it may be, Quine cannot grant the same basis to linguistics without giving up on the entire enterprise. But if there is some relevant difference here, what is it? Why can we not employ the same basis in linguistics to settle questions of truth about the synonymy, analyticity, etc., of expressions?

To the question as to why we cannot meaningfully speak of the truth of hypotheses about the translation of nonlogical expressions within the framework of linguistic theory (a system of analytical hypotheses), just as we *can* meaningfully speak of the truth of hypotheses within the framework of conditioning theory, truth-functional logic, physics, and other sciences, Quine answers:

> To be thus reassured is to misjudge the parallel. In being able to speak of the truth of a sentence only within a more inclusive theory, one is not much hampered; for one is always working within some comfortably inclusive theory, however tentative.... In short, the parameters of truth stay conveniently fixed most of the time. Not so the analytical hypotheses that constitute the parameter of translation. We are always ready to wonder about the meaning of a foreigner's remark without reference to any one set of analytic hypotheses, indeed, even in the absence of any; yet two sets of analytical hypotheses equally compatible with all linguistic behavior can give contrary answers, unless the remark is one of the limited sorts that can be translated without recourse to analytical hypotheses (pp. 75–76).

Accordingly, what for Quine differentiates psychology, logic, and physics, on the one hand, from linguistics, on the other, is that in the former cases we are permitted to have a tentative theory within which competing individual hypotheses can be compared and evaluated on the grounds of predictive adequacy, simplicity, systematic coherence, explanatory power, etc., while in the latter case we are not permitted a tentative theory of language within which individual competing analytical hypotheses about linguistic universals can be compared and similarly evaluated. But, again, we have a distinction without a difference to justify it. The fact that we may always be prepared to wonder about the meaning of sentences from a foreign language shows no more than that, *as yet*, we have no comprehensive theory that settles the question of their translation. The appeal to inductive uncertainty is irrelevant if the uncertainty is simply normal inductive uncertainty and is question-begging if it is indeterminacy of radical translation. Without a difference, Quine's doctrine of indeterminacy can be applied to physics, psychology, and logic at stages when these fields lacked a comprehensive and compelling theory, thereby showing that truth in these fields is not better off than truth in linguistics.

Others, notably Chomsky (1968), have also been unable to find a difference of the sort that Quine's thesis requires and have drawn the same conclusion, namely, that there is no special problem of indeterminacy in linguistics. But Quine (1968) still insists that the parallelism fails. "Theory in physics," he claims, "is the ultimate parameter. There is no legitimate first philosophy, higher or firmer than physics, to which to appeal over physicists' heads" (p. 275). This is true, even though physicists and philosophers actively discuss the conceptual foundations of quantum mechanics. But it is the impressive body of comprehensive and compelling theory in physics as it now stands that makes it the final arbitrator. There was a time when physics did not enjoy this status. Why not suppose that linguistics, through the development of a comprehensive and compelling theory, may someday also become the final arbitrator on linguistic matters?

Quine's answer is not helpful:

> The point about indeterminacy of translation is that it withstands even all this truth, the whole truth about nature. This is what I mean by saying that, where indeterminacy of translation applies, there is no real question of right choice; there is no fact of the matter even to *within* the acknowledged underdetermination of a theory of nature (p. 275).

This begs the question. Instead of citing some difference between physics and linguistics to defeat the alleged parallelism, Quine simply asserts that indeterminacy of translation remains no matter how much we may know about nature. We can agree that, if indeterminacy of translation exists, then "there is no fact of the matter," but the question is what reason there is for thinking it does exist.

When Quine's basic reason for thinking that such indeterminacy will exist no matter how much we come to know is brought to the surface, the fundamental and deepest circularity of his argument emerges. After the previously quoted passage from *Word and Object* (1960b), Quine says:

> Something of the true situation verges on visibility when the sentences concerned are extremely theoretical. Thus who would undertake to translate 'Neutrinos lack mass' into jungle language? If anyone does, we may expect him to coin words or distort the usage of old ones. We may expect him to plead in extenuation

that the natives lack the requisite concepts; also that they know too little physics. And he is right, except for the hint of there being some free-floating, linguistically neutral meaning which we capture in 'Neutrinos lack mass', and the native cannot.... The discontinuity of radical translation tries our meanings: really sets them over against their verbal embodiments, or, more typically, finds nothing there (p. 76).

This brings us round full circle. To refute the intensionalist position that meaning can be vindicated as a theoretically viable notion using a standard of propositional identity framed in terms of a synonymy relation for eternal sentences in each language, Quine urges the indeterminacy of radical translation. Indeed, of the various arguments that he cites against a standard of propositional identity and "the whole idea of positing propositions," the indeterminacy of radical translation argument is the one he himself takes to be central.[32] This argument purports to show that "the very question of conditions for identity of propositions presents not so much an unsolved problem as a mistaken ideal" (p. 76). But now when we go back from the application of the argument in his Section 42 to its formulation in Section 16, we find that at bottom there is nothing to back up the indeterminacy thesis but Quine's bare claim (p. 76) that there are no meanings, no sufficient body of linguistically universal propositions, in effect, no standard of propositional identity. Thus, the whole bootstrap operation collapses.

The assumption that excludes a theory of meaning is just the assumption that no notion of meaning beyond stimulus meaning is acceptable, from which it follows, of course, that semantic relations like synonymy must be graded, not absolute, and thus there can be no standard of propositional identity based on the synonymy relation. But now it is clear that this assumption, like the thesis of indeterminacy of translation itself, is a wholly a priori doctrine about the nature of language. Accordingly, we may conclude that there is no argument against a theory of language containing a specification of the conditions of identity for propositions.

It seems clear that if someone rules out the possibility of a theory of semantic relations but nonetheless accepts linguistic intuitions of speakers about such relations, as Quine does, then his account of these relations must take the form of reports of the judgments speakers make in expressing such intuitions, where these reports reflect all such gradations (between doubt and certainty) found in the judgments themselves. Quite consistently, then, Quine talks about semantic relations in terms of stimulus meaning, a notion so defined that judgments representing every degree of doubtfulness indicated by the same speaker at different times or different speakers enter into the linguist's statements about meaning, his analytical hypotheses, on an equal footing with unequivocal judgments of assent and dissent. Thus, graded concepts become an indispensable feature of the descriptions of an approach whose starting assumption is that there can be no theory. But if we adopt the opposite approach and assume that a theory of semantic relations is possible, we can introduce absolute concepts as idealizations, as is done in other sciences. Thus, it will be possible to admit that synonymy and analyticity judgments

---

[32] Quine (1960b) says, "The difficulties cited earlier in the present section are merely by the way" (p. 206).

are graded, without having to admit further that the theoretical concepts of synonymy and analyticity are also graded. Judgments expressing a degree of doubt on the speaker's part can be handled as comparable cases are handled in other sciences. That is, we can base our application of idealized (absolute) concepts on clear cases, if they collectively constitute strong enough confirmation, and if not, if we encounter cases where the intuitions of speakers are weak, conflicting, or non-existent, then we can obtain our application of such concepts by a theoretical extrapolation, that is, by extending generalizations from cases where intuitions are sufficiently strong. This, in fact, is the special virtue of theories—to provide the theoretical interconnections among generalizations that allow such extrapolation. And it is just this that semantic theory is designed to do in applying idealized concepts like synonymy, analyticity, and entailment. Therefore, Quine's refusal to countenance absolute concepts in semantics is of a piece with his refusal to countenance the possibility of a theory in this area.[33]

In the final analysis, it is difficult to see which way Quine wants to run the argument. Does he start with a refusal to countenance theories of language that posit abstract entities and end up with graded constructs, or does he start with some methodological doctrine (e.g., behaviorism *cum* operationalism) that excludes absolute constructs and end up by refusing to countenance such theories? Either way the underlying motivation would seem to stem from old-fashioned empiricist qualms of the sort that found expression in behaviorist psychology and taxonomic linguistics.[34]

[33] It should be noted that if Quine's basis for rejecting nongraded notions of synonymy, analyticity, entailment, etc., were sound, it could also be used to show that there can be no nongraded notion of logical consequence, since, obviously, intuitions about whether or not one sentence is a logical consequence of another (which are the basis for explicating the notion of logical consequence) grade off as much as do intuitions about semantic relations.

[34] I have tried to clarify this matter somewhat in Katz (to appear), where I argue that Quine's question-begging assumption that there are no meanings "over against their verbal embodiments" comes from his adoption of Bloomfieldian structuralism whose taxonomic model of grammar provides no place for meaning in the grammar of sentences.

Temporal specification, state, process, and the converse relation

Science arises from the discovery of Identity amidst Diversity.

W. S. Jevons

        In this chapter, we shall be concerned with a special case of the synonymy relation, namely, the converse relation. Our aim will be to provide a definition of the converse relation that captures the manner in which expressions and sentences that are synonymous by virtue of being instances of this relation obtain their meaning (hence their status as synonyms) as a compositional function of the meanings and syntactic organization of their constituents.[1]
        The synonymy of complex constituents can arise in different ways. Compare in this regard (7.1a,b) and (7.2a,b):

(7.1)   (a) Someone is a wife of someone
         (b) Someone is a husband of someone

(7.2)   (a) Someone is a bachelor
         (b) Someone is an adult unmarried male human

        [1] The treatment of converses in this chapter is a development of a proposal made in Katz (1967a, pp. 170–173).

In the latter case the synonymy is felt to result from the sense of "bachelor" being built up from the senses of "adult," "unmarried," "male," and "human" by a straightforward compositional process. In the former case, however, the synonymy is felt to result from a relation between "is a wife of" and "is a husband of." This relation is the converse relation.

In logic, the converse relation is treated as a relation that holds of two relations H_1 and H_2 just in case $(x)(y)[H_1 x, y \equiv H_2 y, x]$.[2] For example, $<$ and $>$ are converses, since for any x and y, $x < y$ and $y > x$ are equivalent statements. The concept of a converse relation has found its way into linguistics as a convenient means of describing a certain grammatical relation between expressions and between sentences in natural languages.[3] In this application of the terminology of logic, a relation is given by a verb or verbal construction, adjective, adverbial, etc., and the terms are given by the noun phrases that appear as subject, direct object, indirect object, etc. Consider, for example, (7.3)–(7.5):

(7.3) (a) John *saw* Bill
       (b) Bill *was seen by* John

(7.4) (a) John *is taller than* Bill
       (b) Bill *is shorter than* John

(7.5) (a) John *runs faster than* Bill
       (b) Bill *runs slower than* John

The italicized constituents of (7.3a,b), (7.4a,b), and (7.5a,b) are usually considered *converses*; the occurrences of the noun phrases "John" and "Bill" in each of these pairs are usually taken as the *terms* of these converse relations.

The fact to be explained here is that the members of such pairs and of pairs such as (7.1a,b) are synonymous. Their synonymy explains their necessary equivalence, that is, it explains why if one is true, so, necessarily, is the other, and if one is false, so, necessarily, is the other. But the synonymy itself is unexplained. The difference between pairs like (7.1a,b) and (7.2a,b) points up the need for such an explanation. And simply calling pairs of sentences "converses," though it suggests that the synonymy of these cases has something to do with a grammatically characterizable relation between the verbal constructions in them, does not explain what it is about such verbal constructions that makes the sentence pairs paraphrases. Reference to the definition of the converse relation in logic is only a way of saying that converses have the same truth conditions. It does *not* say which cases in language are equivalent because they are converses or why they are synonymous; it does not say why they have the same truth conditions but merely that they do.

There are two ways to approach a genuine explanation of such synonymy

---

[2] We will be concerned with the case where such statements are necessary by virtue of their grammatical structure alone, that is, by virtue, essentially, of the sense of the words expressing the relations H_1 and H_2.

[3] See Lyons (1963, p. 72).

relations. One is to follow the direct lead of logic. This approach assumes that sentences like (7.4a,b) and like (7.5a,b) are converses because, although they have different senses, these senses are relations that bear the converse relation to one another. The crux of the matter here is that the converse relation holds between distinct senses of linguistic constructions. The linguistic constructions are converses only by virtue of expressing senses of which the converse relation holds, so that our problem is to explicate this relation. In contrast, the other approach assumes, as we have implicitly assumed in taking the converse relation to be a special case of synonymy, that sentences like (7.4a,b) and like (7.5a,b) are converses because they are synonymous; and they are such by virtue of a certain way in which their senses are compositionally formed from the senses of their constituents, a way which distinguishes these sentence paraphrases from other types of synonymy. Thus, instead of trying to explain the mutual deducibility of converse sentences on the grounds that their distinct senses bear the converse relation to each other and that this relation supports deducibility both ways, we try to explain it on the grounds that their senses are identical and thus are each entailed by the other. Both approaches offer the prospect of an explanation—the former by an account of the hypothesized relation that explains how it supports mutual deducibility and the latter by an account of the compositional genesis of the particular class of paraphrases that are converses.

We shall adopt the latter approach, that is, we shall try to explain the special case of converse synonymy on the model of the general case of synonymy. The desirability of this form of explanation is suggested by (7.3) and other cases of active-passive pairs: in these cases the explanation of sameness of truth conditions is, quite plausibly, sameness of meaning rather than a special relation between distinct senses of the active and its corresponding passive.[4] The question, then, becomes one of whether cases like (7.4) and (7.5), as well as other converses, can be accommodated under this form of explanation, whether their account can somehow be modeled on the account of the paraphrase relation between actives and passives.

The difficulty that immediately arises is that active-passive cases can legitimately be regarded as different from other types of converse cases in an essential respect. In the active-passive cases the *same* verb or converse constituent occurs in both sentences, whereas in the other types a *different* verb or converse constituent occurs in each sentence as in (a) and (b) of (7.4) and (a) and (b) of (7.5). The explanation in the active-passive case is based on the principles that the underlying phrase marker(s) of a sentence contain all the semantically relevant syntactic information and grammatical markers such as 'Passive' have no semantic content.[5] From these principles, it follows that the semantic interpretation for

---

[4] See Katz and Postal (1964) and Katz and Martin (1967).

[5] That is, as described in the references cited in note 4, the semantic component operates exclusively on the underlying phrase marker(s) of a sentence, which are generated by the base of the syntactic component, and syntactic symbols like 'Passive' have no entry in the dictionary. Consequently, an active and its corresponding passive will be assigned the same set of readings because they have the same constituents, as far as those bearing lexical readings are concerned, and the constituents bear the same grammatical relations to one another in the two cases.

an active sentence and the semantic interpretation for its corresponding passive represent them as having the same sense(s). But this pattern of explanation cannot be carried over to other types of converse pairs since they simply do not exhibit the formal relation between the source underlying phrase markers that obtains in active-passive cases. Whereas active-passive pairs differ at the level of deep structure only by virtue of a semantically empty grammatical marker, the other cases differ by virtue of nongrammatical morphemes which characteristically contribute semantic content to the meaning of sentences, as, for example, "tall" and "short" in (7.4) and "fast" and "slow" in (7.5).

Therefore, to explain the synonymy of converse linguistic constructions that have different, nongrammatical morphemes in their deep structure, it will be necessary to examine such cases directly rather than to try to subsume them under the active-passive paradigm.

1. The general problem

The constituents with which we will be predominantly concerned are pairs of verbs such as "buy" and "sell," "give" and "receive," "borrow" and "lend." The reason for choosing these as the central cases here has to do not only with their inherent suitability but also with the place they have occupied in certain recent discussions of the nature of semantic theory.[6]

Consider the sentences (7.6) and (7.7):

(7.6)   John sold the book to Mary

(7.7)   Mary bought the book from John

These sentences are paraphrases: both assert the occurrence of the same event, namely, the sale of a certain book wherein John relinquishes possession of it and Mary gains possession in exchange for some definite but unspecified sum of money. Accordingly, the grammar of English has to mark (7.6) and (7.7) as having a sense in common. The semantically interpreted underlying phrase marker assigned

---

[6] See Lyons (1963). Also, Bar-Hillel (1967) and Staal (1967). There is no need to reply explicitly to the latter two papers since the discussion in this chapter does so quite effectively. However, one or two comments about these papers are in order here. Both claim that cases like the synonymy of (7.6) and (7.7) cannot be accounted for on my conception of semantic theory. Of course, if the present chapter does what it sets out to do, then so much for these claims. But it may be worthwhile to indicate where Staal and Bar-Hillel have gone wrong. Staal's mistake is to view the relation underlying the synonymy of cases like (7.6) and (7.7) as syntactic, on the model of passivization. He never considers the question of whether this can be so, nor does he explore the alternative of a purely semantic relation but simply rules it out a priori (see his p. 68). Bar-Hillel's mistakes are, first (p. 409), to accept Staal's mistake, second (p. 413), to add his own a priori claims about the limitations of dictionary entries in expressing semantic relations, and, third (the section titled *Postscriptum*), to fail to supply argument where argument is needed.

to (7.6) and the one assigned to (7.7) have to have the same reading in the set of readings assigned to their highest sentence nodes.

One way to try to obtain this result would be to attempt to structure the syntactic component so that it provides the same underlying phrase marker for (7.6) and (7.7). Another would be to try to formulate lexical readings for "sell" and "buy" that yield the same derived reading for (7.6) and (7.7) by the operation of the projection rule applied to different underlying phrase markers. In the former case we have a syntactic solution to the problem of converse relations, and in the latter case a semantic solution. In this section we shall try to rule out the possibility of a syntactic solution, and in the following sections we shall attempt to develop a semantic solution.

A syntactic solution could try to obtain a common reading for (7.6) and (7.7) in the same manner that stylistic variants like (a) and (b) of (7.8) receive the same reading:

(7.8)   (a) John looked up the address
         (b) John looked the address up

Both sentences would be assigned the same underlying phrase marker by the base of the syntactic component. The semantic component, therefore, would operate on the same syntactic object in each case, thereby assigning these sentences the same reading and thus representing them as paraphrases.

However, this treatment requires that one of the two sentences in question be taken as more basic than the other, that is, as closer in its surface form to the string of terminal symbols in their common underlying phrase marker. In this sense, (a) of (7.8) is more basic than (b). The rationale is that the surface structure of sentence (a) retains more of the constituent structure common to both cases than does the surface structure of sentence (b). In (a), as opposed to (b), the full verb constituent "look up" occurs as a continuous substring in its surface form, and the sentences are otherwise no different. Accordingly, since the underlying phrase marker for (a) and (b) must mark each of the constituents by a labeled bracketing of a continuous substring of its string of terminal elements, it follows, within present transformational theory, that the transformational development of sentence (b) begins like that of (a) but subsequently, unlike (a), includes a transformational permutation that positions the noun phrase object "the address" between the verb "look" and its particle "up." Therefore, if one tries to obtain a common reading for (7.6) and (7.7) in something like the way a common reading is assigned to (a) and (b) of (7.8), he will be required to justify taking one of the sentences as more basic. With such a justification, the solution to the problem of marking the paraphrase relation between (7.6) and (7.7) would be purely syntactic, taking the form of a set of base rules that gives both sentences an underlying phrase marker modeled on the more basic of the two and a set of transformational rules that derives the less basic one by a permutation akin to the exchange of subject and object in the derivation of passive sentences.

But a syntactic solution of this type assumes, falsely, that either (7.6) or (7.7) differs from the other in a manner similar to that in which (a) of (7.8) differs from (b). Such a solution must choose between the following alternatives: either (7.6) is more basic and (7.7) comes from a permutation of subject and indirect object with compensating switches of "sell" to "buy" and "to" to "from" or (7.7) is more basic and (7.6) comes from a permutation of subject and indirect object with compensating switches of "buy" to "sell" and "from" to "to." But there can be no rationale for choosing between these alternatives because they, and the sentences in question, are perfectly symmetrical. Any argument that might be proposed to establish that one of these alternatives is preferable would encounter another argument of equal cogency to establish that the other is preferable. Thus we can conclude that neither of the sentences in question can be justifiably taken as more basic than the other.

Another option exists for someone who seeks a purely syntactic solution since accepting the conclusion just reached does not preclude the possibility of deriving (7.6) and (7.7) from the same underlying phrase marker. Thus, one might propose to derive them, transformationally, from an underlying phrase marker representing a common abstract deep structure. That is, it might be argued that (7.6) and (7.7) have a common underlying phrase marker of an abstract sort such that the sentences are of a roughly equal degree of basicness at this level and both can be derived from this phrase marker by means of transformational derivations of roughly equal complexity. This underlying phrase marker would have to represent the verbs "buy" and "sell" in terms of some abstract morpheme neutral between them and belonging to the category 'Verb', and it would have to represent "to" and "from" in a similar way. Thus, one set of transformations would give the surface structure of (7.6) by realizing these abstract morphemes as "sell" and "to," and another set would give the surface structure of (7.7) by realizing these morphemes as "buy" and "from."

Besides its ad hoc character, there are a number of serious difficulties associated with this proposal, some of which are decisive against it. First, as Chomsky has pointed out,[7] the simplicity metric for selecting an optimal grammar must penalize the use of any abstract constituent that is language-specific. Thus, the use of an abstract verb spanning just "buy" and "sell" will lower the evaluation of the grammar. Second, although this solution can avoid the symmetry objection in connection with morphemic differences between (7.6) and (7.7), it fails to avoid this type of objection in connection with differences in grammatical relations. Let us assume the definitions (7.9a,b) of the relations 'subject of' and 'indirect object of':

(7.9)   (a) X is the subject of the sentence S just in case X is the substring of the terminal string in S's underlying phrase marker that satisfies the function [NP, S].

            (b) X is the indirect object of the sentence S just in case X is the substring

[7] In conversation.

of the terminal string in S's underlying phrase marker that satisfies the function [NP, Prep P, VP, PP, S].

With respect to (a) and (b) of (7.9), or indeed any other definitions of the same kind, it is clear that there can be no rationale for choosing between the alternative of an abstract underlying phrase marker in which "John" is the subject and "Mary" the indirect object of both (7.6) and (7.7) and the alternative of an abstract underlying phrase marker in which "Mary" is the subject and "John" is the indirect object of both sentences. Any argument for arranging the domination relations within the underlying phrase marker for these sentences so that "John" satisfies [NP, S] and "Mary" satisfies [NP, Prep P, VP, PP, S], because of the complete symmetry of (7.6) and (7.7), would be matched by an argument of exactly equal cogency for arranging them so that "Mary" satisfies [NP, S] and "John" satisfies [NP, Prep P, VP, PP, S].

In the case of verbs, prepositions, or other sentential constituents, it is possible to hypothesize abstract morphemes spanning some very small subset of morphemes in the category. But in the case of grammatical relations, no such hypothesis is possible. Such notions, being relational, cannot be given in the form of substantive elements introduced into the terminal or nonterminal part of the vocabulary of syntactic theory. Their characterization must be given by a formal relation among such substantive elements labeling nodes in underlying phrase markers and the domination relations specified by those nodes and their branches.

The arbitrariness of this choice is seen to reach absurd proportions when it is realized that whichever of the alternatives is adopted for (7.6) and (7.7), the other will have to be adopted for (7.10) and (7.11):

(7.10)   Mary sold the book to John

(7.11)   John bought the book from Mary

For one thing, (7.10) and (7.11) are synonymous, and, for another, they are exactly parallel to but *not* synonymous with (7.6) and (7.7), i.e., (7.6) is not synonymous with either (7.10) or (7.11), nor is (7.7) synonymous with either (7.10) or (7.11). The absurdly arbitrary choice is now that of which of the alternatives just presented is to be adopted for the pair (7.6) and (7.7) and which is to be adopted for the pair (7.10) and (7.11). Thus, again, we have a choice where any argument for one decision is faced with an equivalent argument for the opposite one. But if one alternative cannot be shown to be preferable, (7.6) and (7.7) cannot be assigned the same underlying phrase marker and, consequently, their synonymy cannot be explained on syntactic grounds.

Another point worth mentioning in this connection is that the proposal we have been considering conflicts with clear-cut linguistic intuitions that "John" is the subject of (7.6) and (7.11), that "Mary" is the subject of (7.7) and (7.10), that "John" is the indirect object of (7.7) and (7.10), and that "Mary" is the indirect object of (7.6) and (7.11). To put the matter another way, the simplest account of grammatical relations such as 'subject of' and 'indirect object of' would not distinguish (7.6) from (7.12a) or (7.7) from (7.12b).

(7.12)   (a) John sang a song to Mary
         (b) Mary stole the idea from John

Finally, there is one further argument. Sentences such as (7.6) and (7.7) express the occurrence of a transaction in which the possession of an object is transferred from seller to buyer in exchange for a certain sum of money which is transferred from buyer to seller. Since both these aspects of the meaning of such sentences will have to be accounted for syntactically on any syntactic solution for the synonymy of cases like (7.6) and (7.7), the putative common underlying phrase marker for these sentences will have to be considerably more complex than thus far supposed. It will have to take the form of a labeled bracketing of a compound string which is something like (7.13):

(7.13)   John sold the book to Mary *in exchange for Mary's paying a sum of money to John*

But such an underlying phrase marker for (7.6) and (7.7) is out of the question since it would be necessary to suppose that the italicized portion had been deleted in the derivation, and such a transformational operation would be a violation of the principle of recoverable deletion.

Let us consider this point further. It is clear that there must be a condition on deletion operations insuring the recoverability of what is prevented from appearing in surface phrase markers. If there were no such condition, transformations could remove any constituent whatever. Surface phrase markers could then receive any number of different underlying phrase markers, and the results would be, first, that any sentence could mean almost anything, and, second, that the grammar could give no explanation of ellipsis. Chomsky (1965) has proposed a condition to restrict the range of deletion operations to avoid these results:

> a deletion operation can eliminate only a dummy element, or a formative explicitly mentioned in the structure index (for example, *you* in imperatives), or the designated representative of a category (for example, the *wh*-question transformations that delete Noun Phrases are in fact limited to indefinite Pronouns . . .), or an element that is otherwise represented in the sentence in a fixed position (pp. 144–145).

In the case in question, the constituent that has to be deleted is not a dummy element. Nor can it be regarded as mentioned in the structure index of a transformation since there would then have to be a different transformation for every similar case, for example, one for " buy," another for " trade," still another for " bargain." Nor can it be taken as an indefinite pro-form or as an element that is otherwise represented, as is the case with the deleted deep structure verb phrase " plays one-minute chess " in the sentence (7.14):

(7.14)   John plays one-minute chess better than Sidney

Here the deleted phrase is otherwise represented by the verb phrase of the sentential structure in which "John" is the subject. But clearly the italicized constituent of (7.13) is not identical with any other part of the terminal string of the underlying phrase marker. Thus, by Chomsky's account, trying to handle the problem by a deletion operation involves a violation of recoverable deletion. Of course, one can propose some ad hoc solution, such as assigning a feature to the verbs "buy" and "sell" that encodes the information that the portion of the underlying phrase marker for (7.6) and (7.7) represented by the italicized part of (7.13) can be optionally deleted. But this is undesirable in a number of ways. First, it would be necessary to introduce a fairly large number of such features, since there are other verbs that are like "buy" and "sell" in the relevent respect, each with a different covert constituent requiring deletion. Second, it would rob linguistic theory of the principle that explains ellipsis, namely, the principle, embodied in Chomsky's conditions, that ellipsis coincides with an underlying constituent identity. Hence, the conditions on recoverable deletion also preclude a syntactic solution because they are violated by deletion of the constituent introduced to account for the information that the buyer pays a sum of money.

We thus conclude that the paraphrase relations we are considering cannot be explained on syntactic grounds but, rather, must be explained on semantic grounds. We shall try to supply such an explanation in the next sections. But first let us briefly consider the advantages for syntax of turning this problem over to semantics.

In the first place, cases like (7.6) and (7.7) can be given different underlying phrase markers by the rules of the base in the syntactic component, and these phrase markers can be intuitively quite plausible ones, as, for example, (7.15) for (7.6) and (7.16) for (7.7):

(7.15)

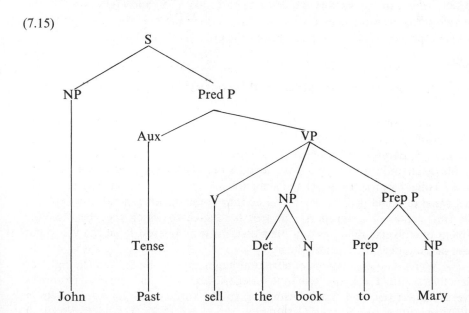

(7.16)

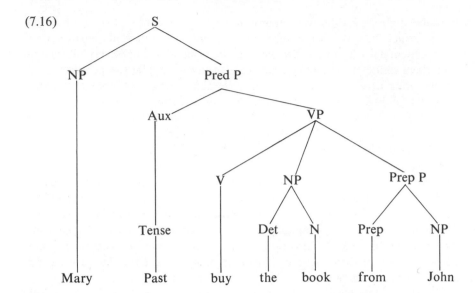

Moreover, assigning cases like (7.6) and (7.7)—and there will be a very great number of them—different underlying phrase markers means that language-specific abstract constituents are not required for them, which raises the value of the grammar in a simplicity evaluation. The syntactic component avoids arbitrary choices, and there will be no necessity to contradict clear-cut intuitions about subject and indirect object relations or, worse yet, give up simple generalizations about their nature that are obviously true of indefinitely many straightforward cases and that provide a uniform account of these relations by extending their characterization in straightforward cases to cases like (7.6) and (7.7). Finally, the principle of recoverable deletion is met, thus preserving the ability of grammars to explain phenomena like ellipsis without the addition of ad hoc apparatus.

2. The concepts 'state' and 'process'

In this section, we begin our attempt to formulate a semantic explanation of the paraphrase relation in cases like (7.6) and (7.7). Here we will set up the general conceptual apparatus. In subsequent sections, this apparatus will be developed in suitable detail and further apparatus added. Along the way toward a solution, very many auxiliary problems about the semantic structure of natural languages will arise, some of which will be dealt with as they come up. In general, the depth of their treatment will be proportionate to the degree to which they bear on the problem of converse relations and their own intrinsic interest from the viewpoint of the development of semantic theory.

Words and expressions of a natural language may be divided (though not exhaustively) into the major semantic categories of *state* and *process*. Examples of verbs, adjectives, and nouns belonging to the former category are given in (a), (b), and (c), respectively, of (7.17).

(7.17)   (a) sleep, live, suffer
         (b) sick, healthy, bankrupt
         (c) sickness, boredom, death

Examples of verbs, adjectives, and nouns belonging to the latter category are given in (a), (b), and (c), respectively, of (7.18):

(7.18)   (a) grow, dry, melt
         (b) dying, growing, drying
         (c) recovery, disappearance, birth

Sentences using words belonging to these categories bring out clearly the intuitive difference between the concept of a state and that of a process. For example, compare the meaning of (7.19) with that of (7.20):

(7.19)   John is asleep (sick, bankrupt)

(7.20)   John is growing (dying, melting)

We can express the nature of the difference by saying that a state is a condition of something (be it a person, place, thing, or whatever) at a given time or during a given time interval, while a process is a change or transition from one state to another over a given time interval. The explication of this difference is crucial to the development of the conceptual apparatus to be brought to bear on the problem of converse relations.

Such an explication must take the form of devising appropriate semantic markers. This treatment follows automatically from the manner in which other cases of the same sort are handled within semantic theory. To say that a word in a language falls into a category is to say that the complex of concepts that forms its sense includes that category as one of its component concepts. Therefore, the category of state, under which the examples in (7.17) are subsumed, must be one of the concepts in their sense; likewise, the category of process, under which the examples in (7.18) are subsumed, must be one of the concepts in their sense. Since each concept in a sense is represented by a semantic marker in the reading that represents that sense, it thereby follows that the category concepts of state and process must each be explicated by a semantic marker that will form part of the reading of some sense of every word that falls under the category.

In previous discussions of semantic theory,[8] the distinction between state and process words was marked by entering cases like those in (7.17) in the dictionary with a lexical reading containing the semantic marker '(State)' and entering cases like those in (7.18) with a lexical reading containing the semantic marker '(Process)'. No effort was made to characterize the nature of this distinction by suitably defining these semantic markers since we were concerned exclusively with questions which required reference only to the distinction between state and process words. For that purpose the use of the undefined semantic markers '(State)' and '(Process)' was sufficient. Now, however, we are concerned primarily not with

---

[8] For example, Katz and Fodor (1963, p. 501).

the existence of this distinction but with its nature. Hence, our problem is to explicate it, not simply to indicate it.

We may start, then, by regarding the semantic markers '(State)' and '(Process)' as, ultimately, defined terms of semantic theory. We seek now to eliminate them, through definition, in favor of some construction built out of other, more primitive semantic markers. They should be defined away on the basis of definitions whose formal structure represents the internal structure of the concepts of state and process, so that it is possible to capitalize on the features of such definitions to explain interrelations between the meanings of state and process words, as, for example, the relation between the state words in (a) of (7.21) to the process word in (b):

(7.21)   (a) liquid, solid
         (b) freeze

and the relation of words like (a) and (b) of (7.22) to state words like (c) and (d), respectively, which express components of the sense of the former:

(7.22)   (a) alcohol
         (b) dope
         (c) drunk
         (d) stoned

and the semantic relations of state and process words to other words in sentences. An example of the last case is the relation of the temporal adverbial and tense constituents to the process words in a sentence like (7.23), were the former determine the period in which the process occurs:

(7.23)   The ice froze yesterday during the cold spell

Our aim, therefore, is to define 'state' and 'process' in such a manner that interrelations and relations that depend on aspects of the internal structure of these concepts, and which thus cannot be accounted for by the undefined semantic markers '(State)' and '(Process)', can be captured in terms of the formal representation of the structure of the concepts as provided in their definitions.

Given that the concept of a state is that of the condition of something at a given time or during a given time interval, we define the semantic marker '(State)' as in (7.24):

$$(7.24) \quad ((\text{Condition}), (\,), \ldots, (\,) \text{ of } \overset{[\,]}{\underset{\langle\,\rangle}{X}} \text{ at } \overset{[\,]}{\underset{\langle\,\rangle}{X}})$$

'(Condition), ( ), ..., ( )' indicates a set of semantic markers representing a condition of some sort. In any instance of (7.24), that is, in any particular state semantic marker occurring in the lexical reading of a specific morpheme, the part '( ), ..., ( )' represents the unique condition contained by the state concept expressed by that morpheme. Thus, for the adjective "drunk," for example, this part of the state semantic marker in its lexical reading would represent the condition of being intoxicated with liquor or other strong drink. This part of the lexical reading of "drunk" would, accordingly, be different from the comparable parts of "sick," "asleep," "dead," etc. Hence, in '( ), ..., ( )' we find represented what it is about the particular state that differentiates it from other states.

In terms of the discussion of categorized variables in Chapter 3, the first variable in (7.24) will be one whose values are readings that refer to the person, place, or thing whose condition is specified by '( ), ..., ( )'.[9] The second variable in (7.24) will be one whose values are readings of the tense constituent in the auxiliary, together with, when applicable, readings of temporal adverbials. This will be explained in detail in Sections 3 and 4 of this chapter.

The concept of a process is, as previously indicated, that of a transition from one state to another through time, as, for example, the process of recovery is a transition from the state of sickness to that of health. Thus, we can define the semantic marker '(Process)' in terms of the definition given in (7.24) for the semantic marker '(State)', as in (7.25) and (7.26):

(7.25)   A singulary process semantic marker has the form:

$$\left(\left(\left(\text{(Condition)}, (\,), \ldots, (\,) \text{ of } X_{\langle\,\rangle}^{[\,]} \text{ at } X_{\langle\,\rangle}^{[\,]}\right)\right), \ldots,\right.$$

$$\left.\left(\text{(Condition)}, (\,), \ldots, (\,) \text{ of } X_{\langle\,\rangle}^{[\,]} \text{ at } X_{\langle\,\rangle}^{[\,]}\right)\right)$$

(7.26)   An *n*-ary process semantic marker has the form:

$$\left(\left(\begin{bmatrix}\text{(Condition)}, (\,), \ldots, (\,) \text{ of } X_{\langle\,\rangle}^{[\,]} \\ \text{(Condition)}, (\,), \ldots, (\,) \text{ of } X_{\langle\,\rangle}^{[\,]} \\ \vdots \\ \text{(Condition)}, (\,), \ldots, (\,) \text{ of } X_{\langle\,\rangle}^{[\,]}\end{bmatrix} \text{ at } X_{\langle\,\rangle}^{[\,]}\right), \ldots,\right.$$

$$\left.\left(\begin{bmatrix}\text{(Condition)}, (\,), \ldots, (\,) \text{ of } X_{\langle\,\rangle}^{[\,]} \\ \text{(Condition)}, (\,), \ldots, (\,) \text{ of } X_{\langle\,\rangle}^{[\,]} \\ \vdots \\ \text{(Condition)}, (\,), \ldots, (\,) \text{ of } X_{\langle\,\rangle}^{[\,]}\end{bmatrix} \text{ at } X_{\langle\,\rangle}^{[\,]}\right)\right)$$

which, for certain purposes, we may abbreviate as ((Process)$_1$ & (Process)$_2$ & ... & (Process)$_n$)

[9] For ease in reading, "of" is used instead of bracketing in (7.24) and elsewhere as a way of indicating the application of the concepts represented by the semantic markers '( ), ..., ( )' to the referent of the value of $X_{\langle\,\rangle}^{[\,]}$ at $X_{\langle\,\rangle}^{[\,]}$. See also note 21.

In (7.25) a process is represented as a transition of states by the representation of a process semantic marker as a sequence of state semantic markers. In (7.26) we allow that a process may be a single process, a double process, a triple process, etc. This will permit us to distinguish between a single process like that expressed by "give" or "receive" and a double process like that expressed by "sell" or "buy." Since the second categorized variable in each state semantic marker of a process semantic marker will have a reading that expresses a time designation as its value, we can specify the *initial state* of a process as the one represented by the state semantic marker with the lowest time designation of any state semantic marker in the process semantic marker and the *terminal state* of a process as the one represented by the state semantic marker with the highest time designation of any state semantic marker in the process semantic marker. The dots between the state semantic markers that represent the initial and terminal states indicate the possibility of intermediate states in the process. Any semantic marker whose time designation is greater than that appearing in the semantic marker that represents the initial state but is less than that appearing in the semantic marker that represents the terminal state will be a semantic marker that represents an *intermediate state*. If the possibility of intermediate states is precluded by the meaning of the process word, we write the process semantic marker for that word in the form shown in (7.27):

(7.27) $((\text{State})_1, (\text{State})_2)$

If the meaning of a process word inherently involves a particular intermediate state, for example, "relapse" in the sense of slipping back into a former state after a change from it to another, as in becoming ill again or reverting to evil ways, we write the connection between the initial and terminal states in the form shown in (7.28), where the time designation in '$(\text{State})_i$' is greater than that in '$(\text{State})_1$' and less than that in '$(\text{State})_n$':

(7.28) $((\text{State})_1, \ldots, (\text{State})_i, \ldots, (\text{State})_n)$

3.   Linguistically expressed time relations

This section develops some theoretical apparatus for expressing time designations which is necessary to complete the definition of state semantic markers and process semantic markers. The section also deals with certain semantic problems arising in connection with the way that time relations are expressed in sentences of a natural language and with the determination of semantic properties and relations of sentences where they turn on aspects of how the time relations are expressed in sentences. We do not hope to provide a comprehensive theory of the semantic representation of temporal relations in sentences, but we do hope to make a start, that is, to offer enough of this theory, first, to show how one can be constructed, second, to illustrate the application of the apparatus introduced, and, third, to provide independent motivation for the employment of this apparatus in the discussion of converses in Section 4.

The fundamental way in which a sentence relates the things about which it speaks—the states, processes, occurrences, actions, activities, achievements, etc.—is in terms of their relation to one another in time. Not all sentences express time relations, however, as illustrated by sentences (7.29)–(7.32):

(7.29) The number two is the only even prime

(7.30) Implication is a transitive relation

(7.31) Idealism is a philosophical theory of reality

(7.32) The owl is a nocturnal bird

But, except for sentences about abstract objects and generic sentences, the expression of temporal relations is a ubiquitous semantic feature of the grammar of sentences.[10]

A sentence does not temporally relate the things it is about to one another directly. Rather, it first relates them each to a fixed reference point and then relates them to one another indirectly by virtue of their relations to the reference point. This reference point is the origin of a time dimension, which extends infinitely in both directions. Each event or thing that a sentence is about is related to the reference point, the origin of the time dimension, by being accorded a position on this dimension, i.e., by being assigned to a point on it. Thus, each event or thing is automatically related to others by their respective relations to the reference point, such relations being specified by the distance between points and their direction with respect to the origin. Accordingly, the time relation holding between two things is given by a sentence in terms of the distance between their positions on the time dimension and the direction of each from its origin.

In order to establish an origin for the time dimension, we think of the sense of the tense constituent as indexical in the way that ordinary pronouns are. Take, for example, the sentence (7.33):

(7.33) I am in John J. Smith's house

The occurrence of the first person pronoun "I" here refers to different persons when (7.33) is uttered by different speakers. The tense constituent is also indexical since the present tense constituent in (7.33) refers to different times when the sentence is uttered on different occasions. But this variation in reference of the present tense constituent in utterances of (7.33) is restricted within limits set by the meaning of the constituent in the sentence type. Such a restriction on tokens is parallel to the restriction of ordinary first, second, and third person pronouns to referents belonging to a class fixed in advance by their meaning. Thus, just as "I" can refer only to the speaker, "you" to the person(s) addressed, and so on, so the

[10] This is what was meant when we said earlier that time relations are the fundamental way in which sentences relate the events that they are about. It is not necessary that the events spoken of in a sentence be related spatially, causally, etc. Whether they are related in one of these ways or not is a matter of what the speaker wants to say. But if he is going to talk about something other than abstract objects, he has no choice but to relate his topics temporally.

present tense constituent can refer only to the time at which the utterance of the sentence occurs, the past tense constituent to some time earlier than the utterance point, and the future tense constituent to some time later than the utterance point. Accordingly, the sentence (7.34) is about the single event of the man's entering the house, and this event is located at the utterance point itself:

(7.34)   The man is entering the house

Sentence (7.35) locates the man's entering the house at some unspecified time in the past relative to the utterance point, and sentence (7.36) locates this event somewhere in the future relative to the utterance point:

(7.35)   The man entered the house
(7.36)   The man will enter the house

Natural languages thus divide time, basically, into two parts, past and future, the point of division being the moment at which the speaker utters the sentence.

This leads naturally to our taking the origin of the time dimension to be the utterance point, the points to the left of the origin to be past times, and those to the right to be future times. More complex tense constituents will pick out points and intervals on this dimension in terms of the interpretation of its origin as the utterance point and of past and future as its left and right segments, respectively. The readings of tense constituents will take the form of designations of positions on this dimension.

When two or more events are spoken of in a sentence, their temporal relation is expressed by means of some time adverbial, such as " before," " after," "simultaneous with," which introduces a clause containing the description of one or more of the events. Often, then, events are temporally interrelated as illustrated in (7.37) and (7.38):

(7.37)   I entered the room before John arrived
(7.38)   I will enter the room before John arrives

In (7.37) my entering the room and John's arrival are related to the utterance point by their both being located in the past relative to it, but they are related to each other by virtue of the former event's being located at a point some distance further from the utterance point than that at which the latter is located. In (7.38) my entering the room is still specified as occurring earlier than John's arrival but both events are now specified as future relative to the utterance point.

Facts such as these constitute the basic semantic features of sentences that the theoretical apparatus to be developed here must represent. But it is equally important that the readings of sentences that represent these features enable us to mark the semantic properties and relations of sentences that depend on the time relations expressed in them. Examples of some of the semantic properties and relations that must be dealt with are illustrated by the sentences (7.39)–(7.48).

(7.39)   The truth of the statement lasted only three days

(7.40)   Implication is a transitive relation every three minutes

(7.41)   An hour is a longer period of time than a minute

(7.42)   He worked for an hour during the last minute

(7.43)   (a) John slept for an hour
         (b) John slept longer than a minute

(7.44)   (a) John arrived before Bill
         (b) John arrived at the same time as Bill

(7.45)   He rested for a minute

(7.46)   He rested for sixty seconds

(7.47)   He rested a longer time than she

(7.48)   She rested a shorter time than he

Sentences (7.39) and (7.40) are both semantically anomalous. Sentence (7.41) is analytic, and (7.42) is a contradiction. Sentence (7.43a) entails (7.43b). Sentences (7.44a) and (7.44b) are inconsistent. And (7.45) is a paraphrase of (7.46), as is (7.47) of (7.48).

It is a constraint on semantic theory, as we have framed it, that definitions of semantic properties and relations already set up in semantic theory to predict semantic anomalies, analyticities, contradictions, etc., arising from semantic structures having nothing to do with the expression of temporal relations be sufficiently general to enable us to predict semantic properties and relations arising from semantic structures that do express temporal relations.[11] It therefore follows that the representational apparatus that we introduce to describe temporal relations in sentences must also provide the proper domain for the application of such definitions. Hence, the aspects of the readings of sentences like (7.39)–(7.48) that reflect their temporal designations must also mark the semantic anomaly of (7.39) and (7.40) on the basis of an assignment of a null set of readings to them, the synonymy of (7.45) and (7.46) on the basis of an assignment of the same reading to them, and so on. This, then, places a strong constraint on the apparatus one may introduce to present linguistically expressed time relations.

Since the semantic component of a grammar requires a specification of constituents and their grammatical relations in order to provide semantic interpretations, the first step in developing a scheme for representing time relations is to determine what types of constituents in an underlying phrase marker have to do with time relations and what grammatical relations obtain between them. We can use the following rough test. We ask whether the replacement of a constituent by a nonsynonymous constituent of the same type changes the time relations expressed in a sentence. If such a replacement, by itself, does change time relations, then

---

[11] That is, the same definitions used to mark semantic anomaly, analyticity, contradiction, entailment, synonymy, etc., in cases where time relations do *not* underlie a sentence's having one or another of these semantic properties or relations must also suffice to mark them in cases where time relations are involved.

that type of constituent is involved in the expression of time relations. If there is no change, then that type of constituent does not contribute to the expression of time relations. Compare, for example, sentences (7.49) and (7.50):

(7.49) The man will arrive after the girl sees the foolish boy

(7.50) A woman will arrive after the children see the lazy dog

The change from (7.49) to (7.50) preserves the time relations: both sentences say someone's arrival follows upon the seeing of something by some one or more persons. If we were to apply this test to each type of constituent, it would turn out, generally speaking, that nouns in simple noun phrases (within subjects, objects, indirect objects, etc.), articles or other components of the determiner system, descriptive adjectives, adverbials of manner, locatives, and so on may be replaced by others without altering time relations. The sentence that results from such replacements will express the same time relations but for a new n-tuple of events and/or objects and/or states of affairs, etc. Thus, not unexpectedly, the constituents that turn out to be relevant to the expression of time relations are the verbs in a sentence, the tense of the auxiliary, and the temporal adverbials, including phrase and clause types. Replacement of any of these characteristically does alter time relations, as is shown by a comparison of (7.49) and (7.51):

(7.51) The man arrived when the girl saw the foolish boy

Thus, the syntactic structure underlying the expression of time relations forms a fairly tightly knit, self-contained system. This being so, it should be possible, without considering any aspects of syntax other than verbs, tenses, and temporal adverbials, to specify the grammatical relations required. To illustrate how they can be specified, we may suppose that the base of the syntactic component contains phrase structure rules of the kind illustrated in (3.79). These rules offer the following analysis of the verbal auxiliary of English: it has a tense constituent, then, option-ally, a modal constituent, and, finally, an aspect constituent, again optionally. If we continue to follow Chomsky's analysis, the first of these constituents is either past or present, the second is one of the elements "can," "will," "may," "shall," "must," etc., and the third is either perfect or progressive.[12] These base rules also characterize temporal adverbials as constituents of the constituent predicate phrase. Thus, such rules suggest that we require one grammatical relation for the auxiliary and the verb or adjective in the same predicate phrase and another for the predicate and its temporal adverbials.

---

[12] See Chomsky (1965, pp. 42–43). Although we are making use of Chomsky's analysis of the English verbal auxiliary system, this should not be construed as a commitment of semantic theory to Chomsky's way of handling the syntactic facts. Should it turn out that another analysis presents a somewhat different constituent analysis of, say, the auxiliary, so long as it still makes it possible to characterize the appropriate grammatical relations, semantic theory will be neutral between them. All that is necessary for this treatment is some set of syntactic distinctions cor-responding to the ordinary distinctions made between tenses, together with an appropriate set of grammatical relations within the tense system, between this system and the verb, and between both and the temporal adverbials.

To begin with, we might have grammatical functions like (a) and (b) of (7.52), which would be used to further specify state and process semantic markers:

(7.52)   (a) [Aux, PP, S]
         (b) [Time Adv, PP, S]

Thus (7.24), the definition of the semantic marker '(State)', might be stated more fully as (7.53):

$$(7.53) \quad ((\text{Condition}), (\,), \ldots, (\,) \text{ of } X \text{ at } \begin{smallmatrix} [\,] \\ \langle\,\rangle \end{smallmatrix} \quad \begin{smallmatrix} [\text{Aux, PP, S}] \vee [\text{Time Adv, PP, S}] \\ X \\ \langle\,\rangle \end{smallmatrix})$$

The disjunction in (7.53) allows either the reading of the auxiliary or the reading of a temporal adverbial or both as values of the second variable.

Clearly, (7.53), as it now stands, is not sufficient, but we may assume that it can be modified so that elements of the auxiliary not relating semantically to temporal relations are eliminated as possible values of the categorized variable by some appropriate further specification of a syntactic category or feature(s) in the analysis of the auxiliary constituent.

Now, given that a semantic marker of the form (7.53) appears in a reading of a constituent C and that the grammatical function of C in its sentence is F, we have the pairs of grammatical functions [[Aux, PP, S], [F]] and [[Time Adv, PP, S], [F]], which define grammatical relations that, respectively, may be called the *inflexional relation* and the *temporalization relation*. These relations supply the necessary information for the projection rule to provide derived readings for constituents on the basis of the readings for verbs, adjectives, and so on whose meaning involves the concepts of state or process and of the readings for the appropriate auxiliary constituent and for time adverbials.

However, the auxiliary contains, besides components that are irrelevant to the expression of temporal relations and are to be eliminated as possible values of the second categorized variable in instances of (7.53), a number of different constituents whose readings have to be combined to form the reading that will serve as the values of the variable for the inflexional and temporalization relations. There is, on the one hand, the basic tenses past, present, and future, where, on Chomsky's analysis of the English auxiliary, the first and second are elements of the tense constituent and the third is an element of the modal, and, on the other, the tense forms perfect and progressive, which, on Chomsky's analysis, are elements of the aspect constituent. Therefore, the aforementioned operation of the projection rule which provides derived readings for the auxiliary constituent presupposes prior operations which combine the readings of these lexical elements that make up the auxiliary constituent.

Our first step must be to construct a notational system for time designations in the form of a suitable set of semantic markers. These will be used as the components of lexical readings for the various components of the auxiliary system that have to do with temporal specification.

We use the symbol 't' to stand for some unspecified position on the time dimension and superscripts on occurrences of 't' to indicate specific positions on this dimension. These superscripts can be either variables or constants. Thus 't' with the superscript constant '0', i.e., '$t^{(0)}$', represents the origin of a time dimension. We interpret the origin of such a dimension as an utterance point, that is, a span of time from the onset to the termination of an utterance of a sentence. Therefore, the occurrence of '$t^{(0)}$' in the reading of a sentence functions as an indexical element referring to the utterance point of tokens of the sentence and thus orienting the time dimension in uses of the sentence. The superscript variables occur with a plus or minus sign prefixed to them and indicate positions on the time dimension. We can take the superscript variables 'n', 'm', 'u', etc., to stand for some unspecified, arbitrary number of units of distance from the origin, with prefixed signs ' + ' and ' − ' indicating the direction from the origin. Given that we let ' + ' stand for "to the right of the origin" and ' − ' for "to the left of the origin," a symbol like '$t^{(+n)}$' determines a point n units to the right of the origin, and a symbol like '$t^{(-n)}$' determines a point n units to the left of the origin. Under our interpretation of the origin as the utterance point, an occurrence of 't' with a variable with a plus sign in its superscript indicates a point somewhere in the future with respect to the time specified by the origin, while an occurrence of 't' with a variable with a minus sign in its superscript indicates a point somewhere in the past with respect to the time specified by the origin.

These symbols are written as superscripts because, in the notation we have set up for semantic representation, superscripts on semantic markers represent their antonymy relations. Given that temporal designations for past, present, and future time are to be represented in the manner just described, and given that we want to mark conceptual incompatibilities found in the temporal relations of sentences like (7.42) or (7.54), considerations of consistency of notation determine that we handle such incompatibilities in the way that other conceptual incompatibilities are handled.

(7.54)   John will arrive a few days ago

The only difference between the representation of conceptual incompatibilities within the system of temporal relations and the representation of conceptual incompatibilities within the other systems we have discussed up to now is that in this new case of antonymy we must recognize the antonymy relation to hold for infinite as well as finite collections of symbols. We cannot get along anymore with antonymous n-tuples but must now introduce *antonymy sets*. However, the condition for a collection of semantic markers being members of the same antonymy set, and so jointly representing a range of incompatible concepts, need not be different from the condition that determined membership in the same antonymous n-tuple, namely, two semantic markers belong to the same antonymy set in case they have the same base symbol and different semantic markers as superscripts.

This notation immediately provides lexical readings for the syntactic symbols 'Past', 'Present', and 'Future'. The lexical readings for these symbols would be simply '$(t^{(-n)})$', '$(t^{(0)})$', and '$(t^{(+n)})$', respectively.

Suppose now (but only for the purpose of convenience) that some rule like (7.55) introduces the syntactic symbols that represent these basic tenses:

(7.55)   Tense → $\begin{Bmatrix} \text{Past} \\ \text{Present} \\ \text{Future} \end{Bmatrix}$

Derived readings for constituents dominating inflexionally related constituents, for example, a tense constituent and a verb or adjective, would be formed by the projection rule substituting the reading of the tense constituent for the occurrence of the variable in the reading of the verb or adjective that is categorized by the function '[Tense, Aux, PP, S]'. Consider, in this regard, an underlying phrase marker like (7.56):

(7.56)

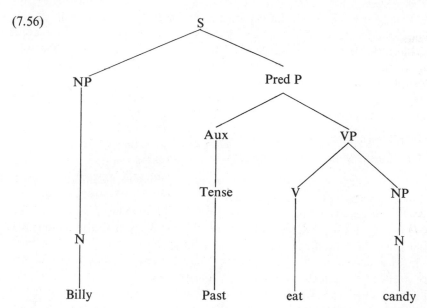

Note that the substitution of the reading of the tense constituent in such an underlying phrase marker does not occur until the compositional process of forming derived readings reaches the level of the predicate phrase. On the basis of the constituent structure in such a case, the order in which the categorized variables in the lexical reading for "eat" are replaced by their values is that shown in (7.57):

(7.57)   (a) [NP, VP, PP, S]
                 X
                 $\langle \rangle$

      (b) [Tense, Aux, PP, S]
                 X
                 $\langle \rangle$

      (c) [NP, S]
                 X
                 $\langle \rangle$

Thus, the categorized variables (b) and (c) appear in the derived reading for the verb phrase of (7.56) and the categorized variable (c) appears in the derived reading for the predicate phrase of (7.56).

Let us examine, in these terms, the time relations represented in the readings of simple, one-event sentences like (a), (b), and (c) of (7.58):

(7.58) (a) John is hungry
        (b) John was hungry
        (c) John will be hungry

Sentence (7.58a) specifies that, for any statement made by the utterance of (7.58a) at a time T, it is asserted that John experiences hunger at T, that is, contemporaneous with the utterance of (7.58a) that makes this statement; the reading of (7.58b) specifies that, for any statement made by the utterance of (7.58b) at a time T, it is asserted that John experiences hunger at a time prior to T, that is, antedating the utterance of (7.58b) that makes this statement; and the reading of (7.58c) specifies that, for any statement made by the utterance of (7.58c) at a time T, it is asserted that John experiences hunger at a time after T, that is, postdating the utterance of (7.58c) that makes this statement.

We now consider cases of sentences that express temporal relations between two or more events. The sentences (7.59) and (7.60) are examples:

(7.59) John kissed Mary before Bill arrived

(7.60) John kissed Mary after Bill arrived

Both the events described in (7.59) are past relative to the utterance point, but John's kissing Mary antedates Bill's arrival. In (7.60), the events are again past relative to the utterance point, but now Bill's arrival antedates John's kissing Mary. Clearly, since the tense constituent of the auxiliary in both sentences is 'Past' and since the only difference between them is the switch of "before" and "after," it must be the meaning of "before" and "after" that accounts for the difference between the temporal ordering of the two events with respect to each other in (7.59) and (7.60). We explain this introduction of temporal ordering by supposing that (a) and (b) of (7.61) are the lexical readings for "before" and "after," respectively:[13]

(7.61) (a) $v[T^s] \rightarrow (v[T^m] + (+r)), \langle\ \rangle$
        (b) $v[T^s] \rightarrow (v[T^m] + (-r)), \langle\ \rangle$

The symbol '$v[\ldots]$' is to be understood as the value of a variable '$\overset{[\ ]}{\underset{\langle\ \rangle}{X}}$' in a sentence. The symbols 'T^s' and 'T^m' are to be understood as abbreviations, respectively, for the variable categorized for the inflexional relation in the sub-

---

[13] We note that this is an example of rules appearing as lexical readings. Other examples include the antonymy rules that comprise the lexical reading for "not" and other negative constituents, and the lexical reading (7.189). Gross misinterpretations of semantic theory, such as that of Bar-Hillel's referred to at the end of note 6 of this chapter, derive, I think, from a failure to see that a syncategorematic sense of a lexical item is still a sense of a lexical item and as such is to be represented in a lexical reading.

ordinate (or dependent) clause and the variable categorized for the inflexional relation in the main clause. Thus, '$v[T^s]$' stands for the reading of the tense constituent in the predicate phrase of the subordinate clause of a complex sentence, while '$v[T^m]$' stands for the reading of the tense constituent in the verb phrase of its main clause. The symbol 'r' stands for some definite but arbitrary number of units on the time dimension less than the absolute value of the superscript on '$v[T^m]$'. We shall see how the rules (7.61a,b) work after we consider their selection restrictions.

The selection restriction in both (a) and (b) of (7.61) is that the readings of the main and subordinate clauses contain, respectively, the semantic markers $v[T^m]$ and $v[T^s]$, that neither of them is $(t^{(0)})$, and that they are identical. The first of these requirements says, in effect, that neither clause can be generic or express a timeless sense. It serves to mark the semantic anomaly of sentences such as those in (7.62) and (7.63):

(7.62)　(a) John kissed Mary before (after) the owl is nocturnal
　　　　(b) The owl is nocturnal before (after) John kissed Mary

(7.63)　(a) John kissed Mary before (after) two plus two is four
　　　　(b) Two plus two is four before (after) John kissed Mary

The second of the requirements serves to mark the semantic anomaly of sentences such as those in (7.64):

(7.64)　(a) John is sick before (after) Bill is well
　　　　(b) John kisses Mary before (after) Bill kisses Jean

The sentences that form the clauses in (7.64b) do not have the ordinary sense of a present tense sentence such as (7.56). Instead, such sentences can have one or another of a rather special set of senses, including what is called the *habitual present* (e.g., "John smokes cigars"), the *dramatic present* (e.g., cases where a speaker uses the present tense in the context of a narrative recalling some past event so as to make the event seem more vivid, as if it were happening now, right before his eyes), and what is called the *future present* (e.g., "I dine with the Smiths tomorrow"). I shall have nothing to say about these interesting cases here, except to point out that, at least in the first case, it will be necessary to have a special lexical reading.

The third of the requirements in the selection restriction of (7.61) serves to mark the semantic anomaly in sentences like those in (7.65):

(7.65)　(a) John will kiss Mary before (after) Bill arrived
　　　　(b) John kissed Mary before (after) Bill will arrive

As suggested by the lexical readings for "before" and "after" in (7.61), the reading for expressions such as "contemporaneous with," "simultaneous with," "at the same instant as" may be given as the rule (7.66), where the selection restriction is the same as that in (7.61a,b):

(7.66)　$v[T^s] \rightarrow (v[T^m]), \langle \rangle$

Let us now explain the operation of the rules (7.61a,b) and (7.66). Consider the sentences (7.67) and (7.68):

(7.67)   John will kiss Mary before Bill (will) arrives

(7.68)   John will kiss Mary after Bill (will) arrives

The basic idea behind rules (7.61a,b) and (7.66) is that the pastness or futureness of the propositions expressed by the clauses of complex sentences like (7.67) and (7.68), as well as (7.59) and (7.60), is fixed by their tense, but that the event referred to in the main clause and the event referred to in the subordinate clause are ordered temporally with respect to each other by the time adverbial. These rules express such an ordering by replacing the reading of the time designation found in the reading of the subordinate clause with a reading that is a function of the reading of the time designation found in the reading of the main clause. In the case of "before," the function is the addition of some fixed number of units on the time dimension to the value of the variable categorized for the inflexional relation in the main clause. The rule (7.61a) says that the result of this operation replaces the value of the variable categorized for the inflexional relation in the subordinate clause. In the case of "after," the function is the addition of some negative quantity to the value of the variable categorized for the inflexional relation in the main clause. The rule (7.61b) says that the result of this operation replaces the value of the variable categorized for the inflexional relation in the subordinate clause. In the case of adverbials like "contemporaneous with," "simultaneous with," and "at the same instant as," the function is identity. The rule (7.66) thus simply replaces the value of the variable categorized for the inflexional relation in the subordinate clause with that of the variable categorized for the inflexional relation in the main clause.

We may illustrate the application of these rules in connection with the temporal relations in the sentences (7.59), (7.60), (7.67), and (7.68), and similar cases. In (7.59) and (7.60), $v[T^m] = (t^{(-n)})$; in (7.67) and (7.68), $v[T^m] = (t^{(+n)})$; in (7.59) and (7.60), $v[T^s] = (t^{(-m)})$; in (7.67) and (7.68), $v[T^s] = (t^{(+m)})$. Let us introduce the symbol '§' as a variable over the signs '+' and '−' prefixed to superscripts. Then, the reading (7.61a) says that $(t^{(§m)})$ is rewritten as $(t^{(§n+(+r))})$ and (7.61b) says that $(t^{(§m)})$ is rewritten as $(t^{(§n+(-r))})$. Since the addition of signed elements proceeds in accord with the conventions for adding (and subtracting) signed numbers in algebra,[14] the temporal relations between the events in the sentences (7.59) and (7.67), i.e., the sentences with "before," are represented as in (7.69):

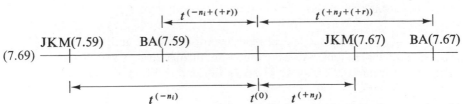

[14] These conventions can be regarded as having the same status as the general mathematical apparatus available to linguistics for the definition of syntactic constructs such as 'string.'

The temporal relations between the events in the sentences (7.60) and (7.68), i.e., the sentences with "after," are represented as in (7.70):

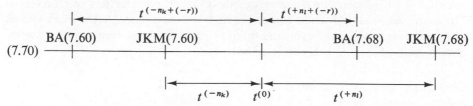

Now, comparing (7.59), (7.60), (7.67), and (7.68) with (7.71), (7.72), (7.73), and (7.74), respectively, we see that they are pairwise paraphrases, i.e., (7.59) is synonymous with (7.71), and so on:

(7.71)   Bill arrived after John kissed Mary

(7.72)   Bill arrived before John kissed Mary

(7.73)   Bill will arrive after John kisses Mary

(7.74)   Bill will arrive before John kisses Mary

Applying the lexical readings (7.61) in the semantic interpretation of (7.71)–(7.74) as was done in connection with (7.59), (7.60), (7.67), and (7.68) results in the assignment of the events in (7.71) to the same positions as those to which the events in (7.59) are assigned in the diagram (7.69), the assignment of the events in (7.72) to the same positions as those to which the events in (7.60) are assigned in the diagram (7.70), and so on for sentences (7.73) and (7.67) and sentences (7.74) and (7.68) with regard to the diagrams (7.69) and (7.70). Hence, each of these four pairs will be marked as paraphrases.[15]

---

[15] It is sometimes claimed that certain occurrences of "and" have a temporal sense, expressing a temporal ordering of the events referred to in the conjoined sentences. (See Strawson (1952, pp. 79–82).) There is certainly much room for doubt about this claim, but if it is right, the apparatus set forth here provides a natural way to handle the phenomenon. Consider the following sentences:

(a) Mary became pregnant and got married
(b) Mary got married and became pregnant

Suppose that these are not interpreted as asserting simply the occurrence of the two events, as if either one of them was an equally good, equivalent response to "Name two things that happened last year." Suppose that they are not synonymous, since the temporal order of the events is opposite: (a) is synonymous with (c) while (b) is synonymous with (d):

(c) Mary became pregnant before she got married
(d) Mary got married before she became pregnant

A very natural way to mark this temporal sense of "and" is to include the lexical reading in (7.61a) for "before" as one lexical reading for "and." This will have the effect of predicting that any sentence in which a pair of constituents are conjoined by "and" has a sense expressing temporal order just in case those constituents have readings that satisfy the selection restriction in (7.61a). Consider, for instance, sentence (e):

(e) Drinking and driving don't mix

It will be predicted that (e) has a sense in which drinking before driving is proscribed, since "drinking" and "driving" are nominalizations of verbs and so contain the categorized variable for the inflexional relation in their readings. But now consider sentence (f):

(f) Oil and water don't mix

The apparatus developed here will also predict that (f) does not have a sense involving temporal order since "oil" and "water" do not come from verbs and hence lack the requisite semantic markers.

In the case of sentences like (7.59) and (7.60), each of the events that are temporally ordered with respect to one another is picked out on the basis of a constituent whose meaning characterizes the event in more or less specific terms. The event temporally ordered earlier in (7.59) and later in (7.60) is described as John's kissing Mary. In (a), (b), and (c) of (7.75), one of the events that are temporally ordered is completely undescribed:

(7.75)   (a) John has won the game
         (b) John had won the game
         (c) John will have won the game

In the sentence (7.75c), for example, there are two events that are temporally related: John's winning the game (at some future time) and another event that is left uncharacterized by the speaker (or in the sentence). This event serves as an additional point of orientation for the described event beyond the speech point (although it might be the event of the utterance of the sentence in some instances of the use of the present perfect). We will take the perfect aspect of the auxiliary to indicate the bare fact of such an event having taken place and the position of the event in time relative to the other event(s) described in the sentence.

Let us refer to this "undescribed event" as 'P' and to the event or events that are described and positioned in time relative to it as 'E'. Using these letter designations, we may schematize the temporal relations in sentences like (a), (b), and (c) of (7.75) as in (7.76):

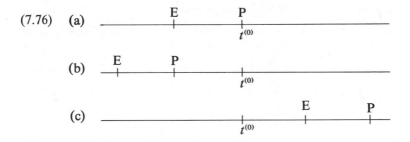

(7.76)   (a)

         (b)

         (c)

The sense of the sentences (a), (b), and (c) of (7.75) are represented by (a), (b), and (c) of (7.76), respectively, if 'E' is the event of John's winning the game. And (a), (b), and (c) of (7.76) represent the sense of the present, past, and future perfect tenses, respectively.

Let us now provide a lexical reading for the syntactic symbol 'Perfect Aspect'. What we want to do is, on the basis of the lexical readings for the simple present, past, and future tenses given previously and the lexical reading for the perfect aspect, provide derived readings expressing the temporal relations presented in (7.76). Thus, we must define a function K such that, given a lexical reading of a simple tense, we obtain via K a reading relating E and P as indicated in (7.76). First, observe that we can write (7.76) in the form (7.77).

(7.77)

LEXICAL READING OF SIMPLE TENSES	READING OF E	READING OF P
$(t^{(0)})$	$(t^{(-n)})$	$(t^{(0)})$
$(t^{(-n)})$	$(t^{(-n+(-r))})$	$(t^{(-n)})$
$(t^{(+n)})$	$(t^{(+n+(-r))})$	$(t^{(+n)})$

Thus the function K is, informally, (7.78):[16]

(7.78) Given that $(t^{(\delta)})$ is the lexical reading of the simple tense, make the reading of the event P be $(t^{(\delta)})$ and make the reading of the event E be $(t^{(\delta+(-r))})$.

The first step in the formalization of (7.78) consists in turning it into a lexical reading such as (7.79) for the symbol 'Perfect Aspect':[17]

(7.79) $(t^{\underset{\langle\ \rangle}{\overset{X}{[\text{Tense, Aux, PP, S}]}}})$, $((\text{Event})\text{ at }(t^{\underset{\langle\ \rangle}{\overset{X}{[\text{Aspect, Aux, PP, S}]}}+(-r)}))$

The last step in our formalization consists in writing the selection restriction under the variable categorized for the inflexional or temporalization relation in instances of (7.53) (that is, the definition of '(State)') and other appropriate cases so that it includes a conjunction requiring that the reading to be the value of this variable not contain a semantic marker that contains the semantic marker '(Event)'. That is, the angles under the second categorized variable of (7.53) should have a condition of the form '$\langle\ldots \& (\ldots\overline{(\text{Event})}\ldots)\rangle$'. Thus, only the instances of the first marker schema of (7.79) will be values of these categorized variables. The instances of the second schema of (7.79) will simply become one of the semantic markers in the reading for the whole sentence, thereby indicating that there is some event P such that the event described in the sentence is earlier than P.

What we have been referring to as "undescribed events" can, of course, come in for description if a perfect aspect sentence contains an appropriate time adverbial, as in (7.80):

(7.80) John $\begin{Bmatrix}\text{had}\\\text{will have}\end{Bmatrix}$ earned the money $\begin{Bmatrix}\text{by Christmas}\\\text{by the time Bill demands it}\end{Bmatrix}$

The time adverbials in (7.80) say that the "undescribed event" posited by the perfect aspect of the sentence is, in the first case, the arrival of the day celebrating the birth of Christ and, in the second case, the moment when Bill calls the loan in. Therefore, we must represent the reading of the perfect aspect so that the meaning of such time adverbials can descriptively specify the event P. This might be accomplished by replacing the semantic marker '(Event)' in (7.79) by '$\underset{\langle(\text{Event})\rangle}{\overset{([\alpha])}{X}}$'. The

---

[16] I wish to thank my friend and colleague M. V. Miller for help in developing this analysis of the perfect aspect.

[17] Note that there is nothing incorrect about using categorized variables as superscripts since these variables can go wherever semantic markers or readings can go.

grammatical function α would be the one required to pick out the relevant class of time adverbials in the sentence. Given this change, either there is no time adverbial of the proper sort in the sentence and so, by the condition (3.77), the value of the categorized variable is just the semantic marker '(Event)', as in our original formulation (7.79), or there is such a time adverbial in the sentence and so, by the operation of the projection rule, its reading is the value of the categorized variable, as desired.

We have been dealing up to now with the representation of temporal relations among events located at a particular point in time. Of course, not all time relations are of this sort. Consider those expressed by sentences such as (7.81)–(7.83):

(7.81)   John is eating soup

(7.82)   John was (has been) eating soup

(7.83)   John will be eating soup

Here the progressive form of the tense constituent appears, and John's act of eating soup is not located at a point but is spread over a segment on the time dimension. That is, in such sentences the event is said to occur over an interval of time, to be ongoing through that interval. In past progressive sentences like (7.82), the event is described as in progress from some undesignated point in the past to some later undesignated point in the past, and in future progressive sentences like (7.83) the event is described as in progress from some undesignated point in the future to some later undesignated point in the future. This is clear. But in the present progressive case the situation is not so clear. Is the event referred to in a sentence with a present progressive tense, that is, in a sentence like (7.81), described as ongoing throughout an interval which is *included* in the interval bounded by the onset and termination of the utterance of that sentence, or is the event described as ongoing throughout an interval which *properly includes* the interval bounded by the onset and termination of the utterance of that sentence? To give an affirmative answer to the latter question is to say that in any utterance of (7.81) that makes a true statement the eating referred to *must* have begun before the onset of the utterance and gone on after its termination. But, although this is usually the case with activities such as eating, it is not at all necessarily the case. Consider for example (7.84) and (7.85):

(7.84)   I am uttering an English sentence

(7.85)   You are listening to me speaking this sentence

It is perfectly clear that there can be utterances of these sentences which make true statements and which, by the nature of the case, must describe activities that are included (though not properly, of course) in the interval bounded by the onset and termination of the utterance. Moreover, it seems possible to answer affirmatively to the first question even in cases like eating soup, for one can imagine that John is a notoriously fast soup eater and the speaker is an extraordinarily slow speaker.

Thus, as John sits down to his soup the speaker begins to utter (7.81), but before the speaker finishes the sentence John has finished eating the soup. Accordingly, we introduce (7.86) as the lexical reading for 'Progressive' in the auxiliary:

(7.86) $(t^{(\S u)}) \rightarrow ((t^{(\S u + (-r_1))}), \ldots, (t^{(\S u)}), \ldots, (t^{(\S u + (+r_2))}))$

The symbol '$(t^{(\S u)})$' is the value of the variable categorized for the inflexional relation, the reading of 'Present' or 'Past' or 'Future', and 'r' is, again, some arbitrary number of units on the time dimension less than the absolute value of the superscript 'u' (where differently superscripted cases can be different numbers).

Let us see how (7.86) marks the time relations in (7.81)–(7.83). In (7.81) the tense constituent contains 'Present', and so $(t^{(\S u)}) = (t^{(0)})$. Thus (7.86) converts it into $((t^{(0 + (-r_1))}), \ldots, (t^{(0)}), \ldots, (t^{(0 + (+r_2))}))$, which, by the algebra of signed numbers, reduces to $((t^{(-r_1)}), \ldots, (t^{(0)}), \ldots, (t^{(+r_2)}))$. In (7.82) the tense constituent contains 'Past', and so $(t^{(\S u)}) = (t^{(-n)})$. Thus (7.86) converts it into $((t^{(-n + (-r_1))}), \ldots, (t^{(-n)}), \ldots, (t^{(-n + (+r_2))}))$. In (7.83) the tense constituent contains 'Future', and so $(t^{(\S u)}) = (t^{(+n)})$. Thus (7.86) converts it into $((t^{(+n + (-r_1))}), \ldots, (t^{(+n)}), \ldots, (t^{(+n + (+r_2))}))$.

Next we consider sentences that temporally relate two events which span an interval of time, as, for example, (7.87) and (7.88):

(7.87) John was eating soup while Bill was eating bread

(7.88) John will be eating soup while Bill is eating bread

Compare (7.87) and (7.88), respectively, with (7.89) and (7.90):

(7.89) John was eating soup and Bill was eating bread

(7.90) John will be eating soup and Bill will be eating bread

In the cases of (7.87) and (7.88), but not in the cases of (7.89) and (7.90), we can infer that the progress of the events spoken of in the main and subordinate clauses occurs over overlapping time intervals. That is, "while" identifies a sub-interval of the time interval over which the first event takes place with a subinterval of the time interval over which the second event takes place, whereas "and" leaves open the matter of whether or not the events spoken of in the conjoined sentences share a common time interval.

We can account for this semantic difference on the basis of a suitable definition for "while" and a general convention that requires us always to choose a different subscript for the variable in the semantic marker appearing as the superscript of 't' for each lexical reading of the tense constituents 'Past' and 'Future'. The convention may be stated as in (7.91):

(7.91) For each pair of semantic markers $(t^{(\S u_i)})$ and $(t^{(\S u_j)})$ assigned to the tense constituent 'Past' or 'Future' in an underlying phrase marker, i and j must be chosen so that $i \neq j$.

By thus insuring that the indexing subscript on each signed variable appearing as the superscript of an occurrence of 't' (in the same reading of a nonsimple sentence) is a different numeral, we reflect the fact that no inference can be made from a sentence like (7.89) or (7.90) to some positive conclusion about the overlap of the events.

The lexical reading for "while" may be given as the two rules in (7.92):

(7.92) (a) $v[\text{T}^m] = ((t^{(\S u_1 + (-r_1))}), \ldots, (t^{(\S u_1)}), \ldots, (t^{(\S u_1 + (+r_2))}))$

$\quad\quad v[\text{T}^m] \rightarrow ((t^{(\S u_1 + (-r_1))}), \ldots, (t^{(\S u_2 + (-s_1))}), \ldots, (t^{(\S u_2 + (+s_2))}),$

$$\ldots, (t^{(\S u_1 + (+r_2))}))$$

(b) $v[\text{T}^s] = ((t^{(\S u_2 + (-r_3))}), \ldots, (t^{(\S u_2)}), \ldots, (t^{(\S u_2 + (+r_2))}))$

$\quad\quad v[\text{T}^s] \rightarrow ((t^{(\S u_2 + (-r_3))}), \ldots, (t^{(\S u_1 + (-s_3))}), \ldots, (t^{(\S u_1 + (+s_4))}),$

$$\ldots, (t^{(\S u_2 + (+r_4))}))$$

where $s_1 \leq r_1$, $s_2 \leq r_2$, $s_3 \leq r_3$, and $s_4 \leq r_4$

On the basis of the lexical reading in (7.92), the time relations in the main and subordinate clauses of sentences like (7.87) and (7.88) are represented by a symbolism that specifies that a portion of the interval over which the event referred to in the main clause occurs coincides with a portion of the interval over which the event referred to in the subordinate clause occurs. The first clause of rule (a) and of rule (b) of (7.92) says that these rules operate on the reading that is the value of the variable categorized for the inflexional relation (obtained by the operation of (7.86) on the reading of the tense constituent). The second clause of (a) and of (b) of (7.92) specifies the change that is necessary to convert representations of the intervals over which events occur into representations of intervals of occurrence with portions that coincide. Note, furthermore, that by the assignment of different numerals in cases like (7.89) and (7.90), rules (7.91) and (7.92) do not indicate that the intervals of occurrence *have* to be nonoverlapping but only that they *can* be nonoverlapping.

Now consider the sentences in (a) and (b) of (7.93):

(7.93) (a) John is eating soup while Bill is eating bread
$\quad\quad$ (b) John is eating soup and Bill is eating bread

Here there is no contrast such as that between (7.87) and (7.89) or between (7.88) and (7.90). The events in (a) of (7.93) progress through a common time interval, and so also do the events in (b). This can be accounted for on the basis of the fact that no superscript variables are involved. In both clauses of both sentences the present tense occurs, and in the lexical reading of 'Present' the superscript on 't' is the *constant* '0'. Convention (7.91) applies only to superscripts of 't' that are variables; thus, it does not apply in the semantically interpreted underlying phrase markers for (a) and (b) of (7.93). Hence, in the case of (a), the reading for "while" replaces $v[\text{T}^s]$ by $v[\text{T}^m]$, which is just replacing '$((t^{(0 + (-r_1))}), \ldots, (t^{(0)}), \ldots, (t^{(0 + (+r_2))}))$' by itself. Accordingly, the semantic representation of (7.93a) describes John's eating soup and Bill's eating bread as occurring over the same interval. In the case of (7.93b), there being nothing to index differently since the superscript on each occurrence of 't' is the constant '0', the semantic representation describes John's eating soup and Bill's eating bread as occurring over the intervals designated by '$((t^{(0+(-r_3))}), \ldots, (t^{(0)}), \ldots, (t^{(0+(+r_4))}))$' and '$((t^{(0+(-r_5))}), \ldots, (t^{(0)}), \ldots, (t^{(0+(+r_6))}))$'. This says that these events are asserted by (7.93b) to be ongoing at the utterance point, but the starting and stopping points of the intervals they span can be different.

Now consider the sentences (7.94)–(7.97):

(7.94)   John was eating soup before Bill was eating bread

(7.95)   John was eating soup after Bill was eating bread

(7.96)   John will be eating soup before Bill will be eating bread

(7.97)   John will be eating soup after Bill will be eating bread

These cases can be handled parallel to (7.59), (7.60), (7.67), and (7.68). What is required is that '$v[T^s]$' in (7.61a,b) be understood to be the semantic marker '$(t^{(\S u+(-r_i))})$' in the reading for a progressive form. Thus, for example, John's eating soup in (7.94) is described as occurring over the interval specified by '$((t^{(-n+((-r_1)+(-r_3)))}), \ldots, (t^{(-n)}), \ldots, (t^{(-n+(+r_2))}))$', whereas Bill's eating bread in this sentence is described as occurring over the interval specified by '$((t^{(-n+(-r_1))}), \ldots, (t^{(-n)}), \ldots, (t^{(-n+(+r_4))}))$'.

There are two additional types of relations that must be considered here— first, the type involving the location of an event at a particular point within an interval and, second, the type involving the location of an event spanning an interval within an interval. Consider (7.98) and (7.99):

(7.98)   John kicked George during the time Bill was sleeping

(7.99)   John was eating soup during the time Bill was sleeping

In the former case, John kicked George at some point in time within the interval through which Bill's sleeping occurred. In the latter case, the interval through which John was eating soup is included within (but not necessarily properly included in) the interval through which Bill was sleeping. These types of time relations can be handled on the basis of a lexical reading for words like "during" which effect the insertion of an event within an interval. Thus, as paradigmatic, we introduce the reading for "during" (7.100), where the selection restriction is the same as in (7.61):

(7.100) $v[T^s] = ((t^{(\S u+(-r_i))}), \ldots, (t^{(\S u)}), \ldots, (t^{(\S u+(+r_j))}))$
$v[T^s] \rightarrow ((t^{(\S u+(-r_i))}), \ldots, v[T^m], \ldots, (t^{(\S u+(+r_j))})), \langle \; \rangle$

According to this rule, (7.98) is represented as saying that John's kicking George is located at the point specified by '$(t^{(-n)})$' and that Bill's sleeping is spread over the interval '$((t^{(-m+(-r_1))}), \ldots, (t^{(-n)}), \ldots, (t^{(-m+(+r_2))}))$', and so the former event is specified as occurring within the interval through which the latter event occurs. Sentence (7.99) is represented by (7.100) as saying that John's eating soup spans the interval '$((t^{(-n+(-r_1))}), \ldots, (t^{(-n)}), \ldots, (t^{(-n+(+r_2))}))$' and that Bill's sleeping spans the interval '$((t^{(-m+(-r_3))}), \ldots, (t^{(-n+(-r_1))}), \ldots, (t^{(-n)}), \ldots, (t^{(-n+(+r_2))}), \ldots, (t^{(-m+(+r_4))}))$'. This, then, says that the interval through which the former event occurs is within the interval through which the latter occurs.

Consider, finally, (7.101):

(7.101)   John's eating soup occurred during Bill's nap which occurred during Sam's trial which occurred during Mary's holiday trip which occurred during ...

The iteration of interval inclusion, as illustrated by this sentence, is quite naturally accounted for by (7.100).

We can now turn our attention to the semantic representation of temporal relations that locate events with respect to intervals whose size is fixed linguistically. Consider the sentences in (7.102)–(7.106):

(7.102)   John has been eating jam in the last hour

(7.103)   John has been eating jam for the last hour

(7.104)   John ate (eats, will eat) cake yesterday (today, tomorrow)

(7.105)   John ate cake a (three) minute(s) ago

(7.106)   John will see George an hour ago

The meaning of time adverbials like those in (7.102)–(7.106) involves a number concept, a unit concept, and a direction concept. Sometimes these concepts are differentiated by the words that make up the adverbial, as in (7.105) and (7.106), and sometimes not, as in (7.104). Semantically, then, the only difference between cases like "two days ago," "one hour hence," "the last six days," "a second from now," "in a day's time" and cases like "yesterday" and "today" is that in the former the complex concept is compositionally formed from the concepts of number, unit, and direction that are assigned lexically to morphemes while in the latter the complex concept is itself lexically assigned. We shall not say anything about the number concept, since it is not special to the representation of time relations and involves enormous complications. Thus, we focus our attention on the concepts of unit and direction.

To define the unit concept on the basis of a reading, we must institute some division of the time dimension into basic units. I choose the "second" as the basic unit of time because it is the smallest temporal unit for which there is a simple name in common speech. I recognize, of course, that natural languages contain names of smaller units, such as "microsecond," but their compositional structure shows that the second is basic: "microsecond" means 'one millionth of a second'. Given that the units larger than a second are definable in a straightforward way in terms of the "second" unit—a minute is sixty seconds, an hour is sixty minutes, a day is twenty-four hours (although, of course, not any twenty-four hour period), a week is seven days, and so on—it will be possible to provide lexical readings for each of the morphemes that express these larger units in terms of multiples of the basic unit "second." Accordingly, (7.45) and (7.46) will automatically come out to be synonymous.

The number concept can be taken as just a coefficient of the unit concept, that is, it can be treated as its multiplier, since "sixty minutes" and "an hour," "twenty-four hours" and "a day," etc., are synonymous.

The direction concept indicates the direction from the origin, left in the case of past and right in the case of future. Thus, except for "now," which can be represented as the origin itself, we can take the direction concept to attach either a plus or a minus sign to the result of multiplying the number concept by the unit concept—a plus in the reading of an expression like "one day hence" and a minus in the reading of an expression like "one day ago." Accordingly, the derived reading for "two minutes ago" would be '$(-((2) \times (60)))$' or '(-120)'.

Hence, the derived readings for these temporal adverbials are *constants* representing a fixed number of basic units and a direction from the origin. This is as it should be, since, generally, the semantic effect of these temporal adverbials is not to change any time relations already determined by the tense constituent but only to make such relations more determinate, as, for example, to specify precisely the span of the interval in which some event is said to occur, as in (7.102), or the span of the interval over which some event is said to occur, as in (7.103). Examples (7.106) and (7.42) show that the semantic effect of such adverbials can be to produce incompatible temporal designations, resulting in sentences that are contradictions. But even here no change in the time relations specified in the tense constituent is brought about. This suggests a natural way of forming derived readings from the readings of temporal adverbials and the readings of the verb after the reading of the tense constituent is substituted: substitute a reading of the temporal adverbial for the appropriate occurrences of the variables appearing as superscripts on 't' within the reading of the verb.

Given this projection rule operation, let us examine the time relations in the sentence (7.107):

(7.107)   John kicked Bill two minutes ago

First, we form the time representation determined in the auxiliary, '$(t^{(-n)})$'; second, we substitute it for the appropriate categorized variable in the reading of the verb; and then we substitute '(-120)' for '$(-n)$'. Thus, John's kicking Bill is represented in (7.107) as located 120 basic units to the left of the origin of the time dimension.

There are two slight complications to be considered. First, we must distinguish between temporal adverbials and adverbials of duration and frequency. Consider the contrast between (7.108) and (7.109) and the contrast in (7.110):

(7.108)   John was eating cake for one minute

(7.109)   John was eating cake one minute ago

(7.110)   John was eating cake for one minute one minute ago

There is a syntactic basis for this semantic distinction which is provided by the syntactic component in the form of a phrase structure rule such as (3.79h).[18] The effect of such a rule, together with the other phrase structure rules of (3.79), is to provide the sort of phrase marker illustrated in (7.111):

(7.111)

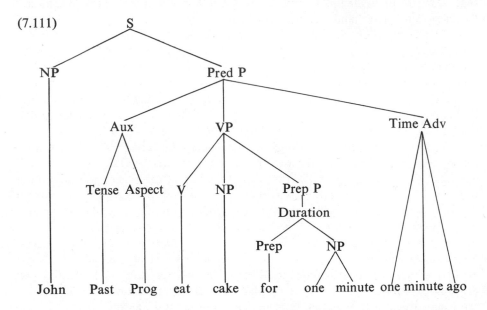

In such a phrase marker there is a basis for distinguishing the temporalization relation from the grammatical relation that holds between the verb and an adverbial of duration or frequency. In terms of this distinction, we can introduce two projection rule operations, one of which applies to cases where the verb is modified by a temporal adverbial and the other to cases where it is modified by an adverbial of duration or frequency. In the former case, the derived reading is formed, as already suggested, by substituting the constant in the reading of the time adverbial for the superscript variable on occurrences of 't' in the reading of the verb. The latter case divides into two subcases, that of duration adverbials and that of frequency adverbials. In the first the derived reading for the verb is formed by substituting the constant in the reading of the duration adverbial for a certain variable in a reading formed from the reading of the verb. Notice that (7.108) and (7.112) are synonymous:

(7.112)   John ate cake for one minute

This means that part of the role for combining the reading of the verb with the reading of an adverbial of duration is a rule for turning the reading for the past into the reading for the past progressive. This we give as the reading (7.113) for "for," i.e., for the preposition that introduces such adverbials.

[18] Chomsky (1965, p. 107).

(7.113) $(Z, \ldots, (t^{(\S u)}), \ldots, W) \rightarrow ((t^{(\S u + (-r_1))}), \ldots, (t^{(\S u)}), \ldots, (t^{(\S u + (\S r_1 + \Phi))}))$

where 'Z' and 'W' may both be null or where 'Z' = '$(t^{(\S u + (-r_1))})$' and 'W' = '$(t^{(\S u' + r_2))})$',

Given the operation of (7.113), the combining of the reading of the duration adverbial with the reading of the verb—in which the time designation is now of the form given to the right of the arrow in (7.113)—consists simply in substituting the constant in the reading of the duration adverbial for the variable 'Φ'.[19]

Finally, consider (7.114)–(7.116):

(7.114) John praised Sally repeatedly

(7.115) John praised Sally again and again (and again ...)

(7.116) John praised Sally over and over (and over ...) again

The derived reading for the verb phrase in these sentences is obtained from the derived reading formed from the reading of the tense and the reading of the verb together with the reading of the adverbial of frequency. This reading would be the rule in (7.117):

(7.117) $(t^{(\S u_i)}) \rightarrow (t^{(\S u_1)}), (t^{(\S u_2)}), \ldots, (t^{(\S u_i)}), \ldots, (t^{(\S u_k)})$

We have constructed part of a representation system for time designations and some rules that assign representations from this system compositionally: as the result of the application of the projection rule (to lexical readings in the system) dealing with such grammatical relations as the inflexional relation and the temporalization relation, derived readings are assigned to sentences as an abstract representation of the time relations among the events spoken of in them. Such examples as (7.39), (7.41), and (7.106) show that the time relations described in this system also underlie semantic properties and relations of sentences, such as semantic anomaly, analyticity, and contradictoriness. Let us now turn to a brief examination of this point.

Consider, first, (7.106) and the sentence (7.118):

(7.118) John kicked Bill one minute from now

---

[19] For example:

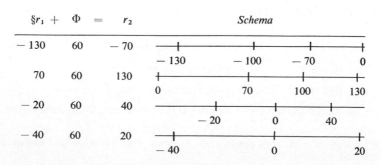

$\S r_1$ +	Φ	=	r_2	Schema
− 130	60		− 70	
70	60		130	
− 20	60		40	
− 40	60		20	

These sentences are both contradictions on a sense because they express incompatible temporal locations for the event which is described in them. In order for us to be able to mark such cases of contradiction by general definition, we require a convention governing the substitution of constants, i.e., readings of the time adverbials in a sentence, for superscript variables on occurrences of 't' when the sign of the superscript variable differs from the sign on the constant. Thus, the former convention of substituting the constant for the variable is to be regarded as applying only when the signs are the same. The full convention can be stated as in (7.119):

(7.119) The result of substituting ' $\S N$ ' for ' $\S u_i$ ' in ' $(t^{(\S u_i)})$ ' is ' $(t^{(\S N)})$ ' in case the $\S$'s are identical and ' $(t^{(\S u_i,\ \S N)})$ ' in case the $\S$'s are different.

This convention can be regarded as a clause of the projection rule. The time relations in (7.118) will now be represented as ' $(t^{(-n,\ +60)})$ ' and the time relations in (7.106) will be represented as ' $(t^{(+n,\ -3600)})$ '. Since ' $-$ ' and ' $+$ ' are antonymous semantic markers, by the definition of 'contradiction', sentences whose reading represents their condition using a semantic marker of the form ' $(t^{(-n,\ +W)})$ ' and one of the form ' $(t^{(+n,\ -W)})$ ', where ' W ' is either a constant or a variable, as in the case of (7.120), will be marked as a contradiction (on a reading).

(7.120) John will kick Bill some time ago

Thus, (7.106), (7.118), and (7.120) will each be marked a contradiction, thereby representing the fact that the events they refer to are incompatibly located at different points in time. Hence, the machinery developed in this section reflects the principle that one single event cannot occur at each of two incompatible temporal locations.[20]

Notice, however, that not only are (7.106) and (7.118) contradictions, but so also are their negations, (7.121) and (7.122), respectively:

(7.121) John will not see George an hour ago

(7.122) John did not kick Bill one minute from now

Consider the pairs (7.123)-(7.124) and (7.125)-(7.126):

(7.123) John will avoid seeing George an hour ago

(7.124) John will not avoid seeing George an hour ago

(7.125) John did refrain from kicking Bill one minute from now

(7.126) John didn't refrain from kicking Bill one minute from now

---

[20] Which, in turn, corresponds to the principle that a single object cannot be in two places at one time.

Such examples constitute an interesting aspect of the distinction between sentences and their senses, the propositions they express. As these sentences show, the relation of being a 'negation of' is distinct from the relation of being a 'denial of'. The second term of the former relation is a sentence, while the second term of the latter is a proposition. The relation of being a 'negation of' holds of a pair of sentences by virtue of their syntactic form: roughly, one differs from the other only by virtue of an occurrence of "not" in its main verb phrase. 'Denial of', on the other hand, is not a purely syntactic relation but rather a logical one primarily. The denial of a sentence expresses a proposition incompatible with the proposition expressed by the sentence of which it is the denial: if the denial is true, then the sentence of which it is the denial is false, and vice versa. But in the case of two sentences where one is the negation of the other, it does not follow that if one is true, the other is false. Consider, for example, Churchill's famous comment (7.127) in the House of Commons:

(7.127) Half of the ministers are asses

And his "retraction" (7.128) when criticized for this comment:

(7.128) Half of the ministers are not asses

Not every declarative sentence is the negation of its denial. The sentences (7.129) and (7.130) are denials of each other, though neither is of negative form:

(7.129) John is alive
(7.130) John is dead

Nonetheless, the pairs (7.106) and (7.121), (7.118) and (7.122), (7.123) and (7.124), and (7.125) and (7.126) are not counterexamples to the principle in semantic theory, as set forth, for example, in Katz (1964a), that the *denial* of a contradictory proposition is analytic because the members of these pairs are not cases of contradictory sentences (i.e., ones that express propositions whose presupposition and truth condition are inconsistent) but contradictions. If they were contradictory sentences, then one of their inconsistent temporal specifications would have to appear in their (truth) conditions and the specification would occur in the scope of the antonymy rules that comprise the lexical reading for 'Neg'. But the readings or parts of readings that represent time relations are *not* in the scope of 'Neg', as can be seen from examples like (7.131), (7.132), and (7.133), as well as the preceding cases:

(7.131) John did not hit Bill at two o'clock
(7.132) John hit Bill at some time other than two o'clock
(7.133) John did not hit Bill at some time other than two o'clock

Sentences (7.131) and (7.133) are consistent, and there can be no entailment of (7.132) by (7.131) since (7.131) can be true and (7.132) false on the condition that John never hit Bill.

By the same token, however, such sentences cannot be ordinary contradictions either since both temporal specifications would have to be in the scope of ' Neg'. Furthermore, it seems wrong to subsume them under the category of indeterminable propositions since they make necessarily false statements ascribing the same event to incompatible temporal locations. Our solution will be to take these cases to be contradictions arising in the propositional type component of a proposition, in the part specifying that the sequence of objects referred to by the readings $r_1, r_2, \ldots, r_n$ sequentially satisfies the relation $\Phi x_1, x_2, \ldots, x_n$. Thus, we take this notion of satisfaction to say that a relation holds for the duration specified in the time designation.[21]

We have been considering one form of contradiction that can arise in connection with the expression of time relations in sentences, namely, that in which different signs occur in the superscript of the same variable 't'. But this is not the only kind of contradiction that can arise, as we shall now see.

Sentences can also be inconsistent in their expression of time relations by virtue of an occurrence of 't' whose superscript contains different constants with the same sign or different variables with the same sign. This, however, is a special case, as can be seen by contrasting (7.134) and (7.135) with (7.136) and (7.137), the latter pair clearly not being a contradiction:

(7.134)   John first kissed Mary an hour ago and a minute ago

(7.135)   John first kissed Mary at one time and then at another

(7.136)   John kissed Mary an hour ago and a minute ago

(7.137)   John kissed Mary at one time and then at another

The second pair here should be handled on the model of adverbials of frequency, discussed previously, since the sentence (7.138) entails the sentence (7.139):

(7.138)   John kissed Mary a minute ago, two minutes ago, an hour ago, and a day ago
(7.139)   John kissed Mary a number of times

Thus, the representation of the time relations of (7.137) will be ' $(t^{(-n_1)})$, $(t^{(-n_2)})$ ' and the representation of those of (7.136) will be ' $(t^{(-360)})$, $(t^{(-60)})$ '. But part of the meaning of "first" (which it shares with "last," for example) is

---

[21] Thus, we regard the notation 'at $\overset{[\,]}{\underset{\langle\,\rangle}{X}}$ ' used in (7.24) and elsewhere as a stopgap measure until the form of the propositional type component of readings is worked out.

the concept of uniqueness. This can be explicated by the rule (7.140), which will be *part* of the lexical reading of " first ":

(7.140) $(t^{(\S n)}) \rightarrow (t^{(\S n, A/\S n+(-r))})$

With (7.140), we can mark (7.134), (7.135), and sentences like them as contradictions on the condition that a single occurrence of 't' has more than one superscript designation (as indicated by their being set off by commas, as opposed to symbols connected by ' + ' or ' − ', which count as one designation).

Another kind of contradiction is found in (7.42), which contrasts with the synthetic sentence (7.141):

(7.141) He worked for a minute during the last hour

Sentence (7.42), as opposed to (7.141), is a contradiction because it includes one time span in another that is smaller than it.

Other kinds of contradictions are exemplified by (7.142) and (7.143) and by mixed cases like (7.144):

(7.142) He will work for a day a day ago

(7.143) He will work for a minute during the last hour

(7.144) He will work for an hour during the last minute

These can be defined on the basis of the representation scheme given for time relations, but they involve complications that we need not go into here.[22]

It is worth noting that, although we get analytic sentences like (7.141), we do not get analytic sentences corresponding to the contradictions (7.106) and (7.118). That is, the sentences (7.145) and (7.146) involve redundancy rather than analyticity:

(7.145) John will see George at some time in the future

(7.146) John kicked Bill at some time in the past

They are more like (7.147) than like (7.148):

(7.147) John is a male bachelor

(7.148) A bachelor is male

[22] One of the complications is, roughly, that the notion of an antonymous *n*-tuple has to be broadened so that we can speak of antonymous semantic markers over an infinite range such as is here involved in the use of natural numbers. There is no special difficulty in this, for we can define two designations of temporal intervals as antonymous just in case either the designation of the initial point or the designation of the terminal point of the included interval determines a location on the time dimension outside the including interval.

This concludes our discussion of time relations. Although there is, certainly, far more to be said,[23] our concern in this chapter with time relations was to develop a general framework for references to them in our discussion of states and processes so that they will have some concrete meaning for the reader.

4. A solution to the problem of converses

The concepts of state and process dealt with in Section 2 of this chapter, together with the framework for representing time relations that was set up in Section 3, provide the apparatus for a semantic solution to the problem of explaining the paraphrase relation in connection with sentences like (7.6) and (7.7). This solution will consist in showing that, on the basis of such apparatus, we can represent the meaning of converse verbs like "buy" and "sell" so that the normal operation of the projection rule will automatically assign the same reading to sentences like (7.6) and (7.7). The procedure we will follow will be that of utilizing one and then another part of the apparatus already constructed to fill out the abstract form of the schemata presented in (7.25) and (7.26) defining the semantic marker '(Process)'.

Categorized variables provide the formal machinery with which to specify the terms of the relation expressed by an occurrence of the verb "buy" or "sell." The functions that define grammatical relations such as 'subject of', 'direct object of', and 'indirect object of', as well as those that define the temporalization relation, the inflexional relation, and others having to do with the time relations in a sentence, provide the information that will be used to state the categorization of the variables appearing in the instances of (7.25) and (7.26) chosen to serve as the lexical readings of "buy" and "sell." Nothing general can be said about the selection restrictions to be used with the variables categorized for 'subject of', 'direct object of', 'indirect object of', and other functions that hold among constituents not most directly involved in the syntactic expression of time relations in sentences. In these cases, the semantic marker content within the angles in categorized variables varies according to the type of process involved: the condition of a particular state semantic marker determines the selection restriction since the question of what the restriction is is answered when it is known what kinds of things can be in that condition. For example, if it makes no sense to say of a corpse or rock or abstract idea that it has recovered from its illness, then the selection restriction on the variable in the reading for "recover" that is categorized for readings of the subject of "recover" must be framed so as to exclude as values the readings of noun phrases whose semantic specification restricts their reference to

---

[23] Of particular importance will be the extension of this work on time relations to more complex tenses and the definition of other temporal adverbials in terms of lexical readings that are specified on the basis of these representations.

nonliving things. On the other hand, something general can be said about the selection restrictions for the variables in instances of schemata (7.25) and (7.26) that are categorized for one or another of the relations holding for constituents most directly involved in the syntactic expression of time relations. In connection with (7.62)–(7.65), we found that time adverbials like "before" and "after" require a reading with a selection restriction that imposes the condition that the readings of the main and subordinate clauses contain either a variable categorized for the inflexional relation or some value substituted for it, which may or may not be further developed by readings of time adverbials. The same restriction is required for a verb like "lasts," as is shown by the contrast between the semantic anomalousness of (7.39) and the nonanomalousness of (7.149):

(7.149) The memory of her statement lasted only three days

Unlike "truth," which must be represented as something timeless, "memory" must be represented as something involving the passage of time. This contrast has nothing to do with the fact that "truth" is a nominalized adjective, while "memory" is a nominalized verb: some verbs, such as "proves," have to be accorded a timeless sense, while some adjectives, such as "sick," have to be accorded a nontimeless sense. The relevant fact here is that the meaning of "memory" is, roughly, the storing of information in the mind for a period of time (or the faculty for such storing). Therefore, since processes are, by definition, things that take place through time, it is clear that the selection restriction which occurs in the readings of adverbials like "before" and "after" (and a verb like "lasts") should be an inherent feature of the process semantic marker.

But, then, it is also an inherent feature of processes that the states of a process succeed each other in time. Accordingly, the time designations in a process semantic marker must determine an interval on the time dimension such that the initiating point is specified by the time designation in the semantic marker representing the initial state of the process and the terminating point is specified by the time designation in the semantic marker representing the terminal state. We therefore need something like (7.150) as a further definition of the semantic marker '(Process)':

$$(7.150) \quad (((\text{Condition}), (\,), \ldots, (\,) \text{ of } \begin{smallmatrix} [\,\,] \\ X \\ \langle\,\,\rangle \end{smallmatrix} \text{ at } \begin{smallmatrix} [\text{Tense, Aux, PP, S}] \\ X \\ \langle(\ldots t \ldots)\rangle \end{smallmatrix} /^{+(-r_1)}), \ldots,$$

$$((\text{Condition}), (\,), \ldots, (\,) \text{ of } \begin{smallmatrix} [\,\,] \\ X \\ \langle\,\,\rangle \end{smallmatrix} \text{ at } \begin{smallmatrix} [\text{Tense, Aux, PP, S}] \\ X \\ \langle(\ldots t \ldots)\rangle \end{smallmatrix} /^{+(+r_2)}))$$

In (7.150) the slash after an occurrence of a variable categorized for the inflexional relation indicates that what is to the left is the variable proper, that is, what is to be replaced in a substitution, and what is to the right is something that enters into construction with the reading that substitutes for the variable: the result of substituting the reading '$( )^{(\alpha)}$' for ' X ' in the context '——$/^{\S(\S r_i)}$' is '$( )^{(\alpha \S(\S r_i))}$'.

This means that the reading of the tense constituent '$(t^{(\S u)})$' becomes '$(t^{(\S u + (-r_1))})$' in a substitution for the first occurrence of the variable categorized for the inflexional relation in an instance of (7.150) and becomes '$(t^{(\S u + (+r_2))})$' in the second occurrence.

   Note, however, that (7.150) does not correctly reflect the temporal relations expressed in sentences like (7.151)–(7.153):

(7.151) The ice just this moment melted

(7.152) The ice melted

(7.153) The ice will melt

The process of the ice changing from a solid to a liquid state is temporally located by (7.150) over the intervals '$(t^{(0+(-r_1))})$', ..., $(t^{(0+(+r_2))})$', '$(t^{(-n+(-r_1))})$', ..., $(t^{(-n+(+r_2))})$', '$(t^{(+m+(-r_1))})$', ..., $(t^{(+m+(+r_2))})$' for the sentences (7.151), (7.152), and (7.153), respectively. But these sentences locate the process as shown in (7.154):

(7.154)

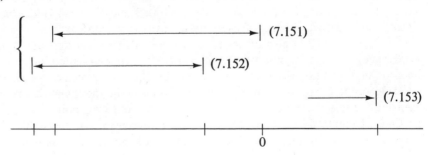

The asterisk in (7.154) indicates that the order of the initial states of the processes referred to in (7.151) and (7.152) with respect to each other is not necessarily as shown. The absence of a symbol designating the point on the time dimension at which the initial state of the process referred to in (7.153) occurs indicates the fact that the sentence does not give this information. (Note, in this connection, that we can say sentence (7.153) even when the ice has not yet begun to melt, for example, when someone has just switched off the electricity for the freezer compartment of a refrigerator.)

   Furthermore, we also want a way of handling progressive aspect sentences such as those in (7.155), (7.156), and (7.157).

(7.155) The ice is just melting

(7.156) The ice was melting

(7.157) The ice will be melting

These sentences locate the process as shown in (7.158):

(7.158)

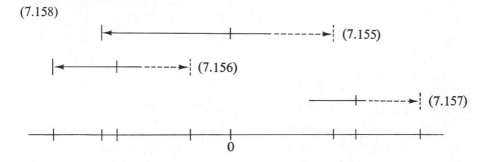

The dashed lines indicate that the sentences do not assert that the final state of the process actually occurs, that is, that the ice melts completely, but only that, if the final state occurs, then it occurs at the point indicated. Accordingly, sentences like (7.151)–(7.153) contrast with sentences like (7.155)–(7.157) in that the former assert that the terminal state of the process takes place whereas the latter assert that the initial state takes place, as well as some intermediary state designated by the point at the middle of each of the lines that represent the intervals in (7.158). In other words, the former sentences say that the process reaches a successful completion while the latter say that it has begun. This contrast is brought out more sharply by comparing (a) and (b) of (7.159):

(7.159) (a) The ice melted a minute ago
　　　　　(b) The ice was melting a minute ago

Sentence (7.159a) says that the *terminal* state of the process took place sixty seconds before the utterance point, and (7.159b) says that the *initial* and *some intermediary* states took place prior to (i.e., the last of the intermediary states occurred at) sixty seconds before the utterance point.

　　　　We note that in the future forms of the simple tense sentences and the progressive aspect sentences there is no indication of whether the initial state occurs in the past, present, or future. In the representational apparatus that we shall now introduce, this fact is indicated by a disjunction of a semantic marker representing some moment in the past, a semantic marker representing the utterance point, and a semantic marker representing some moment in the future.

　　　　We now give (7.160) as the further specification of '(Process)' that is required to assign states of a process to locations on the time dimension in accord with the facts just discussed.

(7.160) (a) $(((\text{Condition}), (\,), \ldots, (\,) \text{ of } \overset{[\,]}{\underset{\langle\,\rangle}{X}} \text{ at } \overset{[\text{Tense, Aux, PP, S}]}{\underset{\langle\,\rangle}{X}} / H_1, H_2, H_4), \ldots,$

$((\text{Condition}), (\,), \ldots, (\,) \text{ of } \overset{[\,]}{\underset{\langle\,\rangle}{X}} \text{ at } \overset{[\text{Tense, Aux, PP, S}]}{\underset{\langle\,\rangle}{X}} / H_3, H_2, H_5), \ldots,$

$((\text{Condition}), (\,), \ldots, (\,) \text{ of } \overset{[\,]}{\underset{\langle\,\rangle}{X}} \quad \overset{[\text{Tense, Aux, PP, S}]}{\underset{\langle\,\rangle}{X}} / H_6))$

(b) $H_1 \quad v[\ldots/] = \begin{pmatrix} (t^{(0)}) \\ (t^{(-n)}) \end{pmatrix} : \quad v[\ldots/] \rightarrow (t^{(\alpha + ((-r_1) + (-r_2)))})$

$H_2 \quad v[\ldots/] = (t^{(+m)}) \quad : \quad v[\ldots/] \rightarrow (t^{(0)})\,(t^{(-n)})\,(t^{(+m)})$

$H_3 \quad v[\ldots/] = \begin{pmatrix} (t^{(0)}) \\ (t^{(-n)}) \end{pmatrix} : \quad v[\ldots/] \rightarrow (t^{(\alpha + (-r_1))})$

$\text{Given}: \quad v[\ldots/] = \underbrace{(t^{(\alpha + (-r_3))})}_{A}, \ldots, \underbrace{(t^{(\alpha)})}_{B}, \ldots, \underbrace{(t^{(\alpha + (+r_4))})}_{C}$

$H_4 \quad \begin{pmatrix} \alpha = (0) \\ \alpha = (-n) \end{pmatrix} : \quad v[\ldots/] \rightarrow A$

$H_5 \quad A \rightarrow \phi \ \& \ C \rightarrow \phi$

$H_6 \quad v[\ldots/] \rightarrow \overset{[\,]}{\underset{\langle\,\rangle}{X}} \| C$

(c)

		INITIAL STATE	INTERMEDIATE STATE	TERMINAL STATE
SIMPLE TENSE	*Present*	$(t^{(0 + ((-r_1) + (-r_2)))})$	$(t^{(0 + (-r_1))})$	$(t^{(0)})$
	Past	$(t^{(-n + ((-r_1) + (-r_2)))})$	$(t^{(-n + (-r_1))})$	$(t^{(-n)})$
	Future	$(t^{(0)}) \vee (t^{(-n)})$ $\vee (t^{(+m)})$	$(t^{(0)}) \vee (t^{(-n)})$ $\vee (t^{(+m)})$	$(t^{(+m)})$

		INITIAL STATE	INTERMEDIATE STATE	TERMINAL STATE
PROGRESSIVE ASPECT	*Present*	$(t^{(0 + (-r_1))})$	$(t^{(0)})$	$\overset{[\,]}{\underset{\langle\,\rangle}{X}} \| (t^{(0 + (+r_1))})$
	Past	$(t^{(-n + (-r_1))})$	$(t^{(-n)})$	$\overset{[\,]}{\underset{\langle\,\rangle}{X}} \| (t^{(-n + (+r_1))})$
	Future	$(t^{(0)}) \vee (t^{(-n)})$ $\vee (t^{(+m)})$	$(t^{(+m)})$	$\overset{[\,]}{\underset{\langle\,\rangle}{X}} \| (t^{(+m(+ r_1))})$

The selection restriction in the occurrences of the variable categorized for the inflexional relation in (7.160a) is the same as in (7.150). As before, the slash after an occurrence of a categorized variable indicates that what is on its left is the variable proper. However, what is on the right of the slash this time is a set of rules (specified in (7.160b)), which take the form of conditionals. The clause to the left of the colon, the antecedent, states the condition of application; the clause to the right, the consequent, states the operation; the symbol '$v[.../]$' is to be read "the value of the variable immediately to the left of the slash." Accordingly, the consequent of a rule is an instruction to transform the value of the variable into the appropriate instance of the reading represented by the symbol configuration to the right of the arrow. The rules are to apply immediately after the substitution of readings associated with the auxiliary constituent (either readings of the tense constituent or of the progressive aspect) for the proper categorized variables in the reading of the process word.

Rules H_5, H_6, and H_2 require special comment. The symbol 'ϕ' is the deletion symbol used in linguistics, so that H_5 says that two operations of deletion are to be performed: first, the semantic marker in the value of the variable that is analyzed as "A" in the structural analysis is erased, and, second, the semantic marker in the value of the variable that is analyzed as "C" is erased. The symbol '$X \begin{smallmatrix}[\,]\\ \| \\ \langle\,\rangle\end{smallmatrix} ...$', where '...' is a semantic marker representing some temporal location, indicates that the state of the process in which this symbol occurs does not necessarily occur but that if it does it occurs at the time indicated by the semantic marker appearing in '...'. Thus, rule H_6 says that the value of the variable is rewritten as indicated on the right-hand side of the arrow, where 'C' is the semantic marker analyzed as "C" in the structural analysis. Rule H_2 rewrites the value of a variable as a disjunction of semantic markers, thereby indicating that it is not known whether the state in question occurred in the past, present, or future.

The operation of these rules yields the representations presented in (7.160c). The top part of this chart accounts for the data in (7.154) and the bottom part accounts for the data in (7.158).

From the general specification of the concept of a process as given in (7.160a,b) we can obtain particular process concepts by introducing different readings to represent the condition in the state semantic markers or by different orderings of the same set of conditions or by both. For example, the process semantic marker for "melt" has a state semantic marker representing the terminal state of the process of melting in which the condition is specified by the semantic marker '(Liquid)', and the process semantic marker for "vaporize" has a state semantic marker representing the terminal state of the process of vaporization in which the condition is specified by the semantic marker '(Gaseous)'. Thus, to distinguish the lexical readings of "buy" and "sell" from those of verbs like "borrow" and "lend" or from that of "auction," we must determine the right conditions for the state semantic markers in the representation of these processes.

We suggested earlier that buying and selling are processes in which possession of something is transferred from one person to another in exchange for a sum of money. The concept of possession that figures in sentences about buying and selling such things as shoes, ships, and sealing wax is, roughly, that of a relation between a person (or perhaps a group of affiliated persons such as a club or corporation) and something which holds in case that person can do with the object whatever he sees fit, that is, can use or dispose of it as he chooses (within certain limits, such as human capability). This relation involves an element of permanence (as contrasted with the relation one has to something one borrows) which holds until something happens to end one's control over the object (as when, for example, it is lost, stolen, given up, or retrieved by its rightful owner). Accordingly, the sense of "buy" and "sell" that we will focus on is to be distinguished from that which applies when referring to the selling done by an auctioneer, a clerk, or a salesman. (In Section 6 we shall briefly consider this latter "proxy sense" of "sell" and "buy.")

That this is the right condition for the processes of buying and selling will be granted, I assume, if we can show that the stronger condition of ownership is not the correct one. Observe, in this regard, that one can buy or sell stolen goods, that is, things that the seller does not own but merely possesses in the sense just characterized. The sentence (7.161) is neither semantically anomalous nor contradictory:

(7.161) John sold some hot merchandise to Mary who only after the sale found out that John did not own it

Hence, it cannot be the case that it is possible to sell and buy only things that the seller owns prior to the sale.

Furthermore, we may say that in the initial state of the process of selling the full condition is that the seller possesses the item he is selling and that in the terminal state the full condition is that the buyer possesses it. In addition, the specifications of the initial and terminal states must include a determination of the article possessed by the seller in the former state and by the buyer in the latter. And what this article is is determined by the direct object in sentences like (7.6) and (7.7). Thus, the semantic markers representing the states have to contain an occurrence of the variable categorized for the grammatical relation of 'direct object of the verb'.

Before proceeding to other features of the formalization that are intended to represent the propositions in question, let us mention something that must be borne in mind in the discussion to follow. Toward the end of Section 1, it was pointed out that sentences like (7.6) and (7.7) express propositions about a transaction in which possession of an article is exchanged for possession of a sum of money. These sentences do not say, nor is our semantic representation of them intended to say, either that the article or the sum of money in question actually changes hands. A sale can occur without the object sold coming into the *physical* possession of the buyer, and a sale can occur without the sum of money coming into the *physical* possession of the seller. To see this, note that neither of the sentences (7.162) or (7.163) is contradictory or semantically anomalous:

(7.162) John sold the book to Mary but she never paid him for it

(7.163) Mary bought the book from John but she never received it

Our claim, then, is that possession (of the article bought and of the sum of money) is exchanged, roughly, in the sense that one intends when one distinguishes possession from physical possession in saying that something belongs to one person even though another happens to have it.

The fact that (7.6) and (7.7) express the claim that possession of an article has been transferred from one person to another and that possession of a sum of money has been transferred from the latter person to the former means that the verbs "buy" and "sell" are to be given readings that are double process semantic markers. That is, their lexical readings will have the form of (7.26), where $n = 2$. The second process semantic marker must be one in which the state semantic marker that represents the initial state expresses the information that the buyer is in possession of a sum of money and the state semantic marker that represents the terminal state expresses the information that the seller is in possession of (although not necessarily physical possession of) that sum of money. Consider sentences like those in (7.164):

(7.164) (a) John sold the book to Mary for twenty cents
         (b) John sold the book to Mary for some money
         (c) John sold the book to Mary for her car

Sentence (b) of (7.164) is redundant, while (c) is anomalous. We must account for these facts and for the fact that in sentence (a) the specifications of the initial and terminal states must include a characterization of the particular sum of money in question. To obtain such a characterization, we must start with the grammatical relation that the noun phrase in prepositional phrases like "for twenty cents" and "for some money" bears to the main verb. We will take such noun phrases to be objects of their verbs and will refer to the relation as 'secondary indirect object of (the verb)'. Our reason for regarding these constituents as objects is that they answer "What?" or "Who?" questions of the sort that are answered by other types of object constituents. For example, with respect to (7.164a), we have the paradigm in (7.165):

(7.165) (a) What did John sell to Mary?   (the book)
         (b) Whom did John sell the book to?   (Mary)
         (c) What did John sell the book for?   (twenty cents)

We can represent the semantic contribution of these constituents by formulating the readings for "buy" and "sell" so that the parts in the second process semantic marker that characterize the initial and terminal states contain an occurrence of the variable categorized for the grammatical relation of the secondary indirect object of the verb. Thus, by the operation of the projection rule, a reading of the secondary indirect object will replace these occurrences of the categorized variable, thereby characterizing the initial and terminal states as ones in which the appropriate persons are specified as possessing the sum of money determined by the sense of the secondary indirect object in a sentence like (7.164a).

As observed in Section 1, however, sentences like (7.6) and (7.7) do not contain a noun phrase that is the secondary indirect object of their main verb, that is, they contain no constituent whose sense provides information about a particular sum of money. Yet the meaning of these sentences contains the information that an unspecified sum of money is possessed by the buyer at the beginning of the transaction and by the seller at the end. These facts can easily be accounted for by having the selection restriction on occurrences of the variable categorized for the secondary indirect object in the lexical readings of "buy" and "sell" require that values of such variables contain the semantic marker '(Sum of money)' and by the principle (3.77). This selection restriction will be necessary anyway to mark semantic anomalies such as (c) of (7.164).[24]

Note that (7.164b) is semantically redundant because it specifies twice the information about there being a sum of money paid to the seller. This, too, can be handled by the use of a selection restriction on occurrences of this categorized variable in the reading of "buy" and "sell" which allows only substitutions of readings that contain the semantic marker '(Sum of money)'. But to handle this fact in a general way we must add a further condition to the definition of the property of 'semantic redundancy', namely, the condition (7.166), which we add to the definition (2.44) as a disjunct:

(7.166)   A constituent C is redundant in a sentence S if C bears a grammatical relation to a constituent C′ of S such that the reading R of C is a value of a categorized variable $X \begin{bmatrix} \ \ \end{bmatrix} \langle (M_1) \ \& \ \ldots \ \& \ (M_n) \rangle$ in the reading R′ of C′ and R is a subset of $\{(M_1), \ldots, (M_n)\}$.

This condition is an obvious supplement to (2.44) which extends the account of semantic redundancy beyond modifier-head relations (e.g., "dead corpse") to the range of cases involving subject-verb, object-verb, etc.

The other selection restrictions required for the readings of "buy" and "sell" are those for the variables categorized for the subject and indirect object (i.e., the constituents that refer to the buyer and seller) as well as one for the variable categorized for the direct object (i.e., the constituent that refers to the article in question). In the former case, the natural hypothesis is that the angles contain the semantic condition '(Human) & (Infant)'; in the latter case, the natural hypothesis is that the angles contain the semantic condition '(Physical object)'. I do not wish to present an extended argument for these choices here, but clear-cut motivation comes from semantically anomalous sentences like (a) and (b) of (7.167):

(7.167)   (a) The $\left\{ \begin{array}{l} \text{rock} \\ \text{newborn infant} \\ \text{snake} \\ \text{number five} \end{array} \right\}$ sold the book to the $\left\{ \begin{array}{l} \text{cloud} \\ \text{bear} \\ \text{noun} \\ \text{chair} \end{array} \right\}$

---

[24] A categorized variable is so defined that in case there is no reading to be substituted from the sets of readings associated with the nodes in a semantically interpreted underlying phrase marker, its value is the semantic markers in its own selection restriction. Thus, in the semantic interpretation of (7.6) and (7.7), the value of the variable categorized for the secondary indirect object is the semantic marker '(Sum of money)', which is the sole semantic marker in its selection restriction. In the sentence "Harold sold the book for six dollars," there is no constituent that is the indirect object of the verb, but the fact that its sense involves a sale to someone can be explained since its reading will represent the concept of a buyer who is human and not an infant.

(b) The man sold the $\begin{Bmatrix} \text{shadow} \\ \text{reflection} \\ \text{number} \\ \text{sharp pain} \end{Bmatrix}$ to the woman

I recognize that we often speak of selling an idea, but it seems to me that what is meant is the selling of the rights to any of its practical uses. Selling uses or services involves something physical, and it seems best in such cases to impose the condition that meaningfulness depends on there being something physical involved. When there is not, as in examples like (7.168) and (7.169), the sentences are semantically anomalous:

(7.168)   John sold the use of his sharp pain to Bill

(7.169)   John hired Bill's reflection

Nothing of any general theoretical import hangs on the total correctness of these selection restrictions, and therefore we shall not consider any of the quite subtle and complicated semantic relationships they involve.

Before presenting the lexical readings for "sell" and "buy," we must consider one further aspect of these verbs. The representation of the process referred to as a "sale" will require a certain intermediary state that represents the information that the buyer and seller agree to exchange possession of the article and the sum of money in question. Otherwise, the reading of a sentence like (7.6) or (7.7) simply says that, at one time, the seller is in possession of an article and the buyer is in possession of a sum of money and that, at some later time, the buyer is in possession of the article that the seller was in possession of earlier and the seller is in possession of the sum of money that the buyer was in possession of earlier. Such an account, however, would not distinguish a genuine sale from an exchange of presents in which one person ends up with, among other things, an article formerly belonging to another person, who ends up with, among other things, a sum of money formerly belonging to the first person. Thus, some appropriate state semantic marker is needed to represent the agreement on the part of the two parties to relinquish possession of the thing belonging to each at the outset of the sale in return for the thing belonging to the other. I shall not try to formalize the state semantic marker that represents the information about this intermediary state. Nor will I try to enter into some subtle questions that arise in connection with such a formalization, like, for example, whether the article sold and the sum of money paid are accepted by the buyer and seller as in some sense equivalent in value. Such a formalization will certainly be required in a complete semantic analysis of "sell" and "buy." Here, however, we are not trying to arrive at such an analysis but are attempting only to provide a treatment of the converse relation.

We now present in (7.170) and (7.171) our partial account of the readings of the verbs "sell" and "buy," respectively.[25]

---

[25] The notation '... Prep = (to, from)-P ...', and '... Prep = (for)-P ...' is employed as a stopgap measure to distinguish between the indirect object and what I have called the secondary indirect object. I realize that it is unsatisfactory as a specification of grammatical functions because, by referring to the specific English morphemes "to," "from," and "for," it defines these functions in a way that is not linguistically universal. At this point, however, I can give no more satisfactory definitions.

(7.170) *sell*; (((((Condition) (Possesses [NP, VP, PP, S] X /⟨(Physical object)⟩) of [NP, S] X /⟨(Human) & (Infant)⟩

at [Tense, Aux, PP, S] X /H$_1$, H$_2$, H$_4$), ..., (... [Tense, Aux, PP, S] X /H$_3$, H$_2$, H$_5$), ..., ⟨(...t...)⟩ ⟨(...t...)⟩

((Condition) (Possesses [NP, VP, PP, S] X /⟨(Physical object)⟩) of [NP, Prep = (*to,from*)-P, VP, PP, S] X /⟨(Human) & (Infant)⟩

at [Tense, Aux, PP, S] X /H$_6$)) & ⟨(...t...)⟩

((((Condition) (Possesses [NP, Prep = (*for*)-P, VP, PP, S] X /⟨(Sum of money)⟩) of [NP, Prep = (*to,from*)-P, VP, PP, S] X /⟨(Human) & (Infant)⟩

at [Tense, Aux, PP, S] X /H$_1$, H$_2$, H$_4$), ..., (... [Tense, Aux, PP, S] X /H$_3$, H$_2$, H$_5$), ..., ⟨(...t...)⟩ ⟨(...t...)⟩

((Condition) (Possesses [NP, Prep = (*for*)-P, VP, PP, S] X /⟨(Sum of money)⟩) of [NP, S] X /⟨(Human) & (Infant)⟩

at [Tense, Aux, PP, S] X /H$_6$))) ⟨(...t...)⟩

4. A solution to the problem of converses **343**

$$
\begin{aligned}
&(7.171)\ \ buy;\ ((((\text{Condition})\ (\text{Possesses} \underset{X}{[\text{NP, VP, PP, S}]} \underset{X}{[\text{NP, Prep}=(to,from)\text{-P, VP, PP, S}]})\ \text{of} \\
&\qquad\qquad\qquad\qquad\qquad\qquad \langle(\text{Physical object})\rangle \qquad\qquad \langle(\text{Human})\ \&\ \overline{(\text{Infant})}\rangle \\[2pt]
&\qquad\text{at}\ \underset{X}{[\text{Tense, Aux, PP, S}]} \qquad \underset{X}{[\text{Tense, Aux, PP, S}]} \\
&\qquad\quad /\text{H}_1,\text{H}_2,\text{H}_4),\ldots,(\ldots /\text{H}_3,\text{H}_2,\text{H}_5),\ldots, \\
&\qquad\quad \langle(\ldots t\ldots)\rangle \qquad\qquad\quad \langle(\ldots t\ldots)\rangle \\[6pt]
&((\text{Condition})\ (\text{Possesses} \underset{X}{[\text{NP, VP, PP, S}]})\ \text{of} \underset{X}{[\text{NP, S}]} \\
&\qquad\qquad\qquad\qquad\qquad\qquad \langle(\text{Physical object})\rangle \quad \langle(\text{Human})\ \&\ \overline{(\text{Infant})}\rangle \\[2pt]
&\qquad\text{at}\ \underset{X}{[\text{Tense, Aux, PP, S}]} \\
&\qquad\quad /\text{H}_6))\ \& \\
&\qquad\quad \langle(\ldots t\ldots)\rangle \\[6pt]
&((((\text{Condition})\ (\text{Possesses} \underset{X}{[\text{NP, Prep}=(for)\text{-P, VP, PP, S}]})\ \text{of} \underset{X}{[\text{NP, S}]} \\
&\qquad\qquad\qquad\qquad\qquad\qquad \langle(\text{Sum of money})\rangle \qquad\qquad \langle(\text{Human})\ \&\ \overline{(\text{Infant})}\rangle \\[2pt]
&\qquad\text{at}\ \underset{X}{[\text{Tense, Aux, PP, S}]} \qquad \underset{X}{[\text{Tense, Aux, PP, S}]} \\
&\qquad\quad /\text{H}_1,\text{H}_2,\text{H}_4),\ldots,(\ldots /\text{H}_3,\text{H}_2,\text{H}_5),\ldots, \\
&\qquad\quad \langle(\ldots t\ldots)\rangle \qquad\qquad\quad \langle(\ldots t\ldots)\rangle \\[6pt]
&((\text{Condition})\ (\text{Possesses} \underset{X}{[\text{NP, Prep}=(for)\text{-P, VP, PP, S}]})\ \text{of} \underset{X}{[\text{NP, Prep}=(to,from)\text{-P, VP, PP, S}]} \\
&\qquad\qquad\qquad\qquad\qquad\qquad \langle(\text{Sum of money})\rangle \qquad\qquad\qquad \langle(\text{Human})\ \&\ \overline{(\text{Infant})}\rangle \\[2pt]
&\qquad\text{at}\ \underset{X}{[\text{Tense, Aux, PP, S}]} \\
&\qquad\quad /\text{H}_6)))
\end{aligned}
$$

The general form of these lexical readings can be simplified as in (7.172) and (7.173), where 'X' stands for the variable categorized for the 'subject-of' relation, 'Y' for the variable categorized for the 'object-of' relation, 'Z' for the variable categorized for the 'indirect-object-of' relation, 'W' for the variable categorized for the 'secondary-indirect-object-of' relation, and 'T' for the variable categorized for the 'inflexional' relation:

(7.172) *sell*; (((((Condition) (Possesses Y) of X at T_i), ...,
　　　　　　((Condition) (Possesses Y) of Z at T_j)) &
　　　　　　(((Condition) (Possesses W) of Z at T_i), ...,
　　　　　　((Condition) (Possesses W) of X at T_j)))

(7.173) *buy*; (((((Condition) (Possesses Y) of Z at T_i), ...,
　　　　　　((Condition) (Possesses Y) of X at T_j)) &
　　　　　　(((Condition) (Possesses W) of X at T_i), ...,
　　　　　　((Condition) (Possesses W) of Z at T_j)))

As the general form of the lexical readings for "sell" and "buy" shows, these readings are exactly the same except that, where the variable categorized for the 'subject-of' relation appears in one, the variable categorized for the 'indirect-object-of' relation appears in the other, and vice versa. This suggests the definition of the 'converse relation' given in (7.174), where x is the image of y if and only if $x \in \{v_1, v_2, \ldots, v_n\}$ & $y \in \{v'_1, v'_2, \ldots, v'_n\}$ and, for $1 \le i \le n$, $x = v_i$ & $y = v'_i$:

(7.174) A constituent C is a converse of a constituent C' (and vice versa) if and only if their readings are the same except for the categorized variables $v_1, v_2, \ldots, v_n$ occurring in the reading of C and the categorized variables $v'_1, v'_2, \ldots, v'_n$ occurring in corresponding positions in the reading of C' (i.e., $v_1 \ne v'_1, v_2 \ne v'_2, \ldots, v_n \ne v'_n$ where $n \ge 1$), and if $v_i = v_j$, then $v'_i = v'_j$, and if $v'_i = v'_j$, then $v_i = v_j$, and, finally, for each v_i and v_j, if $v_j =$ the image of v_i, then the image of $v_j = v_i$, and for each v'_i and v'_j, if $v'_j =$ the image of v'_i, then the image of $v'_j = v'_i$.

We wish now to show that if there are two sentences constructed like (7.6) and (7.7) and if their converse constituents have readings that satisfy the conditions in (7.174), then these sentences are synonymous. Notice, first, that "sell" and "buy" are represented by (7.170) and (7.171) as words whose meaning expresses the same process, namely, the process of someone relinquishing possession of something to gain possession of a sum of money which someone else relinquishes possession of to gain possession of the thing. Notice, second, that the inverse positioning of the categorized variables in (7.170) and (7.171) says that the person relinquishing possession of the item and gaining possession of the sum of money, i.e., the seller, is described by the subject of "sell" and the indirect object of "buy," whereas the person relinquishing possession of the sum of money and gaining possession of the item, i.e., the buyer, is described by the indirect object of "sell" and the subject of "buy." Notice, third, that this inverse positioning corresponds directly to the inverse relations that "John" and "Mary" bear to the verb in (7.6) and in (7.7), as these relations would be picked out on the basis of the underlying phrase markers (7.15) and (7.16): "John" is the subject in (7.15) and the indirect object in (7.16), while "Mary" is the indirect object in (7.15) and the subject in (7.16). Thus, in (7.6) and (7.7) "John" denotes the seller and "Mary" the buyer. Then both (7.6) and (7.7) express the same proposition, namely, that John relinquishes possession of the book to gain possession of a sum of money which Mary relinquishes to gain possession of the book.

The reading representing this proposition expressed by both (7.6) and (7.7) will be assigned to them by the operation of the projection rule on the lexical readings assigned to the lexical items in (7.15) and (7.16). Consider the semantic interpretation of (7.15). Take first the process semantic marker that appears as the first component of the double process semantic marker that is the lexical reading of "sell." The variable categorized for the 'subject-of' relation appears in the semantic marker representing the initial state, and the variable categorized for the 'indirect-object-of' relation appears in the semantic marker representing the terminal state. Thus, the derived reading of the sentence (7.6), which will have the form displayed in (7.172), will contain the reading of its subject in the first state semantic marker of the first process semantic marker and the reading of its indirect object in the last state semantic marker of the first process semantic marker. That is, the reading of "John" will occur where ' X ' occurs in the first conjunct of (7.172) and the reading of "Mary" will occur where ' Z ' occurs in this conjunct. Next, take the process semantic marker that appears as the second component of the double process semantic marker that is the lexical reading of "sell." The variable categorized for the 'indirect-object-of' relation appears in the semantic marker representing the initial state, and the variable categorized for the 'subject-of' relation appears in the semantic marker representing the terminal state. Thus, the derived reading of (7.6) will contain the reading of its indirect object in the first state semantic marker of the second process semantic marker and the reading of its subject in the last state semantic marker of the second process semantic marker. That is, the reading of "Mary" will occur where ' Z ' occurs in the second conjunct of (7.172), and the reading of "John" will occur where ' X ' occurs in this conjunct. Thus, the derived reading of (7.6) will take the form (7.175), where ' R-"..."' indicates the reading of the constituent "...":

(7.175) $(((($ Condition$)$ (Possesses R-" the book ") of R-" John "
$\qquad$ at $(t^{(-n+((-r_1)+(-r_2)))})), \ldots, (\ldots(t^{(-n+(-r_1))})), \ldots,$
$\qquad (($ Condition$)$ (Possesses R-" the book ") of R-" Mary " at $(t^{(-n)})))$ &
$\qquad ((($ Condition$)$ (Possesses (Sum of money)) of R-" Mary "
$\qquad$ at $(t^{(-n+((-r_1)+(-r_2)))})), \ldots, (\ldots(t^{(-n+(-r_1))})), \ldots,$
$\qquad (($ Condition$)$ (Possesses (Sum of money)) of R-" John " at $(t^{(-n)})))$

Now let us consider the semantic interpretation of (7.16). Take first the process semantic marker that appears as the first component of the double process semantic marker that is the lexical reading for "buy." The variable categorized for the 'indirect-object-of' relation appears in the semantic marker representing the initial state, and the variable categorized for the 'subject-of' relation appears in the semantic marker representing the terminal state. Thus, the derived reading of the sentence (7.7), which will have the form displayed in (7.173), will contain the reading of its indirect object in the first state semantic marker of the first process semantic marker and the reading of its subject in the last state semantic marker of the first process semantic marker. That is, the reading of "John" will occur where 'Z' occurs in the first conjunct of (7.173) and the reading of "Mary" will occur where 'X' occurs in this conjunct. Accordingly, the first conjunct in the derived reading for (7.7) will be identical to the first conjunct in (7.175), which is the derived reading of (7.6). Next, take the process semantic marker that appears as the second component of the double process semantic marker that is the lexical reading of "buy." The variable categorized for the 'subject-of' relation appears in the semantic marker representing the initial state, and the variable categorized for the 'indirect-object-of' relation appears in the semantic marker representing the terminal state. Thus, the derived reading of (7.7) will contain the reading of its subject in the first state semantic marker of the second process semantic marker and the reading of its indirect object in the last state semantic marker of the second process semantic marker. That is, the reading of "Mary" will occur where 'X' occurs in the second conjunct of (7.173) and the reading of "John" will occur where 'Z' occurs in this conjunct. Accordingly, the second conjunct in the derived reading of (7.7) will be identical to the second conjunct in (7.175), and, consequently, the reading of (7.7) will be identical to the reading of (7.6), thereby marking (7.6) and (7.7) as synonymous sentences.

Here, then, is our solution to the problem of converse relations and our explanation of why sentences or constituents involving converse relations are synonymous. Though the treatment of the problem was given in terms of only one case, it is easy to see how it could be extended. In Section 6, we shall consider the application of this approach to some other cases.

5. A reconstruction of semantic fields

In this section, we shall sketch the manner in which the ideas about semantic representation developed in the previous section can be used to provide a formal reconstruction of the notion of a semantic field (such as that put forth by neo-Humboldtians like Trier).[26] This notion, stripped down to its linguistic essentials, is that the vocabulary of a language divides into classes of items, each marking off an integrated conceptual domain within which the conceptual space is differentiated into elementary regions whose boundaries delimit and are delimited by the boundaries of others. These elementary regions, either individually or taken together in groups, are labeled by words in a vocabulary, the elementary region or compound region labeled by a word being regarded as its meaning. Different languages label different sets of regions in a conceptual space and so can be compared with one another as we might compare different maps of the same geographic terrain drawn according to diverse cartographical interests. Hjelmslev cites the example of the region of the kinship field corresponding to the concept of the sibling relation which is broken down into the elementary regions 'elder male sibling', 'younger male sibling', 'elder female sibling', and 'younger female sibling', where Hungarian labels each of these elementary regions by a distinct word, English labels the first two together with one word and the second two

---

[26] See Ullmann (1962, pp. 243–253) for a convenient general exposition and Ullmann's footnotes for an extensive bibliography.

together with one word, and Malay labels all four regions together by one word.[27] Other fields studied within this framework are the fields of color names, intellectual qualities, moral properties, and animal terminologies.

After it is stripped of all its speculative trappings,[28] the main deficiency of this work on semantic fields is that it is carried out independently of the general study of the grammatical structure of natural languages and in a manner that is even more intuitive and informal than traditional descriptive work on syntax. But no one, I think, can reasonably doubt that the field theorists have provided interesting semantic problems, along with some helpful, though at times crude and metaphorical, ideas to use in orienting our thinking about these problems.[29] Consequently, persons concerned with developing the theory of generative transformational grammars have to try to incorporate the work of field theorists. The advantages on both sides are obvious. Given the principles of relating semantic interpretation to phonetic form in transformational theory, the problems raised by field theorists can be formulated within a framework far more suitable to their solution. Moreover, the ideas proposed can then be related to more traditional semantic problems in grammar, and the ideas can be expressed formally, without appealing to metaphors or to our intuitive understanding of language. At the same time, transformational grammar increases the range of linguistic phenomena with which it deals.

In taking the first steps toward a reconstruction of the notion of a semantic field, we shall reverse the perspective. Instead of selecting a conceptual domain studied by field theorists and seeking to formalize it within the framework of the theory of transformational grammar, we shall try to show that a formalization of a conceptual domain falls out naturally as a result of the treatment of certain linguistic phenomena within the theory of transformational grammar. The case we shall deal with can then serve as a model for others.

The example we shall use is the treatment of the converses "sell" and "buy" as developed in the previous sections. We shall try to show that this treatment can be extended within semantic theory to account for the conceptual domain that is covered in English by the class including, besides "sell" and "buy," the words "trade," "exchange," "swap," "give," "receive," "lend," "borrow," "inherit," "lease," "hire," "rent," and so forth, that is, the domain in the conceptual space having to do with processes involving transfer of possession.

To obtain such an extension, we start with the account of "sell" and "buy" given in the lexical readings (7.170) and (7.171), respectively, regarding them as defining a region within this domain. We assume that the readings of "sell" and "buy" and the readings of "trade," "exchange," "swap," "give," "receive," etc., have the same general formal structure and that this is what defines the conceptual domain in question. We assume, furthermore, that each of these other words that label regions in this domain can be defined by lexical readings that vary in formal structure from the readings (7.170) and (7.171) but in ways that leave the basic structure of those readings intact.

[27] See Ullmann (1962, p. 247).

[28] I have in mind here speculations about national souls, tie-ins with phenomenology and the Whorf hypothesis about the relations of language to thought, and so on.

[29] Contrast this assessment with Ullman's (1962, p. 250).

One such alteration of (7.170) and (7.171) is to eliminate their second conjunct, i.e., the second process semantic marker in each. This operation results in lexical readings representing a process in which the possession of something is transferred from one person to another without anything being given in return. We thus obtain lexical readings for the verbs "give" (corresponding to "sell") and "receive" (corresponding to "buy"). Since the resulting readings represent "give" and "receive" as converses, they explain why (a) and (b) of (7.176) are synonymous:

(7.176) (a) John gave the book to Mary
(b) Mary received the book from John

Another possible type of alteration involves a change in the semantic markers used to specify the condition of the state semantic markers in the representations of the initial and terminal states of a process. For example, we might replace occurrences of the semantic marker '(Possesses $\overset{[\,]}{\underset{\langle\,\rangle}{X}}$)' in the last of the state semantic markers of the first process semantic marker in (7.170) and (7.171) by occurrences of the semantic marker (a) of (7.177):[30]

$$(7.177)\quad (a)\quad (\text{Possesses } \overset{[\,]}{\underset{\langle\,\rangle}{X}} \text{ at } \overset{[\text{Time Adv, PP, S}]}{\underset{\langle\,\rangle}{X}} \quad /\mathrm{H}_7, \mathrm{H}_8)$$

$$(b)\quad \mathrm{H}_7 \quad v[.../] = (t^{(\alpha)}):$$
$$v[.../] \rightarrow (t^{(\alpha)}), \ldots, (t^{(\alpha+(+r_5))})$$

$$\mathrm{H}_8 \quad v[.../] = (t^{(\alpha+(-r_3))}), \ldots, (t^{(\alpha)}), \ldots, (t^{(\alpha+(+r_4))}):$$
$$v[.../] \rightarrow \overset{[\,]}{\underset{\langle\,\rangle}{X}} \| (t^{(\alpha+(+r_4))}), \ldots, (t^{(\alpha+((+r_4)+(+r_5)))})$$

The readings that result from this replacement represent a process in which someone *temporarily* relinquishes possession of something to someone else who gains possession of it over the time period during which the first person relinquishes possession, the relinquishment of possession being exchanged for a sum of money paid by the second person. Thus, these readings are appropriate lexical readings for the verbs "let" and "hire," respectively. The word "rent" (or "lease" used in the sense where it does not imply that the person acquiring temporary possession has signed a lease) seems to cover either of these cases.

Note, further, that this type of alteration in (7.170) and (7.171) can be made at the same time as the type discussed previously. Thus, if we were to make

---

[30] Actually, the symbol '$(+r_5)$' in (7.177b) is not adequate. What is needed is a categorized variable that will substitute the appropriate component of the reading that is the value of the variable to the left of the slash. This is shown by sentences such as "She borrowed the book until the examination" and "He borrowed the book for one minute," where the terminal point of the period for which the loan was made is designated either descriptively or in terms of a time constant (e.g., '$(+60)$'). The semantic marker in the selection restriction on this categorized variable will be '$(+r_i)$' so that we obtain the correct reading for sentences like "She borrowed the book for a while."

the replacement just described within the lexical readings for "give" and "receive" (obtained by deleting the second conjunct in (7.170) and (7.171)), we would obtain the lexical readings for the verbs "lend" and "borrow," respectively.

Still another kind of alteration involves replacing the semantic markers occurring in a selection restriction by other semantic markers. If, for example, we replace '(Physical object)' in the angles under the variable categorized for the direct object relation in the reading for "hire" by the semantic marker '(Vehicle for transportation)', we obtain the lexical reading for "charter."

To give another example of this type, the selection restriction '⟨(Sum of money)⟩' occurring in the first and last state semantic markers of the second process semantic marker in both (7.170) and (7.171) is what distinguishes the sense of "sell" and "buy" from the sense of "trade," as in (7.178):

(7.178)   Jack traded his mother's cow to a man for some beans

Thus, the lexical reading for "trade" should be identical to that for "sell" given in (7.170) except that where the latter contains the selection restriction '⟨(Sum of money)⟩', the former contains the selection restriction '⟨(Physical object)⟩'. This shows up in an interesting way in sentences like (7.179) and (7.180):

(7.179)   Jack traded the cow for a dollar

(7.180)   Jack traded (an Indian head) penny for a (Confederate) one hundred dollar bill

The sentence (7.179) does *not* have the sense that someone paid Jack a dollar for the cow; rather, it has the sense that a certain dollar bill was exchanged for Jack's cow in a swap. Sentence (7.180) is an even clearer example, having very much the sense of a numismatic transaction. The word "swap" can be given the same lexical reading as "trade," being only somewhat more colloquial, and so can "barter," which is slightly archaic. The word "exchange," aside from its specialized sense of bringing back to a store an item bought there and receiving in return another, more suitable item, seems to have two features that distinguish it from "trade," "swap," and "barter." One is illustrated by the sentences (7.181) and (7.182):

(7.181)   John exchanged toys with Mary

(7.182)   John exchanged his water pistol for Mary's

That is, when exchanging things, possession is only temporarily acquired. Thus, "exchange" is to "trade," "swap," and "barter" as "borrow" and "lend" are to "give" and "receive." It is not absolutely clear that this is indeed a feature of "exchange," but if it is, it can be represented in the lexical reading by giving "exchange" the same reading as "trade" except that in the representation of the terminal states in both conjuncts the semantic marker of the form '(Possesses Y)' is replaced by one of the form '(Possesses Y at $T_j, \ldots, T_{j+k}$)'.

The other feature of "exchange" is that it involves equivalent items. If this is the case, then, while (7.182) is meaningful, (7.183) is to some extent semantically anomalous:

(7.183)   John exchanged his water pistol for Mary's coat

Although this feature can be stated in a lexical reading for "exchange," its status is too dubious for us to give details at this point.[31]

 We have considered three types of alteration of lexical readings that keep their basic structure intact: (a) changing the number of conjuncts, (b) changing the condition specified by state semantic markers, and (c) changing the selection restrictions on categorized variables. Two general questions arise in this connection. First, what are the limits on such changes? Second, what other types of changes can be made to yield other regions of this conceptual space? Although these questions cannot be fully answered at this stage in the development of semantic theory, a brief consideration of them leads to some interesting consequences.

 In the first place, it is clear that, for the conceptual domain we have been considering, we can change the number of conjoined process semantic markers but there must be at least one such semantic marker. It cannot be changed into something that is not a process semantic marker. Furthermore, we can change aspects of the conditions specified in the state semantic markers, as was previously indicated and as would be required even more extensively for "inherit."[32] But we cannot remove the specification of these conditions as having to do with possession, nor can we eliminate the features of the process semantic marker that represent the change of possession. Finally, we can change certain selection restrictions, but, of course, not all. For example, in order that a reading represent one of the concepts in this conceptual domain it is necessary that its categorized variables whose values specify the possessor of the transferred item at the outset and the possessor at the end have a selection restriction that excludes readings for things that are not alive. That is, (7.184) and (7.185) must be semantically anomalous:

(7.184) The corpse sold the book to Mary

(7.185) The mud bought the book from John

However, there are changes in the selection restrictions that are certainly allowable, that is, that lead to other regions, other concepts, but are not required in order to obtain a lexical reading needed by a dictionary. For example, consider the reading that is identical to the reading for "trade" except that the selection restriction under the categorized variable 'W' (that is, the secondary indirect object) is '⟨(Artifact)⟩' instead of '⟨(Physical object)⟩'. This reading represents the concept of giving something over to someone in exchange for some artifact only. Although this concept is not in fact expressed by a word in English, nor perhaps by a word in any other natural language, it is, nonetheless, a *possible* concept: it could be so expressed, but just happens not to be. Thus, semantic theory will reveal—moreover, formally define—concepts which some or perhaps all natural languages contain no word to express. The existence of such cases, as pointed out by field theorists, provides an important way in which languages can be compared semantically. We can ask, relative to full specification of a conceptual domain within semantic

---

[31] Webster supports this feature, as do the intuitions of many speakers of English, but doubts crop up in connection with whether or not the sense of "exchange" in "The salespeople at the store told Joe he could exchange his pants for a baseball glove" is the same as that being discussed here.

[32] Where the procedure by which someone comes into possession of something must refer to the relinquishing of possession as a result of the death of the person who possessed it.

theory, which languages do and which do not map some word onto this, that, or the other particular region in it. The results of charting the regions mapped lexically by different languages and comparing them can be quite significant also for anthropology, which can then ask why, culturally, the languages L_i and L_j differ in their vocabulary for such-and-such a conceptual domain.[33]

Of equal interest will be the discovery of *impossible* concepts, ones that not only happen not to be expressed but also could not be, that is, ones for which the conceptual domain provides no region. The principles that determine the limits on changes taking us from one to another region in a conceptual domain will exclude the selection restriction under the categorized variable 'W' in the reading for "trade" from being '⟨(Introspective object)⟩', for example. A "reading" which has such a selection restriction but which is otherwise identical to that for "trade" will not represent a region of the conceptual domain. Accordingly, there cannot be a word in any language for a process whereby one person exchanges with another person an afterimage, a pain, an ache, a ringing in the ears, etc. Thus, sentences like (7.186) are semantically anomalous:

(7.186) John sold (traded, etc.) his afterimage (pain, ache, etc.) to Bill for ten dollars (Bill's car, etc.)

We might try to explain the impossibility of the concept of selling, trading, etc., one's afterimages, pains, etc., along the following lines. It has been generally recognized that such introspective objects are the content of someone's consciousness and as such belong uniquely to him. No one but John himself can have John's toothache, his sharp pain, or his red afterimage, where these objects are the particular ones in his consciousness. But not only is the relation of possession that holds of someone and his toothache *sui generis*, it is also the only possession relation that anyone can enter into with these particular objects. Accordingly, the object possessed in such cases is not transferable to another person as is required by the meaning of the verbs "sell," "buy," "trade," "give," etc. Furthermore, transferability here involves the termination of possession of something on the part of one person and the gaining of possession of it on the part of another. Therefore, the object in question must continue to exist after the first party no longer possesses it in order that the second party can take over possession of it. In the case of introspective objects, however, the termination of possession implies the nonexistence of the object. Once John no longer has his afterimage, that afterimage ceases to exist, and so it is impossible for Bill to gain possession of it in any sense of possession whatever.

The principles that say what changes can be made in the structure of a semantic marker to form another semantic marker that labels a different region in a conceptual domain and what the limits of such changes are (i.e., which changes are ruled out because they give rise to impossible concepts) can be viewed as conditions that define the notions 'semantic marker' and 'reading'. This is to say that such principles can be thought of as conditions that define well-formedness for the system of semantic representations employed by grammars since no semantic marker should be part of such a system if it represents an impossible concept.

---

[33] Thus, semantics can set certain problems for anthropology, as has, of course, been recognized in the area of anthropological linguistics known as *componential analysis*.

Although these are little understood at present, they will, of course, be a central part of semantic theory.[34]

Abstract or schematic semantic markers, like the marker which represents a process in which possession of something is transferred from one person to another, provide an account of the general form of one conceptual domain and distinguish it from other domains in the full semantic field underlying natural languages. Given such a semantic marker, the conditions of well-formedness allow it to be developed, combinatorially, by changes of the types illustrated previously, thereby giving rise to semantic markers that represent the individual regions in the domain, such as the lexical readings of "sell," "borrow," etc.

Now suppose that in this manner semantic theory recursively specifies a particular conceptual domain in terms of a set of readings. Then, the dictionary in a grammar of a particular language L maps the lexical items of L (its morphemes and idioms) onto some of the regions of the domain by associating each complex symbol in the lexicon of the syntactic component with one or more readings in the set. In this way, certain of the concepts in such a space of possible concepts are associated with certain phonological representations as their lexical meaning, and no phonological representation can be associated with an impossible concept.

But the dictionary is not the full grammatical mechanism for labeling regions in a conceptual domain. Syntactically complex, nonidiomatic expressions are associated with such regions by the operation of projection rules. This is one respect in which a reconstruction of the notion 'semantic field' such as the one presented here far outstrips the theoretic potentialities of the work of field theorists.

Consider the word "resell." In the first place, its meaning is included in the conceptual domain that we have been working with in this section. Second, this word is not a lexical item, but, rather, a syntactically composite form made up of a prefix and a stem morpheme, i.e., "re-" and "sell." Each of these elements must be entered in the dictionary as a separate lexical item, since, if "resell" itself were entered, there would be no explanation in the grammar of how the meaning of this syntactically complex constituent is a compositional function of the meanings of its parts. Moreover, the existence of a very large number of other forms with the same prefix, such as "re-enlist," "relight," "reopen," "refuel," shows that listing each of these forms as a separate lexical item, as opposed to listing each stem morpheme but "re-" only once, would enormously complicate the dictionary and would miss an important generalization about the language.

We now illustrate how the projection rule of the semantic component associates expressions in English with regions in a conceptual domain by showing how to form a derived reading for "resell" from the reading of "sell" and a reading for "re-." The lexical reading for "sell" is given in (7.170). The derived reading for "resell" should then be that in (a) of (7.187), where '$v[.../H_i, ..., H_j]$' is the reading that results when the substitution is made for the variable '...' and then the rules $H_i, ..., H_j$ apply.[35]

---

[34] Note here and previously the close analogy to phonology, as in the similarity of the notions 'possible concept' and 'impossible concept' to 'possible word' and 'impossible word'. But note also the differences: for example, there is no semantic parallel of 'possible word of L_i' and 'impossible word of L_i' (that is, if effability holds).

[35] The occurrence of '(7.170)' at the end of this reading simply abbreviates the whole of the reading given in (7.170).

(7.187) (a) $\left(\left(\left(\left(\text{Condition}\right)\left(\text{Possesses}\ {\overset{[\text{NP, VP, PP, S}]}{\underset{X}{}}}\right) \text{ of } {\overset{[\quad]}{\underset{X}{}}}\right.\right.\right.$ $\langle\langle\text{Physical object}\rangle\rangle$ $\langle\langle\text{Human}\rangle\ \&\ \langle\overline{\text{Infant}}\rangle\rangle$

at ${\overset{[\text{Tense, Aux, PP, S}]}{\underset{X}{\langle\ \rangle}}}$ ${/H_1, H_2, H_4/H_9), \dots, (\dots} {\overset{[\text{Tense, Aux, PP, S}]}{\underset{X}{\langle\ \rangle}}}{/H_3, H_2, H_5/H_{10}), \dots,}$

$\left(\left(\left(\text{Condition}\right)\left(\text{Possesses}\ {\overset{[\text{NP, VP, PP, S}]}{\underset{X}{}}}\right) \text{ of } {\overset{[\quad]}{\underset{X}{}}}\right.\right.$ $\langle\langle\text{Physical object}\rangle\rangle$ $\langle\langle\text{Human}\rangle\ \&\ \langle\overline{\text{Infant}}\rangle\rangle$

at ${\overset{[\text{Tense, Aux, PP, S}]}{\underset{X}{\langle\ \rangle}}}{/H_6/H_{11}\right)\ \&}$

$\left(\left(\left(\text{Condition}\right)\left(\text{Possesses}\ {\overset{[\quad]}{\underset{X}{}}}\right) \text{ of } {\overset{[\quad]}{\underset{X}{}}}\right.\right.$ $\langle\langle\text{Sum of money}\rangle\rangle$ $\langle\langle\text{Human}\rangle\ \&\ \langle\overline{\text{Infant}}\rangle\rangle$

at ${\overset{[\text{Tense, Aux, PP, S}]}{\underset{X}{\langle\ \rangle}}}{/H_1, H_2, H_4/H_9), \dots, (\dots} {\overset{[\text{Tense, Aux, PP, S}]}{\underset{X}{\langle\ \rangle}}}{/H_3, H_2, H_4/H_{10}), \dots,}$

$\left(\left(\left(\text{Condition}\right)\left(\text{Possesses}\ {\overset{[\quad]}{\underset{X}{}}}\right) \text{ of } {\overset{[\quad]}{\underset{X}{}}}\right.\right.$ $\langle\langle\text{Sum of money}\rangle\rangle$ $\langle\langle\text{Human}\rangle\ \&\ \langle\overline{\text{Infant}}\rangle\rangle$

at ${\overset{[\text{Tense, Aux, PP, S}]}{\underset{X}{\langle\ \rangle}}}{/H_6/H_{11})), \dots, (7.170)}$

(b) $H_9 \quad v[..\,/H_1, H_2, H_4] = (t^{(\alpha)}): \quad v[..\,/H_1, H_2, H_4] \rightarrow (t^{\alpha + (((-r_4) + (-r_5) + (-r_6)))})$

$\ H_{10} \quad v[..\,/H_3, H_2, H_5] = (t^{(\alpha)}): \quad v[..\,/H_3, H_2, H_5] \rightarrow (t^{(\alpha + ((-r_4) + (-r_5)))})$

$\ H_{11} \quad v[..\,/H_6] = (t^{(\alpha)}): \quad v[..\,/H_6] \rightarrow (t^{(\alpha + (-r_4))})$

Thus, "resell" expresses a process where something sold once before is sold again, but where the previous seller and buyer can be different from the present seller and buyer and where the sum of money paid in the former transaction can be different from the sum paid in the resale. Thus, consider (7.188):

(7.188)   John resold the book to Mary

Sentence (7.188) refers to the second (or third or fourth, etc.) sale. Let us suppose (7.188) to be represented by an instance of (7.187a). Then, the grammatical function '[NP, VP, PP, S]' in the variable within the semantic markers representing the condition of the initial (intermediary) and terminal states of the process semantic marker representing the earlier sale marks the fact that it is the same book that is sold. The dashes in place of a categorization in (7.187a) mark the fact that the former buyer and seller need not be the present ones (John and Mary in (7.188)), that, in fact, they are left unspecified.[36]

The lexical reading for "re-," therefore, should combine with (7.170) to produce a reading equivalent to (7.187). Let us suppose that we have a definition of the relation that obtains between a verbal prefix like "re-" and its verb stem such that the function '[Stem, V, VP, PP, S]' is the first term of this relation. Then the lexical reading for "re-" can be given as in (7.189):

$$(7.189) \quad re\text{-}; \psi \left(\begin{array}{c} [\text{Stem, V, VP, PP, S}] \\ X \\ \langle\ \rangle \end{array} \right), \dots, \left(\begin{array}{c} [\text{Stem, V, VP, PP, S}] \\ X \\ \langle\ \rangle \end{array} \right)$$

The operator 'ψ' in (7.189) transforms the reading that is the value of the first occurrence of 'X' according to the principles in (7.190).[37]

---

[36] Dashes are not really sufficient. In (7.190a) we introduce the use of Greek letters within brackets to indicate that the person who possesses the book initially is the one who gets the money and vice versa. Actually, intuitions conflict as to whether (a) the seller in the previous sale has to be the same person who is selling the article on this occasion in order to say that the present seller is reselling the article, or (b) the present seller need only have been the buyer in this or some previous sale. In either case the change required is trivial. (My thanks to J. F. Thomson for pointing this out.)

[37] It is interesting to note that the lexical reading for "re-" as given in (7.189) and (7.190) is a transformational rule, as would be the lexical reading for "un-," which would switch antonymous initial and terminal state semantic markers in process semantic markers such as in the reading for "freeze." Antonymy of the initial and terminal state semantic markers would have to be part of the selection restriction in the lexical reading of "un-" since constructions like "unbuy" are meaningless. Further, the need for such transformational rules in the semantic component does not seem to point the way to a deeper level of linguistic organization, and therefore they do not appear to have the profound significance that transformational rules in syntax had.

In certain cases with "re-," the original agent must be the same as the present agent. Consider the following sentences:

(a) John rethought the problem
(b) John re-entered the house
(c) Sam was readmitted to the hospital
(d) Bill was forced to relearn the list

One possible explanation is that verbs with this property do not take indirect objects.

(7.190) (a) Every grammatical function within brackets, except cases of 'NP, VP, PP, S', is replaced by a small Greek letter, identical grammatical functions by the same Greek letter and different ones by different Greek letters.

(b) The rules in (b) of (7.187) apply to the variables in the conjunction of process semantic markers that are categorized for the inflexional relation after the rules H_1, H_2, H_3, H_4, H_5, and H_6 apply; the range of each of the rules in (b) of (7.187) is the reading resulting from the rules named at the right of the slash in the antecedent of the rule.

The selection restriction in (7.189) is that the semantic markers that represent the terminal and initial states of the process semantic markers that are the reading of the verb stem must be different at least in their categorized variables. It is characteristic of the meaning of verbs such as "wait," "stay," "sleep" that the same agent appears in both the initial and the terminal states, and no change in this state comes about with the passage of time. Thus, the selection restriction in (7.189) accounts for the semantic anomaly of sentences such as (7.191):

(7.191) John $\begin{Bmatrix} \text{rewaited} \\ \text{restayed} \\ \text{reslept} \end{Bmatrix}$ in the house

Our reconstruction outstrips the theoretic potentialities of informal work by field theorists in another respect, namely, that it formally represents the regions in a conceptual domain so that they fall in the range of the definitions of semantic properties and relations. Hence, the traditional concern of semantics with these properties and relations is integrated with the description of the semantic structure of conceptual domains. As an illustration, consider the description of the conceptual domain developed here. On the basis of this representation scheme, we are able to mark the synonymy of (7.6) and (7.7), and, furthermore, we can mark the synonymy of (7.188) and (7.192):

(7.192) Mary rebought the book from John

Moreover, we can mark the semantic anomaly of (7.183), (7.184), (7.185), and (7.191), and the semantic redundancy of sentences like (7.193) and (7.194):

(7.193) John sold the book for a sum of money
(7.194) John gave the book to Mary for nothing

6. Suggested extensions

We will now suggest some directions in which the ideas presented in the previous sections can be extended.

Consider the sentences (7.195) and (7.196):

(7.195) John intentionally sold the book to Mary
(7.196) Mary intentionally bought the book from John

These are not synonymous: the first means that *John* entered into the sale with the intention of exchanging his book for Mary's money while the second means that *Mary* entered into the sale with the intention of exchanging some of her money for John's book. Moreover, the sentences (7.197) and (7.198) are synonymous with (7.195):

(7.197)   Intentionally, John sold the book to Mary

(7.198)   John sold the book to Mary intentionally

And the sentences (7.199) and (7.200) are synonymous with (7.196):

(7.199)   Intentionally, Mary bought the book from John

(7.200)   Mary bought the book from John intentionally

The obvious generalization is that the person to whom an intention is ascribed in such sentences is the person to whom the grammatical subject of the sentence refers.

Such facts about difference in meaning can be accounted for in a natural way by incorporating this generalization into the lexical reading of adverbs like "intentionally," "inadvertently," "deliberately," "voluntarily," "begrudgingly," etc. Since such adverbs occur in deep structure as modifiers of the main verb, they will be treated by the projection rule (3.86) in the same way as regular descriptive adjectives such as "female" are treated in constructions like "the female cab driver." That is, their reading(s) will be included in the reading of the head constituent that they modify as a proper subset. Accordingly, if the lexical readings of these adverbs take the form $(( ), ( ), \ldots, ( )(\begin{smallmatrix} [\text{NP, S}] \\ X \\ \langle \rangle \end{smallmatrix}))$, where '$( ), ( ), \ldots, ( )$' represents the meaning of the adverb and the value of $\begin{smallmatrix} [\text{NP, S}] \\ X \\ \langle \rangle \end{smallmatrix}$ determines the individual to whom the intention is ascribed, then the difference in meaning between (7.195), (7.197), and (7.198), on the one hand, and (7.196), (7.199), and (7.200), on the other, will be explained. In the former cases "John" is the grammatical subject, that is, the NP dominated by S, while in the latter cases "Mary" is the grammatical subject.

Another direction in which this work can be extended involves what I shall call *proxy cases*. Consider the sentences (7.201) and (7.202):

(7.201)   John sold the book to Mary for Bill

(7.202)   Mary bought the book from John for Bill

These are synonymous with (7.203) and (7.204), respectively:

(7.203)   John acted as proxy for Bill in the sale of the book to Mary

(7.204)   Mary acted as proxy for Bill in the purchase of the book from John

In a proxy case such as (7.201), the grammatical subject is not the person who possesses the article at the initial state. Rather, the person who possesses it at the initial state is the person referred to by the constituent we may call the ternary indirect object, namely, "Bill" in examples (7.201) and (7.202). The person referred to by the subject of the sentence is just that person's proxy. The proxy is someone who negotiates the terms of the sale with the other party on behalf of the real buyer or seller. Accordingly, we shall have to construct a new lexical reading for "buy" and a new lexical reading for "sell" that represent their proxy senses, and these readings will have to ascribe possession of the article referred to by the direct object to the proper persons in the initial and terminal states by using the appropriate categorized variables in the appropriate state semantic markers. Furthermore, these readings will have to include a formalization of the concept of negotiating the terms of a sale or purchase. This will have to be done in connection with an analysis of the semantic similarities and differences within the word family "proxy," "agent," "factor," "deputy," "attorney," etc., since the readings we want are ones that will explain the synonymy of (7.201) and (7.203) and the synonymy of (7.202) and (7.204) and that will exhibit the differences in meaning between (7.201) and (7.205) and between (7.202) and (7.206):

(7.205) John acted as Bill's attorney in the sale of the book to Mary

(7.206) Mary acted as Bill's attorney in the purchase of the book from John

The next extension has to do with making broader use of the central feature of the solution to the problem of converse relations, namely, the idea of positioning categorized variables one way in the reading of one of a pair of constituents and the reverse way in the reading of the other member of the pair so that, by the operation of the projection rule, the reverse order of other constituents grammatically related to them is compensated for in the process whereby the readings of the sentences are obtained. We wish to see how this idea can be applied to another type of case, one that does not involve conversely related constituents. This is the case of two phonologically identical but syntactically distinct lexical items that are not converses in the sense of the definition (7.174).

Consider the transitive and intransitive forms of the verb "open" as they occur in (7.207) and (7.208):

(7.207) John opened the door

(7.208) The door opened

One semantic fact to be accounted for here is that (7.207) entails (7.208) but not the other way around. We can account for this without denying the further syntactic fact that the constituent "the door" is the direct object of "open" in (7.207) and the subject of "open" in (7.208) if we employ the lexical readings (7.209) and (7.210) for the transitive and intransitive forms, respectively.[38]

---

[38] The dash in (7.210) stands for the grammatical relation in which the constituent "room" stands to "door" in a sentence like "The door to the room opened."

(7.209) *open* [+ —— NP, ...] ; ($\genfrac{[}{]}{0pt}{}{\text{[NP, S]}}{X}$ $\langle$(Physical object) ∨ (Physical event)$\rangle$ (Causes)

(((Condition) (Positioned to prevent passage between inside and outside

$\genfrac{[}{]}{0pt}{}{\text{[NP, Prep P, VP, PP, S]}}{X}$ $\genfrac{}{}{0pt}{}{}{/H_1, H_2, H_4)}$ of $\langle$(Enclosure)$\rangle$ $\langle\langle(..t...)\rangle\rangle$ $\genfrac{[}{]}{0pt}{}{\text{[NP, VP, PP, S]}}{X}$ $\langle$(Barrier)$\rangle$

at $\genfrac{[}{]}{0pt}{}{\text{[Tense, Aux, PP, S]}}{X}$ $\langle\langle(..t...)\rangle\rangle$ $\genfrac{}{}{0pt}{}{}{/H_3, H_2, H_5),...,}$

(((Condition) (Positioned to allow passage between inside and outside

$\genfrac{[}{]}{0pt}{}{\text{[NP, Prep P, VP, PP, S]}}{X}$ $\genfrac{}{}{0pt}{}{}{/H_1, H_2, H_4),...,(...}$ of $\langle$(Enclosure)$\rangle$ $\langle\langle(..t...)\rangle\rangle$ $\genfrac{[}{]}{0pt}{}{\text{[NP, VP, PP, S]}}{X}$ $\langle$(Barrier)$\rangle$ at $\genfrac{[}{]}{0pt}{}{\text{[Tense, Aux, PP, S]}}{X}$ $\langle\langle(..t...)\rangle\rangle$ $\genfrac{}{}{0pt}{}{}{/H_6)))}$

(7.210) *open* [—— NP, ...]; (((Condition) (Positioned to prevent passage between inside and outside

$\genfrac{[}{]}{0pt}{}{[\quad]}{X}$) of $\genfrac{[}{]}{0pt}{}{\text{[NP, S]}}{X}$ $\langle$(Enlosure)$\rangle$ $\langle$(Barrier)$\rangle$

at $\genfrac{[}{]}{0pt}{}{\text{[Tense, Aux, PP, S]}}{X}$ $\genfrac{}{}{0pt}{}{}{/H_1, H_2, H_4),...,(...}$ $\langle\langle(..t...)\rangle\rangle$ $\genfrac{[}{]}{0pt}{}{\text{[Tense, Aux, PP, S]}}{X}$ $\langle\langle(..t...)\rangle\rangle$ $\genfrac{}{}{0pt}{}{}{/H_3, H_2, H_5),...,}$

(((Condition) (Positioned to allow between inside and outside

$\genfrac{[}{]}{0pt}{}{[\quad]}{X}$) of $\genfrac{[}{]}{0pt}{}{\text{[NP, S]}}{X}$ at $\genfrac{[}{]}{0pt}{}{\text{[Tense, Aux, PP, S]}}{X}$ $\genfrac{}{}{0pt}{}{}{/H_6))}$ $\langle$(Enclosure)$\rangle$ $\langle$(Barrier)$\rangle$ $\langle\langle(..t...)\rangle\rangle$

In connection with these lexical readings, note that the semantic marker '(Barrier)' will be a common member of the readings of "door," "gate," "lid," "cover," "hatch," "barricade," etc., and the semantic marker '(Enclosure)' will be common to the readings of "room," "fence," "jar," "hall," "wall," "office," etc. Note also that in the lexical reading for the intransitive form of "open" the process semantic marker is not a part of a semantic marker expressing a causal operation. The reason is that (7.210) does not imply the existence of a cause of the process's occurrence, unlike, say, (7.211a), which should be taken as a short passive of a sentence structure whose underlying phrase marker has an indefinite subject, a transitive form of "open," and "the door" as its object. The absence of a semantic marker representing the concept 'cause' in the reading for the intransitive verb "open" seems clear on the basis of evidence like the fact that (7.211b) is not an affirmatively self-answered question but (c) is. Correspondingly, (d) is not inconsistent but (e) is:

(7.211) (a) The door was opened
         (b) Is there a cause of the door opening?
         (c) Is there a cause of the door being opened?
         (d) The door opened but without anyone or anything doing it
         (e) The door was opened but without anyone or anything doing it

Thus, the intransitive "open" of (7.208) cannot be derived from the transitive "open" of (7.207) by an operation of object deletion.

It is interesting to note that the simple notational scheme illustrated in (7.212) which abbreviates the lexical readings in dictionary entries like (7.209) and (7.210) completely undermines Fillmore's strongest simplicity argument for case grammars.

$$(7.212) \quad ((\ldots \underset{\langle\rangle}{\overset{[NP, S \gimel NP, VP, PP, S]}{X}} \ldots)(\text{Causes})((\ldots \underset{\langle\rangle}{\overset{[NP, VP, PP, S \gimel NP, S]}{X}} \ldots),$$

$$\ldots, (\ldots \underset{\langle\rangle}{\overset{[NP, VP, PP, S \gimel NP, S]}{X}} \ldots)))$$

The notation in (7.212) is understood as follows. The values of a categorized variable of the form $\underset{\langle\rangle}{\overset{[\alpha \gimel \beta]}{X}}$ occurring in a reading R can be readings of constituents that bear either the relation α or the relation β to the constituent to which R is assigned. But if a reading R has a pair of categorized variables $\underset{\langle\rangle}{\overset{[\alpha \gimel \beta]}{X}}$ and $\underset{\langle\rangle}{\overset{[\beta \gimel \alpha]}{X}}$, then the first variable is equivalent to $\underset{\langle\rangle}{\overset{[\alpha]}{X}}$ and the second is equivalent to $\underset{\langle\rangle}{\overset{[\beta]}{X}}$ (that is, the first occurrence of a function takes precedence over the second) just in case there is both a constituent that bears α to the constituent to which R is assigned and a constituent that bears β to the constituent to which R is assigned and the entire semantic marker in which the first occurs, namely, '$(\dots \underset{\langle\,\rangle}{\overset{[\alpha \downharpoonleft \beta]}{X}} \dots)$' and the symbol '(Causes)', is erased just in case there is no constituent that bears β to the constituent to which R is assigned.

Fillmore's claim is that case grammars make it possible to write one dictionary entry instead of two in situations like the transitive and intransitive forms of "open," but this cannot be a unique advantage of case grammars insofar as (7.212) enables us to collapse (7.209) and (7.210) into one entry (in which "open" is unmarked for syntactic transitivity or intransitivity). In the interpretation of (7.207), the occurrence of the variable categorized by [NP, S⌐NP, VP, PP, S] will be replaced by a reading of the subject "John," and each occurrence of a variable categorized by [NP, VP, PP, S⌐NP, S] will be replaced by a reading of the object "the door"; in the interpretation of (7.208), the part of the semantic marker (7.212) that has the form '$(\dots X \dots)$ (Causes)' is deleted (thus accounting for the previously discussed fact that the intransitive occurrence of "open" involves no implication of agency),[39] and each occurrence of a variable categorized by [NP, VP, PP, S⌐NP, S] will be replaced by the reading of the subject "the door."

Certain semantic markers so far taken as unstructured can be structured with respect to some of the ideas in the representation scheme for time relations. The need for such structuring crops up in terms of examples like (7.213), where the pronoun "him" is a pronominalization of the direct object of "married" and hence is co-referential with it:

(7.213)   Joan married a bachelor a year ago and was divorced by him today

Since it is impossible for a bachelor to divorce someone, the reading of "bachelor" cannot contain a semantic marker representing the concept 'unmarried' that is time-independent. That is, the sentence (7.213) is surely not semantically anomalous, as is the sentence (7.214):

(7.214)   Joan divorced a bachelor

Moreover, (7.213) does not entail (7.214). This situation can be handled easily if the semantic marker '(Unmarried)' has the structure '(Unmarried at $\underset{\langle\,\rangle}{\overset{[\text{Tense, Aux, PP}]}{X^{+(-r)}}}$)'. The other semantic markers in the reading of "bachelor" can, of course, be left as representations of time-independent properties.

---

[39] Note that we will have to add a clause to the definition of 'agent' (see Chapter 3, Section 9) that says that in semantic markers of the form '(( )(Causes)( ))' the semantic marker to the left of '(Causes)' is the agent of the process, event, etc., represented by the semantic marker to the right.

Finally, the approach taken here makes it possible to define some new semantic relations. Consider the semantic relation that holds among the ordered triples in (7.215) and among the ordered triples of expressions in (7.216):

(7.215) (a) sick, well, recovers
      (b) knows, doesn't know, forgets
      (c) asleep, not asleep (awake), awakens
      (d) alive, dead, dies

(7.216) (a) well, sick, becomes ill
      (b) doesn't know, knows, learns (comes to know)
      (c) not asleep (awake), asleep, falls asleep
      (d) dead, alive, is resurrected

We call this relation a *conversion triple* and define it as in (7.217):

(7.217) Three words or expressions form a conversion triple just in case two of them have readings that are state semantic markers belonging to the same antonymous *n*-tuple and the third has a reading that is a process semantic marker whose initial state semantic marker is one of the aforementioned state semantic markers and whose terminal state semantic marker is the other.

7. Time and type

Throughout this chapter temporal designations have been positioned within the propositional content portion of semantic markers. This served simply as a means of avoiding additional formalism unrelated to the topics of state concepts, process concepts, and the converse relation. Now, however, we must indicate the proper place of temporal designations in the reading of a sentence.

Temporal information in propositions is part of the propositional type; therefore, temporal designations will occur inside double parentheses. The reason is that such information specifies the period of time over which the object(s), couples of objects, etc., referred to by the readings inside heavy parentheses (i.e., the clauses of the presupposition) have to sequentially satisfy the condition of the propositional content. Thus, this information plays a role in the conversion of the condition of a proposition into the appropriate truth, answerhood, compliance, etc., condition. Take, for example, an assertive proposition like the one expressed by (7.218):

(7.218) A woman kissed a man

Here, the condition 'x kisses y' is converted into the truth condition that the objects denoted by the readings for "a woman" and "a man" sequentially satisfy 'x kisses y' at the time specified in the reading of the tense constituent, namely, at some time earlier than the speech point. Now consider (7.219) and (7.220):

(7.219) A woman is kissing a man
(7.220) A woman will kiss a man

In these cases the conversions effected by the propositional types are as follows. The condition '*x* kisses *y*' in (a) is converted into the truth condition that these objects sequentially satisfy '*x* kisses *y*' at the speech point itself, and in (b) it is converted into the truth condition that the objects sequentially satisfy '*x* kisses *y*' at some time later than the speech point.

Now take the case of pure requestive propositions, as in (7.221):

(7.221) Put on twenty pounds!

The speaker's request is represented here as that of asking the addressee to perform some act or acts to bring about satisfaction of the compliance condition. Thus, the propositional type of (7.221) converts the condition into the compliance condition that the object denoted by the reading for the addressee satisfy '*x* is twenty pounds heavier at some time later than the speech point than at the speech point itself'.

In the case of an erotetic proposition, such as (7.222), the request is represented as that of asking the addressee to provide the interrogator with a token of a specified sentence type (see Chapter 5, definition (5.48)) that makes a true statement:

(7.222) What is the meaning of life?

Thus, the propositional type of (7.222) converts the condition into the answerhood condition that the object denoted by the reading for the addressee satisfy '*x* provides the speaker with a true possible answer to the question at some time following the speech point of the question'.

Hence, the variables categorized for the inflexional relation, the temporalization relation, and any others relevant to the linguistic expression of time relations will occur within double parentheses, at the point in the reading expressing the propositional type where the information from the sense of the tense constituent, temporal adverbials, and so on is needed to specify the conversion of the condition. This proposal requires us to add a further clause to the definitions of semantic properties and relations like 'analyticity', 'contradictoriness', and 'semantic entailment'. Compare the sentences of (7.223) that result from choosing a verbal with the same tense from each pair of braces, on the one hand, and with different tenses, on the other:

$$(7.223) \quad \text{John} \begin{Bmatrix} \text{wants} \\ \text{wanted} \\ \text{will want} \end{Bmatrix} \text{to have what he} \begin{Bmatrix} \text{desires} \\ \text{desired} \\ \text{will desire} \end{Bmatrix}$$

The former are analytic, while the latter are synthetic. Accordingly, the definition (4.113) needs a clause requiring identity between corresponding temporal designations in the satisfaction condition of the propositional type of the including proposition (*viz.*, the one represented by r_i—see (b) of (4.113)) and in the satisfaction condition of the propositional type of the included proposition (*viz.*, the one represented by the part of R meeting (b) and (c) of (4.113)). Similar clauses will be required in the definitions (4.120), (4.141), and others.

Syntax, semantics, deep structure, and the prospects for a theory of surface structure interpretation

Part of the difficulty with the theory of meaning is that "meaning" tends to be used as a catch-all term to include every aspect of language that we know very little about. Insofar as this is correct, we can expect various aspects of this theory to be claimed by other approaches to language in the course of their development.

Noam Chomsky

In this chapter we shall be concerned with the distinction between syntax and semantics and its implications for the concepts of deep and surface structure. A failure to understand the basis of this distinction has caused much confusion in contemporary linguistics, confusion which is as unnecessary as it is unfortunate since the distinction in question can be drawn in a clear-cut way within the framework set up here in the first few chapters.

1. Syntax and semantics

When scientific fields undergo the change from description in terms of ordinary terminology to description in terms of technical terminology, distinctions arise that mark off parts of the fields that have not been satisfactorily demarcated previously. The separation of syntax and semantics rests on just such a distinction.

With the growth of a theory within a scientific field, ordinary concepts from the everyday language that formerly served as a descriptive vocabulary are replaced by a system of technical constructs specially designed to make description more precise and explanation more encompassing. Often the phenomena to be described and explained by the theory are not homogeneous but break up into several kinds, each kind having its own structure. In such cases, concepts from the everyday language are found to contain an admixture of features from phenomena of different kinds. Sometimes such mixed concepts can survive, with a bit of polishing, to serve as descriptive apparatus for the areas of interconnection. But more often it is necessary to replace ordinary concepts by technical ones, each referring exclusively and unequivocally to aspects of one kind of phenomenon, in order to sort out such admixtures.

The latter process is more characteristic of the recent growth of linguistic theory. Ordinary concepts from everyday language and traditional grammar are, by and large, being replaced by technical constructs that better serve the purposes of formal description: " noun," " article," " diphthong," " subject," " ambiguous," " part of speech," etc., are in the process of being replaced or redefined to obtain a suitable technical vocabulary for formal description and explanation within generative grammars. The rationale for such replacement or redefinition, as can be seen from a historical perspective, is that grammatical phenomena break up, broadly, into three kinds—phonological, syntactic, and semantic—while the ordinary concepts are a blend of more than one kind. Thus, as work in the field more sharply separates each kind from the others and creates heavier demands on the theory to provide apparatus to describe new complexities found in the internal structure of each kind of phenomenon, the need to differentiate the phonological, syntactic, and semantic elements blended together in the ordinary grammatical concepts becomes greater. For example, the concept of a noun inherited from everyday language and traditional grammar is that of a category of words that name persons, places, or things, as opposed to actions, qualities, etc., that take articles and limiting modifiers, and so on. This, however, is an admixture of semantic and syntactic elements. Accordingly, grammarians face the problem of having to differentiate these elements and redefine the concept to arrive at a technical construct suitable for the purpose of syntactic analysis within a generative transformational grammar.

But such replacement and redefinition must clearly recognize the proper distinguishing features of grammatical phenomena of different kinds. That is, an adequate technical vocabulary of syntactic constructs must reflect the ways that syntactic phenomena differ from semantic phenomena, on the one hand, and from phonological phenomena, on the other; an adequate technical vocabulary of semantic constructs must reflect the ways that semantic phenomena differ from syntactic phenomena, on the one hand, and phonological phenomena, on the other.

To specify what these differences are, we return to the discussion in the first chapter of this book. The obvious first approximation toward an answer is, in terms of that discussion, that syntactic phenomena have to do with the arrangement of phonetic or orthographic objects in concatenations constituting well-formed linear sequences and with the relations underlying them, that semantic phenomena have to do with the conceptual content or meaning of such sequences and their parts, and that phonological phenomena have to do with their pronunciation. But, although this answer is obviously right, it is nowhere near complete or specific enough by itself to be used in making decisions about the replacement or redefinition of particular grammatical concepts. What it does do is point us in a direction which, if pursued, can lead us to our goal.

If syntactic phenomena have to do with the kinds of arrangements just described, then they consist of such things as the division of sentences and their constituents into segments that comprise their natural parts, the categorization of these segments into types (noun, verb, adjective, etc.), ellipsis, pronominalization, apposition, agreement, nominalization, regular word order, inversions of word order (as in actives and their related passives, for example), case, clausal structure, and inflection. If phonological phenomena have to do with the pronunciation of these arrangements, then they consist of such things as sound distinctions of the sort that differentiate "bin" from "pin," distinctions like that between vowels and consonants, morphophonemic alternations such as in "meter"/"metric," stress, tone, syllable structure, rhyme, alliteration, and metric structure. And if semantic phenomena have to do with conceptual content, then, as we have argued at length, they consist of such things as synonymy, semantic ambiguity, meaningfulness, meaninglessness, analyticity, redundancy, contradiction, antonymy, and entailment.

Thus, just as we have taken this last set of properties and relations to circumscribe the domain for semantic theory, so we can take the former two sets of properties and relations to circumscribe, respectively, the domains for syntactic theory and phonological theory. On the basis of the notions 'syntactic phenomena', 'phonological phenomena', and 'semantic phenomena', specified in terms of these sets of properties and relations, it is possible to formulate a sufficiently precise principle on which to make decisions about whether a particular concept belongs inherently to syntactic theory, phonological theory, or semantic theory. Since these theories are themselves identifiable by their concern with explaining syntactic, phonological, or semantic phenomena, the concepts that provide them with explanatory apparatus must also be identifiable with reference to the kind of phenomena into whose theoretical explanation they enter.

This principle emerges directly from considerations of how the representations (or descriptions) of syntactic, phonological, and semantic structure must differ in order that the explanation of phenomena of all three kinds be achieved in the best possible way. It can be illustrated by an example from phonology where the distinction between what belongs to syntactic representation and what belongs to phonological representation is quite uncontroversial. Consider the case of distinguishing allomorphs of the same morpheme. If the grammar of English did not state the fact that [z], [s], and [əz] indicate allomorphic variants of the plural morpheme, it would fail to explain the different pronunciations of the plural construction in words like "boys," "cats," and "buses." But, on the other hand, if these phonological distinctions were allowed to play a role in syntactic representation, we would be unable to use a single plural morpheme to state syntactic regularities and the grammar of English would fail to explain phenomena of agreement in the simplest and most revealing way. All this is so obvious that the principle underlying a decision like that of making the concepts [z], [s], and [əz] the exclusive property of phonological theory is not explicitly recognized.

Once we do explicitly recognize the principle operating in such decisions, it can be generalized and given a formulation that makes it directly applicable to any question about which component of the grammar a concept belongs to. We propose the formulation in (8.1) of the principle for determining whether a concept belongs to syntactic or semantic theory:

(8.1)   (a) If the representation of syntactic structure must contain a certain gram-matical concept ϕ in order that one or another syntactic phenomenon be explained in the simplest and most revealing way, but the representa-tion of semantic structure cannot contain ϕ because its appearance would prevent one or another semantic phenomenon from being ex-plained in the simplest and most revealing way, then ϕ belongs ex-clusively to the vocabulary of syntactic theory.

   (b) If the representation of semantic structure must contain a certain grammatical concept ϕ in order that one or another semantic phenom-enon be explained in the simplest and most revealing way, but the representation of syntactic structure cannot contain ϕ because its appearance would prevent one or another syntactic phenomenon from being explained in the simplest and most revealing way, then ϕ belongs exclusively to the vocabulary of semantic theory.

   (c) If the representation of both syntactic and semantic structure must contain a certain grammatical concept ϕ in order to explain their respective phenomena in the simplest and most revealing way, then ϕ belongs to both syntactic and semantic theory.

Decisions about whether a concept is syntactic or semantic are not nearly so easy to make as decisions about whether a concept is syntactic or phonological or whether a concept is phonological or semantic. In the case of making decisions about whether a concept is syntactic or phonological, our intuitive grasp of the difference upon which the distinction rests is better than it is in the case of decisions about whether a concept is syntactic or semantic. What makes this so is that there is a fairly good literature about the difference between the formal relations out of which a sentence is built and the constitution of the elements out of which it is built (i.e., the constitution of the syntactic atoms in terms of articulatory features), and, in general, the constitution of such elements does not interact systematically with the formal relations among them that constitute the syntactic organization of a sentence.[1] In the case of decisions about whether a concept is phonological or semantic, our intuitive grasp of the difference is also better than in the case of decisions about whether a concept is syntactic or semantic. Here, again, there is a fairly good literature about the difference between the substantive elements out of

---

[1] Bresnan (1971) suggests that phonological rules can be ordered within the transforma-tional cycle. Part of the initial interest of this suggestion is, surely, that it conflicts with a well-motivated hypothesis about the absence of systematic interaction between syntactic and phono-logical rules.

which sound patterns and meanings are formed, and there is an essentially arbitrary correlation between sound and meaning so that properties of phonetic shape do not predict properties of propositional form and vice versa. On the other hand, our intuitive grasp of the difference between syntax and semantics is relatively weak: syntax and semantics are not arbitrarily correlated, and the literature concerning the difference upon which the distinction rests not only is unilluminating but positively obscures the distinction. Accordingly, in this case, there is a critical need for an explicit formulation of a principle that sets out the criteria for making decisions about which component of a grammar a concept belongs to.

The kind of difference between syntax and semantics that we believe will be brought out by the use of the principle (8.1) can be illustrated most easily by an analogy between a highly simplified artificial language and a natural language. As it stands, (2.5) may be regarded as the syntactic component of a grammar that specifies the set of strings Z in the vocabulary "a" and "b." The sentences of this artificial language, "ab," "$aabb$," "$aaabbb$,"..., are meaningless concatenations of uninterpreted symbols. But the sentences of (2.5) become a language (of sorts) if they are given an appropriate interpretation on which they express statements about some domain. For example, we might provide the interpretation (8.2):

(8.2)　　(a) Let an occurrence of the symbol "a" or "b" designate the number "two."

　　　　(b) Let the concatenation of n occurrences of "a" with m occurrences of "a" or the concatenation of n occurrences of "b" with m occurrences of "b" stand for the addition of the numbers designated by the symbols concatenated.

　　　　(c) Let the concatenation of a full string of "a"'s with a full string of "b"'s stand for the relation of numerical identity between the sums designated by the full string of "a"'s and by the full string of "b"'s.

On the basis of (8.2), the strings "ab," "$aabb$," "$aaabbb$,"... express the statements $2 = 2$, $2 + 2 = 2 + 2$, $2 + 2 + 2 = 2 + 2 + 2$, ... Of course, this interpretation is but one of the indefinitely many that (2.5) can be given. On other interpretations, the strings in Z will make different classes of statements; but under any possible interpretation of (2.5), it is the same syntactic system that undergoes interpretation, the same generated set of formal objects "ab," "$aabb$," "$aaabbb$," etc., that express different classes of statements.

Just as the same syntactic system can be open to many different semantic interpretations, so, conversely, the same semantic interpretation can be placed on different syntactic systems. Here no special example is required, since this is a familiar case in the study of formal logic.

The conception of semantics that emerges from this sort of analogy is that of an interpretation of independently specifiable sets of meaningless strings of inscription types (or sound types) by virtue of which they, or at least some subset of them, come to express concepts and propositions (i.e., are associated with conditions that determine when they are true or false, complied with, answered, etc.). Semantic principles are something over and above the principles of concatenation that determine well-formed sequences of symbols which by themselves are meaningless and open to indefinitely many incompatible interpretations. We are thus imagining that, if the syntax of a natural language were stated formally and completely, it would have the form of an uninterpreted set of symbols and combinatorial relations, vastly more complicated than but otherwise no different from (2.5). But this is not to say that the structure of the syntax does not place severe constraints on the possible semantic interpretations, nor that a knowledge of essential aspects of the semantic interpretation appropriate to a natural language does not place severe constraints on the syntactic systems of which it can be an interpretation.

In adopting the principle (8.1), we take the position that what distinguishes the syntactic and semantic components is, fundamentally, their technical vocabularies and not, for example, the types of rules that are used in these components or the conditions that restrict the operation of the rules. The reason is the obvious one that these components often use rules of the same type (as, for instance, transformational rules, which appear in the semantic component—(7.160), for example—as well as in the syntactic component), and, therefore, they could easily impose the same kinds of restrictions on the operation of such rules. Moreover, a distinction based solely on the organizational structure of these two components—one making no appeal to the difference in the vocabularies required for each—is of no interest whatever, since such organizational differences can be found between subcomponents of the same component (as, for example, between the base and transformational subcomponents of the syntax).

Few are tempted to think that syntactic markers like 'NP' inherently carry semantic information. This is partly because the property of being a noun phrase is not lexical in the vast majority of cases, that is, the property is not ascribed to a constituent by an independent specification in the lexicon, and partly because it is clear that there is no semantic property that all noun phrases have in common. But, unlike such characteristics of phrases, the syntactic concepts of masculine, feminine, and neuter gender, of mass and count, of animate, of human, and others that are formalized as syntactic features, all specify properties of lexical items and often have a distribution that, at least initially, makes it plausible to think that they are associated with certain definite semantic information. The tendency, then, is to take such correspondence in distribution to be evidence that these concepts inherently carry semantic information. The supposition is that such syntactic features can play a dual role, serving, on the one hand, as information that determines which transformations apply to the phrase markers that contain lexical items having the feature in question and what form their surface phrase markers will take and, on the other hand, as information that determines semantic properties and relations. The motivation for this supposition seems to be that one grammatical construct does the job of two, so that there is a simplification of the grammar. This is certainly a plausible position. Whether it is correct depends on whether or not such syntactic features must be distinguished from semantic constructs on the basis of (8.1).

We start on this question with the syntactic concepts of masculine, feminine, and neuter gender. They play their role in determining agreement between different constituents in a sentence, between nouns and pronouns, articles and nouns, adjectives and nouns, etc. The semantic constructs of maleness, femaleness, and sexlessness, which in many languages have a distribution similar to that of the syntactic features, play their role in determining semantic properties and relations such as analyticity, synonymy, and entailment. Assuming that agreement is a syntactic phenomenon while analyticity, synonymy, entailment, etc., are semantic phenomena, we can establish a distinction between the two triplets of concepts under discussion, a distinction that assigns the former to the vocabulary of syntactic theory and the latter to the vocabulary of semantic theory, if, in accord with (8.1), we can show that without such a separation the grammar will either fail to explain cases of agreement or fail to explain cases of analyticity, synonymy, entailment, etc.

The gender concepts are represented by syntactic features (i.e., syntactic symbols), regarded as unanalyzed marks, representing the possession of one of an n-tuple of properties, the full range of the n features providing an exhaustive set of categories for the classification of lexical items. The traditional classification of gender into masculine, feminine, and neuter can be expressed, as suggested by Chomsky (1965, Chapter 4, Section 2), by the features '1 gender', '2 gender', and '3 gender', respectively. If the lexical entry (D, C) for a morpheme D contains one of these three features, it is specified for gender; otherwise, it is not. For example, the lexical entry for the morpheme "boy" will take the form '(*boy*; [+N, +Det——, +Count, +Animate, +Human, 1 Gender, ...])', the entry for the morpheme "girl" will take the form (*girl*; [+N, +Det——, +Count, +Animate, +Human, 2 Gender, ...])', and the entry for the morpheme "stone" will take the form '(*stone*; [+N, +Det——, +Count, −Animate, 3 Gender, ...])'. Thus, each of these morphemes is specified for gender, unlike, for example, the morphemes "mutilate," "very," "of," and so forth, which belong to syntactic categories that do not figure in the gender system of English.

Whatever means we choose for specifying gender, the grammar must also account for the fact that (8.3), (8.4), and (8.5) are all grammatically well-formed:

(8.3)   The baby drank its bottle

(8.4)   The baby drank her bottle

(8.5)   The baby drank his bottle

The facts illustrated in (8.3)–(8.5) show that there cannot be a single lexical entry for "baby" in which only one of the gender features occurs. One natural way of specifying gender amounts to equipping the lexicon with three entries for "baby," each of which contains a different one of the three gender features, or perhaps one entry that is a suitable abbreviation of the three. Another approach involves a lexical entry for "baby" of the form (8.6), where we think of the pronominalization rule as able to select one of the three gender features in determining the surface form of the possessive pronoun in cases like (8.3)–(8.5).

(8.6)   (*baby*; [+N, +Det——, +Count, +Animate, +Human, 1 Gender, 2 Gender, 3 Gender, ...])

The first approach generates underlying phrase marker components like those shown in (8.7):

(8.7)   (a)

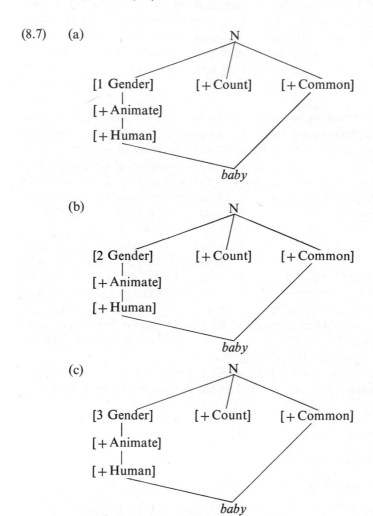

Case (a) of (8.7) would be the feature specification of "baby" in (8.5); (b) of (8.7) would be the feature specification of "baby" in (8.4); and (c) would be the feature specification of "baby" in (8.3). The second approach would ascribe all three gender features to the occurrence of "baby" in the underlying phrase markers of (8.3)–(8.5).

But, regardless of which approach is used to account for the grammaticality of the sentences (8.3)–(8.5), the distribution of gender features required to explain agreement relations will prevent us from explaining certain semantic relations if it is assumed that gender features also express their corresponding sex concepts.[2]

On the first alternatives we would fail to mark the fact that (8.3) entails (8.8):

(8.8)   A male or female infant drank its bottle

We would also get the false prediction that (8.9) and (8.10) are each contradictory, since such sentences would receive an interpretation on which they are asserting that some infant both has and does not have sexual organs:

(8.9)   A male infant drank its bottle

(8.10)   A female infant drank its bottle

Furthermore, it would be implied that the question (8.11) cannot be answered in the affirmative:

(8.11)   Is the baby with its thumb in its mouth female?

On the second approach to gender specifications, there are these difficulties plus further ones. First, the concept of a baby becomes internally contradictory because it must involve maleness and femaleness and the possession of a natural sexual character and the lack of it. Second, as a consequence, the sentences (8.3)–(8.5) must all be taken as expressing indeterminable propositions. Third, expressions like those in (8.12) and (8.13) must be considered redundant:

(8.12)   female baby

(8.13)   male baby

This means that we can no longer distinguish such cases from genuine cases of semantic redundancy such as those in (8.14) and (8.15):

(8.14)   female girl

(8.15)   male boy

[2] The arguments to be given here should be taken together with those given in Chapter 3, Section 4, on the same point. In connection with this discussion, note that the (semantic) sex concepts require a representation that expresses the information that maleness is the property of naturally having organs whose function is that of begetting offspring, that femaleness is the property of naturally having organs whose function is that of bearing offspring, and that sexlessness is the property of not having either type of organ. (We bypass the case of hermaphroditism, the case of naturally having both organs, as this would involve an unnecessary complication of our arguments.)

Elaborations on this type of argument to show that gender features have to be free of inherent semantic specification are rather easy to come by. Consider the sentence (8.16):

(8.16)   Now that Jones's baby has become a brother, it does not want to drink from a bottle

Clearly, this sentence entails (8.17):

(8.17)   A male does not want to drink from a bottle

If we wanted to account for this entailment without giving up the assumption that gender features also encode semantic information, we would have to say that "baby" in (8.16) receives a marker for masculine gender from "brother" and its relation to "baby," this marker being inherently specified for the property of maleness. One difficulty is that such a treatment implies that adjectives enter into the gender system in English, but this may be allowed to pass. However, "baby" must receive this marker *after* pronominalization occurs, since "baby" is pronominalized by "it" in (8.16). The implication, then, is that the referential aspects of such sentences determined by the syntactic relations holding between a constituent and a pronoun, the relations that underlie the anaphoric or nonanaphoric character of the pronoun, are in no way affected by the relations that underlie such entailments. But this is simply not so. Consider the sentences in (8.18):

(8.18)   (a) Now that Jones's baby has become a brother, she doesn't want to drink from a bottle
           (b) Now that Jones's baby has become a brother, he doesn't want to drink from a bottle

The pronoun "she" in (8.18a) is not open to an anaphoric interpretation (although it is open to a nonanaphoric one), whereas the pronoun "he" in (8.18b) *is* open to an anaphoric interpretation (as well as a nonanaphoric one).

The inverse of the difficulty with regard to (8.3) and (8.8) is found in (8.19):

(8.19)   (a) John moved his queen to King's Rook-4 and she was captured on the next move
           (b) A female was captured

In this case, identification of the concept of femaleness with that of feminine gender will lead to the false prediction that (8.19b) is entailed by (8.19a).

Rosenbaum (1967, p. 108) suggests the possibility of marking lexical items such as "likely," "sure," and "certain" for the application of the transformation he calls Pronoun Replacement (often referred to now as *It*-Replacement). Let us suppose that there is some appropriate syntactic formalism for classifying these items, such as assigning to them the syntactic feature [+Pro Replacement]. We will then obtain derivations in which surface phrase markers such as (b) of (8.20) are generated from underlying phrase markers such as (a):

(8.20) (a)

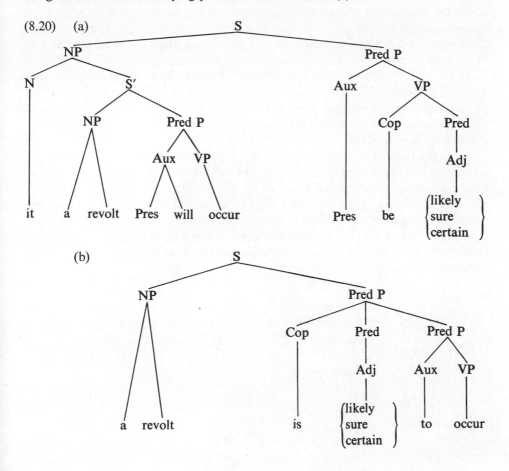

(b)

A phrase marker like (8.20a) underlies cases (b) and (d) of (8.21) as well as (a) and (c):

(8.21) (a) It is likely that a revolt will occur
       (b) It is probable that a revolt will occur
       (c) That a revolt will occur is likely
       (d) That a revolt will occur is probable

But a surface phrase marker like (8.20b) does not give us a well-formed sentence in the case of "probable," as we see from (8.22):

(8.22) A revolt is probable to occur

Thus, unlike "likely," "sure," and "certain," the word "probable" must be marked [−Pro Replacement] (or there must be some equivalent formalism to block the application of the Pronoun Replacement transformation) in order to prevent the generation of (8.22). But this syntactic feature, which tells us that "likely," "sure," and "certain" can appear where they do in structures like (8.20b) but "probable" cannot, can express no semantic information because "likely" and "probable" are synonymous. That is, since the assumption that [±Pro Replacement] carries a semantic distinction predicts that there is a difference in meaning between the synonymous words "likely" and "probable," it follows that this assumption must be false and that the feature in question belongs exclusively to the vocabulary of syntactic theory.

We next turn to the syntactic concepts of count and mass, which are represented by the features '[+Count]' and '[−Count]', respectively. They play their primary role in the statement of co-occurrence relations between determiners and nouns and between nouns and singularity and plurality. Count nouns can occur with predeterminers like "three," "seventeen," "a dozen," "many," "several," "few," whereas mass nouns cannot. For example, the expressions in (8.23), which involve mass nouns, are ungrammatical, as opposed to the expressions in (8.24), which involve count nouns:

$$(8.23) \quad \text{three (several)} \begin{cases} \text{blood} \\ \text{silver} \\ \text{water} \\ \text{bread} \\ \text{rice} \\ \text{fog} \end{cases}$$

$$(8.24) \quad \text{three (several)} \begin{cases} \text{boys} \\ \text{houses} \\ \text{crimes} \\ \text{ideas} \\ \text{days} \\ \text{toes} \end{cases}$$

Connected with this is the further fact that mass nouns do not pluralize, except in a very special case. Plural forms of mass nouns—"bloods," "silvers," "breads," and so on—are interpretable only as cases where the counting ranges over types or kinds. This is especially clear in a contrast like "much fruit"/"many fruits," where the former construction refers to (abundant) quantity and the latter to different kinds. And it is brought out further by contrasting cases like "some bread"/"some raisins," where the former construction means an unspecified quantity and the latter means an unspecified number. Consequently, we find ambiguities like that in (8.25):

(8.25) Mary had a little lamb

And similar ambiguities will be found in connection with a large number of nouns that are both count and mass, as, for example, those in (8.26):

(8.26)   lamb, fish, noise, cheese, oak, paper

Thus, it is clear that the features that formally express the distinction between count and mass words are essential to the syntactic component in order for it to account for such co-occurrence relations. But it is equally clear that these features cannot be taken to carry semantic information because there are many cases of synonymous constructions that differ syntactically in that one is mass and the other count. Consider (a)–(e) of (8.27):

(8.27)   (a) fog / ground-level clouds
          (b) hail / lumps of ice produced naturally in the atmosphere
          (c) footwear / articles of wearing apparel for the feet
          (d) arms / weapons
          (e) camping gear / artifacts for use in camping

Were '[+Count]' and '[−Count]' to carry semantic information, they would express a semantic distinction, and that distinction would differentiate the meaning of each of the mass nouns in (8.27) from that of the adjacent count nominal. But, since it is clear that each of these mass nouns is synonymous with its paired count nominal, it must be concluded that '[+Count]' and '[−Count]' do not express a semantic distinction of any sort.

It is sometimes supposed that 'countness' coincides with the semantic property of a thing's having a fixed shape or precise spatial or temporal limits.[3] Such an account is put forth to try to explain why count nouns refer to countables and mass nouns do not. The idea is that only things having a fixed shape, or precise spatial or temporal limits, are discernible in the way that is required for objects to be put into a one : one correspondence with natural numbers. But the initial plausibility of this supposition disappears when we recognize that among the count nouns are words that refer to things that are not of fixed shape, nor spatially limited, nor temporally locatable, as, for example, the count nouns in (8.28):

(8.28)   theorem, idea, number, mistake, meaning

If it is replied that there are concrete cases that fall under such abstract notions which have a fixed shape and are spatially and temporally limited (e.g., inscriptions, instances, numerals) and that they enable us to consider the abstract notions which they exemplify as indirectly locatable, then the semantic distinction alleged to coincide with the count–mass distinction can no longer be maintained, for the same thing can be said about mass words like those in (8.29).

---

[3] Jespersen (1933, p. 206), among others, takes this view.

(8.29)   knowledge, idleness, traffic, music, noise

> Quine (1960b) observes that "shoe," "pair of shoes," and "footwear"
>
> all ... range over exactly the same scattered stuff, and differ from one another
> solely in that two of them divide their reference differently and the third not at
> all (p. 91).

Quine's point is that reference in the case of mass nouns is collective, while in the case of count nouns it is distributive. Thus, like one of the senses of "all," as opposed to the senses of "each" and "every," mass nouns do not distribute predication individual by individual, as is done in (8.30):

(8.30)   Each (every) man is fallible

In this sentence predication is understood to ascribe the property of fallibility to each individual man, as opposed to sentence (8.31), where the predication is collectivized, that is, the predication is understood to attribute fallibility to whatever is collected together under the subject category:

(8.31)   (All) Men are fallible

But whether or not reference is divided, as in the subject of (8.30) but not in that of (8.31), the meaning of the plural of a count noun (e.g., "verses," "fruits," "candies," "whiskeys") and the meaning of the mass form of the same noun (e.g., "verse," "fruit," "candy," "whiskey") are the same. Thus they determine the same extension.

This is not to say that there is no difference in meaning between sentences like (8.32), on the one hand, and sentences like (8.33), on the other:

$$(8.32) \quad \text{This store has} \left\{ \begin{array}{l} \text{fruits} \\ \text{candies} \\ \text{whiskeys} \end{array} \right\} \text{to sell}$$

$$(8.33) \quad \text{This store has} \left\{ \begin{array}{l} \text{fruit} \\ \text{candy} \\ \text{whiskey} \end{array} \right\} \text{to sell}$$

But the difference has to do with distributivity and number versus collectivity rather than with something derivative from any semantic difference inherent in the syntactic distinction between mass and count. The difference between (8.32) and (8.33) emerges more clearly if we observe that a store that had only one piece of fruit (or candy) to sell could not truthfully advertise its ware by a sign on which (8.32) appears but could by one on which (8.33) appears. It can be explained in terms of a distinction between distributivity of reference and number in connection with (8.32) and collectivity of reference in connection with (8.33), where these aspects of the mode of reference can be plausibly accounted for as coming from constituents other than the count and mass nouns in question.

This account begins with the observation, already made, that distributivity is expressed by the meaning of the determiner constituents "each" and "every" and collectivity is expressed by "all." "Some" is also able to express these meanings, as in the sentences (8.34) and (8.35):

(8.34)   I had some candies

(8.35)   I had some candy

Furthermore, suppose that '[+Count]' is always selected by a distributive feature of the pre-article constituent and '[−Count]' is always selected by a collective feature. This means that we require the features '[+Distributive]' and '[−Distributive]' and a rule of the form (8.36):

(8.36)   Pre-article → [±Distributive]

But it seems clear that this is required anyway since pre-articles are divided according to whether they are distributive ("three," "each," "every," "many," "several," etc.) or collective ("much," "a good deal," "a little more," "a little," etc.) and since there is, in fact, selection with respect to these properties and the properties of countness and massness. For example, we have (8.37) but not (8.38):

(8.37)   three (many, several, etc.) girls

(8.38)   much (a good deal of, a little more, etc.) girls

And we have (8.39) but not (8.40):

(8.39)   much (a good deal of, a little more, etc.) butter

(8.40)   three (many, several, etc.) butter

A pre-article like "some" can be both distributive and collective, as in "some bread" versus "some raisins."

All that is now required is a selectional rule prohibiting complex symbols under the category 'Noun' from having the feature '[+Count]' in environments in which the pre-article is marked '[−Distributive]' and prohibiting them from having the feature '[−Count]' in environments in which the pre-article is '[+Distributive]'.

Now, we already know that plurality co-occurs with '[+Count]' but not with '[−Count]', except in cases where types, kinds, brands, etc., are involved, as in (8.41) versus (8.42):

(8.41)   I had whiskeys (whiskey) of other kinds (brands) but I prefer rye (Four Roses)

(8.42)   I had whiskeys (whiskey) but I'm still sober

Thus, we can account for the fact that a store with only one piece of fruit or candy cannot truthfully advertise using (8.32) but can using (8.33): in (8.32) we take the features representing distributivity and plurality to determine reference to more than one object in the extension of "fruit," "candy," or "whiskey," whereas in (8.33) collectivity determines reference to an unspecified number of objects in the same extension.

The syntactic properties of singularity and plurality determine the agreement of verbs with the noun phrase subjects. For example, (8.43) and (8.44) are both well-formed, but (8.45) and (8.46) are not:

(8.43)   The boy in the room is sick

(8.44)   The girls in the room are sick

(8.45)   The boy in the room are sick

(8.46)   The boys in the room is sick

If we were to attempt to make singularity and plurality carry the semantic information about the number of things involved, we would either fail to handle agreement relations or fail to account for certain valid inferences. For example, words like "trousers" or "pants" are syntactically plural and require a plural form of the verb, as shown by the fact that (8.47) is well-formed while (8.48) is not:

(8.47)   The pants I am wearing are dirty but everything else I am wearing is clean

(8.48)   The pants I am wearing is dirty but everything else I am wearing is clean

But from (8.47) we can infer (8.49):

(8.49)   Only one thing I am wearing is dirty

Or consider the fact that the sentences (8.50) and (8.51) are synonymous:

(8.50)   John is six feet $\left\{ \begin{array}{l} \text{tall} \\ \text{ten inches} \\ \text{ten} \end{array} \right\}$

(8.51)   John is six foot $\left\{ \begin{array}{l} \text{tall} \\ \text{ten inches} \\ \text{ten} \end{array} \right\}$

And so, also, are (8.52) and (8.53):

(8.52)   Ten cannon were brought up to the front overnight

(8.53)   Ten cannons were brought up to the front overnight

Furthermore, consider (8.54), where the subject is plural but nonetheless refers to one thing.

(8.54) The houses (books, etc.) to be sold are (amount to, number, etc.) one dwelling (volume, etc.)

Finally, there is no relevant semantic difference in connection with the nouns in (8.55) even though there is a singular-plural difference:

(8.55) Measles are not hard to cure today but cancer is

In Chapters 4 and 7 we set forth an account of how certain logical properties of relations might be represented, among which were the properties of reflexivity, irreflexivity, and nonreflexivity. It might be claimed, however, that their representation in the grammar can be more simply handled by employing the pair of features '[+ Refl]' and '[− Refl]', with reflexive verbs receiving the former feature, irreflexive ones the latter, and nonreflexive ones neither.[4] Thus, the argument might continue, the feature [− Refl] would serve to differentiate the grammaticality of the (a) case of (8.56) and of (8.57) from the (alleged) ungrammaticality of the (b) cases:

(8.56) (a) self-incrimination
        (b) self-assassination
(8.57) (a) John incriminated himself
        (b) John assassinated himself

It could be further argued that the feature [+ Refl] differentiates the grammaticality of (8.58a) from the ungrammaticality of (8.58b):

(8.58) (a) John perjured himself
        (b) John perjured his mother

Someone taking the position we are considering would then go on to argue that if the syntactic feature '[− Refl]' marks verbs like "assassinate" so that they cannot take reflexive objects, if '[+ Refl]' marks verbs like "perjure" so that they must take reflexive objects, and if the absence of marking in terms of either of these features allows verbs like "incriminate" to take a reflexive object or not, then '[− Refl]' may also be construed as encoding the semantic information that the activity expressed by a verb receiving this feature is one that the agent cannot perform on himself and '[+ Refl]' may be construed as encoding the semantic information that the activity expressed by a verb receiving this feature is one that the agent can perform only on himself. According to this position, then, these syntactic features not only serve to mark syntactic deviance but also determine the logical properties of reflexivity, irreflexivity, and nonreflexivity. However, such a

---

[4] Thus we might introduce lexicon entries like the following:

(*perjure*; [+V, +——[NP, +Refl, +Human, ...], ...])
(*assassinate*; [+V, +——[NP, −Refl, +Human, ...], ...])
(*kill*; [+V, +——[NP, +Animate, ...], ...])

See Postal (1966) for a discussion of the feature '[± Refl]'.

position cannot be maintained without incorrectly predicting some semantic properties and leaving others unexplained.

Consider the sentences in (8.59):

(8.59) (a) A mother has assassinated her $\begin{Bmatrix} \text{husband's only spouse} \\ \text{child's female parent} \end{Bmatrix}$

     (b) The only king alive today has just assassinated the single living male monarch

     (c) A mother has perjured her $\begin{Bmatrix} \text{husband's only uncle} \\ \text{child's male parent} \end{Bmatrix}$

     (d) The only king alive today has just perjured the single female monarch

     (e) A mother has assassinated her $\begin{Bmatrix} \text{husband's only uncle} \\ \text{child's male parent} \end{Bmatrix}$

     (f) The only king alive today has just assassinated the single living female monarch

     (g) A mother has perjured her $\begin{Bmatrix} \text{husband's only spouse} \\ \text{child's female parent} \end{Bmatrix}$

     (h) The only king alive today has just perjured the single living male monarch

There is no way to mark syntactically the noun phrase objects of the sentences in (a) and (b) of (8.59) as identical to their respective subjects. Similarly, there is no way to mark syntactically the noun phrase objects of the sentences in (c) and (d) as different from their respective subjects. Therefore, the cases in (a) and (b) of (8.59) cannot be distinguished syntactically from those in (c) and (d), and (c) and (d) cannot be distinguished syntactically from the cases in (g) and (h), in which the objects of the verb are identical to the subjects. Accordingly, the features '[+Refl]' and '[−Refl]' cannot exclude the ill-formed examples in (a)–(d) (and allow the well-formed examples in (e)–(h)). Yet, it is clear that (a)–(d) of (8.59) are grammatically deviant in exactly the same way that (8.57b) and (8.58b) are: like the sentence (8.57b), the sentences (8.59a,b) express an assertion that someone has performed an act upon himself or herself that cannot be performed on oneself, and like the sentence (8.58b), the sentences (8.59c,d) express an assertion that someone has performed an act upon another that can only be performed on one-self. Hence, the grammatical deviance in these cases will have to be explained as semantic anomaly, by the introduction of appropriate selection restrictions. But if such selection restrictions are added to the readings of verbs like "assassinate" and "perjure," it is no longer clear that the syntactic features '[+Refl]' and '[−Refl]' are needed. The [±Refl] distinction now seems to have no role in the semantic representation of the logical properties of reflexivity, irreflexivity, and nonreflexivity.

The next case we shall consider is that of the syntactic distinction between proper and common nouns. The properties represented by '[−Common]' and '[+Common]' in syntactic theory play their primary role in determining the co-occurrence of certain determiner elements and of relative clauses with nouns and noun phrases. Roughly, we can say that proper nouns do not take articles when they are singular but require them when plural and that the occurrence of restrictive relatives on a proper noun normally demands that the noun have an article. Given, then, that proper noun versus common noun constitutes a necessary syntactic distinction, we can ask whether a semantic distinction coincides with it, that is, whether these nominal features contribute to the senses of sentences or simply determine surface structure differences.

      If there is a coinciding semantic distinction, then it will be the case that the senses of proper nouns share some semantic element(s) which each has by virtue of being a proper noun and which will be represented in the grammar by '[−Common]'. If there is nothing that the senses of all proper nouns share, there can be no coinciding semantic distinction. Accordingly, one can demonstrate that there is no such corresponding semantic distinction if one can show that proper nouns have no meaning at all, since this of course implies that there is no semantic element(s) common to all proper nouns.

      We shall try to show this by arguing that there is no analytic sentence whose subject is a proper noun, that is, no sentence whose predicate explicates the sense of a proper noun. One group of candidates is represented by those classes of things to which we assign names and those of their attributes we consider in assigning names. For example, we assign names to people and normally take their sex into account in choosing a person's name. But proper nouns like "George," "Hillary," "Jessie," "Beverly," "Jean," though usually used to refer to a person of one sex, can also refer to a person of the other sex as well. We would certainly be surprised to hear of a woman named "John" or a man named "Mary," but there would be no inclination to refuse to believe it. What we would say is that the person has a "man's (or a woman's) name." Similarly, proper nouns like "Tom," "Dick," "Harry," or "Mary Ann" usually refer to human beings, yet they can also be names of cats and dogs, and even of inanimate things like cars and boats. Furthermore, the names of cities and countries—for example, "Wales," "Washington,"—can also serve as names of people. Even names we ordinarily associate with a day of the week or with a month—for example, "Tuesday" and "June"—can be names of people. The words that we customarily consider in giving names do not give rise to analytic sentences with proper nouns as their subject, since predications of "female," "human," etc., to the referent of a name like "John," "Mary Ann," etc., can be false, but an analytic sentence cannot.

      There is another group of candidates, typified by sentences whose subject is a proper noun 'N' and whose predicate says of N's referent that it named 'N'. But even these fail to yield analytic sentences because their subject can succeed in referring on the basis of any one of a large number of denotative relations other than that expressed by the verb chosen for the predicate. Consider (8.60a):

(8.60)   (a) John is named "John"
        (b) He was known to us as "John Wells" but his name was "Fritz Schultz"

This sentence cannot be analytic because it expresses a false statement if the subject successfully refers on the basis of some denotative relation other than 'name of' and the referent is not named "John." For instance, the referent of the subject of (8.60a) might be *called* "John" but his name might be "Samson." "Superman" and "Batman" are not the names of the characters to which they refer but, rather, what they are called under certain circumstances. Again, the denotative relation might be 'nickname of', as in a case where someone bears the nickname "Tubby" because of his shape, or it might be 'alias of' or 'assumed name of', as in the case where the alias or assumed name is adopted to conceal the person's real name. For example, someone in a World War II British intelligence team might utter (8.60b) in such a case. Or, the denotative relation might be 'pen name of', as in the case of "Mark Twain." The point is that when the subject of such a sentence succeeds in referring it is not necessary that it does so by virtue of standing to its referent in the denotative relation expressed in its predicate.

The fact that there are analytic sentences such as (8.61a) is of no significance to the question under consideration because such cases are also found with common noun subjects, as in (8.61b):

(8.61) (a) "John" refers to (designates, etc.) John
(b) "Tables" refers to (designates, etc.) tables

Further support for our claim about the semantic vacuity of proper nouns comes from the fact that those that are multiple names are not intuitively judged to be semantically ambiguous, that is, to have more than one sense, in the way that common nouns like "seal" are. For example, "Bulgaria" is the name both of a country and a mushroom, and "Washington" is the name of the first president of the United States and the name of its capital city, yet these words are not intuitively judged as having multiple senses. Furthermore, pairs of proper nouns like "Mark Twain" and "Samuel Clemens" name the same individual, but we are not tempted intuitively to recognize them as synonymous, as having the same sense. Finally, aside from the very special use of "meaning" employed in books on what to name a new baby, we intuitively treat proper names as devoid of sense. For example, we do not ask someone who has used an unfamiliar word that we recognize as a proper noun, "What does it mean?" Rather, we ask about the nature of its referent. With regard to common nouns in the same situation, on the other hand, we do ask, "What does it mean?" Since this question presupposes that its subject does have a meaning, we may then assume that speakers of English do not take this presupposition to be satisfied in connection with proper nouns.

The last case we shall take up is that of the syntactic construct '[± Possessive]' utilized in the derivation of genitive forms. This is virtually the opposite of the preceding case. With regard to the proper-common distinction, there is a multitude of syntactic constructions classifiable as proper, but none has semantic content. Here, on the other hand, there is a small number of syntactic constructions —e.g., the "'s," the "of" in examples like "the teacher of Plato," and the several forms of pronouns in the genitive case—but a multitude of distinct senses in connection with each construction.

Besides the ordinary possession as illustrated in the meaning of (a) of (8.62), there are other relations expressed by genitives, as illustrated in (b)–(g).

(8.62) (a) John's tree (dog, land, etc.)
      (b) John's death (birthday, Bar Mitzvah, etc.)
      (c) John's shadow (reflection, mirror-image, etc.)
      (d) John's doctor (milkman, mother, etc.)
      (e) John's vase (table, coat, etc.)
      (f) John's book (article, poem, etc.)
      (g) John's photograph (picture, statue, etc.)

In these cases grammatical form is quite misleading as to logical form, grouping together cases under one type of construction that diverge significantly in meaning. The constructions in (8.62d), although open to the interpretation that John possesses a doctor, milkman, or mother in the sense that he can use or dispose of them as he sees fit (i.e., in the sense in which they are his slaves), also have another sense. We can see what this is if we first look at the adjective "good" in connection with nouns like "doctor," "milkman," and "mother." "Good doctor" means 'a doctor who gives his patients adequate medical care and treatment'; "good milkman" means 'a milkman who delivers milk and other dairy products to his customers in an efficient and reliable manner'; "good mother" means 'a mother who takes care of the needs of her children and cares for them adequately'. Notice that in each case the meaning involves two roles, one of which is the role of the individual who is referred to (the doctor, the milkman, and the mother) and the other of which is a reciprocal role (the patient, the customer, and the children). On the basis of previous studies of the meaning of "good,"[5] we know that its sense is syncategorematic, and from this we can conclude that the specification of the role and its reciprocal is an inherent aspect of the meaning of the nouns in question. Given this, we can form a quite natural hypothesis about the senses of these cases: the first case of (8.62d) has the sense that John is a patient of the doctor; the second, that John is a customer of the milkman; and the third, that John is a child of the mother. The common semantic content of the sense of such genitives is that the referent of the subject of the underlying form occupies the reciprocal role to the role specified in the sense of the predicate.

There is no notion of role in the meaning of the cases in (c) of (8.62), but there is something that can be considered the parallel of a role and also something that can be considered the parallel of a reciprocal. Consider the noun "shadow." By definition, a "shadow" is 'an area of shade on an illuminated surface produced by the interposition of an object between a light source and the surface which blocks the light from falling on the area'. Here we have an effect and its cause corresponding to the role and its reciprocal. Accordingly, adopting the previous treatment as our paradigm, we can say that the first case in (c) has the sense that John is the interposed object that blocks light to produce the shadow (as an effect).

In the cases in (e) of (8.62), where the predicate nominal of the underlying form has a sense that contains the concept of an artifact, we have genitives which have a sense in which the referent of the subject is the artificer. Similarly, in the cases in (f) and (g) we find a sense in which the referent of the subject is the author

---

[5] See Katz (1964c; 1966, pp. 288–317).

(the writer or the artist) of the referent of the predicate nominal. Of course, the cases in (g) are open to another interpretation where the referent of the subject is what the photograph, picture, or statue represents, but this, we can conjecture, is because the sense of the nouns in question involves the relation of depiction.

Finally, in cases like those in (b) of (8.62), we have nouns whose meaning expresses an event in which some one person is principally involved, and, accordingly, these genitives specify John as the principal figure.

From these observations, it is quite reasonable to think that '[± Possessive]' does not itself determine the meaning of and the differences in meaning among the various genitive types, but, rather, that their meaning and their differences in meaning are determined by aspects of the semantic structure of their component constituents alone. On this view, the '[± Possessive]' that occurs in the underlying form of genitives has no meaning itself but serves only to provide a proper base structure for the derivation of related surface structures.

The preceding arguments cannot, of course, be considered exhaustive. It is neither practical nor even possible for us to consider every case of a syntactic element found to be necessary in the syntactic component and to argue that none can do double duty as symbolic formulations of semantic as well as syntactic properties. The particular arguments presented, however, can be reasonably taken as making a strong case for the existence of a division (in accord with (8.1)) of the theoretical vocabulary for representing nonphonological properties of lexical items into a set of syntactic but nonsemantic constructs and a set of semantic but nonsyntactic constructs.

2. Deep structure and its interpretation[6]

The conception of the organization of grammars and of deep structure in Katz and Postal's *An Integrated Theory of Linguistic Descriptions* (1964) and Chomsky's *Aspects of the Theory of Syntax* (1965) (which we will refer to in this section as "CKP") has recently come in for criticism from certain linguists within the transformationalist framework. They challenge the thesis that natural languages have a level of deep syntactic structure but on grounds quite different from those on which taxonomic linguists would do so. The transformationalist critics agree with other transformationalists that a single phrase marker representing the surface form of a sentence is not an adequate account of its grammatical structure. In particular, they share the view that natural languages have a level of grammatical structure underlying surface form and from which surface form comes transformationally. However, they deny that this underlying level of grammatical structure has the characteristics that it is said to have in CKP.

---

[6] Most of the material in this section was previously published, although in a somewhat different form, as Katz (1970). The author regrets the oversight that led to the omission of an acknowledgment to Manfred Bierwisch in that article. It was through a discussion with Bierwisch that I came to understand how to formulate lexical substitution operations so that a grammar of the type set forth in Chomsky (1965) can handle any lexical facts that can be handled by a grammar of the rival type to be discussed here.

McCawley (1971) appeared too late for me to include here a discussion of his replies to my criticisms. See Katz (in preparation) for this discussion.

In this section we offer a defense of CKP by seeking to show that none of the criticisms can be sustained and that the alternative proposed by the critics is a less adequate conception of the organization of grammars. In exploring this challenge, we shall find ways to amplify the account of deep syntactic structure in CKP, and this amplification will lead to an hypothesis about the aspects of deep syntactic structure that constitute linguistic universals.

Lakoff (1968) proposed what is now a fairly widespread misconception about CKP's characterization of deep syntactic structure. He wrote that CKP claims that the level of deep syntactic structure is defined by the four following conditions:

(I) Basic grammatical relations (e.g., subject-of, object-of, etc.) are represented at this level in terms of grammatical categories (e.g., S, NP, N, V, etc.)

(II) The correct generalizations about selectional restrictions and cooccurrence can be stated at this level.

(III) Lexical items are assigned to their appropriate categories at this level.

(IV) The structures defined at this level are input to the transformational rules (p. 4).

Lakoff, as he himself makes amply clear, takes (I)–(IV) to be separate conditions, each embodying an independent empirical assumption, which must be jointly true for the truth of CKP's thesis about deep structure to be maintained.

> It ought to be borne in mind that it is an empirical assumption that there is a single level of linguistic analysis defined by (I)–(IV). It is an extremely strong assumption and one which might well be eventually falsified by empirical evidence. For example, it may be the case that the level defining the input to transformational rules may not be the same level as that on which the correct generalizations about selectional restrictions can be stated (p. 5).

There was never any question about CKP's thesis about deep structure being an empirical hypothesis since it arose as an alternative to the taxonomic conception of grammatical structure, which held that a description of the surface structure of sentences could fully explain their grammatical properties and relations. But the formulation of this thesis as (I)–(IV) is a misrepresentation which, when coupled with the stress Lakoff puts on its empirical character, makes the thesis appear less systematic, more ad hoc, and more susceptible to falsification than in fact it is. In the form of the conditions (I)–(IV), CKP's conception of deep structure seems somewhat dubious because its truth appears to depend on the joint satisfaction of four independent conditions, none of which gives any indication of why the conditions should be jointly satisfied. But the appearance of dubiousness is created by casting the thesis in a form which suppresses some of its actual assumptions and presents its logical consequences as independent conditions.

CKP's thesis about deep structure should instead be stated in the form of an hypothesis that there is a level of syntactic structure for which the best account is a set of phrase markers K that satisfy the conditions in (8.63) and (8.64).

(8.63)   K is the full input to the transformational component of the grammar (i.e., the members of K and only these phrase markers have no rule of the transformational component in their history).

(8.64)   K is the full input to the semantic component of the grammar (i.e., the members of K give the syntactic information required for a compositional semantic interpretation of sentences).

The condition (8.64) embodies the two principles stated in (8.65):

(8.65)   (a) The semantic component is an interpretive system that operates on phrase markers independently generated by the syntactic component to assign them a compositional semantic interpretation.
   (b) The phrase markers on which the semantic component operates are just those in K.

According to (8.65b), rules of the transformational component do not contribute to the grammar's account of meaning. This principle, too, has recently come in for criticism. Chomsky (1970a) has argued that surface structure information also plays a role in determining semantic representation, and I have tried to answer some of his arguments in Section 4. But, in the present context, (b) of (8.65) is not at issue. Rather, the issue here centers around (a), which expresses the doctrine of interpretive semantics.

   Condition (8.63) is the same as Lakoff's (IV). It rightfully appears as an independent clause in any definition of deep structure since it explicitly denies the taxonomic view that the syntactic level which determines phonetic representation also determines every other aspect of grammatical form, replacing it by the view that the syntactic level of deep structure which determines constituents and grammatical relations determines aspects of phonetic representation. But none of Lakoff's other conditions are required as independent clauses in CKP's definition of deep structure. And (8.64), which is the heart of the theory in Katz and Postal (1964) and which is adopted in Chomsky (1965), does not appear among his conditions. What we wish to show now is that (8.63) and (8.64) together enable us to derive Lakoff's conditions (I)–(III), given only certain generally accepted assumptions about linguistic methodology and certain reasonable assumptions about some of the constructs involved. Such deductions remove the specious claim that the CKP hypothesis about deep structure is as extremely strong and thus as open to falsification as the formulation (I)–(IV) implies.

   Consider (I). The semantic component accounts for the meaning of a sentence and its complex constituents as a compositional function of the meanings of their parts and grammatical relations. It thus follows that, for (8.63) and (8.64) to be jointly satisfied, each grammatical relation on which a (compositionally formed) derived sense depends must be definable over the members of K. But, further, as we argued in Section 9 of Chapter 3, no relation definable over the members of K is a genuine grammatical relation unless it plays a role in determining how derived readings are formed from lower order readings. Given this, the claim that grammatical relations are represented at the level of deep structure follows from (8.63) and (8.64). The term "grammatical relation" does not refer to any relation formally definable over the members of K but only to those relations that determine compositionally derived readings. Thus, the set of relations that must be definable at the level of deep structure in order for (8.63) and (8.64) to be satisfied is the set of grammatical relations, and so their satisfaction implies that the level of grammatical analysis whose phrase markers are input to both the syntactic and semantic components is sufficient to define the grammatical relations.

Consider (III) next. From the compositional character of the semantic component, it follows further that for (8.63) and (8.64) to be satisfied the rules that generate underlying phrase markers must introduce lexical items into syntactic derivations. These phrase markers are the objects that undergo semantic interpretation, and, therefore, the underlying phrase markers assigned to a sentence must contain all the constituents of the sentence that have a sense which contributes to the derived sense of its other meaningful constituents. If these phrase markers did not contain the lexical items in the sentence, not only would some of the meaningful parts of the sentence, namely, its lexical items, not be available for semantic interpretation, but, because the lexical items are the elements out of which all the other constituents of a sentence are built, no other constituent could have its meaning explained as a compositional function of the meanings of its components. Therefore, the satisfaction of (8.63) and (8.64) implies the satisfaction of (III), and the latter is a consequence of the former.

It comes as no surprise that conditions (I) and (III) follow directly from the principle that a compositional analysis of meaning must be given in terms of phrase markers that are the input to the transformational component. The argument that this is so is, of course, essentially the argument of Katz and Postal (1964). It will be recalled that Postal and I used the fact that transformations characteristically destroy the representation of constituent structure in phrase markers (i.e., the marking of the constituents of a sentence and the domination relations that represent their grammatical relations) to show that semantic interpretation must operate before transformations in order to have the representation of constituent structure required for a compositional analysis of meaning. Thus, the argument in that book for restricting semantic interpretation to underlying phrase markers is also an argument for having these phrase markers contain complete specifications of lexical items and the domination configurations over which grammatical relations are defined. Accordingly, (I) and (III) are not required as independent assumptions in the definition of underlying phrase markers if these phrase markers are already defined as the proper objects of semantic interpretation.

Finally, let us consider (II). This condition is a direct consequence of (8.63) and (8.64) together with methodological considerations of the sort that have always been part of the development of generative grammar. The argument that demonstrates this is, in fact, one frequently used by transformational grammarians against the taxonomic approach.[7]

---

[7] See Chomsky (1957), Lees (1957), and Postal (1964a).

Given that an underlying phrase marker of a sentence contains its lexical items, the syntactic selectional and co-occurrence restrictions governing the appearance and arrangement of these items in surface structure should be stated in the rules that generate underlying phrase markers, since then they need be stated only once. The proper selectional and co-occurrence relations that they introduce will then be automatically carried over to the derived phrase markers that result from transformational development. If, on the other hand, these restrictions are not stated in the rules that generate underlying phrase markers, some of them will have to be stated more than once, producing an unnecessary complication of the grammar. Therefore, given that transformations have the property of preserving such restrictions so that they are automatically imposed on any phrase marker resulting from the application of transformations, simplicity considerations make (II) a consequence of (8.63) and (8.64).[8]

We may now ask whether the statement of the deep structure hypothesis in the form (8.63) and (8.64) gives an indication of why these two conditions should be jointly satisfied by a single level of linguistic analysis. Besides (8.63) and (8.64), which relate the syntactic and semantic components of a grammar, the theory in CKP contains a third condition, (8.66), relating the syntactic and phonological components:

(8.66) The phrase markers that have a greater number of transformations in their history than any other phrase marker in their T-marker (i.e., the superficial or final derived phrase markers) are the full input to the phonological component of the grammar (that is, the syntactic information required for the phonological interpretation of a sentence is given by its superficial phrase marker).

We note that (8.63) and (8.64) together with (8.66) express an hypothesis about how sound and meaning are correlated within a natural language: the transformational connection between the superficial phrase marker and the underlying phrase markers expresses the correlation between the pronunciation and the meaning of a sentence. The superficial phrase marker is the object that receives an interpretation in terms of pronunciation and the underlying phrase markers are the objects that receive an interpretation in terms of meaning, and these interpretations are correlated by virtue of the transformational connection between the objects that receive them.

The fact that (8.63), (8.64), and (8.66) together express this hypothesis about the correlation of sound and meaning makes these conditions defining the level of deep structure seem far more systematic, less ad hoc, and less susceptible to accidental empirical disconfirmation than Lakoff's conditions (I)–(IV). Our reason for expecting them to be jointly satisfied is, then, the reason for expecting their account of the correlation between sound and meaning to be true.

The criticisms of CKP's conception of grammar with which we are concerned here take the form of objections to (8.64) and, in particular, to (8.65a). They are not isolated disagreements, constituting (in the minds of their proponents)

---

[8] For further discussion see Katz (1971, pp. 320–322).

a set of unrelated puzzles about the adequacy of CKP. Rather, they are taken as supporting a different conception of the relation of the semantic component to the syntactic component. Thus, these criticisms should be examined as part of the case made by the advocates of an alternative conception of the relation between sound and meaning.

This alternative theory is called *generative semantics*. Its name was chosen, presumably, to reflect the fact that the theory denies that semantic representations are assigned as interpretations of syntactic structure, claiming, instead, that they are independently generated. Accordingly, the advocates of this theory refer to CKP's conception of semantics as *interpretive semantics*. However, "generative semantics" is, in one sense, an ill-chosen label. Any conception of semantic interpretation must, as part of a generative grammar, be generative in the sense of Post (1944). That is, the grammar itself must be a formal system, and the assignment of readings to constituents must be computable in the grammar. Chomsky (1957; 1959) has stressed this technical sense of "generative" as the term is used in contemporary linguistics, and he has complained, quite rightly, about its misconstrual when taken to indicate that "sentence-generating grammar(s) consider language from the point of view of the speaker rather than the hearer" (1959, pp. 137–138, note 1). It is my impression that those who misinterpret sentence-generating grammars in this way are thereby encouraged to be more favorably disposed to a conception of grammatical theory that makes representations of meaning the logically prior objects in the grammar, those from which sentence construction proceeds. With this caution, we may use this term in accord with the technical sense generative semanticists introduced, as a label referring to the theory of grammar in which a system of semantics takes the place of the base component of the syntactic component as the generative source of a grammar.

The central thesis of this theory is that the semantic component provides the input to the transformational component either directly or after the output of the semantic component has received some or full formative specification. Therefore, on this proposal, the relation between the syntactic and semantic components expressed in (8.64) is reversed. Instead of a purely syntactic base component whose output provides the input to both the semantic and transformational components, there is a component that generates semantic representations which are the input, directly or indirectly, to a transformational component that maps them onto surface structure representations.

This issue between the interpretive and generative conceptions is thus a controversy about which of two *organizational universals* should be included in linguistic theory. By "organizational universal" I mean an hypothesis that orders the components of a grammar with respect to one another, which provides directionality in the process of sentence generation. Such universals state that a component A is prior to a component B because the information in the output of A is necessary for the operation of the rules in B (i.e., the rules of B are stated, in part, in terms of this information). Thus, in this sense of directionality, the transformational component is prior to the phonological component, insofar as information about segmentation in surface structure is necessary for the operation of phonological rules. Hence, the two organizational universals in question can be schematically represented in the following ways. Interpretive semantics presents the organization of grammars illustrated in (8.67) (where $K_1, \ldots, K_n$ are the underlying phrase markers for the sentence with the surface phrase marker S), whereas generative semantics presents the organization of grammars shown in (8.68) (where $I_1, \ldots, I_n$ are the semantic representations of the sentence with the surface phrase marker S):

(8.67)

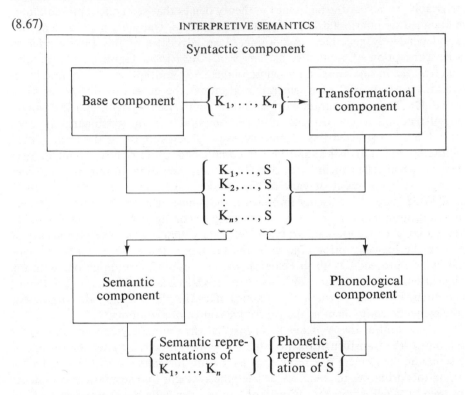

INTERPRETIVE SEMANTICS

It can be seen from (8.68) that a grammar built on the model of generative semantics relates semantic representations of sentences to superficial phrase markers and, ultimately, to phonetic representations by transformational rules, without the intervening level of underlying phrase markers. Generative semantics thus differs from CKP in eliminating both the generative base component and a semantic component formulated as a system for interpreting the objects generated by the base. Phrase markers are not independently generated by phrase structure rules of a CKP base and lexical insertion. Since there is no base, and consequently no underlying phrase markers, there are no syntactic objects to be interpreted semantically, and hence the semantic component cannot be interpretive. Accordingly, the explanation of how sound and meaning are correlated assumes that sound is derived from meaning: the relation of sound to meaning is essentially like the relation of surface structure to deep structure in CKP.

This difference between the generative and interpretive conceptions of the organization of grammars is the *only* real point of controversy. It is sometimes suggested that another point at issue is whether syntactic transformations utilize

(8.68)

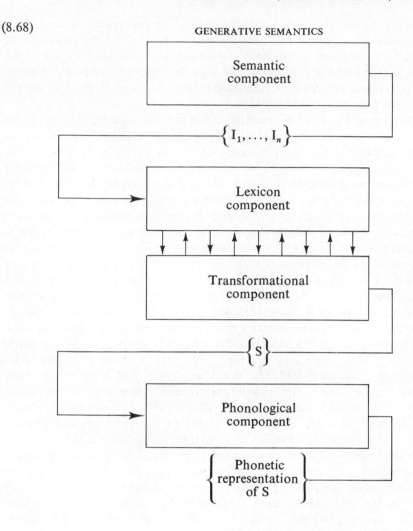

GENERATIVE SEMANTICS

semantic information. I have often argued that they do not, while advocates of generative semantics invariably argue that they do. But, logically, both the interpretive and the generative conceptions of the organization of grammar are independent of any claim about the type of information transformations utilize. On the interpretive conception, the question of whether transformations avail themselves of semantic information is left open since transformations can be written that apply either to underlying phrase markers or to semantically interpreted underlying phrase markers, and the process of transformational development can be made logically posterior to the process of interpreting underlying phrase markers. On the generative semantics conception, the question is also left open because the lexicon component can be formulated so that the semantic symbols in the I's are replaced by lexical items and syntactic symbols before they reach the transformational component. Of course the interpretive conception has been framed on the basis of the view that the rules of the base do not use semantic information, and the generative conception has been framed on the basis of the view that the rules of lexical substitution and transformation do use semantic information. But since both conceptions can incorporate the view on which the other was framed, there can be no issue between them about the nature of the information utilized in the structure indices of transformations.

Advocates of generative semantics claim that, on their theory, operations inserting lexical items are interspersed among transformational operations, so that lexical substitution can occur at various points in a transformational derivation. (The arrows going back and forth between the lexicon component and the transformational component in (8.68) are intended to represent this claim.) However, free interspersal of lexical insertion is also not a point of controversy between the theories of generative semantics and interpretive semantics. Grammars fashioned on the model of generative semantics could restrict lexical substitution to a pretransformational stage. Grammars fashioned on the model of interpretive semantics could allow interspersal of operations inserting lexical items among transformational operations. If grammars of the latter type were to permit such interspersal, the semantic component would have to apply to some phrase markers outside of K, namely, to those derived phrase markers where lexical items not present in the underlying phrase markers make their appearance. As a consequence, we would be forced to reject (8.65b). But this is logically independent of whether or not we accept (8.65a), which states the theory of interpretive semantics and which can be maintained together with free interspersal of lexical items in the transformational process. Whether insertion of lexical items is free or constrained, and, in particular, constrained pretransformationally, is really an issue about whether derived constituent structure contributes to semantic interpretation and, as such, has no place in the present discussion. (See Katz (1971, pp 320–322).)

Apart from the logic of the situation, as just sketched, it is clear that much of the motivation for generative semantics stems from the supposition that the formal apparatus for constructing semantic representations is the same, or nearly the same, as that required for syntactic objects that undergo transformational development. McCawley (1969a), who is perhaps the chief proponent of generative semantics, writes:

> I believe ... that syntactic and semantic representations are objects of the same formal nature, namely, ordered trees, whose non-terminal nodes are labelled by syntactic category symbols, and that in each language there is a single system of transformations which convert semantic representations of sentences into their superficial form (p. 55).

McCawley's claim has two parts. First, he contends that the formal apparatus for grouping the components of semantic representations is the same as that used for grouping the terminal elements of phrase markers in syntactic representation. Second, he contends that the components of semantic representations so grouped can be properly categorized as nouns, noun phrases, verbs, verb phrases, adjectives, and so on. The former claim is trivial and very likely true. The latter is nontrivial and very likely false.

The first claim is certainly one that no advocate of interpretive semantics could argue with, since the apparatus of trees (or parenthesization) has been used by interpretive semanticists to formulate semantic representations. Since it has been the position of interpretive semantics all along that this apparatus is common to both syntactic and semantic description, the truth of McCawley's first claim shows nothing about the merits of his theory. The utility of such apparatus seems to be a very general matter insofar as trees (or parenthesization) is relevant in every subject where hierarchical structure has to be described, as in biological taxonomies, genealogy, and electronic circuitry.

The second claim, however, says that the concepts and propositions represented by the components of semantic representations are correctly classified as nouns, noun phrases, verbs, etc. This makes sense only if it is true that all and only those concepts and propositions classified as nouns (or as noun phrases or as verbs, etc.) share some semantic property. This is the thesis Weinreich (1966) put forth when he wrote:

> the major classes are nouns, verbs, adjectives, and adverbs; ... All members of a major class uniquely share a distinguishing semantic feature.... We intend the distinguishing feature of each major morpheme class, e.g., [+Noun], to be taken as semantic in the full sense of the word; more revealing names might be 'thingness' or 'substantiality'; 'quality' (for [+Adjectival]), and so on (p. 432).

But it is amply clear that a great many of the nouns (or noun phrases) of a language do not have the concept of thingness (or substantiality) as part of their meaning. For example, the English nouns "virtue," "truth," "zero," "pain," "itch," "image," "theorem," "space," "time," "thrift," "hole" are enough to definitely refute Weinreich's thesis and, further, to show that there is nothing semantic common to the meaning of every noun (or noun phrase).

The other claim of Weinreich's, that the concept of quality is part of the meaning of every adjective, is, for all intents and purposes, unintelligible. The concept of quality intended cannot be Aristotle's category of quality, since many adjectives express relations. Nor can it be the ordinary notion of an inherent attribute of a thing. Adjectives such as "fictional," "mythological," "real," "fake," "counterfeit," "genuine," "possible," "probable," "necessary," "complete," "permanent," "tentative," "different," "similar," "familiar," "esoteric" do not necessarily express attributes of the things of which they are predicated.

The more fundamental claim of generative semantics is not that major categories like noun, verb, adjective involve semantic information but rather that their subcategories (mass noun, proper noun, etc.) do. This claim receives its strongest formulation in the thesis that the vocabulary for semantic representation is identical to, or included in, the vocabulary for syntactic representation at the lexical level.

Let us consider some counterexamples to this aspect of the thesis that the formal apparatus for contructing semantic representations is essentially the same as that for syntactic analysis. McCawley (1968b) puts the claim in the form of the thesis that all selection in the grammar is accomplished exclusively in terms of semantic constructs. He says:

> I maintain first that any piece of information which may figure in the semantic representation of an item may figure in a selection restriction and secondly that no other information ever figures in selection restrictions (p. 134).

There is no need to consider McCawley's argument for the first part of this claim, since, if sound, it supports interpretive and generative semantics alike. The second part, however, requires careful examination, since it would support generative semantics against interpretive semantics.

This part of McCawley's argument must be construed to be about selection restrictions, not in the narrow sense in which this term has been used to describe the formal device in an interpretive semantic component which prevents certain derived readings from being formed, but in the broad sense in which it refers to any constraint that prevents the generation of a grammatical, nonphonological deviance. Thus, as long as neither this second claim nor its denial is established, it remains an open question whether information that figures in semantic representations can also figure in syntactic selection. Granted that such information figures in selection, it may only figure in semantic selection (i.e., enable us to mark semantic anomalousness rather than syntactic ill-formedness), while syntactic selection is accomplished by information that figures only in syntactic representations. McCawley's (1968b) case for this second claim is the following:

> Regarding my second assertion, that only semantic information plays a role in selection, I maintain that the various nonsemantic features attached to nouns, for example, proper versus common, grammatical gender, grammatical number, and so on, play no role in selection. All verbs which have suggested themselves to me as possible counter-examples to this assertion turn out in fact to display selection based on some semantic properties (p. 134).

I take it that McCawley's admission that features such as gender and number, which he regards as playing no role in selection, are purely syntactic is already a concession to the view that the vocabularies of syntactic and semantic theory are not the same.

McCawley gives two examples of cases where it might be supposed that a certain form of syntactic selection governs a co-occurrence but where it can be shown that semantic selection is really involved. He writes:

> For example, the verb "name" might at first glance seem to have a selectional restriction involving the feature [proper]:

(8.69)   (a) They named their son John
(b) *They named their son that boy

> However, there are in fact perfectly good sentences with something other than a proper noun in the place in question:

(8.70)   They named their son something outlandish

> The selectional restriction is thus that the second object denote a name rather than that it have a proper noun as its head (p. 134).

The second, and only other, example he gives is the verb "count":

> Regarding grammatical number, verbs such as "count" might seem to demand a plural object:

(8.71) (a) I counted the boys
        (b) *I counted the boy

> However, there are also sentences with grammatically singular objects:

(8.72) I counted the crowd

> The selectional restriction on "count" is not that the object be plural but that it denote a set of things rather than an individual (pp. 134–135).

What McCawley says about these cases cannot be accepted without question. Sentence (8.70) is unquestionably well-formed, and its second object "something outlandish" consists of the pronoun head "something" modified by the adjective "outlandish" coming from a reduced relative clause construction. But the fact that this object is not itself a proper noun does not show that the selection restriction is that the second object must denote a proper name. The original question was whether the selection restriction on the second object involves the syntactic feature '[+ Proper]' (or '[− Common]'). Regardless of the fact that "something" is not a proper noun, we can still hold that the syntactic feature '[+ Proper]' is involved by arguing that the requirement in question is that the second object of "name" be a constituent whose underlying form is marked '[+ Proper]'. The point that McCawley has missed is that the underlying form of a surface constituent can be marked '[+ Proper]' without the surface constituent itself being a proper noun. Given what we are supposing, namely, that the deep structure form of "something" is marked '[+ Proper]' here, the selection restriction that "name" imposes on its second object will be satisfied in a case like (8.70).

Evidence for the position just stated comes from the fact that the pronoun "something" in (8.70) is the same as the one from which the interrogative pronoun in (8.73) arises:

(8.73) What did they name their son?

We know that the possible answers to a question are restricted by the syntactic features assigned to the *wh*'d pro-form(s) in the underlying structure of the question. For example, (8.75) and (8.76) are possible answers to the question (8.74):

(8.74) Who loves us?

(8.75) Jesus loves us

(8.76) Mother loves us

But (8.77) and (8.78) are not possible answers to (8.74):

(8.77) The car loves us

(8.78) Truth loves us

And the possible answers to the question (8.73) include (8.69a) but not (8.69b).

Thus, we can argue that the pronoun " something " in (8.70) is marked ' [+ Proper] '. Hence, rather than being a counterexample to the claim that the selection restriction of " name " involves the feature ' [+ Proper] ', McCawley's case actually supports it.

But even if what McCawley says about these cases could be accepted, his conclusion would not follow:

> I accordingly conclude that selectional restrictions are definable solely in terms of properties of semantic representations and that to determine whether a constituent meets or violates a selectional restriction it is necessary to examine its semantic representation and nothing else (p. 135).

Assuming that his examples show that syntactic selection does not operate in sentences of the sort he considers, they cannot show that it does not operate anywhere else. Being a general claim about selection, McCawley's claim cannot be established by a few examples that conform to it. But it can be refuted by one that does not.

Let us recall from the previous section some cases of syntactic features that are clearly selectional in function but can be shown *not* to carry semantic information. One such case involves the syntactic features representing the two nominal subcategories mass and count, i.e., ' [− Count] ' and ' [+ Count] '. These selectional features have already been shown not to embody a semantic distinction found among the nouns to which ' [− Count] ' and ' [+ Count] ' must be assigned in a correct syntactic analysis. The members of the pairs in (8.27a–e) are the same in meaning, but the first member in each case is a mass noun while the second one is count. If the syntactic features ' [− Count] ' and ' [+ Count] ' were also to represent a semantic distinction, then the correct syntactic assignment of these features would falsely predict that the members of pairs like those in (8.27a–e) are not synonymous.

Another counterexample to McCawley's speculation about the restriction of grammatical selection to conditions that are definable in terms of semantic representations is the proper-common distinction. As we have shown, the distinction cannot be taken to be semantic. In the previous section, we showed that proper nouns are devoid of a sense and so cannot have any semantic property by virtue of being proper nouns, and in the preceding discussion, we showed that there is nothing that the senses of common nouns share which only they have. Accordingly, we can conclude that the selectionally useful syntactic distinction represented by ' [− Common] ' and ' [+ Common] ' plays no role in semantic representations.

These cases, together with the other cases discussed in the previous section, where syntactic distinctions function in selection but are nonsemantic, refute McCawley's general claim about selection and also provide strong evidence that the lexical constructs in the vocabulary of semantic theory and those in the vocabulary of syntactic theory form disjoint sets.

The present evidence does not disprove the theory of generative semantics, but it does severely weaken its case by showing the best hypothesis to be that these sets are disjoint or that the lexical constructs common to them, if there are any, are few and in some way special. We shall explain shortly how this hypothesis enables us to construct arguments that show that grammars built on the interpretive model are simpler.

If the situation were the other way around, the case for interpretive semantics would be severely weakened, but, again, there would be no disproof. The reason we would not obtain a disproof either way involves not only the fact that the class of lexical constructs is not yet fully known, so that no argument at the present time could be exhaustive, but, more importantly, the fact that, logically speaking, both theories accommodate both extreme possibilities with respect to the relation between the vocabularies of syntactic and semantic theory.

Let us suppose that the evidence indicates that the lexical constructs in question belong to both the vocabulary of syntactic theory and the vocabulary of semantic theory. It would still be possible to organize the grammar on the model of interpretive semantics. In this situation, we could take the view that, instead of a lexicon subcomponent of the base in the syntactic component and a dictionary in the semantic component, there is just a dictionary, or, if the inclusion is not full, a dictionary and a lexicon subcomponent with a far smaller job to do (i.e., it would introduce syntactic features that have no semantic significance, if there are such). We could then have transformations operate on semantically interpreted underlying phrase markers, as suggested previously. On the other hand, if the evidence indicated, as it in fact does, that the vocabularies of the syntactic and semantic components are, in effect, disjoint, generative semanticists could take the view that, prior to transformational operations, the lexicon component replaces the lexical readings in the I's generated by the semantic component with phonologically represented lexical items *and* their full specifications in terms of nonsemantic, syntactic features. The appropriate syntactic information would, then, appear in the objects to which transformations are applied. Therefore, neither extreme situation, disjointness or proper inclusion, is conclusive for one theory and fatal for the other.

At this point, it cannot help but appear that the theory of generative semantics might not be a real alternative to the theory of interpretive semantics but, instead, a trivially equivalent system. Appearances are *not* misleading in this case. When we strip the theory of generative semantics of certain superficial differences and formulate it in a way that enables it to satisfy certain conditions of adequacy on semantic representation, it turns out to be a mere notational variant of CKP.

A word or two needs to be said about how we understand the term "notational variant." What we mean when we say that one theory is a notational variant of another is that both theories handle the same range of grammatical facts, no more and no less, and also that they handle these facts on the basis of the same principles. The only difference between the one theory and the theory of which it is a variant is a difference in the way these principles are formulated. An example in recent literature is Harman's (1963) "phrase structure" grammar, which purports both to be a system without transformational rules and not to suffer from the deficiencies that lead to the introduction of transformations. As Chomsky (1966b, pp. 40–49) has shown, Harman's system embodies the principles of transformational grammar in a form where they are disguised to look like phrase structure rules. In effect, Harman's system uses rules that carry indices along in a derivation so that at each stage there is an index coding information about the structure of the previous stages in a way that makes it possible for transformational operations to be performed with respect to the properties of the linear context of symbols.

What I shall try to show here is that generative semantics is just another example of a "new" linguistic theory whose novelty rests on a mere terminological trick. To demonstrate this, we will have to show that any version of generative semantics that specifies grammars meeting proper conditions of adequacy on semantic and syntactic representation cannot fail to express the core principle of interpretive semantics, namely, that stated in (8.79):

(8.79)   The association of semantic representations with sentences and their constituents is determined, in part, by syntactic information about the constituents of sentences, their grammatical relations, and their syntactic classification.

Generative semantics can be a genuine alternative theory to interpretive semantics, rather than merely an alternative way of expressing the principles of interpretive semantics, only if it makes no use of such syntactic information in, or in the application of, the rules by which it associates semantic representations with sentences and their constituents.

Before we can present arguments to demonstrate the point with which we are concerned here, we must consider two things—first, the proper conditions on semantic and syntactic representation and, second, the way in which generative semantics-type grammars describe the grammatical structure of sentences.

On both the conceptions of how grammars ought to be organized being considered here, semantic representations must successfully accomplish the task of semantic representation. That is, the output of the semantic component must provide the simplest, most revealing account of the conceptual structure of the sentences of the language. To be revealing, the account must take the form of semantic representations whose formal structure makes it possible to determine, on the basis of general definitions and in a mechanical fashion, the semantic properties and relations involved in the sentences and constituents to which these representations are assigned. That is, the semantic representation(s) assigned to a constituent must, together with definitions of semantic properties and relations, provide an adequate formal basis to allow us to mechanically determine if the constituent is meaningful, ambiguous, synonymous with another, analytic, redundant, contradictory, and so on.

Both views must lead to the construction of grammars whose semantic component satisfies the following conditions:

(8.80)   (a) For every sentence S of the language L, and every constituent C of S, there is a set R of semantic representations such that R contains exactly one member for each sense of C and no member of R represents a sense that is not a sense of C. (We are assuming, of course, that the whole sentence is one of its own constituents.)

   (b) Each member of R must be such that we can mark the semantic properties and relations of the C to which it is assigned, using definitions in semantic theory.

Condition (a) of (8.80) rules out any grammar whose semantic component fails either to produce a semantic representation for each sense of each whole sentence or to provide a semantic representation for each sense of each of its constituents. It is important to stress this condition because, as we shall see, theories of generative semantics give little indication of how they will produce semantic representations for each of the subsentential constituents of a sentence. Unless these theories do give a reasonable account of this, they will have to be rejected on the grounds that they leave unexplained the speaker's knowledge of the meanings of infinitely many constituents. Condition (b) rules out any grammar which does not assign the same semantic representation to synonymous sentences, more than one semantic representation to semantically ambiguous sentences, and so on.

We anticipate the objection that the use of the notion 'constituent C' in (8.80) begs the question at issue: it does not make reference to constituents of surface structure but to constituents of some deeper, more abstract syntactic structure, and it might be argued that the existence of such a deeper, more abstract structure is just what the generative semanticist has called into question. The objection is not sound, but it leads to an important clarification. What advocates of the theory of generative semantics have called into question is the existence of a *level* of deep structure, not the existence of more abstract syntactic structures underlying surface structure on the basis of which the constituents of sentences can be marked. They deny that there is any special system of rules in a grammar (such as the base of a CKP grammar) whose job is to generate a set of phrase markers that provide the domain on which some specific class of syntactic properties and relations are to be defined. However, the existence of such a system of base rules is *not* assumed by our use of the notion 'constituent C'. Rather, we assume only that underlying a surface phrase marker of a sentence S in a generative semantics-type grammar are a set of derived phrase markers Y such that the full set of constituents of S can be formally determined in terms of continuous subsequences of formatives appearing as terminal symbols of the members of Y. This assumption must be correct if generative semantics-type grammars are to be syntactically adequate transformational grammars.

Now consider how a generative semantics-type grammar describes the grammatical structure of sentences. McCawley (1969a) proposes to derive surface phrase markers from the I's that provide their generative source in a manner that is illustrated by the following case. Consider the sentence (8.81):

(8.81)   John killed Bill

According to McCawley, the I underlying this simple sentence is, roughly, as in (8.82) (see page 400).

Note that the terminal elements of (8.82) are enclosed within parentheses to go along with McCawley's conception of these as bundles of semantic constructs, not lexical items. Note, further, that within the grammar of Chomsky (1965, Section 2.3), (8.82) could not underlie (8.81) because lexical insertion must be one : one from lexicon entries to terminal nodes of a preterminal string. Gruber (1967, Section 2.3.3.1), however, has argued that this restriction is incorrect and that

(8.82)

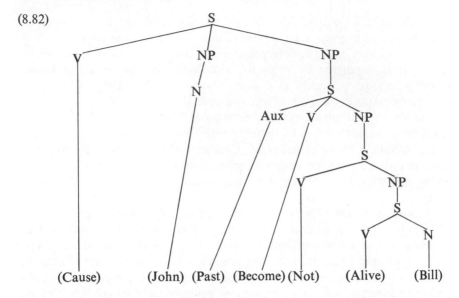

a lexical item can be attached to more than one node of a preterminal string. We do not have to weigh the pros and cons of this argument, since by dropping Chomsky's restriction and replacing it with Gruber's we still stay within the framework of CKP. Nor is it necessary to enter into the discussions of the particular conditions under which a sequence of nodes can be joined by the introduction of a single lexical item. Presumably, such attachment will be governed by the condition that the joined nodes be exhaustively dominated by a single higher node.

We can thus suppose that the lexical item "kill" can somehow be attached, once the elements '(Cause)', '(Become)', '(Not)', and '(Alive)' are collected together in the form of a single constituent. McCawley accomplishes this by a prelexical transformational operation referred to as "predicate-raising," namely, the daughter-adjoining of a node labeled 'V', together with any other nodes it dominates, to the next higher node similarly labeled, applying from the bottom to the top of a tree diagram. The result of applying this operation successively to (8.82) would be as shown in (8.83):

(8.83)

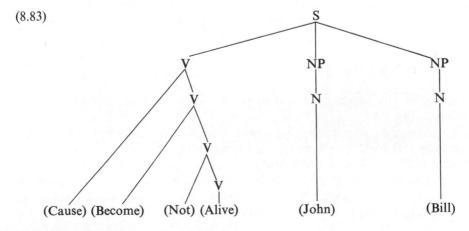

This process is not without its inherent problems, but I will ignore them, having faith that proponents of generative grammar can find solutions.

Now lexical insertion can take place, yielding the phrase marker in (8.84), which, in turn, can undergo transformational development, resulting in the surface phrase marker in (8.85) for the sentence (8.81):

(8.84)

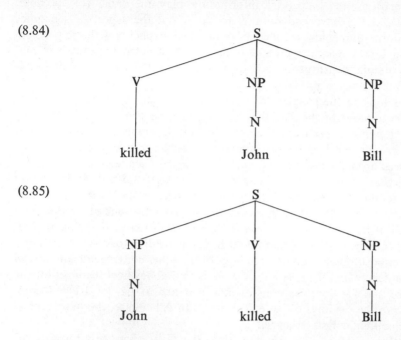

(8.85)

Given this illustration of the derivation of (8.81), we now consider arguments to show that generative semantics-type grammars which satisfy (8.80) must be notational variants of grammars of the CKP type.

In two respects an adequate grammar built on the theory of generative semantics expresses the principles of an interpretive semantics-type grammar: it uses full information about the constituents of a sentence to associate semantic representations with them, and it uses information about the features of lexical items to replace their corresponding lexical readings in I's. The lexicon component of a generative semantics-type grammar is nothing more than an inversely structured lexicon of the CKP type. We shall now try to show that an adequate generative semantics-type grammar also expresses the principle that information about grammatical relations determines the association of semantic representations with constituents. If we can show this, it follows that generative semantics expresses the core of the interpretive theory and is, therefore, a notational variant of it. As we see it, the picture is this: generative semantics inverts the way in which interpretive semantics puts the relation between the syntactic and semantic components of a grammar, and it inverts lexicon and projection rules, the net effect being that the latter inversions cancel out the former and we end up with the same theory we had all along.

All that needs to be shown, then, is that generative semantics-type grammars, if they are to satisfy the conditions in (8.80), must make the same use of grammatical relations as interpretive semantics-type grammars in correlating semantic representations to constituents. We cannot, however, look to what generative semanticists have said on this topic to find out whether information about domination relations and categorial information play the same role because, strangely enough, they have had nothing to say about the aspect of semantics where such information comes in. They have not dealt explicitly with the problem of determining how semantic representations are constructed for sentences and complex subsentential constituents compositionally from the semantic representations of their parts.

Let us look at the problem of how generative semantics-type grammars can provide an account of the way the meaning of each constituent beyond the level of lexical items arises from the meaning of its component constituents. Initially, this is quite unclear because the theory of generative semantics, as so far stated, leaves open the question of what the strings of semantic constructs are that constitute the terminal strings of configurations like (8.82) and (8.83). Should they be understood as the reading of the whole sentence, or should they be understood as a sequence of readings, each member of which is the semantic representation of the lexical item that is to replace it by the operation of the lexicon component? If the former, nothing is said about how this reading for the sentence was constructed compositionally from the readings of the other constituents and lexical items in the sentence; and if the latter, nothing is said about how readings for the whole sentence and for complex constituents in it are to be constructed compositionally from the readings of its lexical items. In either case, the most critical problem of semantic analysis is begged.

Nonetheless, we can fill this gap, since the theory implicitly answers the question just asked. Insofar as the proper substrings of the terminal string in configurations like (8.83) are replaced by lexical items, and insofar as this is done on the basis of lexicon entries in which the item is paired with a representation of the string it can replace, the theory, most naturally interpreted, says that these substrings are, individually, the lexical readings of the minimal constituents of the sentence.

But if the chunks of the semantic representation in (8.83) that are replaced with lexical items to obtain (8.84) are the readings of the lexical items that replace them, then semantic representations like (8.82) are the readings of sentences like (8.81). This being so, the rules that define a derivation like that of (8.83) from (8.82) are simply projection rules applied in reverse. And such a derivation is the inverse of a projection rule derivation in the sense that, instead of combining the semantic representations of the constituents to build up the semantic representation of the whole sentence, it correlates sentences and their constituents with semantic representations (as demanded by (8.80)) by breaking up the semantic representation of the whole sentence and distributing its component semantic representations to its constituents. Moreover, such an inverse projection rule derivation ends up with (*modulo* the interspersal of lexical and nonlexical transformations) the operation of lexical insertion rather than beginning with it (again, *modulo* the interspersal of lexical and nonlexical transformations).

Now, it is clear that the parts of the semantic representation that these reverse projection rules map onto the constituents "John," "Bill," and "kill(ed)" of (8.81) as their readings are determined by the structure indices of the rules (e.g., Predicate Raising) and the structures like (8.82) on which they operate. Hence, whether the semantic representation of the (surface) subject of a sentence like (8.81) is actually correlated with the subject constituent or with the object or with the verb—that is, whether the right correlations take place or not—depends on information about the node domination of substrings in phrase markers like (8.82) and about node labels. Although the configurational information made use of by these reverse projection rules might not define exactly the same set of grammatical relations as in Chomsky (1965), they do define grammatical relations in the same sense (see Chapter 3, Section 8 of this book).

Consider another example of how information about grammatical relations is used to construct inverse projection rule derivations in generative semantics-type grammars. Postal (1970) provides a paradigmatic case of a derivation ing such reverse projection rules as Predicate Raising, Subject Raising, an· Movement. He considers the verb "remind" on the sense it has in sentences ιικ. (8.86a), as opposed to (8.86b):

(8.86) (a) Harry reminds me of Fred Astaire
        (b) Harry never misses an opportunity to remind me of my faults

He argues that this verb does not arise from a single underlying constituent but is derived from different components of the semantic representation of the sentence· in which it occurs as a surface verb. According to Postal, the semantic representation of (8.86a) has the form of a two-place predicate, roughly, 'x perceives y', where the variable "x" ranges over persons (or perhaps sentient beings) and "y" ranges over resemblances (of one sort or another) between two things. A particular resemblance is represented by another two-place predicate, roughly, 'z similar w', where both "z" and "w" range over persons, places, and things generally. Accordingly, the semantic representation of (8.86a) is as shown in (8.87):

(8.87)

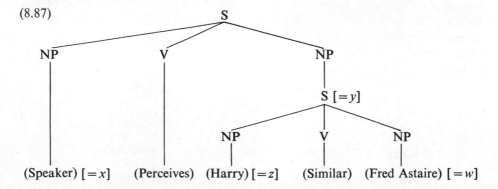

The sequence of phrase markers (a), (b), and (c) of (8.88) illustrates the derivation of (8.86a) from its semantic representation (8.87) to the point at which lexical substitution occurs:

(8.88) (a)

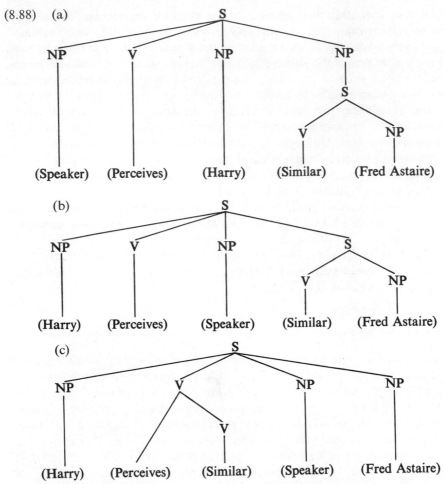

The phrase marker (8.88a) comes from (8.87) by Subject Raising; (8.88b) comes from (8.88a) by Psych Movement; and (8.88c) comes from (8.88b) by Predicate Raising. The surface phrase marker of (8.86a), namely, (8.89), comes from (8.88c) by operations of lexical insertion:

(8.89)

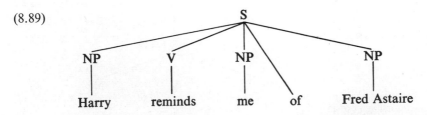

As we have already observed, transformations like Predicate Raising that map semantic representations onto the constituents of sentences as their readings are simply projection rules applied in reverse. Here, for example, Psych Movement extracts the component readings of the reading (8.87) that are the values of the variables "x" in the relation '$(Perceive)_{x,y}$' and "z" in the relation '$(Similar)_{z,w}$' and positions them so that they are replaced by the lexical items "me" and "Harry," respectively, when lexical insertion occurs. Thus, the operation of Psych Movement helps to get the proper readings assigned to these constituents. This, however, is exactly the reverse of what a projection rule would do to obtain the same result.[9] Let us assume an underlying phrase marker for (8.86a) that is something like (8.90a) and a dictionary entry for "remind" that is something like (8.90b), where "Z" is a variable categorized for the 'subject-of' relation and "X" is a variable categorized for the 'direct-object-of' relation:

(8.90) (a)

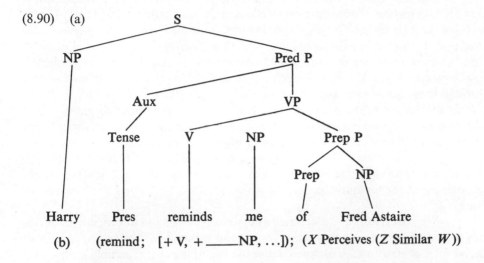

(b)   (remind; [+ V, + _____NP, ...]); $(X$ Perceives $(Z$ Similar $W))$

Given (a) and (b) of (8.90), a projection rule corresponding to Psych Movement would substitute the lexical reading of the subject "Harry" for "Z" and the lexical reading of the direct object "me" for "X."

Not only are transformations like Psych Movement nothing more than projection rules applied in reverse, but the derivations generated by their application are inverses of projection rule derivations. For example, the derivation (8.87)–(8.89) is the inverse of the one that would by defined by a sequence of dictionary entry plug-ins into (8.90a) followed by a sequence of projection rules such as the one just described. Moreover, both derivations would provide the same pairing of constituents of (8.86a) with semantic representations, namely, "Harry reminds me of Fred Astaire" with '$(Perceive)_{x,y}$ & $x = (Speaker)$ & $y = (Similar)_{z,w}$ & $z = (Harry)$

---

[9] Note that such a projection rule is only a device I am using for the sake of argument. It implies no endorsement of Postal's account of the meaning of (8.86a). In fact, I think there are a number of counterexamples to Postal's account. For example, a sentence like (8.86a) cannot be true unless the speaker has had some acquaintance with the referent of "Fred Astaire" but any corresponding 'strike-as-similar' (or 'perceive-as-similar') sentence can be true without such past acquaintance. Moreover, as is clear from the discussion of projection rules in Chapter 3, Section 10, such operations would actually no longer be formulated as the Type I projection rules of Katz and Fodor (1963).

& w = (Fred   Astaire)', ..., "Harry" with '(Harry)', "remind" with '(Perceive)$_{x,(Similar)_{z,w}}$', "me" with '(Speaker)', and "Fred Astaire" with '(Fred Astaire)'. Thus, CKP grammars obtain the pairings to satisfy (8.80) by starting with lexical readings assigned to occurrences of lexical items in (underlying) phrase markers and then applying projection rules to combine readings to form derived readings for complex constituents, whereas generative semantics-type grammars start with the reading of the whole sentence and use projection rule inverses to break up this reading into its component readings and distribute them to the simpler constituents, ending with the lexical items.

Furthermore, derivations in a generative semantics-type grammar must rely on information about constituents and grammatical relations to satisfy (8.80). Labeled bracketing which gives this information, such as in the nonterminal portions of "semantic representations" like (8.82) and (8.87), is required in order that the correct pairings of readings and constituents is obtained. For example, the application of Psych Movement used to generate (8.88b) requires information that distinguishes the subject and object of the verb "remind" in (8.86a) from the subject and object of the prepositional phrase or from the object of the verb and object of the prepositional phrase. Without such information, the transformational derivation of (8.86a) could make arbitrary exchanges of semantic elements dominated by 'NP' (for example, the permutation of '(Harry)' and '(Fred Astaire)'), thereby giving an incorrect pairing of semantic representation and sentence (as in the pairing of the semantic representation (8.87) with "I remind Fred Astaire of Harry").

We now return to the central issue, namely, the claim of generative semantics to provide grammars that relate sound and meaning without using a level of deep syntactic structure. As pointed out at the beginning of this section, such a level is defined by the two conditions (8.63) and (8.64). Thus, any structures that are jointly input to the semantic rules and input to the syntactic transformations that generate the derived phrase markers representing surface structure (in the former instance to provide information about grammatical relations required in the correlation of constituents and readings and in the latter to provide the structures which, after transformational deformation, become the proper input to the phonological component) comprise a level of deep syntactic structure. But the nonterminal portions of representations like (8.82) and (8.87), as we have seen, serve exactly this function: the reverse projection rules and the rules of lexical insertion in a generative semantics-type grammar use information about grammatical relations in the nonterminal portion of such representations to separate the reading of a sentence into its component readings and to distribute the component readings among the subconstituents of the sentence; and the same nonterminal structures, with their terminal strings converted by lexical substitution into strings of lexical items and themselves deformed transformationally, provide the input to the phonological component. Thus, since these nonterminal structures provide the same information and perform the same function as underlying phrase markers, grammars designed on the model of generative semantics also define a level of deep syntactic structure, regardless of whether the objects at this level are written as if they were parts of semantic representations.

We conclude, therefore, that either generative semantics says nothing about the main problem of semantic analysis and is thus inadequate because it fails to meet the conditions in (8.80), or it satisfies these conditions and thus the grammars that it specifies contain rules that are essentially the same as those in a CKP-type grammar and the alleged alternative to interpretive semantics merges into the theory it was originally designed to supersede.[10]

I shall now try to show that, even though generative semantics is a notational variant of interpretive semantics, the choice between them is not a free one because the theory of generative semantics is a less adequate way of organizing grammars. Of course, the argument for its being so cannot be based on considerations purporting to show that generative semantics-type grammars cannot handle facts that interpretive semantics-type grammars can. Rather, it must be based on methodological considerations showing that the rules of the game of theory construction which preclude unnecessarily complex grammars constrain us to choose grammars built on the model of interpretive semantics.

As we recall, the unique feature of generative semantics is that, in grammars built on this theory, the semantic component is the generative source. The rationale for constructing grammars to have this feature has to be that, by according the semantic component this special position, we obtain a better input to the transformational component. This could not be so were it not the case that the formal objects that do the job of semantic representation also provide the best input to the transformational process that produces surface structure representations. If the output of the semantic component or some converted form given by the lexicon component is the optimal structure on which transformational operations can apply, this can only be because these objects contain the appropriate information for the process of producing surface phrase markers. Therefore, the motivation for generative semantics stems from the assumption that the information that determines semantic properties and relations is carried by markers like 'NP', 'N', 'V', '[+Count]', '[+Proper]', which also determine surface phrase markers.

We argued previously that this assumption is false. If it is indeed false, then this fact ought to be reflected in the form of one or another methodological inadequacy in grammars built on the theory of generative semantics. That is, if the information coded in semantic representations is essentially the same information that transformations require to generate proper surface structures, then the natural organization of the grammar is to have transformational development proceed as directly as possible from semantic representations, and such an organization ought to yield the simplest, least ad hoc grammars; whereas if the information coded in semantic representations is only information about the conceptual structure of propositions, and includes little or no information of the sort required by transformations, then the natural organization of the grammar is to have transformational development proceed from underlying phrase markers, and this organization ought to yield the simplest, least ad hoc grammars. If the

---

[10] The reader will find this argument for the equivalence of generative and interpretive semantics discussed in some further detail in Katz (1971).

vocabularies of syntactic and semantic theory are essentially different, then grammars built on the model of generative semantics will use syntactic constructs in their representations of semantic structure that play no role in stating facts about the meaning of sentences. Therefore, the arguments given previously that constructs such as 'NP', 'N', 'Adj', '[+Count]' and '[−Count]', and '[+Common]' and '[−Common]', constructs clearly required for the representation and derivation of syntactic structure, do not carry semantic information show that generative semantics-type grammars incorporate elaborate syntactic apparatus into their semantic representations when such apparatus does not serve to represent semantic structure. Hence, because such grammars are more complex and ad hoc, the theory of generative semantics does not provide the most natural way to organize grammars.

We may consider two such methodological arguments against the theory of generative semantics.

Part of the semantic component in grammars based on either of these theories must be a list of the elementary semantic representations. In grammars based on the model of generative semantics, these are the semantic representations that will occur as the terminal elements of the I's that underlie sentences. The list can be thought of as an enumeration of pairings, each pairing consisting of a (set of) semantic representation(s) and a specification of the configurations in formal objects like (8.82) in which these elementary semantic representations can occur. It does not matter whether these pairings are formulated as rewrite rules, such as in (8.91),[11] or in another way:

(8.91)   V → (Cause)
       V → (Become)
       ⋮
       N → (John)

Nor does it matter that some of these representations might be formed from a "short list" by appropriate expansion rules.

Thus, the semantic component of a generative semantics-type grammar must contain some list of elementary semantic representations. But such grammars also require a further list of pairings in which the same elementary semantic representations appear. This additional list is required in the lexicon component of grammars modeled on the theory of generative semantics in order for semantic representations, appearing as terminal elements in the output of the semantic component, to be replaced by formatives (specified as phonological matrices). Each of the entries on this second list will look something like (8.92):

(8.92)   (Cause) (Become) (Not) (Alive) → kill

Such entries enable grammars to replace the semantic representations that occur as subparts of the terminal string of an I (like (8.83)) by the formative on the right-hand side of the arrow in case such a semantic representation matches the one on

---

[11] Of course these rules may assume a more sophisticated form. For one thing, the familiar apparatus for abbreviation can be used to reduce their number, and, for another, they may use subcategory specifications. None of these sophistications, however, is relevant here.

the left-hand side of the arrow. Thus, these rules are the ones that state the senses of the lexical items of the language and are simply inverses of CKP dictionary entries: instead of introducing readings on the basis of the occurrences of lexical items in syntactic objects, they introduce lexical items on the basis of occurrences of readings in semantic objects.

The reason that grammars fashioned on the theory of generative semantics require two distinct and separate lists for the insertion of readings and lexical items is that the points in a derivation at which these two classes of listed elements are introduced are different and must be so by virtue of the fact that a highly complex process of collection intervenes to transform the structures in whose production rules like (8.91) figure into ones to which rules like (8.92) can apply. Without such a process of collection, generative semantics-type grammars could not account for synonymy relations among sentences.

Generative semantics cannot use one list twice, once within the semantic component to produce I's and once within the lexicon component to insert lexical items. If one list were to do double duty in this way, generative semantics could no longer explain the synonymy of different sentences in terms of their being derived from the same underlying I. It would not be possible to derive paraphrases from the same object in the output of the semantic component by different processes of collection without the wide variety of differences between the organization of the terminal elements in objects like (8.82) and the organization of the terminal elements in objects like (8.83), and such differences require that the grammar contain both entries like (8.91) and entries like (8.92).

But grammars fashioned on the theory of interpretive semantics do *not* require two lists for the insertion of readings and lexical items since in these grammars both classes of listed elements are introduced at the same point in derivations. Because interpretive semantics allows for synonymy in cases where sentences are not derived from the same underlying syntactic object and because the points of insertion for lexical items and lexical readings coincide, grammars of this type require only a single list consisting of entries something like the example in (8.93).[12]

---

[12] The use of this example of a dictionary entry is not to be taken as an endorsement of the analysis it presents. It is used only as an illustration of what a corresponding dictionary entry in an interpretive semantics-type grammar would be. The analysis is, of course, a false account of the meaning of the formative "kill," which is here represented as synonymous with such expressions as "cause to become not alive," "cause to die," "cause to cease living." As a counterexample, we can offer a case where someone is the cause of another's death but is not the person who killed him. Suppose that the sheriff of an Old West town is to fight a gun duel with an infamous badman at high noon. Suppose also that, so as not to take any unnecessary chances, the sheriff goes to the local gunsmith to have his trusty six-shooter put in top working condition. Suppose, furthermore, that the gunsmith, who is a friend of the outlaw's, installs an old, rusty firing pin in the sheriff's gun and tells him that the newest and best available pin has been put in. Now, when the gun duel takes place, the sheriff, who draws first, is unable to fire his gun because the defective firing pin prevents it from discharging, and the outlaw then shoots and kills the sheriff. Clearly, the gunsmith caused the death of the sheriff, but, equally clearly, the gunsmith did not kill him. Another counterexample was suggested to me by V. Valian (in conversation). The sentence in question is "He [the owner of a French inn where the writer was staying] had caused a fire to be lit in the huge fireplace of our salon bedroom ..." (Stern (1927, p. 227)). Here is a case where a 'cause *x* to be *y*' construction excludes the interpretation that the subject is the one who did the *y*-ing. Thus, the owner of the inn did not light the fire.

(8.93)   *kill*; [+N, +Det——, +Count, ...]; (Cause) (Become) (Not) (Alive)

      Comparing item-by-item specification in grammars of these types, we see that, although a given lexical item, its major category, and its subcategories need only be specified once in both types of grammars, generative semantics-type grammars must specify the semantic constructs that represent the sense of a lexical item twice, whereas interpretive semantics-type grammars need only specify such semantic constructs once. Since the cost of such duplication will be sizable owing to the range of cases involved, CKP-type grammars will be considerably simpler in this respect than generative semantics-type grammars.

      Last, let us mention an ad hoc feature of the semantic component of generative semantics-type grammars. It can be argued that such grammars are unable to characterize the notion of semantic anomaly independently of the notion of syntactic deviance and that these grammars are therefore inadequate because semantic anomaly is independent of syntactic deviance. Such an argument could run as follows. First, if the output of the semantic component consists of all and only representations of meaningful sentences, then the input to the lexicon and transformational components cannot contain representations of "senses" involving a conceptual incoherence. Since these components can assign surface phrase markers only to some items of their input and withhold them from others, the only form of deviance that can be marked within such grammars are cases where some I receives no surface phrase marker. Thus, although generative semantics-type grammars can easily account for sentences that are meaningful but not (fully) well-formed syntactically, the opposite case, sentences that are not (fully) meaningful but are syntactically well-formed, can no more be handled in such grammars than surface structures that have no deep structure underlying them can be handled in CKP-type grammars. In both situations, there would be nothing from which to derive the representations of the admittedly existing surface form. Second, there are cases of syntactically well-formed but not fully meaningful sentences. The existence of cases that satisfy all of the conditions on syntactic well-formedness but fail to satisfy some condition on meaningfulness is established by previously discussed considerations which show that selection in a grammar is neither purely syntactic nor purely semantic but involves requirements of both kinds. McCawley himself provides us with a sentence that meets all the conditions of syntactic well-formedness but fails at least one condition of meaningfulness, namely, (8.71b). This sentence has to be taken as semantically anomalous by virtue of just the semantic constraint McCawley cites, that is, that the meaning of the object of the verb "count" must specify reference to a set of things rather than an individual, yet it violates no syntactic restriction and so cannot fall into the category of syntactically deviant sentences, which includes, for example, (8.94):

(8.94)   I bought several (six, many, etc.) footwear

Other examples of purely semantic deviance are given in (8.95–8.98).

(8.95)   John sold his afterimage to Robert

(8.96)   Mary's reflection is waterproof

(8.97)   Bills' footsteps are better than the number twenty

(8.98)   The floor is tall

Since there are no grounds on which to claim that these sentences violate a syntactic restriction, it follows that they meet the conditions for syntactic well-formedness and so must be counted as syntactically nondeviant sentences. Therefore, we can conclude that generative semantics-types grammars cannot account for cases of semantically anomalous sentences like these which are syntactically well-formed.

The generative semanticist can reply to this argument that the semantic component can be designed to generate representations of senses involving forms of some conceptual incoherence. The way out is to design the semantic component to generate two sets, one a set of representations of fully meaningful senses of sentences, and the other a set of representations of non-senses, including various degrees of conceptual garble. Since the members of the latter set are available to be fed into the lexicon and transformational components, there is now a way of deriving surface structures for semantically anomalous sentences.

But this reply leads to a strongly ad hoc feature. As we have seen, one of the original motivations for generative semantics is the assumption that grammatical selection, which determines what objects a grammar will generate, proceeds on the basis of semantic information exclusively. On this assumption, it is reasonable to make the output of the semantic component the direct input to the lexicon and transformation components. But the assumption proved false, as is shown by the existence of semantically anomalous but syntactically well-formed sentences. As the reply under consideration suggests, the form of a generative semantics-type grammar is to be maintained but provision is to be made for handling such sentences. But, insofar as representations at the semantic level are assigned to semantically anomalous sentences as well as semantically nonanomalous sentences, the definition of the notion 'S is a semantically anomalous sentence' cannot be framed in terms of the absence of a reading. This requires constructing a semantic component that is not simply a recursive definition of the notion 'proposition' or 'sense of a sentence' but is a recursive definition of a set H that properly includes the set P of all and only the propositions. Without semantic representations of the members of H, there would not be the source I's required in the generation of the class of grammatical sentences. Thus, the semantic component is made to recursively define a broader set than P in order to prevent grammars built on the principles of generative semantics from failing to satisfy syntactic conditions of adequacy. But the set of semantic representations of the members of H, the output of the semantic component, is itself inappropriate to predict semantic anomaly unless a criterion is found that picks out the semantic representations of P from the set of semantic representations of H. There will have to be some formal property of these semantic representations that differentiates those in the former set from those in the latter, so that it will be possible, on the basis of this property, to predict which sentences are semantically anomalous from their semantic representation. Hence, instead of recursively defining the set P directly, as can be done in a CKP grammar, a generative semantics-type grammar must take a roundabout route, first to H and then back to P via a criterion framed in terms of the formal property of semantic representations that differentiates representations of the members of P from representations of the members of the complement of P with respect to H. This roundabout route was made necessary because generative semantics-type grammars are organized to reflect the false assumption that there is but one kind of selection, and so one kind of deviance, in nonphonological grammatical structure. The ad hocness becomes clearly apparent when we realize that the semantic representations of the members of H that are not semantic representations of members of P do *no* work in explaining or predicting semantic properties and relations that is not already done by semantic representations of the members of P. Nonetheless, these superfluous representations comprise part of the level of semantic representation, contrary to the obvious methodological requirement that a level of grammatical representation should contain the minimal set of representations needed to explain and predict the relevant linguistic properties and relations.

We have now tried to show the following. If generative semantics is a genuine alternative to interpretive semantics, if the grammars that it specifies do not use information of the sort found in representations of deep structure in the way that CKP grammars do, then interpretive semantics is empirically inadequate because it fails to satisfy the conditions in (8.80). If, on the other hand, this theory satisfies these conditions, then it is not a genuine alternative to interpretive semantics but only a notational variant. In this case, however, we argued that it is less adequate than interpretive semantics on methodological grounds. We tried to show that the uneconomical formalism and ad hocness of generative semantics-type grammars arose from a false thesis about language, namely, that the information in semantic representations is required for the syntactic derivation of surface structure representations. This thesis, expressed as the organizational universal that the output of the semantic component is the best input to the lexicon and transformational components, was shown to lead to cases in which general methodological constraints are violated.

3.   A rationale for deep structure

I will now try to say something about the concept of deep syntactic structure based on what we have learned from our examination of a theory that attempts to do without it. We will seek to answer the following question, which is often asked nowadays:[13] "Why should natural languages have a level of deep syntactic structure?" From a certain perspective, this is a very good question to ask. Asking it presses the demand for a general hypothesis about language to explain the existence of the level of deep syntactic structure. Historically, Chomsky posited this level on the basis of the failure of taxonomic grammars to handle certain

---

[13] See Ross and Lakoff (undated).

linguistic data. These data provided good reason to claim that there is such a level, but, as any theoretically minded scientist recognizes, besides wishing to know *that* there is something, one wishes to know *why*. Accordingly, we must now try to discover a reason that makes sense of the existence of the level of deep syntactic structure by showing that it has some function essential to natural language.

Base rules generate underlying phrase markers in which substructures of two kinds are systematically related. One kind is the domain of the semantic component, which uses information from these substructures to assign readings to constituents. The other is the domain of the transformational component, which uses information from these substructures to generate surface phrase markers. Since these surface phrase markers are the input to the phonological component which assigns them a phonetic representation, semantic representations are correlated with phonetic representations by virtue of the systematic interrelations, found within underlying phrase markers, that connect these two kinds of substructures. Given that this is so, one kind of substructure must encode information relevant to the combinatorial process whereby the senses of complex constituents are formed from the senses of their parts, and the other kind must encode information relevant to the process whereby deep structure constituents are realized in their proper form and position in utterances.

We can add two further assumptions to the hypothesis of interpretive semantics, both of which are quite plausible on current evidence. The first is that semantic representations are linguistic universals, that is, they represent linguistically universal concepts and propositions. The second is that phonetic representations and surface phrase markers are highly language-specific, that is, they represent language-particular forms of pronunciation. Given these further assumptions, we observe that one side of the correlation of meaning and sound is linguistically universal while the other side is highly language-specific. This makes it necessary for languages to have some principles that provide mediating connections that relate language-universal semantic structures to language-particular phonetic structures. That is, the universal semantic representations for all grammars are not directly correlatable with the different sets of phonetically represented surface phrase markers encountered from grammar to grammar without some intermediate level in each grammar whose rules interlace the universal elements of the former representations with the specific elements of the latter.

Clearly, the properties of deep syntactic structure are just those required to do this job. The kind of substructures in underlying phrase markers that encode information relevant to determining the compositional assignment of readings and the kind of substructures in these phrase markers that encode information relevant to determining the form and arrangement of elements in surface structure are, respectively, the domination relations and the (clause, phrase, and major word) category markings, and the distinctive feature matrices representing lexical items, their syntactic features and their order and grouping in a terminal string. The base subcomponents of the grammars of different languages blend the former and latter substructures in unique and different ways from language to language because of the wide latitude for variation in aspects of the latter substructures allowed by the abstractness of the grammatical relations.

Taking deep syntactic structure to be the level on which to state the mediating connections that systematically relate language-invariant semantic representations with the language-variant surface structure representations has the following consequence. The syntactic substructures at this level that determine the universal semantic representations will have to be linguistically universal, too, whereas those that determine the highly particular surface representations will have to be strongly language-specific. But this consequence seems well supported. For the domination relations and category markings that define grammatical relations are language-universal whereas the distinctive feature matrices that represent lexical items, their feature specifications, and the order and grouping of these items in the terminal string, the latter two being things that express information about the form and position of these items in surface structure, are largely language-specific.[14]

Why do natural languages have a level of deep structure? Because deep structure, as explicated by underlying phrase markers in CKP grammars, embodies the complex network of connections between the language-universal and the language-particular syntactic structures necessary to link sound and meaning in natural languages.

4. Surface structure and its interpretation

In the previous section we tried to establish the validity of (8.65a), the thesis that the semantic component of a grammar operates interpretively on the phrase markers in K. In this section we shall give support for the further thesis (8.65b), that the semantic component operates exclusively on phrase markers in K.

We cannot really establish this thesis, however, since the situation at the present stage in grammatical research is such that arguments seeking to establish (8.65b) as well as arguments seeking to refute it will be highly inconclusive. Confirmatory and disconfirmatory evidence both depend on points about which it is only reasonable now to be quite open-minded. For instance, the examples that figure most prominently in arguments on behalf of or against the thesis (8.65b) are almost invariably of a type about which one's intuitions are not absolutely clear and which are thus problematic. Moreover, the area in which relevant data

---

[14] If this hypothesis is right, the so-called "universal base hypothesis," which claims that the base component of a transformational grammar is universal, is false. That there are independent reasons for thinking that the universal base hypothesis is false is thus further support for our hypothesis. Such reasons include the following. First, the lexical items of different languages differ extensively in their deep phonological form. Second, the syntactic features assigned to them to determine agreement, declension, and distribution in surface structure also differ extensively from language to language. Third, aspects of constituent structure, such as the order of lexical items and phrases, their bracketing, and their syntactic categorization, also vary significantly. What appears to be invariant from language to language is the domination relations and category constructs and the relations between them that determine the grammatical relations. If we make the natural generalization from these facts, we are led to viewing these latter structures as universal and the former ones as particular, which is exactly what our hypothesis says in claiming that whatever semantic interpretation is based on, namely, grammatical relations and lexical readings, is universal, and whatever phonetic interpretation is based on, namely, idiosyncratic lexical items, their idiosyncratic feature assignments, etc., is particular.

are to be sought has been so little studied that new examples, both pro and con, are likely to pop up unexpectedly. Still another factor is that there are a number of different conceptions of the proper form for underlying phrase markers and transformations,[15] so that what appears to be a counterexample to (8.65b) on one conception can appear to be a supporting instance on the other, and vice versa. Therefore, neither the advocate of (8.65b) nor the critic can afford to take too dogmatic a stand.

Before trying to support the thesis in question, let us review briefly some of the reasons for its original adoption.[16] On the earliest view of transformational grammar,[17] a set of phrase structure rules, with a subset for introducing lexical items under major categories, generates the set K of underlying phrase markers. These are connected with surface phrase markers by transformational rules, which produce a large number of intermediate derived phrase markers from underlying phrase marker to surface phrase marker. Given that the meaning of a sentence is a compositional function of the meanings of its constituents and their grammatical relations, the account of compositional meaning provided by the semantic component takes the form of an interpretation of some set of phrase markers in the syntactic description of a sentence. Thus, the question naturally arises as to *what* set of phrase markers is interpreted in the account of the meaning of a sentence. Is it all the phrase markers in the syntactic description? Is it the proper subset consisting of just the underlying phrase marker(s)? Is it this set plus some of its derived phrase markers?

In Katz and Postal (1964) we posed this problem and offered a solution. We argued in favor of having the semantic component operate exclusively on the underlying phrase markers in the syntactic description of a sentence. Initially, this is a natural choice. Assuming that semantic interpretation proceeds, first, by an assignment of lexical readings from the dictionary to the atomic constituents of a sentence and, then, by an assignment of derived readings to each syntactically complex constituent by the operation of the projection rule upon the readings of its component parts, it is natural to semantically interpret the underlying phrase marker since, generally speaking, this is the only one that contains a specification of its atomic constituents, its complex constituents, and their grammatical relations. We pointed out that the other phrase markers either duplicate some of this information or lack some of it or both. We argued this on the grounds that transformations characteristically use deletion and rearrangement operations that destroy structure, so that derived phrase markers give less information about constituency and grammatical relations than do their underlying phrase markers. Since such information in its full form is indispensable for semantic interpretation, we concluded that the semantic component interprets all and only underlying phrase markers.

However, transformational theory at the time Katz and Postal (1964) was written, namely, the theory of *Syntactic Structures* (1957) and other early

---

[15] For one example see Chomsky (1970b).

[16] See Katz and Postal (1964) and Chomsky (1965).

[17] See Chomsky's early publications, particularly (1957) and (1962).

publications of Chomsky's, was inconsistent with the claim that the semantic component interprets only underlying phrase markers. For, on that theory, sentences with the same underlying phrase markers can differ in meaning, while, on our claim, they must be the same in meaning. The issue was whether transformations that "change meaning" should be allowed in grammars. To support our view that they should not, we tried to show that the transformations that violated our claim were incorrectly formulated and could be shown to be so in terms of purely syntactic evidence. We also tried to show that, when correctly formulated, they made no semantic contribution. Considerable evidence of this kind was presented in the course of our discussion.

On the basis of the thesis (8.65b), it was possible to make certain interesting speculations about the function of transformational processes in natural language. For example, Chomsky and Miller (1963) pointed out that, because transformational processes destroy constituent structure, transformations can be regarded as performing an indispensable function in speech production. By removing large portions of the highly complex constituent structure in underlying phrase markers, transformations produce surface phrase markers that are structurally relatively simple and so better adapted to being the syntactic input to articulatory processing. Underlying phrase markers must be highly complex in constituent structure in order for all of the syntactic distinctions required for semantic interpretation to be contained in them, but just such complexity makes them ill suited to serve as the syntactic input to articulatory processing since the storage capacity of such processing mechanisms is severely limited. Accordingly, one function of transformational rules is to relate objects well suited to carry meaning but poorly suited for articulatory processing to other objects that are well suited for articulatory processing but poorly suited to carry meaning. The surface phrase markers thus need not be adapted to carry meaning since they are connected transformationally to suitably complex objects.[18]

Since the original presentation of (8.65b), new syntactic phenomena have come to the attention of grammarians, and, in many cases, these have made it necessary to try to write new transformations to explain them. In the majority of such cases, it has been possible to formulate transformational rules in accord with the principle that transformations do not contribute semantically relevant syntactic distinctions. In some cases, however, this has proved difficult, and the difficulty has led some grammarians to think that such phenomena might be handled by transformations that violate the principle, that is, transformations that introduce semantically relevant syntactic distinctions. Thus, some linguists now claim that the semantic component cannot operate exclusively on underlying phrase markers.

It should be noted that this objection is not a claim that the principle of

---

[18] This, we may observe, is another reason for rejecting the taxonomic model of grammar. If there is only one level of syntactic structure, the grammar cannot play its proper role in an explanation of speech production, for the phrase markers on that level must be either sufficiently complex for semantics or sufficiently simple for articulation. In the former case, they are not suitable as an account of the syntactic input to articulation, and in the latter, they are not suitable as an account of the input to the semantic component.

the semantic neutrality of transformations is wholly false, but, rather, a claim that in certain situations the semantic component must consider derived phrase markers, particularly surface phrase markers, in addition to underlying phrase markers.[19] We will examine some of the phenomena typical of those on which such an objection can be based. First we will try to show that, when properly understood, these classes of cases do not constitute genuine counterexamples to the principle. Then we will assume, for the sake of argument, that some of these phenomena might, in the final analysis, turn out to be counterexamples, and we will reformulate the principle so that it excludes such possible counterexamples and also preserves what is significant in the original.

4.1. Rhetorical interpretation

In the class of cases that we are going to examine first, we readily concede that deep syntactic structure is not sufficient to provide the needed syntactic information. We admit that, in the cases to be discussed, the phenomena in question here are genuine surface structure phenomena, and we thus agree that their representation involves transformationally introduced distinctions. But we shall argue that such phenomena are *not* semantic. That is, we shall claim that such transformationally introduced distinctions in no way reflect aspects of logical form and, thus, there is no reason to consider them semantic in the sense of the domain for which we have been trying all along to erect a theory. Therefore, if we can show that such surface structure phenomena have nothing whatever to do with meaning, on the notion of "meaning" where it is logical form in the broad sense (i.e., has to do with semantic anomaly, synonymy, analyticity, entailment, etc.), then the fact that transformational rules are required to account for these phenomena cannot be an objection to (8.65b). For Katz and Postal (1964) bases its claim for the truth of (8.65b) on this notion of meaning.

Before developing this line of argument, there is a contrary approach that should be dealt with. This position stems from an extreme form of the use theory of meaning, one which asserts that any grammatical feature of a sentence type that plays a role in the way that speakers use utterances (or inscriptions) of that type is ipso facto semantic. But the position is unsound because the assertion on which it rests is false, conflicting with a host of clear facts and implying unacceptable limitations on transformational theory. Almost any pair of distinct sentences that are synonymous will be a counterexample to this assertion because the surface structure features that distinguish them will suit them for different uses in some speech contexts or written discourses. Consider E. B. White's (1959, p. 53) "version" in (8.99) of Paine's "These are the times that try men's souls":

(8.99) Soulwise, these are trying times

And consider also the two forms of the limerick in (8.100).

---

[19] Chomsky (1970a) writes that "insofar as grammatical relations play a role in determining meaning, it is the grammatical relations of deep structure that are relevant (as before)."

(8.100) There was a young man who said, " God
      must find it exceedingly odd
      that this sycamore tree
      should continue to be
      when there's no one around in the quad(rangle)"

The alternate forms of the limerick show that the assertion in question leads to the absurd conclusion that phonological features such as rhyme and meter are semantic because they can make a difference in the way that sentence tokens are used by speakers. Similarly, obscenity becomes a semantic category, since the use of sentences with four-letter words is clearly different from that of paraphrases with multi-letter scientific equivalents. As further examples, there are sentences with the same deep structure but different surface structures which determine different sets of uses, such as the sentences (8.101) and (8.102):

(8.101) If I ever use a sentence in which the last word is a separated particle of a verb, I'll give your money back

(8.102) If I ever use a sentence in which the last word is a separated particle of a verb, I'll give back your money

Clearly, (8.101) but not (8.102) could be used as a reason to return the money. Again, a sentence like (8.103) cannot be used with the same stylistic effect in a story-telling discourse as the synonymous sentence (8.104):

(8.103) The mouse ran back to its hole

(8.104) Back ran the mouse to its hole

These examples show that surface structure differences can be the basis for differences in use. Thus, were the identification of meaning with use accepted in the theory of transformational grammar, it would no longer be possible for transformational grammars to explain the synonymy of sentences on the basis of their syntactic derivations.

One who holds that any nonphonological and nonsyntactic grammatical feature of sentences that determines some aspect of their use also determines an aspect of their meaning fails to consider the possibility that there might be other categories of grammatical phenomena besides phonology, syntax, and semantics.[20] We should take this possibility seriously, however, since if we find such a category, we may also find that surface structure features which *prima facie* appear to contradict (8.65b) belong to this category. We will then be in a better position to prove that such surface structure features do not contradict (8.65b) than we would be were we to argue only that they are nonsemantic.

---

[20] This failure is endemic to use theories of meaning. The slogan that meaning is use, if it means anything, means that differences in use reflect differences in meaning. This implies that the advocate of the theory is restricting his analysis of the factors that contribute to the way sentences are used to factors of one sort, semantic factors. Thus, the possibility of nonsemantic factors that play a role in use is, essentially, ruled out.

Given that the significance of such surface structure features must lie elsewhere than in the domain of logical structures in language, it is natural to resurrect the traditional distinction between logic and rhetoric and to consider the possibility that the category of rhetoric might be the further category of interpretation we seek. The thesis we shall now explore is that surface structure phenomena of the sort under consideration, although they have no logical significance, are rhetorically significant, in the sense of "rhetorical" where it refers to properties and relations having to do with the expressive form of sentences, with matters of style in the broadest sense. To sharpen this formulation somewhat, we can say that rhetorical and stylistic features of language include whatever grammatical structures can be utilized by speakers in choosing one sentence over synonymous ones to achieve some effect upon an audience beyond the communication of a certain meaning. Rhetoric and style thus concern the manner of saying (or writing) what is said (or written) and semantics its information content.

Expressing the traditional conception of style, Sledd (1959) writes:

> Style in language is possible because all of us, fortunately, command more than one kind of English and because, even with a *single* kind of English, there are synonymous expressions from which we may make our choice (p. 263).

After discussing dialectal illustrations, Sledd turns to the effects of different choices among different ways of saying the same thing:

> Why do we bother to make a choice among synonymous expressions... ? That we do bother to choose is plain, and for a very good reason: different ways of saying the same thing may produce effects which are even more strikingly different. For example, both /párk/ and /páərk/ can refer to the same expanse of lawn, covered with shrubs, trees, and couples lying on newspapers; they can point to the same thing. That is not to say that the total effects of the use of these two forms will also be identical. To the quaint people who dislike or pretend to dislike the "Midwestern *r*," both might be objectionable when compared to an elegant /pá:k/; but of the two, /párk/ might be the more painful. Or, if this example seems far fetched, we need only remember the consternation which "I ain't got none" would cause in circles where "I haven't any" is expected, or the anguish which a four-letter word would cause to people who never blink an eye at its scientific synonym. Unless we know how to say the same thing in different ways, some of our efforts at communication are bound to fail, we will lose influence and make enemies (p. 264).

The position I am going to defend here is that, for a large range of the cases cited as counterexamples to the claim that transformations make no contribution to meaning, we can admit that such cases are surface structure phenomena exclusively. But we can argue that this proves nothing because they are rhetorical (or stylistic) in character and that such phenomena therefore cannot be counterexamples to the claim that transformations do not contribute to the *meaning* of the sentences in whose derivations they occur.[21] This position will be defended by an attempt to sketch a theory of surface structure interpretation based on the

---

[21] Of course, some aspects of deep structure are rhetorical, too, as some of Sledd's examples show. But this has no bearing on the issue at hand.

thesis that surface structure features are rhetorically significant. I shall try to show that, on this thesis, surface structure phenomena receive a coherent, general interpretation in terms of the central concept of rhetorical significance in much the same way that deep structure phenomena receive a coherent, general interpretation in terms of the central concept of logical or cognitive meaning. What I am proposing, then, is that the theory of grammar requires a new subtheory, in addition to the phonological, syntactic, and semantic subtheories, namely, a theory of rhetorical form, and, further, that grammars require a new component to express the rhetorical interpretation of superficial phrase markers. I cannot, of course, give the details of this theory, but many of its features will be quite explicit in our treatment of examples. Moreover, it possible to indicate the area of potential application of such a theory. Sledd remarks:

> We must recognize that if we want to talk about a man's style, we must know both how he said things and how he *might* have said them but chose not to; and we must also recognize that no one can *cultivate* his style unless he somehow knows enough about the resources of his language to choose which he needs (pp. 264–265).

As this suggests, a knowledge of a language's resources for stylistic variation is indispensable for the study of someone's style. If one consults the best works on style and rhetoric, one finds that grammarians and literary critics know a considerable amount about these resources. But their knowledge is mostly intuitive, much like the knowledge of syntactic structure with which classical grammarians worked. Accordingly, if generative grammar can elaborate a formal reconstruction of this knowledge, it will be able to offer the practicing grammarian or literary critic just the formal distinctions and concepts he requires to pursue his study of style in a more formal and general manner.

That there is a set of features, definable on surface structure representations, which are systematic on the principle that they are rhetorical in import, that they form a distinct system from the semantically significant features of deep structure, and that these former features are the ones that writers on rhetoric and style utilize we shall now try to establish by considering some examples of rhetorical analysis. As already mentioned, the formulation of a new interpretive component for grammars, one that operates on surface structures to provide a representation of their rhetorical potentialities, is a matter we shall leave for future research.

It has long been recognized by those who study stylistics that the constituents of a sentence occur in a natural order and that changes in this order change emphasis. Whitehall (1964) states two general rules which partly characterize the notion of natural order in English. These are presented in (8.105) and (8.106):

(8.105) In the subject-predicate sentence, the subject, the verb, any inner complement, and any outer complement occur in a fixed 1, 2, 3, 4 order.

(8.106) Single-word modifiers normally precede, and word-group modifiers follow, the words they modify.

A particularly striking example of the stylistic effect of departures from the natural constituent order is the Dickens line (8.107), where the natural order is as shown in (8.108):

(8.107) Talent, Mr. Micawber has; money, Mr. Micawber has not

(8.108) Mr. Micawber has talent; Mr. Micawber has no money

The effect of the shift in emphasis in (8.107) is to direct special attention to the contrast between the richness of Micawber's natural gifts and the poverty of his financial resources.

Another example given by Whitehall is the second sentence in the discourse (8.109), which uses the order 3, 1, 2, 4, instead of the natural order 1, 2, 3, 4 as in (8.110), to increase the continuity of thought in the transition from the first to the second sentence:

(8.109) Certain persons resisted his military regime; those persons he called "pseudo-internationalists"

(8.110) He called those persons "pseudo-internationalists"

As examples of the shift in emphasis resulting from a departure from (8.106), Whitehall gives cases (8.111), where the movement of the modifier from its natural position gives it the principal stress:

(8.111) soldiers three, water enough, the day following, the journey inland

Strunk (White (1959, p. 27)) points out that almost any element of a sentence other than its subject becomes emphatic when taking first position, as in (8.112) and (8.113):

(8.112) Deceit or treachery he could never forgive

(8.113) Home is the sailor

Strunk also observes that the subject gains special emphasis by taking the position of the object, as in (8.114):

(8.114) Through the middle of the valley flowed a winding stream

A well-known case of the same sort is found in active-passive pairs, where the subject and object exchange positions, as in (8.115)–(8.116):

(8.115) The man in the green hat burned the coat

(8.116) The coat was burned by the man in the green hat

Related cases are shown in (8.117) and (8.118).[22]

[22] Also, "For one to hit home runs with long bats is easy."

(8.117) (a) Long bats are easy to hit home runs with
         (b) Home runs are easy to hit with long bats

(8.118) (a) I heard John sing the song
         (b) It was John whom I heard sing the song

Each member of these pairs is synonymous with its co-member, having the same deep subject and deep predicate. Yet each differs from its co-member in rhetorical potentialities. In every case the difference depends on the placement of one of the deep structure constituents in the position of the leftmost noun phrase in the surface structure of the sentence. It has long been recognized that the noun phrase occupying this position has a special import, the nature of which can be brought out by considering the case where the sentence starts a discourse. In this context, the leftmost noun phrase in the surface structure of the sentence normally conveys the topic of the discourse, unless some special device is used to deviate from this rule for some clear stylistic purpose. Thus, if a discourse starts with (8.115), we expect it to be about a man in a green hat, whereas if it starts with (8.116), we expect it to be about a coat. Furthermore, coherence in discourses often depends upon the use of the proper noun phrase as the leftmost one in succeeding sentences. For example, a straightforward discourse about how to hit home runs that ends with (8.117a) (or the sentence in note 22) would be stylistically inferior to one that ends with (8.117b). Once the topic of a discourse is fixed, the sentences that follow must not introduce an abrupt change of topic without an appropriate rationale. Accordingly, we can derive the fact that the leftmost noun phrase of a sentence conveys the topic of the previous sentences of the discourse from the fact that an abrupt switch reduces the stylistic quality of the discourse.

Let us consider a literary case.[23] The first sentence of Kafka's *The Trial* is quoted in (8.119) and the first sentence of his *Metamorphosis* in (8.120):

(8.119) Someone must have been telling lies about Joseph K., for without having done anything wrong he was arrested one fine morning

(8.120) As Gregor Samsa awoke one morning from a troubled dream, he found himself changed in his bed to some monstrous kind of insect

Kafka could instead have written the sentences in (a) and (b) of (8.121), respectively:

(8.121) (a) Lies must have been being told about Joseph K., for without having done anything wrong he was arrested one fine morning
         (b) As Gregor Samsa awoke one morning from a troubled dream, he found that someone (or something) had changed him in his bed to some monstrous kind of insect

But he did not, and for good reason. Sentences (8.119) and (8.121a) are synonymous, but the use of the active sentence (8.119) focuses attention on the existence

---

[23] Thanks are due to my colleague A. Kibel for these examples and for his observations on their significance.

of the anonymous liar from the very outset of the novel. This is stylistically necessary, since the entire book is about Joseph K.'s attempt to resist the fate imposed
on him by finding out the identity of his malefactor. The use of the passive sentence
(8.121a) would not bring out this theme. On the other hand, the use of the passive
sentence (8.120) instead of the active paraphrase (8.121b) rightly de-emphasizes
the agent or agency by which Gregor Samsa was transformed. This is stylistically
necessary here since, unlike the former work, this one does not deal with the quest
to discover the agent responsible for the hero's misfortune but rather with Gregor
Samsa's attempt to live with his metamorphosis.

Thus, the notions of surface subject and surface predicate, or *Topic* and
Comment as they have come to be called, have an interpretation in terms of rhetorical use. Although we have done little more than suggest some aspects of their
rhetorical significance, nonetheless it is clear that their grammatical function is
quite different from that of the notions of deep subject and deep predicate. The
latter refer to syntactic information utilized in the process of determining the meaning of a sentence from the meanings of its constituents, while the former refer to
syntactic information utilized in according stylistic preference, with respect to
certain speech situations or discourse contexts, to certain of the forms in which
meanings can be expressed.[24] Therefore, it becomes worse than pointless to try,
as some grammarians have, to derive both members of pairs such as those in
(8.115)–(8.118) from underlying phrase markers in which the deep subject is the
same as the surface subject. Such an analysis would not explain how these sentences
are paraphrases and yet have different rhetorical potentialities, and it would fail
to express the generalization that, other things being the same, sentences with the
same Topic are the same in their rhetorical potentialities.

We may mention one further example of surface order used as a stylistic
device. The first sentence of Tolstoi's story *The Death of Ivan Ilych* is (8.122):

(8.122) Ivan Ilych's life had been most simple and most ordinary, and therefore,
        most terrible

The same proposition could be expressed by the sentence (8.123):

(8.123) Ivan Ilych's life had been most terrible because it had been most simple
        and most ordinary

But (8.123) has little of the dramatic impact of (8.122), which first informs the
reader of the simplicity and commonplaceness of Ivan Ilych's life, thereby creating
expectations that serve to make the revelation that comes at the end unexpected
and hence all the more dramatic. Sentence (8.123) is like a badly told joke in which
the punch line is given away at the beginning.

[24] It remains for the generative grammarian to provide a precise explication of these
notions, which may then be connected with a fuller account of their rhetorical uses supplied by
literary critics, rhetoricians, etc. Chomsky, on a suggestion of Kiparsky's, proposes that the topic
of a sentence S be defined as the leftmost NP in its surface phrase marker that is dominated by a
major category and by S. Various refinements are required, such as those that would result from
taking order into account in connection with certain cases. See Chomsky (1965, p. 221).

Having considered some examples of the rhetorical consequences of the order of constituents, let us turn to examples of another grammatical phenomenon with important rhetorical consequences, namely, the phenomenon of the natural answer.[25]

Given a strictly logical property or relation, one can often expect to find that matters of style classify cases so that some rank higher than others on a scale of stylistic preference. Such is true with regard to the logical relation 'is a possible answer to', as explicated in the definition (5.48). Given the set of all and only the possible answers to a question Q, not all the members of the set will be natural answers to Q. Consider the examples in (8.124)–(8.126):

(8.124) (a) What is the house above?
         (b) What is the stream below?
         (c) The house is above the stream
         (d) The stream is below the house

(8.125) (a) Who is John taller than?
         (b) Who is Mary shorter than?
         (c) John is taller than Mary
         (d) Mary is shorter than John

(8.126) (a) Whom did John precede?
         (b) Whom did Mary follow?
         (c) John preceded Mary
         (d) Mary followed John

In each of these cases, (c) and (d) are possible answers to both (a) and (b). This is perfectly clear. Each (c) and (d) are converses, and so synonymous, as indeed are the questions (a) and (b). Accordingly, if either (c) or (d) provides the information requested in (a) or (b), then they both do. However, it is equally clear that (c) in each case is the natural answer to (a) while (d) is the natural answer to (b), and not the other way around. These cases are the same as those in (8.127), where (c) and (d) are possible answers to either (a) or (b), but (c) and (d) are not natural answers to (b), and (e) and (f) are possible answers to (a) and (b) but are not natural answers to (a):

(8.127) (a) Did John sell the book to Mary?
         (b) Did Mary buy the book from John?
         (c) Yes, John sold the book to Mary
         (d) No, John didn't sell the book to Mary
         (e) Yes, Mary bought the book from John
         (f) No, Mary didn't buy the book from John

At this point we come to some examples that have been put forth as counterexamples to (8.65b). Chomsky (1970a) has proposed a number of different

---

[25] I am indebted to P. Postal for this point.

types of examples in order to support the view that in some cases semantic interpretation requires surface structure information not available in deep structure.
The first type concerns the notion of natural answer that we have just discussed.
He points out that such responses to (8.128) as (8.129) (under normal intonation)
are natural answers to the question, whereas responses like those in (8.130) are not:

(8.128) Is it John who writes poetry?

(8.129) No, it's Bill who writes poetry

(8.130) No, $\begin{cases} \text{it's short stories that John writes} \\ \text{John writes only short stories} \end{cases}$

Chomsky argues that the natural answer in such cases is determined by the *focus*
of the question, the constituent in the question that receives the main stress and
that serves as the point of maximal inflection of the pitch contour. In (8.128) the
constituent "John" is the focus. Thus, (8.129) is a natural answer while (8.130)
is not because the former is parallel to (8.128) except for a constituent that appropriately contrasts with its focus while the latter is not. Another example of
Chomsky's is given in (8.131) and (8.32):

(8.131)

Was it $\begin{cases} \text{an ex-convict with a red shirt} & \text{(a)} \\ \text{a red-shirted ex-convict} & \text{(b) that he was warned to look out for?} \\ \text{an ex-convict with a shirt} \\ \quad \text{that is red} & \text{(c)} \end{cases}$

(8.132)

No, he was warned to look out for $\begin{cases} \text{an ex-convict with a red tie} & \text{(a)} \\ \text{a red-shirted automobile salesman} & \text{(b)} \\ \text{an ex-convict with a shirt that is green} & \text{(c)} \end{cases}$

The foci of (a), (b), and (c) of (8.131) are, respectively, "shirt," "ex-convict,"
and "red." Accordingly, the sentences (a), (b), and (c) of (8.132) are, respectively,
natural answers to the three questions in (8.131) because in these pairings the
question and its answer have the proper parallel structure and contrasting foci.
The answers in the other possible pairings, by the same token, are not natural
answers.

Admitting that the notion of focus cannot be determined fully in deep
structure without modifying the conception of deep structure in a highly artificial
way and that it can be determined naturally in surface structure, we can, nonetheless, deny that cases of natural answer relations provide evidence for the claim that
aspects of the assignment of readings depend on properties of surface structure.
We can treat the distinction between natural and unnatural answers to questions
like (8.128) or (8.131) as of rhetorical significance only, and so the difference
among such questions does not have to be accounted for in terms of a relevant
difference in their semantic interpretations. Such a treatment is superior, since an

account in the latter terms would imply that each question in a case like (8.131) has different logical properties, particularly different logical relations to other questions.[26] But this implication is false. For instance, any question that (a) of (8.131) entails is entailed by (b) and (c); any question that (b) of (8.131) entails is entailed by (a) and (c); and any question that (c) of (8.131) entails is entailed by (a) and (b). The same is true in the case of their corresponding statements, given in (8.133):

(8.133)

It was $\begin{cases} \text{an ex-convict with a red shirt} & \text{(a)} \\ \text{a red-shirted ex-convict} \\ \text{an ex-convict with a shirt} \\ \quad \text{that is red} & \text{(c)} \end{cases}$ (b) that he was warned to look out for

    Our claim, then, is that the intuitively felt difference among questions like (a), (b), and (c) of (8.131) is the same as that between (a) and (b) of (8.124), between (a) and (b) of (8.125), and between (a) and (b) of (8.126), and that the intuition can be accounted for without assuming a logical difference between the cases. Accounting for the natural answer relation on rhetorical grounds says that the occurrence of an unnatural pairing in a discourse (for example, (8.131c) followed by (8.132a)), without some stylistic motive, introduces an arbitrary shift that does not repay the reader for his effort.

    Closely related to the notion of focus (in fact, given surface structure, interdefinable with it) is a notion that Chomsky (1970a, pp. 70 ff.) calls *presupposition*. Roughly, this notion of presupposition is that which results from the replacement of the focus by a variable. Accordingly, the presuppositions of (a), (b), (c), (d) of (8.134) are (e), (f), (g), (h), respectively:

(8.134) (a) $\begin{cases} \text{It is} \\ \text{Is it} \end{cases}$ John that writes poetry in the garden(?)

        (b) $\begin{cases} \text{It is} \\ \text{Is it} \end{cases}$ poetry that John writes in the garden(?)

        (c) $\begin{cases} \text{It is} \\ \text{Is it} \end{cases}$ in the garden that John writes poetry(?)

        (d) John writes poetry in the garden

        (e) Someone writes poetry in the garden
        (f) John writes something in the garden
        (g) John writes poetry somewhere
        (h) Someone writes something somewhere

    Chomsky argues that this notion of presupposition belongs to surface structure and that, since an account of meaning must include an account of presupposition, the semantic component must operate on surface structure representa-

[26] That is, as this notion of logical properties and relations of questions is understood in Chapter 5.

tions to obtain the syntactic information it requires to specify the presuppositional aspect of meaning.

Chomsky himself (1970a, p. 77, note 27) observes that the term "presupposition," as he uses it, "covers a number of notions that should be distinguished," and he goes on to say, first, that a sentence like (8.134a) expresses a presupposition like (8.134e) "in the sense that the truth of the presupposition is a prerequisite for the utterance to have a truth value" and, second, that

> when we replace one of the foci of 'John gave Bill the BOOK' by a variable, it is not at all clear that the resulting expression determines a presupposition in in the same sense, though it does characterize 'what the utterance asserts' and to which utterances it is a proper response, when so understood (p. 77, note 27).

First, we observe that any proposition entailed by the presupposition of a sentence is also a presupposition of that sentence, that is, a condition whose satisfaction is necessary for the sentence to express a determinate proposition. Thus (e)–(h) of (8.134) are each presuppositions of the sentences (a)–(d). Accordingly, we can easily account for sentences like (8.134a) having presuppositions like (8.134e) in the Fregean (logical) sense without our having to refer to surface phenomena like foci. Second, we observe that Chomsky's remark about the possibility of other senses of "presupposition" is beside the point because his argument for the semantic relevance of surface structure phenomena like foci cannot be based on anything but the logical sense of this term. We can therefore say that, as far as the content of (e)–(h) is concerned, the sentences (a)–(d) presuppose the same thing, namely, that there is someone (to whom the noun "John" refers) and some place (which has the properties specified in the meaning of "garden").

But it is clear that there is something more to be said about the linguistic significance of the "it is" constructions. Jespersen (1969) says that

> the construction *it is* serves as a demonstrative gesture to point at one particular part of the sentence to which the attention of the hearer is to be drawn especially (p. 76).

The significance of the fact that one particular part of the sentence has been singled out in this way is, I think, that that part, the constituent in focus position, somehow indicates that its referent is unique in being or doing what the "that" clause of the cleft sentence predicates. Thus, the use of the interrogative variant of (8.134a) expresses a question which implies that the speaker takes it that there is some *one* particular person who writes poetry in the garden and that he requests the hearer to state whether that person is John.

The issue is, therefore, as follows. Does the indication of the referential uniqueness of the constituent in focus position figure as part of the Fregean presupposition of the sentence? Or does it figure, rather, in some rhetorical and hence nonlogical aspect of the sentence? I think the answer to the first question is negative and the answer to the second affirmative. It seems to me mistaken to say that if there is more than one person or thing that is (or does) what the "that" clause of the cleft sentence predicates then the sentence can make no statement, that it expresses an indeterminate proposition. But more than an argument on behalf of this view is required.

We begin by distinguishing between the *presupposition* of a sentence, understood as discussed in Chapter 4, and what we will call the *presumption* of a sentence. We understand this latter notion to refer to something the hearer is entitled to take the speaker to believe by virtue of the manner in which the speaker has chosen to express what he or she wants to say. To pin this notion down further, let us consider pairs of questions such as those in (8.135).[27]

(8.135) (a) Will you pass the dessert?
       (b) Won't you pass the dessert?
       (c) Are you coming home?
       (d) Aren't you coming home?
       (e) Did you take it?
       (f) Didn't you take it?

The discussion of questions in Chapter 5 shows that such cases have the same deep structure and are therefore synonymous. This accords well with our semantic intuition that both members of the pair (a)–(b) of (8.135) are requests to the person addressed, asking that he pass the dessert to the speaker. But the surface structure difference between these two questions is clearly one that speakers capitalize on when using them. Question (b) of (8.135), unlike (a), conveys the speaker's presumption that the person to whom his request is addressed has some reason for wanting to withhold the dessert from him.

Clearly, there is no difference between (a) and (b) of (8.135) with respect to what is requested, of whom it is requested, or for whom it is requested. But one might argue that there is a difference between the presuppositions of the two requests. This, however, is not the case, as can be seen if we compare the presumption of (8.135b), that the person addressed has some reason to withhold the dessert, with a genuine presupposition such as that of (5.34), that the person addressed has been beating his wife. In the latter case, if the speaker who utters a token of (5.34) knows that the addressee never beat his wife, the presupposition is false and the utterance does not succeed in expressing a question. But, in the former case, if the speaker knows full well that the person addressed has no reason to keep the dessert from being passed, still the utterance succeeds in expressing a request (or asking a question about the addressee's willingness to pass it), though, of course, a rather rude one. Accordingly, we cannot consider the presumption conveyed by (8.135b) to be a presupposition of that question but must take it to be something we are normally entitled to presume that the speaker believes and to presume that the speaker wants us to know that he or she believes. The presumption has the status of a "don't-believe-a-word-of-it" wink. In both cases, if it turns out that we are factually wrong in accepting the presumption to be true, we can justly

---

[27] Strictly, these cases are simple nexus-interrogatives, requiring a straightforward "yes" or "no" answer, and we will take them as such. But they may of course also be construed as cases that express requests. For the present discussion, it does not matter which way they are taken.

accuse the speaker of misleading us, whereas in a case where the presupposition is false, the sentence as well as its speaker comes in for " blame."

The conception of the rhetorical interpretation for the foci of (a)–(c) of (8.134) parallels the rhetorical account of the surface negative in cases like (8.135b): in both types of cases we are dealing with a presumption, not a presupposition. The general form of the presumption associated with the foci in (8.134a–c) is that the hearer is entitled to take the speaker to believe that the person or thing referred to by the constituent in focus position is unique in being or doing what the " that" clause of the cleft sentence predicates. Hence, we take it that (a), (b), and (c) of (8.134) differ in presumption: (a) carries the presumption that the speaker believes that John is *the* person who writes poetry in the garden; (b) carries the presumption that what John writes in the garden is restricted to poetry; and (c) carries the presumption that the garden alone is the place where John writes poetry.

To see that these are presumptions, not presuppositions, note that if there is more than one person, place, or literary activity that has the property predicated by the " that" clause of the cleft sentence, then, if there is nothing else in the context to indicate that the speaker is " up to something," the utterance is odd situationally but not indeterminate. This is shown also by the fact that (8.136) can express a determinate proposition:

(8.136) It is not John that writes poetry in the garden but his brothers Sam and Harry

In the case of interrogatives like those in (8.131), the general form of the presumption is slightly different, reflecting the fact that sentences of this type request information. Question (a) of (8.131) allows the hearer to presume that the speaker is confident that the person someone was warned to look out for was an ex-convict wearing something red but that the speaker is uncertain that it was a shirt. Question (b) allows the hearer to presume that the speaker is confident that the person someone was warned to look out for was wearing a red shirt but that the speaker is uncertain that this person was supposed to be an ex-convict. Question (c) allows the hearer to presume that the speaker is confident that the person someone was warned to look out for was an ex-convict with a shirt of some color but that the speaker is uncertain that the color was red. Accordingly, (8.132a) is the natural answer to (8.131a) because its use as a response expresses the recognition that the answer the speaker wants is the one most directly addressed to the uncertainty the speaker indicated by the particular choice of question. The same is true of (8.132b) and (8.131b) and of (8.132c) and (8.131c). Similarly, "You bet I won't!" or "I'll pass the dessert; why in the world shouldn't I?" are natural responses to (b) of (8.135) but not to (a). Nonetheless, they are answers to (8.135a), albeit irascible ones. Their naturalness as responses to (8.135b) derives from the fact that the presumption of the request justifies them.

In the cases (8.124)–(8.127), natural answers preserve the vocabulary of the questions to which they are responses. Therefore, unnaturalness must have something to do with the vocabulary switch. If this is so, the unnaturalness ought to be quite dramatic in sentential contexts where good style demands that there be no arbitrary change in the form or content of the relevant constituents, that is, contexts where parallelism is required.[28] Consider the cases in (8.137):

(8.137) (a) When I was asked who John preceded, I answered that Mary followed John
        (b) When I was asked who John preceded, I answered that John preceded Mary
        (c) Abe preceded Bill, Bill preceded Carl, and Donald followed Carl
        (d) Abe preceded Bill, Bill preceded Carl, and Carl preceded Donald
        (e) Was it both a red-shirted ex-convict and an ex-sailor with a shirt that is blue that we were warned to look out for?
        (f) Was it both a red-shirted ex-convict and a blue-shirted ex-sailor that we were warned to look out for?

Clearly, someone who wrote or uttered (a), (c), or (e) of (8.137) instead of (b), (d), or (f) would be rightly criticized for poor style due to faulty parallelism. The rationale for the stricture against faulty parallelism is clear. The writer or speaker has the obligation to the reader to convey his or her meaning in the most direct, simple, and unencumbered manner possible within the limitations of the subject matter so that the reader does not have to experience unnecessary difficulties in understanding what the writer wants to say. This is violated, for example, in the case of (a) or (c) of (8.137) since the reader would have to try to figure out why there is a change in the positions of the nouns from where they would be in the parallel constituent and would end up with nothing for his labor. The good stylist realizes that readers tacitly proceed on the assumption that the stylistic conventions are being adhered to and thus expect that such additional labor will be properly rewarded. If this reward is forthcoming, as it would be were the sentence (8.137a) to be followed in the discourse by sentences that went on to talk about how slavish a follower Mary is, or were the sentence (8.137c) to be followed by sentences that went on to talk about how slavish a follower Donald is, then the reader would not begrudge the extra steps in decoding. Instead, he would find them justified as an anticipation[29] and hence not at all pointless. On the other hand, if the extra effort needed in such cases is not rewarded, if the vocabulary switch is merely an empty promissory note, then the labor is pointless. In this case, the author sins against the canons of style.

Similar considerations apply in cases where no switch in vocabulary occurs. The unnaturalness of (8.130) as an answer to (8.128) can be explained on the grounds that the answer does not preserve the presumption. The rationale for

[28] My use of the term "parallelism" is the same as the one with which we are familiar from courses on "proper grammar." "Faulty parallelism" refers to unnecessary or arbitrary shifts (i.e., shifts without a stylistic motive) from one type of syntactic construction or from one repeated vocabulary element to another.

[29] Compare this case with (8.119)–(8.121). Had Kafka started *Metamorphosis* with (8.121b) instead of (8.120), critics would have complained that his opening sentence focused attention on the agency of the transformation, thereby creating the expectation that it would figure significantly in the plot, but that, contrary to what one was led to expect, the plot had nothing to do with the agency.

parallelism of presumption is the same stylistic canon just given. The reader of the question (8.128) picks up the presumption that the answerer is assumed to have picked up too, namely, that the person who asks the question is confident that someone writes poetry but is uncertain that it is John. The reader obtains this presumption and supposes that the answerer does also because he is aware of the wide range of stylistic variants from which the speaker made his choice. But if the answerer's response is (8.130), although this certainly answers the speaker's question, it has a different presumption, namely, that it is only short stories that John writes. As an answer, then, (8.130) is not the one most directly addressed to the uncertainty that the speaker indicated in his choice of the question. As readers, we conjecture that something out of the ordinary is to follow. If our expectations are unsatisfied, the complexity in the transition from question to answer was pointless and thus a case of poor style; but if our expectations are satisfied in a novel or interesting way, the complexity in transition had a point and is admired as an instance of stylistic skill.

Another rhetorical phenomenon is the use of language to express or excite emotions. One example of this is intonation used to convey surprise, as in (8.138), where a curved line over a constituent indicates a "surprise" intonation contour:

(8.138) (a) John is reading the newspaper

      (b) John is reading the newspaper

      (c) John is reading the newspaper

Thus, these sentences can be rendered in slightly exaggerated form, as in (a), (b), (c) of (8.139), respectively:

(8.139) (a) By God, John, of all people, is reading the newspaper
      (b) By God, John is, of all things, reading the newspaper
      (c) By God, John is reading, of all things, the newspaper

Although the sentences in (8.138) certainly differ markedly in rhetorical force, they are synonymous with one other. Each states the same assertion about John, regardless of the fact that each differs in terms of what it is that the speaker finds surprising.

Again, someone who wants to say that such sentences differ in meaning has to claim that they have different presuppositions. But, as in the previous examples about presumption, there is good reason to deny this. If it turns out that the speaker of one of these sentences is not really surprised at anything and never expected anything else, then, however situationally inappropriate the utterance may be, still it can make a statement (if its subject and object expressions properly refer). The statement is true if the referent of the subject expression is reading the referent of the object expression, and the statement is false if not. Since the speaker's not being surprised at the relevant aspect of the event in question does not render the proposition expressed by the sentences (8.138) indeterminate, the speaker's being surprised cannot be a presupposition.

Suppose, for example, that someone utters a token of (8.138a) although he knows full well that John is the most likely person around to be reading the newspaper. Constrast such a case, again, with one where someone says that John has stopped beating his wife although the speaker knows that John never indulged in this practice. If we find out that the speaker in the second case knew that John had never been beating his wife, we can claim that the speaker's utterance of the sentence failed to make a statement, since it cannot be true that John stopped the practice or false that he stopped it if he never indulged in it. If, on the other hand, we find out that the speaker in the first case knew that John was quite likely to be reading the newspaper, we can only accuse the speaker of trying to mislead or deceive us. In this case, the assertion's truth or falsity does not depend on the truth of the proposition that the speaker believes that John is an unlikely person to be reading the newspaper. In cases of presupposition, the assertion is about something or a state of affairs whose existence is claimed by the presupposition, but, clearly, the assertion of (8.138a) does not depend on the truth of this proposition about the speaker's beliefs.

Surface structure properties of the sort we have considered cannot be counterexamples to the principle (8.65b) because they are rhetorical and stylistic properties and so irrelevant to it. The semantic component explains semantic properties and relations, namely, those that fall out of an analysis of the question "What is meaning?" The properties and relations asked about in the questions that this question is analyzable into concern the logical form of sentences, that is, they have to do with the aspects of the grammar of sentences that determine their inference potentialities. The properties and relations just discussed, on the other hand, are independent of the logical form of sentences. Typically, they differentiate synonymous sentences in terms of rhetorical or stylistic effect, thus making available to speakers a variety of options to choose from when deciding how to express a proposition. Therefore, it is no mere matter of terminology whether they are called "semantic" or "rhetorical." If the properties and relations found only in surface structure are shown to have rhetorical significance, they are not ones that the semantic component is responsible for. They are, then, irrelevant to the issue of whether the semantic component must operate on some class of surface phrase markers.

The notion that the principle (8.65b) is vulnerable to "counterexamples" of this sort stems from a too loose and all-encompassing notion of semantics, which, in turn, stems from a vague notion of linguistic use. If we start with an undifferentiated notion of use, on the one hand, and an uninterpreted, formalized description of syntactic and phonological structure, on the other, we easily slip into thinking of "semantics" as covering every aspect of the way in which the syntactic and phonological features of sentences formalized in the grammar are related to the uses speakers make of these sentences. The result is that every formal property of a sentence is taken as semantic.

But there is no compelling reason to start with so vague a notion of use or to tolerate so loose and all-encompassing a notion of meaning. We can proceed, as we have in this book, by trying *first* to explicate the properties and relations central to semantics as this field is traditionally understood in grammar and lexicography and as it is seen from the pretheoretical viewpoint of the speaker's intuitions about meaning. Semantic representations can then be constructed within the framework of the constraints imposed by the explications of semantic properties and relations, and the relation between these representations and the syntactic structures they interpret can be determined on the basis of what information from syntax is required to assign them compositionally in the grammar. Once we have made some progress along these lines, we can raise the question of how linguistic use and linguistic structure are related. We are then in a better position to make sense of the notion of use. For the grammatical distinction between features of propositional form and features of rhetorical form which emerges from this line of approach leads naturally to a distinction among uses, between those having to do with cognitive matters such as rational argument and those having to do with stylistic matters such as the factors underlying a speaker's choice of a particular sentence from a set of sentences which are the same in meaning.

A secondary conclusion I wish to draw from these reflections is that there needs to be a new interpretive component in grammars, one that assigns a rhetorical interpretation to a sentence that marks the sentence's range of stylistic potentialities on the basis of principles that explain the grammatical structures on which stylistic canons rest. The development of this component lies outside the scope of the present book, but, nonetheless, certain of the general characteristics of the component can be described here.

This component will operate primarily on surface structure representations (i.e., final derived phrase markers) with their phonetic representation, since the differences that grammatically determine differences in rhetorical and stylistic use are found at this level. The component will assign a rhetorical interpretation that marks such properties and relations as Topic, Comment, and presumptive belief. Such interpretations will employ the same vocabulary of representation as semantic interpretation does and so must be distinguished from semantic interpretations to keep logical and stylistic matters separate. For example, if what we have said about a case like (8.135b) is correct, then the aspect of its rhetorical interpretation that represents the presumption of the speaker—namely, that the person addressed is, for some reason, unwilling to pass the dessert—cannot be represented in the reading of this sentence. Consider, on the other hand, a sentence like (8.140):

(8.140) Will those of you whom I believe to be unwilling for some reason to pass the dessert to me please pass it to me?

Here, what is only presumptive belief in (8.135b) is part of the presupposition, since an utterance of (8.140) fails to make a request if none of the people around is unwilling to pass the dessert to the speaker. Being part of the presupposition of (8.140), this proposition is part of its reading. But, since the content of the presumptive belief in the case of (8.135b) is the same as the content of the presupposition in the case of (8.140), that is, the information itself is the same, it is natural to utilize semantic markers to represent it in the former case as well as in the latter. If semantic readings and rhetorical representations are formulated in the same vocabulary and often take the same form, they have to be differentiated on some other basis to keep apart the grammar's account of such things as presumption and presupposition. Since we cannot differentiate them on the basis of a difference in the form of the readings or a difference in some aspect of their content, we must do so on the basis of some difference in the type of syntactic objects semantic and rhetorical representations are assigned to. The difference seems to be that underlying phrase markers are the objects in the former instance and superficial phrase markers are the objects in the latter.

Another secondary conclusion I wish to draw is that such a new component will have important applications in two areas in the study of language. First, it will contribute to the explanation of why languages have transformational structure by providing a supplement to the Chomsky-Miller (1963) hypothesis that transformations have the function of reducing the structural complexity of underlying phrase markers so that the phrase markers that are input to the mechanism of articulation are sufficiently simple.

Although this hypothesis explains a wide range of transformations, it still leaves other transformations unexplained, since not all have the effect of appreciably reducing structure. But if our account of rhetorical force is even roughly right, we may add that transformations also have the function of introducing nonsemantic properties of surface structure on which depends much of the possibility of stylistic variation within a language. This will provide a function for those transformations that do not appreciably reduce structural complexity, as well as for a portion of those that do, although, of course, the matter of what other functions transformations may perform is still open.

Second, the development of a rhetorical component for grammars will also make a contribution to the study of stylistics proper. Thus, it will connect grammar with still another scholarly discipline. Transformational grammar has already established significant interdisciplinary relations with philosophy and psychology in recent years as a result of the development of the concept of deep structure, a concept which has proven directly relevant to problems in these other areas. Now we can expect that, with further study of the relation between formal features of surface structure and stylistic principles, transformational grammar may succeed in establishing an interdisciplinary relation with literary criticism. The rhetorician and literary critic could then obtain the formal statements of just the grammatical concepts with which they now work in an informal and intuitively grasped form. Furthermore, I think that the rhetorician and literary critic will benefit not only by having formalized concepts to work with where formerly they had to rely on unexplicated ones, but also by being made aware of a variety of rhetorically relevant grammatical features whose existence they might not otherwise have discovered. Such features might not come to light without formalization and systematization of the sort one finds in the construction of generative grammars. Beyond this, we can hope that transformational analysis may make it possible to define certain general principles in stylistics such as those of Whitehall's (see (8.105) and (8.106)) about the natural order of constituents in sentences.[30]

[30] That such a definition might be possible on the basis of transformational analysis is suggested by the fact that the various orders of constituents that are not natural in Whitehall's sense appear, in general, to arise from fairly standard permutation transformations. But, such matters must be left for future study.

4.2. Nonrhetorical cases

We have examined a number of purely surface structure phenomena and have argued that none are matters of logical form; they are more plausibly taken to be matters of rhetoric or style. We conclude, then, that there is no basis for considering any of these phenomena to be semantic in the sense that this term has in the principle (8.65b) and so none can be construed as providing a counterexample to (8.65b).

But there are a number of cases proposed by Chomsky (1970a) and others where it is plausible to think that the phenomena cannot be represented in the grammar's account of deep structure and where they are clearly not rhetorical but logical in significance. Among them are the case of the positions of certain adverbs like "even" and "only," the scope relations between occurrences of "not" and certain occurrences of quantifiers, and certain pronominal relations that appear to be a function of stress or surface positioning of elements like "each." These cases cannot be dealt with by the strategy of trying to subsume them under rhetoric.[31] Indeed, the strategy for these phenomena must be to attack the soundness of the "facts" or question the validity of the argument that semantically relevant syntactic information is transformationally introduced into derived phrase markers.[32] We cannot reply to all the arguments that can be constructed with respect to such cases, but we will consider a few typical ones.

One such argument, to which Chomsky (1970a) refers, is due to Jackendoff (1969). Jackendoff considers the three sentences (8.141)–(8.143):

(8.141) Many of the arrows didn't hit the target

(8.142) Not many of the arrows hit the target

(8.143) It is not the case that many of the arrows hit the target

He observes that (8.142) is synonymous with (8.143) and that (8.141) is not synonymous with either (8.142) or (8.143). Consider, now, the passive of (8.141) and (8.142), namely, (8.144):

(8.144) The target wasn't hit by many of the arrows

Jackendoff argues that the principle of the semantic neutrality of transformations is false on the grounds that it would predict that (8.144) is ambiguous between the sense of (8.141) and (8.142) but (8.144) has only the sense of (8.142). To bolster his claim, Jackendoff suggests that these sentences be compared with those in (8.145).

---

[31] Nonetheless, by getting focus, natural answer, etc., out of the way as rhetorical, we significantly reduce the strength of the case against (8.65b): now it must be made with just the phenomena which remain, where the facts are less clear-cut and the arguments more vulnerable.

[32] Such an argument was put forward in Ziff (1966), where it was claimed that certain active sentences involving quantifiers and pronouns are not the same in meaning as their passive forms. A reply to Ziff's arguments has already appeared in Katz and Martin (1967).

(8.145) (a) Many of the arrows didn't hit the target, but many of them did hit it
       (b) Not many of the arrows hit the target, but many of them did hit it
       (c) The target wasn't hit by many of the arrows, but it was hit by many of
          them

He claims that (b) is fully contradictory, while (a) is not, and, further, that (c) is fully contradictory. From this he concludes that the only sense of (8.144) is the one on which it is synonymous with the sentence (8.142).

Both this argument and the arguments used by Ziff (1966) are fallacious if passive sentences have the type of deep structure that they are given in Katz and Postal (1964, pp. 71–74) and Chomsky (1965, pp. 103–106), where the underlying phrase marker of a passive sentence contains a manner adverbial whose realization is 'Passive', an element that makes the passive transformation apply obligatorily. For the principle of the semantic neutrality of transformations says only that sentences with the *same* underlying phrase marker are synonymous. It does not say that sentences with different underlying phrase markers are synonymous, and an active sentence's underlying phrase marker differs from the underlying phrase marker of its corresponding passive by at least the dummy element 'Passive'. Hence, even granting for the sake of this argument that Jackendoff is completely correct about the linguistic facts he cites, since the principle (8.65b) does not entail that a passive is fully synonymous with its active counterpart, it does not follow that (8.65b) is committed to the consequence that (8.144) is ambiguous between the senses of (8.141) and (8.142). To reach Jackendoff's conclusion that surface structure is relevant to semantic interpretation in these cases, a further premise is required, namely, that in (8.146):

(8.146) The dummy element 'Passive' has no reading, i.e., makes no contribution to the semantic interpretation of passive sentences.

For if the underlying phrase markers of two sentences are the same except for an element in one that does not appear in the other, and that element makes a contribution to semantic interpretation, then the sentences need not be full paraphrases.

But, now, it is open to the supporter of (8.65b) to deny (8.146). It is indeed true that Postal and I accepted (8.146), but we did so solely because we accepted the empirical generalization that actives and their corresponding passives are the same in meaning. To incorporate this generalization in our theory required a special proviso in the case of the dummy element 'Passive', namely, that, unlike 'Q', 'Imp', and 'Neg', it carries no semantic information. Assuming now that we are convinced that Jackendoff is right about the empirical facts concerning actives and passives with quantifiers and negation, we naturally drop the principle (8.146), which was never more than an ad hoc feature of our theory, and we simply give 'Passive' a lexical reading that specifies the scope of negation appropriately. Actually, this is an improvement in our theory because it brings the passive element in line with our position with regard to the elements 'Q', 'Imp', and

'Neg'. That is, if this replacement is made, then we have the generalization that any universal element that makes a transformation obligatory and determines a sentence type will carry semantic information.[33]

In the event that the passive underlying phrase marker can be formulated without 'Passive' or that a lexical reading such as would be appropriate for 'Passive' cannot be assigned, Jackendoff's case is as strong as his evidence for the claim that (8.144) does not have the sense of (8.141). Thus, it is worthwhile to examine just how strong this evidence is.

Suppose that we have a film showing the arrows in the quiver prior to their being shot at the target, showing them being shot, and, finally, showing the target with arrows sticking in it and arrows lying around it (where all the arrows that did not hit the target appear). Let us imagine that we draw a circle around the arrows in the quiver (as shown in the first frame of our film) and label this set 'A'. We next draw a circle around the arrows sticking in the target and call that set 'H' and then draw a circle around the arrows lying on the ground and call that set 'M'. We assume that H + M = A. Furthermore, let us explicate the relation 'many of x are y' as a relation between a set x and a set y that holds just in case a sizable number of the members of x are members of y. Now, consider (8.142). On the basis of our assumptions, this sentence says (8.147):

(8.147) The set H does not contain a sizable number of the members of the set A

(We leave open the question of whether (8.142) also says that some A's are H's, since this aspect is not relevant to the point at issue.) Consider, next, (8.143), which says (8.148):

(8.148) ~(There is a B, such that B is a subset of A and B contains a sizable number of the members of A and B = H)

According to Jackendoff, (8.141) is not synonymous (on a sense) with (8.142) or (8.143). On our analysis, (8.141) says (8.149):

(8.149) There is a B, such that B is a subset of A and B contains a sizable number of the members of A and B = M

[33] Of course, there is the problem of constructing a lexical reading for 'Passive' that states the appropriate relation between quantifiers and negations. But this question is not one that needs to be considered here since, as we shall argue, there is no reason to think that the facts warrant such a reading. But that such a reading is possible is enough to invalidate Jackendoff's argument. It is no argument against such a lexical reading that it is exceptional insofar as it involves specific information precluding a VP scope for 'Neg' in the context of a quantifier, since the alternative is to tolerate just as bad an exception, namely, an exception to the generalization that the scope of semantic rules is just the underlying phrase markers. Also, there appears to be no need for a general surface structure rule to cover other cases of NP permutation in connection with quantifiers and negation. Fodor (in conversation) has pointed out that in other cases, such as the dative permutation of direct and indirect objects, the transformation clearly does not change meaning.

In fact, the claim made by Jackendoff that (8.145a) is not contradictory strongly supports this analysis of (8.141), since if it had the sense of either (8.142) or (8.143), it would be contradictory in the way that (8.145b) is or in the way that (8.150) is:

(8.150) It is not the case that many of the arrows hit the target, but many of them did hit it

Let us now look at (8.144). This sentence says (8.151):

(8.151) The target wasn't hit by some things

We can take the things referred to in (8.151) to form a set, call it 'B', such that B is a subset of A. Clearly, (8.144) also says that B contains a sizable number of the members of A and that the members of B are misses. Hence, (8.144) says that there is a subset B of A such that B contains a sizable number of the members of A and B = M, that is, (8.144) says (8.149). Thus, contrary to Jackendoff, (8.144) is synonymous with (8.141) rather than (8.142).

We have taken the analysis of Jackendoff's cases a step further than he did by looking not only at intuitions about synonymy relations but also at the meaning of the sentences in question. As a result, we have found their synonymy relations to be different from what Jackendoff assumed. If we are right, then he must also be wrong about the contradictoriness of (8.145c). Jackendoff claims that (8.145c) is a contradiction and that this conclusively shows that "the only possible reading of the passive [(8.144)] is the one synonymous with [(8.142)]" (p. 224). If we can show that this sentence, too, is not as Jackendoff claims, then, by the same token, we have conclusively shown that his argument is fallacious.

The synonymy of (8.142) and (8.144) is supposed to be reflected in the fact that both (8.145b) and (8.145c) are contradictions. Sentence (8.145b) is a contradiction because its first conjunct asserts (8.147) and its second conjunct asserts the denial of (8.147). Now, if a conjunction is a contradiction because its conjuncts are inconsistent, then it will remain so when the conjunction "but" is replaced by "and." This is the case with (8.145b), as we see from the contradition in (8.152):

(8.152) Not many of the arrows hit the target and many of them did hit it

But (8.145c) fails this test, as we see from (8.153):

(8.153) The target wasn't hit by many of the arrows and it was hit by many of them

Example (8.153) is not a contradiction. It simply says that there were a lot of both hits and misses. Thus, the formulation (8.145c) is misleading because of the use of the conjunction "but" (rather than "and"). "But," as we saw in Chapter 6, requires a logical contrast between the assertions conjoined. As (8.153) shows, the assertions conjoined in (8.145c) are that there are a sizable number of hits and there are a sizable number of misses. Thus, the requirement that the conjoined sentences in (8.145c) contrast logically is violated. This violation produces some form of semantic deviance, and it is this semantic anomaly that is mistaken for contradictoriness. Thus, the intuitions of speakers that seem at first blush to support Jackendoff's position can be better accounted for as intuitions about semantic anomaly that are wrongly interpreted.

We thus conclude that (8.144) is the passive of (8.141), that (8.144) is not the passive of (8.142), and that the passive of (8.142) is (8.154) or (8.155) (depending on whether the former is accepted as being well-formed):

(8.154) The target was hit by not many of the arrows

(8.155) The target was hit by few of the arrows

We observe that (8.156) is a contradiction, as is predicted by our analysis:

(8.156) The target was hit by $\begin{Bmatrix} \text{not many} \\ \text{few} \end{Bmatrix}$ of the arrows and it was hit by many of them

Therefore, we find nothing in Jackendoff's discussion to warrant a rejection of (8.65b).

We shall not consider additional actual or possible criticisms of (8.65b). Our aim cannot be to defend it against every criticism. Rather, we wish to reflect the present situation with respect to the status of (8.65b) by indicating the kinds of replies that can be made to some of the most serious criticisms. My assessment of the situation is that, with respect to a certain range of cases, namely, those that cannot be subsumed under the category of rhetorical phenomena, it is reasonable to doubt (8.65b), but the arguments based on these cases are by no means conclusive. As I see it, the present situation is muddled. In the first place, linguistic intuitions about the critical sentences are often nowhere as clear and unproblematic as they should be. In the second, our present understanding of the phenomena in question (e.g., quantifiers, negative constituents, and pronominalization) is very poor indeed, so that there often appears to be a number of equally plausible ways in which to account for the syntactic structure of the critical sentences. These considerations, of course, cut both ways, and this means that neither those who wish to make a case for (8.65b) nor those who wish to make a case against it can be too confident of their ground.

Thus, for the time being at least, I think it is fruitless to try either to prove (8.65b) by attempting to knock down every criticism or to refute it by adding further criticisms of the same sort. There is, however, an additional question, one which has so far not been considered in the debate about surface structure and semantic interpretation but which has to be dealt with by critics of (8.65b) if they are to provide a conclusive argument against this principle. This is the question of why transformations ought to introduce certain syntactic relations that are semantically significant. Given, for the sake of argument, that the evidence shows that transformations do introduce certain features of surface structure that provide information required for semantic interpretation, what explains it? We recall that there are two general functions of transformations, two answers to the question of why natural languages have transformational structure. One is that transformations reduce the structural complexity of deep structures, thereby making available structures that are more suited to the limitations of the articulatory process, and the other is that they provide the stylistic and rhetorical richness of natural languages. Both these hypotheses indicate that transformations do not have anything to do with providing the syntactic distinctions on which aspects of meaning depend. Moreover, as yet there has been offered no general reason why deep structure should not be capable of including all such syntactic distinctions. Therefore, we need some rationale, either in terms of a further function of transformations or in terms of some necessary limitation on deep structure, or in terms of both, to explain why transformations should be in the business of defining the object of semantic interpretation together with the base component. Only when we have such a rationale will we be in a position to make a conclusive case against (8.65b).

Though it is at present unclear that (8.65b) is false, we may ask what the consequences are if it is shown that certain syntactic relations among quantifiers, negation, and pronouns appear in surface structure but are absent in the deep structures underlying them. Clearly, even if surface structure determines the aspects of meaning that depend on these syntactic relations, the semantic component still has to operate on underlying phrase markers, and for exactly the reasons put forth in Katz and Postal (1964) to justify (8.65b), namely, the following. Since a wide range of transformations destroy constituent structure, so that derived phrase markers typically contain less information about the constituents of a sentence and their grammatical relations, the underlying phrase marker(s) of a sentence provide the full account of its constituents and the account of most, if not all, of their grammatical relations, which is what the semantic component needs in order to provide a compositional analysis of the meaning of the sentence. Now, on the supposition that certain syntactic relations among quantifiers, negation, and pronouns are not found in deep structure, the semantic component would *also* have to operate on certain aspects of the surface phrase markers of certain sentences to fill in information about grammatical relations not available in deep structure. The logical question to ask at this point is to what aspects of propositional structure is such information relevant. What is the semantic difference between the information that the semantic component gets from deep structure and the information that, on our present supposition, it gets from surface structure?

If arguments of the sort that Jackendoff has proposed can be carried through, then, in a certain range of cases, the scope of the operations defined in the lexical entry for 'Neg' will have to be specified in terms of a grammatical relation given by the order of quantifier and negation in surface structure. Chomsky (1970a) argues from some recent work by Dougherty concerning the syntactic relations of quantifiers like "each" to anaphora that in special instances the scope of a quantifier can be determined by properties of surface structure. Also, Anderson (to appear) argues that the parts of sentences that constitute the scope of "even" cannot be specified without reference to derived phrase markers. Supposing such arguments turn out to be sound, we can conjecture, at this point, that the information that the semantic component receives from surface phrase markers is concerned with scope relations.

On the basis of this conjecture, we might rephrase (8.65b) as in (8.157):

(8.157) (a) The semantic component operates on the phrase markers in K to determine the sense of the logical particles, the terms, and the predicates that enter into propositions, to determine the relations between connectives and the concepts or propositions they connect, and to determine the relations of terms to predicates.

(b) The semantic component operates on the phrase markers in K to determine the scope relations between quantifiers and variables, between operators (like negation) and quantifiers, and between adverbials like "even" (and "only") and the constituents they can modify.

If it turns out that (8.65b) fails to account for the sort of case that is in question, one can hold that it fails because (8.157b) is not, in general, true. The cases under discussion disconfirm (b) of (8.157) but not (a). But (a) is, in fact, the heart of the principle (8.65b) and indeed the only part of it that the evidence which Postal and I put forth actually supports. Thus, by reformulating (8.65b) in terms of (8.157a,b), we can argue that the core of this principle remains intact, while granting, if necessary, that its first formulation was wrong. We will have to admit that certain transformations contribute to the semantic representation of sentences, but this, from the present perspective, is a minor concession. Moreover, we are not in the embarrassing position of being faced with two bodies of evidence that suggest conflicting hypotheses. Still we face the question of why syntactic information about the scope of elements such as quantifiers, negation, etc., should be determined by features of surface structure.

5.   Some reflections on what meaning is not

In Chapter 1, I argued that the subject matter of semantics can be circumscribed only pretheoretically in terms of the properties and relations asked about in the questions to which "What is meaning?" gives rise. This situation we took to be typical of the earliest stage of any science. In the course of the book, I have tried to set forth the sort of theory that could account not only for the properties and relations with which we began, but also for others whose semantic character emerged as a result of the way the theory was able to interrelate the phenomena with which it started. For example, the converse relation, the symmetry relation, and the reflexivity relation were found to be specifiable within the same theoretical system originally devised to account for semantic anomaly, semantic ambiguity, synonymy, analyticity, and so on. When the development of a theory leads to the explanation of phenomena it was not initially designed to explain, the theory can be credited with having shown that these phenomena actually are of the same kind as those to which the theory was directed. As semantic theory came to be extended and large numbers of new relationships among phenomena that seemed unrelated pretheoretically were revealed, the domain of semantics, first identified in terms of a small set of clear-cut semantic phenomena, came also to be identified by the theory itself. The theory became a specification of what it means for a linguistic property or relation to be semantic by virtue of specifying the connection between the initial set of clear-cut cases and the further properties and relations whose semantic character came to light in the process of theory construction. Consequently, we can expect that the further we push theory construction in semantics, the better we will understand what semantics is. Fodor (1968b) expressed this sort of point quite nicely in speaking about the same kind of process in psychology:

> There is, then, an important sense in which a science has to discover what it is about: it does so by discovering that the laws and concepts it produced in order to explain one set of phenomena can be fruitfully applied to phenomena of other sorts as well. It is thus only in retrospect that we can say of all the phenomena embraced by a single theoretical framework that *they* are what we meant, for example, by the presystematic term "physical event," or "chemical interaction," or "behavior" (pp. 10–11).

At our present stage in semantics, we are, of course, very far from the point at which we might answer our original question "What is meaning?" in anything approaching a complete form. Nonetheless, I think it is fair to say that in the course of this study many things have come to light about the nature of meaning. They do not add up to a full explanation of meaning, but there should be nothing unsettling about the fact that the answer to so fundamental a question has to await the results of empirical investigations that will provide a more complete statement of the theory.

On the other hand, it is certainly possible, and desirable, to consider some of the things that, on the basis of the progress made thus far in semantic theory, it is apparent that meaning is not. We have already indicated some of these things. For example, we have shown that meaning is not use in the broad sense of this term, where it concerns the conditions under which it is appropriate for speakers to employ words and sentences in real speech situations. Moreover, we have also shown that attempts to narrow the term "use" so as to avoid counterexamples to the 'meaning is use' thesis (such as the "bunny" versus "rabbit" case) require an independent specification of the grammatical features of linguistic types that differentiate uses whose differences are semantically irrelevant from those whose differences are semantically relevant. Since such a specification is a semantic theory, the use side of the 'meaning is use' equation is vacuous.

We have shown, furthermore, that meaning cannot be identified either with extension in the simple traditional sense or with extension in the more complex Goodmanian sense. And we have shown that meaning is not to be equated with the physical conditions under which verbal responses are elicited. I have nothing to add now to the arguments against either of these positions given earlier. But I would like to consider two further things that have been confused with meaning.

There is a large amount of discussion at present about whether meaning is or is not a property of utterances as well as of sentences. On the one hand, "means" in ordinary English is used in reference to the utterances that communicate a speaker's message to hearers in actual speech situations. We talk about the speaker's and/or the speaker's utterance's meaning, without much sense that such uses are metaphorical or homonymic. On the other hand, there is a clear distinction between meaning in connection with utterances and meaning in connection with the sentence types of which they are the tokens: in the former case, we speak of the meaning in a context, and in the latter we speak of the meaning in the language. This distinction may be illustrated by many examples, one of which is the case where someone " condemns (another) with faint praise." In such cases, the sentence means one thing while its utterance (in context) means another.

I think that the way to clarify this confusion is to realize that there is no incompatibility. From the viewpoint of representation, meaning is the same whatever it is we are talking about—sentences, speakers, utterances, etc. We can correctly say that some utterance as used by some speaker in some context has the same meaning as some sentence type. On the effability hypothesis the point can be put yet another way: the same class of semantic representations or readings suffices both for the analysis of senses of sentence types and for their tokens in actual speech situations. On the other hand, from the viewpoint of the theory of how sentences and utterances obtain their meaning, there are important differences in the way that meanings are determined, differences that are sufficient to make the semantic account of sentence tokens (utterance-context pairs) fall outside the theory of the meaning of sentence types. The meaning that " damns" someone who has been only faintly praised can be accounted for only if it is taken as a function of both the compositional semantic structure of the sentence type that expresses the " praise" and the contextual features that license the equation of such faint commendation with reproof.

We based our study of the meaning of sentence types on an idealization that allowed us to focus exclusively on linguistic meaning by abstracting away every aspect of language use that does not reflect pure grammatical competence. We observed early in the book that even a complete theory of the meaning of sentences and other constituent types is a far cry from a full theory of linguistic communication, that a semantic theory, in our sense, is only part of such a broader the orydevoted to the ways language is used. We claimed, however, that in one respect semantic theory is logically prior to a theory of linguistic communication, namely, the former theory is a proper part of the latter and provides information required by the principles that assign semantic representations to utterances. Our position is this. In a large variety of situations, what someone says, asserts, asks, requests, etc., is different from the literal meaning of the sentence type used to perform the speech act. The utterance token of the sentence type expresses some proposition that is incompletely or wrongly specified by the information in the meaning of the sentence type. Yet, the further information required to specify this proposition depends on the meaning of the sentence type as well as features of the context in which the token occurs (so that the relevant features of the context can be picked out only on the basis of the semantic structure of the sentence type). Therefore, we have assumed that a theory of linguistic communication involves principles of contextual interpretation that go well beyond the scope of semantic theory but that these principles require antecedently specified semantic representations of the sentences of the language.

We have said almost nothing in previous studies of linguistic theory about such extra-grammatical principles beyond what had to be said to distinguish them from the grammatical principles of semantic interpretation. The reason was that very little could be said of a theoretical nature since very little was known about how they are related to grammatical principles and on what basis they might be theoretically systematized.

Due to H. P. Grice's efforts to construct a theory of conversational implicature, work on a theory of linguistic communication has taken its first step beyond the theory of grammar.[34] By saying this, I do not mean to underestimate the importance of the work done by philosophers who tried to develop a theory of speech acts nor to overestimate the extent to which Grice has so far been able to carry the construction of his theory. The work of speech act theorists, particularly Austin, and Searle after him, was necessary and highly significant. Grice's theory, moreover, is still in the very earliest stages of its development. Yet, in my opinion, Grice's theory is a significant advance toward an understanding of the complex factors underlying our ability as speakers to produce and comprehend speech.

I will briefly sketch Grice's theory here, starting with the way in which it can serve to link up ideal grammars of sentence types with the construals that speakers place on their tokens in real speech situations.

Grice bases his theory on a set of distinctions that cover the total content of the construal a sentence token receives in context. He distinguishes, in the first place, between *what is said in uttering the token* and *what is implicated in uttering it* (on the occasion and in the circumstances). The former category is analyzed into *the conventional meaning of the sentence type* (of which the utterance in question is a token) and *the statement, etc., that the token makes in the context.* This category provides the hook-up between this theory and the grammar of the language. Grice explains that what is said is related to the sentence's conventional meaning (or, in our terminology, the literal, linguistic meaning) by two factors, the identification of the referents of the referring expressions and the identification of the time points of the temporal designations. He points out that the construal of an utterance is its conventional meaning if we know no more about the speech situation than that the speaker was speaking the language and speaking literally. Consider Grice's example (8.158):

(8.158) He is in the grip of a vice (vise)

The utterance of (8.158), according to Grice, would be construed as expressing the statement that at the speech point some male was caught in the jaws of a device

---

[34] Parts of the account of Grice's theory to be given here are based on published works of his. Where this is so, I have indicated the source. But other parts are based on Grice's 1967–68 William James Lectures at Harvard, which have not been published. In these cases I have relied on memory, notes, and on some manuscript of the William James Lectures which, I am told, Grice used in his seminars. I am sorry not to be able to document some of my statements with quotations from these lectures, but, under the present circumstances, this is impossible. Thus the reader is cautioned not to take certain details of what is said about Grice's theory to be necessarily a perfect rendition of the points in question.

for holding work or the statement that at the speech point someone's behavior was under the control of some failing in his moral character. Hence, to know what is said in an utterance of (8.158), it is necessary to know not only this ambiguity of the sentence type, but also the identity of the individual referred to and the time at which the speaker made the reference.

This conception is very close to that presented in Katz and Fodor (1963), where the purpose was to draw an upper limit on what a grammar concerned with the linguistic meaning of sentence types should account for. We wrote:

> consider a communication situation so structured that no information about setting can contribute to a speaker's understanding of a sentence encountered in that situation. Any extragrammatical [in the narrow sense, including only syntax and phonology] ability a speaker can employ to understand the meaning of a sentence in such a situation will *ipso facto* be considered to require semantic explanation. The type of communication situation we shall consider is the following: a number of English speakers receive an anonymous letter containing only the English sentence S. We are interested in the difference between this type of situation and one in which the same anonymous letter is received by persons who do not speak English but are equipped with a completely adequate grammar of English [again, in the narrow sense].... Suppose S is the sentence "The bill is large." Speakers of English will agree that this sentence is ambiguous, i.e. that it has at least two readings: according to one, it means that some document demanding a sum of money to dispense a debt exceeds in size most such documents, and according to another, it means that the beak of a certain bird exceeds in bulk those of most similar birds (pp. 484–485 of 1964 reprint).

Grice's notion of conventional meaning, as far as it goes, is therefore the same as ours (both views take the conventional meaning or linguistic meaning to be the set of senses of a sentence or other constituent type), and Grice's notion of what is said coincides with our notion of setting selection (both views take the problem to be that of picking out one of the senses of the sentence type on the basis of contextual information about the referents of the indexical elements and information about the time of utterance). Thus, the hook-up of a grammar to a theory of contextual construal is quite direct: the upper limit of semantic interpretation in a grammar concerned with conventional or linguistic meaning is the starting point for a theory of contextual construal.

The latter category, namely, what is implicated in the uttering of a sentence, provides the domain for Grice's theory. Grice divides this category into two subcategories, *what is conventionally implicated* and *what is conversationally implicated*. I shall ignore the former subcategory because I am unable to see why the kinds of cases that are included in it are really anything more than part of the meaning of the sentence type in question. One of Grice's few examples of the membership of this category is (8.159):

(8.159) He is an Englishman; therefore he's brave

Grice holds that someone who utters this sentence under standard conditions "commits himself" (by virtue of the conventional meaning of (8.159)) to its being true that the person in question's being brave is a consequence of his being an Englishman but that the speaker does not say this. I agree that the fact that a word like "because" may have a conventional meaning expressing a 'consequence-of' ('reason-for') relation is not sufficient to claim that this semantic information contributes to what the speaker says when uttering a token of (8.159) under standard conditions; however, I find no difference between cases like (8.159) and cases like (8.160):

(8.160) The reason he is brave is that he is an Englishman

The category of what is conversationally implicated contains cases where the construal of a token of a sentence type in a context is not determined exclusively by what is said but also by inferences from what is said based on certain very general principles of communication. It is these principles that form Grice's theory of conversational implicature. The kind of situation that shows the need for such a category in the general theory of linguistic communication is one where, on the one hand, the speaker of an utterance U can be held responsible for implying something by producing U in the situation but, on the other hand, the meaning of the proposition(s) grammatically associated with U in no way itself licenses this implication. One of Grice's (1961) examples of this is the following:

> If someone says "My wife is either in the kitchen or in the bedroom" it would normally be implied that he did not know in *which* of the two rooms she was (p. 449 of 1965 reprint).

It is perfectly clear that the occurrence of this utterance in a situation where there is no reason to think that the speaker is just not saying which room his wife is in even though he knows commits the speaker to endorsing the truth of the statement that he does *not* know which is the room. Furthermore, this statement to which he commits himself is not a logical consequence of, cannot be inferred from, the relevant standing proposition(s), since otherwise the speaker's ignorance would be a precondition of the truth of his assertion that his wife is either in the kitchen or in the bedroom. Grice offers a convincing argument to show that it is not a precondition:

> Suppose (a) that the speaker knows that his wife is in the kitchen, (b) that the house has only two rooms (and no passages, etc.). Even though (a) is the case, the speaker can certainly say truly "My wife is in the house"; he is merely not being as informative as he could be if the need arose. But the true proposition that his wife is in the house together with the true proposition that the house consists entirely of a kitchen and a bedroom, entail the proposition that his wife is either in the kitchen or in the bedroom. But if to express the proposition p in certain circumstances would be to speak truly, and p, together with another true proposition, entail q, then surely to express q in the *same* circumstances must be to speak truly (p. 449).

Therefore, the implication about the speaker's ignorance of the truth values of the disjuncts of his assertion about his wife's location cannot be explained by any of the considerations of grammar or reference to which we may appeal in connection with conventional meaning or what is said.

Such implications are thus to be distinguished from those in the first two categories by being put in the category of what is conversationally implicated. The explication of this notion will then provide the general model and the conceptual apparatus for the explanation of such particular implications. We may conceive of the situation with which a theory of linguistic communication deals in the following way. A speaker produces an utterance which is a token of some set of sentence types. The first step in understanding the speaker is to associate this token with the set of sentences of which it is a token and the senses of these sentences (i.e., the propositions they express). This step is accomplished by making use of the principles of the grammar of the language. The next step is to reduce the range of ambiguity by choosing a single proposition and to determine the designata of its indexical elements, thereby associating the grammatically obtained set of senses with a single standing (or eternal) proposition. This is accomplished by making use of some as yet unknown principles of the theory of reference (or pragmatics). Finally, the resulting standing proposition must be associated with some other standing proposition(s) that convey what the speaker has conversationally implicated by his utterance. This last step is to be accomplished by the principles of Grice's theory of conversational implicature. Thus, using the previous example, his theory can be viewed as an attempt to specify the principles that enable us to associate a standing proposition that says that some definite person's wife is, at some definite time, either in the kitchen or in the bedroom of some definite house with a standing proposition that says that the person in question, at the time of his utterance, does not know which of the two rooms his wife is in.

We may now give a very brief sketch of Grice's theory. Grice starts with the theoretical assumption that the discourses he is to investigate are part of a cooperative activity in which each participant's speech is designed to help achieve the purpose of the activity. The basic principle on which Grice's theory relies is what he calls the *Cooperative Principle*, which says, in effect, that one is obligated to make one's contribution to a conversation appropriate in terms of its aim and direction. The notion of appropriateness is to be fleshed out by the specification of a set of maxims.

The import of adopting such a principle is that it provides an assumption about the participants in a conversation, roughly, that they are following mutually known and accepted rules, which fact enables them to infer various things about the proper ways to construe a speaker's utterance in connection with what it conveys beyond what the speaker has said. There is, of course, a problem with specifying the aim of a talk exchange, since the purposes vary from one talk exchange to another. Grice handles this by making the simplifying assumption that, generally, regardless of the nature of the ultimate purpose of talk exchanges, they have the prior purpose of achieving a "maximally effective exchange of information." Thus, for example, even if we are trying to influence or direct the behavior of others, we normally have the prior, instrumental purpose of exchanging information in the maximally effective way.

On the basis of the Cooperative Principle and this notion of the purpose of a talk exchange, Grice states four maxims that attempt to spell out the rules that it can be assumed participants have agreed to follow in making their verbal contributions: (a) "the maxim of quantity," which says that the contribution one makes to a conversation ought to be as informative as required in the situation, neither too informative nor too uninformative, (b) "the maxim of quality," which says that one ought to try to make a true contribution, (c) "the maxim of relation," which says that one ought to make a relevant contribution, and (d) "the maxim of manner," which says that one ought to avoid creating confusion as a result of obscurity, ambiguity, etc., and try to be clear and concise.

Grice's explanation of the fact that the utterance of the disjunctive sentence about the whereabouts of the man's wife implicates that the speaker was ignorant of the truth values of its components is, roughly, as follows. The components of a disjunction give more information than the disjunction itself. According to maxim (a) one does not make a less informative statement than one is in a position to make unless there is good reason to. Accordingly, if we assume the man is following the Cooperative Principle and its associated maxims, we can infer that he had good reason for not making the stronger, more informative statement. The obvious reason in a situation where it may be supposed that the stronger statement is appropriate is that the person is simply unable to make it without violating maxim (b). Therefore, we may draw the conclusion that the man lacked the information he needed to assert one of the disjuncts. The man also commits himself to this conclusion (i.e., implicates it) by virtue of the fact that he knows that we are entitled to expect him to behave in accord with the cooperative principle and its maxims.

Conversational implicatures thus arise from the assumption on the part of all the participants in a talk exchange that speakers will adhere to the Cooperative Principle, that they endorse the purpose(s) of the talk exchange and are prepared to obey the rules insofar as they are able to do so. Accordingly, conversational implicatures are implications of a very different nature from semantic entailments or logical implications.

Among the cases where conversational implicatures arise, Grice identifies one where a conversational implicature arises through an apparent violation of a maxim, one where a conversational implicature arises through an obvious unavoidable violation of a maxim, and one where a conversational implicature arises through the deliberate violation of a maxim. In each of these cases the existence of a conversational implicature enables us to preserve the assumption of adherence to the Cooperative Principle by supposing that the violation (or apparent violation) has been produced to help achieve the purpose of the talk exchange. If, in the final analysis, this assumption cannot be preserved, we must take it that the speaker has "opted out" (as, for example, if the speaker says he is not at liberty to say more).

Roughly speaking, in saying *p*, a speaker implicates *q* if, first, the speaker can be presumed to be observing the Cooperative Principle and its maxims, second, the speaker and the audience each think that the others think that the speaker could not be presumed to be observing the Cooperative Principle unless the speaker thought that *q*, third, the speaker has done nothing to indicate that the audience should not think that he thinks *q*, and, fourth, the speaker believes that the members of the audience can be reasonably expected to figure all of this out themselves.

The example of the man who said that his wife was either in the kitchen or in the bedroom is an illustration of the case where a conversational implicature arises through an apparent violation of a maxim. We will now illustrate the case where a conversational implicature arises through a deliberate, blatant violation of a maxim. Grice refers to this case as one in which a maxim is exploited (by the speaker) because the violation is designed to achieve a certain effect in the context.

Let us suppose that Smith, who is known to regard Jones as one of the worst scoundrels in the world, says that Jones is a prince of a fellow. We at once see this remark as a blatant violation of the maxim (b), which prohibits saying what one knows or believes to be false. We reason that, since it is clear that Smith has said something that he does not believe, and since he knows we know this, either he is opting out or else he is trying to convey something other than what he has said. We reason further that there is no basis on which to assume he is opting out and every reason to think he is not, so that we are forced to interpret Smith's remark about Jones in a way different from what was said in making it. The simplest hypothesis available to us that uses the information that first led us to think that Smith said something he did not believe is that he was trying to convey his very low opinion of Jones's moral character. Accordingly, we take the remark to be ironic, that is, to mean the exact opposite of what it says. We conclude that Smith has conversationally implicated that Jones is the very opposite of a prince of a fellow, since we can assume that Smith foresaw that we could draw this conclusion and did nothing to stop us from doing so, and, moreover, the rhetorical effect of the irony is especially appropriate in the light of Smith's intensely negative attitude toward Jones's character.

Before concluding this very brief discussion of Grice's theory, I think it necessary to point out that the line between what is said and what is implicated is not clear at all. Suppose someone publicly utters (8.161):

(8.161)   Richard M. Nixon steals candy from babies

He is then prosecuted for slandering the President of the United States. The defense lawyer argues that the defendant did not actually refer to the President at all but to the local grocer, whose name turns out to be "Richard M. Nixon" (and who is a locally notorious candy thief who preys on children). It seems clear that such a defense would probably fail and ought to fail to convince the court. The court would reason that the speaker must have known or can be assumed to have known that a national audience would inevitably take the occurrence of "Richard M. Nixon" to refer to the President and thus he ought to have employed a qualifying expression (e.g., "who runs the grocery store in my neighborhood") to make the statement that he says he intended to make. If the court convicts him of slander, it does so because what he said (contrary to what he may have intended to say) was that the President steals candy from babies. Here the reasoning depends on the assumption that the speaker was obeying the Cooperative Principle, in particular, that he was not violating maxim (a) by saying less than is required. Since identification of the referent of the subject of (8.161) can depend on maxims like (a) and on the pattern of argument for implicatures, determining what is said depends on the principles for working out what is implicated.

Given, therefore, that the machinery of Grice's theory enters into not only what is conversationally implied but also into what is said, it is clear that, in general, Grice's theory is necessary in order to determine the statement made (the question asked, etc.) by the utterance of a sentence in a speech situation. Not only do we need such a theory to determine the statement in a case like the example of Smith's ironical remark about Jones, but we also need it even where no conversational implicature is involved. Thus, going back to our discussion of propositions and statements at the beginning of Chapter 4, we can now suggest that the problem of identifying the nonoccasion propositions that express the statements speakers make is one that is to be dealt with by the joint contributions of grammar and the theory of conversational logic. Grammar explicates the structure of the propositions and their connections to sentences; conversational logic explicates the connection between propositions and utterances in real speech situations.

Now, we shall try to differentiate sense and meaning from another notion with which it is often confused, particularly by those philosophers who think that no distinction can be drawn between the speaker's beliefs about the world and his or her principles of semantic competence. We explicated the meaning of a word or expression as the sum total of its senses, and we took a sense to be a concept linguistically connected with a word or expression and thereby providing its referential conditions or the contribution it makes to the truth conditions, answerhood conditions, etc., of the sentences in which it can occur.[35] But there is another notion of concept in both ordinary and philosophical usage and this has caused much confusion. This is a broader notion. It corresponds, roughly, to the notion of someone's or some group's conception of something.[36] We may illustrate the difference between the *narrow notion of a concept* and the *broad notion of a concept*, as we shall refer to them, in terms of an example. The dictionary sense of "Martian," the narrow concept of a Martian, is that of a rational creature who is an inhabitant of the planet Mars. But the average person's conception of a Martian, the broad concept of a Martian, might be that of a little green humanoid creature with a plasticlike skin, luminous eyes, bobbing antennae, telepathic powers, and an intelligence vastly superior to ours. The former concept contains the properties that we as speakers of English commonly use to identify the primary, secondary, etc., extension of the term "Martian." The latter is a frequent stereotype, containing properties culled from our experience with science fiction. This difference in the status of the properties that make up the concept emerges clearly when we use them to form explicative judgments about Martians. Thus, (8.162) is analytic but (8.163) is not.

[35] We allow, of course, that a concept which is the sense of a linguistic construction can also be apprehended apart from words, expressions, and sentences of natural language, as, for instance, in the case of nonverbal (e.g., deaf) people or animals. That is to say, their stock of concepts can be largely the same as that of fluent adults. Some concepts, then, are apprehended first and then become senses (in someone's idiolect) when they are subsequently wedded to a linguistic construction in the process of language acquisition. We have to say this since there are countlessly many cases where a nonverbal person first demonstrates the ability to perform tasks that presuppose a knowledge of the concept and then later learns the word whose sense is this concept.

[36] An interesting discussion of very much the same distinction can be found in Ware (1965, chapter 10, section iv).

(8.162) Martians are creatures who inhabit Mars

(8.163) Martians are telepathic (green, etc.)

The broad notion of a concept is the one we have in mind when we talk about the European's concept of an American, the businessman's concept of an airline hostess, the American Southerner's concept of a Negro, the scientist's concept of an atom, or Wittgenstein's concept of philosophy. It is also the notion we have in mind when we talk about how our concept of transportation, surgery, international relations, the woman's role, etc., has changed in recent times. In such cases, we are talking not about the meanings of words but about contingent properties that certain people or groups of people think belong to the referents of words like "airline hostess," "Negro," "atom," "transportation."

Ware (1965, pp. 220–221) makes a further distinction. He points out that there is no such thing as a narrow concept being wrong, false, or mistaken, but that a broad concept (a conception) can be any of these things. Of course, the concept of a rational creature who is an inhabitant of the planet Mars may not be the right concept in an attempt to define "Martian" (perhaps because it is not definitional that Martians are rational), but the concept cannot be wrong in application in the sense in which the racist's sterotype of the Negro is by virtue of the incorrect predications that it entails.

Thus, the mistake that is made when someone takes the question "What is meaning?" to be answered by a correct statement of what the word "meaning" means is to ask for too little understanding of the subject. The understanding we seek in trying to answer this question is not to be found in the meaning of "meaning," any more than an understanding of the nature of water is to be found in the meaning of "water" or an understanding of the nature of Martians, should there be any, is to be found in the definition of "Martian." Our question is about the referent of "meaning"; its answer must, accordingly, be a scientifically acceptable *broad* concept of meaning, a theory of meaning. Knowing the meaning of "meaning" (even tacitly) enables us to pin down the thing we want to learn about, just as knowing the meaning of "water" enables the physicist to pin down the thing he wants to learn about. But there is more to learn about meaning than what things pick meanings out for study, just as there is more to learn about water than knowing what things pick water out for study. In the latter case, we want to know the answers to questions such as why water expands when it freezes when other substances do not. In the former, we want to know the answers to questions such as (1.1)–(1.15). In neither case will the answers we want come from the definitions of the words in question. Thus, the confusion that underlies the claim that to understand meaning we should look at what "meaning," "means," etc., mean is the confusion involved in thinking that the question "What is meaning?" is about the narrow concept when actually it is a question about the broad concept.

Very early in the twentieth century philosophy took a decidedly linguistic turn.[37] Philosophers hoped to locate many of the difficulties that plagued classical philosophy in the basic character of natural languages or in how speakers misuse

---

[37] See Rorty (1967).

them. Growing up in the middle of the twentieth century, my philosophical outlook was strongly conditioned by this linguistic turn. But I soon acquired the conviction that if the linguistic approach to philosophical questions was to prove fruitful it would have to proceed on the basis of a scientific theory of linguistic structure. This, of course, meant turning to linguistics for the theories. When I discovered that linguistics had no theory of semantic structure, I tried to construct one.

In the early stages of the attempt, it seemed that almost any philosophical question might be dealt with within the framework of linguistic theory if only that theory became sophisticated enough. Now, however, I've come to think that this optimism is based on a false assumption that I acquired from the prevailing linguistic outlook of this century, namely, that the classical questions of philosophy are to a significant extent linguistic in nature, that they are in some important sense about the meanings of words. It now seems to me that, although certain aspects of any philosophical question may be illuminated by some of the ideas that linguistics has to offer or will have to offer, the truly important questions of explication in philosophy are questions about *broad* concepts for which *philosophical* theories are needed. If this is so, philosophical understanding of such concepts as that of justice, moral obligation, freedom, knowledge, rationality, and truth will come in the form of theories of these broad concepts.

Accordingly, the quote from Austin appearing at the beginning of this book is doubly apt. It not only expresses the aspirations of the infant science of semantics, but it also rightly assures philosophers that, once the question of language has been kicked upstairs, more than enough philosophical work will be left to do in order to gain a deeper understanding of the good, the true, and the beautiful.

Bibliography

Anderson, S. R. (1970), "On the linguistic status of the performative/constative distinction," The Computation Laboratory of Harvard University, Report no. NSF-26.

Anderson, S. R. (1971), "On the role of deep structure in semantic interpretation," *Foundations of Language*, 6:197–219.

Anderson, S. R. (to appear), "How to get *even*."

Austin, J. L. (1961), "Performative Utterances," in J. O. Urmson and G. J. Warnock, eds., *Philosophical Papers*. London: Oxford University Press.

Austin, J. L. (1962), *How to Do Things with Words*, J. O. Urmson, ed. Cambridge, Mass.: Harvard University Press.

Bach, E., and R. T. Harms, eds. (1968), *Universals in Linguistic Theory*. New York: Holt, Rinehart & Winston.

Bar-Hillel, Y. (1967), "Dictionaries and meaning rules," *Foundations of Language*, 3:409–414.

Bierwisch, M. (1967), "Some semantic universals of German adjectivals," *Foundations of Language*, 3:1–36.

Bierwisch, M. (1969), "On certain problems of semantic representation," *Foundations of Language*, 5:153–184.

Bloomfield, L. (1933), *Language*. New York: Holt, Rinehart & Winston.

Bloomfield, L. (1936), "Language or ideas?" *Language*, 12:89–95.

Bolinger, D. L. (1965), "The atomization of meaning," *Language*, 41:555–573.

Bresnan, J. W. (1971), "Sentence stress and syntactic transformations," *Language*, 47:257–281.

Bromberger, S. (1966), "Questions," *The Journal of Philosophy*, 63:597–606.

Carnap, R. (1937), *The Logical Syntax of Language*. London: Routledge & Kegan Paul.

Carnap, R. (1954), "On Belief Sentences," in MacDonald (1954).

Carnap, R. (1956), rev. ed., *Meaning and Necessity*. Chicago: University of Chicago Press.

Cartwright, R. (1962), "Propositions," in R. J. Butler, ed., *Analytic Philosophy*. Oxford: Basil Blackwell & Mott.

Chafe, W. L. (1968), "Idiomaticity as an anomaly in the Chomskyan paradigm," *Foundations of Language*, 4:109–127.

Chomsky, N. (1957), *Syntactic Structures*. The Hague: Mouton.

Chomsky, N. (1959), "On certain formal properties of grammars," *Information and Control*, 2:137–167.

Chomsky, N. (1962), "A Transformational Approach to Syntax," in A. A. Hill, ed., *Proceedings of the Third Texas Conference on Problems of Linguistic Analysis in English, 1958*. Austin: The University of Texas. Reprinted in Fodor and Katz (1964).

Chomsky, N. (1964), *Current Issues in Linguistic Theory*. The Hague: Mouton.

Chomsky, N. (1965), *Aspects of the Theory of Syntax*. Cambridge, Mass.: M.I.T. Press.

Chomsky, N. (1966a), *Cartesian Linguistics*. New York: Harper & Row.

Chomsky, N. (1966b), *Topics in the Theory of Generative Grammar*. The Hague: Mouton.

Chomsky, N. (1968), "Quine's empirical assumptions," *Synthese*, 19:53–68.

Chomsky, N. (1969a), "Comments on Harman's Reply," in Hook (1969).

Chomsky, N. (1969b), "Linguistics and Philosophy," in Hook (1969).

Chomsky, N. (1970a), "Deep Structure, Surface Structure, and Semantic Interpretation," in R. Jakobson and S. Kawamoto, eds., *Studies in General and Oriental Linguistics*. Tokyo: TEC Corporation for Language Research.

Chomsky, N. (1970b), "Remarks on Nominalization," in Jacobs and Rosenbaum (1970).

Chomsky, N., and M. Halle (1968), *The Sound Pattern of English*. New York: Harper & Row.

Chomsky, N., and G. A. Miller (1963), "Finitary Models of Language Users," in R. D. Luce, R. R. Bush, and E. Galanter, eds., *Handbook of Mathematical Psychology*, vol. 2. New York: Wiley.

Church, A. (1943), "Notes on existence and necessity," *The Journal of Symbolic Logic*, 8:45–47.

Church, A. (1954), "Intensional isomorphism and identity of belief," *Philosophical Studies*, 5:65–73.

Church, A. (1956), *An Introduction to Mathematical Logic*, vol. 1. Princeton, N.J.: Princeton University Press.

Cohen, M., and E. Nagel (1934), *An Introduction to Logic and Scientific Method*. New York: Harcourt Brace Jovanovich.

Copi, I. (1961), *Introduction to Logic*. New York: Macmillan.

Davidson, D. (1967), "Truth and meaning," *Synthese*, 17:304–323.

Fillmore, C. J. (1968), "The Case for Case," in Bach and Harms (1968).

Fillmore, C. J., and D. T. Langendoen, eds. (1971), *Studies in Linguistic Semantics*. New York: Holt, Rinehart & Winston.

Fodor, J. A. (1968a), "The appeal to tacit knowledge in psychological explanation," *The Journal of Philosophy*, 65:627–640.

Fodor, J. A. (1968b), *Psychological Explanation: An Introduction to the Philosophy of Psychology*. New York: Random House.

Fodor, J. A., and J. J. Katz, eds. (1964), *The Structure of Language: Readings in the Philosophy of Language*. Englewood Cliffs, N.J.: Prentice-Hall.

Fraser, B. (in preparation), "Sentences and Illocutionary Forces."

Frege, G. (1952a), "On Concept and Object," in Geach and Black (1952).

Frege, G. (1952b), "On Sense and Reference," in Geach and Black (1952).

Frege, G. (1952c), "Negation," in Geach and Black (1952).

Frege, G. (1953), *The Foundations of Arithmetic*, 2nd ed., trans. J. L. Austin. Oxford: Basil Blackwell & Mott.

Frege, G. (1956), "The thought: A logical inquiry," *Mind*, 65:289–311. Reprinted in E. D. Klemke, ed. (1968), *Essays on Frege*. Urbana: University of Illinois Press.

Frege, G. (1963), "Compound thoughts," *Mind*, 72:1–17.

Frege, G. (1967), *Begriffsschrift*, in J. van Heijenoort, ed., *From Frege to Gödel*. Cambridge, Mass.: Harvard University Press.

Geach, P. (1950), "Russell's Theory of Descriptions," in MacDonald (1954).

Geach, P., and M. Black, eds. (1952), *Translations from the Philosophical Writings of Gottlob Frege*. Oxford: Basil Blackwell & Mott.

Goodman, N. (1951), *The Structure of Appearance*. Cambridge, Mass.: Harvard University Press.

Goodman, N. (1952), "On Likeness of Meaning," in Linsky (1952), MacDonald (1954).

Goodman, N. (1965), *Fact, Fiction, and Forecast*. New York: Bobbs-Merrill.

Gregory, R. K., and J. G. Wallace (1963), *Recovery from Early Blindness*, Experimental Psychology Society Monographs, no. 2.

Grice, H. P. (1961), "The Causal Theory of Perception," *Proceedings of the Aristotelian Society (Supplementary Volume)*, 35. Reprinted in R. Swartz, ed. (1965), *Perceiving, Sensing, and Knowing*. New York: Doubleday.

Grice, H. P. (to appear), *Logic and Conversation*.

Gruber, J. S. (1967), *Functions of the Lexicon in Formal Descriptive Grammars*. Santa Monica, Calif.: Systems Development Corporation.

Halle, M., and S. J. Keyser (1971), *English Stress: Its Form, Its Growth, and Its Role in Verse*. New York: Harper & Row.

Harman, G. (1963), "Generative grammars without transformational rules: A defense of phrase structure," *Language*, 39:597–616.

Harman, G. (1967), "Psychological aspects of the theory of syntax," *The Journal of Philosophy*, 64:75–82.

Harman, G. (1968), "Three levels of meaning," *The Journal of Philosophy*, 65:590–602.

Harman, G. (1969), "Linguistic Competence and Empiricism," in Hook (1969).

Henry, D. P., ed. (1964), *The De Grammatico of St. Anselm*, The Notre Dame Publications in Mediæval Studies, vol. 18. Notre Dame, Ind.: University of Notre Dame.

Herzberger, H. (1965), "The logical consistency of language," *Harvard Educational Review*, 35:469–480.

Herzberger, H. (1970), "Paradoxes of grounding in semantics," *The Journal of Philosophy*, 67:145–167.

Herzberger, H., and J. J. Katz (in preparation), *The Concept of Truth for Natural Languages*.

Hintikka, J. (1970), *Models for Modalities*. Dordrecht, Holland: Reidel.

Hook, S., ed. (1969), *Language and Philosophy*. New York: New York University Press.

Jackendoff, R. (1969), "An interpretive theory of negation," *Foundations of Language*, 5:218–241.

Jacobs, R., and P. Rosenbaum, eds. (1970), *Readings in English Transformational Grammar*. Waltham, Mass.: Ginn.

Jespersen, O. (1933), *Essentials of English Grammar*. New York: Holt, Rinehart & Winston.

Jespersen, O. (1969), *Analytic Syntax*. New York: Holt, Rinehart & Winston.

Katz, J. J. (1964a), "Analyticity and Contradiction in Natural Language," in Fodor and Katz (1964).

Katz, J. J. (1964b), "Mentalism in linguistics," *Language*, 40:124–137.

Katz, J. J. (1964c), "Semantic theory and the meaning of 'good'," *The Journal of Philosophy*, 61:739–766.

Katz, J. J. (1964d), "Semi-sentences," in Fodor and Katz (1964).

Katz, J. J. (1965), "The relevance of linguistics to philosophy," *The Journal of Philosophy*, 62:590–602. Reprinted in Rorty (1967).

Katz, J. J. (1966), *The Philosophy of Language*. New York: Harper & Row.

Katz, J. J. (1967a), "Recent issues in semantic theory," *Foundations of Language*, 3:124–194.

Katz, J. J. (1967b), "Some remarks on Quine on analyticity," *The Journal of Philosophy*, 64:36–52.

Katz, J. J. (1968a), "The Logic of Questions," in B. Van Rootselaar and J. F. Staal, eds., *Logic, Methodology, and Philosophy of Science*, vol. 3. Amsterdam: North-Holland.

Katz, J. J. (1968b), "Unpalatable recipes for buttering parsnips," *The Journal of Philosophy*, 65: 29–45.

Katz, J. J. (1970), "Interpretative semantics vs. generative semantics," *Foundations of Language*, 6:220–259.

Katz, J. J. (1971), "Generative semantics is interpretive semantics," *Linguistic Inquiry*, 2:313–331.

Katz, J. J. (1972), *The Underlying Reality of Language and Its Philosophical Import*. New York: Harper & Row.

Katz, J. J. (forthcoming), "Compositionality and lexical substitution."

Katz, J. J. (in preparation), "Interpretive semantics meets the zombies."

Katz, J. J. (in press), "On the Existence of Theoretical Entities," in T. Bever and W. Weksel, eds., *The Structure and Psychology of Language*. New York: Holt, Rinehart & Winston.

Katz, J. J. (to appear), "Logic and Language: An Examination of Recent Criticisms of Intensionalism."

Katz, J. J., and J. A. Fodor (1963), "The structure of a semantic theory," *Language*, 39:170–210. Reprinted in Fodor and Katz (1964).

Katz, J. J., and E. Martin (1967), "The synonymy of actives and passives," *The Philosophical Review*, 76:476–491.

Katz, J. J., and P. M. Postal (1963), "Semantic interpretation of idioms and sentences containing them," *Quarterly Progress Report*, no. 2, 275–282. Cambridge, Mass.: Research Laboratory of Electronics, M.I.T.

Katz, J. J., and P. M. Postal (1964), *An Integrated Theory of Linguistic Descriptions*. Cambridge, Mass.: M.I.T. Press.

Klima, E. S. (1964), "Negation in English," in Fodor and Katz (1964).

Lakoff, G. (1968), "Instrumental adverbs and the concept of deep structure," *Foundations of Language*, 4:4–29.

Lakoff, G. (1969), " Presupposition and relative grammaticality," *Studies in Philosophical Linguistics*, Series One. Reprinted by The Computation Laboratory of Harvard University (1970), Report no. NSF-24, 51–68.

Lakoff, G., and S. Peters (1966), "Phrasal conjunction and symmetric predicates," in *Mathematical Linguistics and Automatic Translation*, The Computation Laboratory of Harvard University, Report no. NSF-17, VI-1–49. Reprinted in D. A. Reibel and S. A. Schane, eds. (1969), *Modern Studies in English: Readings in Transformational Grammar*. Englewood Cliffs, N.J.: Prentice-Hall.

Langendoen, D. T., and H. B. Savin (1971), "The Projection Problem for Presuppositions," in Fillmore and Langendoen (1971).

Lees, R. B. (1957), Review of Chomsky (1957) in *Language*, 33:375–407.

Leibniz, G. (1951), in P. P. Wiener, ed., *Leibniz Selections*. New York: Scribner.

Lemmon, E. J. (1966), "Sentence, Statements, and Propositions," in B. Williams and A. Montefiore, eds., *British Analytical Philosophy*. New York: Humanities Press.

Lewis, D. K. (1969), *Convention: A Philosophical Study*. Cambridge, Mass.: Harvard University Press.

Lindauer, M. (1961), *Communication Among Social Bees*. Cambridge, Mass.: Harvard University Press.

Linsky, L., ed. (1952), *Semantics and the Philosophy of Language*. Urbana: University of Illinois Press.

Linsky, L. (1967), *Referring*, International Library of Philosophy and Scientific Method. London: Routledge & Kegan Paul.

Lyons, J. (1963), *Structural Semantics: An Analysis of Part of the Vocabulary of Plato*. London: Oxford University Press.

McCawley, J. D. (1968a), "The base component of a transformational grammar," *Foundations of Language*, 4:243–269.

McCawley, J. D. (1968b), "The Role of Semantics in a Grammar," in Bach and Harms (1968).

McCawley, J. D. (1969a), "Meaning and the description of languages," *Kotoba no uchū*, 2.

McCawley, J. D. (1969b), "Lexical Insertion in a Transformational Grammar Without Deep Structure," in W. J. Darden, C.-J. N. Bailey, and A. Davison, eds., *Papers from the Fourth Regional Meeting of the Chicago Linguistic Society*, University of Chicago.

McCawley, J. D. (1971), "Interpretive semantics meets Frankenstein," *Foundations of Language*, 7:285–296.

MacDonald, M., ed. (1954), *Philosophy and Analysis*. New York: Philosophical Library.

Mates, B. (1952), "Synonymity," in Linsky (1952).

Nagel, E. (1961), *The Structure of Science*. New York: Harcourt Brace Jovanovich.

Nagel, T. (1969), "Linguistics and Epistemology," in Hook (1969).

Post, E. L. (1944), "Recursively enumerable sets of positive integers and their decision problems," *Bulletin of the American Mathematical Society*, 50:284–316.

Postal, P. M. (1964a), *Constituent Structure: A Study of Contemporary Models of Syntactic Description*. The Hague: Mouton.

Postal, P. M. (1964b), "Underlying and superficial linguistic structure," *Harvard Educational Review*, 34:246–266.

458 Bibliography

Postal, P. M. (1966), *On So-called "Pronouns" in English*, Monograph Series on Languages and Linguistics, no. 19. Washington, D. C.: Georgetown University, Institute of Languages and Linguistics.

Postal, P. M. (1970), "On the surface verb 'remind'," *Linguistic Inquiry*, 1:37–120. Reprinted in Fillmore and Langendoen (1971).

Prior, M., and A. N. Prior (1955), "Erotetic logic," *The Philosophical Review*, 64:43–59.

Quine, W. V. (1941), *Elementary Logic*. Waltham, Mass.: Ginn.

Quine, W. V. (1953a), "Notes on the Theory of Reference," in *From a Logical Point of View*. Cambridge, Mass.: Harvard University Press.

Quine, W. V. (1953b), "The Problem of Meaning in Linguistics," in *From a Logical Point of View*. Cambridge, Mass.: Harvard University Press.

Quine, W. V. (1953c), "Reference and Modality," in *From a Logical Point of View*. Cambridge, Mass.: Harvard University Press.

Quine, W. V. (1953d), "Two Dogmas of Empiricism," in *From a Logical Point of View*. Cambridge, Mass.: Harvard University Press.

Quine, W. V. (1955), rev. ed., *Mathematical Logic*. Cambridge, Mass.: Harvard University Press.

Quine, W. V. (1959), *Methods of Logic*. New York: Holt, Rinehart & Winston.

Quine, W. V. (1960a), "Carnap and logical truth," *Synthese*, 12:350–374.

Quine, W. V. (1960b), *Word and Object*. Cambridge, Mass.: M.I.T. Press.

Quine, W. V. (1963), "Comments," *Boston Studies in the Philosophy of Science*. Dordrecht, Holland: Reidel.

Quine, W. V. (1967), "On a suggestion of Katz," *The Journal of Philosophy*, 64:52–54.

Quine, W. V. (1968), "Reply to Chomsky," *Synthese*, 19:274–276.

Reichenbach, H. (1947), *Elements of Symbolic Logic*. New York: Macmillan.

Rorty, R., ed. (1967), *The Linguistic Turn*. Chicago: University of Chicago Press.

Rosenbaum, P. (1967), *The Grammar of English Predicate Complement Constructions*. Cambridge, Mass.: M.I.T. Press.

Ross, J. R. (1970), "On Declarative Sentences," in Jacobs and Rosenbaum (1970).

Ross, J. R., and G. Lakoff (undated), "Is Deep Structure Necessary?" circulated by the Indiana University Linguistics Club.

Russell, B. (1905), "On denoting," *Mind*, 479–493.

Russell, B. (1957), "Mr. Strawson on referring," *Mind*, 66:385–389.

Ryle, G. (1955), "Categories," in A. G. N. Flew, ed., *Logic and Language*, second series. Oxford: Basil Blackwell & Mott.

Sapir, E. (1958), "Language," in D. G. Mandelbaum, ed., *Selected Writings of Edward Sapir in Language, Culture, and Personality*. Berkeley: University of California Press.

Searle, J. (1965), "What is a Speech Act?" in M. Black, ed., *Philosophy in America*. Ithaca, N.Y.: Cornell University Press.

Searle, J. (1969), *Speech Acts*. Cambridge: Cambridge University Press.

Skinner, B. F. (1957), *Verbal Behavior*. New York: Appleton-Century-Crofts.

Sledd, J. (1959), *A Short Introduction to English Grammar*. Chicago: Scott, Foresman.

Staal, J. F. (1967), "Some semantic relations between sentoids," *Foundations of Language*, 3:66–88.

Stern, G. B. (1927), *Bouquet*. London: Chapman and Hall.

Strawson, P. F. (1952), *Introduction to Logical Theory*. London: Methuen.

Tarski, A. (1952), "The Semantical Conception of Truth," in Linsky (1952).

Tarski, A. (1956), *Logic, Semantics, and Metamathematics*. London: Oxford University Press.

Teller, P. (1969), "Some discussion and extension of Bierwisch's work on German adjectivals," *Foundations of Language*, 5:185–217.

Ullmann, S. (1962), *Semantics: An Introduction to the Science of Meaning*. Oxford: Basil Blackwell & Mott.

Von Frisch, K. (1953), *The Dancing Bees*. New York: Harcourt Brace Jovanovich.

Ware, R. (1965), *A Philosophical Investigation of the Relativity Thesis of Language*, unpublished Ph.D. dissertation, Oxford University.

Weinreich, U. (1966), "Explorations in Semantic Theory," in T. A. Sebeok, ed., *Current Trends in Linguistics*, vol. 3. The Hague: Mouton.

White, E. B. (W. Strunk, Jr.) (1959), *The Elements of Style*, rev. ed. New York: Macmillan.

Whitehall, H. (1964), "Modification and Shift of Emphasis," in P. C. Wermuth, ed., *Modern Essays on Writing and Style*. New York: Holt, Rinehart & Winston.

Whitehead, A. N., and B. Russell (1935), *Principia Mathematica*, vol. 1. London: Cambridge University Press.

Wilson, N. L. (1967), "Linguistic butter and philosophical parsnips," *The Journal of Philosophy*, 64:55–67.

Wittgenstein, L. (1922), *Tractatus Logico–Philosophicus*. London: Routledge & Kegan Paul.

Wittgenstein, L. (1953), *Philosophical Investigations*. Oxford: Basil Blackwell & Mott.

Ziff, P. (1966), "The nonsynonymy of actives and passives," *The Philosophical Review*, 75:226–232.

Subject Index

N.B.: A reference by chapter and section numeral—e.g., " Analytic truths, Ch. 4.6 "—indicates that the entire section is a discussion of the topic.

Lexicon, 65
 component, accounts of, 399–402
Linguistic communication, 443ff
Linguistic dispositions, 14ff
Linguistic theory. *See also* Theory of
  language, 12, 31
 general features, Ch. 2
 structure of, 29ff
Linguistic truth, Ch. 4
 truths, Ch. 4.6
 scope of, Ch. 4.6
Logic
 nature of, 225ff
 of requests, Ch. 5.5
 of exclamations, Ch. 5.5
 vs. rhetoric, 419
Logical form, 57, 76, 118, 157, 184, 187
Logical particles, 118
Logical truth, 110, 183, 200

Mass nouns, 374ff, 396
Maxim of quantity, 448–450
 quality, 448–450
 relation, 448–450
 manner, 448–450
Meaning
 concept of, 1ff
 dispositional theory of, 8
 image theory of, 8
 referential theory of, 7ff, 234ff
 speaker, 443ff
 subquestions of, 4ff
 use theory of, 8
Meaningfulness, 5
Meaning inclusion, 49, 192
Meaning postulates, 185ff, 246ff
Metalinguistic truth, 110, 198ff

Natural language
 vs. animal communication systems, 22
 vs. artificial languages, 22
 universality of, 136
Negation, Ch. 4.4
 vs. denial, 329ff
 sentential, 169ff
 and presupposition, 135–136
Notational variants, 397

Opacity. *See* Referential opacity

Paraphrase, 5
Performative verbs, 153ff
Petitio principii, 191–192
Philosophical (universal) grammar, 30
Phonological theory, 31, 34n
Phonetic representation, 32
Plurality, 378ff
Polysemy, 59
 vs. homonomy, 68–70
Predicate-raising, 400, 404
Presumption (of a sentence), 429ff

Presupposition, 6, Ch. 4.2, 167, 173, 426ff
 Frege's view *vs.* Russell's, 130ff
Processes, 230, Ch. 7.2
 semantic marker, 305, 333, 335–337
Pro-form, 89–90, 94
Pronoun Replacement Transformation, 374
Projection rules, 33, 36, 45, 67, 68,
  Ch. 3.10
Proper nouns, 380ff, 395–396
Propositional content, Ch. 4.3, 174
Propositional type, Ch. 4.3, Ch. 7.7
Propositions, 38ff, Ch. 4.1
 determinable, 126, 145, 149
 determinate, 126, 143
 eternal, 125ff
 indeterminable, 145, 149
 indeterminate, 126, 143
 occasion, 125ff, 149
 standing, 125ff
 Quine's arguments against, Ch. 6.3.8

Q-element, 205
Quantification theory, 185ff
Question arguments, 204
Questions
 contingently answerable, 223
 determinable, 222
 focus of, 425ff
 evasion of, 210ff, 213
 indeterminable, 222
 linguistically answered, 215–220
 nexus, 207
  complex, 217ff
  simple, 217ff
 presupposion of, 134, 210ff
 rejection of, 210ff, 213
 self-answered, 6, 217
 theoretical, 3
 x-, 207

Reading. *See also* Semantic representation,
  37, 72
 derived, 37, 42, 72
 lexical, 37, 42, 72
Reading schema, 175
Redundancy, semantic, 6
Redundancy rules, semantic, 44ff, 99
Redundant constituent, 50
Referential opacity, Ch. 6.3
 translucency, 275ff
 transparency, 262
Relations, logical properties of, 193ff
Rhetorical component, 433ff
Rhetorical interpretation, Ch. 8.4.1
Rhetorical relations, 113
Rules
 linguistic, 15ff
  internalized, 15ff
  vs. dispositions, 16ff

Selected complement, 161

Name Index

72 73 74 75 76   9 8 7 6 5 4 3 2 1